October 2013

Dear Duncan,

I am delighted to forward you an advance copy of the long awaited publication from Tony on the history of the Bar — a labour of love which he commenced some nine years ago + in true Tory fashion covers every meticulous detail imaginable!

Enjoy!!

m Regards,

Mark Mulholland QC.

Adrian Colton QC

# A History of the Bar and Inn of Court of Northern Ireland

A.R.Hart

The General Council of the Bar of Northern Ireland 2013

ISBN 978 1 909751 04 0

Printed by J.C. Print Ltd.

# Dedication

To the memory of those members
of the Inn of Court of Northern Ireland
who lost their lives upholding the rule of law.

# Acknowledgements

This book has been an inordinate time in its preparation, and that it was completed at all is in part due to the invaluable help that I was given by so many individuals and institutions.

My thanks are due to my fellow benchers of the Inn of Court of Northern Ireland who agreed to my undertaking this work, gave me unrestricted access to the records of the Inn, gave permission to quote from them, and have made a generous contribution to the publication costs. I am equally indebted to the Executive Council of the Inn of Court for giving me access to, and permission to quote from, their records.

Throughout my researches I have been encouraged and supported by successive chairmen of the General Council of the Bar of Northern Ireland, and have been given access to the records of the Bar by the Bar Council. Without its generous support, and its decision to publish this book, it would never have seen the light of day, and I am greatly in their debt.

A number of institutions and individuals gave permission for photographs and paintings to be reproduced in the book, or on the cover. I am most grateful to them all, and they are individually acknowledged in the list of contents. Ivan Ewart of the Marketing and Creative Services department of the Queen's University of Belfast has again been able to reproduce and improve several of the older photographs and drawings with his customary skill.

Sir Robert Caswell, lord chief justice, and Sir Declan Morgan, lord chief justice, were most supportive, and gave me access to, and permission to quote from, original correspondence in files in their office relating to the construction of the Royal Courts of Justice, as well as other records in their custody. The benchers of King's Inns also kindly gave access to, and permission to quote from their records. I received nothing but kindness from Mrs Camilla McAleese, the under treasurer, and Jonathan Armstrong, the librarian, of King's Inns in response to my requests to trace various documents. Other bodies that gave permission to quote from their records are the General Council of the Bar of Ireland, the Council of Legal Education (Northern Ireland), the Public Record Office of Northern Ireland and the governors of the Royal Belfast Academical Institution.

Sir John MacDermott and Andrew Babington each gave permission to quote from the unpublished reminiscences of Lord MacDermott and Sir Anthony Babington, and His Honour Judge Graham Jones gave permission to quote from the autobiography of Sir Edward Jones. The National Archives at Kew gave permission to quote from the unpublished memoir of Mr Justice W.E. Wylie, and Dr John Emberson gave permission to quote from an annotated transcript of that memoir. As will be apparent I have drawn heavily on all of these. It is only right that I should also acknowledge the debt I owe to those without whose invaluable earlier histories of the North East Circuit, and the early days of the Northern Ireland Bar, this work would have been much the poorer. George Hill Smith KC's *The North East Bar, a sketch historical and reminiscent*, and his *Sketch of the Supreme Court of Judicature of Northern Ireland* preserved much valuable, indeed irreplaceable, information on life at the Bar on the North East Circuit before 1921, as did His Honour William Johnson QC in his *History and customs of the Bar and Circuit of Northern Ireland* for the years immediately after 1921.

Sir John MacDermott was also one of those who gave freely of their time to answer questions about their time at the Bar, as did Lord Hutton, Lord Carswell, the Rt Hon Turlough O'Donnell, Sir Donald Murray, Sir Anthony Campbell, Sir Robert Porter QC and the late Sir Frank Harrison QC.

Many other people took the trouble to answer questions and seek information, and space prevents me from naming everyone, but Master Charles Redpath, the clerk of the crown for Northern Ireland, and Mrs Karen Wray, executive assistant to the lord chief justice of Northern Ireland, gave invaluable assistance, as did the Rev. Robert Marshall, Jennefer Aston, and Mrs Pauline Rodway. Brendan Garland, then the chief executive of the Bar, and Andrew Trimble, the present chief executive, provided much helpful advice throughout. Mrs Lynn McMonagle and Mrs Lisa Mayes of the Bar Council staff were unfailingly helpful in finding time among their many other duties to answer my endless requests for information, and in tracing files and documents.

At the beginning of this project I received a great deal of help from Mrs Collette Simmons. She typed some early chapters and made a significant contribution to the compilation of the list of calls to the Bar in Part Two. His Honour John Martin QC read the entire work in draft, and his comments and suggestions did much to improve the text, as did those of my daughter Fiona Hart, who performed the unenviable task of proof-reading the final text. Barry Valentine also read the text and prepared the Index. I owe a great debt of gratitude to each of them, and any errors, imperfections and omissions that remain are my responsibility.

A.R. Hart
23 June 2013.

# Contents

# List of illustrations

Illustrations appear between pp 85 and 92 and 189 and 196

1.  William Carlisle Henderson QC, Father of the North West Bar 1869-1872
2.  Acheson T. Henderson QC 1812-1909. By John Butler Yeats.
3.  Robert Murray, last Father of the North East Bar.
4.  George Hill Smith QC, first Father of the Bar of Northern Ireland.
5.  Barney Donaghy, 'bagman' in Londonderry.
6.  Members of the North West Bar, probably in the summer of 1921.
7.  The first judges of the Supreme Court of Judicature of Northern Ireland, October 1921.
8.  Legal Golf competition, 1924.
9.  Circuit dinner menu, 1926.
10. Bar dinner menu 1938.
11. View of possible exterior of the proposed Royal Courts of Justice. By Charles Terry Pledge ARIBA.
12. View of exterior as adopted of the proposed Royal Courts of Justice. By Charles Terry Pledge ARIBA.
13. The Old Bar Library.
14. The Atrium, New Bar Library.
15. Interior view of the New Bar Library.
16. Exterior view, front of the New Bar Library.
17. The Inn of Court.

## CREDITS

No. 1: Courtesy of the Lord Chief Justice of Northern Ireland; No. 2: Courtesy of the Trustees of National Museums Northern Ireland and Estate of Jack. B. Yeats, all rights reserved, DACS 2013. No. 7: Courtesy of Sir William Moore, Bt. No. 11 and No. 12: Courtesy of the Northern Ireland Court Service. No. 13 and No. 17: courtesy of Paul Megahey. No. 14, No. 15 and No. 16: Courtesy of Chris Hill sales@senicireland.com.

# List of Abbreviations

| | |
|---|---|
| AC | Appeal Cases |
| AG | attorney general |
| All ER | All England Reports |
| *Anal. Hib.* | *Analecta Hibernica, including the reports of the Irish Manuscripts Commission* |
| Babington, *Reminiscences* | Sir Anthony Babington, *Personal Reminiscences* |
| Ball, *Judges* | F.E. Ball, *The judges in Ireland, 1221-1921.* 2 Vols. |
| Baker, *Serjeants at law* | J.H. Baker, *The order of the serjeants at law* |
| Baker, *The common law* | J.H. Baker, *The common law tradition: tradition lawyers, books and the law* |
| Brand, 'The judges of the Lordship of Ireland' | Paul Brand, 'The birth of a colonial judiciary: the judges of the lordship of Ireland, 1270-1377' in W.N. Osborough (ed.), *Explorations in law and history Irish Legal History Society discources, 1988-1994.* |
| Brand, 'The legal profession in the lordship of Ireland' | Paul Brand, 'The early history of the legal profession of the lordship of Ireland', in Daire Hogan and W.N.Osborough (ed.), *Brehons, serjeants and attorneys: studies in the history of the Irish legal profession* |
| BCM | Minutes of the General Council of the Bar of Northern Ireland |
| BM | Benchers' Minutes |
| C | Conservative, or Lord Chancellor |
| *Cal. Pat. rolls Ire.* | *Calendar of the patent rolls of Ireland* |
| *Cal. S. P. Ire.* | *Calendar of the state papers relating to Ireland* |
| CB | chief baron of the exchequer, or companion of the Order of the Bath |
| CBE | Companion of the Order of the British Empire |

| | |
|---|---|
| Clarendon, *State Letters* | *The state letters of Henry, earl of Clarendon.* 2 vols. |
| Cmd. | Command Paper |
| Cmnd. | Command Paper |
| Delaney, *Christopher Palles* | V.T.H. Delaney, *Christopher Palles, lord chief baron of her majesty's court of exchequer in Ireland 1874-1914, his life and times* |
| DPP | director of public prosecutions |
| *DIB* | *Dictionary of Irish Biography* |
| DL | deputy lieutenant |
| DSC | Distinguished Service Cross |
| DSO | Distinguished Service Order |
| DUP | Democratic Unionist Party |
| E | Easter Term |
| EC | European Community |
| ECM | Minutes of the Executive Council of the Inn of Court of Northern Ireland |
| EEC | European Economic Community |
| Ferguson, *King's Inns Barristers* | K. Ferguson (ed.) *King's Inns Barristers 1868-2004* |
| FRCS | Fellow of the Royal College of Surgeons (England) |
| FRIBA | Fellow of the Royal Institute of British Architects |
| FRS | Fellow of the Royal Society |
| FRSE | Fellow of the Royal Society of Edinburgh |
| GCB | knight grand cross of the Order of the Bath |
| Hand, *English Law in Ireland* | G.J. Hand, *English Law in Ireland, 1290-1324* |
| Hart, *The king's serjeants at law in Ireland* | A.R. Hart, *A history of the king's serjeants at law in Ireland: honour rather than advantage?* |
| H | Hilary Term |
| Hill Smith, *Supreme Court of Northern Ireland* | G. Hill Smith, *Sketch of the Supreme Court of Judicature of Northern Ireland* |
| Hill Smith, *The North East Bar* | G. Hill Smith, *The North East Bar a sketch historical and reminiscent* |
| Hogan and Osborough (ed.), *Brehons, serjeants and attorneys* | Daire Hogan and W.N. Osborough (ed.) *Brehons, serjeants and attorneys: studies in the history of the Irish legal profession* |
| Hogan, *the legal profession in Ireland* | D. Hogan, *The legal profession in Ireland 1789-1922* |
| IFS | Irish Free State |

| | |
|---|---|
| *IHS* | *Irish Historical Studies* |
| *Ind* | Independent |
| *Ir Jur* | *Irish Jurist* |
| *ILT & SJ* | *Irish Law Times & Solicitors' Journal* |
| J | Justice |
| Jones, *Jones LJ his life and times* | E.W. Jones, *Jones LJ his life and times- the autobiography of the Rt Hon Sir Edward Jones* |
| KBE | knight commander, Order of the British Empire |
| KC | King's counsel |
| KCB | knight commander of the Order of the Bath |
| Kenny, *King's Inns* | C. Kenny, *King's Inns and the Kingdom of Ireland: the Irish inn of Court 541-1800* |
| Kenny, *Tristram Kennedy and and the revival of Irish legal training.* | C. Kenny, *Tristram Kennedy and the revival of Irish legal training, 1835-1885* |
| KG | knight of the Order of the Garter |
| KI | King's Inns |
| *King's Inns Barristers* | Kenneth Ferguson (ed.) *King's Inns Barristers 1864-2004* |
| KIBMB | King's Inns Benchers Minute Book |
| L | Liberal |
| LAB | Labour |
| LCJ | lord chief justice |
| *Liber mun. pub. Hib.* | Rowley Lascelles, *Liber munerum Publicorum Hiberniae*. 2 vols. |
| LJ | lord justice of appeal |
| *LQR* | *Law Quarterly Review* |
| M | Michaelmas Term |
| MC | Military Cross |
| MGM | Minutes of General Meetings of the Bar of Northern Ireland |
| MLA | member of the legislative assembly |
| MRCP | member of the Royal College of Physicians (England) |
| NA | National Archives |
| NCBM | Northern Committee Benchers' Minutes |
| NI | Northern Ireland Law Reports |
| NICA | Northern Ireland Court of Appeal |
| NILQ | Northern Ireland Legal Quarterly |
| NIQB | Northern Ireland Queen's Bench |
| OBE | officer of the Order of the British Empire |

| | |
|---|---|
| *ODNB* | *Oxford Dictionary of National Biography* |
| W. N. Osborough (ed.) *Explorations* | W.N. Osborough (ed.) *Explorations in law and history in law and history: Irish Legal History 1988-1994* |
| *PL* | *Public Law* |
| PRONI CAB | Public Record Office of Northern Ireland - Cabinet Minutes |
| PRONI WORK | Public Record Office of Northern Ireland - Office of Works |
| QC | Queen's Counsel |
| RIC | Royal Irish Constabulary |
| RM | resident magistrate |
| RNVR | Royal Naval Volunteer Reserve |
| RUC | Royal Ulster Constabulary |
| SC | Senior Counsel |
| *Sel. Comm. Leg ed.* | *Report of the select committee on legal education, together with the minutes of evidence, 1846* |
| SG | solicitor general |
| SDLP | Social Democratic and Labour Party |
| Smyth, *Law officers of Ireland* | C.J. Smyth, *Chronicle of the law officers of Ireland* |
| SRO | Statutory Rule and Order |
| Sullivan, *Old Ireland* | A.M. Sullivan, *Old Ireland, Reminiscences of an Irish KC* |
| TAVR | Territorial Army and Volunteer Reserve |
| T | Trinity Term |
| *Thom's Irish Directory* | *Thom's Almanac and Official Directory*, later *Thom's Official Directory of Great Britain and Ireland* |
| TNA | The National Archives |
| U | Unionist |
| UKUP | United Kingdom Unionist Party |
| UUP | Ulster Unionist Party |

PART ONE

# CHAPTER ONE:

# The early history of the Irish Bar

With the coming into force on 1 October 1921 of the provisions of the Government of Ireland Act that provided for a separate Supreme Court of Judicature in Northern Ireland'[1] Ireland was now divided into two distinct legal, as well as political, jurisdictions, although for a time the High Court of Appeal for Ireland and King's Inns provided links between both jurisdictions. As we shall see, these links were not to survive for long, and in October 1921 the Bar of Northern Ireland came into existence as a separate bar. However, the Northern Bench and Bar, whilst emphasising that the legal system in Northern Ireland was entering a new era, recognised that both were the inheritors of the high traditions of their predecessors.[2] Those traditions were an integral part of a legal system that evolved over many centuries, and so it is appropriate to examine the history of the Irish Bar in order to understand the origins of the Bar of Northern Ireland.

The importation of the common law into Ireland as a consequence of the Norman invasion in 1169, happily described as 'the first adventure of the common law' by W.J. Johnston (a former member of the North East Circuit[3]) resulted in the spread of royal courts across the lordship of Ireland.[4] By the middle of the thirteenth century there is some evidence that itinerant royal judges were holding courts at various locations, and by the end of the century a number of individuals have been identified as

---

1   1920 c. 67, s. 38.

2   G. Hill Smith, The Supreme Court of Judicature of Northern Ireland, (Belfast, 1926), pp 11-17.

3   W.J. Johnston, 'The first adventure of the common law', *LQR*, xxxvi (1920), 11. W.J. Johnston (1869-1940): called to the Irish Bar 1892, joined the North East Circuit 1893, KC 1911. County court judge for Monaghan and Fermanagh 1911-21, a judge of the high court of the IFS 1924-39, and of the supreme court 1939-1940. See M. Kotsonouris, *The winding up of the Dail Courts, 1922-1925: an obvious duty* (Dublin, 2004), pp 250-51, and *ILT&SJ* lxxiii (1939), p. 16 for his career.

4   G.J. Hand, *English Law in Ireland 1290-1324* (Cambridge, 1967), and P. Brand, 'The birth and early development of a colonial judiciary: the judges of the lordship of Ireland, 1210-1377' in W.N. Osborough (ed.), *Explorations in law and history: Irish Legal History Society Discourses 1989-1994,* (Dublin, 1995).

appearing before the various royal and local courts and acting on behalf of clients on a regular basis, some of whom were appointed to act on behalf of the king, a development that would suggest that they were familiar with court procedures. At a very early stage there emerged two distinct classes of lawyer, the attorney and the pleader. The difference between their respective functions has been described by Sir John Baker as 'the distinction between the pleader and the attorney in its most basic form represents the difference between the intellectual or scientific function and the mechanical or ministerial function',[5] although this distinction may not always have been observed in every case in the early stage of the development of the legal profession, and there were instances where the same individual appears to have acted as an attorney and as a pleader at different times.

Initially the attorney's function was to answer on behalf of his client on those occasions when the case was called in court, because if the litigant was not present, then, if he was the plaintiff, his case would be dismissed and his sureties amerced (fined). However, it became common for the attorney to perform a number of procedural tasks on behalf of his client, such as obtaining the correct writ to initiate the action, delivering the writ to the sheriff, and ensuring that the necessary entries showing that the litigant had been represented were made in the court records. Although it was common for an attorney to be recorded in the plea rolls of the court as acting in that capacity only on a single occasion, by the middle of the thirteenth century in England many attorneys can be identified as acting more than once, often for a variety of clients, which would suggest that they had demonstrated some experience in court procedures. The paucity of contemporary court records for this period makes it difficult to draw firm conclusions as to when professional attorneys came into existence in the courts of the lordship of Ireland, but Paul Brand has identified a small number of individuals who appear to have acted in that capacity as between 1290 and 1320.[6]

The forensic process not only required the litigant to select the appropriate writ and to be present, either in person or by his attorney, at the various

---

5    J.H. Baker, *The order of the serjeants at law*, Selden Society, supp. series 5 (London, 1984), pp 21-27.

6    P. Brand, 'The early history of the legal profession of the lordship of Ireland, 1250-1350' in D. Hogan and W.N. Osborough (eds.), *Brehons, serjeants and attorneys: studies in the history of the Irish Legal profession*, (Dublin, 1990), pp 37-41.

stages of the litigation, but to pronounce a formal complaint (or 'count' in Norman French) or to make a formal defence to the complaint. This was a vital step, as a failure to use the correct formula could be fatal to the case. The litigant could therefore employ someone 'ad narrandum', that is to recite the appropriate form of words. Such a person need not have acted in such a capacity before, but, as in the case of the attorneys, some individuals can be identified as acting in this capacity for several clients. At an early stage, the function of the pleader developed from that of simply pronouncing the appropriate formula to the more intricate process of advancing his client's case by formulating points of law, which would be decided by the judge, or to define issues of fact, which would be answered by the jury. It is likely that in due course one of the functions of an attorney would be to advise his client who should be retained to plead on his behalf and inform the pleader of the facts of his client's case.

In Ireland in the thirteenth and fourteenth centuries a variety of terms were used, apparently interchangeably, to describe a pleader. 'Serviens' (serjeant), 'narrator' or 'serviens narrator', and 'countor' are all found. However, whilst in England the term 'serjeant at law' came to be confined to those pleaders who were entitled to practice in the common pleas,[7] a separate order of serjeants never developed in Ireland, where the term 'serjeant at laws' came to be confined to those pleaders who were retained by the king and called the king's serjeants.[8] The term pleader is therefore used in this account to describe all those referred to at this time as serjeants, narrators or counters. However, the modern barrister in both England and Ireland is descended not from the serjeants at law who had a monopoly of practice in the common pleas in England, but from another group of pleaders called the apprentices of the law who eventually eclipsed their senior colleagues in importance.[9]

Brand has identified 48 pleaders in Ireland between 1290 and 1350,[10] and by the end of the thirteenth century we can see that pleaders were to be found regularly appearing throughout the lordship in both the royal and

---

7   J.H. Baker, *The order of the serjeants at law*, pp 21-27.

8   A.R. Hart, *A history of the king's serjeants at law in Ireland: honour rather than advantage*, (Dublin, 2000), pp 9-10.

9   P. Brand, *The origins of the English legal profession*, (Oxford, 1992), pp 110-14; Baker, *The order of the serjeants at law*, p. 109.

10   Brand, 'The legal profession in the lordship of Ireland', pp 48-50.

local courts. At this stage some of the royal courts were itinerant in nature, for example the judges of the Dublin bench also went on circuit as eyre justices, carrying out what were national visitations of the various counties in Ireland. By the death of Edward I in 1307 the lordship had reached its apogee with twelve shires: Dublin, Waterford, Cork, Kerry, Louth, Limerick, Tipperary, Connacht, Roscommon, Kildare, Meath and Carlow. In addition, there were the liberties of Kilkenny, Wexford, Trim and Ulster where, although justice and the courts were in the hands of the lords of the liberty, some pleas were reserved to the crown.[11] As a result, pleaders would find themselves appearing before courts held in widely dispersed locations.

Whilst the nascent legal profession was very different to the profession in later centuries, nevertheless there are similarities between the legal profession of the early period in Ireland and the legal profession as it ultimately evolved. It was already split into two branches, pleaders and attorneys, and the pleaders would, on occasion, travel to appear before royal or other justices at many different locations throughout much of Ireland. In addition, the crown retained its own pleaders, with the office of king's serjeant dating from c. 1261-65, and that of the king's attorney (later to become the attorney general) from 1313, although it is not until 1504 that there is a reference to the king's solicitor, who later became the solicitor general.[12]

The legal system of the lordship also resembled that of more recent times in that a close link between the pleaders and the bench can be seen developing by the closing years of the thirteenth century, when we see several of the king's serjeants and other pleaders being appointed royal justices, John de Ponz in 1294 being the earliest. However, not all judges had been pleaders earlier in their careers, and many do not appear to have had any legal experience before their appointment.[13] As was to remain the case until the 1840s, Irish pleaders did not have a monopoly of appointment to Irish judicial appointments, with many of those appointed at this time having no previous connection with Ireland.[14] Not all of those who were appointed were without blemish, and in at least one case a judge was appointed who

---

11    A.J. Otway-Ruthven, *A history of Medieval Ireland*, 2nd ed. (London, 1980), pp 174-77, and Hand, *English Law in Ireland*, p. 59.

12    Hart, *The king's serjeants at law in Ireland*, pp 7, 15 and 27.

13    Ibid., pp 15-16. Brand, 'The judges of the lordship of Ireland', pp 35-37.

14    Brand, 'The judges of the lordship of Ireland', p. 35. F.E. Ball, *The judges in Ireland, 1221- 1921*, i, viii-ix.

had been considered unfit for appointment to a similar post in England. Adam de Stratton, dismissed from the exchequer of England for forgery and fraud in 1279, became a baron of the exchequer in Ireland in 1311.[15]

By a gradual process the courts of the Irish lordship evolved into a structure resembling in some respects that familiar to practitioners in succeeding centuries. The judicial functions of the justiciar (chief governor) of the lordship were increasingly delegated to specially appointed justices, and the justiciar's court became known as the chief place, the forerunner of the court of king's bench. The Dublin bench became the common place or common bench, later known as the common pleas, and the barons of the exchequer also performed judicial functions. However, these were not the only central, as opposed to local, courts because litigants frequently petitioned parliaments, councils or great councils[16] when they were unable to obtain speedy or satisfactory remedies in the royal courts. There were also the itinerant justices who went on commissions of eyre, assize, gaol delivery, and oyer and terminer.

In addition there were many local courts, particularly the county courts and the courts of the liberties (such as those of Ulster, Desmond and Thomond where great magnates had extensive judicial powers over extensive areas), as well as the many franchises of individual lords or communities with the right to administer justice in various ways. These jurisdictions differed greatly in size and importance, from the liberty of Ulster and its own itinerant justices, to that of the fair of Any, Co. Limerick.[17] Although the evidence is exiguous, professional pleaders appear to have practised in at least some of these local courts at the beginning of the fourteenth century to judge by examples in the court of the liberty of Kilkenny in 1302 and in the county court of Co. Louth in 1306.[18]

During the later part of the fourteenth, and much of the fifteenth, centuries the area of effective royal jurisdiction in Ireland gradually shrank until it was limited to the Pale, that is the medieval counties of Dublin, Louth, Meath and Kildare, and ports such as Wexford, Kinsale, Cork and Galway,

15   F.E. Ball, *The judges in Ireland, 1221-1921*,(London, 1926), i, pp 26, 63. *ODNB*.
16   For the distinctions between parliaments, great councils and councils, see H.G. Richardson
     and G.O. Sayles, *The Irish parliament in the Middle Ages* (Philadelphia, 1952) ch. 7, passim.
17   Hand, *English Law in Ireland*, ch. vii passim and p. 134.
18   Brand, 'The legal profession in the lordship of Ireland', pp 43-44.

although from time to time there were periodic commissions outside the Pale. One took place in May and June 1483 when the second justice of the king's bench and the king's serjeant went on commission through Kerry, Kilkenny, Limerick, Tipperary, Waterford and Wexford.[19] We may surmise that the role of the pleaders in representing their clients before the various courts in which the common law was administered resembled that which had become established by the beginning of the fourteenth century.

What evidence is there that the pleaders of this period received a legal education, either in Ireland or elsewhere, and what was the nature of any such education? In any discussion of this topic it has to be borne in mind that the available evidence as to the form which legal education took in England, as well as in Ireland, before the early fifteenth century is sparse, as the earliest extant records of the inns of court start with the Black Books of Lincoln's Inn in 1422, and there are no records for the other inns before 1500. Nevertheless, modern scholarship has uncovered some evidence that casts a certain amount of light upon the education of pleaders in Ireland and England.

As one might expect, given the relationship of the lordship of Ireland with England, some at least of those who wished to practice, or already practised, law in the lordship received some form of legal education in London, either before they came to Ireland, or, if they lived in Ireland, because they went to London to study. As early as 1287 Robert de St Michael of Ireland had royal permission to stay at Westminster 'for the purpose of learning in the Bench'. Indeed, he is the first person known to be a student of the common law in either England or Ireland.[20] In subsequent years there are occasional references to law students from Ireland studying in England, not all of them complimentary. In 1344 there is a reference to three apprentices of the bench, two of whom were Irish (Richard of Cardiff and John Barry), who were alleged to have lain in wait at night to rob passers by.[21] It is not possible to identify how many Irish men travelled to England to study law at this period, but that this was a regular occurrence might be inferred from the exemption conferred upon serjeants and apprentices of law from a statute of 1413 requiring all Irishmen to leave the kingdom of England on pain of

---

19  S.G. Ellis, *Reform and revival: English government in Ireland, 1470–1534*, Royal Historical Society studies in history, 47 (London, 1986), pp 136–42.

20  Brand, 'The legal profession of Ireland', p. 25.

21  Ibid.

life and limb.[22] Nevertheless, that obstacles were placed in the way of those who wished to travel to London to study law at this time is evident from a complaint to the king from 'the community of Ireland' in 1421 that certain inns of court would no longer receive Irish law students as they had in the past, and that this should be remedied 'that your laws may be perpetuated and not forgotten in your said land'. A similar complaint was made to Henry VI by the Dublin parliament in 1429.[23] However, these complaints do not appear to have resolved the problem. Some years later the chancellor of Ireland, Thomas Chace, whilst on official business in England, made successful efforts to have Irishmen admitted to the inns as freely as their English counterparts.[24] Certainly the records of Lincoln's Inn record at least 11 individuals born in Ireland who were admitted as members, nine of whom subsequently became judges there, and references have survived to others who were granted licences to leave Ireland to study law in London.[25]

Whether there was some form of indigenous legal training in the common law in Ireland before the sixteenth century is impossible to state because of the lack of contemporary records, however Paul Brand has pointed to two important English treatises that contain references to Ireland. The treatise *Natura Brevium* (written not long after 1285) refers to proceedings before the chief justiciar,[26] and in one of the versions of the pleading manual *Novae Narrationes*[27] Irish place-names and personal names were substituted for English originals. At the very least the incorporation of specifically Irish material and examples in treatises or manuals originally produced for an English audience suggests that the authors realised that an audience also existed in Ireland for instruction in the common law, and it seems not unreasonable to infer that at least part of that audience would be members of an emerging legal profession in the lordship of Ireland.

However, whilst a number of individuals may have had some form of education in the common law in England, that was not the case for everyone. Although some pleaders travelled to England to study, or improve their knowledge of, the common law, it may have been the case that others acquired a degree of

22   C. Kenny, *King's Inns and the Kingdom of Ireland: the 'Irish inn of court', 1541–1800*, p. 16.
23   Ibid., pp 16-17.
24   Ibid., pp 18-19.
25   Ibid., p. 19, n. 5 where a list is given of those who can be identified.
26   P. Brand, 'Ralph de Hengham and the Irish common law', *Ir Jur*, xix (1984), 107 at n. 6.
27   P. Brand, 'Ireland and the literature of the early common law', *Ir Jur*, xvi (1981), 112.

legal knowledge by simply watching pleaders arguing cases before the judges and acquiring legal skill as a result of acting for a number of clients over the years, particularly when the inns of court in London were not admitting Irish students in the early fifteenth century. In any event, not all those who practised in the Irish courts at this time had a common law background, and it was to be quite some time before the pleaders, whether of English or Irish origin, gained a monopoly of judicial appointments.

To judge by his title, only Master David le Blund may have held a university degree, a unique qualification for a pleader at this time in either Ireland or England.[28] However, prior to 1341 a significant proportion of the Irish judiciary had a clerical or administrative background, either in England or Ireland, prior to their appointment to the bench.[29] Whilst the professional pleaders established a monopoly over appointments to the chief justiceship of the Dublin bench by 1377,[30] it was not until the beginning of the sixteenth century with the appointment of Richard Nagle as a baron of the exchequer in 1505 that we see the last clerical appointee as a judge of the common law courts, although even he had been admitted to Lincoln's Inn in 1485 and so may well have had a common law background.[31] However, clerics were appointed as chancellor or master of the rolls until a much later date. To what extent any canon law training or experience may have influenced those clerics appointed as judges when they discharged their duties in the common law courts in Ireland at this period must remain a matter of speculation.

In England by the early years of the fourteenth century there are references to apprentices receiving instruction from the judges in court.[32] Although there is no evidence of this in Ireland, it seems not unreasonable to speculate that there may have been a similar practice, albeit at a later date. That there may have been a tradition of aspiring lawyers receiving some instruction from leading practitioners in Dublin in the later part of the fifteenth century is suggested by an account recorded by the king's attorney in 1517–18 of the manner in which two men who later achieved considerable prominence in the lordship spent their time in Dublin in 1482-83.

28  Brand, 'The legal profession of Ireland', p. 34.
29  Brand, 'The judges of the lordship of Ireland' is the definitive study of the backgrounds of those appointed as judges in the lordship of Ireland between 1210 and 1377.
30  Ibid., p. 47.
31  Ball, *Judges*, i, pp 161, 191.
32  Brand, *The origins of the English legal profession*, pp 110-12.

William Darcy, later to become under-treasurer, and Thomas Kent, later king's serjeant and then chief baron of the exchequer, were described as learning their tenures and *Natura Brevium* in the home of John Estrete (or Stret) who was the king's serjeant at law at the time and who later served in a number of senior posts, including becoming a privy councillor in England.[33] We do not know whether this involved some form of formal relationship of master and pupil, or whether such a practice was generally adopted, but that someone as prominent as Estrete was prepared to devote time to the instruction of those who were themselves to become eminent lawyers is striking. Not only did Darcy and Kent study under Estrete, but on holy days (holidays) they went to the home of the chief justice, accompanied by their 'companions', where they 'learnt to harp and dance', thereby practising the social and cultural skills which would be useful to them when they went to study in London. Darcy is known to have done so, as he appears in the records of Lincoln's Inn in May 1485.[34]

The foundation of King's Inns in 1541 was a significant event in Irish legal history because, even though there had been complaints from time to time about the need for lawyers in Ireland to have greater skill and learning, the newly formed institution did not make any provision for legal education in Ireland. Instead, in 1542 the Irish parliament enacted what became known as the Statute of Jeofailles. This stipulated that any person who wished to act as a pleader in any of the 'King's four principal courts' (i.e. chancery, king's bench, common pleas and exchequer) had to have resided and studied at one of the inns of court in London, although it seems that the statute did not prescribe a minimum number of years for which this was to be done.[35] For almost a century the requirement was limited to those who wished to practise at the four courts and did not extend to other courts, although the statute, which remained in force until 1885,[36] naturally exercised a profound effect upon Irish pleaders, ensuring that all those who wished to practise had to study in London, and, as we shall see, the requirement was reinforced in the seventeenth century.

Whilst this ensured that they were grounded in the common law of

---

33   For details of Estrete's career, see Hart, *The king's serjeants at law in Ireland*, pp 24-25, 147.
34   Kenny, *King's Inns*, pp 21-22, where the relevant extract from NAI, Ferguson MS 1 a. 49 , 136, f 52 is quoted.
35   The text of the statute is discussed in detail in Kenny, *King's Inns*, pp 41-46.
36   The Barristers Admission (Ireland) Act, 48 & 49 Vict (1885), c. 20.

England, which also applied to Ireland, it meant that students wishing to study law in London incurred considerable expense, and, from time to time, hostility. Given that royal control did not extend over the whole kingdom of Ireland, as the lordship became in 1541, and the legal profession at that time was in all probability small in numbers, it was understandable that it was thought desirable that those who wished to practise law should study at the inns of court in London. However, whilst the judges and lawyers who signed the petitions of 1541 and 1542 which set out the reasoning behind the foundation of King's Inns made passing reference to education, they

> ...saw themselves as providing a new governing elite for the whole island of Ireland. Their King's Inns was a special institution, a hybrid of serjeants' inns, inns of court, inns of chancery and the recently proposed 'king's graces house', for the education of an English governing class in civil and Christian renaissance principles.[37]

That Irish students were not always welcome in London is apparent from the quota system restricting the numbers of Irish students exercised by the inns for a considerable period. Whilst it is unclear whether there was a quota in operation in Lincoln's Inn before 1542, there was in that year, as only four Irish-born students were permitted at the inn at any given time, and they had to reside in the chamber called the 'Dovehouse'. The rules of the Middle Temple excluded Irish students at this time, and there are references to Irish students lodging together at Gray's Inn in 1556 and 1568-69.[38] In any event, whilst the requirement was to study in London, it does not seem to have been essential for a barrister to be called by one of the inns before returning to practise in Ireland, because although some had been called, others had not. Nor does it appear that upon their return there were any readings, moots, or any other exercise whereby practitioners could keep abreast of legal developments, provided by or under the auspices of King's Inns.[39]

As the records of the inns of court are much more extensive during the reigns of Elizabeth I and James I it is possible to identify Irish students

---

37  Kenny, *King's Inns*, p. 39.

38  P. Brand, 'Irish law students and lawyers in late medieval England', *IHS.* xxxii (2000-2001), 169; Kenny, *King's Inns*, pp 49-50.

39  Kenny, *King's Inns*, p. 67.

who attended each inn with much greater accuracy. It has been estimated by D.F. Cregan that during that period at least 284, and perhaps as many as 306, Irish students enrolled in the four inns.[40] Of those who can be firmly identified as Irish no fewer than 132 were admitted to Gray's Inn, and it is interesting to note that, particularly in Elizabeth I's reign, a significant proportion of all the Irish students (with the exception of those admitted to the Inner Temple where this information is not recorded) are shown as having not only Irish place names of origin, but were also recorded as being of one of the inns of chancery. Those shown as being of Staple Inn or Barnard's Inn entered Gray's Inn, those from Furnivall's Inn went to Lincoln's Inn, and those from New Inn to the Middle Temple.[41]

The inns of chancery were of lesser status than the inns of court, and whilst in the fifteenth century they were mainly used by clerks and attorneys who were not admitted to the inns of court, they were also used by younger students who wished to study the rudiments of procedure. By this period, the inns of chancery had become subordinated to the inns of court, some of which were also their landlords,[42] for example Gray's Inn acquired Staple Inn in 1528, and Lincoln's Inn acquired the site of Furnivall's Inn in 1548.[43] The frequency with which Irish students appear to have joined an inn of chancery before being admitted to one of the inns of court might suggest that membership of the former was seen as a form of initial instruction before a student proceeded to the latter, although the practice appears to have become much less common from the latter part of Elizabeth I's reign onwards. Nevertheless, as late as 1625 the principal of Staple's Inn identified to Gray's Inn four Irishmen who had been at Staple Inn within the last three years.[44]

At the beginning of this period, as one might expect, almost all of those identified by Cregan came from the Pale, although a few came from towns

40 D.F. Cregan, 'Irish catholic admissions to the English inns of court 1558-1625', *Ir Jur* v (1970), p. 99. To Cregan's figure of 275 (and possibly up to 297) Old Irish and catholic students have to be added a further 9 he identified as New English protestants at p. 97, a total of at least 284, and possibly as many as 306, Irish students.

41 Ibid.

42 J.H. Baker, *An introduction to English legal history*, 3rd. ed. (London, 1990), pp 183-84.

43 J.H. Baker, 'The inns of court and chancery as voluntary associations' in *The legal profession and the common law: historical essays* (London, 1986), pp 56-7.

44 *Cal. S. P. Ire., 1615-25*, p. 581.

in the South East such as Wexford. Later in Elizabeth I's reign more from Munster and Leinster were admitted, and towards the end of the reign of James I students from Galway started to be admitted in significant numbers. However, only a few came from Connacht or Ulster, which would be broadly consistent with these areas being the last to be brought within the effective control of the English government and so subject to the common law.

In 1623 we find a suggestion in the privy council that the king make an allowance of £20 a year to Maurice Eustace, who later had a distinguished political and legal career in Ireland,[45] whilst he studied at Lincoln's Inn. Interestingly, in support of the recommendation it is stated the king 'has usually allowed exhibitions to some one of that nation who studied the laws here'.[46] It is not possible to say how often this happened, but this isolated reference would suggest that some form of financial support was given by the English government to at least some Irish students at the inns of court in London, presumably those who, like Eustace, might be expected to support the administration in the future.

During Elizabeth I's reign there were increasing pressures upon all her subjects in both England and Ireland to conform to the official, protestant, church. These pressures affected catholic Irish students studying at the inns of court, as can be seen from a letter in 1581 from Christopher Robinson to his father, the king's serjeant, explaining that he had temporarily withdrawn from his studies at the Middle Temple to avoid being detected as a recusant.[47] Early in the reign of James I the government started to remove catholic judges from the bench, and replace some of them with appointees from England, and by 1613 all the Irish judges were protestant, or had conformed to the protestant faith.[48] Although this policy closed off advancement to the bench to catholic lawyers, for a time they were admitted as members of King's Inns following its revival under Lord Deputy Chichester in 1607, and remained as members in 1613. However, in that year the Irish parliament required all lawyers to either conform or be excluded from practice, and to ensure that this requirement was enforced the chancellor was required to

45    For Eustace's career, see Hart, *The king's serjeants at law in Ireland*, pp 57-58, 169.
46    *Cal. S. P. Ire., 1615-25*, p. 424.
47    *Cal. S. P. Ire., 1574-85*, p. 286; Hart, *The king's serjeants at law in Ireland*, p. 44.
48    H.S. Pawlisch, *Sir John Davies and the conquest of Ireland: a study in legal imperialism* (Cambridge, 1985), pp 41-42; Kenny, *King's Inns*, pp 51-52.

administer the oath of supremacy to practitioners from that time.[49]

Those who did not conform were prevented from practising until 1628, when Charles I issued the Graces, instructions to the Irish administration in which many of the grievances of his catholic subjects in Ireland were addressed. Article 15 not only provided that all lawyers who took the oath of allegiance could be readmitted to practice, but for the first time specified that potential barristers had to have been students at one of the inns of court for five years, and '...shall bring any attestation sufficient to prove the same'.[50] After the Restoration, catholics were allowed to practise until the eighteenth century, when the right of catholic lawyers to practise law preserved by the articles of Limerick and Galway was restricted, and then removed, by a series of statutes, although the rigour of these and other statutes aimed at the catholic population in general was evaded to some degree by practitioners officially converting to the protestant faith.[51] Nevertheless, it was not until the passage of the Catholic Relief Act of 1792 that almost all of the restrictions upon catholic lawyers practising law were removed. One prohibition that remained was that no catholic 'could hold or enjoy the place or office of King's Counsel',[52] and it was only with the passing of the Catholic Relief Act of 1829 that the bar to catholics holding judicial and other legal offices was removed, except for the office of lord chancellor where the bar remained until 1868.[53] The comment of the late Professor Delaney on the impact of the Penal Laws on the legal profession in Ireland is a just one. 'The operation of the Penal Laws prevented Irish Catholics from entering the legal profession; and this exclusiveness had the inevitable effect of degrading it'.[54]

At this point it is appropriate to say something further about the nomenclature used to describe those who pleaded before the courts, and particularly the king's courts. As we have seen, in the thirteenth and fourteenth centuries a variety of terms were used, apparently interchangeably. By the early years

---

49  *Cal.pat.rolls Ire., Jas* I, p. 255; Kenny, *King's Inns*, pp 91-92.

50  A. Clarke, *The Old English in Ireland, 1635-42* (Cornell, 1966), pp 242-43.

51  For a detailed study of this question see T.P. Power, 'Conversions among the legal profession in Ireland in the eighteenth century' in Hogan and Osborough (eds) *Brehons, serjeants and attorneys*, and Kenny, 'The exclusion of catholics from the legal profession in Ireland, 1537-1829', *IHS*, xxv (1986).

52  Kenny, 'The exclusion of catholics from the legal profession', p. 356; D. Hogan, *The legal profession in Ireland 1789-1922*, (Dublin, 1986), p. 20.

53  The Offices and Oaths Act, 1867 (c.75), s. 1. Ball, *Judges*, ii, p. 302.

54  V.T.H. Delaney, *Christopher Palles*, (Dublin, 1960), p. 31.

of the seventeenth century it was usual to describe those pleading before the superior courts as counsel or counsellor, not as barristers. Sir John Baker has pointed out that the term barrister was originally confined to internal use in the inns of court, and had no direct connection with the bar of any court, with the older term 'apprentice' being used for formal purposes and in court.[55] Whilst the term 'utter barrister' came into use in England from the late sixteenth century onwards, the term 'councell', or more commonly 'counsellor (or 'counsellor at law'), was still generally used at this time to describe those who had trained at the inns of court,[56] and was to remain in common use in everyday parlance in Ireland until recent times.[57] In his preface to his *Reports* published in 1615, Sir John Davies referred to 'a learned Councellor' when describing the nature of the honorarium given to counsel.[58] No. XXIX of the directions given for the conduct of the Irish courts in 1622 contains a reference to '…the party whom it concerns, or his Councell or Sollicitor',[59] and in the common pleas rules issued in Ireland in 1671, at rule vi relating to the admission of attorneys the expression 'practising counsellor' is used.[60] The use of the word 'counsel', which derives from the Latin 'homo consiliarius', found in the plea rolls,[61] was a recognition that the role of the pleader had long ceased to be confined to the process of pleading and arguing in court, and now included the wider function of giving advice on all legal matters out of court, whether on a particular occasion, or because he was subject to a general retainer from his client.

55   J.H. Baker, 'Counsellors and barristers', *Cambridge Law Journal*, 27 (1969), pp 205-29, reprinted in *The legal profession and the common law: historical essays* (London, 1986), at pp 109-11. Baker, 'The degree of barrister' in *The common law tradition: lawyers, books and the law* (London, 2000), pp 69-76 passim.

56   Baker, *The legal profession*, pp 101, 111-12. In *The state of the protestants in Ireland under the late King James' government* (3rd. ed. London, 1692), at pp 244 and 266 Archbishop King refers to John Eaton and Nehemiah Donnellan respectively as 'Counsellor at Law'.

57   An unusual example of both terms being used together occurred in 1662 when Major Elllis Goodwin was created a 'counsellor and barrister at law', as well as king's counsel, by letters patent. *Liber munerum publicorum Hiberniae*, ed. R. Lascelles (2 vols. London, (1852), I, pt. 2, p. 76. For an eighteenth century example, see A.R. Hart, 'Fighting Fitzgerald: mad, bad and dangerous to know, an eighteenth century murder trial', *NILQ* 49 (1998), p. 231.

58   J. Davies, *Le Primer Report des Cases en les Courts del Roy en Ireland*, (Dublin, 1615).

59   G.J. Hand and V.W. Treadwell, 'His Majesty's Direction for ordering and settling the Courts within the Kingdom of Ireland, 1622', *Anal. Hib.*, 26 (1970), p. 204.

60   Quoted in W.N. Osborough, 'The admission of attorneys and solicitors in Ireland, 1600-1866' in Hogan and Osborough (eds.), *Brehons, serjeants and attorneys*, p. 110.

61   Baker, 'Counsellors and barristers', p. 101

In 1594 a new rank of counsel was created in England with the appointment of Francis Bacon as the queen's 'learned counsel extraordinary, without payment or fee', an appointment confirmed by James I in 1604 when he authorised the issue of letters patent by which Bacon was appointed 'our counsellor at law, or one of our counsel learned in the law'.[62] The new rank or office of king's counsel was in time to eclipse the order of serjeants at law in England in importance. The first appointment to this new office in Ireland was that of William Hinton on 26 January 1613.[63] Whilst only the date of Hinton's appointment as king's counsel survives, with the appointment of Walter Archer in 1614 we learn something more of the reasons for, and the terms of, Archer's appointment because he was appointed 'in respect of his conformity and knowledge of Irish which the rest of our learned counsel there do want'. His patent is described as containing 'a clause of Place and Praecedence in the King's Courts or elsewhere, but with a proviso that this should not derogate from any office before granted by the king or his predecessors'.[64] In 1619 Archer's appointment was ratified when he received an express appointment 'of the place of one of His Majesty's learned counsel at large in Ireland during pleasure, and to assist in finding offices, and soliciting His Majesty's causes before the Commissioners for Wards, according to certain instructions attached'.[65] Why another counsel was required in 1613 when the king already had the services of three counsel, namely the king's serjeant, the attorney general and the solicitor general, is unknown, but it would seem that one of the reasons, if not the principal reason, for Archer's appointment in 1614 was that he could speak Irish, and in 1619 it was felt necessary to have the services of another counsel who could devote time to representing the crown before the Court of Wards. Archer received 100 marks for his fee,[66] but the traditional fee of £40 granted to king's counsel in England upon their appointment (although probably not paid)[67] does not appear to have been a feature of Irish grants.

Thereafter appointments as king's (or queen's) counsel appear to have been relatively infrequent in Ireland, although on a few occasions several were made on the same occasion, as in Hilary Term of 1714 when five were admitted, and between 1711 and 1721 16 were admitted.[68] In all, it would

---

62  'The rank of Queen's Counsel', in Baker, *The common law tradition*, pp 89-92.
63  *Liber mun. pub. Hib.*, I, pt. 2, p. 76.
64  Ibid.
65  *Cal. S. P. Ire., 1615-25*, p. 265
66  *Liber mun. pub. Hib.*, I, pt. 2., p. 76. One mark=13s  4d
67  Baker, 'The rank of Queen's Counsel', p. 92.
68  *Liber mun. pub. Hib.*, I, pt. 2,  pp 76-78.

seem that at least 90 king's or queen's counsel (although the word 'council' was generally used until well into the 1800s) were probably appointed between 1613 and 1768. Whilst 83 are listed in *Liber munerum* there are references to a further seven in official correspondence of the 1680s and 1690s, and so it would seem that the list in *Liber munerum* is incomplete. In 1686 the earl of Clarendon, the lord lieutenant, referred to barristers named Nugent and Nihill as being king's counsel,[69] and in 1690 the earl of Nottingham wrote to the lords justices in Dublin to inform them that the king had appointed Sir John Meade, Mr Rochester and Mr Donnellan 'to be his counsel at law'.[70] Rochester and Donnellan are not included in *Liber munerum*, but Donnellan is referred to as one of the king's counsel by Sidney, the lord lieutenant, in a letter to Nottingham in 1692.[71] In 1695 the then lord lieutenant, Lord Capel, informed the duke of Shrewsbury that he had appointed William Porter, and intended to appoint two others, Ormsby and Wingfield, as king's counsel.[72]

Whilst many of those appointed as king's or queen's counsel between 1613 and 1768 were at the forefront of the Bar, and later became judges, this was not invariably the case. Sometimes the rank was conferred for political or other reasons, as in the case of Sir Thomas Longueville. In 1686 we find Clarendon, writing to Lord Sunderland to support the appointment of Longueville, saying that 'he is an old cavalier decayed in his fortune, he picks up a little livelihood by following the law, and the character of being of the king's council will both give him reputation, and bring him, out of the crowd, within the bar, where he may sit down; which will be a great ease to his old age'.[73] Longueville was duly appointed shortly afterwards.[74]

In an era when cases were heard on the basis of the seniority of the counsel concerned, appointment as king's counsel, and the mark of royal favour it represented, was of considerable value to the recipient, conferring both professional and social prestige, including admission as a bencher of King's Inns.[75] It is therefore surprising to find that Redmond Morris, who was

69   *The state letters of Henry, earl of Clarendon*, (2 vols., Oxford, 1765), I, p. 33, and II, p. 6.
70   4 Dec. 1690. *Cal. S. P. dom., 1690-91*, p. 181.
71   9 Nov. 1692. *Cal. S. P. dom., 1695 (Addenda 1689-95)*, p. 219.
72   17 Dec. 1695 *Cal. S. P. dom., 1695*, p. 129.
73   Clarendon, *State Letters*, p. 57.
74   *Liber mun. pub. Hib.*, I, pt. 2, p. 77.
75   Kenny, *King's Inns*, p. 166.

appointed a king's counsel in 1744, resigned from that office in 1768.[76] This is a unique occurrence, and the reason for it is unknown.

It is difficult to arrive at anything other than a rough approximation of the number of practising barristers in Ireland in the seventeenth, eighteenth and the first half of the nineteenth centuries. The admissions records of King's Inn are incomplete, and when admissions are recorded it does not necessarily follow that each individual entered practice. Nevertheless there is some evidence as to the size of the Irish Bar at various points during this period. Kenny's analysis of the King's Inns records identified 172 barristers admitted between 1607 and 1649,[77] and a study of the indexes of bills filed in chancery and of the equity division of the exchequer led Barnard to conclude that in the later part of the seventeenth century the Irish Bar 'certainly exceeded 200'.[78]

Recent research in the chancery bill books between 1667 and 1698 by Hazel Maynard, who has also studied the admissions of Irish students of the inns of court over the same period, has identified 12 barristers from Ulster practising in the chancery court, and a further eight who entered the inns of court during the same period, three of whom were admitted by King's Inns. The great majority of the 12 practitioners came from Eastern Ulster, with three from Carrickfergus, three from Co. Down, one from Belfast, and one from Co. Armagh, compared to one from Co. Tyrone. The pattern amongst the eight admitted to the inns of court is the same, with only one (from Co. Londonderry) from the Western part of the province. Some of the names, such as Richard Dobbs of Carrickfergus, and Henry and Robert Echlin, both of Co. Down, are names of prominent families in those areas.[79] Whilst the figures are small, nevertheless they are an indication that the number of those going to the Bar from Ulster was increasing when compared with the early 1600s.

Evidence as to the earnings of the Irish Bar in the seventeenth century is slight, but some figures have survived which would suggest that the most successful practitioners could earn substantial sums. The most extensive records are those of Sir John Temple, who was solicitor general from 1660

---

76  *Liber mun. pub.Hib.*, I, pt. 2, p. 77.

77  Kenny, *King's Inns*, p. 274.

78  T.C. Barnard 'Lawyers and the law in later seventeenth – century Ireland', *IHS* xxviii (1993), p. 263.

79  I am indebted to Mrs Maynard for this information.

to 1689, and attorney general between 1690 and 1695. Returning to Ireland in 1653, by 1665 his earnings from practice (as opposed to those as solicitor general) were £1166 10s, and in the next twenty years (apart from 1670 when he was in England for over three months) his annual earnings never fell below £1000, and usually were in the region of £1500 to £1600.[80] In November 1693 Alan Brodrick, who had already been third serjeant for a short period, and was to become the dominant figure in Irish legal and political life over the next three decades, said that he had made £200 10s in the 20 working days of the law term starting on 5 November, which he considered 'very fair'. Considering that at the time the salary of an Irish puisne judge was £400 a year, together with a circuit allowance of £100, the incomes of practitioners such as Temple and Brodrick were sizeable.[81] Nevertheless, as Barnard has pointed out, although Temple's earnings were large by Irish standards, they were modest when compared with the earnings which leading counsel could command in England at that time.[82] Whilst the customary fee for each appearance was £1, some who were particularly in demand could command fees of £3, and although it was said in the 1660s that fees in Dublin matched those in London,[83] it is probable that the average practitioner earned less than his English counterpart. Nevertheless, if a member of the Bar was fortunate enough to be promoted to one of the law officerships, then the financial rewards could be considerable, with the attorney general receiving £2000 or more, and the prime serjeant £1600 or £1700 in a good year, by the end of the eighteenth century.[84]

Almanacs published in Dublin from the 1760s onwards frequently contain lists of barristers, and these are an important source of information about the membership of the Irish Bar at this period. *Wilson's Dublin Directory* of 1761 lists 316 barristers, 14 of whom were judges or masters in chancery, but the compiler of the directory observed that many of the remaining 302, nine of whom were 'king's council', 'are since retired'. In addition seven advocates were listed separately as practitioners in the courts of delegates and the prerogative, admiralty and consistory courts, although some of the advocates, such as Francis Stoughton Sullivan,[85] who was a

---

80    Barnard, 'Lawyers and the law', p. 275, Table 2.
81    Hart, *The king's serjeants at law in Ireland*, p. 72. For details of Brodrick's career see pp 164-65.
82    Barnard, 'Lawyers and the law', p. 276.
83    Ibid., pp 267-72.
84    Hart, *The king's serjeants at law in Ireland*, pp 71-80, and 185-89.
85    Francis Stoughton Sullivan (1719-1779). *ODNB*.

distinguished jurist and academic at Trinity College, were also members of the Bar. The size of the Bar may well have increased somewhat above the 200 or thereabouts of 60 years before, but it is likely that the number in active practice in the mid eighteenth century was below 300 judging by the comment above that many of those listed in 1761 had retired.

At this time we also have some anecdotal evidence of the income a successful practitioner might achieve. Chief Baron Willes, who came to Ireland as chief baron in 1757 having practised mostly on the Midland Circuit in England,[86] wrote that whilst he had been told that two or three of the leading counsel earned £2000 to £3000 a year, in general earnings at the Irish Bar were small. He gave a number of reasons for this. Firstly, there were more counsel than the available business would support, and at many venues on circuit more than 12, and sometimes more than 20, counsel were present. Secondly, attorneys moved many interlocutory motions themselves, with a substantial loss of business to the Bar as a result. However, this was offset to some degree by charging higher fees, and by retaining many more counsel than would be the case in England, partly to ensure that enough counsel were present to deal with the case when it came on as some would be engaged in other courts.[87] A notable example of this tendency was the celebrated trial in 1743 of the ejectment action in *Annesley v Anglesey* where the plaintiff was represented by 13 counsel and the defendant by 14. In the subsequent perjury proceedings in 1745 there were twelve counsel for the prosecution and fifteen for the defendant.[88]

Willes' impressions are supported by the estimate of Henry Grattan junior that Anthony Malone's professional earnings were 3000 guineas a year.[89] As the foremost advocate of his day, Malone would have commanded very high fees.[90] However, impressions though these estimates may be, they may be broadly accurate to judge by the earnings of John Hely-Hutchinson, prime serjeant from 1761 until he became provost of Trinity College in 1774. His fee books

86  For Willes's career, see J. Kelly, (ed.) '*The letters of Lord Chief Baron Willes to the earl of Warwick 1757-62: an account of Ireland in the mid-eighteenth century* (Aberystwyth, 1990) pp 4–10.

87  Edward Willes 'Miscellaneous observations on Ireland, 1750-60', PRONI, T. 2855/1, pp 10 and 20.

88  Ball, *Judges*, ii, 134-35.

89  *Memoirs of the life and times of the Rt Hon Henry Grattan* (5 vols., London, 1839-46), I, p. 61. Henry Grattan, who was called in 1775, made £85 in his first year, £132 in the second, and was making £1000 a year within five years. J.R. O'Flanagan, *The Irish Bar*, (2nd. ed. London, 1879), p. 66.

90  Anthony Malone (1700-1776). Called 1726, an MP 1727-76. Prime serjeant 1743-53, chancellor of the exchequer 1757-61.

for the period from 30 October 1762 to the end of November 1772 record total earnings of £31456 8s 9d, an average of £3119 a year. Although he was prime serjeant throughout this period, these earnings appear to be only his barrister's fees, and he was said to earn a further £1200 a year as prime serjeant. Hely-Hutchinson's fees in 1762 and 1763 were mostly less than £5, with frequent refreshers at £1 2s 9 and retainers at £2 5s 6d, with very few above £10. A fee of £20 was exceptionally high, and fees of this level meant that a successful counsel such as Hely-Hutchinson had to be briefed in a very large number of cases to command an income of £2000–£3000 a year. Outstanding juniors such as John Fitzgibbon, later Earl of Clare and lord chancellor, and John Philpott Curran, soon earned over £1000 a year, Fitzgibbon earning £1066 19s 1d in his fifth year after call, and Curran at least £1038 10s in his fourth.[91]

The Bar appears to have greatly increased in size in the last four decades of the eighteenth century, and by 1798 there were no fewer than 818 barristers listed in *Wilson's Dublin Directory*, although this included several judges. However, many of these were not in active practice, and the number of practising barristers was certainly much less, possibly in the region of 300. That might be surmised from two contemporary indications of the size of the practising Bar. In 1792 the benchers of King's Inns considered draft rules for the government of the profession, and ordered 300 copies to be printed for those barristers who wanted one,[92] which would suggest that the benchers estimated that this figure represented the number of practitioners likely be affected. Another indicator is that at the famous general meeting of the Bar held in 1798 to oppose the projected Act of Union 198 actually voted.[93] No doubt there were some who did not attend for a variety of reasons, but this was a matter of the greatest controversy and one may reasonably infer that a substantial proportion of the active Bar attended.

In the eighteenth and early nineteenth centuries, the Bar occupied a position of great importance in Irish political and parliamentary life, leading the then

91   Hart, *The king's serjeants at law in Ireland*, pp 78-80. John Hely-Hutchinson (1724-94). Called 1748, KC 1758. MP 1759-94, provost of TCD 1774-94. *ODNB*. J.R. O'Flanagan, *The Munster Circuit. Tales, trials and traditions*, (London, 1880), pp 114, 120-22.

92   Hogan, *The legal profession in Ireland 1789-1922*, p. 20. However, in 1868 Denis Heron said that in 1800 there were about 500 practising barristers in Ireland. Quoted in K. Ferguson (ed.) *King's Inns Barristers 1868-2004* (Dublin, 2005), p. 117. Heron took a keen interest in statistical matters, and was vice-president of the Statistical and Social Inquiry Society of Ireland 1871-81. For an account of his career Hart, *The king's serjeants at law in Ireland*, pp 130-32 and 172. *DIB*.

93   O'Flanagan, *The Irish Bar*, p. 129.

lord chancellor, Lord Redesdale, to write in 1805 that 'There is no body now in Ireland which has so much influence in public opinion as the bar'.[94] Throughout the eighteenth century barristers comprised a significant element in the Irish house of commons, and it has been estimated that at the Union of the 300 MPs, 67 were barristers, of whom 42 were in active practice.[95] Many of the leading political figures in the Irish commons were barristers, such as Anthony Malone, John Hely-Hutchinson, John Scott, John Fitzgibbon, Henry Flood, Hussey Burgh, Henry Grattan and Barry Yelverton, to mention only some of the outstanding figures of the second half of the century.

However, it cannot be said that their forensic ability was the product of a comprehensive system of professional education or training. Still compelled to join one of the inns of court in London and remain there for five years, a requirement reaffirmed by the benchers of King's Inns as recently as 1779,[96] the collapse of an organised and effective system of professional education in the inns of court during the Civil War[97] meant that thereafter students in London were left to their own devices to acquire such legal learning as they could by attending the courts and by private study. In such circumstances few were likely to have displayed the persistence of William Plunket, a future lord chancellor of Ireland,[98] whose grandson wrote of his studies in London that

> …he applied himself to the drudgery of legal preparation with unflagging zeal and accuracy. The note-books which he filled at this time afford a curious record of the manner in which he acquired his exact and well-arranged knowledge of the great principles of jurisprudence, and trained his matchless memory for the performance of the intellectual feats which so often astonished those who met him in after life.[99]

94  Quoted, Hart *The king's serjeants at law in Ireland*, p. 106
95  G.C. Bolton, *The passing of the Irish Act of Union: a study in parliamentary politics.* (Oxford, 1966), pp 80-81.
96  Kenny, *King's Inns*, p. 179.
97  W.R. Prest, *The Inns of Court under Elizabeth I and the Early Stuarts 1590-1640*, (London, 1972), pp 132-36.
98  W.C. Plunket, Lord Plunkett (1764-1854). Called 1787, KC 1797. Solicitor general 1803-05, attorney general 1805-07 and 1822-27. Declined the office of master of the rolls in England in 1827 because of the objections to his appointment by the English Bar, chief justice of the common pleas in Ireland 1827-30, lord chancellor of Ireland 1830-34 and 1835-41. Created Baron Plunket of Newtown, Co. Cork in 1827. *DIB*.
99  99 D. Plunket, *The life, letters and speeches of Lord Plunket*, (London, 1867), I, p. 40. Plunket was not unique in taking this approach, Thomas Lefroy and Francis Blackburne devoted themselves to private study in the same way. C. Kenny, *Tristram Kennedy and the revival of Irish legal training 1835-85* (Dublin, 1996), pp 191-92.

Such accounts as have survived suggest that the lure of social or political interests in London often proved more interesting than study of the law. Henry Grattan devoted much of his three years in London to reading poetry and history, as well as attending parliamentary debates. Despite declaring that he would break 'the neck of the law by a course of sustained reading' a year or so after he entered the Middle Temple, his admission after he was called to the Bar that he would have to spend a vacation reading law would suggest that his earlier plan had not been carried through.[100] Those who had attended Trinity College, Dublin would not have fared any better as teaching of the common law, other than by Francis Stoughton Sullivan in the eighteenth century, was almost non-existent,[101] and it was not until well into the nineteenth century that a more satisfactory system of legal education in Ireland came into being.[102]

On being called to the Bar Grattan and his contemporaries would have frequented the Four Courts, which had been located in the precincts of Christ Church cathedral since 1608, and were to remain there until the opening of Gandon's new Four Courts in 1796. The four courtrooms were housed in a small and simple structure about 80 feet by 50 or 60 feet in size, with each court open to the hall.[103] The building, which was located on what is now the garden immediately south of Christ Church and part of the street that is now Christ Church Place, was surrounded by a warren of narrow streets, and set above 'cellars let out to toyshops and tippling houses, and one of the main entrances was approached through an insalubrious Hell'.[104] Hell was the name given to one of the lanes by which the Four Courts were approached and where many barristers and solicitors had their chambers, leading to the advertisement 'To be let, furnished apartments in Hell. They are well suited for a lawyer'.[105]

100 R.B. McDowell, *Grattan, a life* (Dublin, 2001), pp 19-20.

101 V.T.H. Delaney, 'Legal studies in Trinity College, Dublin, since the foundation', *Hermathena*, lxxxix, no. 3.

102 Kenny, Tristram Kennedy and the revival of Irish Legal training, ch. 7 and 8, passim.

103 C. Kenny, 'The Four Courts at Christ Church, 1608-1796' in W.N. Osborough (ed.) *Explorations in Law and History*, (Dublin, 1995) pp 127-28. This was a feature of Gandon's original design of the new Four Courts, with the Round Hall initially open to the courts. T. Clancy, 'The Four Courts building and the development of an independent Bar of Ireland', in C. Costello (ed.) *The Four Courts: 200 years* (Dublin, 1996), p. 85.

104 E. McParland, 'The Old Four Courts, at Christ Church' in C. Costello (ed.) *The Four Courts: 200 years*, p. 31.

105 O'Flanagan, *The Munster Circuit*, p. 71.

The courts and their location were regarded as unsatisfactory, Grattan writing in 1772 'the Four Courts are of all places the most disagreeable'.[106] For many years there had been concern about the security and inconvenience of the arrangements for the storage of public records which were held in a number of different offices scattered throughout Dublin,[107] and efforts had been made on a number of occasions to provide a single home for them. Eventually in 1776 the foundation stone was laid for a new building designed by Thomas Cooley for this purpose on a site owned by King's Inns at Inns Quay. The building was only partially completed when Cooley died in 1784 and a decision was made to extend the scheme to include a new Four Courts. The task of adapting Cooley's design for this new purpose was given to James Gandon, who transformed and extended Cooley's design to produce the magnificent Four Courts, which were opened in November 1796.[108]

Unfortunately, despite the modernity of the new courts, with the exception of robing rooms in cellars directly underneath the Round Hall, no provision was made for the accommodation of the Bar in the original building. The cellars were 'dark, cold and had a predilection to flooding'.[109] It was not until 1838 that a Law Library was completed at the rear of the building when the Nisi Prius and Rolls Courts were also built.[110] The reason why no provision was originally made for a Law Library at the Four Courts may well be because the benchers of King's Inns were at the time planning to build new premises for the society, which had nowhere to meet at the time because of its decay in previous decades. In 1793 the society's charter had been revoked and new regulations were introduced for the governance of the society, one of which was that every barrister and attorney (the attorneys being governed by King's Inns at the time) was required to pay a deposit for chambers 'to be allowed when the gentlemen shall purchase from the society chambers or ground to build chambers on'. In the event, no chambers were ever built, and the benchers abandoned a plan to build new premises on the south side of the Liffey between the river and James' Street because it

106 Kenny, 'The Four Courts at Christ Church', p. 128, n. 75.
107 C.P. Curran, 'Cooley, Gandon and the Four Courts' in C. Costello (ed.) *The Four Courts; 200 years*, p. 108.
108 Ibid., p. 109; E. McParland, 'The early history of James Gandon's Four Courts' in C. Costello (ed.) *The Four Courts: 200 years*, pp 119 & 125.
109 T. Clancy, 'The Four Courts building and the development of an independent Bar of Ireland', in C. Costello (ed.) *The Four Courts: 200 years*, p. 94.
110 C. Griffin, 'Post Gandon at the Four Courts', in C. Costello (ed.) *The Four Courts: 200 years*, p. 236.

was too expensive, deciding instead to build on a site about a mile away on Constitution Hill at the top of Henrietta Street, where King's Inns stands today. The foundation stone for the new building, also designed by James Gandon, was laid in 1800.[111]

Despite the brilliance of so many outstanding orators, the Irish Bar in the second half of the eighteenth century was also notable for heavy drinking and duelling, albeit that these habits were by no means confined to the Bar. An English attorney called Howard attacked the Irish Bar in 1750 for its intemperance, saying that many '..seemed to do nothing but walk the courts the whole morning, and devote whole evenings to the bottle'.[112] W.C. Plunket, who wrote to a friend shortly after his return to Dublin in May 1786, made a similar criticism of his colleagues.

> I have not been able to read a word since I came home, and, indeed, it is almost impossible for any man who shares in the dissipation that prevails amongst the legal men here to do so. The taste for idleness and debauchery which pervades the whole profession would, in my opinion, alone be sufficient to account for the difference between the legal information of the two countries. I have for my part been obliged to make a serious resolution against supping out and sitting up late, for besides the time lost in it, it leaves me in a state of entire stupefaction the entire next day.[113]

Duelling was endemic in Ireland at this time, barristers and judges were as willing as anyone else to take part, and many such encounters took place. Two examples will suffice. John Egan, chairman of the Co. Dublin quarter sessions, fought with Jerry Kelleher at the Waterford assizes on a point of law,[114] and when the *Belfast Newsletter* reported the imminent trial of Colonel Robert Fitzgerald (Fighting Fitzgerald) at the Castlebar assizes in 1786 it remarked without surprise: 'It is expected a number of duels will take place at Castlebar, among the gentlemen employed in the prosecution and defence of Mr Fitzgerald'.[115]

Although members of the Bar were usually based in Dublin where the principal courts were situated, much business was transacted upon assize

---

111 Kenny, *King's Inns*, pp 255-57.
112 O'Flanagan, *The Irish Bar*, p. 55.
113 D. Plunket, *Life and speeches of Lord Plunkett*, I, pp 46-47.
114 Ibid.
115 Hart, 'Fighting Fitzgerald', p. 232.

when the judges went on circuit. As we have seen, the practice of the judges travelling throughout the country can be traced back almost to the earliest days of the common law in Ireland. By the 1570s assizes were being held in some of the Leinster counties, and in the 1590s assizes were held in Cavan, Monaghan, Down and Cavan. The establishment of presidency courts for Munster and Connacht in 1569 created separate provincial systems of courts for those areas. However, it was not until after 1603 that a system of assize circuits covering the remainder of the country was established.[116] Whilst the length of the circuits fluctuated depending upon the conditions of the time, they could occupy considerable periods of time. In the summer of 1613 Serjeant Beare spent 68 days on circuit in Munster, and in 1615, having spent 50 days on assize earlier in the year, starting on 11 July he spent a further 42 days in 'Longford, Leitrim and other counties'.[117] Whilst these may have been unusually long circuits, as the country was divided into five circuits (six from 1796 when the Home Circuit consisting of Counties Meath, Westmeath, Kildare, Carlow, Queen's County and King's County was created), each of which visited by two judges twice a year, circuits could last for several weeks at a time. It was usual for barristers who wished to go on circuit to attach themselves to a circuit with which they had some family or other connection. For example, W.C. Plunket joined the North West Circuit as it included Enniskillen, the place of his birth,[118] while John Scott (subsequently Lord Clonmell, chief justice of the king's bench), Hugh Carleton (later Viscount Carleton, chief justice of the common pleas), and Barry Yelverton, (later Lord Avonmore, chief baron of the exchequer), all of whom were natives of Munster, chose the Munster Circuit.[119]

Given that each circuit covered several counties, and that the judges and the Bar travelled together from assize town to assize town, members of each circuit would spend a great deal of time in each others company, and as a result each circuit developed a spirit of camaraderie amongst its members that it is difficult to envisage today. It is not known whether each circuit had its own rules and code of conduct prior to the nineteenth century as no records of the circuits of that time have survived. Nevertheless, as we shall see in the next chapter, it is likely that some, albeit rudimentary, rules were developed by each

---

116 J. McCavitt, "'Good planets in their several spheares'-the establishment of the assize circuits in early seventeenth-century Ireland", *Ir. Jur.* xxiv (1989), 249 and 254.
117 Hart, *The king's serjeants at law in Ireland*, p. 50.
118 D. Plunket, *Life and speeches of Lord Plunket*, I, p. 59.
119 O'Flanagan, *The Munster Circuit*, p. 105.

circuit. In 1904 the Connaught Bar was able to publish a list of its members from 1604, using the old circuit books (which were therefore presumably still in existence at that time) and Burke's *Anecdotes of the Connaught Circuit*, also contained a list of members from the same date, although it recognised that the list was not complete. The existence of records of this type would suggest that there was some form of society of members of the Bar in existence on that circuit before the nineteenth century.[120]

Before improvements in the roads meant that carriages could be used the judges and the Bar travelled together around each circuit on horseback, as much for safety as for pleasure. The judges would be met at the county boundary by the high sheriff, and members of the grand jury and others would ride out to welcome the party some miles from the assize town. The spectacle described in the following passage from the *Anecdotes of the Connaught Circuit* would have been a familiar sight throughout Ireland.

> The holsters in front of the saddle were filled with loaded pistols, the outside coat was strapped in a roll behind, while the dragoon-like regularity of pace at which they advanced gave the party a certain military appearance. The servants followed, mounted like their masters, and watchful of the saddle-bags, which, containing the Circuit wardrobe and Circuit library, dangled from their horses' flanks. A posse of fellows too, well-mounted, bearing wine and other luxuries, followed close behind. At the head of the nomadic caravan rode the High Sheriff of the county with his halberdmen, armed with javelins, which they grasped in the centre, while a troop of horse brought up the rear.[121]

When the roads improved and the use of carriages, both public and private, became common, it appears to have been the rule, at least on the Connaught Circuit, that members of the Bar were prevented by professional etiquette from travelling in a public coach lest they come in contact with attorneys or witnesses, and as a result unless a barrister could afford his own carriage, or share the expense of one with his colleagues, he might have to walk from assize town to assize town,[122] and as we shall see in Chapter Three impecunious barristers still did so on occasion at the beginning of the

---

120 O.J. Burke, *Anecdotes of the Connaught Circuit from its foundation in 1604 to close upon the present time* (Dublin, 1885), xv–xxiv. R.J. Kelly; 'The Connaught Bar from 1604 to 1904', *Journal of the Galway Archaeological and Historical Society*, Vol iv (1905), pp 51-54.
121 Burke, *Anecdotes of the Connaught Circuit*, p. 135.
122 Ibid., p. 222.

twentieth century. In these circumstances there was a need to transport luggage around the circuit, and the Connaught and North East Circuits purchased wagons for this purpose, and it was not until 1836 that the North East Circuit finally disposed of its wagon.[123]

The assizes were the occasion of great social, as well as legal, activity, the town crowded with parties, witnesses and jurors. As quarter sessions (other than in Co. Dublin) had a very limited criminal jurisdiction, the result was that the bulk of criminal business was dealt with at the assizes, and a significant proportion of the cases were comparatively trivial offences, such as assault and trespass.[124] Much of the time of the judges was devoted to dealing with civil business. Writs (known as records) were tried on circuit, but a great deal of the civil business took the form of civil bills, often for small sums. These were dealt with in huge numbers, in 1760 Chief Baron Willes wrote that 2300 were heard on the Munster Circuit,[125] and on the North West Circuit of the same year 1529 were entered, and decrees or other orders were made in 1124 cases.[126] Whilst the fees charged by the judges on each process represented a considerable source of income for them, the number of cases was so great that the judges could not possibly deal properly with them, and eventually in 1796 parliament stepped in to remedy the situation by transferring civil bill business to quarter sessions, where the judicial post of assistant barrister had been created in 1787 to improve the administration of criminal business. An assistant barrister was appointed for each county, and the position was the direct predecessor of the modern county court judge.[127]

The great volume of business did not, however, mean that the assizes were lucrative occasions for the Bar because counsel's fees were beyond the means of many defendants and litigants, and it would seem unlikely that counsel were retained in more than a small minority of civil bills. Thus, in the six counties of the North East Circuit in the Lent Assizes of 1760 counsel were engaged in only 112 out of 959 civil bills in which decrees

---

123 Hill Smith, *The North East Bar*, p. 29.
124 N. Garham, *The courts, crime and the criminal law in Ireland, 1692-1760* (Dublin, 1996), p. 80.
125 J. Kelly, *The letters of Lord Chief Baron Edward Willes to the earl of Warwick, 1757-1762* , p. 73.
126 Hart, *The king's serjeants at law in Ireland*, pp. 76-77. The definitive account of the development of the civil bill is to be found in D.S. Greer, 'The development of civil bill procedure' in J. McEldowney and P. O'Higgins (ed.), *The common law tradition: essays in Irish legal history* (Dublin, 1990).
127 36 Geo. III, c. 25 (Ir.). Greer, 'The development of civil bill procedure', pp 53-54.

were made.[128] Counsel were competing for whatever briefs were available, Chief Baron Willes saying that many more counsel went on circuit than the available business would suggest were necessary. In most venues there were more than 12, and, in some cases, more than 20, counsel present, with six going round the entire circuit.[129]

---

128 Greer, 'The development of civil bill procedure', p. 57. The counties were Louth, Down, Antrim, Armagh, Monaghan and Meath.
129 Edward Willes, 'Miscellaneous observations on Ireland, 1750–60', p. 10.

# CHAPTER TWO:

# The Irish Bar from the Act of Union to 1921

The Act of Union of 1800 did not formally affect the legal system in Ireland, although an immediate and significant consequence was that there were fewer barristers in the House of Commons at Westminster than at College Green because there were fewer constituencies. Apart from this the Irish Bar and legal system continued unchanged for some time. However, as the nineteenth century progressed there were significant changes in the legal system which affected the Bar.

The first was in legal education. As we have seen in the previous chapter, by the eighteenth century there was nothing in the way of a structured or formal system of legal education which members of the Bar had to undergo before they were called, and it was not until the 1830s that there were signs of any change. Until then, an aspiring barrister was still required to join one of the Inns of Court in London after joining King's Inns, but it was still the case that he was left entirely to his own devices to acquire any legal knowledge. In the words of the House of Commons select committee on legal education in England and Ireland which reported in 1846

> …it may therefore be asserted, as a general fact to which there are very few exceptions, that the student, professional and unprofessional, is left almost solely to his own individual exertions, industry, and opportunities, and that no Legal Education, worthy of the name, is at this moment to be had in either country.[1]

This damning assessment of both university and professional legal education was well deserved. Unfortunately, as we shall see, it was some years before the situation was improved in any way. The 1846 select committee was set up in the aftermath of the demise of the Dublin Law Institute, a pioneering attempt by Tristram Kennedy to provide a systematic and comprehensive course of professional legal education. Before describing Kennedy's efforts, it is appropriate to describe what an aspiring barrister had to do before he

---

1 *Report from the select committee on legal education, together with the minutes of evidence, 1846*, H.C. 1846 (686), x, lvi.

could be called to the Irish Bar in the early Victorian era.

First of all, he had to enrol as a student of King's Inns and pay the necessary fee of £16 5s. 4d, as well as stamp duty of £25.[2] On admission he had to state whether he intended to commence his studies at King's Inns immediately, or 'repair to one of the Inns of Court in England for the space of time required by law'.[3] He was now required to keep eight terms in London, and nine terms at King's Inns.[4] The requirement to keep terms in London meant that a student had to dine for three nights in each term, and some satisfied this requirement by going over only to dine. Whilst this meant that it was possible to avoid the expense of living in London, for example, by keeping the last three days of the Easter Term and the first three days of the Trinity Term, thereby keeping two terms in about three weeks,[5] nevertheless the expense of travelling to London to keep terms was considerable, even though it was common for terms to be kept by proxy, that is getting someone to dine in one's place.[6] In addition, if the Irish student did not have a degree, it was apparently necessary to deposit 100 guineas with the Inn he wished to join in London.[7]

Students were left to their own devices to acquire some legal instruction. They could read and study privately, but in the absence of guidance as to what books to read this was difficult. An alternative was to go into the chambers of a practitioner, but it was apparently not very common for Irish students to go into chambers of a conveyancer or a special pleader in England.[8] Two who did were Joseph Napier, a pupil of John Patteson, and James Whiteside, who was a pupil of Joseph Chitty.[9] Even if a student sought to acquire instruction in this way it was not without its disadvantages. First of all, the customary fee for a year was 100 guineas,[10] together with the expense of living in London. Secondly, differences between English and Irish statutes and forms of pleading could lead the student into error

---

2    *Sel. comm. leg. ed.*, q. 2269.
3    Rules of the King's Inns, Rule X, quoted in Hogan, *The legal profession in Ireland*, p. 32.
4    C. Kenny, *Tristram Kennedy and the revival of Irish legal training, 1835-1885*, (Dublin, 1986) pp 192-93.
5    *Sel. comm. leg. ed.*, q. 1612.
6    Ibid., q. 1600.
7    Ibid., q. 1641. The figure of £100 was also given, see q. 1639.
8    Ibid., q. 1880.
9    *ODNB*. For details of their careers see below.
10   *Sel. Comm. Leg. ed.*, q. 1647.

when he embarked on practice in Ireland.[11] In any event, pupils did not usually receive much attention from their masters, and, as Sir John Baker has observed, 'The general character of pupillage seems, however, to have been little more than self-help pursued on the edge of real practice'.[12]

However, even if a student wished to prepare himself by studying in Dublin, there were few barristers who were prepared to take pupils. Giving evidence to the select committee in 1846, J.A. Lawson, who had a brilliant academic career at Trinity College, Dublin, where he was at the time professor of political economy, and who was later to be a judge of the common pleas and then of the queen's bench,[13] described how a student could gain some knowledge of the law.

> Then there are no facilities in Dublin for going into a lawyer's chambers, for there are, I may say, scarcely any; there are only two or three barristers who take pupils, and the course usually adopted by law students is to try and supply some instruction for themselves. The course that is adopted, is to go to a barrister in practice, with whom you are acquainted, and to work in his chambers for him, for instance, and make yourself as useful as you can, and by that means gather up a knowledge of your profession; of course there is no remuneration, and therefore with respect to a barrister, unless he is a friend of yours, there is very little inducement to him to take the trouble of instructing you, which he must do for some time, before you are of any use to him.
>
> 1881. Was it not the case with the late Master of the Rolls, Mr O'Loghlen; did he not attend Mr O'Connell's instruction for a period? –Yes; and almost all the students who have a friend at the bar, who will take the trouble with them, and who are anxious to proceed and avail themselves of that mode, do so; it is almost the only mode that they can take.
>
> 1882. Is it not the habit in Ireland, as it respects chambers, on the part of barristers, that they have not chambers separate in their own houses? They have not; they do business in their own houses.[14]

In his evidence, Michael Barry said that he only knew of three who would

---

11   Ibid., q. 1663 and q. 1880.
12   Sir John Baker, *Legal Education in London 1250-1850* (Selden Society, 2007), p. 24.
13   For Lawson's career, see Ball, *Judges* ii, 367-68.
14   *Sel. comm. leg. ed.*, q. 1880 *et seq.*

take pupils, although they would have three to five.[15]

It was in an effort to remedy this deplorable state of affairs that Tristram Kennedy opened the Dublin Law Institute in 1839. The story of Kennedy's ultimately unsuccessful efforts to provide a comprehensive system of professional legal education in Ireland has been told elsewhere by Dr Kenny,[16] and it is only necessary to refer briefly to it here. Having been apprenticed to, and then admitted as, an attorney in 1826, Kennedy was called to the Irish Bar in 1834. He therefore had recent experience of preparing himself for entry into both branches of the profession. In the autumn of 1839 his prospectus to establish a Dublin Law School, or 'Institute' as it soon came to be known, announced that 'the great purpose of the course proposed is to elevate the standard of professional knowledge, to cultivate diligence and provide for regular and permanent benefits by a system more intended for utility than display'.

Courses were initially provided in common law, equity, real property, conveyancing and medical jurisprudence; introductory lectures in criminal law and nisi prius practice were also given, as well as occasional lectures in the law of master and servant, and in procedure. The lecturers included a future lord chancellor (Napier) and chief justice of the queen's bench (Whiteside),[17] and the lectures in medical jurisprudence were given by Thomas Brady, a doctor and professor in the College of Physicians. Despite the obvious need for such instruction to provide intending barristers with some grasp of the principles of their intended profession (Napier was to tell the select committee that total ignorance of criminal law was professionally quite acceptable as the criminal law was held in so little regard by practitioners), the courses were not particularly well supported. This was hardly surprising as there was no requirement by King's Inns that students attend, and so attendance was entirely voluntary. Despite

---

15  Ibid., q. 1650-55.
16  Kenny, *Tristram Kennedy and the revival of Irish legal training,* and 'Adventures in training-the Irish genesis of the 'remarkable and far-sighted' Select Committee on legal education, 1846' in P. Brand, K. Costello and W. N. Osborough, (ed.) *Adventures of the Law-proceedings of the sixteenth British Legal History Conference 2003,* (Dublin, 2005). The passage in the text is based upon Dr. Kenny's work.
17  Joseph Napier (1804-1882). Called 1831, joined NE Circuit 1832, QC 1844, MP (C) Dublin Univ 1848-1859, AG 1852, C 1858-59. James Whiteside (1806-1876). Brother in law of Napier. Called 1830, joined Connaught Circuit but transferred to NE Circuit 1833. QC 1841, MP (C) Enniskillen 1851-1859, Dublin Univ 1859-1866. SG 1852, AG 1858-59, 1866, CJQB 1866-1876. Ball, *Judges,* ii, pp. 361-62 (Napier) and 364-65 (Whiteside), both in *ODNB.*

support from a wide cross-section of the Bar, of members of parliament and the press, the Institute only received modest financial support from the benchers of King's Inns, and Kennedy was unable to gain the support of the government or the heads of the judiciary. This, and the hostility shown by the solicitors' profession whom Kennedy had neglected to cultivate, meant that despite widespread initial support for the Institute and the lectures delivered there, it was unable to continue and develop without funding from King's Inns, which was not prepared to continue its modest initial grant. The Institute closed in 1842, although it briefly resumed operation in 1845, and a further, unsuccessful, attempt was made to revive it in 1846.

However, Kennedy's visionary efforts were not entirely wasted. He had a significant ally in Thomas Wyse MP, who drew upon the experience of the Dublin Law Institute when he moved in the House of Commons in April 1846 for the appointment of a select committee to enquire into the state of legal education in Ireland, and how it might be improved and extended. The motion was passed, and soon afterwards its terms of reference were extended to include the state of legal education in England. The select committee's report, which has already been referred to, no doubt played a major part in persuading the benchers of King's Inns that they had to respond to the criticism levelled at them for their failure to provide any system of instruction whatever for entry into what was regarded as a learned profession.

In 1850 King's Inns established a school of legal education and appointed two professors. At the same time, partly because of an approach from the benchers that they should cooperate in setting up an effective school of law, Trinity College reorganised its courses and raised the qualifications for its two professors.[18] Henceforth students of King's Inns had to attend lectures at four courses over three years, two of the courses being provided at Trinity (one on civil law and general jurisprudence, the other on equity and real property), and two at King's Inns (one on constitutional and criminal law, the other on personal property, pleading, practice and evidence), although attendance at all four was only compulsory for non-graduates, and there were no examinations. A voluntary final examination was introduced in 1864, although, following the example of the English inns of court, those who sat the examination were not obliged to attend the lectures, and attendance

18   R.B. McDowell & D.A. Webb, *Trinity College Dublin 1592-1952 an academic history* (Dublin, 2004), p. 193.

predictably declined. However, attendance at lectures and sitting the final examination were both made compulsory in 1872. As Dr Kenny points out, as graduates of a chartered university need only attend two of the four courses and could do so in two, rather than three, years, and only had to keep six terms at King's Inns and six in London, whereas non-graduates had to keep nine and eight respectively, this was 'a modest incentive to attend university'. Nevertheless, it represented a sea change in the provision of professional legal education in Ireland. Not only did the new system introduced in 1850 predate similar changes in England by two years, but it involved a longer period of study and the attendance at lectures was compulsory in part. In its final form the scheme was in advance of that in England as it involved a link with a university law school and made attendance at lectures compulsory, something that was not required in England.[19]

Important though these changes were, they did not address the continuing requirement to keep terms in one of the English Inns. There were several unsuccessful attempts in parliament to repeal the Statute of Jeofailles between 1842 and 1878, but it was not until the passing of the Barristers Admission (Ireland) Act, 1885[20] that the requirement that Bar students enrol at one of the English inns of court and keep terms there was removed. Whatever advantages by way of enabling Irish students 'to become familiar with the law of England and the manner and justice of its administration'[21] may have been derived from the requirement, it imposed considerable financial burdens on generations of students, and its removal was long overdue, particularly when King's Inns had instituted its own system of instruction for its students.

As has long been recognised, a system of post-call education is essential to supplement pre-call lectures and exercises. As Lawson pointed out to the select committee in 1846 in the passage quoted earlier, only a few members of the Irish Bar were prepared to take pupils, and so even when a system of lectures and examinations were put in place by King's Inns, most of those who wished to learn how to apply what they had been taught to the requirements of practice had no real means of doing so unless they underwent a period of pupillage after call. Some did enter into a formal arrangement

---

19  Kenny, *Tristram Kennedy and the revival of Irish legal training*, pp. 163-68 and 173-74.
20  48 &49 Vict., c.20. Kenny, *Tristram Kennedy and the revival of Irish legal training*, Ch. 9.
21  Lord Fitzgerald speaking in the second reading debate on the Barristers Admission (Ireland) Bill in the house of Lords in 1882, quoted in K. Ferguson (ed.) *King's Inns Barristers* (Dublin, 2005), p. 26.

with an experienced member of the junior Bar who, in return for a fee allowed his pupil or 'devil' to study his papers, draft opinions, accompany him to court and consultations, and generally make himself useful to his master. This would enable the pupil to learn the practical techniques of pleading and advocacy, although the latter might not always be achieved. When Edward Carson was called to the Bar in 1877, his master was George Price, an equity practitioner who, according to Carson's biographer, was tongue-tied in court, although his conveyances were works of art.[22] Other pupils of Price who were to achieve professional eminence were Charles O'Connor, later master of the rolls, and John Ross, later Mr Justice Ross and, as Sir John Ross, the last lord chancellor of Ireland.[23] Peter O'Brien, later lord chief justice and Lord O'Brien of Kilfenora, was the last pupil of Christopher Palles, later Chief Baron Palles, before Palles took silk in 1865.[24] However, although Ross said this was the usual practice, it was not always done, probably because the parents of the barrister could not afford the fee. In the 1870s the fee was 50 guineas, but it seems to have increased as Anthony Babington's father paid £100 to Robert Osborne,[25] and the pupillage in his case was for a year, although it continued on a voluntary basis after the year was up.[26] Judge John Adye Curran KC, writing in 1915, said that although his father was a member of the Bar, he could not afford the fee. However, for six months before his call in 1860, Curran was able to frequent the office of a successful solicitor who was a friend of his father, and so learned much of the practical work of the profession.[27] This would suggest that although pupillage was the custom, it was neither required nor always embarked upon. Presumably someone who, or more realistically, whose parents, could not afford the fee, and did not have such connections to fall back on, had to do what they could to pick up the elements of their profession by watching experienced practitioners in court, although the disadvantage might have been ameliorated by the tradition in the Law Library that anyone, however junior, could ask a member for advice, a request that was seldom, if ever, refused.[28] However, that such advice was

---

22  E. Marjoribanks, *The life of Lord Carson* (London, 1932) i, p. 23.

23  J. Ross, *The years of my pilgrimage* (London, 1924), p. 23.

24  V.T.H. Delaney, *Christopher Palles*, pp 107-08.

25  Sir Anthony Babington (1877-1972). Called 1900, KC 1917, attorney general for Northern Ireland 1925-37, knighted 1937, a lord justice of appeal 1937-49. *DIB*. Robert Osborne, (1861-1939). Called 1886, recorder of Londonderry 1919-37.

26  Sir Anthony Babington, *Personal Reminiscences* (1966), pp 31 and 34.

27  J.A. Curran, *Reminiscences of John Adye Curran KC*, (London, 1915), p. 9.

28  Ross, *The years of my pilgrimage*, p. 26, Marjoribanks, *The life of Lord Carson*, p. 22. A M. Sullivan, *Old Ireland reminiscences of an Irish KC* (London, 1927), p. 104.

readily available lead to suggestions that members of the Irish Bar did not receive as thorough a grounding in the law as their English contemporaries. In 1920 J.A. Strahan commented dismissively upon the tradition.

> Moreover, the ease with which difficulties can be overcome without study makes some men rely on so overcoming them; and so what at the beginning is a great help becomes in the end a great hindrance. If many an Irish barrister long in practice is not a sound lawyer, he has often to thank for that the assistance which at first enabled him to do his work without learning his law.[29]

Although born in Carrickfergus and a graduate of Queen's College, Belfast where he was Professor of Jurisprudence and Roman Law from 1909 until 1926 (by which time it had become The Queen's University of Belfast), Strahan was not a member of the Irish Bar, having been called to the English Bar in 1883, where he enjoyed a distinguished academic law career.[30] It might therefore be thought that his criticism could not be grounded in experience, despite his teaching experience at Queen's. Nevertheless, Strahan's criticism was echoed by Babington, who recalled that Sir Denis Henry[31] said that the 'general run of English barristers were much better instructed, as they practised by the book, whereas the Irish practised by ear'. Babington continued

> There is more than [a] grain of truth in this, for our Library system has compelled all barristers to work together in the same room, and makes it easy for a young man to walk across the floor and ask some acknowledged expert for his opinion on the problem he is wrestling with and the help is rarely refused. This is a practice to be avoided by every young barrister and should never be resorted to at any rate until the books have all been exhausted and the answer still eludes the student.[32]

The nineteenth century saw the development of the Law Library, a distinctive feature of the Irish Bar (although one shared by the Scots Bar with its Advocates' Library) whereby members of the Bar practised not

---

29   'The bench and bar of Ireland' in *Blackwood's Edinburgh Magazine*, January 1920, p. 98.
30   (1858-1930), Reader in Equity at the Inns of Court 1897-1929, and author of several legal textbooks (including *The Law of property*, which ran to several editions and for which J.S. Baxter wrote an Irish section, a work that was for many years relied upon by Irish students and practitioners). For an account of Strahan's career see *The Nabob, a tale of Ninety Eight*, (Dublin, 2006), pp 164-69.
31   Denis Stanislaus Henry (1864-1925). Lord chief justice of Northern Ireland 1921-25.
32   Babington, *Reminiscences*, p. 218.

from chambers, but from their homes and a common library to which they subscribed, and at which they could be found daily when the courts were sitting, unless of course they were absent on circuit, and around which the Bar came to be centred. As has been noted in the previous chapter, no provision had been made in the new Four Courts for communal accommodation for the Bar, other than a robing room. Although a library was created in the King' Inns, partly as a result of King's Inns being a copyright library between 1801 and 1836, and thus entitled to a copy of every book published in the United Kingdom free of charge,[33] in the early years of the nineteenth century the books were not readily available until the present library in Henrietta Street was completed in 1830. Before 1830 the books were originally stored in double-locked deed boxes in the basement of the courts, and thereafter in wooden sheds, with some in what is now the Benchers' Room in King's Inns, until the library was completed.[34] As the benchers accepted in 1822, there was no catalogue for the books and 'there are large parcels of miscellaneous books upon the floor and heaped upon each other for want of room'.[35]

There was therefore an obvious need for practitioners to have ready access to law books in the Four Courts themselves. Serjeant Sullivan[36] set out what was generally believed to be the origin of the Law Library.

> An enterprising merchant bought a law library, put it on movable stalls, and set it up daily on the quay opposite the courts. Hence books could be hired when wanted for a shilling or sixpence. This was such a convenience that a committee of the bar fitted up a small unused room, in the building, let the huckster ply his trade there, and on his death bought his books and carried on the business for the bar. Larger apartments were given by the authorities as the library and its subscribers increased until the system developed with all its delightful consequences.37

The same tradition was recorded by Lord Shandon, formerly Sir Ignatius

---

33  C. Kenny, *King's Inns and the battle of the books*, 1972- *cultural controversy at a Dublin library*, (Dublin, 2002), pp 23-24.

34  D. Hogan, *The Honorable Society of King's Inns* (Dublin, 1987), pp 17-18.

35  Minutes of Benchers, 16 June 1822, quoted in Hogan, *The legal profession in Ireland*, 1789- 1922, p. 26.

36  Alexander Martin Sullivan (1871-1959). The last surviving king's serjeant at law in Ireland. See Hart, *The king's serjeants at law in Ireland*, p. 182. *ODNB*. *DIB*.

37  Sullivan, *Old Ireland*, p. 105.

O'Brien lord chancellor.[38] However, as Hogan has pointed out, whilst there may be an element of truth in this story, it is not wholly accurate.[39] In his evidence to the 1846 select committee on legal education, Acheson Lyle, by then a bencher and second remembrancer, gave a somewhat different account of the origins of the library. He said that it was in being when he was called in 1818, and he thought that it had not been in existence for many years before that. Lyle described the library in 1818 as being 'a small octagonal room that I do not think was more than 14 or 15 feet, certainly not more than 22 feet across, in one of the angles of the building at the Four Courts'.[40] The library appears to have been in existence in 1813 as it appears on a plan of that year.[41]

It seems that before 1816 one Valentine Delaney had provided a library at his own expense, because at a general meeting 'of the subscribers to the Law Library in the Four Courts' held on 17 February 1816 a committee was appointed to purchase 'such of the books in the present Law Library as they think proper at a fair valuation', and that Delaney 'be continued as Librarian at a salary of £80 a year'. The committee was to 'manage the affairs of the Subscribers at large'.[42] The committee brought forward regulations at a further meeting of the Subscribers on 11 May 1816 providing for the management of the Society and the employment conditions of the librarian. It would seem that the existing accommodation of the Library was inadequate, the committee suggesting that 'an application being made to the benchers for the purpose of obtaining for the Establishment of a large and more commodious apartment than the present one',[43] and as the Bar grew in size the room soon proved to be too small, although requests made to the benchers in 1818 and 1822 for a larger room were rejected. By 1820 there were 236 subscribers, and in 1826 the Law Library Society minutes

---

38   *The reminiscences of Lord Shandon*, p. 110. Ignatius O'Brien (1857-1930). Called 1881, 1881, QC 1899, second serjeant 1911, SG 1911-12, AG 1912-13, C 1913-18. Created a baronet 1916, and Baron Shandon 1918. Ball, *Judges*, ii, 383. Described as 'a person of no significance either as a lawyer or a politician', O'Brien suffered the humiliation of being told by Lord Birkenhead LC that he could not sit as a law lord as the others would refuse to sit with him. R.F.V. Huston, 'Legal history and the author: some practical problems of authorship' in W.N. Osborough, (ed.) *The Irish Legal History Society: Inaugural Addresses*, Dublin, 1989), pp 28-30. *ODNB.*

39   Hogan, *The legal profession in Ireland*, p. 55.

40   *Sel. comm. leg. ed.*, q. 2245-48.

41   A copy of the plan is to be found in *King's Inns Barristers*, p. 56.

42   Law Library Minute Book 1816-36.

43   Ibid.

refer to a new building having been built for the Society by the benchers. The number of subscribers continued to grow, and there were 427 by 1832,[44] and a further request that year for additional accommodation was more sympathetically received,[45] and plans were put in hand to build a new library as part of a larger scheme to provide new rolls and nisi prius courts. The new library was completed in 1838, by which time the numbers had increased still further. In 1835 there were 650 subscribers,[46] and at a general meeting at the end of 1840 it was noted that 'the number of subscribers now on the list exceeds six hundred, and there has been expended since the foundation in the purchase and binding of Law Books a sum of £3400'.[47]

The new Law Library was a large, handsome room in three bays with a gallery on each side top-lit by three large domes. Serjeant Sullivan described it as a 'wonderful place. The main room was about 60 feet long and 30 feet wide'.[48] The original room was retained, and another octagonal room and two other rooms were secured, as can be seen from a plan included in the 4th Annual Report of Public Works, Ireland, 1836. Unfortunately it seems that no photographs of the 1838 Law Library have survived, but Carson's biography contains a vivid description.

> The main room was rectangular, with narrow galleries round the sides, under which were the bookshelves, a small octagonal room at each corner [in fact two of the rooms were square], and another room, the 'Long Room', running at right angles and opening off one side. The entrance used was through one of the small rooms, which became an ante-room in which solicitors and their clerks could speak to counsel. The barristers sat on forms at long desks, or at the 'Round Table', a large table in the centre of the main room and opposite the chief fireplace (where twelve men sat), or at small round tables or separate desks in the corner rooms, or occupied any other available space. The accommodation was quite insufficient for the number requiring it, and the Bar were packed like children in a poor school of the bad old days, but with far more discomfort than would now be tolerated in such a place. But it will easily be seen that at such close quarters the members of the Bar were a much closer association than their brethren in London, that jealousy and backbiting were so uncomfortable as to

---

44  Ibid, 12 Jan. 1832.
45  Hogan, *The legal profession in Ireland*, pp 55-56.
46  Law Library Minute Book 1816-36, 26 Nov. 1835.
47  Law Library Treasurer's Accounts 1837-43, meeting of 9 Dec. 1840.
48  Sullivan, *The last serjeant*, (London, 1952), p. 24.

become really impossible, and that friendship and good-fellowship were not only general but necessary in such conditions.[49]

In the event, the 1838 Library proved inadequate in size and facilities, and although efforts were made from time to time to have the facilities improved, it was not until 1894 that these efforts were successful. The Four Courts Library Act[50] of that year provided that the Library should be enlarged and altered, and the accommodation, furnishings and fittings improved, £15000 from the unclaimed suitors fund being used for this purpose. The work was completed in 1897, although surprisingly a year later it was found necessary to replace much of the gallery floor when it was found to be in a dangerous condition.[51] The new Law Library consisted of the two top floors of the east wing of the Four Courts and was a large and impressive structure, with three large stained glass windows at the east end. Along both sides were alcoves with books from floor to ceiling, with the galleries reached by two fine staircases below the windows. As in the 1838 Library members sat at long desks, with the desks protruding from the alcoves and forming a central aisle.[52]

Until the Four Courts, were destroyed in June 1922[53] this was not just the physical home of the Irish Bar, but the environment that did much to create its unique character, consolidating the sense of camaraderie fostered by the enforced fellowship involved in going on circuit. Reminiscences and memoirs of the period contain many passages where the Library was fondly recalled. It was sometimes referred to as a club, Judge Bodkin, a former MP, describing it as the best club in Europe, the House of Commons being second-best.[54] Serjeant Sullivan defined its camaraderie somewhat differently.

> It was not the life of a club. No self-respecting club would permit the familiarity
> with which strange young juniors treated grave old seniors around the fireplace
> of the Law Library. At a club a man may keep to himself. At the Irish Bar life
> would have been intolerable to any man who did not school himself to accept

49  Majoribanks, *The life of Lord Carson*, p. 19.
50  57 and 58 Vict. (1894) c. 4.
51  *ILT&SJ*, xxxii, (1898), p. 256.
52  Babington's description in S.C. L/23.
53  Ronan Keane, 'A mass of crumbling ruins: the destruction of the Four Courts in June 1922' in C. Costello, (ed.) *The Four Courts: 200 years*, p. 159
54  M. McDonnell Bodkin (1850-1933). Called 1877, QC 1894, MP (N) 1892-95. County court judge for Clare, 1907-24. *Recollections of an Irish Judge* (London, 1914), p. 86.

in good humour the free and witty criticism of himself that was levelled at him sometimes with malicious candour during the gossip of the lunch hour. The most popular were addressed by their Christian names, unless they had nicknames. The men in active practice lived on terms of personal intimacy. Promotion to the bench could not break the habits formed by years, and judges continued to be spoken of (though not addressed in court) by the courtesy titles that they had borne among their brethren before promotion. Whatever personal antipathies existed, to manifest them before the other members of the profession brought down upon the offender such punishment of incessant ridicule, that the few foes who were amongst us, had to behave as friends.[55]

Sullivan, although an old friend and journalistic colleague of Bodkin, unsuccessfully tried to have his appointment as a county court judge quashed on the basis that Bodkin had not been in active practice, having been an active journalist and not in practice at the Bar.[56] An example of the mordant humour so characteristic of the Library was Tim Healy's[57] comment to D.M. Wilson when Bodkin was occasionally attending the Library before his appointment to show that he was in active practice by being available to take a brief. Bodkin had an unusual cough, and hearing it one day Healy said to Wilson, 'What county court judge is dead now'? Wilson replied, 'Why do you ask that'? Healy replied in sepulchral tones, 'I hear the cough of the Banshee'.[58]

It was into this atmosphere that a new barrister made his entrance, having been called in open court by the lord chancellor as chairman of the benchers of King's Inns. In the nineteenth century it was the custom of members of the Bar to don their wigs and gowns on arrival at the Four Courts, and wear them throughout the day, whether appearing in court or working in the Library. Serjeant Sullivan claimed that a century before the Irish barrister robed at home and then walked or drove in his wig and gown to the Four Courts, his uniform being a protection against arrest for debt until imprisonment for debt was abolished in 1870.[59] Because of their exclusive right of audience in

---

55  Sullivan, *Old Ireland*, pp 103-04.
56  Ibid. pp 153-55. Sullivan's nephew, Maurice Healy gives an amusing account of the proceedings in his *The Old Munster Circuit*, (3rd impression, London and Dublin, 1948), pp 174-182. Adams courageously remained in post in Co. Clare until his retirement in 1924, despite being in great danger.
57  Timothy Healy (1855-1931), journalist, parliamentarian and major political figure, first governor general of the Irish Free State, 1922-28. Called 1884, QC 1889, treasurer of Gray's Inn 1929. *ODNB*.
58  Babington, *Reminiscences*, p. 78.
59  Ibid., p. 105.

the superior courts and on assize barristers were immune from arrest when going to and from court to ensure that their clients' cases could be heard,[60] and several cases where the privilege was successfully claimed are to be found in the Irish law reports.[61] Whilst there may be an element of truth in Sullivan's claim, it is more likely that the practice stemmed from the period before the opening of the 1838 Library when counsel were to be found in the Round Hall of the Four Courts when they were in not in one of the courts. Everyone who had business in the courts and many who did not, resorted to the Hall, which was thronged with large numbers of witnesses, jurors, litigants and attorneys. In his 'Hall of the Four Courts' published in the 1820s Richard Lawlor Sheil described how, in what appeared at first to be a scene of inextricable confusion, the leading counsel of the day would be found near the entrance of the court into which they were shortly to be called to attend to their cases, whilst around the Hall would be gathered groups of junior counsel, some employed, many more hoping that their turn would come as they 'trudge the Hall'.[62] In such a melee wig and gown were essential to allow members of the Bar to be identified, and for the recently called to advertise themselves to attorneys and show that they were available to be briefed.[63]

For the new barrister to make a start in his profession was notoriously difficult if he did not possess family or other connections amongst the solicitors' profession, and the lean years that most suffered were a familiar theme in memoirs of the time. The difficulty was often thought to be exacerbated in Ireland by the large numbers of barristers. In his *Sketch* referred to above, Sheil commented upon the 'enormous excess they bear to the professional occupation which the country can by possibility afford'.[64] Throughout the 121 years from the Act of Union of 1800 to the Government of Ireland Act of 1920 the number of those called to the Irish Bar remained reasonably constant at around 30 a year, although there were fluctuations from time to time. Compared to an average call of just over 20 per year between 1800

---

60  Pigot CB in *Dubois v Wyse* 5 Ir. Comm. Law Rep. 300.
61  See the cases collected in T. Brunker, *Digest of cases in the courts of common law in Ireland*, (Dublin, 1865), pp 254-55.
62  *Sketches of the Irish Bar*, (edited by R.S. Mackenzie, New York, 1854), i, 58-59. Richard Lalor Sheil (1793-1851). Called, 1814. Went the Leinster Circuit. QC 1830. With William Henry Curran, son of John Philpott Curran, published the *Sketches* between 1822 and 1829. MP 1831-50. In his early political career Sheil was a close associate of Daniel O'Connell, but later held various posts in Whig governments, and was appointed ambassador to Florence in 1850, where he died. *ODNB*.
63  Bodkin, *Recollections*, p. 85.
64  Sheil, *Sketches of the Irish Bar*, i, 62.

and 1810, the 20 years from 1831 to 1850 saw an average of 67.6 between 1831 and 1840, and 48.5 between 1841 and 1850.[65] The fluctuations in the late 1830s and early 1840s were particularly marked, with 97 being called in 1838 and 1839, 107 in 1840, but only 43 in 1844.[66] Not all of those called intended to practise, and it is very difficult to estimate how many barristers were in active practice because the almanacs continued to list those who had ceased practice, and many of those who were still nominally practising did not actively do so, either because they had private means or because they were earning a living elsewhere. Reference has already been made to the number thought to be practising at the Irish Bar at the time of the Union, and we have seen how the number of the subscribers to the Law Library Society increased from its foundation in 1816. It can safely be presumed that virtually all, if not all, those who held themselves out to practise were subscribers to the Library Society, and that the records of the Society provide an accurate indication of the numbers at the Irish Bar.

The number in practice appears to have declined from 1850 onwards. Although the Law Library Society Minute Book survived the burning of the Four Courts, it was extensively damaged by fire and has not been examined by the author because it is in such a fragile state. Writing to the *Times* in 1868, Denis Caulfield Heron said that whereas in 1850 there were 690 subscribers to the Law Library, for the last few years it had been about 427.[67] It seems likely that the number at the Bar remained at about this level until the end of the nineteenth century, and that there was then a small rise to 447 subscribers in 1910, but a dramatic fall by 1920, as can be seen from the figures extracted from the *Annual Balance Account Law Library* set out below. It also appears that there was a high level of natural wastage as the overall number of subscribers remained relatively stable despite the number of new calls paying entrance fees.

|      | Subscribers | Entrance Fees |
|------|-------------|---------------|
| 1890 | 431         | 23            |
| 1891 | 425         | 23            |
| 1892 | 424         | 26            |
| 1893 | 418         | 25            |
| 1900 | 441         | 23            |
| 1910 | 447         | 33            |
| 1920 | 330         | 10            |

65  Hogan, *The legal profession in Ireland*, Table 1, p. 163.
66  *Sel. comm.* leg. ed., q. 2271.
67  Quoted in *King's Inns barristers*, p. 117.

Sullivan, referring to the Library of the pre First World War era, said that there were about 270 subscribers, with seating for about 70.[68] In 1910 *Thom's Directory* gives a total membership of 315 for all five circuits, and it has to be borne in mind that there were a number of practitioners who did not join a circuit, and that not all members of the Library were still in active practice. Writing in 1966, Babington recalled an attendance of 200 to 300 members, and the same figure was given by Healy.[69] Whilst the recollections of Sullivan, Babington and Healy are significantly at variance with the subscriber figures given above and which are a more reliable, though not necessarily exact, indicator of the number of active practitioners, it is very difficult to identify with any degree of precision how many subscribers to the Law Library at any given time were in active practice. The most that can be said is that in the early years of the twentieth century the number of active practitioners was between 300 and 400, many who barely scraped a living, even if they kept up their modest subscription to the Library.

In 1856 the subscription had been fixed at one guinea,[70] and by the beginning of the twentieth century it had doubled to two guineas. In addition a fee of one guinea was due to the robing room, for which wig and gown were minded and mended when necessary, and clean bands left out each morning. If necessary robes were sent by parcel post to assizes or quarter sessions from the robing room, and could then be sent back by the same means.[71] If a barrister joined a circuit, then a subscription was payable on joining, fixed at two guineas in the case of the North East Circuit.[72] Although there was also the cost of going on circuit, given that members of the Irish Bar did not employ clerks and did not have to rent chambers, it was a remarkably economical way to practise a profession.

Each day during Term time members of the Bar went to the Library where they would be found between 10.30 am and 4.30 pm, unless they were in court. Consultations were usually held at night at the house of the leading counsel in the case, although by 1921 consultations at the courts had become more common. Brief bags were collected from their houses before 9 am in the morning and delivered to the Library, where they were to be found on their owner's desk by 10 am. The Library closed at 5 pm

---

68   Sullivan, *Old Ireland*, p. 93.
69   Babington, *Reminiscences*, p. 75. Healy, *The Old Munster Circuit*, p. 44.
70   Clancy, 'The Four Courts Building', pp 90–91. Healy, *The Old Munster Circuit*, p. 43.
71   Healy, *The Old Munster Circuit*, p. 4.
72   The laws and rules of the Society of the North East Bar (1875), rule 4.

when the bags were collected and returned to the owner's home an hour or so later in time for him to work on his papers that night.[73] Until the 1880s or thereabouts this task was performed by the 'bagwomen' who carried the bags on their backs or wheeled them in makeshift perambulators. Despite their dire poverty, these women were completely honest. However, some years after Carson's call in 1877 they were replaced by two horse-drawn vans known as the 'Legal Express'.[74]

The Library was far from being a tranquil place judging by the description contained in an article in the *Irish Law Times & Solicitors' Journal* in December 1893 by Michael Douthwaite.[75]

> The first thing to strike the visitor is the Babel of tongues, sufficient one would think, to make consultation difficult and work impossible. There is a throng of barristers running to and fro, some to seek places at the crowded, littered tables, others to search for missing bags or books, others in answer to the stentorian hale of the doorkeeper, who announces that a visitor seeks an interview....The outside world is not admitted here; the solicitor, though he be the bearer of a brief, must have his barrister summoned to him and adjourn to the Hall for further discussion.

A similar description of the din was given by Majoribanks, who said that 'the place seemed more like pandemonium than a place to work',[76] but a member of the Library soon learned to hear nothing in the noisy room but the sound of his own name.[77] The solicitor or his clerk would give the name of the counsel he sought to the doorkeeper, who would consult the list of the destination of all members leaving to go to court, such as the common pleas or the rolls. He would then shout out the name in a voice that carried through the hubbub to the farthest reaches of the Library, and if the member did not appear then the enquirer was directed to the appropriate court.[78] As juniors waited for the briefs to arrive, they would often sit in court and watch their experienced brethren in action, or walk

73  Clancy, 'The Four Courts Building', p. 104. Healy, *The Old Munster Circuit*, pp 46–47.
74  Marjoribanks, *The life of Lord Carson*, p. 21.
75  *ILT&SJ*, xxvii (1893), p. 653. Douthwaite was librarian to the King's Inns. C. Griffin, 'Post Gandon at the Four Courts', *The Four Courts: 200 years*, p. 237.
76  Marjoribanks, *The life of Lord Carson*, pp 20–21.
77  Sullivan, *Old Ireland*, p. 104.
78  Ibid.

about the Round Hall as their predecessors had done in Sheil's time. By the 1890s the scene in the Hall did not differ greatly from its appearance when Sheil described it seventy years before. Then it had been the resort of the political idlers of the town, who dropped by to pick up the rumours of the day, as well as being populated by from a throng of litigants and lawyers.[79] In 1893 it was still the market place of the litigant, but 'the man about town no longer comes there to give and receive a budget of news'.[80] However, the Hall was now ringed by six statues;[81] one of Sheil, the others being of Plunket,[82] O'Loghlen,[83] Joy,[84] Whiteside,[85] and O'Hagan.[86] No fewer than four of these were members of the North East or North West Circuits, Plunket being a member of the North West, whilst Joy, Whiteside and O'Hagan were members of the North East.

However, except for the fortunate few who had private means or for whom family connections or university friendships meant that some briefs soon arrived, it was necessary for the new barrister to find some means to support himself and advance his career. The opportunities for outside earnings were very limited, as teaching or writing in some form were the only other occupations permitted by professional etiquette.[87] Some dabbled

79   Sheil, *Sketches of the Irish Bar*, i, 59.
80   *ILT&SJ* xxvii (1893), p. 653.
81   C.P. Curran, 'Figures in the Hall', *The Four Courts: 200 years*, pp. 173-76.
82   William Conyngham Plunket (1764-1854). Called 1788. KC 1797. MP Charlemont 1797-1800. MP Midhurst 1807, and for Dublin Univ. 1812-27. SG 1803-05, AG 1807 and 1822-27. Created Baron Plunket 1827 as compensation for refusing the post of master of the rolls in England in the face of the hostility of the English Bar at the post being offered to a member of the Irish Bar. CJCP 1827-1830. Lord Chancellor of Ireland 1830-34, 1835-41. Ball, *Judges*, ii, 343-45. C. Kenny, 'Irish Ambition and English preference in chancery appointments, 1827-1841: the fate of William Conyngham Plunket' in W. N. Osborough (ed.) *Explorations in law and history* (Dublin, 1995), p. 133. *ODNB*.
83   Michael O'Loghlen, (1789-1842). Called 1811, KC 1830, third serjeant 1831-32, second serjeant 1832-34. SG 1834. MP (L) Dungarvan 1835-36. SG 1835, AG 1835-36. A baron of the exchequer 1836-37, master of the rolls 1837-42. Created a baronet 1838. Ball, *Judges*, ii, 349-50. *ODNB*.
84   Henry Joy (1763-1838). Son of Henry Joy, owner of the *Belfast Newsletter*. Called 1788, KC 1808, third serjeant 1814-16, second serjeant 1816-17 and first serjeant 1817-22. SG 1822-27, AG 1827-31, CB 1831-38. Ball, *Judges*, ii, 347.
85   See fn. 17 above.
86   Thomas O'Hagan, (1812-1885). Called 1836. QC 1849, second serjeant 1859-60, SG 1860- 61. AG 1861-65. MP (L) Tralee 1863-65. JCP 1865-68, Lord Chancellor 1868-74 and 1880-81. Created Baron O'Hagan 1870 and a knight of St. Patrick 1881. J.F. McEldowney, 'Lord O'Hagan (1812-1885): a study of his life and period as lord chancellor of Ireland (1868-1874)', *Ir Jur*, xiv, (1979), 360. *ODNB*.
87   Hogan, *The legal profession in Ireland*, pp 74 -75.

in journalism[88], others wrote reports of cases for newspapers. John Adye Curran wrote circuit reports for several newspapers, the accepted rate at the time being 10s and 6d.[89] At the end of the nineteenth century times were equally hard. W.E. Wylie[90] gave 'grinds' most evenings from 7 to 9.30 pm at three shillings an hour, as well as taking classes for honours exams at Trinity College, charging each student one shilling an hour.[91] This form of teaching may have been a frequent resort for struggling barristers. T.K. Overend, who was called in 1874, earned £75 for giving grinds in his first year, compared to £25 in professional fees.[92]

One way of becoming known, or of enhancing one's reputation, was to write a textbook. Some of these became established works, others enjoyed little or no success. Osborne's *County Courts practice in Ireland* first appeared in 1890 and became an established work, and Babington, who as we have seen had been Osborne's pupil, prepared the second edition in 1910.[93] Other members of the North East Circuit who published legal works included W.G. Huband,[94] and William Johnston, who with H.M. Fitzgibbon,[95] wrote *The Law of Local Government in Ireland* (1899). The law of workmen's compensation proved a fertile subject for members of the North East, with Henry Hanna, Thomas J. Campbell, and Samuel Porter publishing on the topic.[96] Hanna's book ran to a second edition, but S.S. Millin's digest of decisions on petty sessions failed to be reviewed in the *Irish Law Times &*

88  One who combined journalism with practice at the Bar was Bodkin, who became chief leader writer to the *Freeman's Journal* to supplement his income at the Bar after retiring from Parliament. *Recollections*, p. 244.

89  Fifty two and a half pence. *Reminiscences*, p. 39.

90  (1881-1964). Called 1905, KC 1914. Prosecuted in courts martial arising out of the 1916 Rebellion, judge of the Land Commission 1920-36, and of the High Court of the IFS. A leading figure in the Royal Dublin Society. *King's Inns barristers*, pp. 320-21. 1 shilling = 5 pence.

91  TNA 30/89/2, *A memoir by the Honourable William Evelyn Wylie KC* (1939), p. 5.

92  Thomas Kingsbury Overend. (1846-1915). Called 1874, joined the North East Circuit 1875. QC 1885, Recorder of Londonderry and county court judge of Co. Londonderry 1892-1912, when he resigned due to ill-health. Died 1915.

93  It remained in use for many years as it was the only work on county court equity practice. Osborne presented the copyright to Babington as a wedding gift. Babington, *Reminiscences*, p. 63.

94  William George Huband, (1845-1912). Called 1869, joined the North East Circuit 1872. *A practical treatise on the law relating to juries in Ireland*, (London, 1910). By the time his treatise appeared he was the private secretary to the lord chancellor. *King's Inns Barristers*.

95  Henry Macaulay Fitzgibbon (1855-1942). Called 1879. *King's Inns Barristers*.

96  Henry Hanna and Thomas D. Kinghan, *The law of workmen's compensation with the Irish rules and forms*, (2nd. ed. Dublin, 1907). Thomas Joseph Campbell, *Workman's Compensation Acts*, Samuel Clarke Porter, *Employer's liability and Workman's compensation*.

*Solicitor's Journal.*[97] In 1912 J.B. Lee[98] of the North West published (with
H.J. Moloney) what was for many years the standard book on criminal
injuries, as well as a work on the Shops Act of 1912.[99]

Details of the earnings of members of the Irish Bar in the nineteenth and
early twentieth centuries are meagre, but such information as there is
suggests that for many, if not the great majority, the first few years were lean.
Overend made £1500 in his fourth year, but he was unusual in making such
rapid progress, taking silk in 1885, 11 years after call.[100] Others were less
fortunate, and struggled for some time to become established, and of course
some never did. A fairly typical example in some respects was probably
George H. Brett who was called in Trinity Term 1898, and as one of three
probationers on the North East Circuit went on the Summer assizes in July
of that year. Brett, who joined the North East as a full member the next year,
held two briefs in Belfast on his first assize, whereas his fellow probationer
D.M. Steen held only one and Charles Weir had none.[101] Despite being
the son of Charles Brett of L'Estrange and Brett, one of Belfast's leading
firms of solicitors, Brett did not find life in the law either straightforward
or remunerative at first. Having served his articles as an apprentice in the
family firm it was felt the firm could not support all of the family, so he was
sent to Dublin to qualify as a barrister. Brett eventually became moderately
successful, 'but until he was over thirty required more financial support
from home than was convenient'.[102]

Babington and Wylie, who were very close friends on the North West Circuit,
earned very little for several years, a situation that probably reflected the

97  Samuel Shannon Millin, (1846-1947). Called 1894, joined the North East Circuit 1895. *A Digest of
    the reported decisions of the superior courts relating to the petty sessions in Ireland* (Dublin, 1898). Millin
    was a prolific writer, and his published works include *Sidelights on Belfast History* (Belfast and
    London, 1932) and *Additional sidelights* (1936). King's Inns Barristers. I owe the information about
    the *Digest* to Sir Peter Froggatt.
98  See Anthony P. Quinn, *Wigs and guns: Irish barristers in the Great War* (Dublin, 2006), pp 98-99.
99  *The Law relating to compensation for criminal injuries to person and property* (Dublin, 1912), *Shops
    Act, 1912, and the Irish regulations, notices and forms* (Dublin, 1912).
100 Details of Overend's earnings are taken from a letter written in 1975 by his son, a distinguished
    Dublin solicitor, who had seen his father's fee book. I owe the information about Overend to Robert
    Marshall who kindly provided a copy of the letter.
101 These figures reflect references to counsel by name in reports in the *Belfast Newsletter* in July 1898.
    It may well be that briefs were held in other cases that were not reported in the local newspapers.
102 Sir Charles Brett, *Long Shadows Cast Before, nine lives in Ulster*, 1625-1977 (Edinburgh, 1978),
    pp 120-21.

experience of most newly called barristers in the nineteenth and twentieth centuries. Babington, called in 1900, was fortunate to have an allowance of £120 a year from his father, and earned five guineas in his first year, ten in the second and 20 in the third, and when he earned £100 in his fourth believed that he was on the road to success.[103] Wylie, who was called in 1905, had an equally slow start, and recalled that he made £40 in his first year, £60 in his second, and £90 in his third,[104] although he recalled that his income jumped from £90 to £1000 in one year following his success in obtaining a manslaughter verdict for a husband and wife, who were charged with murder of their son by neglect in a highly publicised trial at Londonderry,[105] and he took silk in 1914, nine years after being called. His fee books have survived and are to be found amongst his papers in the National Archives[106] in London, and, as we shall see, broadly support his recollection of his earnings.

For many the early years were spent going round quarter sessions and assizes in an effort to become known. Wylie went to sessions in one town 22 times before anyone spoke to him, and recalled how he and Babington travelled third class on night trains, 'staying in 4th class country hotels and getting nothing to do'.[107] Babington's description of the gruelling travelling, with train fares and hotel bills consuming much of his meagre earnings, probably reflects the experience of the great majority of newly-called juniors of his era who sought work outside Dublin.

> I have caught the early workman's train on a Monday morning at Mount Street Bridge at 5.30, the Northern Mail from Amiens Street at 6.5 and the Letterkenny train from Strabane about 10.30, arriving in Letterkenny some time after 11.0 a.m., then a day's work there, leaving in time to catch the night mail again from Derry to Dublin at Strabane, some time after 10.00 pm, arriving at Dungannon about 1 a.m. Two day's work there and then the night mail train to Cavan. Two days work there and the night mail to Belfast on Friday and the early train to Coleraine on Saturday. A full day there leaving about 7.0 p.m. to catch the night mail from Belfast to Dublin, arriving there at 5.0 a.m. One such trip I remember well. I had forty-two guineas for the week less hotel charges and train fares. Not lucrative, but great training, and

103 Babington, *Reminiscences*, p. 41.
104 Wylie, *Memoir*, p. 5.
105 Ibid., pp 9-10.
106 TNA 30/89/13-14
107 Wylie, *Memoir*, p. 5.

it eventually produced fairly good results.[108]

However, in his early years, Babington, like Adye Curran and many of his colleagues on the Home Circuit 40 years before,[109] often went from town to town on foot, on at least one occasion walking the entire North West Circuit from Mullingar to Londonderry via Longford, Cavan, Enniskillen, Omagh and Lifford.[110]

Fees were generally small, even for well-established practitioners. A leading equity practitioner such as Thomas Lefroy at the height of his success in 1829 rarely received a fee of more than 10 guineas, and most fees were for amounts of less than five guineas, although these are for each item of work, rather than for the entire case.[111] Babington recalled how he sometimes appeared in the county court for half a guinea, three guineas being quite a good fee. He drew deeds of all kinds and settled conditions of sale at two guineas a time, and got an occasional high court action or the defence of a prisoner on circuit.[112] Seniors often did not do much better, with fees of two or three guineas in a civil bill appeal being common, and one guinea for the junior if there was one, as seniors often did an appeal without a junior.[113] Carson's experience had been similar, frequently having briefs marked half a guinea, and even when he was addressing juries behind two seniors, fees of two guineas were common.[114]

Wylie's fee books, which cover the eight years from his call until March 1913, provide an interesting insight into the nature of the work which a junior might expect to do, and the fees he might receive. In the nine months from his call until the end of 1905 he marked 24 fees totalling 37 guineas, although the total may have been less as four are stroked out, whilst one of the latter is marked paid. Nineteen in all were marked paid, amounting to 26 guineas.[115] In 1906 he was much busier, recording 77 briefs totalling 106 guineas, although not all fees were paid, with only 53 marked 'paid', making a

108 Babington, *Reminiscences*, pp 38–39.
109 Curran, *Reminiscences*, p. 40
110 Babington, *Reminiscences*, p. 31.
111 Hart, *The king's serjeants at law in Ireland*, pp 191-94.
112 Babington, Reminiscences, p. 55.
113 Ibid., p. 44.
114 Majoribanks, *The life of Lord Carson*, p. 41.
115 TNA 30/89/13.

total of 76 guineas actually received.[116] In January of that year he recorded 10 fees, three in February, eight in March and eight in April. By the end of 1907, by which time he had been less than three years in practice, he recorded 238 fees for that year for a total of 362 guineas. However, despite the increase in size of his practice, it seems his income did not increase proportionately. Of the 238 entries, only 72 were marked paid, amounting to 119 guineas, and as there is an entry to being overpaid £2 2s 0d, presumably his net income was 117 guineas for that year, somewhat greater than he recalled much later.

Of the 238 entries in 1907, the great majority were for one guinea, with the highest being one of six guineas, five of five, two of four and the remainder for two or three guineas. Even in the last three month period before the last entry on 27 March 1913 the picture remains unchanged. The majority of the fees were for one guinea, the remainder being for two or three guineas, except for one of four and one of six guineas. In that period his fee book records 21 fees for pleading in the king's bench division, four for the chancery division, two before the lord chancellor, four for probate matters, and two before the master of the rolls.[117] The fees, and the distribution of work across common law, equity and some probate, were probably fairly typical of a successful junior at that time. By 1908 the proportion of unpaid fees had fallen dramatically, although it appears to have risen again in subsequent years. Thus in 1912 there were 502 entries of which only 191 were marked paid. However, this may give an somewhat inaccurate impression, as sometimes Wylie records that he was paid 'on account' and on others he records 'clear to date', and so he may have received more money than the number of entries marked paid would suggest. In any event, by 1913 he was clearly doing very well because in April of that year he compiled a list of share purchases amounting to £1100 14s-3d.[118]

It has been estimated that by the end of the nineteenth century a junior would be doing well if his annual income exceeded £1000 after a decade in practice, and, with a few exceptions, the earnings of most seniors would be in the range of £3000-£5000.[119] So far as juniors are concerned, Wylie's career would seem to substantiate that estimate. However hard the early days at the Bar were, they provided an invaluable training ground for the

116 Ibid. Two more have been marked '?' and are excluded from this total.
117 TNA 30/89/14.
118 Ibid. The fee book contains a note in Wylie's hand dated April 1913 on notepaper headed 7 Upper Fitzwilliam Street, Dublin.
119 Hogan, *The legal profession in Ireland*, pp 81-85.

young barristers. The variety of cases to which they had to turn their attention, whether on circuit, the assizes, or in the Four Courts, meant that they necessarily gained a wide range of experience. In Ireland complete specialization was rare, and generally confined to more experienced practitioners.

In due course the ambitious junior would consider whether he should become a 'silk' by being appointed a king's (or queen's) counsel. As we have seen in the previous chapter, the first king's counsel in Ireland had been appointed in 1613. For some time the appointment was not frequently made, only 84 being appointed from 1613 up to and including 1768, when no fewer than seven were appointed, including Hugh Carleton, later Viscount Carleton and chief justice of the common pleas; John Scott, later Earl of Clonmell and chief justice of the king's bench, and Frederick Flood.[120] In the late eighteenth century their number appears to have increased, and by 1800 there were 36. Thereafter the number was relatively stable until 1833, when there were 52. By 1845 there were 75, and in 1900 about 66, although the latter figure represented a larger proportion of the Bar, which had shrunk since 1850.[121] In the eighteenth century the decision as to who should be made 'one of his majesty's counsel' was that of the lord lieutenant, although the lord chancellor could expect to be consulted. For example, in February 1795 Lord Fitzwilliam requested Lord Chancellor Fitzgibbon to call eight new king's counsel, and Fitzgibbon, who felt that there were already too many, was only partially successful in influencing the actual appointments by ensuring that three of his nominees were included in the list.[122] During the nineteenth century the decision seems to have become entirely that of the lord chancellor, and although political considerations almost always played a part, it was not uncommon for representations on behalf of a particular candidate to be pressed on the lord chancellor from his brother judges and others.[123] In the 1880s and 1890s there was a general, though not invariable, practice that some years would elapse between calls

---

120 *Liber. Mun. pub. Hib.*, ii, 76–78.

121 Hogan, *The legal profession in Ireland*, p. 79, gives 74, the total shown in *Thom's Directory*.
     However, several were no longer in practice. Carton and Curran were county court judges. Carson,
     Arthur Houston, and Seymour Bushe were in practice in England, and Lord Rathmore and
     Thomas DeMoylens were also listed as honorary benchers of King's Inns. E.H. Edge was an
     assistant legal land commissioner. The figure in the text takes these into account.

122 D.A. Fleming & A.P.W. Malcomson, (ed.), *'A volley of execrations' The letters and papers of John
     FitzGibbon, Earl of Clare 1772–1802* (Dublin, 2005), pp 206–08.

123 Hogan, *The legal profession in Ireland*, pp 85–88.

to the inner bar. However, from 1904 to 1915 there were calls every year, even though only one person was called in 1905. Although three were called in November 1914, and two in March 1915, no further calls took place until February 1918. Ignatius O'Brien, who was lord chancellor from 1913 to 1918, said that this was at the request of the Bar.[124] Babington gives a similar account, saying that the senior juniors on the North West Circuit agreed that they would not take silk until the younger members who had volunteered for war service came home, but that they had to follow suit when the other circuits said that they must have silks.[125]

The decision whether to apply for, or to accept silk if it were offered, was a difficult one to make. Whilst it provided a means of escaping from the drudgery of drafting pleadings and going round sessions, and the prospect of increasing one's income, it was not without risk, and sometimes a candidate might decline until he felt the time was more propitious.[126] A few juniors took silk after only a few years at the Bar. Issac Butt[127] and John David Fitzgerald[128] were both 31 when they did so; Palles, William Keogh[129] and W.E. Wylie 33 (the latter a day past his birthday).[130] These were the exceptions, as most had been at the Bar for about 20 years when they were called to the Inner Bar.[131] Once established as a senior, for those who had the ability and determination, it was generally a successful move. For example, Babington recalled that after one thin year he doubled his income, and doubled it again by 1921.[132]

Appointment as a king's counsel meant that the holder wore a silk gown, in contrast to the 'stuff' gown worn by a member of the Outer or Junior Bar, and sat within the bar of the court, or in the front row if the court did not have a bar. The holder was called within the bar by the lord chancellor in

---

124 This passage is based on the details given in *King's Inns Barristers*, pp 403–05.

125 Babington, *Reminiscences*, p. 57.

126 Hogan, *The legal profession in Ireland*, pp 86–87 gives examples.

127 Issac Butt (1813–79), called 1838, QC 1844. MP (C) 1852–57, (L) 1857–65, (Home Ruler) 1871–1879, chairman of the independent Irish parliamentary party. *ODNB*.

128 John David Fitzgerald (1816–1889). Called 1838, KC 1847. SG 1855–56, AG 1856–58 and 1859–60. JQB 1860–82, a lord of appeal in ordinary 1882–89. Ball, *Judges*, ii, 363. *ODNB*.

129 William Nicholas Keogh (1817–1878). Called 1840, QC 1849 SG 1852–55, AG 1855–86. JCP 1856–78. Ball, *Judges*, ii, 359. *ODNB*.

130 Delany, *Christopher Palles*, p. 47. *King's Inns Barristers*.

131 Hogan, The legal profession in Ireland, p. 77.

132 Babington, *Reminiscences*, p. 168.

the chancery court, and took precedence after his predecessor. As 'His/Her Majesty's Counsel learned in the law' a KC or QC who wished to appear against the crown, most commonly by defending a prisoner, was obliged to pay a fee to the Treasury, a practice that was not abolished until 1901.[133]

Although precedence was determined by the date and order in which calls to the Inner Bar took place, it was subject to the precedence which the law officers enjoyed over all counsel. From 1805 when the ancient office of prime serjeant at law in Ireland was abolished, the attorney general of the day was *ex officio* head of the Bar and enjoyed precedence over all others. After him came the solicitor general, and then the first, second and third king's serjeants at law in that order. All were party political appointments, but whilst the attorney general and solicitor general left office upon a change of government, a serjeant retained his position and would normally be promoted second or first serjeant upon a vacancy, irrespective of his political allegiance.[134] This meant that the attorney general and the solicitor general reverted to their previous precedence at the Bar unless they had been appointed to a vacancy on the bench in the interim. Equally, if appointed to either position, they assumed their new precedence, even if this meant a change in the order of representation in a current case. Thus in November 1892 the appointment of The MacDermott QC as attorney general and Serjeant Hemphill as solicitor general meant that they now led Edward Carson QC and John Atkinson QC, who had previously led them at an earlier stage of the Wicklow Peerage case.[135]

Another means of obtaining precedence was by a patent of precedence granted by the Crown by virtue of the royal prerogative, the patent conferring upon the barrister named therein specified precedence in the courts. Patents of precedence were regularly granted in England and a number of British colonies,[136] and the last patent granted in England was to Walter Phillimore (later Mr Justice Phillimore) in 1883.[137] Patents of precedence were rare in Ireland, and were usually granted to a former prime serjeant or attorney general to enable him to maintain his former

133 *ILT&SJ*, xxxv (1901), 392.

134 Hart, *The king's serjeants at law in Ireland*, ch. 5 passim.

135 *ILT&SJ* xxvi (1892), 608.

136 Such as Ontario. See *A G for Canada v A G for Ontario* [1898] AC 297.

137 Sir John Sainty, *A list of English law officers, king's counsel and holders of patents of precedence* (Selden Society, 1987), pp 275-76.

precedence, or confer upon him such precedence as might be specified therein. Thus Anthony Malone was granted

> Pre-audience, Place and Precedence of His Majesty's Prime Serjeant at Law, AG and SG, and all his Majesty's Council (sic), with full liberty of sitting and practising within the Barr, as well in all the Courts as elsewhere in Ireland, as any of his Majesty's Council did or might.[138]

This procedure was utilised to confer precedence after the king's second serjeant upon Daniel O'Connell in October 1831,[139] thereby enabling him to have the professional standing within the Inner Bar that he would have had were he made a king's counsel, standing demonstrated by his being entitled to wear a silk gown without him having to become 'one of His Majesty's counsel' which would have been politically embarrassing as he had publicly pledged that he would not accept any office from the government.[140] No further patents of precedence appear to have been issued in Ireland after that granted to O'Connell,[141] compared to 71 in England.[142] Of the five patents known to have been awarded to Irish barristers, two were granted to William Saurin, the first in 1798, and the second in 1822 after he had ceased to be attorney general.[143]

It is convenient at this stage to consider the governance of the Bar as a profession. The benchers of King's Inns controlled admission to the Bar and exercised a degree of control over professional standards, as well as exercising the ultimate power to disbar a person, thereby preventing him from practising. Disbarment was comparatively rare, and appears to have been exercised by the benchers only when the person concerned had been convicted of a crime, as in 1850 when the barrister concerned had been convicted of stealing books from the library of King's Inns. Other cases

---

138 *Lib. Mun. pub. Hib*, ii, p. 78.

139 Maurice O'Connell (ed.) *The correspondence of Daniel O'Connell*, (Dublin, 8 vols.) iv, pp 360-61. O'Connell was admitted to the inner bar on 4 Nov. 1831.

140 O'Connell sought the grant of a patent of precedence for a decade, and it was not granted until his career as a barrister was effectively over. Patrick M. Geoghegan, *King Dan The rise of Daniel O'Connell* 1775-1829 (Dublin, 2008), pp. 198, 244-55.

141 C. J. Smyth, *Chronicle of the law officers of Ireland*, (London and Dublin, 1839), p. 205 states that one was granted to Francis Blackburne upon his ceasing to be attorney general in 1835. This is incorrect. In his *Life of the Right Hon. Francis Blackburne, late lord chancellor of Ireland* (London, 1874), at pp 195-99, his son states that the grant was withheld from Blackburne due to O'Connell's influence.

142 Sainty, *A list of English law officers*, pp 275-282.

143 Smyth, *Law officers of Ireland*, pp 204-05.

involved forgery and bigamy. Lesser penalties in the form of censure or admonishment were imposed in less serious cases, as in 1847 when one G. Donleavie was admonished for interviewing accused persons in prison without being instructed by an attorney.[144] Hogan has observed that 'By the middle of the nineteenth century the benchers had ceased to be a dynamic element in the legal profession and were playing much more of a passive or defensive and responsive role',[145] and as the nineteenth century progressed the Bar became a more organised profession, with its own representative and governing bodies, although the process was a slow one.

The ultimate form of collective decision making and authority was a general meeting of the Bar, such as that which was held in 1792 when the Bar rejected a charter obtained by the benchers.[146] General meetings were held for a variety of purposes, some of a social nature as when an address of congratulation would be passed to mark the promotion of a member of the Bar, other were more controversial, such as the meeting held in June 1841 to protest at the appointment of John Campbell, the attorney general of England and a member of the English Bar, as lord chancellor of Ireland, when a resolution was passed that 'inasmuch as all judicial appointments in England are made from the English Bar, so all judicial appointments in Ireland ought to be made from the Irish Bar'. Despite this protest Campbell was appointed lord chancellor, a post he held for six weeks before resigning upon the fall of the government.[147] Other meetings were convened from time to time to deal with a variety of topics, such as fees. A general meeting held in 1864 adopted rules prohibiting senior counsel from signing pleadings in law or equity unless a junior counsel also signed; requiring junior counsel to appear on either side on a summons to settle issues (a practice said to be enforced by the judges of the common law courts), as well as eight rules relating to general and special retainers of counsel.[148] Other matters discussed from time to time were professional discipline, matters of internal organisation, and the relationship between the Bar and the benchers. The latter topic was the subject of a meeting on 5 June 1869, when the

---

144 Hogan, *The legal profession in Ireland*, pp. 37–38.
145 Ibid.
146 Hogan, *The legal profession in Irleand*, Ch. 5 on which this part of the text is based.
147 For a description of this episode see C. Kenny, ' Irish ambition and English preference in Chancery appointments, 1827-1842: the fate of William Conyngham Plunket' in W. Osborough (ed). *Explorations in Law and History* pp 154-63, and Ball, Judges, ii, 284-86.
148 Brunker, *Digest of cases*, pp 257-58.

Bar sought that the composition of the benchers should be remodelled. Eventually the benchers accepted the need for greater representation of the practising Bar amongst the benchers, resolving in 1872 that at least half of the Bench should be practising members of the Bar, and that (except for a lord chancellor) every judge who was a bencher *ex officio* should cease to be a bencher upon vacating his office.[149]

Although general meetings continued to be held until 1921, this was an unwieldy form of professional governance, and during the nineteenth century other bodies came into existence designed to meet specific organisational needs of the Bar. We have already seen how the Law Library Society came into existence in 1816 and was primarily responsible for the management of the Law Library, employing a librarian and other staff, gathering subscriptions and purchasing law reports, as well as other, more mundane matters. The Law Library Society appears to have been 'a highly efficient controlling committee who were at the very heart of the profession and its immediate needs at the Four Courts'.[150]

Despite the indispensable role of the Law Library Society in managing the facilities of the Law Library, there was an obvious need for a body to represent the Bar as a profession, and in sometime in the 1880s a Bar Committee was formed. It is known to have been in existence by 1889, when the Committee submitted its annual report and the Committee for the following year was brought into being. The five law officers (the attorney general, the solicitor general and the three serjeants) were *ex officio* members; and the elected members consisted of six QCs and 18 junior counsel. It was particularly active in pressing for improved accommodation for the Bar, efforts which led to the passing of the Four Courts Library Act in 1894 and the construction of the new Library to which reference has already been made.[151]

The Bar Committee, or the Bar Council as it came to be called, was itself replaced by a new body called the General Council of the Bar of Ireland which was brought into existence as the result of a general meeting of the Bar on 9 June 1897. The new body, also known as the Bar Council, was to be

---

149 Hogan, *The legal profession in Ireland*, pp 60-62.
150 Thomas Clancy, 'The Four Courts Building and the development of an independent Bar of Ireland' in Caroline Costello (ed.) *The Four Courts: 200 years*, pp 89-93.
151 Hogan, *The legal profession in Ireland*, pp 63-65.

'the accredited representative of the Bar, and its duties shall be to deal with all matters affecting the profession and to take such action thereon as may be expedient'.[152] Ten years later another general meeting of the Bar passed a resolution which remodelled the responsibilities and composition of the Bar Council. The three serjeants were no longer to be *ex officio* members, although they were reappointed some years later, together with the king's advocate (who represented the crown in admiralty proceedings).[153] The members of the Council were the law officers and any former law officers (so long as they remained in actual practice at the Bar), seven practising barristers, and no fewer than ten practising members of the Bar to be elected by the circuits, with two from each circuit, one of whom had to be a member of the junior bar. That the Bar Council was solely responsible for representing the interests of the Irish Bar was made clear by Regulation Two of the regulations adopted at the 1907 meeting.

> The Council shall be the accredited representative of the Bar, and its duty shall be to consider and report upon, and to make such representations as may be necessary in all matters affecting the profession, and particularly the conduct and arrangement of the business of the profession, etiquette and professional practice, the relations between the Inner and Outer Bar, the relations between the Bar and the Judicial Bench, right of audience, the claims of the Bar in relation to the maintenance and disposal of offices, legislation, or alterations in the system of administration, and all the matters in which the Irish Bar is professionally concerned.[154]

However, extensive as the powers of the Bar Council were, it was as much a representative as a governing body, and the ultimate authority of the Bar remained the general meeting of the Bar, although the Bar Council gradually assumed several of the functions of the latter. For example, in 1912 it published a set of 'approved' rules as to the privileges of junior counsel, and in 1914 with the outbreak of the Great War it published resolutions designed to preserve the practices of those barristers who had enlisted in the armed forces. Nevertheless, counsel's fees were dealt with at general meetings, as in February 1920 when a scale of minimum fees for High Court and conveyancing work was adopted.[155]

---

152 Ibid.
153 Ibid.
154 *ILT&SJ* xli (1907), 176-77.
155 Hogan, *The legal profession in Ireland*, pp 66-67.

# CHAPTER THREE:

## Circuit life before 1921

Before considering the role of the circuits in the life of the Irish Bar, it is appropriate to refer at this stage to the extent of specialisation at the Irish Bar. There was relatively little complete specialisation at the Irish Bar, although there were many who practised largely in the courts of equity or other non-common law courts. For example, in the early nineteenth century Thomas Lefroy was a leading equity practitioner, although he became a serjeant at law and in that capacity acted as an assize judge, before becoming a baron of the exchequer in 1841, and chief justice of the queen's bench in 1852.[1] Hugh Law, a member of the North East Circuit who became solicitor general, attorney general and then chancellor from 1881 until his death in 1883, was also primarily an equity practitioner.[2]

In addition to those barristers who practised before the courts of equity, there were a small number of individuals who studied civil law to qualify as advocates and who then practised before the high court of admiralty, the prerogative court, the consistorial court of Dublin and the high court of delegates. These courts were progressively abolished in the Victorian era, commencing with the abolition of the testamentary jurisdiction of the ecclesiastical courts and the creation of a new court of probate in 1857,[3] and their jurisdictions transferred to the high court created by the Supreme Court of Judicature Act (Ireland), 1877.[4] This process was not complete until February 1893 when the death of the admiralty judge, Judge Townshend, resulted in the extinction of the admiralty court and the transfer of its functions to the supreme court of judicature. So far as the admiralty jurisdiction was concerned, the volume of business does not appear to have been very great, at least to judge by the comment of one anonymous writer in 1890 who observed that 'the suits are so few that the office of Judge is

---

1    For details of Lefroy's career see Hart, *The king's serjeant at law in Ireland*, pp. 112-117, 174 and 191-194. *ODNB, DIB*.

2    Born 1818, educated at Dungannon Royal School and Trinity College, Dublin, called 1840, QC 1860, law adviser 1868, SG 1868, AG 1874 and 1880-81, chancellor 1881-83 when he died. Ball, *Judges*, ii, pp. 373-74. *ODNB, DIB*.

3    By the Probate and Letters of Administration Act, 1857, 20 & 21 Vict. c. 79.

4    40 & 41 Vict., c. 57, hereafter 'the Judicature Act'.

almost a sinecure'.[5] The accuracy of that assessment is borne out by the appointment of Mr Justice Johnson to exercise the admiralty jurisdiction of the high court after Townshend's death, the jurisdiction being assigned to the probate and matrimonial division.[6] As the law administered by these courts consisted of, or was at least strongly influenced by, civil and canon law,[7] those who practised as advocates had to be doctors of law. As almost all those who qualified as doctors of law did so at Trinity College, Dublin where the 'exercises' required for qualification had 'degenerated to very perfunctory formalities',[8] to become a doctor of law was hardly an onerous requirement.

The number of those qualified to act as advocates in Ireland never seems to have been large, with seven recorded in 1761.[9] By 1855 the number had increased to 28,[10] although by 1865 it had shrunk to 21,[11] possibly as a result of the creation of the court of probate in 1857. However, it seems unlikely that more than a handful, if any, of the advocates practised exclusively in the civil law courts. Although s. 25 of the Admiralty Court (Ireland) Act 1867 provided that all barristers at law were entitled to practise before that court, before this barristers had no right of audience in the admiralty court, although barristers who were not advocates were occasionally given special leave to appear.[12] Examples of the extent to which those barristers who were also qualified as civilians practised in other courts can be seen from the careers of some advocates who were in practice in 1855. George Battersby QC, surrogate of the vicar general of the consistorial court of Dublin, was also a member of the Home Circuit where he was senior crown counsel for Counties Kildare, Meath and Westmeath. Sir Thomas Staples was the queen's advocate (who represented the crown in admiralty proceedings) and the Father of the North East Circuit, as well as being senior crown

---

5    *Our Judges* by 'Rhadamanthus', (Dublin, 1890), p. 107.

6    J.O. Wylie, *The Judicature Acts*, (Dublin, 1906), p. 12. The probate and matrimonial division was amalgamated with the queen's bench division, as was its admiralty jurisdiction, by s. 5 & 6 of the Supreme Court of Judicature (Ireland) No. 2 Act, 1897.

7    The Admiralty Court in Ireland has now been the subject of an authoritative history by Kevin Costello in *The Court of Admiralty of Ireland 1575-1893*, (Dublin, 2011), but the history of the other courts of civil law has so far been largely ignored and awaits further study.

8    R.B. McDowell & D.A. Webb, *Trinity College Dublin, 1592-1952*, (Dublin, 2004), p. 194.

9    *Wilson's Dublin Directory*, 1761.

10   *Thom's Almanac and Official Directory*, 1855.

11   Ibid., 1865.

12   Costello, *The Court of Admiralty of Ireland*, pp 225-26.

prosecutor on the Circuit. Another advocate at that time was John Thomas Ball QC, who was also a member of the Home Circuit where he was senior crown prosecutor for Co. Carlow and Queen's County. However, Ball practised mainly in the ecclesiastical and probate courts, where he enjoyed considerable success, perhaps because he was prone to theological study. He stood unsuccessfully as a Liberal for Dublin University in 1865, before being elected as a Conservative for the same constituency in 1868, became solicitor general and then attorney general in late 1868. Ball was again attorney general from 1874 to 75, and lord chancellor between 1875 and 1880.[13] With the abolition of the civilian courts and the transfer of their jurisdiction to the High Court by the Judicature Acts, there was no longer a need for a separate profession of advocates, and so the number of barristers who had qualified as doctors dwindled, although they did not disappear entirely. However, by 1896 only two QC's were so qualified,[14] J.O. Wylie and A.W. Samuels,[15] whilst the queen's advocate, Stephen Ronan QC, was not. However, Ronan was one of the most distinguished lawyers of his time and the leader of the chancery bar.[16]

The change in the composition of the Bar Council in 1907 to provide that the majority of the elected members of the Council were to be members of, and elected by, the five circuits was a recognition of the importance of the circuits in the professional life of the Irish Bar, even though that importance was less than it had been in the past. Although the great majority of members of the Irish Bar joined, and practised on one of the circuits, at least in their early years, not everyone did so, some preferring to confine their practice to the Four Courts, particularly the chancery lawyers. Thus in 1865 we find that William Bennet Campion,[17] a leading chancery lawyer who had been called in 1840 and was to take silk in 1868, later becoming successively third, second and first serjeant at law, was not a member of any of the circuits. There were also a small number of barristers who only practised in their own localities, or divided their time between Dublin and

---

13 Ball, *Judges*, ii, pp 306-08 and 370-71, *ODNB* and *DIB*.
14 *Thom's Irish Directory*.
15 J.O. Wylie (1845-1935), called 1872, a member of the North West Circuit, QC 1894, author of a commentary on the Judicature Acts (1895 and 1906), judge of the high court (Irish land commission) 1906-20, being succeeded in that office by his nephew W.E. Wylie. A.W. Samuels (1852-1925), called 1877, a member of the Leinster Circuit, MP (U), Dublin Univ 1916-19, SG 1917-18, AG 1918-19, judge of the high court 1919-24.
16 *ODNB*, *DIB* and Sullivan, *Old Ireland*, p. 67.
17 Hart, *The king's serjeants at law in Ireland*, p. 166.

their local courts, without venturing on the entire circuit. One was Randal Kernan who, having served in the militia for several years, was called to the Bar and practised in Dublin and his native Enniskillen until his death in 1844.[18] Another was Frederick Lindsay, who was member of the North West Circuit from 1817 until 1834, yet apparently never held a brief other than in Omagh and Dungannon.[19]

Nevertheless, the great majority of those setting out to practise at the Irish Bar did choose to join one of the circuits, although some might wait for a year or two and avoid incurring the expenses of travel, hotel and mess bills until they had a chance of getting some work. One who chose to wait for a couple of years was Ignatius O'Brien, later lord chancellor and Lord Shandon.[20] It was not necessary to be a member of a circuit to practise at the county court or quarter sessions on that circuit,[21] probably because members of the Bar did not go regularly to many of the smaller or more remote courts, and hence there was no need for any collective presence in those areas in the manner that inevitably occurred at the assizes. George Hill Smith (sometimes known as Hill Smith) refers to an abortive attempt on the North East in 1846 to extend the idea of a bar mess to quarter sessions, saying that the idea of a 'Mess' at any of the towns 'would be more than absurd'.[22] As the circuit bars were voluntary societies, it was theoretically possible for a barrister to practise on a circuit without being a member of that circuit, although this would be difficult in practical terms as such a person would be excluded from the bar mess. Indeed the North East Circuit Rules of 1875 provided that a member 'shall not act professionally in the Civil Court on circuit with Barristers who are not members, except with Probationers, and in the usual manner with Counsel specially retained'.[23] However, a few may have done so, and Hogan records that one who did was Gerald Fitzgibbon, who practised on the Connaught Circuit for five years after he had been refused election before he was eventually elected.[24] It would seem that Eugene Sheehy practised in Dundalk, Newry, Downpatrick and

18  S. MacAnnaidth, *Fermanagh Books, Writers & Newspapers of the Nineteenth Century*, (Enniskillen and Belfast, 1999), pp 44-46. Whilst he was a militia officer Kernan (1774-1844) escorted Wolfe Tone and the French prisoners to Londonderry gaol after their capture in October 1798.
19  Hogan, *The legal profession in Ireland*, pp 51 and 70.
20  *Reminiscences of Lord Shandon, lord chancellor of Ireland*, (n.d.), p. 216. *DIB.*
21  Hogan, *The legal profession of Ireland*, p. 43.
22  Hill Smith, *The North East Bar*, pp 35-36.
23  Rule VIII 3.
24  Hogan, *The legal profession in Ireland*, p. 43.

Belfast after his call in 1910 until the outbreak of the First World War in 1914, although he does not appear to have joined the North East Circuit.[25] Interestingly, Sheehy recalled that the Bar did not wear wig or gown in the county courts of Co. Down, thereby no doubt making it even more difficult for a young barrister to attract the attention of the local solicitors, and also revealing his youth to his clients.[26]

Where there was sufficient business heard before the local courts, small local bars grew up, whose members practised largely, if not exclusively, in their local court and at the assizes when the latter sat in that locality. In the 1840s and 1850s only Cork was of sufficient size and prosperity to support a small local bar, with three main practitioners.[27] However, the rapid industrial growth of Belfast in the Victorian era, and the prosperity of the surrounding parts of the North East, provided the impetus for the development of a local bar based in Belfast. By 1898 there were eight members of the Bar listed in the *Belfast and Ulster Directory* as practising in Belfast and the surrounding area. Six had chambers in Rea's Buildings at 142 Royal Avenue, Belfast;[28] one, F.J. Robb, had chambers in 13 Royal Avenue, and one, Samuel Keightley, appears to have practised from his home. Given that there were 124 solicitors or firms of solicitors listed in the *Directory*, the majority of whom were single practitioners, there were obviously opportunities for the Bar in the local courts. Some barristers who restricted their practice in that fashion enjoyed a degree of local success, but either through choice or because they did not achieve greater success, did not practise to any material extent outside Belfast and the surrounding area. Others, although practising as part of a local bar, did not confine their work to Belfast, and enjoyed wider professional success. W.M. McGrath took silk in 1904, and W.M. Whitaker did so in 1907. Henry Hanna, only two years at the bar in 1898, took silk in 1911, and ultimately became third serjeant at law and one of the first judges appointed to the high court of the Irish Free State.[29] J.S. Baxter, who took silk in 1922, simultaneously held

---

25  Eugene Sheehy (1883-1958), *May it please the court* (Dublin, 1951), pp 60-62. Although Sheehy describes choosing the NE, he only refers to appearing in the county courts, and is not included in the list of those who joined after 1909 in Hill Smith, *The Supreme Court of Judicature of Northern Ireland* (Belfast, 1926), pp 48-50.

26  Sheehy, *May it please the court*, p. 60.

27  O'Flanagan, *The Irish Bar*, pp 407-09.

28  W. Whitaker; W.M. McGrath; J.S. Baxter; S.S. Millin; Henry Hanna and Henry Gilbert.

29  For an account of Hanna's career see Hart, *The king's serjeants at law in Ireland*, pp 123, 132-33, 158, and 171. A copy of the King's Inns portrait of Hanna now hangs in the Inn of Court in Belfast.

chairs in law at Trinity College, Dublin and Queen's University, Belfast for 24 years by lecturing on alternate days and travelling between Belfast and Dublin by train.[30] S.S. Millin, although the author of works on local history and other topics, does not appear to have enjoyed much professional success, despite his publication of the digest of decisions on petty sessions mentioned earlier, and in 1907 moved to live in Dublin.[31] Samuel Keightly, although he appears to have had a substantial local practice at that time, and was recorded in Hill Smith's *The North East Bar* as a member of the circuit in 1909, by then principally, if not entirely, devoted his time to writing and politics, becoming a successful historical novelist, a prominent Liberal politician, and being knighted in 1912.[32]

The local Belfast bar continued to grow in size, and by 1912 there were 13 members of the Bar with addresses in Belfast, several of whom were to be prominent figures in the Northern Ireland judiciary and public life after 1921. They included T.W. Brown, KC, MP, who was the last solicitor general for Ireland, then the last attorney general for Ireland, and became one of the original judges of the new high court of Northern Ireland; H.M. Thompson, KC and recorder of Belfast; J.H. Robb, KC, MP, minister of education, leader of the Senate, and county court judge for Counties Armagh and Fermanagh; T.H. Campbell, KC, Nationalist senator and MP and county court judge for Tyrone 1945-46; William Lowry, KC, MP, minister of home affairs, attorney general and a judge of the high court, and J.E. Warnock KC, MP, minister of home affairs and attorney general.[33] By 1919 there were 16 barristers listed in Belfast, although one appears to have been a court official. B.A. Crean, who gave his address as the County Courthouse, joined the Colonial Service in 1920 where he had a distinguished career.[34] Of those listed, most had chambers at Rea's Buildings, although several of those who had been listed in earlier years, including Whitaker, McGrath, Hanna and Warnock, no longer did so, presumably because they were by then primarily based in Dublin.

30  *King's Inns Barristers*, p. 137. His schedule is described in E.W. Jones, *Jones LJ, his life and times*, (Enniskillen, 1987), p. 24. Jones described him as 'a superb lecturer though possibly not pressed for time with other professional commitments'.

31  I am indebted to Sir Peter Froggatt for the information on Millin's career.

32  For an account of Keightley's career see *DIB*.

33  *Belfast and Ulster Directory.*

34  Ibid. Crean (1880-1956) was called to the Irish Bar in Trinity term 1912, and appears in *Thom's Irish Directory* at p. 926 as having an address at 25 Rea's Buildings, Belfast. Chief justice of British Guiana 1934-38, and of Cyprus, 1938-43, and knighted. *King's Inns Barristers*, p. 165.

Between 1796, when the Home Circuit consisting of Meath, Westmeath, Kildare, Carlow, Queen's County and King's County was created, and its abolition in 1885 there were six Circuits, but upon the abolition of the Home Circuit its counties were distributed amongst the remaining circuits, which remained largely unaltered until 1921. The Munster consisted of Clare, Limerick, Kerry and Cork. The Connaught consisted of Roscommon, Leitrim, Sligo and Mayo, to which was added King's County. The Leinster consisted of Kilkenny, the North and the South Ridings of Tipperary at Nenagh and Clonmel respectively, Waterford, Wicklow and Wexford. To these were added Kildare, Carlow and Queen's County. The North East consisted of Louth, Monaghan, Armagh, Down, Antrim and Carrickfergus (at that time a borough), to which was added Meath. The North West consisted of Longford, Cavan, Fermanagh, Tyrone, Donegal, and Londonderry, to which was added Westmeath.

As a result of the changes in local government in Ireland brought about by the creation of county, rural district and urban district councils by the Local Government (Ireland) Act, 1898,[35] when the legislation came into effect in 1900[36] a number of venues ceased to be assize towns, whilst others achieved that status. Tipperary became one county, Carrickfergus ceased to be a borough, becoming an urban council and so losing its assizes. However, Londonderry became a separate county borough, and thereafter separate assizes were held in Londonderry for the city and the county.[37]

The first, and most important, decision an intending member had to make was which circuit to choose. As we have seen in Chapter One, judges in Ireland had been going on assize for centuries, and after the circuits became fixed it seems that societies were formed by those members of the Bar who habitually went on each circuit. When these societies were formed cannot now be established because of the loss and destruction of early records, but that such societies with their own rules were in existence in the eighteenth century at least seems highly probable. In his *The North East Bar*[38] Hill Smith

---

35   61 & 62 Vict. c. 37.

36   The legislation came into force on 8 Aug. 1900. *ILT & SJ* xxxiv (1900), 536. List of assize judges for the North West Circuit from 1820-1925 compiled by Alfred Moore Munn, clerk of the crown and peace for the City and County of Londonderry in the possession of the author.

37   By s. 21(1) and sch. 2 six county boroughs were created which were to be administrative counties (and hence assize venues), namely Dublin, Belfast, Cork, Limerick, Londonderry and Waterford. S. 69(2) provided that Tipperary became a single county.

38   *The North East Bar a sketch historical and reminiscent*, (Belfast, 1910), p. 10.

says that although the minute book containing the records of the Circuit prior to 1801 were lost, a committee was appointed to draw up a new code of rules and regulations for the Circuit, and instructed to 'revive and introduce into the new Code as many of the Ancient Rules and Regulations as be can well authenticated'. The 'revived' Code was submitted to a meeting of the Circuit on 29 May, 1802, and presumably adopted as Hill Smith went on to say that it 'contains the germ of the Code existing on the Circuit to the present day'. The books and minutes of both the North West and North East Circuits were destroyed[39] when the Four Courts were destroyed following the attack on the building when it was seized by Republican forces and then bombarded by artillery fired by the forces of the Provisional Government, heralding the start of the Civil War. Fortunately a copy of the Rules adopted by the North East Circuit in 1875 has survived, and is to be found in Appendix One.

How did an aspiring member join a circuit? Maurice Healy claimed that the Munster Circuit was the only open circuit in Ireland, and all that he had to do was to send a cheque for his entrance fee to the secretary and he became a member, whereas a member of another circuit who wished to transfer to the Munster had to be elected in the usual manner.[40] On the North East under the 1875 rules someone who wished to join had to have been proposed and seconded by existing members of the Circuit. He then became a probationer and had to go on a probationary circuit, during which he had to appear as a barrister in at least three assize towns, and dine with the Bar in each town in which he appeared if there was a Bar dinner in that town. No doubt the other circuits had similar, though not necessarily identical, requirements. For example, the Home Circuit required the probationer to travel the circuit for a year, which must have meant that he had to attend two assizes, compared to the North East's requirement that a probationer complete a single circuit.[41] Once his probationary period had been completed, the candidate had to be balloted for, with one black ball in seven excluding on the North East, compared to one in three on the Home.[42]

Each circuit had a Father who presided over meetings and circuit dinners when present, and in his absence the senior member present took the chair. On the North East the 1875 Rules provided that the Father was to be the member

---

39    Hill Smith, *Sketch of the Supreme Court of Judicature of Northern Ireland*, (Belfast, 1926), p. 47.
40    *The Old Munster Circuit a book of memories and traditions*, (London, 3rd impression Dublin, 1948), p. 89.
41    Hogan, *The legal profession in Ireland*, p. 43.
42    Ibid., Rule 3 of the 1875 Rules.

of longest standing on circuit, or in his absence, the senior member present. Originally the Father had merely been the senior member present, but on 30 January 1836 Robert Holmes was appointed the permanent Father of the Circuit, and held the position until about 1855 when he was succeeded by Sir Thomas Staples who held the position until 1865. It appears that, notwithstanding the provision in the Rules that the Father be the senior member of the Circuit, an attempt was made to make the office an elective one, but a resolution passed on 30 November 1878 confirmed that the office was not to be an elective one.[43] The Father's duties were wide, and in the case of the North East

> All questions arising between Members of the Society in Court or in the Bar-Room on circuit, shall be finally and immediately decided and adjusted by the then present Father; and any member of the Society refusing to abide by, or disobeying the said Father's order or award on such occasion, shall be expelled.[44]

Although the Father was the member of longest standing on the circuit, this did not necessarily mean that the Father was in active practice, nor did it mean that he would be present throughout the entire circuit. Acheson Henderson KC,[45] who was Father of the North East until his death in 1909, had not been in active practice for about 20 years before his death, and indeed had been an honorary member of the circuit from 1907.[46] He did not often appear on circuit, and never outside Belfast, and appears to have been of a somewhat reserved disposition. Hill Smith said that he 'was courteous, quiet, and reserved, fulfilling his duties in strict accordance with the best traditions of the Circuit, but leaving on your mind the idea that, to him, it was a *duty* and not a pleasure'.[47] His successor was Sir James Henderson (no relation), although as James Henderson was the energetic proprietor of the *Belfast Newsletter* and active in public life,[48] he must have been only a

---

43  Hill Smith, *The North East Bar*, pp 31-32.
44  Rule VI.1.
45  (1812-1909), called 1837 and joined the North East Circuit in 1838. He had a small junior practice, chiefly on the North East Circuit. QC 1868.
46  *ILT&SJ* xliii (1910), 48. Hill Smith recorded at p. 103 that Henderson was crown prosecutor for Antrim and Belfast until 1907, but this is incorrect, as he says at p. 82 that Henderson resigned as crown prosecutor in 1892, being succeeded by J.H.M. Campbell QC.
47  Hill Smith, *The North East Bar*, pp 87-88. A copy of his portrait by J.B. Yeats is to be found between pages 85 and 92.
48  (1848-1914) Called 1872. Editor *Newry Telegraph* 1873-83, alderman Belfast Corporation 1894, first lord mayor of Belfast 1898, knighted 1899, first high sheriff of Belfast 1900, managing proprietor of the *Belfast Newsletter* and of the *Belfast Weekly News*.

nominal practitioner, and the other demands on his time suggest that it was unlikely that he acted as Father outside Belfast.

Although the 1875 rules of the North East Circuit made provision for various professional matters, the rules were primarily concerned with the appointment of various officers, such as a treasurer, a standing committee of five, as well as a town steward who was in effect the secretary and was responsible for keeping minutes, preserving records and similar duties, including arranging the annual dinner in Dublin. A circuit steward appointed by the Father was to act as steward for each town, and his duties, in which he was assisted by the junior, involved keeping accounts of expenditure from the bar mess fund for each town.

That the members of each circuit developed a strong feeling of comradeship and pride in the achievements of their most successful members is apparent from the memoirs and histories of several of the circuits written in the nineteenth and early twentieth centuries. An example of this is the way in which the North East Bar gradually acquired busts, portraits and photographs of some of their most distinguished members which were placed in Armagh and Belfast courthouses,[49] some of which are now to be found in the Bar Library together with group photographs of both the North West[50] and North East Circuits. From about the 1860s the North East also kept an album of individual photographs of members and this is in the possession of the Bar of Northern Ireland.

Once the decision to join a circuit had been made, although it was not impossible to change to another circuit later, it was very uncommon. Hill Smith, in his list of those who joined the North East, records only five instances of someone changing to or from the North East between 1800 and 1909. The first, and probably the most striking example in Ireland, was James Whiteside who joined from the Connaught Circuit in 1833. The most famous advocate at the Irish Bar of his day, and 'one of the most brilliant names in the annals of the Irish bar' whose greatest triumph was his speech in the famous case of *Yelverton v Yelverton* in 1861, Whiteside was also an influential political figure and then chief justice of the queen's bench from

49   Hill Smith, *The North East Bar*, Ch. VI.
50   Some photographs of members of the North West Circuit which were formerly in the Londonderry Courthouse are believed to have been appropriated during renovations in the 1950s or 1960s and are now lost. Information from the Rt Hon Sir Robert Porter QC to the author.

1866 until his death in 1877.[51] It is not until 1886 that the next change occurs, with F.W. Denning moving to the Connaught, with others changing to other circuits in 1889 and 1896. Although there are many instances of members being re-elected, presumably having let their membership lapse, in only one instance do we find a member being re-elected having joined another circuit, O.W. Murray being re-elected from the Munster Circuit in 1902. Hogan gives a number of examples of changes on other circuits,[52] quoting Maurice Healy's explanation why Edward Carson's attempt to transfer to the Munster Circuit was unsuccessful.

> But the stern rule of the circuits is the same in England and in Ireland: unless there is a very special reason, a man must stick to the choice he first made, and the mere fact that he would do better on another circuit would be no ground on which to base an application for a transfer.[53]

That such changes on the North East Circuit were so rare is proof of the accuracy of Healy's comment. A member who allowed his membership of the North East to lapse through non-attendance had to be re-elected, and this was a relatively frequent occurrence to judge by the number of such entries in Hill Smith's list of those who joined the North East. In 1860, for example, four were re-elected, and Maziere John Brady was re-elected in 1863 and again in 1866.[54]

As well as travelling together twice a year on circuit, the North East Circuit met regularly in Dublin, and dined afterwards, often with members of the judiciary or one of the law officers as their guests, although the practice of dining after the meeting ceased after about 1859.[55] Until January 1823 the meetings were quarterly, and thereafter twice yearly. Between 1801 and 1860 these meetings were usually held in taverns and then in hotels, although not continuously at one place. For example, 42 dinners were held at Morrison's Tavern in Dawson Street, and 33 at the Gresham Hotel, although in later years many were held in the admiralty court. Convivial social gatherings of this sort must have played their part in preserving and strengthening the feeling of comradeship created as the members travelled around the circuits together. About 1869, or shortly

---

51  *ODNB.* Whiteside was generally regarded as less distinguished as a judge than as an advocate.
52  Hogan, *The legal profession in Ireland*, p. 44.
53  *The Old Munster Circuit*, p. 89.
54  Hill Smith, *The North East Bar*, pp 109–110.
55  This passage is based upon Hill Smith's account of the Circuit.

afterwards, the tradition of dining ceased, and meetings were held in the afternoon at either the Four Courts or King's Inns.[56]

When the judges went out on circuit in March and July they, and the members of the Bar who accompanied them, would be away from Dublin for several weeks at a time depending upon the volume of business. Until the railways spread across Ireland travel was difficult and slow. In 1813 Mr Justice Day recorded that he had completed the North East Circuit in precisely three weeks exclusive of the journey from the last town. He estimated that the North East covered 200 miles, with the North West 264 miles, the Munster 358, the Connaught 301, compared to the Leinster at 182 and the Home at 129.[57] Most of those going on circuit travelled on horseback, although some brought their own carriage, as Bar etiquette meant that they could not use public coaches or conveyances whilst on circuit.[58] To carry the belongings of the Bar from town to town a wagon was purchased, a new wagon being bought in 1812 which was disposed of in 1836.[59] Each circuit probably had its own wagon at one time, as the Connaught Bar purchased one in 1828.[60]

With the spread of the railways it became much easier for members of the Bar to travel from Dublin to each assize town, resulting in a gradual decline in the number of members who went round the whole of each circuit. Hill Smith lamented in 1910  that the number going on circuit had declined, recalling that on his first circuit as a probationer on the Spring assizes of 1878, 45 members of the North East dined in Armagh, whereas by 1910 they seldom exceeded 24.[61] However, well before 1878 it was already apparent that not all members were going round the entirety of each circuit. Lists of those members of the North East Circuit who went on the Spring and Summer assizes of 1872[62] show that many members of the Circuit did not attend at all, or if they did, did not attend every assize town, as can be seen from the following table. The number of QCs is shown in brackets and

56   Hill Smith, *The North East Bar*, pp.19-20.
57   Gerald O'Carroll, *Mr Justice Robert Day (1746-1841) The Diaries and Addresses to Grand Juries 1793-1829* (Tralee, 2004), p. 232.
58   Hill Smith, *The North East Bar*, p. 29.
59   Ibid., pp 30-31.
60   Oliver Burke, *Anecdotes of the Connaught Circuit*, p. 221.
61   Ibid., p. 43.
62   Inn of Court Box 23. These figures are handwritten on the back of the printed North East Bar lists for the Summer Assizes of 1898, and appear to have been compiled at the request of the  assize judges (Palles CB and Fitzgibbon LJ).

is included in the overall total. The assize towns are listed in the order in which their assizes were held.

| Assize | Spring | Summer |
|---|---|---|
| Dundalk | 20 (2) | 18 (6)1 |
| Monaghan | 17 (3) | 21 (5) |
| Armagh | 25 (3) | 38 (4) + 3 probationers |
| Down | 30 (3) | 35 (3) + 3 probationers |
| Belfast | 46 (9) | 41 (10) + 5 probationers |

Of the silks, Hugh Law went to all five of the Spring assizes, but went to none in the Summer, despite his being a native of Co. Down and educated at Dungannon Royal School. However, he may have been preoccupied with other matters, as he became solicitor general on 18 November 1872. At the Summer assizes Hamill went to all five, McMahon, Elrington and Andrews each to four (although not the same assizes in each case).

Reference has been made earlier to the growth of a local bar in Belfast with the increase in prosperity of Belfast in particular and the North East of Ireland, but this prosperity was not confined to the North East as can be seen from the growth of the North West Circuit. As can be seen from the table overleaf, by 1910 the North East had overtaken the Munster Circuit as the largest circuit in Ireland. The North East shrank in size after the First World War, both circuits having the same number of members in 1920. During the same period the growth of the North West, although less than the North East, was proportionately quite high, and brought the North West above both the Leinster and Connaught Circuits in terms of numbers. In the table overleaf the number of silks on each circuit appear in brackets and are included in the total figures for each circuit. The figures have been taken from *Thom's Directory*, and while they may not be completely accurate (because the 1865 figures for the North East in *Thom* are slightly higher than the total of 82 (including four probationers) given on a North East dinner list dated 13 March, 1865),[63] and depend upon how accurate and up to date were the figures supplied by each circuit, nevertheless the figures undoubtedly reflect the changes that took place in the sizes of the respective circuits. Account must also be taken of the distribution of members of the Home Circuit amongst the other circuits after the Home was abolished in 1885, although only four members of the Home joined the North East.[64]

---

63   To be found in the front of the North East Bar photograph album.
64   Hill Smith, *The North East Bar*, p. 39.

| Circuit | 1865 | 1910 | 1920 |
|---|---|---|---|
| Munster | 97 (17) | 81 (15) | 90 (12) |
| North East | 84 (10) | 112 (17) | 90 (18) |
| Leinster | 63 (11) | 52 (11) | 40 (12) |
| Connaught | 42 (7) | 29 (2) | 28 (5) |
| North West | 31 (7) | 42 (6) | 42 (10) |
| Home | 39 (4) | | |

At the beginning of each assize circuit, the members of each circuit set out with the judges appointed to go on that circuit. Each circuit followed a prescribed pattern, although the order in which each assize was held on the circuit might be altered from time to time. The Spring assizes commenced in late February or early March, and the Summer in early July. As we shall see, on these assizes the judges dealt with both civil and criminal business. In addition, by the end of the nineteenth century winter assizes were held in December purely for criminal business, with the assizes held at different venues. Thus in 1892 the Ulster Winter assizes comprised the North West and North East Circuits and were held at Belfast, with sittings in Cork for the Munster Circuit, at Wicklow for the Leinster, and for the Connaught at Sligo.[65] The Winter assizes were not always held in the same venue each year, and in 1891, 1896 and 1912 they were held in Londonderry for the North West and North East Circuits.[66] Presumably this was to lessen the burden on the jurors of the principal towns or counties on each circuit.

At each Spring and Summer assize the judges dealt with both criminal and civil business, and took the business in turn at alternate venues, although when a judge finished his list he helped his colleague with his list. Sometimes the criminal list at a particular venue was so heavy that it could not be completed in the time allotted, in which case the crown judge would usually return at the end of the circuit to complete it. The business varied from place to place. On the 1808 Summer assizes Mr Justice Day noted that there were three records and 14 criminal cases at the Waterford assizes, but that was followed by the Co. Tipperary assizes at Clonmel, which he described as 'formidable' with 32 records and 114 prisoners.[67] A 'record' was a writ which had been set down for trial before a jury at the assizes instead of being tried before one of the common law courts, or, after the

---

65   *ILT&SJ* xxvi (1892), 608.
66   Munn, list of judges on the North West Circuit.
67   O'Carroll, *Mr Justice Day's diaries*, p. 158.

Judicature Act, before the high court, in Dublin. Many actions were tried at assizes. Day noted that at the 1809 Co. Cork Summer assizes there were 75 records, two of which took two days each. He spent from Wednesday 2 August until 5 pm on Friday 11 August on this list, and Chief Baron O'Grady assisted him for one and a half days.[68] This was the culmination of a heavy circuit, with 28 records tried at Ennis; 20 at Limerick, 10 at Tralee, and 16 at Cork City assizes. Lists like these could result in long sittings, which sometimes extended overnight. In 1810 Baron Cusack Smith heard a record where the plaintiff's case ended about 11 pm, and the defendant closed his case about 3 am.[69] Day himself was finally persuaded to abandon a very late sitting at Limerick when he was passed the following note from a member of the Bar close to midnight:-

> Try men by night! My Lord forbear,
> Think what the wicked world will say,
> Methinks I hear the rogues declare,
> *That Justice is not done by Day.*[70]

Such late sittings seem to have been less common as the nineteenth century progressed, but civil jury actions continued to be a major part of assize work, and some were of considerable importance and difficulty. For example, on the 1813 Spring assizes Day tried a record at Dundalk where the jury was the fifth jury to consider the case, but despite being enclosed all night they were unable to agree, and the parties agreed to withdraw a juror to bring the hearing to an end.[71] In 1859 a famous trial establishing a public right of way to the Cave Hill was tried over five days at the Co. Antrim assizes in Belfast before Chief Baron Pigot and a special jury.[72]

Although all the circuits appear to have had a rule requiring members not to appear with counsel from other circuits, this was subject to the exception that it was permissible for a counsel to appear on a circuit other than his own provided that he marked a 'special' fee, and it was quite common for the leading counsel of the day to be brought 'special' to do a case. An example of counsel appearing for a special fee was when W.C. Plunket of the North West Circuit,[73] and one of the outstanding advocates and political figures

---

68  Ibid., p. 167.
69  Ibid., p. 184.
70  J.R. O'Flanagan, *The Irish Bar* (London, 1879), p. 69.
71  O'Carroll, *Mr Justice Day's diaries*, p. 231.
72  John Gray, *The great Cave Hill right of way case* (Belfast, 2010).
73  (1746-1854), Baron Plunket of Newton, Co. Cork, chief justice of the common pleas and lord chancellor of Ireland. Ball, *Judges*, ii, pp. 343-45. *ODNB, DIB.*

of the early nineteenth century, came to Carrickfergus assizes on the North East Circuit in July 1807 at special fee of 150 guineas.[74] Daniel O'Connell was in particular demand, and held briefs on three different circuits outside the Munster Circuit on the Spring assizes of 1824.[75] The Home Bar laid down that the minimum fee was 100 guineas for a silk, or 50 guineas for a junior. [76] That the North East had a practice of requiring special fees to be marked can be seen from the extract from the 1875 Rules quoted earlier, although the amount of the fees to be marked is not known.

That it was considered necessary to regulate the manner in which briefs were to be received, apart from special fees, appears from the provisions in the North East Circuit Rules of 1875 which prevented a member from taking a brief in a record unless a fee has been marked, or from accepting a record brief after the last court had risen on the first day of the sitting in each assize town.[77] As we shall see it was possible to enter cases for hearing right up to the commencement of an assize, and there were occasions when solicitors sent a brief to counsel at a very late stage, seeking out counsel as the assizes were about to commence or actually sitting. Babington recalled one occasion when E.S. Murphy and he were called out of the Bar room at Londonderry by a solicitor 'with a bundle of briefs, which he handed to us'.[78] That these rules existed suggests that there were occasions when some counsel accepted briefs in circumstances regarded by their colleagues as unprofessional.

Whilst inevitably there had been some changes in the assize jurisdiction by the end of the nineteenth century, the general nature of the business, and hence opportunities for the Bar, had not changed a great deal from the assizes described by Mr Justice Day in the early years of the century, as can be seen from newspaper accounts of the North East and North West Summer assizes of July 1898. These assizes have been studied because a dinner list for the North East Circuit has survived, and enables a comparison to be made of those on the list and those who were named as counsel in the detailed newspaper reports of the time. Although the newspaper reports do not refer to every case heard, they are comprehensive and detailed. In

---

74   O'Carroll, *Mr Justice Day's diaries*, p. 91.
75   Hogan, *The legal profession in Ireland*, p. 49.
76   Ibid.
77   Rule VIII (1) and (2).
78   *Reminiscences*, p. 49.

addition, Lord Justice Fitzgibbon, who was one of the going judges on the North East (Chief Baron Palles being the other), took the opportunity to address complaints made on behalf of jurors, and described the nature of the civil business at Belfast in some detail.

The criminal business at Belfast was probably significantly higher than usual, because the centenary of the 1798 Rising resulted in one of Belfast's periodic outbreaks of sectarian rioting on 6 and 7 June, and a number of prosecutions arising out of the riots were heard at the Summer assizes. Of 103 defendants, 58 were charged with riot, two with arson and one with attempted arson, compared to 27 with various offences of dishonesty. Of the remainder, eight were charged with wounding or assault, two with murder, one with manslaughter, one with attempted rape, two with robbery, one with attempted rape, and two with forcible possession.[79] When the assizes opened there were actually 112 defendants on 79 bills, and as there was more than one bill in respect of the same incident in some cases, these represented 13 distinct cases in the county and 33 in the city.[80] Except in cases of murder, where the Crown paid for defence counsel, many defendants were unrepresented. Those who had the means, or whose family or friends raised the money for legal representation, were represented by counsel. The prosecution were represented by the permanent crown prosecutors for Co. Antrim, the senior crown counsel being J.H.M. Campbell QC, MP,[81] and the junior crown counsel was George Hill Smith. The criminal cases, including a private prosecution brought by the Great Northern Railway against, amongst others, some of their employees, which was heard before Lord Justice Fitzgibbon over three days, lasted from 14 to 27 July. The volume of criminal business at Belfast was much higher than elsewhere on the North East or the North West Circuits. For example, there were only three bills at the Co. Armagh assizes,[82] and five at Downpatrick, although three of these were homicides.[83] On the North West, there were nine bills at the Donegal assizes, including one murder where the defendant was

---

79  *Belfast Newsletter*, 7 July 1898 reporting the cases to be heard at the Antrim assizes opening on 14 July.
80  Palles CB charging the Co. Antrim Grand Jury on 14 July. *Belfast Newsletter* 15 July 1898.
81  (1852-1931). Called 1878, QC 1892, MP(U), St Stephen's Green 1898-1900, Dublin Univ 1903-1916, SG 1901-04, AG December 1905, and 1916-17, lord chief justice 1916-18, lord chancellor 1918-21. Created a baronet 1917, and Baron Glenavy 1921. Chairman of the Senate of the IFS 1922-28. Ball, Judges, ii, p. 385. *ODNB, DIB.*
82  *Armagh Guardian*, 8 July 1898.
83  *Belfast Newsletter*, 12 July 1898.

found unfit to plead and ordered to be detained at Her Majesty's pleasure.[84] Such was the peaceful state of Fermanagh there were no criminal cases and the judge received the traditional gift of white gloves.[85] Whilst the crown prosecutors could be well remunerated depending on the volume of business, there was less work for defence counsel. Even where the government paid for the defence costs in murder cases the fees were small.

From the perspective of the Bar, the main source of work was on the civil side. In his address to the Carrickfergus grand jury at Belfast Fitzgibbon explained that at the Antrim Assizes there were 22 common jury records, seven special jury records and two non jury records entered, together with at least 108 civil bills. As cases could still be entered during the next two days, perhaps 110 civil bills could be expected, although ten had been withdrawn.[86] In the event, all the special jury actions were settled,[87] but many of the common jury cases were contested. These cases, and the criminal jury cases, meant a very large number of members of the public attended the assizes, as 250 common and 48 special jurors were required, and it was estimated that the 100 civil bill appeals would involve the attendance of another 50 people.[88]

The civil business at assizes covered a very wide range of work. For example, at Downpatrick the civil bill appeal list involved causes of action as diverse as bills of exchange, a claim for professional fees by a doctor, trespass, title, damage to a house from sparks from a traction engine, and seduction, and there was also a petition for a divorce *a mensa et thoro* (apparently the first of its kind on circuit).[89] At Armagh Chief Baron Palles heard a civil bill appeal involving burial rights in a Presbyterian churchyard.[90] At Belfast the cases reported included breach of promise, recovery of land, charter parties, dishonoured bills of exchange, defamation, wrongful dismissal, breach of contract, assault and battery. In his remarks on the volume of business in his address to the Carrickfergus grand jury Lord Justice Fitzgibbon referred to the priority given to civil bill appeals, and such cases formed a substantial part of the civil judge's list at every venue, although the total number of

84   Ibid., 18 July 1898.
85   *Fermanagh Times*, 14 July 1898.
86   *Belfast Newsletter*, 15 July 1898.
87   Ibid., 28 July 1898.
88   Ibid., 15 July 1898.
89   *Down Recorder*, 16 July 1898.
90   *Belfast Newsletter*, 9 July 1898.

such cases could vary considerably. At the Fermanagh Summer assizes that year there are newspaper reports of 21 civil bill appeals,[91] but the civil bill appeal list at the Co. Tyrone assizes at Omagh was invariably enormous, such was the number of appeals from the decisions of Sir Francis Brady, who was the county court judge.[92]

One of the difficulties for the Bar when such cases were heard on circuit was that text books and law reports were not readily available, although that omission was deliberate. Hill Smith states that 'In the earlier days of the Circuit it was a well-established custom that no Member was allowed to bring a Law book round; and that no one was even supposed, or expected, to quote an authority in court'. Whether that was the case or not, he does quote a resolution of the North East Bar of February 1876 regretting that they were unable to accept an offer of the library of a deceased member of the Circuit on the grounds that to do so 'would necessarily involve the formation of a complete Law Library, continued from the date of Mr Cunningham's Volumes'. The difficulty of keeping up and transporting even a small library around the circuit is obvious, but the need for a library was evident. In later years the North East did form a library of standard text books and digests which were brought on circuit, and no doubt those appearing at the Belfast Summer assizes of 1898 could make use of the Sessional Bar Library established in Belfast by the local bar and solicitors.[93]

Sir Francis Brady merits a brief reference as he features in so many reminiscences of the time. He was the eldest son of Maziere Brady, who was three times lord chancellor of Ireland, and who that held that office for a total of 17 years. Sir Francis, who inherited the baronetcy granted to his father, had what was probably the unique distinction of being called to the Bar, and then to the Inner Bar, and finally being appointed a county court judge, by his father.[94] Prior to the County Officers and Courts (Ireland) Act, 1877 the assistant barristers (who dealt with civil business), and chairmen of quarter sessions (who dealt with criminal business) were part-time judges who generally continued to practise. When the county court judges became full-time appointments (also acting as chairmen of quarter sessions, unlike

91  *Fermanagh Times*, 14 July 1898
92  (1824-1909). Educated at London University, called M. 1846. Joined the Munster Circuit, QC 1860, vice-president of the Royal Irish Academy of Music.
93  Hill Smith, *The North East Bar*, pp 34-35.
94  *ILT&SJ* xliii (1909), 216-17.

their counterparts in England who were purely civil judges), the existing judges were offered the option of becoming full-time judges, and so losing their right to practise, but becoming eligible for a pension; or retaining the right to practise but foregoing the right to a pension. Sir Francis, who held the lucrative post of crown prosecutor for Co. Cork, elected to take the latter option, and so remained both county court judge for Co. Tyrone and crown prosecutor for Cork until his death aged 85 in 1909.[95] Brady, who was an accomplished musician, wrote a number of works, and wrote or arranged several songs, including one for the opera 'The Lily of Killarney'.[96]

His decisions were regarded as being somewhat eccentric, and T.J. Campbell described his court

> ...as at intervals a babel of confusion, he being not the least contributor to it. No one could say in advance how he would decide a case–perhaps as much by rule of thumb as any other rule. Appeals went from him not single spies but in battalions, and on his exit shrunk to skeleton size.[97]

Babington said that he had seen over three hundred appeals from Brady at Omagh. This generated business for the Bar, and he went on to say that 'Denis Henry would be in about half, whilst the juniors got a few, with fees of two or three guineas for a senior and a guinea for a junior'.[98]

Although many of the Bench and Bar were out on circuit, that did not mean that the Four Courts closed down, as the chancery judges did not go on circuit, and as a result there was a good deal of work in Dublin to occupy members of the North East and other circuits who chose not to go on circuit. Thus in July 1898 we find almost daily newspaper reports of cases of Ulster interest in which members of the North East Bar appeared before the master of the rolls, the vice chancellor, the land judge, and sometimes the lord chancellor, as well as Mr Justice Boyd sitting as the vacation judge in the queen's bench division. Indeed, only 66 of the members of the Circuit whose names appear on the printed circuit list were named in the reports in the *Belfast Newsletter* in July 1898, and of these twelve members are reported as only appearing in the Four Courts. Whilst these reports may not have recorded every counsel, and only

95  Ibid.
96  Ibid., 231.
97  T.J. Campbell, *Fifty years of Ulster*, (Belfast, 1941), p. 144.
98  Babington, *Reminiscences*, p. 44.

one month has been analysed in depth, the figures nonetheless suggest that a significant proportion of the North East Bar either did not go on circuit, or if they did, did not get any or much work. Twenty five of those who are recorded as appearing on circuit were not reported as holding more than two briefs. It should also perhaps be mentioned that some of these appearances were in other courts sitting during July 1898, such as the Belfast recorder's bankruptcy court which continued to sit each Saturday at the Crumlin Road Courthouse. This must have posed an accommodation problem when the assizes were also being held in the building.

Whilst on circuit the Bar stayed in local hotels which would provide them with a room, and store their wine. The hotels were not always very satisfactory, Hill Smith recalling that the financial difficulties of the proprietor of one Downpatrick hotel resulted in the gas supply being cut off whilst the Bar were at dinner, and the remainder of the meal had to be eaten by the light of sundry candles placed in improvised holders.[99] One of the duties of the circuit junior was to look after the wine held for each circuit in each circuit town in the hotel, or at a wine merchant.[100] These stocks were augmented from time to time by levies from members of the circuit in the form of 'congratulations' donated by members of the circuit who had been appointed to an office,[101] or by gifts from judges, usually former members of the circuit. The North East Circuit wine book[102] has entries from the Monaghan Spring assizes of 1917 onwards. It records gifts of champagne from Sir James Campbell LCJ on 10 July 1917 at Monaghan (one dozen), and at Belfast (four dozen Ruinart) a week later. Gifts of champagne from H. Jackson KC (master of the king's bench division-two dozen Deutz and Gelderman), Mr Justice Moore, and John McGonigal KC are also recorded, testimony to the generosity and affection for the North East Circuit of its members and former members, as well as their excellent taste in champagne.

Whilst the Belfast assizes in particular may have been busy, not every venue was busy all the time, and there were opportunities for badinage and entertainment at and after dinner. Although gambling was forbidden on the North East Circuit by the 1875 Rules, not all the younger members of the circuits could resist the lure of forbidden activities. On one occasion, whilst

---

99  Ibid., p. 44.
100 Babington, *Reminiscences*, p. 187
101 The scale for the North East Circuit is to be found in Hill Smith, *The North East Bar* at p. 24.
102 Inn of Court Box 26.

staying in Strabane for the Donegal assizes at Lifford, members of the North West attended a cock fight at about four a.m., although the silks and crown prosecutors prudently stayed away.[103] A formal dinner was held on each circuit when the Bar would entertain the judges. On the North West this was usually held in the Court House at Omagh.[104] A dinner was usually held at Armagh by the North East. Hill Smith wrote that by 1910 when the circuit reached Belfast, especially after the first night, members did not dine in any great numbers.[105] Every probationer was expected to entertain his colleagues with a song, whether he could sing or not, and the Father would decide whether he should be given a certificate, thereby absolving him from singing again.[106]

The Irish Bar and the circuits were not immune to the tempests of political events, war and civil war that engulfed Ireland and Europe in what was to prove to be the last decade of the existence of the Irish Bar as a united body. The impact of the Great War on the Irish Bar has been comprehensively chronicled by Anthony Quinn,[107] but no account of the Irish Bar, and of the North West and North East Circuits, would be complete without some reference to those events. With the outbreak of the War many members of both branches of the legal profession joined the armed forces, and members of the North West and North East Circuits were amongst those who did so. By April 1915 13 members of the North West and 10 of the North East were serving.[108] The numbers rose as the War dragged on, and by February 1916 18 members of the North West and 23 from the North East had joined.[109] By the end of the War 33 members of the North East had served.[110] Six members of the North East Circuit, and five members of the North West Circuit lost their lives. Memorials to those who died were erected by the North West Circuit in Londonderry Courthouse, and by the North East in the Crumlin Road Courthouse in Belfast. Fittingly, a joint memorial with the names of those who died from both Circuits was later inscribed on the wall of the Main Hall of the Royal Courts of Justice in Chichester Street.

---

103 *Reminiscences*, p. 296.
104 Ibid., p. 187.
105 Hill Smith, The North East Bar, p. 44.
106 Babington, *Reminiscences*, p. 187. Hill Smith, *The North East Bar*, p. 45.
107 *Wigs and Guns Irish barristers in the Great War*, (Dublin, 2006).
108 *ILT&SJ* xlix (1915), pp 84–85.
109 *ILT&SJ* l (1916), 'War Supplement' between pp 59–60.
110 *ILT&SJ* liv (1920), pp 76–77 reporting the speech of R.D. Murray, Father of the North East Circuit, at the unveiling of the memorial in the Crumlin Road Courthouse to members of the Circuit who had lost their lives in the Great War.

The impact of the War was not confined to those on active service, as many members of the Bench and Bar had members of their families serving. For example, by August 1915, 85 members of the judiciary and Bar had sons serving or had been killed. From the North East Circuit R.F. Harrison KC had one son serving, William Moore KC MP had two, as had James Williamson KC. J.H.M. Campbell KC, MP, by now attorney general, suffered the loss of his third son who was killed in action a month before Campbell was appointed lord chief justice.[111] Not all of those who joined up were young men. From the North West Circuit, Patrick Walsh KC, who was 56 at the outbreak of the war, joined the Donegal recruiting staff. Two of his sons also served, and his daughter served with the VAD (Voluntary Aid Detachment).[112] From the North East, Daniel Wilson KC, 52 at the outbreak of the war and a bencher of King's Inns, served in the Royal Inniskilling Fusiliers until he relinquished his commission in 1916 due to ill-health.[113] Walsh subsequently became president of the district court in Cyprus and then chief justice of the Seychelles, whilst Wilson was MP for West Down, 1918-21, solicitor general from 1919 until 1921, then recorder of Belfast for a few months in the summer of 1921 before being appointed one of the judges of the newly created high court of Northern Ireland in October, 1921.

The political turmoil in Ireland during and after the War did not leave the circuits unscathed. During the 1916 Rising W.E. Wylie KC was serving with the Trinity College, Dublin Officers Training Corps and was directed to prosecute the prisoners before the courts martial set up in the aftermath of the Rising. The prisoners were unrepresented, and included William Cosgrave, later President of the Executive Council of the Irish Free State. Wylie's determination to ensure that they were fairly tried, particularly by taking points on their behalf, was recognised by those he prosecuted.[114] After the War, William McGrath KC of the North East was shot dead by armed raiders at his home in Dublin in January 1921.[115]

As we draw this account of the circuits, and of the North West and North East

---

111 *ILT&SJ*1 (1916) at p. 312 (25 Nov.) reported the death in action of Lieutenant Commander
    Philip S. Campbell, RNVR, of the Royal Naval Division, and at p. 334 (23 Dec.) reported his
    appointment as lord chief justice.
112 A.P. Quinn, *Wigs and Guns*, p. 50.
113 *ILT&SJ*1 (1916), Irish Law Times War Supplement, 4.
114 Leon O'Broin, *W.E. Wylie and the Irish revolution 1916-17*, (Dublin, 1989), pp 23-29.
115 *ILT&SJ*lv (1921), 17.

in particular, to a close, it is perhaps appropriate to refer to one of the members of the North West Circuit whose outstanding legal and parliamentary career demonstrated that the friendships made in the Law Library and cemented on circuit crossed religious lines and defied party affiliations, and who exemplified the apt observation of T.J. Campbell when he wrote of the Irish Bar, 'Lord Justice Holker said that at Circuit in England they had association without friendship. In Ireland we had both'.[116] Denis Henry, who was to become the first lord chief justice of Northern Ireland, was called to the Irish Bar in 1885. A native of Draperstown, Co. Londonderry, he naturally joined the North West Circuit where he rapidly established himself as the leader of the Circuit, becoming a QC in 1896, and then as one of the leaders of the Irish Bar. Despite being a roman catholic, he stood for parliament several times as a unionist, becoming MP for South Londonderry in 1916, solicitor general in December 1918, and attorney general in July 1919. That he inspired friendship and affection from political supporters and opponents alike, as well as respect for his professional abilities is evident. W.E. Wylie wrote 'what do we of the old North West Circuit not owe him. He was the quickest thinker and most brilliant advocate I ever knew'.[117] Babington described him as 'a marvellous advocate and equally at home before all Judges from the House of Lords down and in every class of case', saying that his death when lord chief justice 'was a tragedy for our profession and the Northern Bar'. He said of Henry's abilities that

> In all courts, the extent of his knowledge and his resources as an advocate were astonishing. I have also listened to him on many other occasions, and as he had a fine voice and presence, he generally dominated any court in which he was appearing. He was the least vain of men, mostly because he had a keen sense of humour.[118]

T.J. Campbell KC, a Nationalist member of the Northern Ireland senate between 1929 and 1934, and MP for Belfast Central from 1934 until 1945 (when he was leader of the Nationalist party[119]) and therefore opposed to Henry's political views, thought that he 'was among the wittiest and readiest

---

116  *Fifty years of Ulster*, p. 160.

117  *Memoir*, p. 6.

118  *Reminiscences*, pp 217-18.

119  Whilst Campbell was widely regarded as the 'leader', during his time in parliament the Nationalists had no official leader, nor, it seems, any procedure for appointing or dismissing one. Philip E. Leonard, *The contribution of Thomas Joseph (T.J.) Campbell KC MP (1871-1946) to Nationalist politics in Northern Ireland* (unpublished MSSc Thesis). I am indebted to Tom Campbell Esq., solicitor and grandson of T.J. Campbell, for making this available.

raconteurs in the Law Library'.[120]

Perhaps the most unusual recognition of Henry's outstanding position at the Irish Bar also came from a lawyer, and is to be found in a volume of stories first published in 1917. In 'A settlement by consent' the principal character is Andy McKay, a countryman and connoisseur of litigation, whether as participant or as a witness. In the story there are references to Henry, as when McKay recalls the boundary dispute that 'made Denis Henry's reputation as a junior barrister', and is said to be

> especially proud of the fact that, as he was standing in the Central Hall at the adjournment on one of the days he spent in the Four Courts, no less a personage than 'Dinis Henry, KC', had shaken hands with him and said, 'How are you, Andy? Are you as fond of the law as ever.[121]

There can be few barristers whose fame has been recognised in fiction in this way, certainly in their lifetime. It is a tribute to Henry's standing and the respect in which he was held that the author of the stories, Louis J. Walsh, held political views completely opposed to those of Henry. Walsh was a solicitor who was born in Maghera, Co. Londonderry not far from Henry's birthplace at Draperstown, where Walsh later practised as a solicitor. In 1918 he stood unsuccessfully as a Sinn Fein candidate against Henry in South Londonderry,[122] and was later interned in Londonderry gaol and Ballykinlar.[123]

120 *Fifty years of Ulster.* (Belfast, 1941), p. 142.

121 *The Yarns of a Country Attorney, being stories and sketches of life in rural Ulster,* (Dublin, 1918), p. 10.

122 A.D. McDonnell, *The life of Sir Denis Henry Catholic Unionist* (Belfast, 2000), p. 49.

123 (1880-1942) Born in Maghera, Walsh was a solicitor in Co. Londonderry and Ballycastle, Co. Antrim. He was interned in 1920. On his release he went to live in Southern Ireland, where he was appointed one of the first district justices, serving in Co. Donegal from 1922 until his death in 1942. A prolific writer, newspaper columnist (under a pseudonym) and playwright. *Irish News*, 28 Dec. 1942; *ILT&SJ* lxxvii (1943), p. 4, and Robert Hogan, (ed.) *Dictionary of Irish literature*, (2nd ed. Westport, Connecticut and London, 1996), p. 1222. *DIB*.

William Carlisle Henderson QC, Father of the North West Bar 1869-1872
Courtesy of the Lord Chief Justice of Northern Ireland

Acheson T. Henderson QC 1812–1909. By John Butler Yeats.

Robert Murray, last Father of the North East Bar.

George Hill Smith QC, first Father of the Bar of Northern Ireland.

Barney Donaghy, 'bagman' in Londonderry.

Members of the North West Bar, probably in the summer of 1921.

The first judges of the Supreme Court of Judicature of Northern Ireland, October 1921.

Courtesy of Sir William Moore, Bt.

Legal Golf competition at Scrabo, 1924.

Circuit dinner menu, 1926.

# CHAPTER FOUR:

## King's Inns and the foundation of the Inn of Court of Northern Ireland

Whilst the Government of Ireland Act of 1920 provided that all existing members of the Irish Bar should have a right of audience in the supreme courts of judicature of both Southern and Northern Ireland, the effect of the Act was to create two separate bars when the Act came into force in Northern Ireland on 1 October 1921. By early 1922 the Bar of Northern Ireland was established with its own governing body in the shape of the Bar Council, together with a separate Circuit of Northern Ireland. Nevertheless, the organic link provided by King's Inns between the benchers and bars of Northern and Southern Ireland remained, and at first it seemed that, unlike the remainder of the legal system, this link would not be broken. That at least was the view which Sir John Ross, the last lord chancellor of Ireland, expressed in an address to an audience of bar students in 1921.[1]

The creation of the new Northern Ireland judicial system inevitably meant that King's Inns had to adapt its structures and rules to accommodate this new reality. On 31 October 1921 the benchers passed a resolution with the object of preserving its position as the sole inn of court in Ireland by continuing to be responsible for the education of bar students in both jurisdictions, whilst recognising that the legal system in Northern Ireland was a distinct entity. Given that the Government of Ireland Act sought to preserve a common framework within which both systems would continue to operate by providing for a High Court of Appeal which would hear appeals from the courts of appeal of Northern Ireland and Southern Ireland, this was an understandable attempt to maintain professional unity despite the legal and constitutional changes brought about by the Act. Profound though these changes were for Northern Ireland, they were stillborn in Southern Ireland with the accession to power of the Provisional Government in January 1922, although it was not until 1924 that the tensions inherent in the attempt by King's Inns to preserve a single governing body for the bars of two distinct and politically hostile entities became impossible to ignore and increasingly difficult to resolve.

1  *ILT&SJ*, lv (1921), 269.

The benchers' resolution envisaged a largely autonomous structure in Northern Ireland for the education and discipline of bar students under the auspices of King's Inns, whilst seeking to preserve the ultimate right of the benchers in Dublin to determine any matters in dispute. The judges of either supreme court were to be benchers *ex officio*, and the lord chief justice of Northern Ireland was empowered to nominate a committee of benchers 'to deal with questions of education of students and discipline of students or members of the bar, subject to an appeal to the whole body of the benchers upon any question involving the disbarring or suspension of members of the bar or expulsion of students'.[2]

In addition to himself, Sir Denis Henry appointed a further 11 benchers to his committee, all former members of the North East and North West Circuits. Lord Justices Moore and Andrews, Mr Justice Wilson and Mr Justice Brown, the attorney general for Northern Ireland (Richard Best KC, MP), John Leech KC and E.S. Murphy KC were either judges of the new Northern Ireland supreme court of judicature, or members of the Bar who had decided to practice in Belfast. The remaining nominees never attended meetings of what became known as 'the Northern Committee'. Serjeant Hanna KC, Samuel Brown KC and R.F. Harrison KC continued to practise mainly in Dublin, whilst J.M. Whitaker KC went to practise in London.[3]

The need for books for the Northern Ireland Bar was urgent, and arrangements were made by the benchers of King's Inns to lend some books to the Bar Library. A number of books were sent to Belfast early in 1922 to form what was intended to be 'a branch library of the King's Inn', including the penultimate editions of textbooks.[4] It seems that it had been intended to send a set of the law reports as well, but this was frustrated by the seizure of the Four Courts, by the anti-Treaty faction of the IRA on Good Friday 1922 and the subsequent destruction of the building.[5]

---

2    Northern committee benchers' minutes (hereafter NCBM), p. 1.

3    The Northern committee held its first meeting on 11 Jan. 1922. Mr Justice Brown was appointed a member following his appointment as a judge of the high court of Northern Ireland on 26 Jan. 1922. NCBM, p. 2.

4    C. Kenny *King's Inns and the battle of the books*, 1972, p. 27. On 20 Apr. 1922 the benchers of King's Inns noted a letter of thanks from the Northern Bar Council. King's Inns Benchers' Minute Book 1917-28 (hereafter KIBMB), p. 168. Some 450 books were sent. Memoranda on the setting up of the Supreme Court of Judicature in Northern Ireland 1 Oct. 1921-31 July 1922. PRONI CAB/6/57 para. 32.

5    Hill Smith, *The Supreme Court of Judicature of Northern Ireland*, p. 47.

Provision was also made for the appointment of a professor of King's Inns who would give lectures and conduct examinations (other than the final examination) in Belfast for students of the Inn. The Northern committee immediately set about the task of setting up a system of lectures and examinations for bar students in Belfast, and at its second meeting resolved that students applying for call to the Bar should be introduced to the committee on that day. Library and education committees were set up, and the latter was instructed 'to prepare a scheme and to report on the provision to be made for the admission of law students applying to be called to the Northern Bar so far as not inconsistent with the resolution of the benchers of the King's Inns of 31st October, 1921'.[6]

In an attempt to enable members of the Northern committee to continue to play a part in the affairs of King's Inn, and to ensure that important decisions were not taken in Dublin without them having the opportunity to attend, the secretary was instructed to write to the under treasurer saying that the Northern committee had fixed the date of their second meeting of each term to enable them to attend the second meeting of the benchers in Dublin if necessary, and to express the hope that the benchers of the King's Inns could see their way to transact their more important business, including the election of bencher or professor or any alteration of the Constitution, at their second meeting instead of their first'.[7]

This was rapidly agreed to by the benchers of Kings Inns,[8] and in May 1922 the Northern committee considered a lengthy memorandum from Sir Thomas Molony, lord chief justice of Ireland,[9] relating to the proposals by the standing committee of benchers for the working out of the resolution of 31 October, 1921. As the memorandum revealed, the implications of the resolution for King's Inns were wide-ranging and complex. The benchers recognised that `Northern students' (defined as students who attend the lectures of the King's Inns professor in Belfast and were registered as such with the under treasurer) should be at liberty to attend a two year course to be provided by the benchers in Belfast. Because the two existing King's

6   NCBM, p.4.
7   Ibid., p. 5.
8   Ibid., p. 6.
9   Molony retained the title of lord chief justice of Ireland. See 'The title of the last lord chief justice of Ireland' in W.N. Osborough *Studies in Irish Legal History* (Dublin, 1999).

Inns professors were already fully committed to giving lectures in Dublin,[10] the benchers would appoint a third professor (to be known as the King's Inns professor of common law and equity) to teach the course in Belfast. The benchers would only appoint the professor after applications for the post had been sent to the Northern committee. The Northern Committee would then propose the name(s) of the candidate(s) it considered suitable to the benchers, and the benchers would take the views of the Northern committee into consideration before making the appointment.

Other consequential changes to the rules were proposed, including a reduction for Northern students in the requirement to keep dining terms in King's Inns from twelve to four, which could be kept at any time. It was also proposed that the number of lectures, the time of delivery, and the syllabus 'may from time to time be altered by the Committee of Benchers for Northern Ireland, but subject to the provision that the course shall as near as possible correspond with the course in Southern Ireland'.[11]

These proposals made generous provision for the needs of the Northern students. King's Inns were to pay the new professor's salary of £300 a year, but as the students fees were still paid to King's Inns, and, as we shall see, the fees paid to King's Inns by Northern students far exceeded the cost of the professor, King's Inns were still net beneficiaries. These arrangements effectively gave the Northern committee almost complete autonomy. The necessary changes in the rules were soon made by the benchers.[12] Later that year the Northern committee adopted new regulations for the attendance of students at lectures, and conduct of examinations, by the King's Inns professor of common law and equity, thereby completing the necessary framework to enable Northern students to be taught in Belfast.[13] That the two bodies succeeded in creating this new framework appeared to augur well for the future. The willingness of the Northern committee to contribute to the educational role of King's Inns was demonstrated by two of its members going to Dublin each autumn between 1922 and 1925 to act as examiners during the final exams, a time-consuming task covering several days.[14]

---

10  NCBM, pp 11-12.
11  Ibid.
12  14 Jun. 1922. KIBMB, 1917-18, pp 185-91.
13  NCBM, p. 22.
14  Between Oct. 1922 and Oct. 1925 Andrews LJ acted twice, Wilson J twice, Brown J once and E.S. Murphy KC once. KIBMB, 1917-28, pp 201, 236, 254, 288-89 and 307-08.

In 1922 six former members of the North East Circuit met in Dublin under the chairmanship of Robert Murray, the last Father of the Circuit. They resolved that of the remaining funds of the Circuit, £150 would go to the Circuit of Northern Ireland, together with the Circuit silver and books, and the wine held in Armagh and Downpatrick.[15] By implication the wine in Dundalk and Monaghan, and the balance of the Circuit funds, were to remain at the disposal of the members of the old Circuit in Southern Ireland. The meeting also resolved that the portraits of Holmes and Perrin were to be presented to the Benchers of King's Inns by the old North East Circuit. However, these hung in Armagh courthouse, and it seems that they remained there until they were brought to the Bar Library in Belfast in the 1950s. They now hang in the Bar Library.

The friendly relationship between King's Inns and the Northern committee continued during 1923 when King's Inns elected John McGonigal KC, one of the Northern committee's nominees, as a bencher to fill the vacancy created by the death of Mr Justice Gordon, and presented a copy of an engraving of Lord Justice Fitzgibbon to the Northern Bar.[16] In November 1923 sums of £10 and £5 respectively were granted to the Northern committee as first prizes in the senior and junior class examinations in Belfast.[17] Nevertheless, the strains created by the demands of the different, and often conflicting, political entities in Ireland were to prove too great for King's Inns to contain, let alone reconcile, and the new framework proved to have a short existence.

One of these demands related to the question of stamp duty, on the face of it a somewhat unlikely subject for dispute. Stamp duty was payable to King's Inns on solicitors' articles of clerkship. Whilst the amounts were relatively small, £384 in 1922-1923 and £312 in 1923-24,[18] the Northern government did not wish to have to remit sums to Dublin that had been paid in Northern Ireland. In addition, there were the fees and stamp duty paid by Northern students on admission to King's Inns, and on call, which amounted to a sizeable

15  The minutes of the meeting do not record when it was held, although Murray signed them on 8 Dec. 1922. A valuation certificate of four items of silver dated 5 Dec. 1922 addressed to W.M. Whitaker KC accompanied the minutes, and as he was recorded as being present perhaps the meeting was on 8 Dec. 1922. I am indebted to the Rt Hon Turlough O'Donnell for a copy of the minutes, and to his son Mr Justice O'Donnell who discovered them.
16  18 Apr. 1923, ibid., pp 225-27.
17  10 Nov. 1923, ibid., p. 246.
18  NCBM, p. 114.

sum. In June 1925 the Northern Committee calculated that in recent years King's Inns had received £1214 on the admission of 21 Northern Ireland students, and a further £2267 in fees and duties in respect of 15 Northern barristers called to the Bar of Northern Ireland, far outweighing the cost of the Northern professor paid by King's Inns.[19] In any event, the creation of the Incorporated Law Society for Northern Ireland in 1922 meant that it was anomalous that payments should be made to Dublin when the Law Society in Northern Ireland needed financial support to help it educate its students.[20] The Northern minister of finance, H.M. Pollock, raised the prospect of amending legislation to stop these payments to King's Inns in a meeting with the lord chief justice, Sir Denis Henry, in December 1923. Henry appears to have persuaded Pollock not to pursue the matter for the present, as

> it was agreed that pending the completion of arrangements for the affiliation of the Northern Ireland Bar to one of the Inns of Court in London, steps should not be taken to discontinue these payments to the Society of King's Inns in Dublin. [21]

It seems clear that Henry recognised at that time that it was only a matter of time before King's Inns ceased to have any part to play in the affairs of the Northern Bar. When King's Inns became aware of the Northern government's wish to stop these payments, R.F. Harrison KC wrote on its behalf to the Northern committee, saying the origin of the payments was a payment by the Irish Treasury for the site of the old Four Courts and that the benchers 'cannot afford to have their income cut down'.[22] It cannot be a coincidence that on the same day Serjeant Hanna KC wrote to the Northern committee pointing to the anomalies that were inherent in the present system, which he described as unsatisfactory, and suggesting that the Northern committee 'frame a scheme for a separate Inn, with power to confer with the benchers of King's Inns'. Hanna continued,

> I think that everyone, both in Dublin and Belfast is of the opinion that the present system is quite unsatisfactory. The profession is in fact separate under

19  8 June 1925. NCBM, p. 123.
20  When the Incorporated Law Society of Northern Ireland was founded in 1922 its only assets were £77 14s 3d and the books and furniture belonging to the Belfast Law Club. Memorial of 24 Feb. 1932 by the Incorporated Law Society of Northern Ireland to the minister of finance. S.C. L/24.
21  NCBM, p. 72.
22  27 July 1924, ibid.

the two jurisdictions, though in theory one, and for myself, I can see nothing to be gained by postponing the settlement of the problem.[23]

Whilst nominally a member of the Northern committee, Hanna did not attend its meetings, although he was a regular attender at benchers' meetings in Dublin. With his Northern and Unionist background Hanna was probably more alert to the implications of Northern Ireland's status than many of his fellow benchers in Dublin. He was also an *ex officio* member of the General Council of the Bar of Ireland. His recognition that the profession was in fact divided may well have been influenced by the recent refusal of the Northern Bar to nominate members to the Bar Council in Dublin. The Southern Bar Council included representatives of each of the circuits, and so it invited the Circuit of Northern Ireland to nominate a senior and a junior to sit on the Bar Council. The Northern Bar Council decided not to accept the invitation, directing its secretary to reply:

> that inasmuch as the Circuit is entirely subject to the jurisdiction of the Bar Council in Northern Ireland and so is not in any way subject to the jurisdiction of the Bar Council in Dublin the Council did not consider it right that the Circuit should nominate any representatives to the Bar Council in Dublin.[24]

The Northern ministry of finance again raised the issue of the payment of stamp duties to King's Inns in January and in June 1925, although the Northern committee succeeded in persuading the government not to include a provision altering the position in the projected finance bill on the basis that it was inopportune to pursue the matter, the Northern committee having decided to give King's Inns notice of the Northern committee's intention to terminate what it referred to as the 'agreement' of 31 October 1921 from the beginning of the Long Vacation on 1 August 1925.[25]

Significant though the issue of stamp duty was, this was a subsidiary question, and the precipitating cause of what came to be known as 'the split' was a more politically sensitive issue. This was the decision of the benchers of King's Inns to allow a number of leading politicians and others to be called to the Bar despite their not having passed some or all of the prescribed examinations. This was not unprecedented because on

23  Ibid.
24  22 Jan. 1924. Bar Council Minutes (hereafter BCM), p. 35.
25  NCBM, pp 92, 114 and 117.

several occasions after the First World War the benchers of King's Inns had exempted students from sitting various examinations, including the final examination, on the basis of their war service. For example, at their Trinity Term meeting on 27 May 1921 the benchers permitted Captain John Gillespie, a solicitor, to be called to the Bar without sitting his final examination for this reason, and similar exemptions were granted to two students at the Michaelmas Term meeting on 25 October 1921. Such exemptions were not invariably granted, and at the same time as Gillespie's request was granted, a request for exemption from the entrance examination on the basis of war service was refused.[26]

However, a number of applications for exemptions which came before the benchers in Dublin in 1924 were significant, coming as they did in the context of the changes brought about by the inauguration of the new court system in the Irish Free State created by the Courts of Justice Act 1924. As a result of these changes Sir Thomas Molony retired as chief justice and Hugh Kennedy KC became the new chief justice of the Irish Free State. Kennedy, who had served as law adviser to the provisional government, and then as attorney general, held very different views to many of his fellow benchers. One commentator, Thomas Towey, described him thus.

> Kennedy was an advanced constitutional nationalist who saw dominion status as an avenue to the development of a distinctly Irish, as opposed to English-inspired, structure of the state and its institutions. In his view, institutions based on English tradition were alien accretions.[27]

Kennedy's attitude towards the views of the Northern bench and Bar were therefore almost certainly less sympathetic than those of Molony. As chief justice Kennedy presided *ex officio* at benchers' meetings,[28] and his views would carry great weight, although, as we shall see, they were not always decisive.

The exemptions granted to several individuals by the benchers in late 1923 and in 1924 were a source of great concern to the Northern committee, and set in train the events that led to the rupture between King's Inns and

---

26  KIBMB, 1917-28, pp 141 and 150.
27  Thomas Towey, 'Hugh Kennedy and the constitutional development of the Irish Free State',
    *Ir. Jur.* xii (1977) 355.
28  Before 1923 the lord chancellor presided at benchers' meetings. On 11 Jan. 1923 the benchers
    resolved that henceforth the lord chief justice would do so. KIBMB. 1917-28, p. 213.

the Northern committee. Three of the individuals were granted exemption because of their war service. In November 1923, Major O'Brien-Twohig was permitted to sit the final examination without having attended lectures,[29] although he had earlier been refused permission.[30] In November 1924 he was called to the Bar, as was Leon O'Broin who was to be a distinguished public servant and historian, being secretary to the department of posts and telegraphs 1948-67 and a member of the Royal Irish Academy.[31] Although O'Broin does not appear to have been given exemption, his call was one which caused the Northern committee concern. Another exemption on the ground of war service was that granted to Major Barra O'Briain in October 1924, permitting him to attend first and second year lectures concurrently.[32] As the benchers pointed out when the Northern committee criticised such exemptions in 1925,[33] there were several precedents for such concessions. Nevertheless, that some of the benchers were uneasy about the granting of exemptions on the grounds of military service may be inferred from the terms of a motion tabled at the benchers meeting of 1 November 1924 by Alexander Blood KC.

> That as and from this date, no student's memorial praying for concession or exemption in consideration of military service of any description, be received by the Under Treasurer unless previously certified in writing by two Benchers to be [of] a special and exceptional nature and deserving the consideration of the Bench.[34]

Consideration of Blood's motion was deferred to the next meeting, when it was again deferred.[35] Whilst it was not until 1928 that much stricter rules governing exemption from the educational requirements on the grounds of war service were adopted by King's Inns,[36] the reluctance of the benchers to grasp this nettle in 1924 and 1925 surely suggests that it was considered

---

29   Ibid., p. 258. Commissioned into the Royal Munster Fusiliers in 1913, O'Brien-Twohig served as a regular soldier in the British Army in the First and Second World Wars, and as a king's messenger 1948-57.

30   Ibid., p. 234.

31   Ibid., p. 299.

32   Ibid., p. 293. A judge of the circuit court 1943-59, and president of the circuit court 1959-73. I am indebted to Mr Justice Fennelly for drawing O'Briain's judicial career to my attention.

33   NCBM, p. 122.

34   KIBMB, 1917-28, p. 303.

35   Ibid., p. 304.

36   6 June 1928, ibid., pp 443-45.

impolitic to try to prevent some individuals from relying on war service to gain exemption from the educational requirements of the Inn. That the war service was, in some instances, in the forces opposed to the crown would not have made those exemptions palatable to the Northern committee. Be that as it may, at its meeting of 25 October 1924 the Northern committee considered the future relations between it and King's Inns. Although the matter was deferred to the next meeting, it is clear that the Northern committee felt that the actions of the benchers in Dublin imperilled the system of reciprocity between King's Inns and the English inns of court, whereby each recognised the qualifications of the other as satisfying the requirements for call.

Matters were brought to a head by events in Dublin on the same day, when the benchers resolved 'That in consideration of his high office, the Ceann Comhairle of Dail Eireann, Mr Michael Hayes be exempted from attendance at lectures and be permitted to proceed to his call to the Bar, upon the Honours Examination only'.[37] The Northern committee responded to this development on 7 November by writing to King's Inns that it had decided not to admit to the Bar of Northern Ireland gentlemen called in Southern Ireland without further enquiry, especially as they were anxious to preserve the existing system of reciprocity between themselves as members of King's Inns and the members of the English Inns of Court. The Northern committee decided that until their concerns were met 'no Free State Barrister will, in future, be called here'.[38] In view of this unambiguous statement of their position the Northern committee may well have felt that King's Inns had decided to press ahead regardless of the consequences when they decided in January 1925 to call to the Bar Kevin O'Higgins, the minister of justice in the Irish Free State. Although he had passed the final solicitors' examination, O'Higgins had not been admitted to practice. The benchers unanimously resolved, 'That in consideration of Mr Kevin O'Higgins as Minister of Justice, his educational attainments and the experience of legal matters acquired by him therein and elsewhere Mr O'Higgins' memorial be granted', and he was called that day.[39]

When the Northern ministry of finance again raised the question of stamp duties at the beginning of January 1925, the Northern committee set up

37   Ibid., p. 295.
38   NCBM, p. 122.
39   19 Jan. 1925, KIBMB, 1917-28, p. 311.

a sub-committee to consider this, but that the real issue was the future relationship between the Northern committee and King's Inns was clear from the draft report of the sub-committee signed by Lord Justice Andrews on 15 January 1925. The lengthy report made no reference to the stamp duty issue but reviewed the history of King's Inns and its finances, the origins and constitution of the English inns, and examined in considerable detail exemptions granted by King's Inns, notably those relating to Hayes, O'Briain, O'Broin and O'Brien-Twohig. It concluded that a final rupture with King's Inns was only a matter of time, and proposed that steps be taken to form a separate inn in Northern Ireland, and to enquire from the English inns the conditions upon which the students of such an inn may be permitted to join one of the English inns so that they could take their final examinations in London. It suggested that the Northern committee protest to King's Inns and warn them that the Northern committee would in future decline to call to the Bar of Northern Ireland anyone called to the Bar of Southern Ireland who had been granted special exemption of which the Northern committee did not approve.[40]

A letter was then sent to King's Inns protesting about O'Higgins' call, accompanied by a portion of the sub-committee's report.[41] It was not until 11 May 1925 that King's Inns responded, when it emerged that the benchers had never been shown the Northern committee's letter of 7 November 1924. Why such an important letter was not disclosed to the benchers was not explained, and it must be a matter for speculation whether King's Inns would have made a different decision about calling O'Higgins if they had been aware of the Northern committee's concern. Given the recent precedent of Hayes, it is perhaps unlikely that a different course would have been taken. Nevertheless, the failure to disclose the November letter was a serious blunder which may well have led the Northern committee to conclude that King's Inns had decided to call O'Higgins in full knowledge that to do so could create a serious dispute between the two bodies, when in fact the benchers of King's Inns were unaware of the Northern committee's views.

King's Inns response of May 1925 was unyielding. It claimed that it had complied with all parts of the resolution of October 1921, and pointed to precedents when exemptions for war service had been granted when

40 NCBM, p. 92 et seq.
41 Ibid., p. 99.

members of the Northern committee had been present. Whilst both points were perfectly reasonable, the benchers' assertions that the Northern committee had no right to admit anyone to the degree of barrister at law, or to deny call to anyone admitted to the degree by King's Inns as only it could confer the degree of barrister at law in any part of Ireland, were less so. Whilst the Government of Ireland Act preserved the right of all existing members of the Irish Bar to practise in the courts of Northern and Southern Ireland, as this only applied to existing members it had the effect of creating separate bars for those called thereafter. The lord chief justice of Northern Ireland called candidates to the Northern Ireland Bar on the recommendation of his fellow benchers, and whilst they were still nominally acting as benchers of King's Inns, the reality was that they were acting independently.

The arrangements put in place after the benchers' resolution of October 1921 had been arrived at after discussions between the standing committee of King's Inns and Lord Justice Moore. These discussions appear to have taken place, so far as the Northern judiciary were concerned, on the basis that it was impractical to create a new inn in Northern Ireland, rather than the premise that only King's Inns would have the right to admit students to the degree of barrister at law in either jurisdiction under the new dispensation. That this was the case may be seen from an extract from a lengthy memorandum Moore drew up during the Long Vacation of 1922 for the Northern government which he intended should be published (although in the event it was not). Moore described the many steps that had to be taken to bring the new legal system in Northern Ireland into being, in the course of which he referred to the arrangements agreed 'after considerable discussion in Dublin'.

At an early stage the Chief Justice took into consideration the relations between Bench and Bar. The Benchers of the Inn of Court, at which the barrister has, so to speak, graduated, control him in matters of legal etiquette and discipline. They also make provision for the education of those students for the Bar admitted under their regulations to the Inn as students. All the members of the Bench and Bar on October 1st had, of course, been in some capacity members of the King's Inns, Dublin, which enjoys a certain amount of revenue from fees and investments, and is responsible for the education of students. It was felt to be impracticable at present to form a new Inn in Belfast even if desired, partly from lack of funds, and partly because at first not more than about ten students in the year as a maximum might be expected. It was therefore thought desirable to carry on, if possible, under the King's Inns, and the Chief Justice authorised Lord Justice Moore to attend a meeting of the standing Committee of the Benchers in Dublin and carry through some such arrangements.[42]

It now became clear that neither side was prepared to yield, and that what Serjeant Hanna had termed 'the settlement of the problem' a year before was increasingly unlikely to be achieved by agreement. On 13 June 1925 Hanna, who had been appointed a high court judge a few weeks before, wrote to the Northern committee from Green Street courthouse.

[The] position of [the] Northern Bar in its association with King's Inns is anomalous and illogical. I think they must have a separate establishment and I have only been anxious that the inevitable separation should be carried out with good feeling and without recrimination. In my view there should be a conference between two or three reasonably minded Benchers from either body, instead of a long correspondence.[43]

Unfortunately Hanna's hope that 'the inevitable separation should be carried out with good feeling' was not to be realised. The Northern committee resolved on 2 June to give notice to King's Inns of its intention to terminate the agreement of 31 October 1921, and, despite an exchange of letters in June and July, it was clear that a rupture was imminent and relations between the two bodies worsened. At the beginning of June Anthony Babington KC, who had been elected a bencher of King's Inns in November 1924, resigned, and E.S. Murphy KC informed the benchers that he would be unable to act as a final examiner.[44] King's Inns made it clear that it was not prepared to move from the position that it must remain the ultimate disciplinary and educational authority for both jurisdictions. The Northern committee suggested that a meeting be held to settle all outstanding matters as they were 'anxious that the severance which must now take place should be carried through in an amicable a spirit as possible'.[45] However, when King's Inns stipulated that any such meeting should only consider the

42  PRONI CAB/6/57.
43  13 June 1925. NCBM, p. 128.
44  Babington's resignation was noted on 3 June, and Murphy's letter on 10 June. KIBMB, 1917-28, pp 323 and 327-28.
45  23 June 1925. NCBM, p. 133.

arrangements to be made for students in the following Michaelmas Term,[46] this was not acceptable to the Northern committee and no meeting took place. On 30 July the Northern committee resolved to establish an inn of court at the earliest possible moment, and on 4 August reaffirmed that it had severed relations with King's Inns.[47]

The remainder of 1925 was marked by developments in both jurisdictions which emphasised that the split was irreparable. At their next meeting on 26 October the benchers of King's Inns heard Kennedy report that he had directed that a wreath be sent with their sympathy to Lady Henry following the recent death of the lord chief justice. They then turned to consider a motion by Kennedy to make 'a competent knowledge of the Irish language, of Irish History and of the Constitution and Government of Ireland' a requirement for call to the Irish Bar. This was referred to the education committee, but with an instruction that the committee was not to consider any change in the rules making knowledge of Irish a condition of admission as a student, or to the degree of barrister at law, when they considered if any changes were required.[48]

Whilst a knowledge of Irish was not to be made a requirement for call to the Irish Bar until imposed by the Legal Practitioners (Qualifications) Act, 1929, that such an attempt would be made had been predicted in 1922.[49] A belief that such a requirement would eventually be imposed may well have been an unarticulated factor contributing to the Northern committee's attitude. Whether it was or not, and as we shall see it was referred to after the split, as the split approached the Northern committee decided to contact the Council of Legal Education in London to explore whether it would be possible to establish a link with it. Whilst the response of the Council's chairman, Lord Justice Atkin, was not unsympathetic, he thought that the problem would be seen as 'party political', and suggested that the Northern committee try to arrange a satisfactory agreement with King's Inns.[50] Such was the importance and urgency of the matter, in the absence of Henry on circuit Lord Justice Andrews had immediately gone to London on his own initiative in the Summer of 1925 to see Atkin.[51] Whilst it was not until 1928

---

46   NCBM, pp 138-39 and 144.
47   Ibid., pp 140-45.
48   KIBMB, 1917-28, pp 340-41.
49   W.N. Osborough, *Studies in Irish History*, (Dublin, 1999), p. 275.
50   NCBM, pp 134-37.
51   Ibid.

that the arrangements for Northern students to take the English Bar final examination in London were completed, Andrews and Atkin established that this could be achieved.

Throughout the remainder of 1925 the Northern committee explored how the new inn should be created. One of the possibilities was whether a royal charter of incorporation could be obtained. It is revealing that one of the reasons given by the Northern committee in October 1925 when seeking agreement from the home office to the grant of a charter was the desire 'to keep the practice in Northern Ireland assimilated with the English Inns as closely as possible, valuing as they do the existing rights of exchange between the Irish and English Bars'. In particular, reference was made to Kennedy's recent attempt to make a knowledge of Irish compulsory for students entering King's Inns, and the fear was expressed that if such a requirement were to be adopted in future, which the Northern Committee viewed as quite possible, were King's Inns to remain the sole body through which qualification for the Bar could be achieved '...then there would be very few students from Northern Ireland, or possibly none, to come to the Bar of Northern Ireland'.[52] The Home Office would not agree to the grant of a charter, pointing out that the other inns of court were constituted as voluntary associations and suggesting that the new inn should be formed on a similar basis.[53]

A joint meeting of the bench and Bar was convened for that purpose on 11 January 1926. At that meeting the new lord chief justice, Sir William Moore, explained in some detail why relations had been severed with King's Inns, and perhaps it is appropriate to conclude this survey of these events with an extract from Moore's address in which he justified the decision to sever relations with King's Inns. Having said that the Northern committee had considered whether to set up an inn of court for Northern Ireland by obtaining a charter, or by obtaining an act of parliament from the Northern Government, before deciding to do so by a joint meeting of the Bench and Bar he continued:

> In what I am now about to say I honestly desire to avoid all acrimony. But I have
> seen quotations in the Belfast papers from journals published in the Free State,

52   Letter approved 28 Oct. 1925. NCBM, p. 157.
53   Andrews to Atkin (undated) 1926.

criticising our action, and I would wish to have our position clearly appreciated. Contrary to suggestion it is entirely different from that of the doctors in the Free State, who are now being compelled to join an Irish Register instead of a British one. Rightly or wrongly they are being deprived of a British advantage. We wish to retain our British advantage. The students of any Bar are educated under the tutelage of the leaders of the profession in those Courts in which they wish to practice. If the standard of those Courts and such training is sufficiently high, it is recognised by any other Court, or Inn of Court, in the British Dominions; but when the barrister goes to any other court he must first be called to the Bar practising in that Court. One great advantage that the Irish barrister always possessed while this state of affairs continued was this: That after three years practice in Ireland his admission to call at the English Bar was little more than a formality. The English barrister was similarly treated here. The like would apply to his position in the Colonial Courts of the Empire, and we desire to retain and secure this privilege for members coming to the Northern Bar, which we can only do by seeing that the existing standard of education, corresponding with that of the English Inns of Court, is maintained here. If we remain as an integral part of the King's Inns, and if they adopt a resolution recently proposed there by the Chief Justice of the Free State, that 'Irish' should be a compulsory language for Call to the Bar, we should probably find that the Irish barrister would not be admitted to the English Bar on the present terms once Latin has ceased to be part of the curriculum.

Legislation is differing so much in its tendency in the Free State from that in Northern Ireland, which is approximating as closely as it can to the legislation of the Imperial Parliament, that a new system of jurisprudence differing largely between North and South is steadily growing up. We find fewer and fewer members of the Free State Bar coming North to exercise the right of audience in our Courts, and it is very seldom indeed that a member of the Northern Bar goes into the Free State.

In these circumstances we thought it best to bring before this meeting of the Bench and Bar our proposal to set up a separate Inn. Our friends, the Solicitors' profession, have their own governing body here having broken off from the Incorporated Law Society in Dublin. The Pharmaceutical Chemists have done the same, and in each case without reproach; and I do not see why representatives of the Bench and Bar in Northern Ireland should be criticised for taking steps to become masters of their own house. If and when our new Inn be constituted, we will then have a representative body in the profession in Northern Ireland who, without surrendering in any way control over their internal affairs, will be in a position to enter into friendly working arrangements, if they are desired, with the King's Inns or any other Inn of Court which may appear to be for their mutual benefit.[54]

Moore's references to educational issues were indicative of the great importance which the Northern judiciary and Bar attached to preserving the ability of members of the Northern Bar to practise elsewhere, something which had been of considerable importance to Irish barristers who could not make a living at home, and which was to be equally important in the years to come. But when he referred to the growing divergences between legislative systems of the two jurisdictions he touched upon what Babington, who had succeeded Best as attorney general upon Best's appointment as a lord justice of appeal to fill the vacancy consequent upon Henry's death the previous October, described in his speech seconding the resolution as 'a question of jurisdiction which goes to the very root of our profession'. His opinion was that the creation of a separate Inn 'has been inevitable since the passing of the Free State Treaty Act. It has been forced upon us by the logic of events...'[55]

The logic of events to which Babington referred was, as Serjeant Hanna recognised, that there were now two Bars in Ireland, and the position of King's Inns that they 'do not recognise separate categories of Barrister at Law in Northern Ireland or Southern Ireland or the Irish Free State',[56] despite their understandable wish to preserve the unity of the Irish Bar, was no longer sustainable in the face of inexorable and irreconcilable changes in the political, constitutional and legal frameworks within which the Bar had to exist in each jurisdiction.

54  'Report of the proceedings at a meeting of the bench and Bar in Northern Ireland, held at the Law Courts, Belfast, on Monday, 11ᵗʰ January, 1926, at which an Inn of Court was established', pp 7-8.
55  Ibid., p. 9.
56  Letter of 20 June 1925 from King's Inns. NCBM, p. 131.

# CHAPTER FIVE:

# The construction of the Royal Courts of Justice

The Government of Ireland Act provided for the creation of supreme courts of judicature for both Southern and Northern Ireland, each consisting of a court of appeal and a high court. Appeals from the respective courts of appeal were to lie to the High Court of Appeal for Ireland consisting of the lord chancellor of Ireland, the lord chief justices of Northern and Southern Ireland, and such additional judges as were necessary.[1] Whilst the High Court of Appeal for Ireland and the supreme court of judicature for Southern Ireland could be accommodated in the Four Courts, provision had to be made for the accommodation of the superior courts in Northern Ireland, and the Imperial government undertook to provide this.

In view of the widespread violence and political turbulence which continued throughout Ireland after the passing of the Government of Ireland Act on 23 December 1920, it is not surprising that little thought appears to have been given to the question of where the new courts were to be located, and what accommodation they would require. It seems that it was not until about the time of the appointment of Sir Denis Henry as the first lord chief justice of Northern Ireland on 5 August 1921[2] that these questions were addressed in any detail, and later that month the Northern Ireland government announced that it had purchased the Stormont estate to be the site of the new courts of justice, parliament and ministerial buildings. Although the Government of Ireland Act provided that the supreme court of judicature of Northern Ireland was to consist of a lord chief justice, two lord justices of appeal and two puisne (or ordinary) judges of the high court, when Henry came to Belfast on 8 September 1921 he was 'without a colleague except Mr Justice Moore [who had applied to transfer from the king's bench division in Dublin], or an official, with the duty of seeing that the Supreme Court came into existence fully equipped'[3] by 1 October 1921.[4]

---

1    1920 c.67 s. 34(1).

2    Henry was appointed by royal warrant on 5 Aug. 1921 and sworn in by the lord chancellor of Ireland, Sir John Ross, in the Town Hall at Portrush, Co. Antrim where Ross was on holiday. A.D. McDonnell, *The life of Sir Denis Henry Catholic Unionist* (Belfast, 2000), pp 86-90.

3    'Memoranda on the setting up of the Supreme Court of Judicature in Northern Ireland, and other matters incidental thereto. 1st October 1921-31st July 1922' prepared by Moore LJ during the Long Vacation of 1922. PRONI, CAB/6/57.

4    1 Oct. 1921 was the 'appointed day' under SRO 1921 no 1527 by which s. 38 of the Government

This was a daunting task indeed, and arrangements were immediately made to secure the use of the County Court House on Belfast's Crumlin Road for the new courts until a more permanent solution could be achieved. Whilst not merely the obvious, but the only choice, nevertheless it was far from suitable, even as a temporary expedient. Although its two large courtrooms were excellent, as Henry quickly realised they were insufficient to provide a permanent home for a court of appeal and a high court which was soon to be divided into a king's bench division and a chancery division, with the probability on occasion of at least a minimum of three courts sitting at the same time, apart from the sittings of the high court of appeal, and the need for a smaller court for the use of the chief clerk and the taxing master from time to time. In addition, accommodation was required for the five judges of the supreme court and its 27 permanent staff based in Belfast. The building was already used for two or three assizes, each of about a fortnight at a time, and the Belfast quarter sessions. It also accommodated the offices of Antrim County Council; the clerk of the crown and peace and his staff (whose duties also included the local offices of the land registry); the Belfast bankruptcy court and its offices; the North East Bar, and solicitors. Belfast Corporation rapidly agreed to the transfer of the courts for which it was responsible to Townhall Street, where the recorder's court was renovated and put into proper condition for that purpose.

After what Moore described as many interviews, much correspondence and the good offices of the prime minister, Sir James Craig,[5] and Antrim County Council; which had initially offered the use only of the two courts, two judges' chambers and one other room; agreed to make a proportion of the building available to the supreme court. The Bar, solicitors, clerk of the crown and peace, the chief crown solicitor and the press all played their part by surrendering rooms which they had occupied to enable court staff to be accommodated. However, everyone had to carry out their duties in circumstances which Moore was later to describe, with considerable understatement, as 'cramped

of Ireland Act, 1920 was brought into effect. It was a sign of the extreme pressure under which all concerned were functioning that Henry pointed out that the necessary order in council had not been made, and it was not signed by King George V until 27 Sept. 1921.

5    Sir James Craig, (1871-1940). MP (U) East Down, Mid Down 1918-21, Co. Down 1921-29, North Down 1929-40. A government whip 1916-18, parliamentary secretary, ministry of pensions 1919-20, financial secretary to the admiralty 1920-21, 1st prime minister of Northern Ireland 1921-40. Created a baronet 1918 and 1st Viscount Craigavon of Stormont 1926. Honorary bencher of the Inn of Court of Northern Ireland 1928.

and crowded'.[6] Although Henry proposed to Craig in September 1921 that the County Court House should be purchased and used for the new courts, experience rapidly led him to realise that it was not satisfactory and that it would be more economical to build entirely new courts.

Henry prepared a memorandum setting out in considerable detail the requirements for the new courts, which was sent to the office of works on 15 December 1921. In his covering letter Henry withdrew his earlier suggestion that the County Court House should be purchased.[7] Henry envisaged a building not more than two storeys high with four courts; chancery, king's bench, court of appeal and high court of appeal. All were to be large enough to accommodate three judges, and the king's bench court was to be capable of temporarily accommodating five judges when hearing criminal cases by way of crown cases reserved (the procedure whereby difficult points of law could be 'reserved' by the trial judge by way of case stated and argued before the judges of the supreme court, who would then give their opinion).[8] One of the courts was to be capable of accommodating 600 members of the public. There were also to be two small courts for use by the taxing master and the chief clerk, in addition to the necessary office accommodation for the staff.

Henry proposed a 'Law Library' consisting of one large room with desks to accommodate about 80 barristers and capable of storing a large number of law books; a robing room to accommodate the same number, together with presses and lockers and independent lavatory accommodation. A room to accommodate about 30 solicitors at writing desks, with locker and independent lavatory accommodation, was also to be provided, together with a shared refreshment room for barristers and solicitors with kitchen and storage facilities. He also requested facilities for witnesses, consultation rooms, a room for up to six press reporters, a post and telegraph office, a stamp office and the public record office. Whilst these offices were not strictly part of the courts, Henry recognised that it would be convenient

6   PRONI, CAB/6/57.
7   Henry to Major Williams of the office of works, 15 Dec.1921. S.C. L/23. Henry referred to his
     letter of 14 Sept. 1921 to Craig in which he had suggested purchasing the County Court House.
8   Under 11 & 12 Vic., c. 78. See D.S. Greer, 'A security against illegality? The reservation of crown
     cases in nineteenth century Ireland' in N.M. Dawson (ed.) *Reflections on Law and History Irish
     Legal History Society Discourses and Other Papers, 2000-2005*, (Dublin, 2006). Appeals after 1921
     were rare. J.A.L. McLean 'Some developments in Northern Ireland since 1921-the Supreme Court
     of Judicature in Northern Ireland', (1972) 23 NILQ 84.

to the public to be able to pay judicature fees and purchase official forms at the courts, and suggested that accommodation be provided for the Inland Revenue in connection with death duties and other matters. Finally, a room was to be provided for the under sheriff, who sat with a jury to assess damages in cases where judgment had been marked in default of an appearance by the defendant.

Whilst these proposals seem unexceptionable to later generations, and most of them were ultimately accepted, some proved remarkably contentious. The design of the building was characterised by increasingly bitter disputes between the judiciary and the legal profession on the one hand and the treasury and the office of works in London on the other, disputes which undoubtedly contributed to some degree to a delay in starting construction. These delays were, however, largely due to difficulties caused by the increasingly severe pressure on public finances in the 1920s which led to demands to economise on the cost of the building. Even when construction eventually got underway with the laying of the foundation stone on 19 October 1929, the building workers' strike of 1931 further contributed to the delay in completion.

It was not until October 1922 that the Imperial government responded to Henry's memorandum in a letter from A.P. Waterfield, a senior official in the Treasury seconded to Dublin Castle.[9] Waterfield was critical of many of Henry's proposals, in particular the number and the size of the courtrooms. One objection where the treasury ultimately carried the day was to the size of the king's bench court, which Henry had suggested should be large enough to contain 600 members of the public. Examples of other queries were why it was felt necessary to have a conference room for the judges, or why four rooms were required for witnesses.[10] This letter was a foretaste of what was to be an unsympathetic, and often parsimonious, approach to the whole matter by the treasury, which was determined to ensure that the facilities in the new courts were no better than those in the Four Courts. As a result the building which was opened in May 1933 was significantly

9    Alexander Percival Waterfield (1888-1965). Having taken first class honours at Oxford he entered the Treasury in 1911. Treasury rembrancer in Ireland 1920-22. CB 1923, principal assistant secretary 1934-39, member of the Palestine Partition Commission 1938. Deputy secretary, ministry of information, 1939-40. Knighted 1944, KBE 1951. For Waterfield's time in Ireland see Michael Hopkinson (ed.) *The last days of Dublin Castle: the diaries of Mark Sturgis*, (Dublin,1999).

10   Waterfield to Anderson, 4 Oct. 1922. S.C. L/23.

different in a number of important respects from that which Henry, the judges, the Bar and solicitors originally envisaged.

Henry was absent when Waterfield's letter arrived, and Lord Justice Moore replied on his behalf. The reply was immediate, robust and uncompromising. At his direction, a lengthy letter was sent to Waterfield by A. Newton Anderson, permanent secretary of the supreme court (but almost certainly written by Moore), explaining the reasoning behind the original proposals.[11] Of particular interest is the justification advanced for a king's bench court with accommodation for 600. It was pointed out that in Dublin the courthouse at Green Street had been built for the trial of prisoners because the courts in the Four Courts were small, and the new court house was to combine the purposes of Green Street and the Four Courts. Henry's original memorandum had not expressly stated that the new courts were to accommodate assize business, but the proposal was remarkably far-sighted; as was the judges' desire that the building should be built in such a way as to make allowance for expansion because it was anticipated that the volume of business would increase in the near future. The determination of the judiciary to ensure that the facilities for staff and public were modern and satisfactory was underlined by the tart comment that 'there should be at least similar accommodation for witnesses in the new Court House as in the modern Law Courts in the Strand, and the requirements of 150 years ago as at the Four Courts should not in this instance be taken as a model for Belfast'.[12] The judiciary were very concerned about the treasury's attitude, particularly its unwillingness to commit itself as to whether the proposed building would make provision for any future expansion in legal business. Moore had the correspondence sent to Craig, arguing that it was for the prime minister to see that the Imperial government's obligation to provide accommodation for the courts was enforced.[13]

Waterfield, whose time in Ireland was coming to an end, was due to travel to Belfast to discuss the provision of buildings for the civil departments of the Northern government, and at his request a meeting with the judiciary was

11  Anderson to Waterfield, 11 Oct. 1922. S.C.L./23.
12  Ibid.
13  Anderson to Lt. Col. W.B. Spender, 11 Oct. 1922. S.C. L/23. Lt. Col. Sir Wilfred Spender, KCB, CBE, DSO, secretary to the Northern Ireland Cabinet 1921-25, permanent secretary ministry of finance and head of Northern Ireland civil service 1925-44.

held at the County Court House on Saturday 28 October, 1922.[14] Henry, who insisted that the meeting was 'without prejudice' to his proposals,[15] was accompanied by Lord Justices Moore and Andrews, whilst Waterfield was accompanied by Captain Street of the office of works. The meeting failed to resolve any of the matters in dispute. Waterfield would not be drawn as to whether provision would be made for future expansion, and many of his proposals were described as 'cutting the new arrangements down to their finest limit' by Anderson, when he wrote to Craig at Moore's direction to inform him of the outcome of the meeting, and to seek an assurance that Craig would not approve of any proposals until Henry had been given the opportunity of considering them in detail.[16]

When Waterfield returned to London he prepared a lengthy memorandum taking issue with almost every aspect of Henry's proposals. Some objections were well founded, as when it was pointed out that if it were intended to deal with criminal work (such as was transacted at the Old Bailey in London or at Green Street in Dublin) in the new court that was the responsibility of the county, and not of the state, and so criminal work should continue to be dealt with at the County Court House. It was also pointed out that a court to accommodate 600 would be much larger than any at the Law Courts in the Strand, where the lord chief justice's court would only hold 120 in the well of the court, and 88 in the gallery; and none of the courts in the Four Courts would hold more than 250.[17] As we shall see, although concessions were ultimately made by the judiciary on both points, most of the treasury's counter proposals were quite unacceptable. Henry responded by stating that unless the proposed accommodation was considerably extended the judges would not approve the proposals, and pointed out that the proposals as to the Bar Library (as he now called it) had to be considered by the Bar, and the views of the solicitors' profession and of the chamber of commerce had also to be obtained. Henry sharply refuted a suggestion by Waterfield that he had agreed at the meeting of 28 October to an inquiry into the organisation and conditions of service of the staff of the High Court. Henry said that he was quite satisfied with the manner in which their

14   Waterfield to Anderson, 14 Oct. 1922. S.C. L/23.
15   Anderson to Captain Street, 26 Oct. 1922. S.C. L/23.
16   Anderson to Spender, 30 Oct. 1922. S.C. L/23.
17   Treasury memorandum S. 13107/03, 30 Nov. 1922. S.C. L/23.

duties were performed, pointing out that every one of the offices had only been set up after the closest scrutiny by the Treasury.[18]

Henry's response crossed with a letter of 8 December 1922 from the treasury proposing such an inquiry. Henry refused to agree, reiterating that the treasury had concurred in the establishment of every post 'after careful scrutiny and examination and considerable delay occasioned by the Treasury, and this within the last fourteen months'.[19] However, the treasury continued to press for an inquiry, and in March 1923 Stanley Baldwin, the chancellor of the exchequer,[20] wrote to Henry proposing that the matter be referred to arbitration,[21] suggesting as arbitrator Lord Colwyn, an industrialist whose services were frequently called upon by government.[22] The same year Colwyn was appointed chairman of an arbitration committee to consider whether any alteration in the Northern Ireland contribution to Imperial services (such as defence, the foreign office etc.,) was required. He was therefore an obvious choice to perform this sensitive task. This suggestion placed Henry in something of a quandary. As he pointed out in a letter to Craig, because the obligation of the Imperial government to provide reasonable accommodation for the new courts was one which would be enforced, if necessary, by the prime minister and government of Northern Ireland, Henry felt that he could not enter into such an arbitration without express authority from the Northern Ireland government, indeed he preferred to leave the matter in their hands. Apart from that, as accommodation would be required for the Bar, the solicitors' profession, jurors, witnesses, the public and the press, all of whom had their own independent organisations, their interests would also have to be satisfied. He suggested that the Northern Ireland government arrange to appear before Colwyn, with himself as a witness. This would enable bodies such as the Bar, the Northern Law Society and other interested bodies to

---

18  Anderson to Waterfield, 8 Dec. 1922. S.C. L/23.

19  Anderson to the secretary of the treasury, 20 Dec. 1922. S.C. L/23.

20  Stanley Baldwin (1867-1947). 1st Earl Baldwin of Bewdley, chancellor of the exchequer 1922-23, prime minister 1923-24, 1924-29 and 1935-37.

21  Baldwin to Henry, 14 Mar. 1923. S.C. L/23. This suggestion had probably already been mooted informally because on 28 Feb. 1923 the Bar Council considered whether to appear before treasury officials who, it was believed, would shortly visit Belfast. BCM, vol. 1, p. 22.

22  Frederick Henry Smith (1867-1947). 1st Baron Colwyn. Created a baronet 1912 and 1st Baron Colwyn 1917. Privy councillor 1924. See R J. Lawrence *The government of Northern Ireland public finance and public services 1926-1964.* (Oxford, 1965), for Colwyn's role in the public finances of Northern Ireland in the 1920s.

appear as witnesses, thus relieving him of a certain amount of responsibility.[23]
The government's reply came from Colonel Spender, secretary to the
cabinet, and was probably not entirely to Henry's liking. Spender said
Craig had found Colwyn to be 'admirable as an arbitrator in other matters,
and considers that this proposal will be best [to] enable a decision to be
reached', and continued

> The Prime Minister thinks that all outstanding questions appertaining to the
> Law Courts can advantageously be referred to this arbitration, and he would be
> glad if the Lord Chief Justice took full responsibility for representing the
> interests of Northern Ireland in the matter, arranging with the Bar, Counsel
> (sic), Northern Law Society; etc to put forward their views, should he deem it
> advisable.[24]

Although this gave Henry a free hand, it also meant that he would have
to put forward the views not only of the judiciary, but of other interested
parties, such as the Bar and the Law Society, without having any authority
to bind them. He persuaded Craig[25] that it was preferable that Colwyn
come to Belfast and hold an inquiry, at which the various interested parties,
including the treasury and the judiciary, would put forward their views.
This was to be an informal inquiry, in that no counsel would be allowed,
and Henry anticipated that it should not last more than a day, certainly not
more than two, and wrote to Baldwin accordingly.

Whilst maintaining that the British government was not obliged to formally
consult with the various external interests to whom Henry had referred,
Baldwin conceded that Colwyn should hear from one representative each of
the judges, the Bar and solicitors. He also felt that as the Northern Ireland
government was interested, the ministry of finance should hold a watching
brief. Colwyn was not willing to travel to Belfast but would sit in Liverpool,
and asked for the responses of the judges, Bar and solicitors to the treasury
proposals to be reduced to writing and sent to him.[26]

Baldwin's justification for the interest of the Northern Ireland ministry
of finance in these proposals was that, although the Northern Ireland

23   Anderson to Sir James Craig, 21 Mar. 1923. S.C. L/23.
24   Spender to Anderson, 22 Mar. 1923. S.C. L/23.
25   Spender to Anderson, 28 Mar. 1923. S.C. L/23.
26   Baldwin to Henry, 24 Apr. 1923. S.C. L/23.

government had no responsibility for the administration of the supreme court as it was a reserved service, it was greatly interested to see that the cost, 'including the expenses of maintaining the building, number of staff to be accommodated, etc, is kept as low as possible'.[27] As we shall see, it was not until three years later that the judiciary discovered that the building was to be four, not two, storeys high, with various Northern Ireland government offices occupying the third and fourth floors.[28] It may be that Baldwin's reference to the Northern Ireland government's interest in these matters indicated that a decision had already been made to increase the size of the law courts from the two storey building originally proposed by Henry in December 1921 in order to provide accommodation for some Northern Ireland departments.

Henry agreed to Baldwin's proposals for the form the arbitration was to take,[29] and sent the treasury's proposals to the attorney general (as leader of the Bar) and the Law Society for their proposals, suggesting that a joint meeting of the Bar and Law Society might be prudent before they submitted their responses. A general meeting of the Bar considered Waterfield's memorandum on 13 December 1922, and unanimously approved a memorandum on the accommodation required for the Bar prepared by Anthony Babington KC.[30] A former member of the North West Circuit who was to become attorney general in 1926, Babington was to make a very significant contribution to the design of the new building. Together with Henry, Moore, Andrews, Sir James West, who ultimately designed the building, and R. Ingleby Smith, who prepared some of the early plans, Babington deserves much of the credit for the creation of the fine building which was ultimately to emerge after much travail.

The contents of Babington's memorandum of December 1922 are unknown, but there is no reason to believe that they were materially different from the four page memorandum setting out his proposed evidence to Colwyn sent to the treasury on 21 June 1923, together with memoranda from the lord chief justice and judges of the supreme court, the secretary of the Law Society and the Belfast chamber of commerce.[31] Babington argued for a Law Library

27  Ibid.
28  At a meeting on 29 Mar. 1926. BM, vol. 1, p. 34.
29  Henry to Baldwin, 7 May 1923. S.C. L/23.
30  BCM, vol. 1, p. 16.
31  Davies to F.G. Salter of the Treasury. S.C. L/23.

divided into two compartments, with the larger, outer one, for general use, and an inner one for those engaged in work requiring more privacy and seclusion. In addition there should be an ante-chamber in which interviews could be held without disturbing other occupants of the Library; robing rooms and lavatories, and a separate refreshment room. He described the accommodation provided for the Bar in the Four Courts and King's Inns and the way in which members of the Bar carried on their business, and suggested that four consultation rooms were required.[32] In its memorandum the Law Society sought a library, council chamber and examination hall, lecture theatre, waiting room, refreshment room, lavatory, secretary's office, furniture, office equipment and law books. That the Bar and the Law Society had discussed what ancillary accommodation was required for the proper conduct of business may be inferred from the request for four consultation rooms also made by the Law Society.[33] The Belfast chamber of commerce referred to the accommodation requested by the Law Society and supported its request. The chamber argued that the following were 'essential and indispensible': a grand jury room, a room for common and special jurors, a male witnesses room, a female witnesses room, a female jurors room, ladies and gentleman's lavatories, a public refreshment room with kitchen attached, and at least four consultation rooms.[34]

In their memorandum the judiciary approved the memoranda of the Bar, the Law Society and the chamber of commerce, and made a number of comments on some of the earlier responses of the treasury.[35] The judiciary continued to argue that four courts were required: a court of appeal capable of accommodating three judges and 200 members of the public, a chancery court also capable of accommodating 200, together with two king's bench courts, each not smaller than the existing crown court in the County Court House with a jury room attached, the bench of one to be capable of accommodating at least four judges. An office was necessary for the sheriff to enable him to sit with a jury of six to assess damages where judgment had been obtained by default in unliquidated claims, and to deal with the jury

32  'Memorandum of evidence to be given by A.B. Babington K.C. on behalf of the Bar of Northern Ireland as to the accommodation necessary for the Bar in the new courts of justice Belfast'. S.C. L/23.

33  'Memorandum of the Incorporated Law Society of Northern Ireland as to the necessary accommodation required by the solicitors' profession in the new courts of justice to be erected in Belfast'. S.C. L/23.

34  'Memorial of the Council of Belfast Chamber of Commerce'. 8 May 1923. S.C. L/23.

35  'Northern Judiciary Law Courts: memorandum by Lord Chief Justice and judges of Northern Ireland'. S.C. L/23.

panels and the execution of writs in civil matters in the high court. Suitable courts for the chief clerk and taxing master were also essential. Whilst the judges' memorandum recognised that the abolition of the high court of appeal in Ireland [36] had to be taken into account, and their acceptance that the courts of appeal and chancery need only accommodate 200 might suggest that they were prepared to make concessions on the size of the courtrooms, nevertheless their insistence that two of the four courts be capable of accommodating as many as the crown court at the Crumlin Road courthouse is further evidence that they envisaged the two king's bench courts being used for criminal trials.

Colwyn's response was to seek further information as to the number of judges and staff of the supreme court, as well as statistics showing the business done in the courts. This information was sent on 10 July 1923,[37] and on 17 July Colwyn was informed that Lord Justice Moore would attend at the forthcoming conference in Liverpool in place of Henry.[38] In the event, the proposed arbitration was to prove unnecessary and never took place. The treasury prepared a vigorous response to the various memoranda in a further submission to Colwyn.[39] Whilst a number of concessions were made, it still maintained that the courts were far too large, contrasting them with the courts in the Royal Courts of Justice in the Strand and the Central Criminal Court at the Old Bailey. Even the lord chief justice's court, by far the largest in the Strand, was only 48 feet by 45 feet (2,160 square feet) with seating for 196, with the other courts ranging from 1,020 to 1,665 square feet. The largest court at the Old Bailey was 2,500 square feet. Separate courts for the taxing master and chief clerk were still objected to.

Whilst accepting that the accommodation should be limited to the number of staff presently authorised, the treasury repeated its wish that there be an inquiry into the organisation and conditions of service of the staff, expressing the hope that this would 'suggest possibilities of economy in numbers e.g. by increases of numbers of working hours per diem, reduction of holidays

---

36  The high court of appeal for Ireland had been abolished in Dec. 1922 by the Irish Free State (Consequential Amendments) Act, 1922, sch. 21, para. 6.

37  Davies to Salter. S.C. L/23.

38  Davies to Salter, S.C. L/23. No reason was given for Moore going in place of Henry, but it was quite possible that Henry wished to remain at one remove from the detailed negotiations in case he had to intervene later.

39  'Second Treasury memorandum on the subject of the provision of the new Law Courts in Belfast with reference to the enclosures from the Registrar's letter of 21st June'. 17 Aug. 1923. S.C. L/23.

etc.'. It continued to take issue with the proposal that the sheriff and grand jury be accommodated in the new courts, pointing out that this confused the responsibility of the Imperial government to provide accommodation for the supreme court with that of Antrim County Council for assize and county courts. The memorandum contained an equally emphatic rejection of the claims of the Bar and the Law Society for accommodation, maintaining that neither was entitled to be accommodated at public expense, and that if such accommodation was to be provided it should be paid for by 'Northern Ireland funds'. In effect this meant by the Northern Ireland government as both professional bodies had already emphasised that they had no funds other than the subscriptions of their members.

Uncompromising though this response was on the surface, there were indications that the treasury was preparing to change its position on accommodation for the Bar and Law Society, including consultations rooms and refreshment room, because the memorandum concluded by asking Henry to indicate the size of the rooms requested for these purposes. This was ostensibly to enable Lord Colwyn 'to see exactly what the Northern Ireland proposal involves, both architecturally and in the matter of cost'. However, the inquiry in the covering letter to Henry as to what proportion of the professions in Northern Ireland were represented by the 80 barristers and 30 solicitors for whom accommodation was sought, and whether accommodation could be limited to a certain proportion, coupled with the reference to 'assuming for the sake of argument that the principle is approved providing accommodation on a scale similar to that in the Four Courts',[40] suggested that the treasury might be willing to concede that the Bar and the Law Society should be accommodated in the new courts at public expense, particularly if Henry accepted that the proposed courts could be reduced in size.

The treasury response arrived during the Long Vacation, which caused difficulties for those concerned, for example the Bar Council was unable to meet.[41] However, Henry discussed the treasury proposals with Pollock, the minister of finance, on 12 September and 26 October, and with W.D. Scott of the ministry of finance in November 1923. Pollock was acting as an

40   R.S. Meiklejohn to Henry, 20 Aug. 1923. S.C. L/23.
41   Davies to the treasury, 3 Oct. 1923. S.C. L/23.

intermediary with the full knowledge of the treasury [42] who sent him their 'without prejudice' proposals for consideration by Henry as an alternative to arbitration.[43] Following his meeting with Scott, Henry reached agreement with the treasury on almost all issues, except those relating to the Bar and Law Society, where he insisted that the treasury deal with the professional bodies direct. Henry accepted the treasury proposals for the size of the four courtrooms. The largest (the present nisi prius court) was to be the same size as the lord chief justice's court in the Strand at about 2160 square feet in order to accommodate a minimum of 240 people. The second largest court was to be 1350 square feet, accommodating a minimum of 150, the same size as the largest king's bench court in London. The third and fourth courts were each to be the size of the largest chancery courts in London at 1050 square feet accommodating at least 84 people. A small court of approximately 400 square feet was to be provided for the common use of the taxing master, chief clerk and registrar of titles; as were suitable robing rooms for the judges, an ante room to the lord chief justice's room for meetings, jury rooms and post office.

The treasury also conceded that the building should include a Bar Library (which would include an ante room) of about 2200 square feet, a robing room of about 400 square feet (to include lockers), and a refreshment room which was to be part of the main refreshment room, but partitioned off, also of about 400 square feet, a total about 3000 square feet. There is no record of the Bar Council discussing this proposal,[44] but the actual floor area of the Bar Library as it ultimately emerged is considerably greater than that proposed by the treasury in 1923. Whilst it is not impossible that the Bar persuaded the treasury to agree to a larger area in 1923, there is nothing to suggest that this was the case, and there is evidence to indicate that it was not until the final plans were prepared some years later that the Bar secured a significant increase in the size of the Bar Library. The treasury proposed that the Law Society should not be provided with any accommodation in the new building, and that there should only be a room of about 500 square feet for solicitors, and two consultation rooms, each of 250 square feet, 1000 square feet in total. The Law Society was naturally disappointed with this, although the treasury maintained that its proposal

---

42   Ibid.

43   Ministry of finance to Henry, 29 Oct. 1923 with treasury proposals. S.C. L/23.

44   No minutes of meetings of the Bar Council exist for the period between 25 Feb. and 27 Dec. 1923.

compared 'favourably with the accommodation provided at Dublin, and is in excess of that provided at London'.[45] The Law Society met the minister of Finance on 12 and 15 November 1923,[46] and by 1926 had succeeded in obtaining an increase in its accommodation to 3000 square feet, with the Northern Ireland government contributing £7000 towards the cost of £10500, and advancing the balance as a loan repayable over 50 years. This was still insufficient for the Law Society's needs and, as we shall see, they sought further accommodation in 1932.[47] It would therefore seem that agreement had been reached as to the accommodation which was required in the new courts by the end of 1923, because sketch plans were prepared and transmitted to the ministry of finance for examination by the various parties concerned, the ministry informing the office of works on 3 January 1924 that 'the lord chief justice has provisionally agreed the main principles'.[48]

When the Northern Ireland government announced in August 1921 that the Stormont Estate was to be the site for the new courts of justice,[49] the absurdity of placing the new courts on the outskirts of the city was obvious because of the inconvenience and expense all court users would incur in an age when almost everyone either walked to their destination, or was dependent upon public transport, and the commercial life of Belfast was based in and around the centre of the city. In addition, doubts were immediately expressed as to the constitutional propriety of having parliament and the courts in such close proximity, or even combined in one building, Lord Crawford (the first commissioner of the office of works) writing to Craig in these terms on 16 August 1921.[50] By early October the office of works had obtained the agreement of Belfast Corporation, as joint owners of the County Court House, to enter into negotiations

---

45   Treasury proposals. S.C. L/23.

46   Private secretary of the lord chief justice to Spender, 11 Oct 1932. Inn Box 34.

47   Para. 8 of the memorial sent by the Law Society to the ministry of finance said that the increase was to 2,160 square feet. An undated memorandum sent to the lord chief justice by the office of works on 8 Sept. 1932 said that the Law Society agreed to a further 2000 square feet to be provided at Northern Ireland expense, to which the ministry of finance agreed. On 7 June 1926 Pollock offered to increase the area to 3000 square feet, but only to provide £7500 of the cost of £10000, asking the Law Society to pay the balance, or reduce the area accordingly. S.C L/24.

48   The undated memorandum referred to above. S.C. L/24.

49   *ILT&SJ*, lv (1921), 213.

50   PRO WORK 27/7/1.

for its sale.[51] Although Henry did not formally withdraw his suggestion that the government purchase the building until December 1921, it seems that the government had anticipated that this would occur because it had already made an approach to the governors of the Royal Belfast Academical Institution (R.B.A.I.) to purchase the open ground in front of the school facing College Square. Whilst the governors were reluctant to sell, they felt that they could not refuse the government's request and at the end of November 1921 offered the plot to the government for £80000.[52]

The absence of a decision where the new courts and other public buildings were to be situated gave rise to considerable public concern. In October 1922 Craig held a conference at Belfast City Hall, telling the representatives of the city council that the law courts, and associated offices such as the stamp office and registry of deeds would be located as close to the centre of Belfast as possible.[53] As we have seen Waterfield approached Henry shortly afterwards, and the Imperial government followed up its earlier approach to R.B.A.I. with a counter offer of £50000. However, despite the chairman of the governors telling the government that he would place an offer of £70000 before the board, although without committing himself or it to approve such an offer, there was no response from the government. That the school and the government were in negotiation became public knowledge, and in March 1923 the board, angered by the government's procrastination and suggestions that they had asked an exorbitant price when they were reluctant to sell, decided to withdraw its offer to sell the site to the government.[54]

There matters rested until January 1924, when a meeting was held between the trustees of the school and the ministry of finance, following which the government made a final offer of £60000 for most of the open site fronting College Square, a site fractionally larger than that occupied by the Technical College. Having considered the offer, and recognising that although the school could continue on its present site for a few years with increasing difficulty because of the impact of the construction work, the price was

51 *Belfast News Letter* 4 Oct. 1921.
52 The board decided to sell on 21 Nov. 1921. R.B.A.I. Minute Book 1916-24. PRONI, SCH/524/3A/1/11.
53 *ILT&SJ*, lvi (1922), 242.
54 Board meeting of 19 Mar. 1923. R.B.A.I. Minute Book, pp 414 and 436-37. PRONI, SCH/524/3A/1/11.

insufficient to enable a new school to be built on its property in the suburbs at Osborne and Cranmore, the board decided to reject the offer, the motion being proposed by J.H. Robb KC, MP. Conscious of criticism which might be levelled at the board, its chairman wrote to the newspapers explaining at some length the reasons for its decision.[55]

The delay in the construction of the courts was a considerable embarrassment to the Northern Ireland government, with the ministry of labour in particular very anxious for work to start, presumably because of the employment that would be generated by such a large project. The government knew an alternative site for the new courts was under consideration when the final offer was made to R.B.A.I.,[56] and it must have been with a sense of considerable relief that it learnt at the end of February 1924 that an offer of £55000 had been made to Belfast Corporation for the potato market at the bottom of Chichester Street, an offer which was quickly agreed.[57] Now that the basic specification for the building had been agreed and the site acquired, it must have been hoped by all who so anxiously awaited its completion that matters would proceed much more rapidly than before, but if so they were to be cruelly disappointed. It was not until May 1933, more than nine years later, that the new building was officially opened, having undergone so difficult and prolonged a gestation that what had happened so far seemed relatively straightforward. Despite the site having been acquired and sketch plans drawn up, hopes of rapid progress were dashed almost immediately when the Imperial government warned that it was 'highly probable that the new Law Courts will not be finished prior to 1930' and that it was seeking an extension of its tenancy of the County Court House up to 12 January 1930, with the option of an annual tenancy thereafter, although the possibility of earlier completion was at least kept open with breaks of the tenancy being sought in 1928 and 1929.[58] Henry again sought Craig's support to expedite matters, and Craig agreed with him that the building should be ready for occupation by January 1928.[59]

---

55   Board meetings of 28 and 30 Jan. 1924. R.B.A.I. Minute Book, pp. 488-90. PRONI, SCH/524/3A/1/11. *Belfast Telegraph* 31 Jan. 1924.
56   Cabinet meeting 22 Oct. 1923. CAB/4/92.
57   Cabinet meeting 29 Feb. 1924. PRONI, CAB/11/102. The conveyance was signed on 1 Apr. 1924. S.C. L/23.
58   Sir Arthur Durrant, director of lands accomodation, office of works, to Davies, 20 May 1924. S.C. L/23.
59   Spender to Davies, 13 Jun. 1924. S.C. L/23.

With no sign of progress during the remainder of 1924 the judges and the Bar became increasingly concerned. On 15 April 1925 the Northern committee of benchers passed a resolution deploring the delay, pointing out that the site for the new building had not even been cleared, and strenuously urging the Northern Ireland government to ensure that the Imperial government met its obligations. The difficulties experienced by everyone working in extremely cramped and overcrowded conditions can be seen from the following extract from the resolution.

.... the attempt to carry on the work of four Courts in the two public Courts repeatedly leads to much inconvenience and delay. The judges are repeatedly compelled by force of circumstances to hold Courts in their own private Chambers and in other small rooms quite unsuitable for the purpose; and on one occasion it was found necessary to hold the trial of an Action in a temporary galvanised structure without sufficient floor space to provide even standing accommodation for the litigants and their witnesses.[60]

This may have had the desired effect, for plans were prepared in July 1925 and revised in December of that year. However, these plans were abandoned because of expense. Fresh plans were then drawn up by R. Ingleby Smith, deputy director of works in the ministry of finance. These plans, whilst different in design and much cheaper than the building originally planned, provided the same accommodation as had originally been agreed.[61] Following a meeting between the benchers and representatives of the minister of finance, including Ingleby Smith, the benchers set up a committee to consider the matter and seek professional advice as necessary.[62] They sought the advice of J.E. Croasdaile, a civil engineer, who reported that whilst the original plan was suitable in every way except for an expensive and unnecessary basement below high water level, the other designs were quite unsuitable. Having been warned by Lord Justice Andrews that the Treasury wanted to reduce further the size of the rooms, the benchers resolved that buildings erected in accordance with the second and third designs would be quite inadequate, and decided to send an edited version of Croasdaile's report to the ministry of finance.[63]

60   15 Apr. 1925. NCBM, pp 105-27.
61   BM 1926-33, pp. 12-13.
62   Andrews LJ, Babington KC MP, E.S. Murphy KC and J.H. Munroe KC.
63   At a meeting on 2 Mar. 1926. BM 1926-33, pp 30-32.

That the plans produced after such a long delay were so unsatisfactory was bad enough, but worse was to come when Andrews informed his fellow benchers that he had learnt that it was proposed to allot the two top storeys of the new building to Northern Ireland government departments. This had been discovered by the new lord chief justice Sir William Moore (Henry having died the previous October), and when Pollock pointed out that Henry had agreed to this proposal, Moore responded 'unfortunately my predecessor did not keep any records of discussions, such as you mention, and communicated very little about them to us…' In reply Pollock pointed out that most of the offices were 'those which should naturally be there for the convenience of the legal profession, such as the Stamp Office, Estate Duty Office, Record Office and Registry of Deeds'.[64]

Despite Moore's indignation at what he later characterised as 'the absurdity of superimposing a gigantic Department of Commerce on top of the Courts, and calling the whole building the 'Law Courts'',[65] there was little that could be done as Henry had already agreed to this proposal. When the benchers wrote to Pollock on 31 March 1926 agreeing to a fourth set of plans (which had been prepared by Ingleby Smith) they confined themselves to expressing '… their extreme regret that the New Law Courts should not be reserved exclusively for the administration of justice'.[66]

Unfortunately none of the different sets of plans appear to have survived, but it would seem that the first three sets of plans had one major feature in common which was subsequently abandoned, namely, that the four courtrooms were to be placed at each corner of the central hall, thus consciously replicating the design of Gandon's Four Courts. It seems probable that this was at the suggestion of Henry and his colleagues, because the proposals of 15 December 1921 suggested separate robing rooms for the judges for each court, together with separate lavatory accommodation for each court easily accessible from the robing rooms. This, together with the absence of any reference to other chambers for the judges suggests that the courts were to be laid out in this way. Strange though this may seem to those familiar with the present Royal Courts of Justice, it would be natural to those who had spent their professional careers in the Four Courts to seek to reproduce its features in the new courts in Belfast.

64  Pollock to Moore, 23 Mar. 1926, and Moore's reply 24 Mar. 1926. BM 1926–33, pp 38–39.
65  W. Johnson, private secretary to the lord chief justice, to Spender, 11 Oct. 1932. Inn box 34.
66  BM 1926–33, p. 44.

That this was not to be the case was due to the efforts of Anthony Babington KC, now attorney general and, as such, head of the Bar. His efforts were decisive in preventing what would have been a thoroughly awkward and inefficient layout being adopted for the distribution of the courtrooms in the new buildings. He also played an important part in the design of the courtrooms themselves, as well as ensuring that the accommodation ultimately achieved in the Bar Library was greater than had originally been envisaged. Babington's experience of the Four Courts led him to reject the proposal that the four courts should be placed at the corners of the main hall, and heated arguments ensued with the office of works, which prepared the original plans.[67] The benchers condemned the government's proposals as being

> ...objectionable on many grounds, [the] principle (*sic*) of which were inconvenience in the arrangement of the Courts and Judges apartments, unsuitability and inadequacy of accommodation for the Bar, reduced size of the central hall, and defective lighting of corridors.[68]

They described the plans drawn up by Ingleby Smith as 'infinitely superior' to those that had gone before. When a further set of plans was prepared by the office of works in London the benchers refused to consider those plans unless Ingleby Smith's plans were 'submitted again to the Benchers and negotiations proceed on the basis of their general acceptance'.[69] Ingleby Smith had been asked to prepare these fresh plans by Babington. Aware that new plans were to be prepared following a conference held in London to resolve the matter at which Lord Justice Andrews and Babington represented the interests of the bench and Bar,[70] the benchers adopted a 13 paragraph memorandum on behalf of the bench and Bar on 29 July 1926. This set out requirements which were almost all ultimately incorporated in the building. The principle features of this memorandum, which bears the stamp of Babington's views and Ingleby Smith's plans, were fourfold. The courts were all to be grouped on one side of the central hall, with the judges' chambers and related rooms behind opening off a single corridor with a separate entrance for the judges. The Bar were to have a separate library, librarian's workroom, robing room, luncheon room and lavatories in one,

---

67 Babington, *Reminiscences*, p. 256.
68 Benchers letter to Pollock, 13 July 1926. BM 1926-33, pp 80-81.
69 Ibid.
70 BM 1926-33, pp 82-83.

self-contained, unit with a private entrance, preferably in the interior of the building. All rooms and parts of the building should have adequate natural daylight and lighting. Finally, in keeping with the other public buildings of the city, the outside walls of the entire building should be of Portland or other good cut stone.[71]

Babington described what had happened at the conference.

> I was appointed to look after the interests of the Bar and I found the second plan adopted the lay out of the Four Courts in Dublin with a central hall and a court at each corner. I had considerable experience of the inconvenience of this design and said No. The arguments became quite heated as the Chief Architect or the Principal Officer of the Office of Works, I never knew which, would not give way. Eventually a conference was arranged which took place in Whitehall, presided over by Lord Peel and I went over prepared to argue with anyone. I had taken the precaution of getting some sketch plans drawn by an architect called Ingleby Smith, an officer in the Ulster Works Division. When I was objecting to the proposed plans, I produced these which in their layout are what was finally adopted and Sir George Baine, the Chief Architect, was very angry because Ingleby Smith had been in his office and he did not like him as I afterwards discovered when I asked why Baine was so contemptuous. Finally on the second day of this argument, Ronald McNeill,[72] Parliamentary Secretary to the Chancellor of the Exchequer, then Sir Winston Churchill, turned up with the information that the Chancellor said we were to have whatever we wanted. McNeill thought that the plans should go in the wastepaper basket and the experts told to start again. I was afraid we would be done down and the condemned plans again submitted with some changes, but Sir George Baine went out of the Office of Works to London Transport, and Sir William [sic] West took his place. He was a most satisfactory person to work with and I kept in close touch with him throughout the whole job, thereby securing quite a few amenities and also some spare room for the Bar.[73]

Babington's arguments and Ingleby Smith's plans carried the day and the ultimate internal layout of the building closely followed the benchers' 13

---

71  Ibid.
72  Ronald McNeill, 1st baron Cushendun. MP (U) 1911-18 and 1918-27. Parliamentary under secretary for foreign affairs 1922-24 and 1924-25; financial secretary to the treasury 1925-27, chancellor of the duchy of Lancaster, 1927-29.
73  Babington, *Reminiscences*, p. 257.

point memorandum. New sketch plans were prepared in the autumn of 1926 and agreed by the benchers, so far as they affected the benchers and Bar, on 12 November 1926, following a meeting with Croasdaile, J.M. Davies representing the staff of the supreme court, and the sub-committee of the Law Society.[74] The Law Society, which had also retained its own architect, whilst expressing some reservations as to the size of some of the court offices, agreed to the revised plans on the same day.[75] Two plans for the exterior of the building were prepared, one of brick, and the other of stone, although the latter would cost approximately an additional £25000.[76] Drawings of the proposed exteriors prepared by Charles Terry Pledge of the office of works have survived, and they are strikingly different in design, with the brick version featuring an enormous porch extending the full height of the Chichester Street elevation of the building, together with a mansard roof.[77] On 1 December 1926 the prime minister, now Viscount Craigavon,[78] reported to the Northern Ireland cabinet that on a recent visit to London he had discussed the plans with the chancellor of the exchequer and the financial secretary to the treasury. Craigavon, who had been accompanied by the ministers of finance and labour, felt that stone was 'much more in keeping with the amenities of the surroundings than a building in brick', and it was agreed with the chancellor that the Northern Ireland government should contribute £12500 towards the additional cost, and this was agreed by the cabinet.[79] Work was then put in hand to prepare large-scale plans, which were discussed at a series of meetings in May 1927.[80]

However, progress was still painfully slow, and it was not until 19 October 1929 that the foundation stone was laid by the duke of Abercorn, governor of Northern Ireland. At the ceremony Moore said that as they had waited seven years for the laying of the foundation stone, he hoped they would not have to wait another seven years before it was completed. Babington and the president of the Law Society added their support to these remarks, leading George Lansbury MP (the first commissioner of the office of works) to

---

74  BM 1926-33, p. 115.
75  Memorandum 12 Nov. 1926. S.C. L/24.
76  PRONI, CAB/4/182. The final contribution was £13,500.
77  See plates between pages 189 and 196.
78  Sir James Craig had been created Viscount Craigavon of Stormont in the New Year's Honours List of 1926.
79  CAB/4/182.
80  Undated memorandum sent to the lord chief justice by the Office of Works on 8 Dec. 1932. S.C. L/24.

respond that the building should be completed by the Autumn of 1932.[81] This proved not to be the case as a strike by building workers in 1931 held up the work,[82] and it was not completed until 1933, when the Governor opened the building on 31 May in a splendid ceremony attended by dignitaries of church and state.

The final stages of the construction of the building were not without incident. In 1932 the Law Society made a belated effort to obtain substantially greater accommodation to provide for a lecture hall, four consultation rooms, a common room and a ladies cloakroom, as well as financial support for the provision of furnishings and library. Despite the vigorous support of the lord chief justice, who engaged in an increasingly acerbic correspondence with various Northern Ireland departments over the issue, the Law Society had only partial success, the office of works pointing out that the building was almost complete and so incapable of extension to meet further demand.[83] However, some additional room was made available which the Law Society reluctantly accepted.[84] Moore, whose relations with Pollock and the ministry of finance had worsened considerably, sought to have control over the two lower storeys vested in the lord chief justice, something that was accepted by the office of works.[85]

When completed the new law courts represented a remarkable achievement. Supported on 1153 reinforced concrete piles to an average depth of 40 feet, and with frontages of about 390 feet to Oxford Street and about 260 feet to Chichester Street and May Street, the building was 'in a style intended to convey the dignity and tradition of the Law'.[86] Although the internal walls are faced in brick, the exterior is of Portland stone.[87] The exterior, described at the time as being 'in the traditional Italian style, after the manner of Palladio'[88] has not received universal praise. Sir Charles Brett called it 'an interesting

---

81  Belfast News Letter supplement, 16 Nov. 1932.
82  Ibid.
83  W. Ormsby Gore, MP, first commissioner of the office of works, to the lord chief justice, 10 Jan. 1933. S.C. /24.
84  J.C. Taylor, president of the Law Society, to the lord chief justice, 10 Jan. 1933. S.C. L/24.
85  Ormsby Gore to Moore, 10 Jan. 1933. S.C. L/24.
86  Official Programme for the opening on 31 May 1933.
87  At the cabinet meeting of 1 Mar. 1927 the Northern Ireland government approved a sketch elevation of the new courts, and decided to pay £13500 as a final contribution from Northern Ireland to the extra charge involved. CAB/4/187.
88  *Belfast News Letter*, 16 Nov. 1932.

study in the Recessional-Imperial style of British Architecture', and described the Chichester Street facade as being 'very grim and forbidding', criticising much of the exterior detail, notably the 'obtrusive' and 'very slab-like and unrelated' attic storey. However he praised the magnificent central hall, 140 feet long and 30 feet high, which is panelled in travertine marble, commenting 'in many ways, this is the best room in the city'.[89]

Generations of judges, barristers, solicitors and litigants would surely agree with Brett's description of the four original courts. 'The courtrooms themselves, panelled in teak and floored with cork, are both impressive and practical – even comfortable'.[90] That this is the case is largely due to the collaboration of Babington and West, with Babington providing the practical contribution to the basic layout of the courtroom furnishings, and his account of how the lay out of the court rooms was planned should be required reading for all court room designers.

There appears to be no formula for the design of the Courts, so I got Sir William (sic) [West][91] to lay out the Chief Justice's Court in wooden scantlings and we did some experimental work shifting the seating round until we thought it would do. The position of the Judge, Jury and witness, the room and ease of access provided for Counsel. [There were] no steps and passages, and some other minor improvements were all thought out and the three other Courts followed the design on a slightly smaller scale. Sir William was very particular about lighting. He had designed the Duveen Galleries in the National Gallery at Trafalgar Square, and when we were all lined up for a procession on the opening day, he walked down to where I was posted and said – 'Mr Attorney, can you find a single dark spot in this building'? I was not quite sure but I said 'No' as I knew he would not have asked me if there had been one.[92]

It may be that it was the contrast between the happy conjunction of Babington's practical experience and West's plans and other, far less

89  C.E.B. Brett, *Court houses and market houses of the province of Ulster* (Belfast, 1973), p. 50.
90  Ibid. The cork flooring has been removed in a completely unnecessary safety measure to stop members of the public from slipping. Unfortunately this has considerably impaired the previously excellent acoustics.
91  West, James Grey (1885-1951). CBE 1930, Knt 1936. FRIBA. Entered the office of works 1904, chief architect 1934-40. Designer of RAF College Cranwell, and the catafalque of Westminster Hall for the lying-in-state of King George V, as well as the annexe to Westminster Abbey for the Coronation of King George VI and Queen Elizabeth.
92  Babington, *Reminiscences*, pp 257-58.

successful designs, that Lord MacDermott had in mind when he wrote, although in the context of a criminal trial:

> .. the even handed administration of justice depends, to an extent far greater than most people think, on having the courtroom acoustically good, reasonably heated well-ventilated and the theatre or centre of action small enough to have the judge, jury, witnesses and accused all within easy sight of each other.[93]

After long delays and much travail Northern Ireland obtained courts far superior to those in the Strand, the Parliament House, or the Four Courts. This was due to the efforts of many individuals, notably Henry's determination that the new courts should be modern and suitable in every way. Nevertheless, it was entirely appropriate that at its meeting of 2 June 1933 the Bar Council passed votes of thanks to Babington and West. That to Babington recorded his efforts to secure proper accommodation and facilities for the Bar, and the thought and care he devoted to the task. West was thanked for his 'unremitting attention and high professional skill'... in endeavouring to perfect the arrangement and equipment of the building, and especially in relation to the accommodation set apart for the members of the Bar, as well as 'the courtesy with which he was always ready to consider suggestions made by the attorney general and other members of the profession'.[94] That these were not mere words was demonstrated by gifts to West and Babington.[95] Somewhat surprisingly perhaps, Ingleby Smith's contribution to the ultimate design does not appear to have been acknowledged.[96]

The satisfactory outcome of the lengthy gestation of the new courts represented a considerable achievement for which Henry in particular deserves great credit. Whilst his proposal that some of the new courts should be large enough to accommodate 600 had to be abandoned because the treasury, correctly in accordance with the division of responsibility for civil and criminal courts in both Northern Ireland and England and Wales of the time, insisted that assize work should continue to be heard at the

---

93   MacDermott, *An enriching life*, p. 202.
94   BCM 1921-49, pp 116-17.
95   Babington, *Reminiscences*, p. 258.
96   According to the lore of the Works Division, this was, not surprisingly, a source of some annoyance to him. Communication to the author from Robin McKelvey, principal architect of the Construction Service.

County Court House because it was the responsibility of Antrim County Council to provide courts for this work, Henry's proposal was sensible and farsighted. Had it been adopted, an enormous waste of judicial, professional and public time spent by succeeding generations in travelling to the Crumlin Road from the centre of Belfast could have been avoided. It is ironic that the closure of the County Court House in June 1998 led to some Crown Court cases being heard in the Royal Courts of Justice until the new Laganside Courts came into operation at the beginning of 2002.

Henry and his colleagues, particularly Moore, and both branches of the legal profession were determined that the facilities to be provided for the judiciary, staff and public were to be modern and spacious; and that accommodation be provided for both branches of the legal profession as part of the supreme court of judicature. Their determination, helped by the good offices and financial support of the Northern Ireland government, ensured that the treasury ultimately accepted that Northern Ireland would be provided with law courts well fitted for its needs in the 20th century, although at substantial cost, a contemporary estimate being that the total cost came to over £750000, a considerable amount at the time.[97]

97   *ILT&SJ* lxiii (1933) p. 161.

# CHAPTER SIX:

## Education and the Inn

With the establishment of a separate inn of court in Northern Ireland, provision had to be made immediately for the education of those who wished to be called to the Bar of Northern Ireland. Difficult decisions had to be made about the content of the course of lectures, who was to deliver them, and whether the final examination was to be conducted under the auspices of the Inn itself or another body. In addition, arrangements had to be made for those individuals who had embarked upon a court of study at King's Inns with a view to being called to the Bar of Northern Ireland. One of the first acts of the newly-elected benchers was therefore to set up an education committee. In view of his previous involvement with legal education as an examiner for King's Inns, and his initiative in travelling to London the previous summer to contact Lord Justice Atkin, it was natural that Lord Justice Andrews was appointed chairman. Such was the urgency of the situation that the education committee met for the first time on 26 January 1926.

One of the decisions on that occasion illuminated the complexity of the situation created by the creation of the new Inn, namely the position of Bar students presently attending lectures provided by King's Inns in Belfast. As we have seen in the previous chapter, lectures were being provided for King's Inns students in Belfast by the King's Inns Professor of Common Law and Equity under regulations laid down by the Northern committee. In September 1925 the Northern committee refused permission to sit a supplemental examination to a student who had failed his final year examination in June. The student then applied to King's Inns and was given permission to sit a supplemental exam before the King's Inns professor (Marcus Begley KC). The student had been successful. The education committee refused to give the student credit for this and required him to sit the first year examination again.[1]

Whilst this decision demonstrated the determination of the education committee and the benchers to assert their control over the education of their

1    BM, 1, pp 9-11.

students, in practice it seems that the pre-1926 arrangements continued to function until a completely new system was devised and put in place some years later. In the Summer of 1926 examinations for what were described as 'The Continuous Course Examinations' were held in both Dublin and Belfast, those in Belfast being conducted by Martin G. Ellison. Thirteen students were involved and King's Inns awarded prizes.[2] A supplemental examination was held in October 1926.[3] Similar examinations were held in Belfast in June and October in both 1927 and 1928.[4] On each occasion the examination was conducted by Ellison, and the results reported by him to the education committee of King's Inns. However, the obvious practical difficulties created by this were demonstrated by a letter to the education committee of the Inn of Court of Northern Ireland sent by Begley on 23 January 1926 asking whether he should send the examination papers and results to King's Inns, or to the Inn of Court of Northern Ireland, and although the minutes do not describe exactly how this problem was resolved, it was resolved satisfactorily.[5] Applications for call to the Bar of Northern Ireland were first of all considered by the education committee. It granted applications for call by seven members of the Bar of the Irish Free State at its first meeting, and it was not long before enquiries were being received from members of the Irish, English and other bars seeking to be called to the Bar of Northern Ireland.

Throughout 1926, 1927 and 1928 discussions about the education of the Inn's students continued on two fronts; firstly with Queen's University about the provision of lectures; and secondly with Lord Justice Atkin, as chairman of the Council of Legal Education, to see whether arrangements could be agreed which would enable Northern Ireland Bar students to study in London and sit the English Bar Final there. Whilst both Queen's and the Council of Legal Education were very helpful, the implications for both institutions were significant, and some time was to elapse before the final arrangements were worked out. By June 1926 Andrews was able to respond that discussions with Queen's had established that the University was willing to co-operate with the benchers, and to re-organise its law faculty in a manner which would ensure a more continuous and complete course of instruction so far as preparation for practice was concerned. The ramifications of this

2    KIBMB, p. 371.
3    KIBMB, pp 384–86.
4    BM, 1, pp 14–15.
5    BM, 1, p. 18.

proposal for the University were substantial, requiring as it did an increase in staff and a reorganisation of the syllabus to provide lectures in pleading and practice, as well as conveyancing, for the Bar students only. The University proposed to appoint Professor J.S. Baxter[6] to a new post as head of the faculty, and to appoint an assistant lecturer in these additional subjects, with the benchers paying £150 for these lectures. These arrangements were approved by the benchers on a provisional basis,[7] but in the event they were to provide the basis upon which, with some alterations over the years, Queen's provided courses for Bar students for almost half a century.

These courses were of two kinds. A Bar student could take the three year undergraduate course (which was extended to four years in 1937), as well as the lectures in pleading and practice and conveyancing, and the benchers paid the University a proportion of the fees the student paid to the Inn.[8] Alternatively, a Bar student who was not required to take the undergraduate degree course because he or she possessed an arts degree of a recognised university would only be required to take the lectures in pleading and practice, unless obliged to take lectures in other subjects required for call to the Bar of Northern Ireland which they did not have as part of the degree, such as Irish land law.

Whilst the arrangements for teaching at Queen's were largely agreed by June 1926, those for education and examinations in London were not concluded until June 1928. The benchers were determined to insist upon a high standard of legal education as a condition of call to the Northern Ireland Bar, and required candidates for admission as students to have passed a university matriculation examination, whilst those seeking admission to the Bar had to possess an arts degree of a recognised university.[9] These requirements effectively made the Northern Ireland Bar a graduate profession, as possession of a university degree was not an essential requirement for call either to the Bar of Ireland or the Bar of England and Wales. In this respect the benchers were certainly setting more rigorous standards than had King's Inn, and on 24 January 1927 Gerald Fitzgibbon wrote to Moore from Dublin congratulating the benchers on their decision to require a university degree, commenting

6   See pp 63-64 for details of Baxter's career.
7   15 June 1926. BM, 1, pp 50-51.
8   Report to the benchers by James McSparran KC and George B. Hanna KC. BM pp 771-72.
9   Andrews to Atkin. BM, 1, pp 71-72.

Curiously enough, about a year and a half ago the Chief Justice here discussed with me, and I think at the Education Committee, the possibility of making a similar rule here, but we came to the conclusion that the majority of the Benchers and the general opinion of the Bar would not stand for it.

You are starting from the foundations and can do what you think best.[10]

Fitzgibbon made one pessimistic prediction which fortunately was not borne out, when he suggested

Practice will be your real crux, and I doubt if the young practitioner in Belfast will be able to count on the help of his seniors and contemporaries as we used to be able to do in our early days at the Bar. In a small and close borough like that, competition and the resulting jealousy must make people more shy about imparting knowledge than the old Irish Bar used to be.[11]

The benchers were also anxious to establish a close and formal educational link with the English inns of court. Andrews wrote to Atkin on 16 June 1926, and having described the steps taken to establish the Inn, outlined the framework of the scheme the benchers wished to create.[12] This letter is also important because it set out the reasons why such a link was thought necessary.

At a Meeting held a few days ago the Benchers decided that, if satisfactory arrangements could be made, they would like to establish a closer association with the English Inns of Courts in educational matters than that foreshadowed in my previous letters. Their wishes are:

1. That our students should attend three Terms Commons at one of the English Inns, such attendances to be similar to those required in the case of Oxford and Cambridge Students.
2. That it should be optional for students to take one year of their legal course in England by attendance as Pupils in the Chambers of a Barrister or Conveyancer with attendance for the same year at Lectures of two Professors

10   Inn Bundle S.2. The typed copy wrongly gives the signature as Edward Fitzgibbon, but the writer must be Gerald Fitzgibbon (1866-1942). Called 1891, KC 1908, bencher 1912. TD (Dublin Univ) 1921-23, last holder of the office of king's advocate, judge of the supreme court of the IFS 1924-38.
11   Ibid.
12   Andrews to Atkin, BM, 1, pp 71-72.

of the Inns of Court in London. This privilege is at present accorded to, but, we think somewhat seldom availed of, by, the students of King's Inns.

3. That our students should, before being called to the Bar, pass the Final Examination for Call to the Bar in England in such subjects as may from time to time be approved by the Bench. It was, I think, generally considered that such subjects would include all those comprised in Part II entitled Final Examination in which the law in England and Northern Ireland is more similar than is the case in some of the subjects included in Part I.

We feel that an association of this character with the English Inns of Court would be a matter of supreme importance to our newly formed Inn, and that it would do much to ensure the attainment of a high standard of legal education which we are determined to insist upon as a condition of Call to our Bar. This high standard of education we are also endeavouring to secure by requiring candidates for admission as students to have passed a University Matriculation Examination, whilst those seeking admission to the Bar must possess the Arts degree of a recognised University.

Atkin was very supportive and encouraging in his reply of 21 June 1926, although he drew attention to a number of technical issues. He commented that there might be difficulty were it suggested that students should sit Part II of the English Bar Final in Northern Ireland, although those difficulties might not be insuperable. He also pointed to the requirement for Latin 'to which we attach considerable importance and to which you probably adhere',[13] but thought that there should be no difficulty about the proposal that a student would have the option of spending a year attending lectures provided by the Council of Legal Education whilst a pupil in the chambers of a barrister or conveyancer in London. He did, however, point out that whilst it would probably be possible to keep terms on the same basis as an Oxford or Cambridge student by dining three nights in the term instead of six, this would require a student to join whichever of the four English inns he chose, as had been the rule for Irish students in the past. Although Atkin suggested that this would be advantageous if a student adopted the option of reading in chambers, he also observed that

This certainly was the rule in 1875; it was abandoned later for an optional

---

13  BM, 1, pp 74–75. The benchers had already decided that Latin was to be one of the entrance examination requirements. 29 Apr. 1926. BM, 1, pp 50–51.

admission to an English Inn, I assume for reason of convenience and expense; and no doubt you will consider whether the same considerations may not make it difficult for you to make this proposal compulsory.[14]

It took some time for the necessary changes to be made to the consolidated regulations of the inns of court in London, but in the Summer of 1928 the final touches were put to the scheme whereby students of the Inn of Court of Northern Ireland became members for one year of one of the English inns on payment of one third of the usual fee. They were required to keep three terms' commons by dining three days in each term, and were permitted to attend lectures provided by the Council of Legal Education for the four inns of court in London as an alternative to attending one year of the course of legal education at Queen's University. They were also required to pass Part II of the Bar Final conducted by the Council of Legal Education in London.[15]

The introduction of these arrangements put in place the final part of a tripartite structure of pre-call education for the Bar of Northern Ireland which was to remain largely unaltered until July 1972. This structure was in most respects both pragmatic and visionary, representing as it did an effort to ensure that high educational standards were achieved by a small branch of the legal profession in a separate jurisdiction which was the smallest part of a nation which contained two other much larger and distinct legal systems. By reaching an agreement whereby Queen's educated Inn students, the Inn made a virtue out of necessity because, as Lord Justice Moore pointed out in 1922,[16] it was impractical for the Inn to teach a handful of students each year. In 1921 it had been thought that at most about ten students each year might be expected. However, apart from 1948, it was not until 1970 that the number of students, and hence calls to the Bar, ever reached, let alone exceeded, this figure, as can be seen from the following figures.[17]

(1) In 1926–35 there were 40 calls, an average of four a year, but of the 40, six who were called in Hilary Term 1926 made their careers at the Southern Bar, so the true figure is really 34, or fewer than four each year.

14  BM, 1, p. 74.
15  BM, 1, pp 233–238. Cmd 579, para 4 (Armitage Committee report, hereafter *Armitage*).
16  See p. 104.
17  Tables based on benchers' records and *Armitage*, App. 5, p. 53.

(2) In 1936-45 there were 22 calls, or fewer than three each year.

(3) In 1946-55 there 61 calls, of whom three were members of the English Bar (although G.B.H. Currie was a native of Northern Ireland[18]), so the yearly average was just under six. However, this is somewhat misleading, as there were very substantial fluctuations in the numbers called during this period, with eight calls in 1947 and 16 calls in 1948, and seven calls each year in 1949, 1950 and 1952.

(4) In 1956-65 there were 26 calls, of whom five were members of the English Bar, leaving an average of fewer than three local candidates each year.

Apart from the difficulties created by the small number of students, it was understandable and entirely appropriate for the benchers to require their students to pass Part II of the English Bar Final. This ensured that the standards required of Northern Ireland Bar students would be seen to be as high as those in England and Wales. This was of particular importance as we have seen from Sir William Moore's remarks at the foundation of the Inn quoted in Chapter Four.[19] The English Bar, and the colonial legal service in particular, had long provided outlets for Irish barristers,[20] and as we shall see, the colonial legal service was frequently resorted to by members of the Northern Ireland Bar for many years to come. The alternative would have been to have had a totally self-contained Northern Ireland system, but this would have had to have been entirely, or at least predominantly, provided by practitioners. However attractive such a concept might seem, a system of vocational professional education which relies exclusively on practitioners, however desirable in theory, all too often proves unsatisfactory in practice, something the benchers may well have been aware of given the criticism that had been directed at the King's Inns system of teaching in the past.

Nevertheless there were two respects in which the new structure was open to criticism. The first was that it ignored differences between Irish and English law, although it is probable that this only became apparent with the passage of time as more and more differences developed between the legal

---

18  MP (U) for North Down 1955-70, although educated in Ireland, Currie practised as a member of the Northern Circuit in England. D. Lynch, *Northern Circuit Directory 1876-2004* (Liverpool, 2005), p. 242, and J.F. Harbinson, *The Ulster Unionist Party, 1882-1973 its development and Organisation* (Belfast, 1973), p. 83.

19  See p. 108.

20  Hogan, *The legal profession in Ireland*, p. 37.

systems in England and Northern Ireland, with the result that students had to remember the many differences between the rules and structures of both jurisdictions.[21] In addition, certainly by the 1960s, criminal procedure was not taught at all to Northern Ireland Bar students (other than those who had studied at Queen's) who were left to learn it for themselves, hardly a defensible position! However, this is less a criticism of the system devised in the late 1920s, and more of the failure to revise it in later years to make it suitable for changed times.

This was not the only deficiency identified when the system was reviewed by the committee under the chairmanship of Professor Armitage, then vice chancellor of Manchester University, set up by the Northern Ireland government in 1972. The committee also commented on the requirement to join and keep terms in an English inn.[22]

> Although the arrangements existing for Northern Ireland candidates to take the English Bar final examination are at an end because of the re-organisation of the course following the Ormrod Report we should, in passing, note that these arrangements were not altogether satisfactory. The student had to study largely on his own for the English Bar Final at the same time as he was fulfilling the other requirements of the Inn of Court for Call to the Northern Ireland Bar which involved a separate and simultaneous study of Rules and Statutes peculiar to Northern Ireland. Furthermore in addition to the professional fees required by the Northern Ireland Inn of Court he was also required to pay professional fees to an English Inn of Court and to travel to England to keep terms. Such expenditure, not being educational expenditure and therefore not payable by the local education committee where a discretionary award had been made, bore heavily on the student's financial resources and it may well have been that some persons who might otherwise have entered the Profession were deterred from doing so because they were unable to meet the expense of entry.

In this respect at least the benchers can be criticised without the benefit of hindsight because, as we have seen, Atkin expressly touched upon the implications for Northern Ireland students in terms of expense of requiring them to join an English inn and keep terms by eating dinners. Why was this

---

21  *Armitage*, para 29.
22  Ibid., para. 30

requirement re-imposed when it had been abandoned forty years before?[23] The benchers' minutes do not throw any light on this, but the explanation is probably to be found in Andrews' observation in his letter to Atkin quoted above 'That an association of this character with the English inns of court would be a matter of supreme importance to our newly formed Inn.'[24] Perhaps the benchers thought that the arrangement for their students to sit the English Bar Final, and to have the option of pupillage in chambers, would be more easily achieved if the students were at least placed on the same footing as Oxford and Cambridge students, rather than by seeking a more detached relationship. It may be that they were correct, but Atkins' tactful comment may have contained a hint that a request for the creation of a special category of student for those who only wanted to sit the Bar Final in London might have been worth pursuing. Be that as it may, it was not until 1972 that a completely new educational structure came into being which abandoned the requirement to sit the English Bar Final, and was based entirely upon local teaching and examining directly under the control of the Inn.

Although the education scheme remained substantially unaltered until 1972, for a number of reasons in the 1950s and early 1960s the benchers considered whether significant changes should be made to their scheme. The principal reason was because the law faculty at Queen's wished to reshape its curriculum. As a result of the proposed changes, and their implications for the courses to be studied by Bar students at Queen's, the benchers and the University engaged in protracted, and at times difficult, negotiations extending over almost a decade. These difficulties were due to the tension between the desire of the law faculty to have a modern curriculum which enhanced the study of law as an academic discipline in its own right, and the desire of the benchers to ensure that its students received a thorough grounding in those subjects that they regarded as essential to equip a Bar student for practice, which one may term the vocational approach.

However, the first difficulty which the benchers had to address during this period related to a quite different matter. In 1952 for the first time they became aware[25] of the implications of the provisions of the

23  For an account of this requirement see C. Kenny: *Tristram Kennedy and the revival of Irish Legal Training*, Ch. 9.
24  Andrews to Atkin. BM, 1, p. 73.
25  The 1885 Act had been considered for repeal by the Northern Ireland authorities, and it seems likely that the parliamentary draftsman drew the Act to the attention of the benchers.

Barristers Admission (Ireland) Act, 1885[26] for the rule requiring Bar students to join an English inn of court. The benchers appreciated that this requirement could be illegal under the 1885 Act, and so called into question a fundamental aspect of the scheme created in the 1920s whereby Bar students had to join one of the English inns. A series of meetings were held by the benchers in April 1952 to consider the implications for the inn's requirement that Bar students join one of the English Inns in order to sit Part II of the English Bar Final in London. A division of opinion emerged amongst the benchers as to the utility of the need to join an English inn. Initially Lord Justices Porter and Black, as well as Mr Justice Sheil and Mr Justice Curran, opposed the continuation of the requirement to join an English inn and keep commons there, whilst Lord MacDermott supported it. The preponderance of opinion of the Bar benchers was in favour of requiring students to keep commons in London until such time as facilities were available to keep them in Northern Ireland, and a resolution to this effect of 22 February 1952 was confirmed by seven votes to one on 29 April 1952.[27] Whilst there were differing views among the benchers as to whether the provisions of the 1885 Act did apply, it was recognized that the matter was far from clear, and the decision was taken to seek an opinion from Geoffrey Cross QC in London.[28] Cross advised that the 1885 Act continued to apply.[29] In the event the benchers did not have to have to abandon 'the traditional form of student training which the [1885] Act itself recognises,'[30] because fortuitously an avenue presented itself for the repeal of the 1885 Act in the form of the Repeal of Unnecessary Laws Act (Northern Ireland) 1953[31] passed by the Northern Ireland parliament. As a result of the repeal of the 1885 Act the requirement that Bar students join an English inn, keep terms and sit Part II of the English Bar Final continued for almost a further two decades.

The prospect of significant change in the relationship between the Inn's requirements for the education of Bar students and the Queen's law faculty's courses was first formally mooted on 12 January 1953 when the

26  See Ch. Two at p. 40.

27  BM, 29 Apr. 1952.

28  Arthur Geoffrey Neale Cross (1904-1989). A high court judge in England and Wales 1960-69, a lord justice of appeal 1969-71, and, as Lord Cross of Chelsea, a lord of appeal in ordinary 1971-75.

29  Cross declined to mark a fee for his opinion and was presented by the benchers with a gift of glassware. BM, 1950-54, p. 236.

30  Explanatory memorandum to the Repeal of Unnecessary Laws Bill.

31  1953 Ch. 5.

vice chancellor of Queen's[32] wrote to the lord chief justice raising concerns about the number of courses Bar students were required to take, as well as technical issues relating to examinations.[33] As we shall see, this letter marked the beginning of an extended, and at times difficult, period of discussions between the University and the Inn about the inter-relationship between the Inn's educational requirements and courses for its students and the impact of these on the curriculum and structure of the LL.B course at Queen's. In the event these discussions were not to be satisfactorily resolved for twelve years. A committee of benchers[34] was appointed which met representatives of the University, and it reported to the benchers in a memorandum of 12 February 1953.[35] Amongst the concerns of the University was that the Inn's requirement that Bar students possessed an arts degree meant that some were studying arts and law in two faculties at the same time, and this was felt to be unsatisfactory. Whilst some of these concerns appear to have been satisfactorily resolved by the summer of 1953,[36] Queen's remained unhappy with the extent to which the law faculty was constrained by its willingness to provide courses for Bar students in subjects which it did not provide for the LL.B., such as pleading and practice, at a time when it wished to reshape the LL.B. curriculum. As the vice chancellor put it in a letter to Lord MacDermott of 11 July 1955 '...the overall needs of the profession are very diverse and the purpose of the Faculty is not solely to train practising lawyers'.[37]

Three meetings were held between representatives of the Inn and of the University in January and February 1956 to discuss these matters. The University representatives again raised the Inn's requirement that Bar students should possess an arts degree. They pointed out that legal subjects taken at Cambridge, for example, led to a B.A. and gave exemption from part of the Bar examinations, while the same legal subjects taken at Queen's led to an LL.B. which was not recognised for exemption. The effect of this,

---

32  Eric Ashby (1904-1992). Vice-chancellor of the Queen's University of Belfast 1950-59, master of
    Clare College Cambridge 1959-75, vice-chancellor, University of Cambridge 1967-69. Knt 1956,
    FRS 1963, created Lord Ashby 1973.
33  BM, 1950-54, pp 249-50.
34  Lord MacDermott LCJ, G.B. Hanna QC and C.A. Nicholson QC represented the Inn, the
    vice-chancellor and Professors MacBeath, Montrose and Newark represented the University.
35  BM, 1950-54, pp 280-82.
36  BM, 1950-54, pp 292-95 record a meeting of 3 July 1953 at which decisions were made
    accommodating the University's concerns.
37  Sir Eric Ashby.

as the Inn had recognized in the 1953 discussions, was that Queen's students who took an arts degree first had to spend six years studying before they could be called, whereas students of other universities where an arts degree could be obtained on a legal curriculum could qualify for the Bar in four years.[38] This put the growing number of Bar students studying at Queen's at a serious disadvantage compared to those who studied at universities where law was taught as part of an arts degree, particularly Oxford, Cambridge and Trinity College, Dublin. The university proposed that the Inn's regulations requiring an arts degree should not apply to students who had spent four years on a law degree and a further year in preparation for the Bar Final.

The Inn's representatives recognised that the existing requirement was an anomaly, and recommended to the benchers that the requirement of an arts degree be removed.[39] The benchers discussed the matter and the general feeling was that no one should be admitted as a student unless he was a graduate of an approved university, and thereafter he should pursue a course of legal education of at least two years and before call should pass the English Bar Final.[40] However, although the committee was asked to reconsider its report in the light of these suggestions it did not report, no change was made to the Inn's rules, probably because it seems that Queen's did not pursue the proposed changes to the curriculum at that time.

The issue remained dormant until 1962, when Queen's decided upon a radical revision of the curriculum of the law faculty. The LL.B. course was to become a four year one, with all students studying a number of courses in the first two years, and then electing for one of three honours schools for the final two years. The university was determined to put in place this new curriculum to enable some subjects to be studied in greater depth in the honours schools, whilst at the same time making clear their relationship with other branches of learning. These proposals were viewed with great concern by the Inn because the proposals, if adopted, would render it impossible for a Bar student at Queen's to comply with the existing requirements of the Inn. The benchers were concerned that under the proposed curriculum Bar students would not study a number of subjects in sufficient depth that were important from a vocational perspective. The

---

38  Memorandum to the Education Committee of the Inn 12 February 1953.

39  Report of the sub-committee to discuss the question of legal education with representatives of Queen's University, BM, 1955-64, p. 115.

40  2 July 1956. BM, 1955-64, p. 124.

Law Society was also concerned about the impact of the changes. The university, no doubt mindful of the difficulties which had arisen when it had earlier tried to change its curriculum, only notified the benchers of its intentions when they were in an advanced stage of preparation, and the senate of the university passed the necessary regulations on 25 April 1962. However, the resolution also said that they were not to come into effect until a special sub-committee of the senate had consulted with the Inn and the Law Society to 'consider means by which the said regulations may be adapted to serve the needs of the legal professions in Northern Ireland and to secure recognition'.[41]

The subsequent discussions and negotiations between the benchers (and the Law Society) and the university were difficult and destined to last several years. The Inn suggested several changes to the structure of the new curriculum, but the law faculty was adamant that the suggested alterations were unnecessary and would have the effect of serious limiting the objectives of the new curriculum. The views of the faculty can be discerned from the concluding passage of a lengthy memorandum prepared by Professor Montrose, dean of the Law Faculty, in response to a number of alterations to the curriculum which had been suggested by Lord MacDermott.

> The whole object of the Honours Schools is to ensure that the objectives of legal study which have been proclaimed by law teachers for many years should be effectively achieved. It is necessary for this purpose that subjects should be studied at such depth that their relations with other branches of law should be adequately discerned, and also with other branches of learning. These objectives are not merely those of law teachers, they are those of all who have been concerned with ensuring that the university student is preserved from the evils of a narrow and technical specialisation. Law properly taught can be a means of enlarging perspectives, of serving as a bridge between the sciences and the humanities. The proposals put forward by Lord MacDermott would seriously endanger the attainment of these objectives, and greatly increase the dangers of producing an arid and narrow technician.[42]

Whilst the sincerity of this viewpoint is obvious, by its decision to

---

41 Quoted in BM, 1954-64, p. 636.
42 Undated memorandum sent by the vice-chancellor (Professor Michael Grant) to Lord MacDermott on 9 Feb. 1963. BM, 1955-64, p. 512.

suspend the implementation of the regulations pending discussions with both branches of the profession the university recognised that as many of its law graduates entered the legal profession in Northern Ireland the views of the profession could not be ignored. In the ultimate analysis the profession could withhold recognition from the LL.B. If that happened it would create a gravely embarrassing situation for the university, because its law degree would not be recognised as a means of qualifying for one, or both, branches of the legal profession in Northern Ireland, with the likely result that students who wished to practise in Northern Ireland would not go to Queen's. The benchers (and the Law Society) were not prepared to drop their demands, and the impasse continued until 1965, when the university made some changes to its regulations. The benchers responded by removing the requirement that a student possess an arts degree before call, and thereby effectively recognised the Queen's LL.B. as an approved degree for the purposes of admission to the Bar.[43]

With this change, the 1920's scheme was to continue in being until it was replaced by a completely new system in 1972. Whilst this new system proved to be an interim arrangement, as it was substantially replaced in 1977 by the present system of joint professional education with solicitor students in the Institute of Professional Legal Studies, the origin of the interim system can be traced to the conjunction of a number of developments in the mid to late 1960s. As we shall see, changes in university law courses, and in the context and structure of Part II of the English Bar Final, were developments entirely beyond the control of the Inn, but could not be ignored. Another issue was the need to encourage recruitment to the Bar. The success of these efforts immediately created an urgent need to cope with the unprecedented numbers of Bar students joining the Inn each year. As a result the benchers devoted a great deal of time to grappling with these particularly difficult issues between 1968 and 1972.

The first, albeit modest, recognition of the need for change to the educational qualifications students had to meet came with the decision in 1965 to remove the requirement that a student pass a special examination in Latin if that subject was not included in the student's university matriculation requirement, and substituting English language for Latin. This change was made because although most universities still included Roman Law in

---

43   3 May 1965. BM, 1965-69, p. 45.

their syllabus, it was only optional at Queen's. Other universities, notably Oxford, Cambridge and Trinity College, Dublin, no longer included Latin as a compulsory matriculation subject.[44]

A matter which was to receive considerable attention in later years was the need to improve the standards of pupillage so that newly-called barristers could acquire the tools of their trade from their masters. An early recognition of the need for improvement in this whole area was the unanimous decision by the Bar Council in favour of students who had passed the Bar Final being allowed to use the Bar Library in the company of their future masters before they had been called to the Bar. However, despite the obvious advantages of allowing successful Bar students to do this during the Summer months before call in the Autumn, this proposal was not enthusiastically received by the benchers when it was relayed to them by the attorney general,[45] and it was not pursued.

During the mid-1960s small numbers of students were being admitted to the Inn, with the inevitable result that the numbers being called to the junior Bar were correspondingly small. Between 1960 and 1968 only 12 were called to the Bar. With the exception of 1960 when there were four, in most years two at most, and usually only one, were called, and in 1961 no one was called. Whilst there was some increase in 1968, when six were called,[46] there was considerable concern amongst the benchers about this state of affairs, because the numbers being called were insufficient to replace those who left, resulting in a fall in the number of practising members of the Bar from 67 (18 QCs and 49 juniors) in 1962 to 56 in 1967 (21 QCs and 35 juniors).[47] It was recognised that unless there was a sufficient flow of new junior counsel joining the Bar to replace those leaving practice upon accepting judicial appointments or upon retirement, the number of competent counsel remaining would be reduced, with a consequent weakening of the quality of the Bar.[48] This was raised by Mr Justice Lowry in April 1968, and later that Summer, Mr Justice McGonigal, accompanied by two members

---

44  BM, 1965-69, pp 84-86.
45  BM, 1965-69, pp 307. The attorney general was E.W. Jones QC MP, a high court judge 1968-1972, a lord justice of appeal 1972-1984.
46  *Armitage*, p. 53, Appendix F, 'Rate of intake of Bar students and of new Barristers 1960-1972'.
47  List of practising members of the Bar for years 1962-1978, file 3 (Inn) Royal Commission on Legal Services, 1976-79.
48  17 Apr. 1968. BM, 1965-69, pp 331-32.

of the junior Bar (C.M. Lavery and F.C. Elliott), and the under-treasurer (J.A.L. McLean), addressed a specially-arranged meeting of the students of the Queen's law faculty. This meeting has been popularly credited with causing the great increase in numbers called to the Bar in succeeding years. Whether or not that is correct, it was an unprecedented attempt by the Inn and the Bar to encourage those who were perhaps in two minds to consider choosing the Bar as a career, and to identify obstacles to that choice in the eyes of prospective students.

McGonigal reported to the benchers that the meeting had been very successful.[49] The law faculty had agreed to cancel all lectures to allow all students to attend, and the room was crowded. McGonigal identified earnings as a junior in the years after call, when compared with the financial rewards open to law graduates pursuing a career elsewhere, as the key concern of the students. He stated that graduates with a good degree often had offers of very attractive salaries from competing commercial or industrial firms, whilst a newly-qualified solicitor could hope to be employed as a qualified assistant at £1000 p.a. upwards, with many having prospects of a partnership in the not too distant future.

Against these attractive options he pointed to the cost of qualifying for the Bar. Although living expenses whilst pursuing the Bar course might attract a local authority maintenance grant, the cost of enrolling as a student and of call were in the region of £240 (or £270 for a non-law graduate). To this had to be added the expense of travelling to, and staying in, London whilst eating dinners (and, he might have added, sitting the Bar Final). McGonigal's comments upon the benefit of the prospective barrister of the requirement to join an English Inn and keep terms by dining are worthy of note.

> There appears to be little advantage to a student to attend an English Inn and eat dinners. He derives no educational or worthwhile benefit from it and does incur considerable expense in doing so.

He also emphasised the deterrent effect of cost on those whose parents were not well off.

> There are no social barriers at the Bar; but it is unfortunate if the Bar has to

49   BM, 1965-69, pp 423-25.

be regarded as closed to those whose families have not the mean or the financial backing to enable them to meet these pre-call expenses.

Whilst McGonigal's views about the cost of joining an English inn echo those of Atkin of forty years before, and of Carson many years before that, this was still a minority view. Nevertheless, whilst this cost may have been an important factor in dissuading good candidates from coming to the Bar, it was almost certainly not the only one. The prospect of uncertain or low earnings as a junior for the years immediately after call when compared to greater and more certain earnings elsewhere was surely at least as significant, if not more so. In this context McGonigal's reminder that out of 300 law students at Queen's only eight were students of the Inn must have given his fellow benchers considerable food for thought.

A change in the existing system was both unavoidable and imminent because of the changes to the English Bar Final proposed by the Ormrod Committee, which had been set up to examine the English Bar's educational requirements. A sub-committee of the education committee chaired by Mr Justice Lowry reported on the Inn's educational requirements in June 1969.[50] Whilst the report made nine recommendations, it pointed to three major issues against which the recommendations had to be viewed. The first was the difficulty of recruiting staff of satisfactory calibre and of financing a separate course only for Bar students meant that it was impossible in practical terms for the Inn to provide such a course. Secondly, there was the low rate of recruitment to the Bar. Finally, the lack of any real system of post-call pupillage was seen as a serious defect in any scheme.

Of the nine recommendations, five were of particular significance in the light of later developments.

(1) Students without a law degree would be required to take Part I of the new Bar Final.
(2) All students would be required to attend the proposed 'practicals' in London, and eat the same number of dinners as before.
(3) Whilst close contact would be maintained with Queen's, the provision of courses and lectures by Queen's for the Inn would be discontinued.
(4) Post-call pupillage would be required for either six or twelve months.

50   BM, 1965-69, pp. 452-59. The other members of the sub-committee were McGonigal J and F.A. Reid QC.

The pupil would be required to pay 50 guineas to his master, a practice which had fallen into disuse.

(5)  Two or three bencher tutors would be appointed to help Bar students.

Of these proposals only (1), (2) and (5) were accepted. Before the proposals could be further considered the benchers had to re-consider the situation. The arrangement with the Council of Legal Education in London that Northern Ireland Bar students could be accommodated within the new scheme had been made on the premise that the number of students would be small. However, 18 students were admitted by the Inn in September 1969, a wholly unforeseen development. By February 1970 this number had risen, and it was anticipated that no fewer than 21 would sit the old style Bar Final in May or September of that year. It was initially believed that such numbers would be exceptional,[51] but the Council of Legal Education had doubts about its ability to accommodate Northern Ireland Bar students in such numbers.

With the Inn faced with the immediate need to provide its own courses if the students were not to be admitted to the new course in London, a crisis was averted by the decision of the Council of Legal Education to continue the old-style Bar Final for a further period to provide for English Bar students who had failed earlier Finals. The Inn was then able to arrange with the Council that its students would continue to take the old style Bar Final until September 1972.[52] This interim solution gave the Inn the opportunity to review the position, but the need to have arrangements in place before students were admitted in September 1971 meant that a decision about what course was to be prescribed in the future had to be made by the Summer of that year. Further discussions took place with the Council of Legal Education, and it indicated that, whilst its own future was unclear, it believed that it could take Northern Ireland students on the new Bar Final course if the numbers were not too great. This represented a change in the Council's position, and came as something of a surprise to Mr Justice Lowry and the under treasurer when they discussed the matter with the chairman of the Council in London in May 1971.[53] However, the Inn was now actively considering the option

---

51  Mr Justice Lowry wrote to Lord Diplock (Chairman of the Council of Legal Education) on 4 Feb. 1970 'There are grounds for believing this number to be exceptional and most unlikely to be matched in the foreseeable future'. BM, 1970-73, p 11.

52  Memorandum on Bar Final Examination by the Under-Treasurer 22 June 1971 (hereafter 'Bar Final memorandum') BM 1970-73, pp 169-72.

53  BM, 1970-73, p.148.

of providing its own course and examinations in Northern Ireland, despite having regarded this as impractical two years before.

This change of direction was due to two developments. The first was that, contrary to what had been thought, the number of Bar students continued to be very much greater than in the past, with 17 enrolling in 1970. Admissions did continue at this increased level, with 15 admitted in 1971, and 18 in 1972, so that it would now be feasible for the Inn to provide its own courses and examinations.[54] The second development was the radical suggestion that postgraduate vocational education in Northern Ireland could be provided for both Bar students and solicitors' apprentices in a common institution. The visionary concept of an institute of legal studies appears to have been developed by Professor Twining of the Queen's Law Faculty. It was first discussed by the Benchers at a meeting on 26 March 1971 when Turlough O'Donnell QC reported an approach by the president of the Law Society about the possibility of a common practical training course to be attended by both Bar students and solicitors' apprentices, and in the ensuing discussion Mr Justice Lowry referred to Professor Twining's suggestion of an institute of legal studies.[55]

By the summer of 1971 the Inn had therefore, albeit somewhat reluctantly, come to realise that it was preferable to provide a separate Northern Ireland Bar Final. Divergences between the procedures in the Northern Ireland and English courts were now considerable, and it was recognised that a local examination would enable the Inn to exercise much more control over the teaching for the Bar Final course. Whether in the longer term an institute for common professional training was created or not, it was recognised that participation by the Inn would be essential to the survival of such a body, and so any decision to have a local Bar Final might well be irrevocable, even if the decision were made to run a local Bar Final in conjunction with Queen's for an interim period of two or three years.[56] It was thought that the reciprocity arrangements with the English Bar would not be affected by such a change.

The Inn's decision to make arrangements for its own Bar Final to come into effect from 1 July 1972 was a decisive and historic move. Whilst these were

---

54   *Armitage*, p. 53, Appendix F.
55   BM, 1970–73 p. 117, and later at p. 148.
56   Bar Final memorandum.

avowedly interim arrangements, the framework of the course, and the greater involvement in teaching by practising members of the Bar, foreshadowed much of the philosophy behind the creation of the Institute of Professional Legal Studies. The suggestion of a common teaching institution shared by Bar students and solicitors' apprentices was as yet only an idea, and in 1971 there was no guarantee that it could be successfully developed into a workable concept and successfully brought to fruition. The interim arrangements provided for the entire Bar Final course and examination to take place in Northern Ireland. Students no longer had to incur the expense of travelling to England and joining an English inn, and the papers had the advantage of being based purely on Northern Ireland law, thus avoiding the study of irrelevant English law and procedure. Students were now examined in seven papers designed to be of approximately equal difficulty and scope as the previous English Bar Final. Nevertheless the system, although an interim one, was 'far from adequate as a systematic course of professional training'.[57]

The new Northern Ireland Bar Final comprised the following papers –

(1)  common law, sale of goods (including hire purchase) and negligence;
(2)  equity and administration of estates;
(3)  criminal procedure;
(4)  civil procedure;
(5)  evidence and company law;
(6)  practical conveyancing;
(7)  divorce law and practice.

The law faculty at Queen's provided full, taught, courses for (4), (5) and (6), whilst the Inn provided a course of lectures in criminal procedure. However, no teaching was providing for any part of the paper on equity and administration of estates, and teaching was only provided for part of paper (1). Bar students could avail of the faculty's family law lectures to prepare for the paper on divorce law and practice. As its family law syllabus was somewhat different from that prescribed by the Inn, the Inn provided a course to supplement the lectures given by the law faculty. Examining was undertaken by senior members of staff of the faculty and practising barristers. The faculty's external examiners, and a senior member of the Northern Bar (who acted as assessor), ensured that the standard of marking

---

57  *Armitage*, para. 44.

was fair and of the requisite academic standard.[58] This arrangement could not have been sustained, even as an interim measure, without the willingness of the law faculty to provide courses for Bar students without any increase in its staffing and financial resources.[59] In the event, these interim arrangements were to continue for several years until the Institute of Professional Legal Studies admitted its first students in the Autumn of 1977. That five year period was to witness an unparalleled expansion of the Bar, as can be seen from the figures below.

Students admitted to the Inn 1962 to 1976[60]

| 1962 | 1963 | 1964 | 1965 | 1966 | 1967 | 1968 | 1969 | 1970 | 1971 | 1972 | 1973 | 1974 | 1975 | 1976 |
|------|------|------|------|------|------|------|------|------|------|------|------|------|------|------|
| 1 | 3 | 0 | 1 | 8 | 7 | 5 | 21 | 17 | 15 | 18 | 23 | 30 | 40 | 24 |

In February 1972 the need for a comprehensive review of the entire system of professional education for both branches of the legal profession, and how this could be funded, was recognised by the Northern Ireland government with the appointment by the Minister of Education of a committee to consider these matters under the chairmanship of Professor A.L. Armitage, vice-chancellor of the University of Manchester. A distinguished academic lawyer who had been a member of the Ormrod Committee, Armitage presided over a strong committee with equal membership from the Inn,[61] the Law Society and the law faculty at Queen's. Given his advocacy of an institute of legal studies, it was particularly appropriate that Professor Twining was one of the members nominated by Queen's.

The publication of the report of the Armitage Committee in September 1973 heralded an historic change in the provision of professional legal education in Northern Ireland. Whilst Armitage recommended that the three-stage structure of legal education envisaged by the Ormrod Committee be adopted; namely an academic stage, followed by a professional stage of institutional training and in-training, with the third stage comprising continuing education or training; the professional or vocational stage was

---

58  This passage is drawn from *Armitage*, paras. 43 and 44.
59  The university calculated that the cost to it in 1972-73 of providing courses for 25 Bar students (after deduction of tuition fees) was £11429. *Armitage*, Appendix D, p. 52.
60  Figures compiled by the Inn for the Royal Commission on Legal Services, File 3 (Inn)-Royal Commission on Legal Services 1976-79.
61  Mr Justice MacDermott and Mr Justice McGonigal.

to be organised through a new Institute of Professional Legal Studies. This was to be part of Queen's University, and would receive its initial capital expenditure and recurrent expenditure by way of an earmarked Northern Ireland government grant to the university. The governing body of the Institute was to be the Council of Legal Education (Northern Ireland) made up of representatives of both branches of the profession and the university. Finally, the Institute would assume the powers of both branches of the profession to recognise law degrees for approval for entry to the Institute, as well as the responsibility for providing the academic courses, examinations and assessments which had to be satisfied before call or admission. This was to be achieved by way of revocable delegation by both branches of the profession of their powers and responsibilities to the Institute, although both would retain their powers to decide whether a particular student was a fit and proper person to be admitted into the profession, and students would have to be admitted as students of the Inn or the Law Society before being offered a place at the Institute.

Some aspects of the Armitage report proved controversial, particularly the question of control over admissions, and others have subsequently been extensively modified in detail over the years in the light of experience. Nevertheless, the soundness of the basic concept of the Institute; the imaginative constitutional framework of the Council of Legal Education and its relationship with Queen's; and the thoroughness with which these matters and the content of the Institute's courses were developed in detail, all meant that the Institute has proved to be a success since it opened its doors in September 1977.

The Institute could not have been founded without government funding. Armitage estimated that at 1972 price levels the capital outlay necessary to establish the Institute would be up to £61,500, with some £35,450 required to meet recurrent expenditure, and accepted that the professional bodies did not have the means to make a significant continuing contribution unless an educational levy were imposed on practising members.[62] Whilst there was concern that the government might not be willing to subsidise the education and training of a particular profession,[63] by November 1975 the lord chief justice was able to report to the benchers that satisfactory arrangements for

---

62   *Armitage*, Ch VI, pp32 and 33.
63   20 Sept. 1974, BM, 1974-79, p. 70.

the funding of the Institute had been agreed, and representatives of the Inn were appointed to a provisional council of legal education.[64]

Apart from capital and recurrent funding, Armitage also touched on the question of maintenance. This was of particular importance to Bar students who (unlike solicitors' apprentices who were paid a modest amount by their employers) received no income whilst preparing for the Bar examination. In practice local education committees made discretionary grants which at least covered the cost of study in Belfast, and Armitage stressed the importance of continuing financial support by way of awards during the mandatory year's attendance at the Institute.[65] In the event, there has been a shortfall in the financial support from public funds available for Institute students for much of its existence, although at times this has been compounded by the demand for places considerably exceeding the numbers originally planned. Armitage estimated that present needs of both branches of the legal profession would be met by a vocational course for 50 students, the great majority of whom would become solicitors.[66] The department of education for Northern Ireland initially agreed to provide 50 bursaries for Institute students, which included both tuition fees and maintenance. However, by October 1976 it was apparent that 50 places would be insufficient to meet the demand, and consideration was being given to expanding the number of places to 69.[67] Sixty nine places were made available, but as there were only 50 bursaries, the remaining 19 students had to fund themselves. The number of bursaries was later increased to 70 for the 1979 intake,[68] and was maintained at that level until 1992. When the number of students admitted to the Institute was increased to 90 this was on the basis that the additional places would be entirely self-financed. From 1992 the number and value of bursaries was progressively reduced, and eventually eliminated, and for some time all students have to pay fees to cover the cost of the course, as well as supporting themselves.

When the Institute opened in 1977 there was no quota system reserving places for Bar students. Admissions were decided on the basis of academic merit,

---

64   27 Nov. 1975. BM, 1974-79, p. 288. The representatives were Mr Justice MacDermott, R.D. Carswell QC, and the author.

65   *Armitage*, pp 6 and 38, para. 94.

66   *Armitage*, p. 18, para. 47.

67   Council of Legal Education (hereafter CLE) minutes, 16 Oct. 1976.

68   CLE AC/R/79/7/XV.

with all those having obtaining first or upper second class degrees being admitted automatically, the remaining places and bursaries being awarded on the results of interviews conducted over several days by the admissions committee of the Council of Legal Education.[69] In the event a reasonably stable proportion of Bar students to solicitor students emerged. However, despite Armitage clearly anticipating that the Institute would be the sole means of qualifying for either branch of profession, this was not achieved for some time as both the Inn of Court and the Law Society allowed some students to qualify who had not attended the Institute, and the continued existence of these alternative means of entry became increasingly contentious.

So far as the Inn was concerned the justification for the preservation of these alternative means of entry was that there were still large numbers of students who wished to be called to the Bar, and there were not enough places for them at the Institute. Although the interim system, which, as we have seen, had been set up in 1972, was eventually discontinued in 1980,[70] for several years the Inn allowed candidates to sit an examination marked by the Inn and based upon a syllabus it issued, although no lectures or tuition were provided. Between 1979 and 1984 the numbers called to the Bar by this route each year varied between 8 and 4.[71]

The continued existence of these alternative means of qualifying for the Bar and the solicitors' profession meant that distinct, but nevertheless closely related, issues were not being addressed. These were the question of restricting the numbers admitted to the legal profession and the requirements for admission. The latter question might be more accurately described as the formulation of a method of selecting a limited number of students in a way that was rigorously objective and identified those best suited to practice law, without deciding this solely on the basis of academic performance in the shape of their university degree classification. A great deal of attention was to be devolved to those thorny issues in the mid 1980s.

---

69  Initially about 10 places were reserved for non-law graduates who were first required to take a two year course in the Law Faculty at Queen's. The number of non-law students actually accepted from 1977 to 1984 can be found in *Armitage*, p. 47, Appendix F in the table 'Academic Course'.

70  16 June 1980. BM, 1978-82, pp 266-67.

71  *Report of the Committee on Professional Legal Education in Northern Ireland*, p. 10, Ch 2. 7. The chairman was Professor P.M. Bromley, Professor of Law in the University of Manchester. The Committee reported in April 1985 (hereafter referred to as 'The Bromley Report' or '*Bromley*'). See his obituary in *The Times*, 28 March 2013.

That the department of education was concerned by the continuance of these alternative courses, which were by their very nature less satisfactory than those provided by the Institute at considerable public expense, was obvious. The lack of places was one of the problems identified by the Royal Commission on Legal Services in its otherwise favourable comments on the new system when it reported in 1979, and it recommended that there should be a comprehensive review of the new arrangements in three years time.[72] The appointment by the government of the Committee to review the arrangements for professional legal education in Northern Ireland in September 1983 (the Bromley Committee) was followed by the formation of the Executive Council of the Inn of Court in November of the same year, and so it fell to the Executive Council (which had taken over most of the powers and functions hitherto exercised by the benchers) to consider the issues raised by Bromley. From the Bar's perspective, these might be grouped under seven separate heads, some of which raised questions of greater difficulty than others.

The first, and fundamental question, was whether the concept of providing vocational training for prospective barristers and solicitors in the same institution with a high degree of common teaching was still valid. Although the Executive Council felt that there were many aspects of the Institute's operation which required change, it believed that the arguments accepted by Armitage were still valid and that to depart from the Institute model would be unsatisfactory.

Whether public funding should be continued was an equally crucial question, and again the Inn supported the existing system. The demands upon the Inn's resources were such that it was unable to contribute towards the cost of the Institute, which at that time amounted to approximately £285000, of which some £85000 represented the maintenance element of the 70 bursaries. The increase in size of the Bar had placed a great strain on the Bar Library, and the capital expenditure necessary to improve the facilities of the Library would result in a substantial increase in subscriptions. The number in practice had increased from 61 in 1969 to 128 in 1976, and to 248 in 1983. Of those 248 no fewer than 126 were of less than six years standing, and unable to make a realistic contribution towards the cost of extending

---

72  *Report of The Royal Commission on Legal Services*, Cmd 7648, 42-93. The relevant passages from the report can be found in *Bromley*, Appendix A, pp 40-42.

and improving the Bar Library facilities, let alone bear an educational levy at the rate that would be necessary to defray the level of expenditure inherent in the continued operation of the Institute.[73] The acceptance by the government of Bromley's recommendation that the Institute should remain in being, and receive financial support from public funds, was therefore a wholly satisfactory outcome from the Inn's perspective.

Bromley devoted a considerable amount of attention to two matters which, although treated separately in the report, can be conveniently considered together, namely the position of the Institute as a constituent part of Queen's University, and the role and composition of the Council of Legal Education (Northern Ireland) as the governing body of the Institute. The Institute, as a non-faculty unit within the university, was formally part of the university, and received its finances through the university. However, the desirability of the Institute being part of the university was not universally conceded because of a widespread perception that the Institute had become too academic in its approach and so divorced from the needs of practitioners. The suggestion that the Institute 'become an independent body sponsored by the legal profession' was in part a reaction to this perception, although it gained support from those who believed that control of admission to the legal profession should be exercised directly by the professional bodies. The impetus for an independent Institute came from the Law Society because the Inn, whilst not unsympathetic to the Law Society's reasoning, recognised that the smaller number of Bar students meant that it would be wholly impractical for the Inn to provide a satisfactory system of vocational training on its own. It accepted that the concept of revocable delegation of powers by the professions, together with strong representation by both branches of the profession on the Council of Legal Education, provided an acceptable framework linking the Inn to the Institute. The Inn also recognised that there were other considerations which meant that it was desirable for the Institute to remain within the university structure. This facilitated close liaison with academic lawyers, thereby helping practitioners to keep abreast of developments in other jurisdictions, and allowed the public interest in the maintenance of intellectual standards to be maintained by the academic council of the university.[74]

A closely related issue was the composition and role of the Council of Legal

---

73  Submission by the Executive Committee to the Bromley Committee paras 7 and 8.1.
74  *Bromley* Ch 3.3, p. 14.

Education. As originally envisaged by Armitage, the Inn and the Law Society would each have three members on the Council, and the director of the Institute would also be a member, and by 1983 other Institute staff had been added to the Council. There was a undoubtedly a feeling that the ability of both branches of the profession to influence the operation of the Institute had been diluted, and Bromley referred to the desire of the Law Society for an increase in its representation to reflect the numerical preponderance of solicitors in the legal profession.[75]

One matter to which the Inn raised in its submission to Bromley was the possibility of moving the Institute to a location in the vicinity of the Law Courts. This suggestion, although it was ultimately rejected by Bromley, perhaps inevitably in view of the cost of such a move,[76] represented a strong feeling that a closer and more up to date acquaintanceship with the courts on the part of the Institute and the students was not merely desirable but essential, something that will be considered later in the context of the content of courses at the Institute. The most important issue, and that which gave rise to the most intense debate within the Executive Council when the submission to the Bromley Committee was being drafted, was whether there should be a limitation on the number of Bar students accepted into the Institute each year. A separate issue, but one which was so closely linked to any consideration of numbers that in practice it was considered throughout as part of the numbers issue, was what criteria were to be adopted to select the Bar students for the Institute?

As stated earlier, the number of practising barristers had quadrupled from 61 in 1969 to 248 in 1983. Not only were there 126 members of the Library of less than six years standing, but 78 members had no desk at which to work.[77] The efforts of the Bar Council, and later the Executive Council, to cope with the pressures on the Library system created by the increase in members are considered in Chapter Ten. At this time there was a strong body of opinion on the Executive Council that the time had come to impose some restriction on numbers, at least for a limited period, to prevent the collapse of the Library system. Many feared that if the Library system collapsed barristers might be tempted to form chambers on religious or political lines, or on the basis that

75  *Bromley* Ch 4.9, p. 20.
76  *Bromley* Ch 3.19-23 at pp 17 and 18.
77  Submission of the Inn of Court to the Committee for the Review of Legal Education in Northern Ireland, (hereafter 'Submission of the Inn of Court'), para 7.

only one type of client would be accepted, such as criminal prosecution or defence, plaintiffs or defendants. Such a development would at best impair, and at worst seriously damage, the maintenance of a collegiate atmosphere of mutual trust which contributes to the maintenance of high professional standards by mutual example, within the Bar. There was also a general acceptance that a substantial minority of those already in practice were unable to earn even a modest income, and many were therefore concerned that overcrowding could lead to the erosion of standards if too many people were competing for a limited amount of work.

An equally strongly-held view was that, understandable though these concerns were, they did not justify abandoning the traditional 'open door' approach of the Bar. Those who espoused this view believed that the Bar should be open to all those who achieved the necessary educational and professional standards, and that once these standards were met, all should have the opportunity to prove themselves, and that their survival would be determined by the support of clients in an open and competitive market. To restrict artificially the numbers entering the Bar could, the proponents of the open door policy argued, have the effect of favouring some candidates on the basis of their family background, or their professional or other connections. Consideration was given to proposing that the number of Bar students be limited to ten each year for five years from 1 May 1984. However, in the absence of a consensus, the view was taken that this could not be adopted as the policy of the Inn as it was too restrictive, as was an alternative suggestion that while 20 places at the Institute might be reserved for Bar students, only ten bursaries would be granted to Bar students.

In parallel with the debate about numbers, the need for a change in the method of selecting students for the Institute was also being urgently considered. There was increasing concern that the Institute's policy of awarding places solely on the basis of degree results was not the correct one, partly because it was felt that differences between universities meant that it was difficult to distinguish between candidates with the same class of degree, as some universities were thought to be less rigorous in their marking than others. A related concern was that success in degree examinations did not necessarily mean that the same level of success was being achieved in the final result of the Institute. Support for that concern emerged as the result of an analysis of the relative performance in the Institute final examinations of students who had 2.1 degrees, and so had been admitted automatically, and those with 2.2 degrees, who had been admitted after interview. This revealed that over five years a significant minority of those with 2.2 degrees had been placed in the top half of the results, whilst a significant minority of those with 2.1 degrees had been in the bottom half.[78]

The Inn therefore suggested that Bar students be selected, and bursaries awarded, after sitting an examination consisting of four three-hour papers 'containing problems of a practical nature designed to illustrate the candidates ability to identify and deal with legal problems of a type likely to be met in practice at the Bar'. Candidates would have to have a recognised degree in law of 2.2 standard or above, and be subject to interviews by the Inn's nominees on the Council of Legal Education. Whilst the Inn felt it was difficult to accept that there would be a need for more than 300 members of the Bar in the foreseeable future, it considered that it was undesirable to fix a quota for any given year. Nevertheless, it also argued it was necessary to raise the standards required for entry to the profession, and that this could significantly reduce the intake. The suggested selection procedure for the Bar students had to be viewed in that context as well as in the context of improving standards.

The Bromley Report recommendation that 20 places out of a total of 90 at the Institute be reserved for Bar students effectively formalized the pattern of about 20 calls to the Bar since 1976[79] by way of the Institute and the alternative exam provided by the Inn. This recommendation did not seek to reduce the numbers coming to the Bar at the time, rather it was designed to ensure that they all went through the Institute. In that respect the 'open door' policy was not changed. The recommendation that written tests be set to select students for the Institute when the number of applicants exceeded the number of places available could justifiably be regarded as an acceptance of much of the underlying principle of the Inn's submission that there be a written selection test for Bar students. *Bromley* recognised that 'there is considerable merit in requiring all applicants to undergo a common test of practical competence which must be capable of being objectively evaluated', with the questions designed 'to test a student's ability to apply his knowledge of law in a practical way'.[80]

*The Bromley Report* acknowledged that there was no precedent for such a test, and it also recognised that it would not be easy to devise such a test.

---

78  *Submission of the Inn of Court*, paras 9-11.
79  18 in 1976, 19 in 1977, 1981, 1982 and 1983, 22 in 1978 and 1979 and 28 in 1980. Appendix A, *Submission of The Inn of Court*.
80  *Bromley*, Ch 5.20, p. 26.

That proved to be the case, because it was not until 1987 that the admission procedure emerged broadly in its present form. Recognition of the class of degree is given by attributing a mark which varies according to the degree. In 2013 300 marks will be awarded for a first, 225 for 2.1 down to zero for a pass or general degree. The student will sit two papers with a possible maximum of 1000 marks. The total mark is calculated by adding the degree mark to the result of the written test. Whilst the admission test has been refined and developed over the years, the structure is still broadly that put in place following the Bromley Report. The prescience of the Executive Council in seeking to move from a purely academic criterion to a test sat by all applicants, a test designed so that the practical application of legal knowledge may be seen from the percentages of successful applicants when compared with their degree results. For example, in 2002 74% of firsts, 47% of 2.1s, 10% of 2.2s were successful, but no thirds.[81]

The final area of concern to the Inn, as to the Law Society, was the syllabus and the structure of the course at the Institute. As the Law Society felt that its students should have some office experience before entering the Institute for the one year vocational course, a two year sandwich course ultimately emerged for solicitors, with the Bar students following a one year course starting in the Autumn after graduation. For both groups of students a considerable number of detailed changes were made to the teaching content of the courses to ensure that they continued to be relevant to actual practice. In the decades since the Bromley Report great efforts have been made by the Council of Legal Education and the staff of the Institute to ensure that this is the case. The approximately 200 practising solicitors and barristers who act as part-time teaching assistants, and the contribution by teaching and selecting of specialist practitioners and academics,[82] have a major role to play in ensuring that the constant changes in practice are made known to students.

Whilst there have been dramatic changes to, and improvements in, the system of pre-call vocational training for Bar students over the last thirty years, the system of post-call training through pupillage remained largely unchanged for many years. It has been long recognised that no matter what form of pre-call vocational training Bar students undergo, it is essential that they are required to undergo a form of practical induction after call.

81   CLE/M/02/5.

82   *Report on IPLS Audit on 9-10 March 2000*, 1.6, p. 15.

Traditionally this has been the object of pupillage, with the pupil reading the master's papers, attending consultations and cases, and discussing the points that arise, thereby gaining an essential grounding in the technical and ethical aspects of competently representing clients in court and tribunals of all kinds, although until the late 1960s it was accepted that a newly-qualified barrister, no matter how inexperienced, could represent his or her client, and hopefully be paid for doing so, immediately after call.

By 1970 there was growing awareness that it was necessary to significantly improve the pupillage system, but for a considerable period there was no consensus as to how this should be achieved, as can be seen from the outcome of a general meeting in June 1970 at which the subject was debated. A proposal that students who had passed their Bar Final at the end of June should be allowed to come into the Library over the summer months before their call in late September was defeated, but they were allowed to use a special room as a concession. A more radical proposal put before the same meeting was that there should be a system of compulsory non-practising pupillage if the existing educational system was not changed by January 1972.[83] Whilst this proposal was also rejected, it was symptomatic of increasing concern that the traditional pupillage system was close to collapse because the increase in work available meant that newly-called counsel were regularly appearing in court almost from the date of call, and so were not always being taught the traditional skills and ethical standards. A suggestion made at another general meeting in 1972 that there should be a system of pre-call non-practicing pupillage was left in abeyance,[84] but in March 1974 the Bar Council decided to recommend to the benchers that a period of six months non-practising pupillage should be introduced.[85] The benchers' response was to suggest that pupils with masters should be admitted to the Library for six weeks before call for 1974 only. This suggestion was accepted,[86] and was continued in 1975. However, although this was a form of limited pre-call pupillage, many were never comfortable with pupils being in the Library, and seeing client's papers, before call; and when the benchers requested in 1976 that the arrangement should be continued for at least another two years the request was rejected, no doubt because the Bar felt that this was an inadequate system that was in danger of becoming permanent.[87]

83  MGM 25 June 1970.
84  MGM 19 Apr. 1972.
85  BCM 11 Mar. 1974.
86  MGM 24 June 1974.
87  MGM 24 June 1976.

The Bar Council persisted with its demand that newly-called barristers undergo a period of compulsory non-practising pupillage, and in 1978 the benchers finally agreed to require twelve months post-call pupillage with a practising barrister, of which the first six months was to be non-practising, the master certifying at the end of the first six months that the pupillage had been satisfactory. This was to apply only to those who became students after 8 May 1978,[88] thus avoiding imposing an additional burden on those who had commenced their Bar studies in the belief that they would be able to practice immediately after call. This meant that a pupil could not accept instructions as counsel or conduct a case in court during his or her six month pupillage, and although it imposed an additional financial burden on those who intended to practice by preventing them from earning for their first six months at the Bar, it was felt to be essential to ensure that pupils learnt their trade without learning bad habits because they were devoting time to building their own practices at the expense of time spent with their master. In 1985 the requirement was modified to allow a pupil to appear before a master of the high court after three months of pupillage in a case where his master, or another barrister, has already been briefed;[89] and this remains the position today.

Bromley suggested that consideration be given to a two year pupillage, of which the first year would be represented by the Institute year, and that 'some additional form of supervision or assessment of a pupil's ability should take place during or at the end of the six month period of practising pupillage'.[90] These suggestions were not implemented, although the practice developed whereby a pupil would spend a short time with another barrister whose work was in a different area to his or her master. Whilst highly commendable because this enabled pupils to gain insights into the requirements of different areas of practice in an era of greatly increased specialisation, it was voluntary, and not necessarily followed by all pupils. It remained the case for almost two decades after Bromley that there was no post-call assessment of a pupil's practical ability, nor was there any formal requirement upon practitioners of whatever seniority and experience to undergo additional training of the type Bromley referred to. This lacuna became increasingly difficult to ignore.

The development of the concept of continuing professional development

---

88   BCM 22 May 1978, MGM 26 June 1978.
89   *Bromley*, Ch 2.8, p. 12.
90   *Bromley*, Ch 2.8, p. 13.

(CPD) in other professions naturally influenced the attitude of the Bar to these matters and efforts were made to encourage continuing professional education. However, this was voluntary, and ultimately it was recognised that the Bar needed to provide a compulsory scheme of CPD which could be sufficiently flexible to recognise and accommodate the different ways in which practitioners could ensure that they were keeping up to date with developments relevant to their area of practice, whilst at the same time ensuring that the study or related work engaged upon was relevant and of a sufficient standard to be accepted as providing real benefit to the individual member of the Bar. Throughout 2002 and 2003 considerable efforts were devoted to preparing a scheme which met these requirements, and this came into operation on 1 September 2004.[91]

In brief the CPD regulations require all pupils to undertake compulsory training in both advocacy and Bar ethics by taking part in courses provided by the Bar within 12 months of call. In addition all members of the Bar, irrespective of how long they have been in practice, have to complete a minimum of 12 hours CPD each year after completion of pupillage. There are various ways in which this requirement can be met, and the Bar Council does not provide courses or instruction, but approves instruction provided by other suitable bodies or course providers. Unless the course or activity has been approved it does not qualify. It is for the individual barrister to identify and undertake such study, and to keep a record of what he or she has done and present that to the Bar Council. It is a measure of the importance which the Bar attach to the need for continuing professional development that from its inception the scheme has been embodied in regulations. A failure to comply with the scheme may result in disciplinary proceedings being taken against the barrister concerned, and it has proved necessary to do this in a small number of cases. The conception, implementation, and vigorous enforcement of these regulations, was a recognition by the Bar of the need to ensure that all its members continue to offer a high level of expertise to their clients by ensuring that its members keep abreast of the many and rapid changes in the many areas of law and practice, and other related fields, with which they have to deal.

One area which the Inn and the Bar had not adequately addressed by the start

---

91   Continuing Professional Development Regulations of the Code of Conduct of the Bar of Northern Ireland.

of the twenty first century was the need to provide some form of financial assistance for those who were studying for the Bar by way of awards or scholarships. By 2002 there were only four prizes available to Bar students at the Institute, the most generous of which was the Eoin Higgins Prize worth £250. However, two recent developments have significantly improved the position. By 2003 the benchers were concerned by the impact upon the financial cost on students imposed by the reduction in the number of bursaries at the Institute, the level of fees, and the substitution of student loans for local authority grants. As a result many Bar students accumulated very significant amounts of debt during their studies. The absence of financial support for Bar students contrasted unfavourably with the financial support given to solicitors' apprentices who were paid £150 a week by their masters at the time, rising to £195 a week during the final eight months of their apprenticeship.[92] The benchers therefore initiated a scheme whereby they provided a significant sum from their subscription account on the basis that the Bar would match the amount. As a result scholarships worth £4000 were made available, and by 2008 the total value of these scholarships had increased to £8500 a year. Although these scholarships are awarded on the basis of performance at the Institute, they are post-call scholarships as they are conditional on the recipients entering practice. The support provided in the form of these Inn of Court scholarships has been augmented by private and corporate munificence. For a number of years J.E. Grant QC provided a very generous scholarship, and in 2010 the First Trust Bank provided a generous donation of £5000 which was used to fund five advocacy prizes.[93]

However, these gifts have been exceeded by an unparalleled act of private munificence by a member of the Bar when John P.B. Maxwell donated a six figure sum to Queen's University. This amount is sufficient to produce £10000 a year which is also devoted awarded to post call scholarships awarded to Bar students who have studied at the Institute.[94] The John P.B. Maxwell scholarships, and the Inn of Court scholarships, now provide much needed financial assistance to new entrants to the Bar, and go some way to ease the financial burden on them of studying for call to the Bar.

---

92   Memorandum to the treasurer 11 Dec. 2002.
93   BCM 6 Oct. 2010.
94   BM 12 June 2008.

# CHAPTER SEVEN:

## The early years 1921-1945

During the Long Vacation of 1921 members of the North East and North West Circuits must have given careful thought to the choice which each would have to make that autumn, namely whether to continue to practise in Dublin and in the courts of Southern Ireland, or to move to Belfast to practice in the courts of Northern Ireland. The Government of Ireland Act[1] provided that all existing members of the Irish Bar should have a right of audience in the Supreme Courts of Judicature of both Southern and Northern Ireland, and because this had the effect of creating two separate bars, those who were considering practising in the Northern courts had to weigh up the implications of doing so.

For those juniors who made up the small local bar, most of whom practised from Rea's Buildings in Belfast, the decision would have been straightforward. The new courts could be expected to bring a substantial volume of work to Belfast that had hitherto been dealt with in Dublin. This would provide new opportunities for those who had hitherto practised primarily or exclusively in the local courts in Belfast and the surrounding area, as well as at the assizes at Belfast and Downpatrick. For seniors who had done so as juniors, such as J.H. Robb KC, or whose connections were primarily in the North East, such as R.D. Megaw KC, Marcus Begley KC and William Beattie KC; (all of whom had recently taken silk) the choice would have been equally straightforward.[2] Some had already effectively made their choice when they sought election to the Stormont parliament at the election held in May 1921. Megaw, MP for Antrim,[3] was appointed parliamentary secretary to the Ministry of Home Affairs when the first cabinet of the Northern Ireland government was announced on 31 May 1921.[4] Richard Best KC, MP for Mid Armagh, was appointed attorney

---

1   Para. 4 of Part III of sch. 7, Government of Ireland Act, 1920, and The Government of Northern Ireland (Northern Ireland Bar) Order, 1926 (SRO 1926 No 917).

2   Megaw was called to the Inner Bar in February, Robb and Begley in June, and Beattie in July 1921. *ILT&SJ*, lv (1921), 58, 150 and 176.

3   Megaw, Robert Dick (1869-1947). Called 1893, NE Circuit 1894, MP (U) Antrim, parliamentary secretary to the ministry of home affairs 1921-25. Judicial commissioner, land purchase commission 1927-37, a judge of the high court 1932-1943.

4   St. John Ervine, *Craigavon Ulsterman* (London, 1949), p. 417.

general on the same day.[5] Robb[6] and G.B. Hanna[7] were also elected to the new parliament. Others such as Anthony Babington KC[8] and E.S. Murphy KC,[9] also made the decision to move to Belfast.

For Babington, Murphy and many others, particularly those from the North West Circuit, the decision to come North meant that they had to sell their homes in Dublin and uproot their families to settle in Belfast where they may have had few, if any, family, social or professional connections. Even for those who had such connections, such as T.J. Campbell KC,[10] the prospect of living and pursuing their professional career in Northern Ireland may not have been an attractive one, because of political opposition to the new Northern Ireland state, or because personal and professional ties to Dublin were too strong. A significant number of members of the North East and North West Circuits

5    Ibid. Best, Richard (1872-1939). Called 1895, NE Circuit 1896, KC 1912, Bencher KI 1918. MP (U) Mid-Armagh and attorney general 1921-25. A lord justice of appeal 1925-39.

6    Robb, John Hanna (1873-1956). Called 1898, NE Circuit 1899, KC 1921. MP (U) Queen's University 1921-37. Parliamentary secretary, ministry of education 1925-37, minister of education and leader of the senate 1937-43. County court judge for Co. Armagh 1943-54. Author of *The law and practice of bankruptcy and arrangements in Ireland* (1907), and *The history of the school, Centenary Volume of the Royal Belfast Academical Institution* (1912).

7    Hanna, George Boyle (1877-1938). Solicitor 1901. Called 1920. NW Circuit. MP (Ind U) East Antrim (at Westminster) 1919-22, MP (U) Co Antrim 1921-29 and Larne 1929-37. Parliamentary secretary, ministry of home affairs 1925-37. County court judge for Co. Tyrone 1937-38.

8    Babington, Anthony Brutus (1877-1972). Called 1900. NW Circuit, general secretary of the Bar of Ireland. KC 1918. Bencher KI 1924-25 when he resigned. MP (U) Cromac, and attorney general, 1925-38. A lord justice of appeal 1938-49. Ed., Osborne, *The jurisdiction and practice of county courts in Ireland in Equity and Probate matters* (Dublin, 1910). *DIB*.

9    Murphy, Edward Sullivan (1880-1945). Called 1903. NW Circuit, KC 1918. Bencher KI 1921. Member NI senate 22 Mar. to 11 Apr. 1929 when resigned and elected MP (U) City of Derry 1929-39. A lord justice of appeal 1939-45. The son of Murphy J, he had an outstanding undergraduate career at Trinity College, Dublin, winning first scholarship in classics, a first class moderatorship in logic and ethics, as well as vice-chancellor's prizes for Latin prose and verse, and Greek verse. See E.W. Jones, *Jones LJ his life and times-the autobiography of the Rt Hon Sir Edward Jones*, (Enniskillen, 1987), pp 96-97. *DIB*.

10   Campbell, Thomas Joseph. (1871-1946). Editor *Irish News* 1895-1906 when he resigned to follow a career at the Bar. Called 1900, NE Circuit 1901, KC 1918. Bencher KI 1924. Bencher of the Inn of Court of Northern Ireland 1938, treasurer, 1941. Contested South Monaghan for the Irish Party 1918, then East Belfast 1921 and West Belfast 1931, both as a Nationalist. A Nationalist member of the Northern Ireland senate 1929-34. MP (N) Belfast Central 1934-45, and 'Leader' of the Nationalist Party. This was an informal position there being no election of, or any formal position as, leader). Philip Leonard, 'The contribution of Thomas Joseph (TJ) Campbell, KC, MP (1871-1946) to Nationalist politics in Northern Ireland', QUB MSSc dissertation (1992), pp 63-67. County court judge for Co. Tyrone 3 Dec. 1945, died 3 May 1946. Author of *Fifty Years of Ulster 1890-1940*, (Belfast, 1941). *DIB*.

who came from counties which were now within Northern Ireland continued to be based in the Four Courts, and some were soon to be appointed to the bench in Southern Ireland, such as James Creed Meredith KC,[11] James Murnaghan,[12] and Serjeant Hanna KC.[13] As it transpired, not everyone chose to confine their practice to one jurisdiction only, and for some time members of the former North East and North West Circuits based in Dublin continued to appear in the courts in Northern Ireland.

The courts which comprised the new supreme court of judicature of Northern Ireland were formally opened by the lord chief justice at the beginning of Michaelmas Term on 24 October 1921 in the presence of his fellow judges, the Bar, representatives of the solicitors' profession, the prime minister of Northern Ireland and a large number of guests.[14] Sir Denis Henry led his fellow judges, the attorney general, the recorder of Belfast, king's counsel and junior counsel, all in full costume, into the central hall of the County Court House. Standing under the clock, he then proceeded to hold a Levee; as had been the practice of the lord chancellors of Ireland at the beginning of Michaelmas Term; receiving his brother judges, the leading members of the Bar and the solicitors' profession. Following the Levee, the Bar, solicitors, officials and guests went to the Crown Court. When the judges had taken their places on the bench, and having called the attorney general within the bar, Henry addressed the gathering. In the course of his remarks he referred to the Bar –

> The Bar also to-day enters on a new era. The old Circuits of the North East and North West have disappeared – to be merged in a new one. There will be a Bar to practice here, and they too, as part of the Irish Bar, will have great memories to carry on. Nothing influences the Courts of Justice more than the existence of good advocacy, and of such a high tone of professional instinct among the

---

11  Meredith, James Creed. Litt. D. Called 1901, NE Circuit 1905, KC 1918. A judge of the high court of the IFS 1924-36, and of the supreme court 1936-42 when he died. See Kotsonuris, *Retreat from revolution: the Dail courts*, 1920-24, (Dublin, 1994) for his work in the Dail courts. She described him as an Irish nationalist from a Protestant unionist background (p. 129). *DIB*.

12  Murnaghan, James Augustine (1881-1973). Called 1903, NW Circuit. A judge of the high court of the IFS 1924-25, and of the supreme court 1925-53. *DIB*.

13  Hanna, Henry (1871-1946). Called 1896, NE Circuit 1897, KC 1911, bencher KI 1915. Third serjeant at law 1919-25, a judge of the high court of the IFS 1925-43. Hart, *The king's serjeants at law in Ireland*, pp 132-33 and 171.

14  This passage is based upon Hill Smith, *Sketch of the Supreme Court of Judicature of Northern Ireland*, Ch. 3.

Bar that the court can implicitly rely on statements made by counsel. (Hear, hear.) This is a matter to be regulated by the members of the Bar themselves, and I have no doubt that the Bar of Northern Ireland will fully rise to a sense of its duty and its responsibility.'

As leader of the Bar the attorney general (Richard Best KC, MP) responded to the lord chief justice's remarks –

I was glad to hear the Lord Chief Justice referring to the high traditions of the Bench. The Bar, too, had high traditions, and the Bar of that Supreme Court – made up as it would be of the old North East and North West Bars – would also uphold their traditions. We have men who are prepared to carry on those traditions and to see that honour and faith were kept with the court. It was a mistake to believe that advocates should come in and hide or shield facts from the court. (Applause). Their business was to put forward every consideration for their clients which could properly influence the court, but it was no part of their duty, and I do not believe it will be the case in these courts, that any member should come in and try to hold back from the court any facts of a case or to blind it, because the members of the Bar were equally responsible with the Bench for the pure and undefiled administration of the law, as the Lord Chief Justice has said.

But, after all, the Bench and Bar were only institutions which had a certain purpose in view, and that was that the public should be served in the administration of justice. I have no hesitation in saying that the Supreme Court would administer justice in as fine a way as it ever had been administered in any supreme court, whether in Ireland or in Great Britain. (Applause). They were no longer a local Bench or a local Bar – they were a supreme court: and your Lordships are endowed with as wide powers as those possessed by any supreme court in existence at the present time.

Any little inconvenience which the Bar had suffered in making the necessary preparations for the opening of the courts and the carrying on of their work the Bar has borne most willingly: and I know the same applies to the solicitors' profession. We were all working together that there might be no doubt that justice should be fairly and impartially administered, the work expeditiously done, and that every satisfaction should be given to every suitor, be his belief or his principles what they might.[15]

No doubt the speakers made a deep impression upon those present, with their words encapsulating the high standards expected of the Bar, and the crucial role they play in the administration of justice, as well as emphasising that the Bar of Northern Ireland, as did the Bar of Ireland, inherited the traditions and standards of their distinguished predecessors. Nevertheless, whilst one might reasonably surmise that these words may have given confidence and encouragement, another consideration which may also have been in the minds of these members of the Bar who attended a meeting held in the Crumlin Road courthouse on Wednesday 26 October 1921 was whether the institutions set up under the Government of Ireland Act would survive for any length of time. Although the Northern Ireland government and parliament were in being, four of the five judges of the supreme court of judicature of Northern Ireland had been appointed,[16] and temporary accommodation for the new courts had been acquired,[17] the continuing political upheavals, widespread murder, and disorder throughout Ireland, must have given rise to much uncertainty as to the future of the separate legal system in Northern Ireland.

Whatever their private thoughts and political views may have been, the seven seniors and 14 juniors who gathered at 12.30 pm under the chairmanship of the attorney general put in hand the necessary steps to provide for the 'formation regulation and government of the Bar of Northern Ireland', and the 'provision and management of a library, dressing rooms, and refreshment room and such other facilities as may be necessary or desirable for the advantage and comfort of members of the Bar' by appointing a committee to consider these and any other matters in the interests of the profession. The desire of all those present to work for the good of the Bar was demonstrated by the proposal being put by T.J. Campbell KC, seconded by Megaw KC, and passed unanimously. The members appointed to the committee were the attorney general, John J. Leech KC (NW), John McGonigal KC (NE, who was not present), Robb KC (NE), J.A. Pringle (NE), and James McSparran (NE), with Arthur Black (NE) as secretary. That there was a strong desire to ensure that the interests of the members of the former North West Circuit were properly taken into account was evidenced by the instruction that the committee were 'to pay special attention to the claims

15  Ibid., pp 11 and 14.
16  Their appointments were announced in the *Belfast Telegraph* 1 Oct. 1921.
17  See Ch. 5.

of the late North West Circuit' when exercising their power to co-opt.[18] A provisional bar council was then elected, consisting of the attorney general, Leech KC, Megaw KC, Pringle, James Williamson KC (NE) and Robb KC.

Further meetings in December 1921 and January 1922 resulted in the formation of a Circuit of Northern Ireland, and the election of the Bar Council and a library committee. Whilst these meetings were primarily concerned with taking the necessary steps to frame rules for the future governance of the Circuit and the Bar, fixing subscriptions and the remuneration of staff to take charge of the catering arrangements in Belfast and to assist in the library and dressing room, they were not without controversy. At the second meeting on 12 December 1921 a proposal by T.J. Campbell KC and George Hill Smith KC that the name of the new circuit be 'the Northern Circuit' was defeated, 'the Circuit of Northern Ireland' being chosen instead.[19]

It was not long before an issue was raised with profound implications for the future of the Northern Ireland Bar. One of the recommendations placed before the meeting of 12 January 1922 by the committee appointed on 26 October 1921 was 'that the Committee are in favour of adopting the Library system and hope that that system will be ultimately adopted to the exclusion of the Chamber system'.[20] Until then, as we have seen in the previous chapter, many members of the local bar had chambers in Rea's Buildings, and, if for no other reason than the accommodation for members of the Bar at the Crumlin Road courthouse was so cramped, continued to work from those chambers where they were joined by some others, although most of those who came from Dublin based themselves in the courthouse.[21] Even allowing for 16 with chambers in Rea's Buildings in 1923,[22] the facilities for the Bar at the Crumlin Road courthouse must have been extremely crowded and uncomfortable.

Notwithstanding any such discomfort, the continuation of a chambers system gave rise to considerable concern, and 13 members of the Bar requisitioned a meeting to discuss the matter, a general meeting being convened for this purpose on 27 February 1923. The wording of the resolution placed before the meeting is revealing.

18   BCM, vol. 1, pp 1-2.
19   Ibid., p. 3.
20   Ibid., p. 6.
21   MacDermott, *An enriching life*, pp 156.
22   *Belfast and Ulster Street Directory*, 1923.

That in the opinion of the Bar of Northern Ireland the chamber system is contrary to the traditions and against the best interests of the Irish Bar and that those members of the Bar of Northern Ireland who at present hold chambers should surrender their tenancies in same on the first possible date according to their respect tenancies therein; and this meeting of the Bar of Northern Ireland hereby calls on those members who hold chambers to comply with the terms of this resolution.[23]

It is interesting to note that William Lowry, who proposed the resolution, had chambers in Rea's Buildings in the past.[24] Whilst the minutes do not record whether there was a debate on the resolution, the issue was plainly an extremely divisive one. An amendment adjourning the matter to the second day of the next term, and authorising the distribution of ballot papers among all subscribing members of the library in the interim, was only carried by 17 votes to 16. When the amendment was then put as a substantive motion it was carried by 18 votes to 16. As there is no record of any further meetings until December 1923 it cannot be established whether or not the adjourned meeting was held. Given the division revealed by the voting figures at the meeting in February 1923, the continuing delays in the construction of the new courts of justice considered in Chapter Five, and the severe pressure on accommodation, it is perhaps reasonable to infer that the matter was not pressed to a conclusion in 1923. During the 1920s there was a gradual decline in the number of barristers with chambers in Rea's Buildings,[25] so that by 1933 only one member of the Bar is recorded as practising from there, whereas eight solicitors, or firms of solicitors, had addresses there. When the new Courts of Justice opened in 1933 the Bar moved into the new Bar Library, thus continuing the tradition of the Irish Bar invoked by Lowry in 1923. Had a significant proportion of the practising Bar continued in chambers after 1933, this would undoubtedly have had a detrimental impact upon the cohesion, collegiality and spirit of fellowship of the Bar which have been of crucial importance in developing and maintaining its ethos and effectiveness, thereby enhancing the administration of justice in succeeding generations.

23  BCM, vol. 1, p.21.
24  William Lowry (1884-1949). Called 1907, NE Circuit 1913 on starting practice. KC 1926. MP (U) City of Derry 1939-47. Parliamentary secretary ministry of home affairs 1940-43, minister of home affairs 1943-44, attorney general 1944-47, a judge of the high court 5 June 1947 until he resigned on 11 Oct. 1949, died 14 Dec. 1949. *DIB*.
25  *The Belfast and Ulster Street Directory* lists 10 names in 1926 and 6 in 1929.

Having decided to form a Bar Library, and that each member of the Library was required to sign the membership roll, the annual subscription was fixed at £6 6s for seniors and £5 5s for juniors.[26] These figures were varied in 1924 when the subscription was divided into two elements, presumably to lessen the burden on those who maintained chambers. Henceforth seniors paid £4 4s for the Library and £2 2s for the robing room and luncheon room, with juniors paying £4 4s and £1 1s respectively.[27] Dan Thompson was appointed to take charge of the catering arrangements in Belfast and to assist in the Library and dressing room at £6 5s per month, with an assistant at £1 per week.[28] Not content with providing food, the caterer also sold alcohol, although when it was realised that he did not have a licence the attorney general intervened to stop this.[29]

The need for books for the Bar was an urgent one and arrangements were made by the benchers of King's Inns to lend some books to the Bar Library. A number of books were sent to Belfast early in 1922 to form what was intended to be 'a branch library of the King's Inn', including the penultimate editions of textbooks.[30] The secretary of the Bar Council (Arthur Black) wrote to the Committee of the Law Library in Dublin in December 1921 asking for 'a fair share of the books and assets of the Law Library' for the Bar Library in Belfast. A delegation consisting of McGonigal KC, Baxter and McGookin went to Dublin and met the Law Library Committee on 21 December 1921. The Committee was sympathetic, prepared a list of law reports that could be sent to Belfast, and referred the matter to the Bar Council in Dublin,[31] which decided at its meeting of 16 January 1922 that this was a matter to be decided by a general meeting of the Bar.[32] In the event the seizure of the Four Courts by the anti-Treaty faction of the IRA on Good Friday 1922, and the subsequent destruction of the building, meant that such a gesture was impossible. Even before these tragic events, it had been appreciated in Belfast that whatever books could be provided by

26  BCM, vol. 1, p. 6.
27  Ibid., p. 38.
28  Ibid., p. 5.
29  NCBM, pp 6 and 9.
30  C. Kenny, *King's Inns and the Battle of the Books*, 1972 (Dublin, 2002), p. 27. On 20 Apr. 1922 the benchers of King's Inns noted a letter of thanks from the Northern Bar Council. KIBMB, p. 168. Some 450 books were sent. Memoranda on the setting up of the Supreme Court of Judicature in Northern Ireland 1 Oct. 1921-31 July 1922. PRONI CAB/6/57 para. 32.
31  Minutes of Committee of Law Library, p. 87.
32  Minutes of the General Council of Bar of Ireland, p. 219.

King's Inns would still be insufficient, and in February 1922 it was decided to seek a grant in aid from the Northern Ireland Government towards the equipment and upkeep of the library.[33] A deputation headed by Lord Justice Andrews was appointed to approach the Ministers of Home Affairs and Finance, but it was not until May 1924 that a handsome grant of £4,000 was made by the Ministry of Home Affairs for the purchase of books.[34]

In the courthouse the Bar were accommodated in two rooms. The larger room, where the law reports and text books were kept, was on the ground floor on the east side and became Court No 5 in the 1970s. The smaller room, which in later years was used by the clerk of the crown and peace, was across the corridor and faced onto the Crumlin Road itself. Known as the 'Ladies' Room' because no smoking was allowed and not because it was used by lady barristers, it became the almost exclusive preserve of a few seniors. At the rear of the building there was a room allotted to the Bar as a lunch room, at the back of which was a very cramped robing room.[35] Some time after the Northern Ireland Bar came into existence, a service known as 'the pony express' to collect and return brief bags similar to that in Dublin was set up. This involved a small motor van calling at the houses of the subscribers to the service in the morning to collect their brief bags and take them to the Bar Library, returning them to their homes in the evening.[36]

It is not possible to establish precisely how many barristers regarded themselves as members of the Northern Bar in the first few years as the surviving documentary records and references are not easy to reconcile. Hill Smith listed 72 members (including four 'new' members, i.e. probationers), but this was only for the first circuit in 1922.[37] Membership of the Circuit was not necessarily identical with membership of the Bar, although the great majority of practising barristers were members of both. In any event, of the 72 listed by Hill Smith, three silks and ten juniors were also members of the new Midland Circuit formed to cover those counties formerly in the North East or North West Circuits and now in the Irish Free State, and so presumably regarded themselves as primarily practising in Southern Ireland. Two other prominent silks with strong North East connections,

33  BCM, vol. 1, p. 12.
34  Ibid., p. 39. A vote of thanks was passed by the Bar Council on 16 May 1924.
35  W. Johnson, *History and customs of the Bar and Circuit of Northern Ireland* (Belfast, 1985), p. 7.
36  Ibid. p. 8.
37  Hill Smith, *The Supreme Court of Judicature of Northern Ireland*, pp 48-50.

S.L. Brown KC and Serjeant Hanna KC, continued to be based in Dublin, even though both were on the Northern committee of the benchers of King's Inn appointed in January 1922. In the event neither attended any of the meetings of the Northern committee, Hanna becoming a judge of the high court of the Irish Free State in 1925, and Brown a member of the Senate.[38] However, many of those based in Dublin continued to appear before the courts in Northern Ireland, at least for the first few years. For example, in June 1923 Hanna led Brown in the Court of Appeal when Serjeant Sullivan KC led for the other side.[39] Those who elected to live in Belfast no doubt had occasion to appear in Dublin after October 1921, at least for a while. T.J. Campbell KC was led by Brown for a Belfast plaintiff in a non-jury trial before Molony LCJ in Dublin in December 1922, with E.S. Murphy KC as one of the counsel for the defendant, Belfast Corporation.[40]

A roll of subscribers to the Bar Library was opened on 20 April 1922, and this provides a rather more, but not completely, reliable indication of those who regarded themselves as primarily, or solely, practising before the courts in Northern Ireland, although the manner in which it was kept means that it cannot be regarded as a definitive list of such practitioners at any given time. Whilst the great majority of barristers signed the roll, some did not do so for some time after call and were probably practising before they signed, in several instances for many years before they did so. A number of examples illustrate this. James Reid was present at the first general meeting 'of those members of the Bar who intend to practise in the Courts of Northern Ireland' held on 26 October 1921,[41] but it would seem that he did not sign until sometime between November 1931 and January 1932 as his signature is sandwiched between those of J.S. Steele on 9 November 1931, and Gerard Grant on 25 January 1932, even though Reid's signature is dated 20 April 1922 and his date of call is given as H. 1909. Two calls of Michaelmas term 1930, those of Mary K. Sheil and W.W.B. Topping, are separated by two entries of 1931 calls, one of 1928 and one of 1927 in that order. This rather haphazard record keeping continued at various times

38   Brown, Samuel Lombard (1856-1939). Called 1881,  NE Circuit 1881, QC 1899, bencher KI 1905. A native of Newry, leader of the chancery bar when he retired in 1926. Then served as commissioner of charitable donations and bequests and regius professor of laws at Dublin University. An honorary bencher of the Inn of Court of Northern Ireland 1926. *DIB*.

39   *Macura v The Northern Assurance Co Ltd* [1925] NI 141.

40   Campbell, *Fifty years of Ulster*, p. 148.

41   BCM, 1921-25 p. 1.

over the years, notably in the late 1930s and early 1940s. Perhaps the most dramatic example is that of W.W. McKeown, whose entry appears at the bottom of page two after that of J.S. Baxter of 1 June 1922 and is followed by that of E.S. Murphy at the top of the next page dated 4 December 1922, even though McKeown's entry is dated 14 June 1948! From the mid 1940s the Roll of Subscribers was kept reasonably well until 1966, but none of those called between 1965 and 1975 subscribed until various dates in 1975 and 1976 when an effort was made to bring it up to date,[42] and it was then kept until 1991, when those called in Michaelmas term of that year were the last to sign. William Boles was called in Michaelmas 1925 but only practised for a short time and did not sign the roll,[43] and there may well have been a few others in the same position who cannot now be identified.

In any event, membership of the Bar Library was not a requirement to practise, and at least one person is known to have practised but does not seem to have joined the Bar Library, namely Benjamin Lamb who was called in Michaelmas term 1925. As we shall see, many of those called to the Northern Ireland Bar between 1921 and the start of the Second World War did not enter practice in Northern Ireland at all so far as can be ascertained, and so the Roll of those called to the Northern Ireland Bar does not provide a complete record of those entering practice in Northern Ireland in the early years.

Nevertheless, provided these deficiencies are kept in mind, the Roll of Subscribers to the Bar Library is a useful indicator of those who were in practice at the Northern Ireland Bar in the first years of its existence. On 20 April 1922 23 members signed, with the list headed by the attorney general, Richard Best KC, immediately followed by George Hill Smith KC, and by the end of 1922 44 had signed. Eight more joined in 1923, bringing the total to 52. Three more joined in 1924, and three in 1925, bringing the total to 58. No one joined in 1926.[44] To these should be added those whose signatures came later, or who are known to have practised, namely McKeown, Reid, and Lamb, making 61. We know from the printed report of the proceedings of the meeting on 1 January 1926, at which the Inn of Court of Northern Ireland was established, that there were 70 original members of the Inn,

42  The author commenced practice immediately after his call on 22 Sept. 1969 but did not sign until 24 Oct. 1975, despite having been a member of the Bar Library throughout this period, as were his contemporaries who also did not sign until 1975.

43  BCM, Vol. 2, pp 310-11.

44  Roll of Subscribers to the Bar Library, Robing Room and Luncheon Room.

of whom six were judges and three civil servants,[45] leaving 61 members who one might assume were in practice, even if their practice was nominal because of age or lack of work. However, the number of those entitled to practise was somewhat higher, as the report also contained a statement that 49 counsel who had a statutory right of audience under the Government of Ireland Act[46] had signed the roll of membership of the Inn, and a further 21 who had been called since then had also signed. One might therefore reasonably infer from these figures that the Northern Ireland Bar in the sense of those who were holding themselves out to practice, and regarded themselves as permanently practising, in Northern Ireland, had grown to between 60 and 70 members by January 1926.

However, in the first few years after 1921 it is likely that the number of those practising before the courts was somewhat higher than these figures would suggest, because in October 1923 Sir Denis Henry estimated that there were 86 barristers regularly practising in Northern Ireland, and he said that a 'considerable number' of those entitled to do so because they had qualified before 1920 'do so from time to time as business may require'.[47] As there were only 52 subscribers to the Bar Library by December 1923, Henry's figure of 86 suggests that in the first two or three years after October 1921 at least 30 more barristers based in Southern Ireland appeared before the courts in Northern Ireland from time to time on the basis that they had been called before 1921, and so were entitled to practise in Northern Ireland.

A further complication is that there is a very substantial discrepancy between the number of individuals called to the Northern Ireland Bar after October 1921, and those who signed the Roll of Subscribers to the Bar Library during that time, particularly between 1921 and 1926. Of the 40 individuals called in 1924, 1925 and 1926, only seven signed the Roll of Subscribers, three in 1924[48] and four in 1925.[49] Even when William Boles and Benjamin Lamb are added to this list in 1925, the discrepancy remains

---

45  Sir Arthur Quekett was parliamentary counsel to the government of Northern Ireland 1921-45, knt 1945. F. Redmond and J.F. Caldwell were clerks in the supreme court. Caldwell (1892-1981) was first parliamentary draftsman 1945-58, KC 1946, CB 1952.

46  Sch. 7, para. 4 of the Government of Ireland Act, 1920 provided that all existing members of the Irish Bar became members of the Bar of Southern Ireland and of the Bar of Northern Ireland, and had right of audience in the supreme courts of both jurisdictions, from the appointed day.

47  3 Oct. 1923. J.M. Davies writing on Henry's direction to the treasury. S.C. L/23.

48  William Johnson, John Long and Archibald Stewart.

49  P.A. Marrinan, Maurice Macaulay and J.D. Condy.

striking. The explanation must be that the great majority of those called during that time were barristers who made their careers at the Southern Bar, and who it may be assumed were called in Northern Ireland in the expectation that it would be possible for them to practise on both sides of the new border. That expectation became less realistic with the passage of time, particularly when the connection between King's Inns and the Northern Bar was severed in 1925. It is noteworthy that whilst 17 were called in 1925, eight in 1926 and nine in 1927, of whom five of those called in 1927 signed the Roll of Subscribers to the Bar Library, only seven of the 18 called in 1925 did so. The 1925 and 1926 calls contained some who were to have distinguished careers at the Southern Bar, notably Richard McGonigal,[50] E.C. Micks,[51] and Denis Pringle,[52] but the number of those called who were based in Southern Ireland dried up rapidly and completely after the formation of the Inn of Court of Northern Ireland in January 1926. After a few years it seems that even those members of the Southern Bar who were entitled to practise in Northern Ireland did so very rarely, although a few came on circuit for a time to some of the Assize towns on the old North West Circuit, such as Enniskillen, courts which were readily accessible by train from Dublin in those days.[53] One who did appear in 1942 was Cecil Lavery SC, who represented the defendants charged with the murder of an RUC constable at their trial before Lord Justice Murphy at the Belfast City Commission between 28 and 31 July 1942.[54]

The supreme authority of the Bar was a general meeting of the Bar, as had been the position at the Irish Bar. Eleven general meetings in all were held by the end of 1923, although the day to day governance of the Bar was increasingly in the hands of the Bar Council from 1923 onwards. It was a general meeting that decided to form a Bar Council and a Circuit of Northern Ireland on 26 October 1921, and general meetings held on 12 and 16 December 1921, 12 and 20 January 1922, and 9 February 1922[55] made decisions relating to the name of the Circuit, as well as the arrangements for the Bar Library and the Bar Council. The general meeting of 27 February 1923 considered whether

50   (1902-1964). SC 1940. *DIB*.

51   (1900-1973). SC 1948. *ILT & SJ*, cvii (1973), 311.

52   (1902-1998). High court judge 1969-74. *The Times* , 4 Sept. 1998.

53   MacDermott, *An Enriching Life*, pp 185-86.

54   *Irish News* 29 July 1942. Lavery had been called in 1915, and took silk in 1927. A Fine Gael TD 1935-8, he was attorney general and a senator 1948-50, and a judge of the supreme court 1950-1966. *DIB*.

55   BCM, pp. 1-8, and 10-12

those who had chambers should surrender their tenancies, and at the general meeting of 17 December 1923 amendments of the Constitution of the Bar Council were adopted that were intended to 'secure unity of control over matters relating to the Bar by making the Library Committee and the Circuit Committee committees of the Bar Council'.[56] There is no record of any general meeting being held between 23 February 1925 and 16 November 1940,[57] but four general meetings were held between the meeting of 17 November 1940 and June 1945 to pass resolutions of sympathy upon the deaths of members of the judiciary and of the Bar. For the remainder of the period covered by this chapter the Bar Council was responsible for the governance of the Bar, except for those matters such as disciplinary questions, where the ultimate authority lay with the benchers.

The Circuit Committee, although independent with its own officers, meetings, and accounts, was subordinate to the Bar acting as whole in a general meeting from the beginning. This can be seen from the decision of 17 December 1923, and the general meeting of 12 December 1921 which not only decided that the name of the Circuit was to be 'The Circuit of Northern Ireland', but decided the order in which the Circuit towns were to be held, as well as appointing a committee to 'consider the establishment and constitution of the new Circuit and the drafting of rules therefor'.[58]

Unfortunately the deficiencies in record keeping noted in the Roll of Subscribers of the Bar Library extend to the minutes of the Bar Council, as there are six blank pages between the minutes of the Bar Council meetings of 28 February 1923 and 6 December 1923. Minutes of meetings from then until the end of 1925 have been entered. No minutes have been recorded for any of its meetings after 14 December 1925 until the meeting of 6 February 1931, and there are over 30 blank pages in the minute book between those dates. One can only assume that it was intended that the minutes would be written up later for meetings of the Bar Council held during these years, because, whatever may have been the position between February and December 1923, it is inconceivable that there were no meetings of the Council for over five years.

56   Ibid., p. 32.
57   Ibid., p. 163. The meeting in 1940 decided to co-operate with the Law Society to secure more convenient access to the building.
58   Ibid., pp 2-4.

The members of the Bar Council were elected each year, and the attorney general, who was regarded as *ex officio* head of the Bar, presided at its meetings when he was present. In his absence the senior member of the Bar on the Council took the chair, and this occurred fairly frequently. From its inception the Bar Council was responsible for deciding matters of professional etiquette, resolving at its first meeting on 26 January 1922 that members of the Junior Bar appearing in the courts in the Courthouse in Belfast and on Circuit 'should always where possible sit in the seats assigned to Junior Counsel'.[59] Questions of proper behaviour and etiquette were often interlinked, and on 27 November 1924 the Bar Council was asked by B.J. Fox[60] to consider the propriety of his stating that his client blamed someone else whilst making a plea in mitigation although this was not in the depositions, for which he had been criticised by the trial judge. The Bar Council sought the views of the trial judge, and, having considered them, resolved the next day that counsel should not do so unless this appeared in the depositions. This was coupled this with a submission sent by it to the judge pointing out that Fox's client had insisted that this course be taken, that the practice had hitherto been uncertain, and requesting the trial judge 'favourably to consider a modification of the censure passed by him upon Mr Fox'. Lord Justice Moore, who was the trial judge, subsequently stated in open court that the Council had brought the difficulty of Fox's position before him, and 'that he was satisfied that Mr Fox had acted with absolute bona fides and had not had any intention of transgressing the bounds of legitimate advocacy'.[61]

An important aspect of the Bar Council's function was to protect the interests of the Bar as a whole, and it sought to do this by making representations in the appropriate quarters about a range of matters that were of concern to the Bar. These ranged from the arcane subject of placing of some permanent civil servants ahead of king's counsel in the scale of precedence published in the *Belfast Gazette*, to deciding to tell the lord chief justice that it was the opinion of the practising Bar that silk should only be given on the basis of professional standing and actual practise at the Bar,[62] a matter that was to be of concern to the

---

59  Ibid., p. 9.
60  Recorder of Belfast 1944-59.
61  BCM, p. 44.
62  22 Jan. 1924. Ibid, pp 34-36.

Bar for many years. Proposals for changes in the law were considered where they related to areas of particular interest to the profession, as when the Council responded to a request from the Land Registry in 1936 by approving proposed rules of procedure, and from the mid 1930s the minutes reveal that the Council had to consider proposed legislative changes more frequently. However, in the first ten or fifteen years of the Council's existence, meetings were often infrequent, and, to judge by the sparse minutes when it did meet, its attention was generally focussed on internal and routine business.

One topic that frequently raised its head was the length of the court vacations. At that time the legal year in Northern Ireland, as is still the case in Southern Ireland and England and Wales, was divided into four terms. The Michaelmas term started in late October, the Hilary term in mid January, the Easter and Trinity terms were separated by a short break at Whitsun, and the Long Vacation started on 1 August. In May 1922 the Rules Committee asked the Bar Council for its views on the desirability of reverting to fixed dates for the Easter and Trinity terms, and the Council was strongly in favour of this, suggesting that the Easter term run from 15 April to May 18, and the Trinity term start on 1 June and end on 31 July.[63] The matter was raised again in 1925, when a proposal was brought before the Council to shorten the Long Vacation and abolish the fixed dates for the Easter and Trinity terms so that Easter and Whitsun were included in the terms.[64] A general meeting[65] referred the matter back to the Bar Council, which considered the matter on three occasions, and at the end of 1925 came to the view that at the latest the Long Vacation should end on 15 October.[66]

The Council decided that a general meeting of the Bar should be held to discuss this, but as there are no minutes of any meetings after that until 1931 it is not known whether a general meeting was held. It would appear that no changes were made, because in January 1933 the attorney general raised the desirability of the dates of the Easter Vacation varying according to the date of Easter. The Bar Council deferred the matter,[67] but the Council minutes show that in May 1933 it discussed the shortening of the Long

63   12 May 1922. Ibid., p. 14.
64   16 Feb. 1925. Ibid., pp 45-46.
65   23 Feb. 1925. Ibid., pp 46-47.
66   On 15 May, 2 June and 14 Dec. 1925.
67   12 Jan. 1933. BCM, pp. 99-100.

Vacation because this was again being considered by the Rules Committee. Whilst only one member (C.L. Sheil) was against such a suggestion, three favoured starting the Michaelmas term on 1 October, whilst four (including Sheil) supported 12 October as the start of term.[68]

An essential characteristic of a self-governing profession is that it exercises disciplinary powers over its members. The most serious disciplinary matters were regarded as the responsibility of the Inn of Court because the benchers decided whether to call applicants to the Bar, and retained the ultimate power to expel barristers from the profession by disbarring them from the Inn. No barrister has been disbarred by the Inn of Court of Northern Ireland since its foundation for disciplinary reasons, although on many occasions barristers have been disbarred at their own request so that they can be admitted as solicitors. The Bar Council minutes record a small number of occasions when complaints were made about the conduct of individual barristers. In May 1925,[69] and again in July 1931,[70] complaints were made by solicitors against unnamed members of the Bar. On both occasions the Bar Council concluded no action was necessary. The minutes do not reveal the nature of the 1925 complaint, but the July 1931 complaint related to delay in settling a statement of claim.

More serious complaints were referred by the Bar Council to the Benchers. One such instance occurred in early in 1931, when the benchers concluded in February that a member of the Bar had been guilty of professional misconduct as counsel for the plaintiff by interviewing the defendant about the case in the absence of, and without the knowledge of, the defendant's professional advisers. The benchers notified the Bar Council accordingly. The Council then directed that its earlier resolution to this effect be screened in the Bar Library, and notified the benchers.[71] This meant that the announcement appeared on the notice board which acted as a screen at the doorway into the Bar Library, and so the rebuke to the barrister concerned was publicly communicated to his professional colleagues.

Not all complaints before the Bar Council came from solicitors or the public. From time to time members of the Bar questioned the conduct of their

68   Ibid., pp 106-09.
69   15 May 1925. Ibid., pp. 48-50.
70   9 July 1931. Ibid., pp. 86-88.
71   Ibid., pp 85-86.

colleagues, and in 1928 the attorney general complained about the same barrister who was the subject of the disciplinary action in 1931 mentioned above. The Bar Council felt that it could not take action and suggested that the matter be referred to the benchers.[72] Having considered complaints where the existing practice or rules of conduct were felt to be unclear, the Bar Council often passed a resolution setting out the rule to be applied in future. One such occasion related to G.B. Hanna MP appearing for a client prosecuted by the government department in which he was a minister. The matter was referred to the Bar Council who wrote to Hanna in January 1933, and his reply was considered at its next meeting in March 1933, Hanna having taken silk in the interim on 3 February. The Council resolved that it disapproved of his conduct.[73] It then put in hand the drafting of a rule to prohibit ministers appearing for defendants who had been prosecuted by their departments. It was not until November 1935 that such a rule was introduced, when it was prompted by the Council being informed that, despite Hanna having been informed of the Council's earlier decision, he had appeared for a client in a licensing case which was opposed by the police.[74] In due course the resolutions of the Bar Council covered a wide range of matters of practice and professional conduct, although, as we shall see, the absence of a complete and readily accessible compilation of the resolutions was a problem that was recognised, but not satisfactorily addressed, in years to come.

There is little doubt that many found it difficult to make a living at the Bar because there was not a great deal of work in either the civil or criminal courts. There was no criminal legal aid at all until 1946, and, as we shall see in the next chapter, it was not until 1964 that a system of civil legal aid was introduced. The amount of civil litigation was very small by present day standards, fees in the high court and county courts were low, the scales remaining unchanged for many years. Prisoners in criminal trials who wished to be legally represented had to find the money themselves, or with the help of family and friends. The only exception when the charge was murder. In such cases the prosecution paid the defence fees as well, although the fees allowed were very small.

An indication of the of the level of work for the Bar in the high court and

---

72  Correspondence between Babington AG, the secretary of the Bar Council and the Inn of Court, Apr. 1928. Inn File R2.
73  7 Mar. 1933. BCM, pp 103-04.
74  1 Nov. 1935. BCM, pp 130-31.

Bar dinner menu 1938.

View of possible exterior of the Royal Courts of Justice.
By Charles Terry Pledge ARIBA.

Courtesy of the Northern Ireland Court Service.

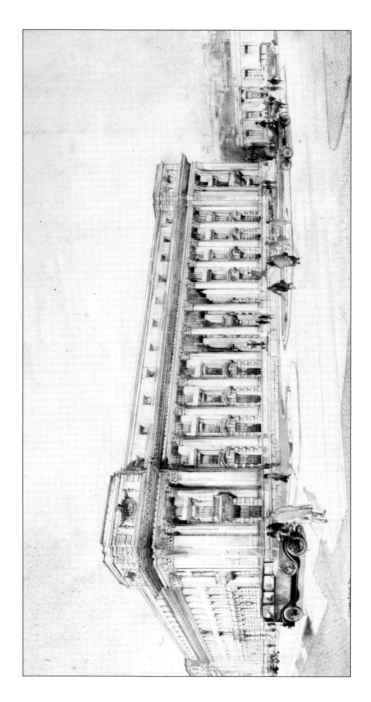

View of exterior as adopted of the proposed Royal Courts of Justice.
By Charles Terry Pledge ARIBA.
Courtesy of the Northern Ireland Court Service.

The Old Bar Library.

Courtesy of Paul Megahey

The Atrium, New Bar Library.

Courtesy of Chris Hill sales@senicireland.com.

Interior view of the New Bar Library.
Courtesy of Chris Hill sales@senicireland.com.

Exterior view, front of the New Bar Library.

Courtesy of Chris Hill sales@senicireland.com.

The Inn of Court.

Courtesy of Paul Megahey

the court of appeal in the 1930s is given by the daily Law List published in the newspapers, as can be seen from an analysis of the lists in January and February 1934 and 1939. On Monday 15 January 1934 there was one case listed in the court of appeal for judgment, one to fix a date, and one for hearing. In the chancery court eight petitions, notices and summonses were listed before Mr Justice Megaw, and there were two matters listed before the chief clerk. In the king's bench Lord Justice Andrews was to give judgment in a civil bill appeal after the court of appeal. On Tuesday 16 January three summonses were listed before Mr Justice Megaw, who also had six motions and one mention in the land purchase commission list. In the king's bench the lord chief justice had one probate and matrimonial summons and one summons. The under sheriff was to conduct a sheriff's inquiry to assess damages, and we know from a newspaper report the next day that J.D. Chambers was for the plaintiff. On Wednesday 17 January there were six civil bill appeals, with the only other business listed consisting of summonses before the chief clerk, the registrar and the taxing master. On Thursday 18 January the court of appeal gave a judgment, and there was no other court of appeal, chancery or king's bench business listed other than summonses before the chief clerk and the taxing master. Friday 19 January saw the court of appeal give judgment. In the king's bench before the lord chief justice there were one summons to fix a date, six motions, one summons and one non-jury action. Mr Justice Brown was listed to deal with bankruptcy matters, and Mr Justice Megaw had 14 land purchase matters in his list. The chief clerk had one summons and the taxing master two. No matters were listed on Saturday, although the courts were open.

The lists for the week of Monday 12 February 1934 reveal a similar level of activity. On Monday 12 February Mr Justice Megaw had five notices and summonses in his chancery list, and in the king's bench Mr Justice Brown had two non-jury actions, and one special jury action, for hearing later in the week, as well as a matrimonial matter and a linked action for criminal conversion for hearing on Friday, all to be mentioned. On Tuesday 13 February the court of appeal heard interlocutory applications, and continued the hearing on Wednesday, when they also heard a workmen's compensation appeal. On Tuesday the king's bench had two settled actions for mention. In the chancery list the chief clerk and taxing master dealt with summonses and motions. Wednesday 14 February saw the court of appeal dealing with one appeal and listing another part-heard case for mention on Friday. The registrar, chief clerk and taxing master had summonses and motions listed. On Thursday 15

February there were two non-jury actions listed in the king's bench.

In the same weeks in January and February 1939 the pattern was broadly similar. Term started on Wednesday 11 January, and one non-jury action was listed in the king's bench, and the chief clerk had two summonses in Chancery. On Friday 13 January the lord chief justice was to hear *ex parte* motions and 19 summonses and motions, with Mr Justice Brown dealing with the bankruptcy list. On Monday and Tuesday of the following week there were to be two actions each day, with one on Wednesday, and one probate, and one non-jury, action on Thursday. In the event on Monday 16 the lord chief justice had one action and a civil bill appeal in his king's bench list, and Mr Justice Brown also had one action. The list for the week beginning Monday 13 February 1939 was even lighter, although the list for Friday 17 February warned of seven actions listed in the following week.

Although the great majority of cases were dealt with by the high court and the court of appeal, there was a good deal of business before the land purchase commissioners and the judicial commissioner arising out of the workings of the Land Purchase Acts in which counsel were engaged, and there are many reports of such cases in the *Northern Ireland Reports* of the 1920s and 1930s. There were also a small number of cases that went on appeal to London, all but one to the House of Lords, where it was the almost invariable practice of the parties to bring in English counsel, and not just in tax cases where English counsel were always instructed. An example is *Lagan Navigation Co Ltd v Lambeg Bleaching, Dyeing and Finishing Co Ltd*, where J.B. Matthews KC was brought in for the plaintiff and F.H. Maugham KC (later lord chancellor) for the defendants, only the Northern Ireland junior counsel remaining from the court of appeal hearing.[75] The only exception to the rule that appeals went to the house of lords was when the matter could be referred to the judicial committee of the Privy Council under s. 51 of the Government of Ireland Act. It seems that this only occurred once when Belfast Corporation challenged the Stormont Government's decision to levy a rate on local county councils to be paid to the Government towards the cost of educational services.[76] There do not seem to have been a great many appeals to the House of

75  The court of appeal decision is at [1926] NI 31, the decision of the house of lords is reported at
    [1927] NI 24.
76  *In re a reference under the Government of Ireland Act*, 1920, (1936) A.C. 352. MacDermott, *An
    enriching life*, pp 227-28.

Lords, only six being reported in the *Northern Ireland Reports* between 1926 and 1938, although there may have been other cases which were not reported in that series, such as *McEvoy v Belfast Bank.*[77]

Although most cases in the court of appeal or the high court were relatively short, some were lengthy with many counsel engaged. Perhaps the most substantial case to be fought out in the Northern Ireland courts before the Second World War was that arising out of the sale of the great Belfast shipbuilding firm of Workman & Clark, with a claim for damages for fraudulent misrepresentation against the directors. At the conclusion of the plaintiff's case the trial judge, Mr Justice Brown, dismissed the case against some defendants. The case lasted 20 days in the high court, and 15 days in the court of appeal.[78] It then went to the house of lords, where it took a further nine days. There were 14 counsel engaged in the court of appeal, of whom 13 were members of the Northern Ireland Bar. In the house of lords there were 11, of whom only four were members of the Northern Ireland Bar.[79]

Whilst these are only snapshots of the volume of business in the court of appeal and the high court, the contrast with the very much larger lists in later decades is striking. Of course, for the junior Bar in particular, the court of appeal and high court were not the only courts because county courts and appeals from the county courts were very important sources of work. Appeals from the county courts went to the high court in cases from the Belfast recorder's court and County Antrim,[80] and to the assizes in all other counties. Criminal cases were dealt with at quarter sessions which were presided over by the recorder or county court judge who was also the chairman of quarter sessions for his county and so exercised a criminal jurisdiction, unlike his counterparts in England and Wales.

It was into the small, and tightly knit, professional world of the Bar Library that a newly-called barrister who intended to practise came upon being called to the Bar. Pupillage was customary, although not it seems compulsory, to judge by the experience of John Clarke MacDermott,

---

77 Reported in the court of appeal at [1934] NI 67, and in the house of lords at (1935) AC. 24.
   MacDermott, *An enriching life*, pp 225-27.
78 [1928] NI 162.
79 [1930] NI 4.
80 Memoranda on the setting up of the Supreme Court of Judicature in Northern Ireland. PRONI
   CAB/6/57.

later Lord MacDermott. He later described how he was unable to arrange a pupillage with any of the established juniors when he was called in November 1921. MacDermott realised that it was up to him 'to absorb by close observation, continual curiosity and further reading' as much as he could of the law in action and the nature of the courts, particularly the Belfast recorder's court, which he had been advised to attend diligently and in wig, gown and bands.[81] However, for the majority, as before 1921, pupillage was the norm. Sir Frank Harrison QC, recalled how, then plain F.A.L. Harrison, it was difficult to obtain an introduction to a master unless one had some connection with a judge or an existing practitioner. He was introduced to L.E. Curran, and recalled that the fee was 50 guineas on starting pupillage, and a further 50 guineas on completion of the first year.[82] A pupil would have the run of his master's papers, prepare draft pleadings and opinions if requested, attend consultations with his master, and make himself generally useful to his master. If the master was conscientious and took a close interest in his pupil's welfare, he would not merely respond to requests for advice but would keep a close eye on his pupil's early appearances in court, offering advice and guidance as necessary. The pupil would be introduced to the master's solicitor clients and, if he impressed, might expect to be handed on some of the briefs his master could not deal with, and eventually succeed to at least some of the master's practice if the latter took silk. The relationship was often a very close one, as may be seen from Sir Edward Jones's description of his pupillage and friendship with his master Desmond Chambers,[83] who was amongst the leading juniors in the late 1930s, together with Curran, James McSparran and Charles (Charlie) Sheil.[84]

It was unusual for a newly-called barrister to make a great deal in his early years, indeed it is believed that the only three members of the Northern Ireland Bar who managed to make the respectable sum of 100 guineas in their first year at the Bar between 1921 and the Second World War were Chambers, Jones and MacDermott. Jones made exactly that sum,[85] (although he does not say whether it was net of travelling and professional expenses), and MacDermott about 180 guineas, which he reckoned came to about 100

81   MacDermott, *An enriching life*, p. 154.
82   To the author on 22 July 2000.
83   Jones, *Jones LJ, his life and times*, Ch iv.
84   Ibid.
85   *Jones LJ, his life and times*, p. 33.

after expenses.[86] Jones continued to meet Chambers' exacting standard of doubling his income each year after the first for the next three years, making £985 in his fourth year before he left the Bar Library to join the Army on 10 November 1939.[87] In general, although those who succeeded could hope to make a decent living by the standards of professional people at the time, work was scarce, and, as we shall see, many left the Bar to seek more secure livelihoods elsewhere.

Although life at the Bar was hard for many, there was tremendous camaraderie, both inside the Bar Library and outside. Golf provided an opportunity for the bench and Bar to mingle socially, and there were Bar dinners on various occasions in leading hotels, and in the summer some of the judges arranged social gatherings for the Bar. Lord Justice Best gave an annual garden party at his home in King's Road, Knock. For many years Lord Justice Andrews hosted an annual cricket match in Comber between the Bar and a Comber team led by his cousin William. Sir William Moore LCJ organised an annual party for the Bar at Moore Lodge, his house overlooking the Bann at Kilrea.[88]

Although during this period the Northern Ireland Bar was almost completely male, a handful of women were called. The first was Frances Christian Kyle, who was called in Dublin on 1 November 1921, and in Belfast shortly afterwards. The first woman to be called to the Bar anywhere in the British Isles, she was a person of very considerable intellectual attainments. After initially studying French, she studied law for the last two years of her degree at Trinity College, Dublin and graduated B.A. and LL.B. in 1916.[89] When the Sex Disqualification (Removal) Act of 1919 removed the barrier to women entering the legal profession, she and Averill Deverell were admitted as students by King's Inns.[90] Kyle's ability was demonstrated by her winning the 1st Victoria Prize, and then gaining first place in her Bar examinations and the John Brooke Scholarship of £50 for three years. This was no mean achievement because J.C. MacDermott, later Lord MacDermott, came second, and Patrick McGilligan, who was to have distinguished career as

86   *An enriching life*, p. 175.
87   *Jones LJ, his life and times*, p. 33.
88   Sir Frank Harrison QC to the author, and W. Johnson, *History and Customs of the Bar and Circuit of Northern Ireland*, p. 16.
89   *Dubl. Univ. Calendar* 1916–17, vol. iii, pp 39, 80 and 108.
90   *King's Inns Barristers*, pp 27–34.

a politician, government minister, academic and barrister in the Irish Free State, came third.[91] Because she was winner of the Brooke Scholarship Kyle was the first barrister to be called in her year, ahead of MacDermott and McGilligan and the others called on the same day, including Miss Deverell. Kyle and MacDermott were both called shortly afterwards in Belfast. She joined the Bar Library and was present at the meeting on January 1926 at which the Inn of Court of Northern Ireland was formed. On 14 June 1922 she was elected a member of the Circuit, when it was recorded that she had appeared as a probationer at two assize towns, and had been excused attendance at a third.[92] Her name remained on the list of members of the Circuit until 1939. On her death in 1959 newspaper obituaries said that she practised for a short time,[93] but Margaret (Peggy) Aiken, who was called in Michaelmas 1928, claimed in 1985 that she became the first woman actually to practise at the Northern Ireland Bar.[94] Aiken had left the Bar by 1932 when she obtained a post in the principal probate registry of the high court, whilst Kyle remained a member of the Circuit until at least 1939. However, Kyle is not recorded as going on circuit after the surviving Circuit records start in 1936, and the most likely explanation is that she may have tried to practise for a short time, and then remained a nominal member of the Bar until the outbreak of the Second World War. During the War she helped to provide support and hospitality for servicemen, using her gift for foreign languages to learn Czech so that she could help Czech airmen who felt lonely in a foreign country.[95]

Averill Deverell was called to the Northern Ireland Bar in Easter 1922, but appears to have confined her career to the Southern Bar, where she practised for forty years, establishing a considerable chancery practice.[96] The next women to be called were Audrey M. McMeekin and Aiken, both in Michaelmas 1928, followed in Michaelmas 1930 by Mary K.A. Sheil, and in Trinity 1931 by Enid M.L. Henry, who was the last woman to be called until after the War. None of the women appear to have found life at the Bar very rewarding, and as noted above Kyle does not seem to have been in active practice in later years, if indeed she ever was. Although she and Mary

91   (1899-1979). For details of McGilligan's career see *DIB*.
92   CM, p. 15.
93   *Belfast Newsletter* 24 June 1958; *Belfast Telegraph* 24 June 1958.
94   Aiken, *Inn of Court Newsletter*, Vol. 1 No.3.
95   *Belfast Telegraph*, and *Belfast Newsletter*, both 24 June, 1956.
96   Averill Katherine Statter Deverell (1893-1979). *DIB*.

Sheil appear on the Circuit list published each year in the *Belfast and Ulster Directory* until the outbreak of war in 1939, and so must have kept up their Circuit membership, Mary Sheil never received a brief, and only stayed in the Library for two years before returning to live in Portadown.[97] Neither she nor Kyle is recorded as going on circuit in the circuit book kept from 1936 onwards. Enid M.L. Henry was called in Trinity 1931, and signed the Roll of Subscribers that year, but by 1935 appears as a second class clerk in the registrar's department of the high court, and she remained on the high court staff until her retirement in the 1970s.[98]

Nothing is known of Audrey McMeekin after she was called in Michaelmas 1928, but Peggy Aiken has left an account of the two years or so she spent at the Bar before she joined the high court staff as a second class clerk.[99] She describes what must have the common lot of a newly-called barrister, going to an inquest in Donnemana, attending Derry quarter sessions, and appearing for three men who pleaded guilty to 'breaking and entering' at the Northern Ireland Winter Assizes in Downpatrick. Whilst she recalled in 1985 that 'everyone seemed anxious to make life as pleasant as possible for the one solitary young girl in their midst', it seems probable that lack of work led her to abandon the Bar for a secure position in the principal probate registry.

Whilst it is a reasonable assumption that solicitors were reluctant to brief a lady barrister because they felt concerned that their clients would be unwilling to have one appearing for them, it has to be remembered that many men also found it difficult or impossible to make a living at the Bar at this time, and throughout the 1920s and 1930s a significant number left to pursue a career elsewhere. One or two left to become solicitors, such as O.W. McCutcheon who was called in Hilary 1931, but disbarred at his own request a few months later to become a solicitor.[100] Gerard P. Torney was called in Michaelmas 1932 and joined Gray's Inn in November 1935.[101] Several joined the colonial legal service. Some appear to have done so immediately after call, although most did so after a few years at the Bar. Between 1923 and 1939 eight of those

97  Sir John Sheil (her nephew) to the author. In the late 1930s her address is given as Portadown in the barristers' section of the *Belfast and Ulster Directory*.
98  *Belfast and Ulster Directory*, 1935.
99  Although called in Michaelmas 1928, she continued to study for her LLB at Queen's until June 1929. She must have left the Bar and joined the staff of the high court in 1931, because she was listed as a second class clerk in the 1932 edition of the *Belfast and Ulster Directory*.
100  He was disbarred on 26 Oct. 1931.
101  He was called in Gray's Inn on 18 Nov. 1935, but died a few weeks later in January 1936.

called later pursued careers abroad, of whom at least four practised for some time in Northern Ireland. J.R. Gregg left in 1929 to become a magistrate in the West Indies; A.A. Cromie was appointed a crown prosecutor in Sierra Leone in December 1927; in 1940 Martin McCall became a crown counsel in the Straits Settlements;[102] and F.A. Reid also left about the same time to go to the Straits Settlements. A number of others went on to have distinguished careers abroad, although it is unclear whether they practised at all, or for any appreciable time, after they were called in Northern Ireland. James Reynolds, who was called in Hilary 1931, became a judge of the high court of Eastern Nigeria,[103] and W.H. Irwin, who was called in Michaelmas of the following year, became a judge of the high court of Western Nigeria.[104] The Bar Council and the benchers were keenly aware of the importance of the importance to the Northern Ireland Bar of the ability of its members to seek employment in the colonial service. In 1938 a committee was set up by the benchers with members of the Bar Council to consider the qualifications required of barristers applying to the colonial service.[105]

Although those who left were young men, one notable exception was James Harvey Monroe KC. He was called to the Irish Bar in 1909, joined the North East Circuit as a probationer that year,[106] and took silk in July 1920. In 1921 he elected to continue his career at the Northern Bar, and was elected a bencher in 1926. Despairing of judicial preferment, he accepted a position as a high court judge in Lahore in India in 1932, when he was elected an honorary bencher of the Inn of Court of Northern Ireland.[107] However, during this period Monroe was unique in leaving Northern Ireland for such a senior judicial appointment. The departure from the Bar Library of one of its members, whether to the colonial service or the bench, was usually marked by a dinner held in one of Belfast's leading hotels or restaurants. Some of the menu cards for these have survived, and are decorated with skilfully drawn and amusing cartoons. Although their creator cannot now

---

102 Now part of Malaysia.

103 Note on Roll of Barristers.

104 W.H. Irwin (1907-74). District magistrate Gold Coast 1936, puisne judge in Trinidad and Tobago 1947-54, and Nigeria 1951-61.

105 1 July 1938. BCM, p. 151.

106 Hill Smith, *The North-East Bar*, p. 127.

107 Died. 21 May 1944. *ILT&SJ* lxxix (1945), 308. In a lecture 'Inst and the Law' (15 Sept. 2010) Lord Carswell recounted that Monroe was disappointed not to be appointed as chancery judge when Megaw was appointed.

be established with certainty, it is likely that they were the work of J.D. Condy, who was killed on active service in the Second World War.[108]

Although much of the life of the Bar was spent in the courts in Belfast, the work of the Bar was by no means confined to Belfast as a great many courts were attended throughout Northern Ireland. Although it was not unknown for counsel to appear in the petty sessions, or inquests,[109] this was relatively unusual at that time, and the Bar largely confined their work to criminal work at quarter sessions and county courts across Northern Ireland. A major feature of professional life for the Bar was the assizes. Two judges of the Supreme Court went on circuit twice a year. A single judge would preside at the Northern Ireland Winter assize, which, as its name implied, was for criminal business alone from all over Northern Ireland. The Winter assize was often held outside Belfast, for example in 1923 and 1925 it was held in Armagh, and in 1924 at Londonderry. Other than the Winter assize, the assizes dealt with both civil and criminal business, the judges taking it in turn to act as the crown and civil judge. The assizes started with the Co. Antrim assizes which were held at the Crumlin Road court house. The only civil business conducted at the Antrim assizes would be the hearing of any records, a record being a writ issued for hearing at the assizes rather than for hearing at the high court. The judges then went to Downpatrick, Armagh, Enniskillen, Omagh, and Londonderry in that order. Because the Northern judiciary was so small, the judges drew up a rota amongst themselves whereby the senior judge was the lord chief justice or one of the two lord justices, and the junior judge was one of the two puisne judges. All the judges took it in turn to preside at the Belfast City Commission (the criminal assize court for Belfast which sat four times a year), and at the Winter assizes, so a substantial portion of their time was devoted to criminal business.[110]

Professional life at the assizes was regulated by the Circuit of Northern Ireland, which, as we have seen, had a separate existence from, although it was ultimately responsible to, the Bar Council. The Circuit was presided over by the Father, had its own secretary and treasurer, and its own rules

---

108 The original drawings of two of these cartoons survive and his name appears on the back of each, together with references to charging against an account. These details may have been recorded by the printer on receipt of the originals. The style of several of the drawings suggests that they are by the same person.

109 Aiken, *Inn of Court Newsletter*, Vol. 1 No 3.

110 G. Hill Smith, *The Supreme Court of Judicature of Northern Ireland*, (Belfast, 1926) pp 26-29.

governing professional conduct at the assizes and social activity. The Circuit of Northern Ireland was formed at a meeting of members of the North East and North West Circuits on 12 December 1921, but unfortunately in 1933 it was discovered that the original circuit account book had been removed, and the first 13 pages of the minute book torn out, by a person or persons unknown 'at or about the time of the opening of the new law courts'.[111] Why this was done, and by whom, is a mystery. Fortunately the minutes resume with a meeting of the Circuit committee on 7 June 1922, and a new Circuit account book was started in 1936, and these records provide a great deal of information about the Circuit and its activities, although unfortunately the names of those attending at each assize town were not invariably entered in the new account book.

The Circuit had its own committee, and general meetings of the circuit were held from time to time. The Circuit replicated the rules and practices of the pre-1921 circuits, requiring new members to attend three assize towns as probationers before being elected. On election an entrance fee was paid, and thereafter an annual subscription. In 1936 the entrance fee was five guineas, and the annual subscription two guineas.[112] It is probable that the influence of George Hill Smith, author of the history of the North East Bar which has been frequently referred to, was instrumental in persuading members of the Bar to form a new Circuit, and he was elected its first Father. His wishes were not always heeded, and on 14 November 1924 he threatened to resign when the Circuit unanimously decided not to hold a dinner in Belfast that year.[113] However, he appears not to have done so and remained Father until his death on 1 April 1926, when he was briefly succeeded by John Leetch KC, who had been the last Father of the North West Circuit.[114] Leetch resigned a month later and John McGonigal KC was elected, defeating T.H. Maxwell KC. As the Rules perpetuated the pre-1921 practices there was little need for the Circuit to have to consider matters of professional conduct. One occasion when it did so was on 4 November 1925 when a general meeting considered the propriety of a senior being briefed in a civil bill appeal without a junior in an appeal to the high court from Co. Antrim, because the new practice was for such appeals to go to the high court and not to the assizes, and so the appeal was not being heard at an assize town.

111 4 July 1933. CM, p. 69.
112 1936 summer assizes, Circuit Book.
113 CM, p. 38.
114 *Thom's Official Directory of Great Britain and Ireland* (Dublin, 1920), p. 934.

It was resolved that the general rule that a senior should not appear without a junior in such cases should be applied.[115]

Most of the Circuit minutes are devoted to the social side of assize life. Following the pre-1921 tradition, a Circuit dinner was usually held, sometimes in Belfast, sometimes in an assize town. The North East Circuit often had a dinner in Armagh, but in 1924, 1925, 1926 and 1934 Circuit dinners were held in Omagh, and Circuit dinners were held in Belfast in 1923, 1930, 1932 and 1944. The going judges of assize and their registrars were usually the guests of the Circuit at such dinners, although occasionally others were invited, as in 1930 when all the judges of the Supreme Court, the attorney general, the recorders of Belfast and Londonderry and Judge Bates were also guests.[116] The old custom of the Bar storing its own wines in each circuit town continued, and in 1926 it was decided that £80 should spent on this. Members plainly did not stint themselves or their guests, it being resolved in 1924 that the judges be entertained in Omagh 'and to supply champagne thereat out of the circuit funds'.[117] However, the purchase and supply of wines could give rise to controversy. At a Circuit meeting on 2 March 1927, a proposal that 20% of the wines purchased should be British Empire wines was defeated, but it was resolved that no whiskey should be opened at any Down assizes (although no reason is given for this, it may be that as members returned to Belfast at night, to drink whiskey at lunch was felt to be undesirable),[118] and this rule was not rescinded until 1951.[119]

That any alcoholic liquor at all be supplied out of Circuit funds was controversial. At a general meeting of the Circuit in 1922 a motion that no alcoholic liquor be supplied out of Circuit funds at Circuit dinners or lunches proposed by J.A. Pringle and seconded by J.H. Robb KC MP was defeated. Pringle, a total abstainer, had been a solicitor in Fermanagh before being called to the Bar. However, his concerns were not without foundation as Lord MacDermott recalled that quite a lot of 'hard liquor' was consumed on Circuit, mostly by the older men.[120]

115 CM, p. 43.
116 Ibid., p. 61.
117 Ibid., p. 34.
118 Ibid., pp 49-51.
119 Ibid., p. 103.
120 *An enriching life*, p. 188.

As each county had two Crown prosecutors, a senior, who was almost invariably a silk, and a junior, they would attend their own county, but the numbers of the Bar attending varied between county depending upon the work that would be expected in that county. On the civil side, record actions were increasingly rare, although some important cases were still tried before a civil jury, at least in the early days. For example, Mr Justice Wilson tried an action in Londonderry in 1925 when a special jury awarded the then very large amount of £6,388 to one of the two plaintiffs.[121] However, in time civil bill and criminal injury appeals came to represent the only business on the civil side. Criminal business might provide a good deal of work at venues such as Antrim, at least for the crown prosecutors, although there was often little or no criminal business at some venues, particularly in Fermanagh. Even where there was rewards could be slim for the Bar as there was no legal aid (except in murder cases).

In the early years of the Circuit most of the Bar travelled by train from one assize town to the next, but as the years went by more and more would travel by car. As the first Circuit account book has disappeared there are no records of who went to each assize before 1936, but the pattern of attendances in the records from 1936 are probably reasonably representative of the years before. The 1938 Spring assizes are the first for which a complete record exists of all those who were members of the Circuit since 1922 because a printed circuit list has survived, and lists 48 members (including 13 silks) and no fewer than ten probationers.[122] Given that not every member of the Library may have chosen to join the Circuit, this suggests that in 1938 there were just under 60 practising members of the Northern Ireland Bar. The entries in the Circuit account book for that year are the first to show who attended each assize town, and the varying levels of attendances are obvious.

Downpatrick: 20 attended, six seniors, nine juniors and five probationers.
Armagh: nine attended, four seniors, four juniors and one probationer.
Enniskillen: five attended, one senior, three juniors and one probationer.
Omagh: 21 attended, five seniors, 12 juniors and four probationers.
Londonderry: 15 attended, six seniors, six juniors and three probationers.

121 *Thompson v Reynolds, Gibson v Reynolds* [1926] NI 131.
122 Inn of Court Box 20 (Circuit of Northern Ireland (General) (A8)).

The figures for the 1938 Summer assizes are very similar, the only significant difference being that ten attended in Enniskillen, three seniors and seven juniors. Probationers, no doubt mindful of the expense involved, seem to have generally confined their attendances to the minimum required to qualify for election to the Circuit. Thus on the 1938 Spring assizes, of the five probationers present at Downpatrick, four attended three assizes each. Agnew and Harrison went on to Omagh and Londonderry; Little to Armagh and Omagh; and Bruce went to Enniskillen and Omagh. Reid, who was the fifth probationer at Downpatrick, did not attend any of the other towns on that occasion, but did attend Downpatrick, Omagh and Londonderry at the Summer assizes that year. At both the 1938 Spring and Summer assizes there was a big turn out at Omagh, with 21 attending at the Spring assizes and 19 the Summer assizes, the explanation possibly being that there was a Circuit dinner there on each occasion.

A town steward was appointed for each town, and was responsible for organising all the social matters. A cess (or levy) was struck for each town to cover the cost of meals and wine, which the town steward was responsible for collecting, together with 'bag money'. Bag money was levied to pay local men who would bring members' bags from the station to where they staying, or, in the days of the North West Circuit, would carry the bags of those who walked from Lifford to Londonderry.[123] The amount paid as bag money varied, sometimes seniors paid more, sometimes less, but the amounts were small. For example, at the Londonderry 1936 Spring assizes the 15 members attending each paid two shillings bag money, and a cess of 25 shillings.[124] To these amounts had to be added the cost of accommodation and travel. Whilst the amounts may seem small by present-day values, the overall expense of going on circuit could be not inconsiderable, particularly for a junior struggling to make a living, if a senior or a junior did not hold a brief at some or all of the venues on the Circuit. This no doubt explains why few seniors or juniors are recorded as going to every town on the Circuit at each assize.

As the pace of professional life was generally less frenetic than today, there was plenty of time on Circuit for enjoyment outside court, some of which could attract judicial ire, as when a message was sent to the

---

123 Sir Robert Porter QC met Edward Donaghy, the Londonderry bagman after the War. Sir Robert
    Porter QC to the author 18 Apr. 2001. The Circuit paid Donaghy £25 in January 1962, possibly as
    a token of their esteem. No explanation for this is recorded. Circuit file.
124 Two shillings=10 pence, 25 shillings =£1.25.

Bar that the judges considered it 'inappropriate' to play pitch and toss on the grass behind the court at Downpatrick. However, this was very much the exception, and other less controversial forms of entertainment were usually found. Time to spare at Armagh in good weather sometimes resulted in a challenge by the Bar to the local cricket club with the match being played in the beautiful surroundings of the Mall. Visits might be paid to nearby sites of historic interest such as Struell Wells near Downpatrick, or Devenish Island on Lough Erne with its round tower. Business was often light at Enniskillen, and the judges were often taken on a trip on the Lough in the police launch. Trips on Lough Erne were not confined to the judges. On one glorious summer evening members of the Bar were delayed in their return from a trip on an underpowered launch which was unable to make sufficient headway against the wind on its return journey. As a result they found themselves returning to their hotel through deserted streets long after the beginning of the curfew then in force. Fortunately, they were accompanied by one of Enniskillen's leading solicitors and no embarrassment befell them.[125]

Whenever the day's work was over, other than at Downpatrick where they returned home to Belfast at night, the Bar returned to their hotel where a private room was reserved for them to dine, whilst the judges returned to their lodgings. Except at Downpatrick, where they took a private suite of rooms at the Slieve Donard Hotel in Newcastle, the judges stayed in private houses which were large enough to accommodate them, their two registrars and two tipstaves, as well as having a suitable dining room and drawing room. They would entertain guests each night, and on one night these would include the senior and junior crown prosecutors for the county. Other members of the Bar might be invited as well, especially probationers. The Bar dined alone, although the judges and their registrars were invited to the Circuit dinners already mentioned. The senior member present acted as Father, and sat at the head of the table, with the junior (as the town steward came to be known) at the foot of the table. The junior said grace, and after dinner, but before coffee was served, toasted the health of the Father and the Circuit. When toasting at Downpatrick and Armagh the junior had to use the toast of the North East Circuit, but at Enniskillen, Omagh and Londonderry it was that of the North West Circuit, which ran as follows:

125 MacDermott, *An enriching life*, pp 184–85.

Junior:   Father are you at home?

Father:   At home Junior.

Junior:   Your health and the health of the Northern Bar.

Father:   Junior your health and the health of the Northern Bar.[126]

After the toasts, the Junior would say 'Father, may your sons smoke?' whereupon the Father would grant the necessary permission. Many years later the request was modified to 'may your sons and daughters smoke'. Despite the presence of women on the circuit, they did not dine with their colleagues at night, and this rule was re-affirmed as being still operative as late as 1951.[127] However, indefensible though this rule appears today, its severity was mitigated, at least in Peggy Aiken's case. She recounted how, after she dined alone, two members of the Bar collected her and took her to the local cinema, where they sat on hard kitchen chairs and a harmonium provided the musical accompaniment.[128] After the toasts had been given, entertainment usually took the form of cards, stories, or songs by those who were known to have a good repertoire. Every probationer was required to sing or recite at their first circuit dinner, and once he had complied, successfully or otherwise, he would be granted a verbal 'certificate' from the Father which absolved him from having to do so ever again unless he wished to do so.[129] If a member was considered to have breached the rules or traditions of the Circuit during the evening the Father could 'fine' the person concerned, the punishment usually requiring the miscreant to provide alcohol or cigars for his colleagues, as at the Armagh Spring assizes in 1946 when Charles Stewart was twice fined five cigars, the first fine for being late for dinner, and the second for being in contempt of the Father.[130]

The outbreak of the Second World War had a considerable effect on the Circuit and on the Bar as a whole. The use of juries in civil cases was suspended because of the demands of the war effort on the population, and some time was to pass after the end of the War before the use of civil juries

---

126 Johnson, *History and customs of the Bar and Circuit of Northern Ireland*, p. 13. The North West toast was given seated. Sir Robert Porter to the author 18 Apr. 2001.

127 At a general meeting held on 26 June 1951. CM, p. 105.

128 Aiken, *Inn of Court Newsletter*, Vol. 3, p. 2.

129 This passage is based upon W. Johnson, *History and customs of the Bar and Circuit of Northern Ireland*, pp 9-14.

130 Circuit of Northern Ireland Account Book.

was reinstated. The work appears to have declined, and wartime travel and other restrictions must have made it much more difficult and unattractive to go round the assizes unless one was assured of some work. In addition, as we shall see, many of the Bar joined the armed forces. No doubt each of these reasons contributed to the substantial fall in the number of members of the Circuit attending each assize town. Whereas 19 attended the 1939 Downpatrick Spring Assizes, only ten did so in 1940, nine in 1942 and 11 (including one probationer) in 1945. Throughout the War it was rare to find more than ten at any venue, indeed, often only five or six attended. The 1942 Summer assizes are a good example of the fall in numbers, with eight attending Downpatrick, five at Armagh, two at Enniskillen, eight at Omagh and seven at Londonderry. It is hardly surprising that at a general meeting of the Circuit in February 1940 the Father (J.H. Robb KC) announced that no Circuit dinner would be held.[131] It was not to be until December 1943 that another general meeting was held. A Circuit dinner does not appear to have been held until March 1944, when it was held in Belfast before the next assizes went out.[132]

Even before the War the Circuit's finances were 'not in a very sound position'. Although various committees were set up, little, if anything, appears to have been done to remedy the situation until the end of 1943. One of the sources of income for the Circuit was 'congratulations' fees, these being the amount payable by a member of the Circuit upon his appointment to a judicial or other position, such as a crown prosecutor, which would improve his financial position. A long-standing tradition of the Irish Bar,[133] congratulations fees had been considered at a Circuit meeting in 1936. At the request of the Bar Council, a committee was appointed to consider them, together with the abolition or reduction of entrance fees, and the amount of the annual subscription. It was not until March 1944[134] that the Circuit adopted a new scale of congratulations fees, which was as follows.

£36 15s. high court judge.
£26 5s. county court judge.

131 CM, p. 83.
132 Ibid., p. 86.
133 Before 1921 the fees were sometimes levied in the form of 'fines' of champagne, as in the Munster Circuit where, for example, taking silk merited a fine of 2 dozen, becoming a high court judge 6 dozen. J.R. O'Flanagan, *The Munster circuit, tales, trials and traditions* (London, 1880), p. 312.
134 CM, p. 86.

£15 15s. resident magistrates, attorney general and the senior crown prosecutor for Belfast.

£8 8s. umpire (ministry of labour).

£7 7s. for other senior crown prosecutors and the junior crown prosecutor for Belfast and deputy umpire (ministry of labour).

£5 5s. member, industrial commission.

£4 4s. junior crown counsel.

£3 3s. member, pension appeal tribunal.

These fees are an interesting reflection of the perceived relationship between the traditional steps of judicial and professional preferment, and their value, as well as the creation of new forms of judicial office as the result of wartime conditions, positions which have since become a significant feature of the legal system in the form of industrial, social security and other tribunals.

The impact of the outbreak of war on the Bar was not confined to the Circuit. Several members left on military service, including J.C. MacDermott QC MP, and L.E. Curran, both of whom had served in the First World War, and W.B. Maginess QC, MP. MacDermott and Maginess were later released from military service and entered the government.[135] Other present or former members of the Northern Ireland Bar who joined up were W. Johnson, J.D. Condy, W.W.B. (Ken) Topping, C.A. (Cyril) Nicholson, E.W. Jones, F.A.L. Harrison, T.A. (Alec) Blair, F.A. Reid and James Reynolds (the last three of whom served in the Far East). On 16 October 1939 the Bar Council decided to inform the Law Society that any member of the Bar at that time would 'act for and on behalf of any absent barrister' who was on active service in order to preserve the practice of such barristers.[136] In May 1940 the Bar Council also decided that members of the Bar on active service would be excused payment of their Library subscriptions.[137] Another echo of the impact of the war is that in November 1940 we find a reference to difficulties being experienced in gaining access to the Bar Library. Although these difficulties are not specified, they were sufficiently acute to result in a general meeting of the Bar.[138] As the war dragged on it was inevitable that the practices of those who were serving in the forces, or otherwise engaged in war work, would be affected by their absence, although efforts were made

135 For Maginess's career see *Belfast Telegraph*, 17 Apr. 1967, and *DIB*.
136 BCM, p. 157.
137 3 May 1940. Ibid., p. 161.
138 Ibid., pp 162-63.

to prevent them from being unduly disadvantaged. In 1942 E.W. Jones, who was on war service, was appointed junior crown prosecutor for Co. Down by the attorney general, who appointed Bradley McCall to discharge Jones's duties in his absence[139] F.A.L. Harrison was appointed to the same post in Co. Tyrone in 1943 although he too was on war service at the time.[140]

At this time the number of active practitioners was further reduced by death and by judicial appointments, and very few new calls took place in the early years of the war. These factors, and no doubt a reduction in the amount of work that we have already seen reflected in the fall in the number going on circuit, meant that the Bar Council also had to deal with a significant deterioration in its finances. It seems from the subsequent report that this was due to the careless way its books had been kept by the then treasurer, although it was accepted that he had satisfactorily accounted for all monies received by him. G.B. Hanna was appointed as treasurer and carried out a thorough investigation into the accounts for 1940, 1941 and 1942. He reported that some barristers had not paid any subscriptions, and that the Bar Library was in debt to the amount of £535, a very considerable figure when compared with the anticipated expenditure for 1944 of £440. New banking and accounting procedures were adopted, and annual subscriptions were raised. Seniors were now to pay £21, and juniors of seven years and upwards £15 15s. For their first three years of membership juniors were now to pay £5 5s, and for the second three years £10 10s. Non-practising members were to pay £5 5s.[141] It was anticipated that these figure would enable the debt to be paid off within five years, and whilst it appears that the financial position did improve, the non-payment of Library subscriptions remained a recurrent problem. Hanna's efforts as treasurer would seem to have been appreciated by his colleagues, because he topped the poll for membership of the Bar Council in 1948 and 1949, and upon his appointment as Minister of Home Affairs in 1953 it was decided to hold a dinner 'in view of his services to the Bar'.[142]

An unusual development during, and just after the end of the war, and one that was hitherto unprecedented in Northern Ireland, but was to be repeated on a number of occasions in the 1960s, 1970s and 1980s,

---

139 *ILT&SJ* lxxvi (1942) 74.
140 Sir Frank Harrison QC to the author on 22 July 2000.
141 BCM. Jan. 1944.
142 BCM 18 Dec. 1953. For details of Hanna's career see *DIB*.

was that a number of former members of the Bar resigned their judicial posts and returned to practice at the Bar. W.F. McCoy KC, who had been appointed a resident magistrate in Belfast in October 1937, was the first to do so when he resigned in January 1943. This caused a considerable stir, although it was later stated in parliament by the government that he had resigned because he regarded the salary as inadequate.[143] The next to do so was J.D. Chambers KC. He had been one of the leading juniors of his era, and had taken silk in 1938 when his practice went from strength to strength. Appointed recorder of Belfast in late 1943 after the elevation of Arthur Black to the high court, Chambers found judicial work uncongenial, and resigned at the end of November 1944. He then returned to the Bar, but died aged 45 on 2 April 1945.[144] The third was Charles Sheil KC. He took silk in June 1943, and was then appointed county court judge for Co. Tyrone in August that year.[145] He resigned in October 1945 and also returned to the Bar. There is nothing in the contemporary records to suggest that the Bar as a body regarded a return to practice after holding judicial office as inappropriate, and their resignations did not adversely affect the careers of those concerned. Sheil was readmitted to the Circuit with his previous seniority,[146] and elected to the Bar Council in January 1946 (defeating McCoy).[147] McCoy, who had taken silk in 1939 when a resident magistrate, was elected as the Unionist MP for South Tyrone at a by-election later in 1943,[148] and later held the lucrative position of senior crown prosecutor for Belfast for many years. Chambers was appointed senior crown prosecutor for Belfast almost as soon as he returned to the Bar.

It is appropriate to conclude this chapter with the end of the Second World War, by which time the Bar had survived two World Wars, the upheavals in Ireland in the 1920s, as well as the Great Depression, remaining a united profession determined to uphold the high standards it had inherited from its predecessors.

---

143 *ILT&SJ* lxxvii (1943) 17 and 111.
144 *ILT&SJ* lxviii (1944) 302 and lxxix (1945) 89. See Jones, *Jones LJ: his life and times*, pp 30-42 for an account of Chambers' ability and character.
145 *ILT&SJ* lxxvii (1943) 200.
146 3 Dec. 1945. CM, p. 91.
147 30 Jan. 1946. BCM, p. 207.
148 Harbinson, *The Ulster Unionist Party*, p. 199.

# CHAPTER EIGHT:

## The post War period, 1945-1969

As we have seen in the previous chapter, the numbers in active practice at the Bar fell during the War when several members joined the armed services. This fall was accentuated by several judicial appointments made during the War: two to the high court; Black KC to be recorder of Belfast and then to the high court in 1943, and MacDermott KC in 1944; and five to the county court, namely Begley KC, McGonigal KC, T.J. Campbell KC, Fox KC and Robb KC (excluding Chambers KC and Sheil KC whose return to practice after short periods on the bench has been referred to in Chapter Seven). The decline in numbers was only partly offset by six new calls between Easter 1941 and Hilary 1945.[1]

With the end of the War, and their gradual release from military service, those who survived the War returned to practice, and the numbers in practice were swollen by a considerable number of new calls in the next decade. This was particularly the case in 1948 when 15 were called,[2] the highest number to be called in one year since 1921. This number was not to be approached, let alone exceeded, until Michaelmas 1970 when 17 were called. Whilst both 1945 and 1946, with three called, were in line with pre-War calls, there were several other years when large numbers were called, with seven in both 1949 and 1950. Thereafter the numbers fluctuated, and were generally lower, with only two being called in 1954 and 1955. A significant proportion of those called during the later 1940s and early 1950s had served during the War, and resumed their legal studies afterwards, such as Brown, McGonigal and Lowry, or embarked upon them immediately afterwards, and at least ten of those called after the War had served.[3] Only two women were called between 1945 and 1974, Sheelagh Murnaghan was the first in 1948, and the other was Kathleen O'Brien in 1952. Whilst Miss Murnaghan[4] remained in practice throughout the period covered by this

---

1  Knox Cunningham, later Sir Knox Cunningham, MP (U) for South Antrim (1955-70), is not included as he had been a member of the English Bar since 1939.

2  G.B. Currie (1905-78), later MP (U) for North Down is excluded from this figure. A member of the English Bar, he practised on the North West Circuit.

3  Dennison, Brown, Lowry, Shaw, McGonigal MC and bar, Rowland, McLean, Porter, Workman and Babington DSC in the armed forces, and Harty in the Merchant Navy.

4  *DIB.*

chapter, Miss O'Brien left Northern Ireland after some years and practised in England, later becoming a law reporter there. She ultimately returned to Northern Ireland, practising here for a period after her return.

The number of ex-servicemen in the Bar Library, whether resuming or embarking upon practice, meant that there was a significant element of older and more mature men amongst those in practice during the first decade after the War, and they rapidly established themselves at the senior and junior Bar. Jones and Harrison resumed their practices, and were two of the three silks appointed in July 1948. Reid, called in 1938, and Brown, Lowry and McGonigal who were called in 1946, 1947 and 1948 respectively, soon established themselves at the forefront of the junior Bar. Their rapid professional advance was recognised when all four were included amongst the six silks appointed in November 1956, despite the short period each had been in actual practice.

By the beginning of 1955 there were 64 practitioners in the Bar Library, 12 seniors and 52 juniors, of whom 22 were of less than eight years standing. There was a sharp increase in 1956, as the Circuit list for the Spring assizes of that year contains 70 members and two probationers. The mid 1950s marked the apogee of the size of the Bar until the 1970s, although the next decade was to see a marked decline in numbers. However, by the mid 1950s the increasing numbers placed a considerable strain on the accommodation in the Bar Library. In 1955 the lord chief justice (whose consent was required as he was responsible for the first two floors of the building[5]) agreed to the provision of two new desks each seating six people, and the Bar Council decided that these be placed in the Smoke Room.[6]

This is an appropriate point at which to consider the cost of studying for, and call to, the Bar of Northern Ireland, and then of practising, in the immediate post War period, as well as the finances of the benchers, the Bar Council and the Circuit. As explained in Chapter 6, following the creation of a separate Inn of Court of Northern Ireland in 1926 the benchers of the new Inn required its students to join one of the English Inns; to attend lectures provided for the Inn of Court of Northern Ireland in Belfast in the law faculty at Queen's University, and to then to take Part II of the Bar Final in London. In 1936

5   See Ch. 5.
6   BCM, 16 June 1955.

the total payable by a student of the Inn in stamp duty and fees (including the stamp duty and fees payable on call) amounted to £216 12s. By 1950 this had increased to £269 7s because of an increase in the lecture fees payable from £15 15s a year for three years to £25 a year for four years. The total cost of a four year course remained £269 7s in 1956, although in both 1950 and 1956 if a student was granted exemptions from certain courses and did the course in three years the cost was £250 17s.[7] These fees remained unaltered until the ending of the requirement to join an English Inn. However, to these fees had to be added the cost of travelling London to eat dinners in one's Inn in order to keep terms there, and to sit the Bar Final. Thus, the total fees paid in 1968-69 by the author to become a student of the Inn, in lecture fees, as well as the cost of joining an English Inn and sitting the Bar Final in London, then being admitted to the degree of barrister at law and called to the Bar in Northern Ireland amounted to £237 14s 2d, to which had to be added the cost of travel to London, and accommodation there, to keep terms by eating dinners and sitting the Bar Final.

The largest elements of these costs were the fees payable to the Inn and the stamp duty paid to the government. On becoming a student of the Inn a fee of £25 and stamp duty of £25 were payable, and on being called the fee to the Inn was £50, with a further £50 stamp duty. These amounts did not go unchallenged, and in 1947 a reduction in the stamp duty payable by Bar students in England and Wales by virtue of the Finance Act of that year led to a plea by Bar students to the Minister of Home Affairs in Northern Ireland for an equivalent reduction in the stamp duty payable in Northern Ireland. The petition was sent by W.P. Doyle on behalf of the 12 signatories to the minister, but to no avail, and the rate remained unchanged.

No doubt that was a matter of some relief to the benchers. When the government enacted the Finance Act (Northern Ireland) 1925 repealing the provision requiring stamp duty to be paid to King's Inns,[8] the benchers and the Law Society reached an agreement with the Northern Ireland government that payments would be made to the Inn and the Law Society instead. This was intended to be by way of financial assistance to each body, and the agreement was that in each year if the stamp duty payable to either body fell below £300 then the actual amount would be payable to that body.

7    Scales of fees prepared by the under treasurer in those years. Inn of Court Reg. No 6.
8    See Ch. 4.

If the amount payable was over £400, then 75% or £500, whichever was less, would be paid. Although the gross amount received between 1922/23 and 1946/47 was only £3980, £5584 15s 0d was paid to the Inn concerned (the amounts paid from 1922/23 and 1925/26 were paid to King's Inns),[9] so the value of this arrangement to the Inn in helping to meet its administrative expenses was obvious as it had no other source of income apart from the fees charged to its students on admission and call.

Once a barrister was called, then it was expected that he would arrange pupillage with an experienced junior. It would seem that pupillage was still not compulsory, because in 1949 the Bar Council concluded that whether a fee should be charged was a matter for the counsel concerned, but if it was it should not be less than 'the traditional fee of 50 guineas'.[10] After call the barrister almost invariably joined the Bar Library and paid the necessary admission fee and annual subscription, as well as joining the Circuit and paying the appropriate fees to it. As we have seen in the previous chapter, during the War the Bar Library had to address the unsatisfactory state of its finances, and because of continuing problems in collecting subscriptions in succeeding years this was to be a recurring problem.

The governance of the profession remained unchanged throughout this period. The benchers were responsible for the admission and education of students, and call to the Bar. These matters occupied most of their attention as we have seen in Chapter 6. The composition of the benchers underwent a slight change with the election of Judge Fox KC, the recorder of Belfast, as a bencher in June 1952. For many years after the foundation of the Inn of Court of Northern Ireland in 1926 Judge Fox was the only county court judge to have been elected a bencher. In 1965 he donated the fund presented to him by the Belfast Jewish community to endow the prize bearing his name which is awarded each year on the results of the Bar examinations.[11]

The lord chief justice was chairman of the benchers *ex officio*, and presided at meetings of the benchers. Although a treasurer was elected each year, with the post alternating between bar and judicial benchers, this was a subsidiary post to the chairman. In September 1969 Lord MacDermott

9    PRONI FIN/18/6. Ministry of finance file on payments to the Inn prepared in 1947 as a result of the petition.
10   20 Apr. 1949. BCM, p. 250.
11   16 June 1965. BM.

LCJ pointed out that in London it was the treasurer who was head of the inn and presided during his year of office, and proposed that in Northern Ireland the treasurer should take a greater part in the Inn's affairs, and preside at meetings of the bench. However, this suggestion did not find favour with his fellow benchers,[12] and the lord chief justice continued to act as chairman of the benchers until the constitutional changes brought about by the creation of the Executive Council in 1983, changes which are discussed in Chapter Twelve.

As had been the position since 1921, the day to day regulation of the Bar, including disciplinary proceedings, was in the hands of the Bar Council, although the final decision in such matters still rested with the benchers, who alone had the power to impose the ultimate sanction of expulsion from the profession by disbarring the barrister concerned. In fact, no barrister in Northern Ireland has been disbarred for disciplinary reasons since 1921, although there have been many occasions when barristers have been disbarred at their own request so that they may become solicitors. Disciplinary proceedings of any kind were almost unknown during this period. When a complaint was made against a barrister, whether by a member of the public, a solicitor, or by another barrister, the pre-War practice continued of the Bar Council considering the matter first. Complaints were rare, and were generally dealt with by the Bar Council drawing the attention of the counsel concerned to an existing rule, or resolving what practice should be followed in future.

One such occasion was in 1955 when Jones QC informed the Council that G.B. Hanna QC, who was minister of home affairs at the time, had appeared for a plaintiff who was an ex-policeman. It appeared that a police doctor had claimed privilege when cross-examined about the plaintiff's medical history, and that a police inspector had been in court, although he was not called to give evidence. The potential for embarrassment by the minister responsible for the police having to examine police officers was obvious, and it was surprising that it was Hanna who had acted in this way, as it was his father whose action in similar circumstances led the Bar Council to pass a resolution twenty years before on this very subject. The Bar Council wrote to Hanna drawing his attention to the resolution of 1 November 1935, and asking for his observations.[13] Having considered Hanna's explanation the

---

12 BM, 23 Sept. 1969.
13 11 Nov. 1955. BCM, p. 112.

Council accepted his *bona fides*, but ruled that the minister responsible for the administration and discipline of the RUC should not appear in a case in which a policeman was likely to be called by either side.

If the matter was considered to be of sufficient gravity the Bar Council referred it to the benchers. This appears to have only happened once during the period covered by this Chapter, and occurred when the Bar Council was informed in April 1946 that a barrister was acting for clients without being instructed by a solicitor, and taking money from clients. Interestingly, the minutes record that the barrister concerned was not a member of the Bar Library, but by taking cognisance of the complaint the Bar Council asserted that someone who was not a member of the Bar Library nonetheless remained subject to its jurisdiction.[14] The allegation was referred to the benchers, and at their request the Bar Council framed specific charges against the individual concerned. The benchers found the allegations proved, reprimanded the barrister, and warned him that any recurrence could result in his being disbarred, and the finding was ordered to be screened in the Bar Library.[15]

The state of the Bar Library finances continued to be a significant problem throughout the 1950s because of the difficulty of collecting subscriptions, and a reference in the Bar Council minutes in June 1952 to problems with arrears was the precursor to repeated attempts to grapple with this continuing problem.[16] In April 1953 there were still problems with subscriptions,[17] with a reference in January to 'a few members being in arrears to the extent of two or more years', and although the amount actually due was approximately £1000, only £797 12s had been paid, a shortfall of almost 20%.[18] A determined effort was made to reduce arrears of both Bar Library and Circuit subscriptions, but with limited success as £252 was still outstanding in March.[19] Increases in the salaries paid to the Bar Library employees in June 1954 exacerbated the problem, and there were also substantial unpaid bills with a number of book suppliers. The pressure on the finances was such that the treasurer had to approach the Council's

---

14   15 Apr. 1946. BCM, p. 217.
15   Inn of Court Box 3, file L.1.
16   27 June 1952. BCM, p. 40.
17   15 Apr. 1953. BCM, p. 50.
18   21 Jan. 1954. BCM, p. 59.
19   4 Mar. 1954. BCM, p. 60.

bank manager for an overdraft. At the end of the year the overdraft was £341, a very substantial sum when compared to the subscription income for 1954 of £1442 16s.[20]

In June 1954 the Bar Council decided to increase the subscriptions, the burden of the increase falling on the seniors whose subscription was doubled, and on the juniors of eight years and more standing, whose subscriptions were increased by two thirds. In his report delivered in March 1955 the treasurer (R.T. Rowland) anticipated that the Bar Council should have a credit balance by the end of the year. Unfortunately his expectations were not realised, because £300 in subscriptions was still outstanding in October. The situation worsened in 1956, with £809 16s outstanding in March, although in less than a month Rowland was able to report that the arrears had been reduced by more than half.[21] The problem of non-payment of subscriptions remained a serious one. In June 1958 the treasurer had to report that the arrears were approximately £1400, and that a number of members were several years in arrears. Whilst the arrears had been reduced to £429 8s a month later, the Bar Council decided to take more drastic action, and explanations were sought from the six members who were in default. When only two responded the Bar Council decided that those in arrears would be excluded from the Library if arrears were not discharged by 31 December 1958.[22] This seems to have had the desired effect because financial problems are no longer referred to in the Council minutes, and subscriptions were not increased again until the end of 1963, which suggests that after the difficulties of the 1950s the finances of the Bar Library were on an even keel for some time. A further significant increase which came into effect in 1966 may well have been necessary because the number of subscribers to the Library declined substantially in the 1960s although expenses grew as pay for the staff also increased.

The problem of persistent non-payment of subscriptions throughout the 1950s was probably symptomatic of the difficulties many members of the Bar were having in making a living at the time. As we shall see several left the Bar during this period, and a constant pre-occupation of the Bar Council was the need to achieve increases in fees payable for both civil and criminal

20 Treasurer's report 1955. BCM, between pp 85-86.
21 BCM, pp 129 and 131.
22 BCM, pp. 193 and 197.

work. Nevertheless, even when the subscriptions were raised, and they were a major, but not the only, expense for those practising at the Bar, they remained low. In addition, fees were reduced for those in the early years of practice, and a graduated rate was a feature of the subscription rates from 1944 onwards. However, the bands were altered in 1966, thereby significantly increasing the amounts payable for juniors after the first year, and for seniors who saw their subscriptions double as can be seen from the rates below.[23]

|  | 1944 | 1955 | 1964 | 1966 |
|---|---|---|---|---|
| Juniors. |  |  |  |  |
| (1944-63 1st three years, 1966 1st year only) |  |  |  |  |
|  | £5 5s | £5 5s | £6 6s | £10 10s |
| (1944-63 4th and 5th years, 1966 2nd to 6th years) |  |  |  |  |
|  | £10 10s | £10 10s | £12 12s | £31 10s |
| (1944-64 6th and 7th years) |  |  |  |  |
|  | £15 15s | £15 15s | £19 19s |  |
| (1955-64, 8 years and over, in 1966 7 years and over) |  |  |  |  |
|  |  | £26 5s | £33 12s | £68 5s |

To these subscriptions have to be added the entrance subscription to the Bar Library upon call, the entrance subscription to the Circuit, and the annual subscription to the Circuit of £2 2s. Nevertheless, for a junior in his or her first few years of practice the annual subscription represented a very modest annual outlay for a base from which to practise, and the services provided therein. The established practitioners each had a desk, although the increase in numbers meant that until the new desks which have already been referred to were added, a pupil or young practitioner might have to squat at his or her master's desk for some years. The Library provided law reports and textbooks which could be consulted and taken into court, but not removed from the building. A small and loyal staff, all of whom served the Bar faithfully, most for many years, looked after the books, answered the telephone, distributed mail and provided stationery and carried out miscellaneous tasks, such as lodging cheques for members.

23  BCM, 1944 p. 179; 10 June 1954, p. 69; 16 Dec. 1963, p. 319; 8 Nov. 1965, p. 23. These have been changed from guineas to £ s d where necessary.

From 1922 the Library facilities were attended to by a caterer, telephone attendant, and a diary attendant (both of whom are unnamed in the records).[24] Thompson carried on his duties as caterer for some years. For many years until his death in 1954 the Library's most important employee was undoubtedly William Eakins. A former sergeant in the RIC, and a son of a head constable in the RIC, Sergeant Eakins was appointed to the staff of the Bar Library in 1924 upon his retirement from the RIC, and served the Bar loyally and cheerfully until his death 30 years later on 24 May 1954. 'The Sergeant' as he was known to both branches of the profession, was a kindly and cheerful man whose principal task was to guard the door of the Bar Library against unauthorised intruders, a task he performed 'like Cerberus' in the words of Sir Frank Harrison QC, and to deal with requests by solicitors or the public to see members of the Bar. The Sergeant was very protective of the junior Bar in particular. Solicitors would seek his advice on who was available, and if a junior did not want to see a particular solicitor, Eakins could be relied upon to tell the solicitor 'that Mr X was in the country doing an arbitration'.[25] It is a sign of the affection and respect in which he was held by the Bar that upon his death a resolution of the Bar Council recorded 'the debt due to his memory by the Profession whose interests he so jealously guarded and whose prestige he so firmly maintained', and placed a copy of his obituary notice in the minutes.[26] In 1959 an inscribed plate was erected in his memory in the foyer of the old Bar Library where it remains. [27]

He was succeeded by Sergeant Breheney, also a former member of the RIC and then the RUC, who proved to be an equally outstanding, dedicated and loyal servant of the Bar. As the older members of the Bar will recall, he was invariably courteous, kindly and tactful, and if someone had gone to Lavery's pub in Chichester Street was known to say to an enquiring solicitor that the barrister was in the court of appeal as Lavery's was known. In the late 1950s the librarian was Frank Over, a former bandmaster in the Warwickshire Regiment.[28] By 1958 he was in poor health, and it was decided to employ his son, a sergeant in the fingerprint and photography department of the RUC, as his assistant. Sid Over duly retired from the RUC to take up the

24   20 Dec. 1922. BCM, pp 16-17.
25   Sir Frank Harrison QC to the author 22 July 2000.
26   BCM, pp 66-67.
27   Letter from the ministry of finance of 2 Jan. 1959 giving permission.
28   Rt. Hon. Sir Robert Porter QC to the author 18 Apr. 2001.

post, and he and his father then sat at opposite desks inside the door of the Library until his father's death on 11 February 1961. After his father's death it was decided to appoint Sid Over as librarian, and in November that year Charles Corr (also a former policeman) was appointed as a further library assistant. He and Sid Over were also to serve the Bar effectively and faithfully for many years. In addition to his duties as librarian, including repairing damaged volumes where possible, for a modest fee Over would bind compilations of statutes and statutory rules and orders relevant to particular areas of the law. One of Over's tasks was to measure those about to be called for wig and gown, which he would then order on their behalf from Ede & Ravenscroft in London. Another task was to lodge cheques for members of the library if they had accounts in the nearby banks.

As noted in the previous chapter, from the inception of the Northern Bar in 1921 the Bar provided its own small servery for the private use of its members. The first caterer was Dan Thompson, assisted by Albert Thompson (presumably his son), a maidservant (only referred to in the minutes as Molly), and he was followed by John Allen. When Allen retired in January 1956 after nine years he was succeeded as manager of the servery by Mrs Betty Steele, who was assisted by two other employees, Mrs Kirkwood and Mrs Hadley.[29] The servery was in effect a club where people had lunch and chatted and gossiped over tea or coffee. Like the other members of staff Mrs Steel was very kind, particularly to new members of the Bar, and in later years kept a scrap book in which she inserted newspaper clippings relating to the Bar.[30]

Although the salaries paid to the various employees of the Library were a substantial part of the cost of running the Bar, the salaries were not unduly generous, no doubt reflecting that the men had police pensions. At the time of his death Sergeant Eakins was paid £9 a month, and Mr Over £12 8s 6d a month. On Sergeant Breheney's appointment in June 1954 he was paid £5 10s a week, and Mr Over's salary was increased to £6 a week. Mrs Steele was initially paid £6 a week, soon increased to £6 10s a week.[31] Although increased from time to time, the salaries remained modest, with Sid Over's salary being increased from £420 to £504 a year in 1963, and

29   11 Jan. 1956. BCM, pp 117-19.
30   Now the property of Sir Richard McLaughlin.
31   Treasurer's report 1955. BCM, between pp 69-70, and BCM, pp 117-19.

those of Sergeant Breheney and Mr Corr from £286 to £360 a year at the same time.[32] Small though these may appear to be, it has to be remembered that at the time wages in general were low by modern standards, and, as we shall see, many young members of the Bar were earning less in their first year or two in practice.

Although the Bar Council was responsible for the day to day running of the Bar Library, representing the interests of the Bar, and matters of professional etiquette, practice and discipline, the ultimate authority remained the general meeting of the Bar, and in the 1950s and early 1960s general meetings were more frequent than had been the case for the previous two decades, often being held at least once a year and sometimes more frequently. Most general meetings were held because of concern about counsels' fees in civil and criminal cases, and these issues, together with debates about the desirability of a civil legal aid scheme, were to be a major concern of the Bar from 1949 until 1964.

Fees in civil cases in the high court were, as now, ultimately determined by the taxing master, but it had long been the custom for the Bar to adopt a scale of fees for pleadings and interlocutory work which was accepted as 'the going rate' by the taxing master. The Irish Bar adopted such a scale in 1920 which remained in force in Northern Ireland until 1939, when it was increased.[33] By 1949 the fall in the value of money led to pressure for another increase in high court fees, and at a general meeting on 31 March 1949 a decision was taken to set up a sub-committee to consider the question. The sub-committee reported in 1950. After discussion at general meetings on 24 February and 31 March, it was decided that the revised scale would come into operation on 1 June 1950.[34]

When an increased scale that would be accepted as the 'going rate' by the taxing master was agreed between the Bar Council and the Law Society in England in April 1958[35] this naturally led the Bar to seek a similar increase in Northern Ireland. A general meeting on 27 November 1959 decided to adjourn the meeting to allow a Bar Council sub-committee to report on the issue. The adjourned meeting was ultimately held on 18 January 1960 when

32  BCM, p. 312.
33  Report presented to a general meeting on 16 Oct. 1964. MGM.
34  MGM 31 Mar. 1950.
35  [1958] 1 All ER 870.

the proposed scale was approved, except for a minimum fee for senior counsel. However, it was not long before there were demands that the 1960 scale be increased, and a general meeting on 26 June 1964 set up a sub-committee to consider the matter. The sub-committee's report was presented by Maurice Gibson QC to a general meeting on 16 October 1964. The report reviewed the history of the practice of the Bar adopting such fees since 1920, and it appears from the minutes of that meeting that there was unhappiness with the approach of the taxing master to the scale of minimum fees. The matter was considered again at another general meeting on 4 December 1964, when it was decided not to seek a further increase in the scale of minimum fees because it had become apparent that the fees sought would be higher than those allowed in England. The minutes also record that there was concern that any increase might have an unfavourable impact on the use of two counsel and the continuation of jury trials in civil cases in Northern Ireland (civil juries had largely disappeared in England and Wales in 1933[36]).

The fees in the high court were not the only source of concern. When they were under discussion, from time to time reference was made to the fees allowed in the county court, where a statutory scale of fixed, *inter partes*, costs has operated since the creation of the county courts in Ireland in their modern form in 1877.[37] The jurisdiction of the county courts was £100 in 1950, and was increased to £300 in 1955.[38] Moving cases out of the high court to a cheaper jurisdiction brought about a loss of income to the Bar because the fees in the county courts were low. In 1943 the amounts allowed to counsel in ordinary civil bills were increased to £4 4s where the amount awarded or claimed was between £50 and £75, and £5 5s where the amount exceeded £75.[39] Following the increase in the county courts' jurisdiction in 1955, a new scale of fees came into force in 1957. The fees prescribed for counsel in ordinary civil bills were now contained in a series of seven bands depending upon the amount awarded or claimed, starting at £1 1s and rising to a maximum of £9 9s.[40] These fees remained unchanged until 1972.[41]

---

36   The Administration of Justice (Miscellaneous Provisions) Act, 1933.

37   By the County Officers and Courts (Ir) Act, 1877. A.R. Hart, 'Complexity, delay and cost- The county courts in Northern Ireland' (2000) 53 *NILQ*, 125.

38   By the County Courts (Northern Ireland) Act, 1955.

39   Direction of the lord chief justice, SRO 1943 No 80.

40   Appendix A of the County Court Costs Rules (NI), 1957. SRO 1957 No 65.

41   When they were replaced by a new scale contained in the County Court (Costs) Rules (NI) 1972, SRO 1972 No 197.

The low level of civil fees was not the only area of concern to the Bar, because from 1946 there was constant unhappiness at the very low fees paid to both prosecution and defence counsel in criminal cases. The Criminal Justice Act (Northern Ireland) 1945 for the first time (except in murder cases where the government already paid for legal representation for the defendant) provided for free legal aid for a defendant's solicitor and counsel in both indictable and summary cases, although subject to certain limitations. The issue of a defence certificate in both indictable and summary cases was in the discretion of the judge or resident magistrate, and in summary cases possible only when it was desirable in the interests of justice 'by reason of the gravity of the charge or of exceptional circumstances'.[42]

The fees payable to defence counsel were prescribed by statutory rules[43] made in 1946, and remained unchanged for indictable cases until 1964,[44] although those payable in summary cases were revised in 1956.[45] The scale fees were modest. In 1946 the fee on the brief for counsel in a murder case was £15 15s for a senior and £10 10s for the junior, or £10 10s if only one counsel was briefed. In all other cases the fee for a senior was £5 5s and £3 3s for a junior, although if the judge thought fit, and the trial lasted more than one day, he could increase the fee for a senior to £15 15s and to £10 10s for the junior. In summary cases the fees were £3 3s and £2 2s respectively, although provision was made for additional fees for cases at courts more than 20 miles from Belfast. There were very few murders in Northern Ireland at this time, and with the passage of time, and the continuing fall in the value of money, the fees were increasingly unrealistic, leading to pressure from the Bar for an increase, something that was only achieved with great difficulty. A meeting of the Bar Council in 1951 considered both defence and prosecution fees. The meeting suggested that defence fees should be doubled in the more serious cases, with significant increases for other cases, and appropriate refreshers. However, no change was made until 1964.

Dissatisfaction with prosecution fees first emerged at a Bar Council meeting in October 1948 where it was noted that prosecution fees had remained unchanged over a very long period (unspecified), and that there were anomalies in the use of one and two counsel. The anomalies were unspecified,

---

42   S. 41 and s. 42.
43   The Poor Prisoners (Counsel and Solicitors) Rules (NI) 1946, SRO 1946 No 62.
44   The Poor Persons (Defence Certificates) Rules (NI) 1964, SRO 1964 No 96.
45   The Poor Persons (Legal Aid Certificates) (Rules (NI) 1956, SRO 1956 No 161.

but probably related to the practice of senior counsel appearing without a junior at the Belfast city commission and at the Belfast quarter sessions before the recorder. This was a practice the Bar Council recommended should cease when it again considered the level of prosecution fees in 1951.

A number of the details of the Bar Council's 1951 recommendations are of interest. First of all, it seems that the junior crown prosecutor, whether in Belfast or elsewhere, was not briefed in every case, because in what were described in the recommendations as 'one-horse cases', (larceny, robbery and receiving), senior counsel directed proofs, drafted the indictment and conducted the case, all for a fee of £4 4s. In ordinary cases a senior was paid £3 3s, and the junior £2 2s, on the brief, and the junior £1 1s for drafting the indictment, the senior receiving £3 3s for proofs. Consultation fees of £2 2s each were only paid if permitted by the attorney general. Whilst the fees were modest, the attorney general had power to certify for higher fees, which no doubt ameliorated the position to some extent.

With fees of this level, and as the criminal lists in some counties could be small, a crown prosecutorship outside Belfast may not have been particularly lucrative. The position in Belfast was different, because the volume of work there was such that to be the senior or junior prosecutor was a valuable post to hold, at least to judge from the Bar Council's view at the time that there should be no increase in prosecutors' fees in Belfast, although increases in fees should be made elsewhere. E.W. Jones relates how, when offered silk by Andrews LCJ in 1948, he said that he was concerned that if he did take silk he would be expected to resign his position as junior crown prosecutor for Belfast. Andrews told him that he had concluded that being a silk was not a bar to holding a junior crown prosecutorship,[46] and Jones continued to be the junior after he took silk. Although we might infer that this was unprecedented, it was not quite as unusual as it may seem. There had been occasions before and after 1921 when juniors had been appointed as senior crown prosecutors, or seniors acted as junior crown prosecutors. For example, as long ago as 1894 Serjeant Dodd KC had been the junior crown prosecutor at the Dublin commission.[47] More recently, in 1920 George Hill Smith KC was the senior in Co. Antrim but the junior in Belfast, and both prosecutors in Co. Fermanagh were juniors, whereas the crown prosecutors

---

46   *Jones LJ his life and times*, p. 62.
47   *ILT&SJ*, xxviii (1894), 123.

for the City and County of Dublin were both silks.[48] L.E. Curran was appointed the senior crown prosecutor in Co. Fermanagh in July 1942,[49] although a junior, and more recently W. Johnson had been appointed the senior for Co. Antrim in February 1946 although he was still a junior[50] and did not take silk until October of that year.

Such was the level of dissatisfaction with crown prosecutors' fees that the matter came before a general meeting in July 1951. The meeting was attended by the exceptionally high number of 52 members, and the Bar Council's recommendations were almost all accepted. This led the attorney general to suggest a new scale to the Bar Council in February 1952, but it was rejected by a general meeting. It appears that this led to the ministry of home affairs, which was responsible for approving the fees, agreeing to a revised scale which seems to have been accepted at a further general meeting in March 1952.[51] At the same time there were similar concerns about the fees payable to defence counsel. However, no progress was achieved on that front, the ministry of home affairs saying that as the fees were the same as those paid in England it could not agree to an increase.[52] The anger of the Bar at the ministry's attitude was such that a general meeting of March 1952 passed a resolution which criticised the fees. Whilst the resolution stated that counsel would not be encouraged to appear in such cases it stopped short of saying that counsel should not appear for the defence in publicly funded cases. It was not until 1956 that an increase in defence fees was accepted as an interim measure until the English scales were increased.[53]

There the matter rested until 1964. By this time the English scale of defence fees in criminal cases had been increased but there had not been any increase in Northern Ireland. Not unnaturally, the disparity caused considerable resentment. A general meeting was requisitioned in February 1964 to consider a proposal that the Bar should not hold a brief in any criminal case 'under the present scale of fees'. It was decided to seek the adoption of the English scale, which can hardly be considered an unreasonable position. It appears that the difficulty in achieving a satisfactory increase was due

48  See *Thom's Irish Directory*, p. 935 for these and other examples.
49  *ILT&SJ* lxxiv (1940) 184.
50  His warrant of appointment is dated 18 Feb. 1946. PRONI D/4022/A/7.
51  MGM, 26 July 1951, 8 Feb., 22 Feb. and 7 Mar. 1952
52  MGM, 22 Feb. 1952.
53  MGM, 26 Oct. 1956.

to the opposition of the lord chief justice, whose consent to the proposed fees was required.[54] At the next meeting it was reported that he was 'quite intransigent', and that 'it appeared that his minimum figure on a scale would be less than was acceptable to the Bar', despite the English scale having been accepted by the ministry of home affairs, the ministry of finance and the Law Society. Why Lord MacDermott took such a hard line when the government was prepared to pay the same fees as in England must be a matter of speculation. However, his position provoked the Bar to resolve from 30 June 1964 that (except in exceptional cases with the consent of the Bar Council) the Bar would not accept anything other than the English scheme, effectively threatening to strike.[55]

This created a very delicate and unsatisfactory situation for the Bar, and placed the attorney general, who had presided at these general meetings is his capacity as head of the Bar, in a very difficult position, both as the person who appointed the crown prosecutors and as a member of the government who paid them. However, fortunately perhaps, on 20 March 1964 Brian Maginess QC MP resigned as attorney general on being appointed as a county court judge, and was succeeded as attorney general by E.W. Jones QC MP.[56] Jones soon suggested a compromise proposal to a general meeting which he chaired on 12 June 1964. His proposal was that there would be an interim scheme, and although the details of his proposal in the minutes are sparse, it would seem that this would involve his certifying fees. This initiative appears to have helped to resolve a dispute that showed every sign of developing into a damaging and public confrontation between the Bar and the lord chief justice. The Bar decided to accept this proposal, and amended its earlier resolution by making the withdrawal of its services contingent upon a further resolution, thereby removing the deadline of 30 June.[57] Shortly afterwards Lord MacDermott gave his consent to new scales which came into effect on 1 July 1964. The new scale provided for fees on the brief of £63 for a senior and £42 for the junior in a murder case, and a fee of between £36 15s and £8 8s for any other case, with daily refreshers of one-third of the brief fee in both categories. There were two other features of the new scheme that were important. The first was that the attorney general would determine the fees in an individual case that fell into the

54   See s. 43(3) of the 1946 Act.
55   MGM, 13 Mar. 1964
56   [1964] NI.
57   MGM, 12 June 1964.

second category before the trial. The second was that the trial judge could increase the brief fee and refresher in either category of case to such amount as he may specify where he certified that the case 'was one of exceptional length or difficulty'.[58]

That these continuing disputes lasted many years is an indication of how difficult it was for members of the Bar to achieve a reasonable income for almost twenty years after the end of the War when fees for interlocutory civil and criminal work were so low. The Bar was united in its approach in these disputes. The same cannot be said throughout the same period when it debated its attitude to the introduction of a scheme for civil legal aid. Although procedures had existed for centuries allowing those who could not afford to pay the cost of litigation to sue *in forma pauperis*,[59] this provided a very limited means of access to justice. During the Second World War a limited scheme known as Poor Persons Divorces had been operated by the Bar and the Law Society as a response to the number of persons of limited means seeking divorces. This scheme was not without its problems because of difficulties about the allocation of cases to counsel,[60] and the reluctance of some counsel to do such work for religious reasons. In any event this was a *pro bono* scheme as neither the solicitor or counsel received any fee. The introduction of an extensive scheme of legal aid and advice in civil cases in England by the Legal Aid and Advice Act 1949 naturally generated considerable interest in the introduction of a similar scheme in Northern Ireland. The resulting debates were to expose markedly different opinions amongst members of the Northern Ireland Bar about the desirability of such a scheme, a debate that was to continue intermittently for over a decade.

The desirability of introducing in Northern Ireland a scheme similar to that in England and Wales was first considered by the Bar at two general meetings in November 1950. Although no vote was recorded, the minutes imply that at the very least a substantial body of opinion within the Bar, perhaps a majority, was opposed to such a scheme. As the Bar Council had already decided to defer consideration of such a scheme for a year to see how effectively the scheme worked in England the matter was deferred.[61] In the event the matter was not considered again until it was debated again

---

58  Poor Person (Defence Certificates) Rules (NI) 1964, SRO 1964 No 96.
59  See 11 Hen 7 ch 12 (1495).
60  BCM, 20 Apr. 1945 and MGM, 28 June 1945.
61  MGM, 16 and 24 Nov. 1950.

at general meetings held in April, June and July of 1953. Although the June meeting recorded that 'a majority of the senior members present were against the introduction of legal aid in civil cases', it was decided to poll all the members of the Bar on the matter. The July meeting was told that a majority of members of the Bar were in favour of such a scheme.

The idea of such a scheme was not raised again until 1958, by which time the government had set up a committee under the chairmanship of General Sir James Steele[62] to report on the desirability of adopting such a scheme in Northern Ireland. It appears that by this time there had been a shift in opinion within the Bar. At a general meeting on 4 December attended by only 27 members it was unanimously decided to reject a resolution supporting the introduction of such a scheme. Nevertheless it was apparent that, despite the opposition to such a scheme in the high court, there was some support for the introduction of legal aid in the county courts and the magistrates' courts. The meeting was adjourned for a week, and then further adjourned to try to get a better turn out. The third meeting lasted from 7.30 pm to 9.45 pm on 17 December 1958, and after much debate and consideration of variously worded resolutions the meeting passed by 18 votes to seven, with nine abstentions, a resolution that the Bar 'does not consider the introduction of a legal aid scheme to be either necessary or desirable in the interests of the administration of justice in Northern Ireland'.

The minutes of the various general meetings of the Bar do not reveal the detail of the arguments made against the introduction of a civil legal aid scheme, although those of the 1958 meeting refer to two concerns. The first was that there were fears that such a scheme would undermine the independence of the Bar, presumably because it was feared that the Bar would become unduly dependent upon public funds for a substantial part of members' incomes, and their relationship with legally-aided clients would be controlled by the legal aid authorities. The other concern was that a legal aid scheme would result in a drop in the volume of litigation, although the meeting was informed that a drop in England was not attributed to the existence in legal aid but to the absence of juries in civil cases; whilst in Scotland, which like Northern Ireland, still had juries in civil cases in the superior courts, the volume of litigation had increased since the introduction of civil legal aid.

---

62   General Sir James Steele, GCB, KBE, DSO, MC, LLD.

The issue did not go away, and in June 1959 another general meeting considered a letter from General Steele, and it was unanimously decided to authorise the Bar Council to prepare a draft scheme for the assistance of the committee. This was a clear indication that the Bar, whilst not accepting the principle of a legal aid scheme, recognised that one was likely to be introduced and had decided to try to influence its provisions. The Bar Council prepared a memorandum which it submitted to the Steele Committee.[63] Whilst not abandoning its objection to any form of legal aid in civil cases, the Bar Council memorandum suggested that a much simpler and cheaper system could be put in place than the English scheme (which was ultimately adopted in Northern Ireland as well) of assessment committees deciding in advance what cases should receive legal aid. This would be achieved by making provision in civil cases where the plaintiff failed and was not in position to pay costs to permit the trial judge to certify that it was reasonable to prosecute the claim, in which case the unsuccessful plaintiff's costs would be paid by the state. In cases where the judge did not certify, the plaintiff could still have recourse to an assessment committee with power to grant state aid for either the whole or part of the plaintiff's taxed costs. The rationale for this suggestion was that there was a willingness on the part of both solicitors and barristers to undertake what the report referred to as 'speculative actions' where it was felt that a plaintiff had a just case, although counsel did not expect to be paid if the action failed, a practice which the Steele Committee recognised existed.[64]

However, the objections of the Bar to the introduction of a civil legal aid scheme remained, and the Report acknowledged that the written evidence from the Bar Council set out 'more fully than any other contribution a case against the introduction of a legal aid scheme in Northern Ireland,' and then recorded the Bar's arguments in the following passage.

> ...whereas in a densely-populated and highly-industrialised society, a person might be denied access to the courts because he is not known to his solicitor and has little or no ready cash or resources, this is not the case in Northern Ireland; it is difficult to find a single authenticated case (except in divorce proceedings, especially by wives) where a client has been denied access to the courts, and no

63   Report of the Committee on Legal Aid and Advice in Northern Ireland, 1960. Cmd. 417, pp 80-84.
64   Ibid, p. 9, para. 29.

member of the Bar will refuse to give his services, if necessary free, where the interests of justice require a case to be made; many impecunious persons are at present being assisted to litigate their causes by reason of the attitude taken by the Bar and the solicitors' profession; this system compares favourably with the alternative presented by the adoption of the English or Scottish schemes; four out of five legally-aided cases in England and Wales are concerned with divorce; there is no compulsory (or any) procedure for reconciliation before the commencement of state-aided procedure; the interests of the children of the marriage are ignored except in the ancillary custody and maintenance aspects of divorce; a maximum of £500 disposable capital would rule out from the scheme many farmers and small shopkeepers, etc., of a type very characteristic in Northern Ireland; the advent of legal aid would make it unlikely that solicitors would take cases after legal aid had been refused; most applicants would require the help of a solicitor in preparing an application for aid if the English scheme were to be adopted; for this the solicitor could not be recouped under that scheme and consequently the solicitor would have to charge the client for time and outlay; many cases which would not qualify for legal aid because the cause of action is too doubtful would be dropped, although under the present system they often result in settlement or a small verdict; there is excessive pressure to save public money through premature settlements; there is acute injustice entailed in the position of the successful unassisted defendant, while the fact that his position has not been remedied is an indication of undesirable rigidity in the scheme.[65]

Notwithstanding the opposition of the Bar, in October 1960 the Steele Committee reported in favour of the introduction of a scheme based on the English model.  It is noteworthy that although one of its members, T.A. Blair QC, accepted the majority of the recommendations in the report because he agreed that in the county courts, courts of summary jurisdiction and tribunals it was not normally possible to obtain the services of a solicitor on a speculative basis, he was one of five members of the Committee who felt that an adequate case had not been made out for the introduction of such a scheme in the Supreme Court. Minority reports were also prepared by R.L.E. Lowry QC and W.F. Patton QC. Whilst their reports put forward different grounds of objection to the proposals of the majority, they strongly supported Blair's observation that no evidence had been forthcoming to show that a single individual had been prevented from bringing an action.

65  Ibid. p.16.

They also pointed to what they believed to be the adequacy of the existing system of speculative action. None of the three Bar members of the committee were impressed by the response of 29.5% of the 203 practising solicitors who replied to a Law Society questionnaire and said that they had experience of litigants having been prevented from prosecuting or defending a prima facie case because of lack of means. If, as Blair speculated,[66] they were individuals whose case either related to divorce or else were appropriate to the lower courts, then it is difficult to see why such individuals were not entitled to state assistance if they were prevented from pursuing their claims through the courts when such individuals were not assisted by the profession's readiness to support speculative actions in the Supreme Court.

Thereafter the matter seems not to have been considered again by the Bar until a general meeting on 27 November 1961. By this time a Law Society committee was engaged in drawing up detailed proposals for the working of such a scheme for submission to the minister, and had indicated informally that if the Bar would send a delegation the committee would be receptive. The decision of the meeting showed that the Bar had to accept that a policy of non-engagement was unwise, and that in order to protect the interests of the Bar it was essential to engage with the Law Society. Two seniors and two juniors were therefore appointed to approach the committee with authority to make decisions on behalf of the Bar.[67] A scheme almost identical to that operating in England and Wales since 1949 was finally introduced in Northern Ireland by the Legal Aid and Advice Act (Northern Ireland) 1965.

Although, as we have seen, much of the time of the Bar Council during the twenty years following the end of the Second World War was devoted to financial matters, it would be wrong to assume that such matters were the only issues with which it was concerned. A perennial topic in the pre-War years had been whether the Long Vacation should be shortened and when the Michaelmas term would start. This was discussed by the Bar Council in 1953 and 1954, starting with a suggestion by Fox in 1953 that the Long Vacation should be altered to cover July, August and the first half of September.[68] Further references to the issue in 1954 suggest that the idea was being actively considered by the judiciary, because it was

66   Ibid, p. 60.
67   MGM, 27 Nov. 1961.
68   8 July 1953. BCM, p. 52.

generally recognised that, with the almost total closedown of many factories and offices for the traditional 'Twelfth fortnight', it was very difficult for the civil courts to do much work in July because of the unavailability of witnesses in all courts, and of jurors in the high court. However, it was not until 1959 that the Rules of the Supreme Court changed the sittings (terms) of the high court and court of appeal from four to three. The Michaelmas sittings were now to start on 15 September and end on 18 December, with a mid-term recess from 29 October to 3 November inclusive. The Hilary sittings started on 11 January and ended on 31 March, and the Trinity sittings started on 15 April and finished on 30 June.

Whilst this change meant that there were now technically only three terms (as the sittings are still almost invariably described) in the legal year, in reality there are still four, with the short mid-term recess at the end of October dividing the legal year into four terms, just as the short Whitsun recess between the Easter and Trinity terms still provides a short break in mid-summer in England and Wales and in the Republic of Ireland. Somewhat surprisingly, the opportunity was not taken in 1959 to make the Easter break dependent upon the date of Easter itself. The structure of the legal year which came into force in April 1959[69] has remained substantially unaltered since, although the terms have been slightly extended in subsequent years. The end of the Hilary term and start of the Trinity term are now fixed each year by the lord chief justice to take account of the date of Easter. There is now a break of a week on either side of Easter Sunday, and the Hilary Term starts on 6 January. The Michaelmas term now starts on 5 September and ends on 21 December, with the mid term recess of one week starting on 25 October, the dates of the recess having recently been moved forward a week by the lord chief justice in order to coincide with school half-term holidays.[70]

As circumstances required the Bar Council commented upon proposed legislation, or considered other matters that impinged upon the Bar. As we have seen in the previous chapter one area of concern to the Bar Council at all times was to protect members of the Bar from what it considered to be unjustified criticism of members of the Bar by the judiciary. There were a number of occasions during this period when it felt that such representations

---

69   The necessary changes to O. 63 of the Rules of the Supreme Court came into force on 15 Apr. 1959 and were made by SRO 1959 No 7.

70   First implemented in 2011.

were necessary. In December 1948 the Bar Council expressed the view that an unnamed counsel had been treated discourteously by Lord Justice Porter who had refused to hear a submission and peremptorily ordered him to sit down. Whether the Council's views were conveyed formally to Porter does not appear, but they may well have been conveyed informally. No doubt there were occasions when a member of the Bar may have felt, whether justifiably or not, that a judge had said something that appeared to reflect upon that counsel's competence or integrity, but did not pursue the matter after a period of reflection.

However, occasionally counsel did feel sufficiently aggrieved to bring the matter before the Bar Council, and the minutes record two occasions when it had to consider such matters. On the first the Council recorded its regret at criticism by Lord MacDermott of a member of the Bar who had not told the court office that an action had been settled although the jury panel would have been required anyway. The Bar Council decided not to pursue the matter.[71] That decision may have taken because it was recognised that the lord chief justice may have been justified in seeking to remind practitioners of the need to avoid the unnecessary attendance of jurors. Be that as it may, in 1963 the Bar Council directed the attorney general to convey to the lord chief justice a copy of its minute recording its anger at his treatment of counsel in court, but the matter was apparently resolved after a meeting between the lord chief justice and O'Donnell, the counsel concerned.[72]

The death of Sir James Andrews on 18 February 1951 after 13 years as lord chief justice marked a significant transition in the history of the Northern Ireland legal system. Appointed a lord justice of appeal straight from the bar in November 1921, during his 29 years of judicial service Andrews had been closely involved in the educational affairs of the Inn of Court. He had a strong affection for the Bar, demonstrated by the magnificent bequest of books from his library to the Bar under his will,[73] and by many other acts of kindness and generosity to the Bar. However, there seems little doubt that under his regime the pace of judicial business was leisurely and left something to be desired. With the return to Northern Ireland of Lord MacDermott from the appellate committee of the house of lords as Andrews' successor on 6 April 1951 there was an immediate quickening in the despatch of

71  7 Mar. 1957. BCM, p. 164.
72  BCM, 23 May 1963 and 16 Sept. 1963.
73  BCM, 31 Oct. 1951.

judicial business in the high court and court of appeal. At a meeting of the Bar Council on 19 April 1951 concern was expressed at the court of appeal setting a case down for hearing at 10.30 am when the customary hours of the court had been to start at 11 am and rise at 4 pm. A deputation made up of the attorney general and four KCs was appointed to speak to the lord chief justice about this. The deputation reported to the Bar Council that the lord chief justice did not intend to depart from the customary hours. However, the same meeting appointed a further deputation to Lord MacDermott because cases were being listed without notice (presumably in the high court) when counsel were involved at the assizes.[74] The issue was discussed at a general meeting of the Circuit on 26 June 1951. The matter was resolved when the lord chief justice agreed that a list of cases with the names of junior counsel would be sent to the Library so that a list of at least eight cases ready for hearing would be selected each week during the assizes, 'and thus enable the courts to dispose of the accumulated cases outstanding'.[75] However, this does not appear to have resolved the matter in the eyes of the Bar, because the subject was raised again at several meetings the following year. James McSparran KC and G.B. Hanna KC were asked to discuss the matter informally with the lord chief justice.[76] In July 1953 the Bar Council again protested to the lord chief justice at his proposal to sit out of term in order to hear the appeal from the enquiry into the *Princess Victoria* disaster.[77] In this instance at least their protest was successful, and the hearing took place over 11 days in September and October 1953.[78]

Lord MacDermott's determination to ensure that judicial business was despatched expeditiously may have been uncomfortable for the Bar, but in at least one instance the Bar was notably and unjustifiably dilatory. Soon after his appointment as lord chief justice in 1951 Lord MacDermott enquired of the Bar Council whether it had any plans for a memorial to Jack Condy, who had been killed in action during the War. The Bar Council replied that they would like to bear the cost of adding his name to the existing Bar memorial to the fallen of the First World War. The council suggested the creation of a suitable memorial scholarship in conjunction with the benchers,[79] however, nothing

---

74   BCM, 22 June 1951.
75   CM, p. 107.
76   BCM, 19 Mar., 3 June and 27 June 1952.
77   BCM, 30 July 1953.
78   [1954] NI 172.
79   BCM 22 June 1951.

appears to have been done. In 1952 the Law Society raised the question of a suitable memorial to its members killed in the War with the ministry of finance as the ministry responsible for the fabric of the Law Courts. The relevant Inn file contains correspondence indicating that there was some difficulty in checking records to see that all relevant individuals had been included, but the tenor of the correspondence suggests that the responsibility for the delay in completing suitable memorials rested principally with the Bar Council. It was not until 4 November 1955 that additional memorials to the members of the Bar and the Solicitors' profession killed in the Second World War were finally unveiled in the Main Hall of the Royal Courts of Justice.[80] As well as the name of J.H. Condy, the Bar memorial also contains the name of D.M. Wilson MC who was killed in Tunisia in 1943. Wilson, the son of Mr Justice Wilson, was a member of the English Bar who had been called to the Northern Ireland Bar in Michaelmas term 1936. Whether D.M. Wilson ever actually practised in Northern Ireland is unknown. As Lord MacDermott only referred to Condy when he enquired about a memorial in 1951 that might suggest that Wilson had not practised in Northern Ireland. Nevertheless Wilson is properly remembered on the memorial as a member of the Northern Ireland Bar.

As we have seen in the previous chapter, the Circuit of Northern Ireland was a separate entity. The Circuit Meeting, when a general meeting of all of the members were entitled to attend and take part, was the governing body. The Circuit committee was charged with the day to day administration of the Circuit. Both were presided over by the Father of the Circuit (who was thereby regarded as the Father of the Bar) elected by the Circuit, although the senior member was usually chosen. T.J. Campbell KC was the father prior to his appointment as a county court judge at the end of 1945, and was succeeded by S.C. Porter KC in December 1946. Porter only occupied the post for a few months as he was appointed a lord justice of appeal in March 1946, and was succeeded as father by James McConnell in April 1946.[81]

The influx of new members of the Bar after the War which has already been mentioned naturally led to an equivalent increase in the size of the Circuit. Forty three probationers joined the Circuit between 6 July 1944 and 5 July

---

80   Inn of Court Box 4, file 'Erection of memorial to Solicitors and Barristers 1939-45'. The Bar
      Memorial cost £75. BCM, 12 Oct. 1955.
81   CM, pp 91-92.

1950, all but two of whom were elected after the War. The number of new members slowed somewhat after that, with 11 joining between 22 February 1952 and 1 March 1954. The increase in the size of the Circuit meant that not all of the accommodation available to it in the past was suitable, and a Circuit meeting in March 1949 decided to approach the Royal Arms Hotel in Omagh (requisitioned during the War) to see if it could accommodate the Circuit as the Cloonavon Hotel in Omagh was too small.[82] The organisation of the transportation of the Circuit wines and books, and arranging accommodation, meals etc, of the Bar in each of the circuit towns during the assizes fell to a junior member of the Bar who was now referred to as the Junior (the terms circuit steward and junior appear to have been used interchangeably). For the Spring assizes of 1950 it was decided that the Junior would be paid an honorarium of 40 guineas ($£42$), and in addition his Bar cess (the cost of food and drink) was to be remitted. R.T. Rowland was appointed as the Junior for that assize. V.A. Care acted as Junior at the next assize, and continued to do so at least until the Spring Assizes of 1954.

The rules of the Circuit required all probationers to be elected to the Circuit upon completion of their probationary attendance. However, doubts arose in 1955 as to whether the practice of nominating probationers at meetings of the circuit committee conformed to Rule Four, which required this to take place at a meeting of the Circuit in Belfast. As a result, a major revision of the laws and rules of the Circuit was carried out at Circuit meetings on 26 October and 9 November 1955. These were mostly of an administrative nature, but two decisions are worthy of note. First, the invalid nominations of 54 probationers between 6 July 1944 and 1 May 1954 were retrospectively validated. Secondly, lady members were admitted as members of the Circuit. It will be recalled that in the 1930s Peggy Aiken was not able to dine with other members of the Circuit, and again in 1951 when Sheelagh Murnaghan raised the matter at a circuit meeting the Father ruled that Rule 45 still applied, and that as a result lady members were unable to attend Bar dinners.[83] As Kathleen O'Brien was called in 1952, it appears that it was at last appreciated that lady members of the Bar should not be excluded from the social life of the Circuit and the Bar.

Another matter raised at the Circuit meetings in late 1955 concerned the

---

82  CM, pp 93, 98-99 and 117.
83  26 May 1951. CM, p. 105.

whereabouts of Circuit property in various assize towns. As we have seen in earlier chapters the North East Circuit in particular had accumulated various portraits and photographs. R.W. Porter informed the meeting that from enquiries at all assize towns except Enniskillen he had established that there were three portraits in Armagh, two of which were of fathers of the North East Bar; and in Londonderry there were a few group photographs and a number of photographs of fathers of the North West Bar. It was decided to enquire about the whereabouts of books, photographs and other property of both circuits. Although the sub-committee is not recorded as having reported, three portraits were brought from Armagh courthouse and now hang in the Bar Library and the judges' corridor in the Law Courts. A number of photographs which were retrieved from Londonderry courthouse now hang in the Bar Library. Two other important items were donated to the Bar during the post War period. One was the photograph album with photographs of a great many members of the North East Circuit presented by Sir James Andrews, to whom it had been given by Mr Justice Hanna, one of the last members of the North East Circuit, and one of the first high court judges appointed in the Irish Free State. The other was the collar of SS belonging to Sir Denis Henry, the first lord chief justice of Northern Ireland. This was presented to the Inn of Court by his family in 1966,[84] and is now also in the safe-keeping of the Bar,[85] as is the collar of SS belonging to Sir William Moore LCJ, purchased from his grandson in 1995.[86] Ninety sixty six also saw the return to the Bar of the busts of Robert Holmes and Thomas O'Hagan from the Ulster Museum where they had been deposited for safe-keeping. This was arranged by E.W. Jones QC MP, the attorney general, and in due course the busts were placed in the specially constructed niches in the corridor between the main hall and the entrance to the Bar Library. [87] The bust of O'Hagan has now been placed on the landing of the entrance to the Inn of Court.

It was the custom for the Bar to be given collective membership of county

84  BM, 13 June 1966.

85  The collar of SS is the chain worn by the lord chief justice as his badge of office. The present chain worn by the lord chief justice was that of Sir James Andrews, who gave his chain in trust to be worn by his successors. Collars of SS have been worn by the chief judges of the superior courts in England and Ireland since Tudor times. See V.T.H. Delaney 'The gold collar of SS of Ireland' (1961) 77 *LQR* 169.

86  ECM 22 Feb. 1995, 24 May 1995 and 21 June 1995.

87  BCM 18 Apr. 1966. Holmes and O'Hagan were both members of the North Eastern Circuit. For details of their careers see the *DIB*.

clubs in some of the county towns throughout the Province, where members of the Bar could use the facilities of the clubs to lunch or dine, and, in the case of the Northern Counties Club in Londonderry, stay overnight. Social facilities such as these were obviously of considerable benefit to the Bar in the days when travelling was difficult, or when it was necessary to stay overnight in Londonderry. For example, before October 1942 the Circuit sent an annual subscription to the Tyrone County Club in Omagh, but, presumably because of a reduction in numbers going to Omagh during the War, were honorary members for the duration of the War. In 1950 a Circuit meeting resolved to offer to again become a subscriber to the club. Many older members have fond memories of the hospitality shown to members of the Bar by the Tyrone County Club, and by the late Arthur Davidson in particular, over many years.[88] In 1956 members of the Circuit became honorary members of the Downpatrick club at an all-in subscription of £7 7s.[89]

Bar dinners continued to be a major feature of Circuit life. A dinner at which the going judges and their registrars were the guests was usually held in the Bar Library at least once a year the night before the Circuit went out.[90] From time to time a dinner was held on circuit, a Circuit meeting resolving in 1951 'that henceforth the Circuit to have a dinner to be held in Londonderry'.[91] Hospitality was occasionally extended to others, as in February 1952 when it was decided not to hold a dinner that term, but to hold a cocktail party in the Library instead, and to invite visiting members of the Southern Bar. Apart from the formal Bar or Circuit dinners, those attending circuit towns on assize dined together in the traditional fashion, and sometimes these dinners were somewhat rowdy affairs.

By the Spring assizes of 1956 the Bar, and the Circuit, had increased to such a size that the circuit list contained the names of 70 members (of whom 11 were silks) and two probationers, although not all were in active practice. Nevertheless, despite its size, there were already unmistakable signs that the Circuit was gradually weakening as an institution and might not survive. Two members of the Circuit recalled to the author how the Circuit was becoming less popular, with members increasingly driving down to the

88    20 Feb. 1950. CM, p. 101.
89    26 June 1956. CM, p. 121.
90    The Rt Hon Turlough O'Donnell to the author 20 Aug. 2009. Such a dinner was to be held on 6 July 1955. It is referred to as the annual dinner. CM, pp 112-113.
91    26 June 1951.

relevant assize town for the day on which their case was on.[92] Concern about this practice was voiced by Turlough O'Donnell, then a member of the Circuit committee. At Circuit meetings in 1955 and 1958 he pointed out that the Circuit committee was very perturbed by the practice which was endangering the circuit as an institution.[93] These comments echo the concerns of George Hill Smith half a century earlier,[94] but, although the Circuit survived as an institution until the early 1970s, it was clear that improved roads, the greater availability of cars, and perhaps less enthusiasm for collective socialising of this nature, meant that the Circuit appeared to destined for extinction despite the efforts of O'Donnell and Porter in particular to nurture and sustain one of the main means of perpetuating the strong sense of friendship and camaraderie that characterised the Northern Ireland Bar of the time. By the mid 1960s the numbers eating together on circuit had fallen considerably, although this may have been in part a reflection of the declining numbers at the Bar by that time. For example, at the 1964 Spring Assizes only 12 lunched in Downpatrick, ten dined in Armagh, nine in Fermanagh, ten in Tyrone, and eight in Londonderry. The numbers at the next assizes that year were even smaller; because although 16 lunched in Downpatrick, only seven dined in Armagh, six in Tyrone, four in Fermanagh and six in Londonderry. In succeeding years the Circuit account book reveals that attendances at most assize towns rarely exceeded ten, often only six or seven, and occasionally as few as four or five attended, with only two dining at the Fermanagh Spring assizes of 1969 (which were held in Omagh as the courthouse in Enniskillen was closed for repair).

It is probably not a coincidence that no general meeting of the Circuit appears to have been held after 27 April 1961, although meetings of the Circuit committee were held regularly until 1963, the last meeting recorded of the committee being held on 11 October 1963, when Alan Comerton was nominated as probationer. The minutes of that meeting were never signed, and no further minutes were entered in the minute book. It therefore appears that the Circuit was only a shadow of its former importance by then, and was rapidly fading away as Turlough O'Donnell had warned might happen.

Although by 1956 the Bar had grown enormously since the end of the

---

92  The Rt Hon Turlough O'Donnell and Sir Robert Porter to the author.
93  2 Feb. 1955 and 15 May 1958. CM, pp 111 and 124.
94  See Ch. 3.

war, and in numerical terms was larger in size than at any time since its creation in 1921, the reality was that there was insufficient work to provide a livelihood for all. In the immediate post-War years the work in the high court seems to have been similar to pre war levels, at least so far as the number of actions in the high court is concerned, with 111 actions disposed of in 1947, compared to 96 in 1937 and 129 in 1927. By 1957 the number of actions disposed of had increased to 420. Of course, civil litigation in the high court, although traditionally the main source of work for the seniors and the senior juniors, was not the only source of work for the Bar. Licensing and public inquiries of various types provided a good deal of work for those who did that type of work, and the county courts continued to provide one of the principal sources of work for newly-called barristers. By the late 1950s and early 1960s it was much more common for barristers, particularly juniors, to appear in the magistrates' courts.

However, as we have seen the fees for interlocutory work and criminal work remained low throughout this period, and county court fees were also modest. From time to time there were major cases (generally referred to as a 'dripping roast') which provided well-paid opportunities for several counsel over a significant period, and the opportunity for individual counsel to establish or enhance their reputations. A notable example was the public inquiry into the loss of the *Princess Victoria*, the passenger ferry which sank off the coast of Co. Down with the loss of 133 lives during a severe gale on 31 January 1953. First of all there was a lengthy inquiry before a court of summary jurisdiction convened under the Merchant Shipping Act, 1894. It was followed by an appeal by the owners of the vessel, the British Transport Commission, and the manager of the vessel, and reference has already been made to the timing of the hearing of the appeal. No fewer than 18 members of the Bar were engaged in the appeal for various parties, and F.A. Reid, appearing as a junior on his own, succeeded in having the findings against his client, the registered manager of the vessel, overturned.[95] Other significant inquiries providing work for the Bar were into the explosion on the steamship *Reina Del Pacifico* whilst it was undergoing trials in Belfast Lough, and into the gangway collapse on the *Juan Peron*.[96]

The most striking feature of the Bar in the decade from 1956 onwards was

95    *The Princess Victoria* [1954] NI 172, and J. Hunter, *The loss of the Princess Victoria* 2nd ed. (Stranraer, 2010).
96    *Jones LJ his life and times*, pp 38-39.

the marked reduction in numbers that took place. Although five were called in both 1956 and 1957, only one was called in 1958; and, with the exception of 1960 when four were called, the pattern between 1958 and 1967 was that only one or two joined the Northern Ireland Bar each year. Leaving out of account members of the English Bar who were called to do a specific case, only one person was called each year in 1958, 1959, 1962, 1963, 1964 and 1966, two were called in 1965 and 1967, but no one was called in 1961.[97] During the post-War period, and particularly from the mid 1950s onwards, there was a steady outflow of members from the Bar for a variety of reasons. Eight were appointed to the high court,[98] eight to the county court,[99] one became president of the lands tribunal, two resident magistrates,[100] and three were appointed national insurance commissioners.[101] Five joined the colonial legal service,[102] five were disbarred at their own request to become solicitors,[103] four died,[104] and six left to go into family businesses or industry.[105] Others took up positions in the courts.

As a result there was steady decline in the number of practising members of the Library, from 67 (18 silks and 49 juniors) in 1962, to 56 (21 silks and 35 juniors) in 1967, although there was an upturn in 1968 and 1969. By 1969 there were 61 in practice, made up of 22 silks and 39 juniors, although by the end of that year 15 of the juniors were of five years standing or less, over one third of the total and a very substantial proportion of the junior Bar. This meant that twenty five years after the end of the War the Northern Ireland Bar was to all intents and purposes approximately the same size as it had been when it came into existence almost half a century earlier. The fall in numbers was particularly dramatic between 1963, when there were 65 members, and 1967 when there were only 56.[106] As we have seen in Chapter Six, this fall in

---

97  Two members of the English Bar were called in 1957, one in 1958, and two in 1963. They
    have been omitted from these figures.
98  Porter QC, Sheil QC, Curran QC, McVeigh QC, Lowry QC, Jones QC, McGonigal QC and
    Gibson QC.
99  Johnston QC, Agnew QC, Hanna QC, Topping QC, Maginess QC, Conaghan QC, Little
    QC and Brown QC.
100  Harrison QC president of the lands tribunal, McBirney QC and Stewart QC resident magistrates.
101  Moody QC, Blair QC and R.W.B. McConnell.
102  Dennison, G. McLaughlin, Pollock and Edwards.
103  Oakey, O'Neill, Bamford, Pollock, J.B. McKee and W.H. McLaughlin.
104  Nicholson QC, T. Wilson, English and Clarke.
105  Hopkirk, Breen, Cinnamond, Harty, Gregg and McQuitty QC.
106  These figures have been taken from figures compiled for the benchers for submission to the Royal
    Commission on Legal Services in 1978.

numbers was source of considerable concern to the benchers.

However, this steep decline was not anticipated. In the early 1960s the first of what was to prove to be a series of much more significant physical expansions of the physical size of the Bar Library took place with the construction of a small room off the corridor leading to the Smoke Room from the lobby (where the staircase which now leads up to the members room and the Inn of Court has been constructed). This was named the Nicholson Room after the late Cyril Nicholson QC, and used for study or dictation when not required for Bar Council meetings.

It was particularly surprising that this dramatic reduction in the size of the Bar occurred just at a time when the volume of litigation was increasing in the high court, leading to the appointment of two additional high court judges in March 1968.[107] There had been a significant increase in the number of high court actions in the decade from 1957, 550 actions being disposed of in 1967, with a dramatic increase to 832 actions in 1968. These increases no doubt reflect the advent of civil legal aid and greater trade union activity during the industrial expansion and increased prosperity that marked the late 1950s and early 1960s in Northern Ireland. However, civil litigation in the county courts declined slightly between 1964 and 1968. In 1964 there were 4,742 defended civil cases of all types in the county courts, compared to 4,428 in 1967, and 4,432 in 1968. These figures include categories such as criminal injuries, licensing applications and adoptions, and counsel would not have been briefed in every case, particularly in those county courts farthest from Belfast. The relative paucity of civil work at the assizes can be seen from the small number of civil bill appeals heard on assize (those from Antrim Down and Belfast went direct to the high court). In 1964 in Northern Ireland there were only 69 such cases heard, of which 11 were in Armagh, five in Fermanagh, 11 in Tyrone, one in the city, and two in the county, of Londonderry. Given that there were two assizes each year these figures show that the civil side of the assizes did not provide a great deal of work for those attending, because by this time records (writs) at the assizes were virtually extinct, and so appeals from the county court were effectively the only civil cases heard on assize.

Criminal work was also relatively stable at this period, with 709 indictable cases dealt with by the assizes and county courts (which now exercised the

---

107 E.W. Jones QC, MP and A.J. McGonigal QC, MC and bar.

indictable jurisdiction formerly exercised by quarter sessions) in 1964, 643 in 1967 and 769 in 1968. However, these cases were divided between the assizes and the county courts, with the majority of cases outside Belfast being dealt with by the county courts. For example, in 1964 Co. Armagh had 11 trials at the assizes, and 51 in the county court. So far as prosecutors were concerned, outside Belfast only Co. Antrim provided a substantial volume of business at the assizes. In the county courts outside Belfast prosecutions were normally conducted in person by the crown solicitor for each county, and so counsel were not usually briefed for the prosecution. County Antrim with 68 cases at the assizes in 1964, and 84 in 1968, provided a fair amount of work for the senior and junior crown prosecutors at each assize, whereas Fermanagh with three cases at the assizes in 1964, none in 1967, and nine in 1968, was almost an honorary position.

Outside Belfast, there was a recognised ladder of promotion from the less busy to the busier counties for crown counsel, but to be appointed a crown prosecutor by the attorney general at that time, whilst professionally significant, was usually less financially rewarding. The exception was Belfast, as the city commission sat four times a year to exercise the assize jurisdiction for the city. The Belfast recorder's court also sat for indictable business four times a year, its sittings alternating with those of the city commission. The volume of business in Belfast was naturally much greater than elsewhere because of the size of Belfast relative to the rest of Northern Ireland. In 1964 there were 166 cases at the commission in 1964, and 104 in the recorder's court. Again the volume of business was relatively static, with 168 and 80 cases respectively in 1968. The crown counsel in Belfast for many years were W.F. McCoy QC MP and D.J. Little MP, and these were more remunerative posts than their counterparts outside Belfast because of the volume of work, even though the fees in each case were modest. On the defence side, as we have seen, the fees were low for many years. Although a number of counsel did a certain amount of criminal work, it was unusual to find someone doing predominantly criminal work, perhaps the main junior who did so in the 1960s, at least in Belfast, was H.G. McGrath.[108]

Those who left the Bar for reasons other than judicial preferment obviously

---

108 The statistics about civil and criminal business in this chapter are taken from the *Report of the Committee on the Supreme Court of Judicature of Northern Ireland* 1970. Cmd. 4292. (The MacDermott Report), p. 25 and App. 9, pp 180-85. See also p. 90 of the MacDermott Report on county court appeals.

did so because they were not, or did not anticipate, making a reasonable living. Until the middle of the 1960s the early years at the Bar for the great majority of young barristers were marked by the traditional features of little work and low earnings. Turlough O'Donnell (called in 1947) marked 100 guineas (£105) in his first year, two hundred guineas (£210) in his second, and four hundred guineas (£440) in his fourth year, although he ruefully recalled that he was not paid all the fees he marked,[109] an experience suffered by most young counsel from time to time, particularly in their first few years. Sir John MacDermott was called in 1949 and made 37 guineas (£38 15s), in his first year, and 64 guineas (£67 4s) in his second.[110] As the traditional fee paid to one's master for pupillage was 50 guineas (£52 10s) on top of the fees paid on call, buying wig and gown, and payment of Library and Circuit subscriptions, few of those starting straight from university would have much, if anything, to show for their labours for the first few years, unless they were fortunate enough to have relatives or other connections in the solicitors' profession who would put work their way. This situation did not change for many years, as can be seen from the experience of Sir Anthony Campbell. He was called in 1960, by which time the pupillage fee was 100 guineas (£105), and earned £201 7s 6p in his first year, and £192 5s in his second,[111] significantly less than Sgt Over was paid as librarian at that time.[112]

Personal injury work was the mainstay of the Bar at that time, although there was some falling off in the immediate post-War period with the abolition of workmen's compensation. Until the abolition of the defences of common employment and contributory negligence it was very difficult to win a workman's case. Judges and jurors were inclined to the view that many workmen injured at work were the authors of their own misfortune, and workmen were reluctant to sue in case that would jeopardize their return to work.[113] With the gradual increase in the number of actions in the late 1950s and 1960s the seniors, and no doubt the established juniors, made a reasonable living. Nevertheless, progress was slow for almost everyone. In the high court newly-called barristers were often given interlocutory applications to move on behalf of their masters. Appearing before Mr Justice Sheil, Mr Justice Jones, or Lord

109 Conversation with the author 20 Aug. 2009.
110 Conversation with the author 9 Aug. 2009.
111 Comments to the author 24 Jan. 2010.
112 See p. 243.
113 Sir John MacDermott to the author.

MacDermott, could be a daunting experience if one's tackle was not in perfect order.

During the 1950s it became more common for barristers to be instructed in the magistrates' courts, although the fees were small. For example in the early 1960s the RAC paid their solicitors £3 3s for a careless driving case, of which counsel got £1 11s 6d.[114] The county courts continued to be the main source of work for many juniors, and, although the fees were small, senior juniors would go to distant courts for fees of £5 5s or £7 7s. There was the added hazard in the county court that the case might not get on the first day, and then be heard over a number of days subsequently, Lord Carswell recalled one instance in Omagh when his case was not heard on the first day, was part heard on the second, and completed on the third, resulting in three train trips to Omagh for one fee.[115] There was also a certain amount of work outside the principal courts for a few counsel, such as appearances before the special commissioners of income tax, planning enquiries, or drafting private bills at Stormont. The creation of the Lands Tribunal in 1964 to deal with matters such as compensation for compulsory purchase of property and valuation appeals provided additional opportunities for some counsel.[116] There were also occasional forays to London to appear before the house of lords. It is a notable feature of this period that it was much less common for English counsel to be brought into a case at that stage than had been the case before the war, although it still happened occasionally, particularly in revenue cases.

Although the Library itself was well-equipped with text books and law reports, it was less well-equipped to deal with a more demanding world. Some changes in traditional practices were resisted, or reluctantly adopted. By the 1960s there were only four telephones, two for outgoing and two for incoming calls, and as we shall see complaints about the inadequacies of the telephone system was to be a recurrent theme for many years to come. By October 1950 ten members were making use of a shorthand typist to type opinions. In November the lord chief justice granted their request that she be allowed to use a room in the law courts, but stipulated that she had to leave by 12.30 on Saturdays, and that 'the room shall under no circumstances

114 Sir Anthony Campbell to the author.
115 To the author 23 Dec. 2009.
116 By the Lands Tribunal and Compensation (NI) 1964.

be used on Sundays'. By the end of 1957 a further request was made that a second typist be permitted, and there was a reference to the use of recording machines. However, not all innovations were well-received, and the Bar was very slow to recognise the need to change its practices in some respects. In 1957, when it was realised that E.W. Jones QC was providing carbon copies of his opinions so that they could be provided to the insurance client without the solicitor having to incur the expense and trouble of typing copies, it was solemnly resolved by the Bar Council that it was undesirable to provide solicitors with 'copies of opinions, pleadings, advices etc'.[117]

A more difficult problem that had to be addressed in the 1960s came about as an unexpected consequence of the advent of commercial television. In 1961 James McQuitty QC wished to become a director of Ulster Television, which had been awarded the commercial television franchise for Northern Ireland. He sought the advice of the Bar Council and the benchers as to the propriety of his doing so. The benchers decided that if he were to become a director of UTV this would constitute 'engaging in a trade or business'.[118] A few days later the Bar Council resolved that 'it would be undesirable for a practising member of the Bar of Northern Ireland to be a member of the board of Ulster Television Ltd'.[119] McQuitty subsequently left the Bar to take up a place on the board of UTV. The rigour of this decision was modified slightly in 1964, when a general meeting of the Bar accepted that barristers could be directors 'without managerial duties in companies of good standing carrying on business of a type which as a general principle is not usually engaged in litigation', provided that one month's notice was given to the Bar Council.[120] This principle has been applied by the benchers in subsequent years when deciding whether to permit members of the Bar to become company directors.

Those who were in the early stages of their careers in the 1950s and 1960s are at one in their recollection of a less frenetic and more leisurely atmosphere in the Bar Library compared to the present day. The tradition of a young member being able to approach another member of the Library, no matter how senior, and ask his advice about a problem had been maintained. Cards were often played in the late afternoons in the Smoke Room. On Saturday

117 3 June 1957. BCM, p. 169.
118 BM, 26 May 1961.
119 30 May 1961. BM, p. 404.
120 16 Oct. 1964. MGM, p. 56.

mornings, although the courts were closed, many members of the Library would come in, sometimes bringing their children with them. During the week it was sometimes possible to find time to lunch in one of Belfast's restaurants, and promotions to the bench continued to be marked by dinners. There also were the Circuit dinners which have already been referred to, and some of the silks and their wives entertained young juniors.[121] Outside the Library the Bar Golfing Society provided an opportunity for the Bar and the judges to meet socially. Founded in 1951, it held its first captain's day at Royal Belfast Golf Cub, Craigavad, on 17 September of that year. Thereafter it was a prominent part of Bar social life, and soon provided an opportunity for the Northern Bar to resume friendly relations with the Southern Bar and judiciary. Starting with a match against the Bar of Ireland Golfing Society at Royal County Down in Newcastle in April 1952, there were regular matches between the two bars at different venues, once as far away as Cork. These meetings went a considerable way towards establishing friendlier relations with the Southern Bar and judiciary, relations having been glacial for many years after 1926. However, as we shall see in Chapter Eleven, this thaw in relations was insufficient to lead to a resumption of formal reciprocity between the two inns for another twenty years. Matches with the Scottish Bar were instituted in 1955.[122] These social visits with the Irish and Scottish Bars undoubtedly helped to foster good relations with the other bars, and to reduce the sense of isolation of the Northern Bar which was the smallest of the bars in these islands.

Another opportunity for members of the Bar to become more closely acquainted with the supreme court judges occurred if a judge appointed a member of the Bar to act as his registrar.[123] Each assize judge was entitled to appoint a registrar for the duration of his assize circuit, and it was customary (but not invariably the case) for the judges to invite young members of the Bar to fill the position. This provided the barristers concerned with the opportunity to spend the two or three weeks of a circuit in the company of the two assize judges. The registrar acted as aide de camp to his judge, inviting guests to dine with the judges, and organising (with the invaluable help of the judge's far more experienced tipstaff) the many details of the judge's activities in and out of court. This provided registrars with an

---

121 Lord Hutton and Sir Anthony Campbell in particular recall the kindness shown to them in this fashion.
122 Minutes of the Bar Golfing Society.
123 The equivalent of a judge's marshal in England.

invaluable opportunity to see the judge at close quarters on and off the bench. As well as being fed and accommodated at the public expense, the registrar also received the statutory fee of £183 12s 4p, or 'two hundred pounds Irish'.[124] Despite the fall in the value of money, for many years this remained a useful addition to a struggling junior's income.

In the middle of the 1960s the Northern Ireland Bar was therefore a small, closely knit, profession in which standards of professional conduct were maintained as much by, if not more so, the force of collective opinion and conventions as by written rules. In the decades since the end of the Second World War it had expanded dramatically in size for the first ten years, and then equally dramatically contracted during the next decade, and, as we have seen, ending the second period of its independent existence approximately the same size as it had been when it came into existence as a separate Bar in 1921. Outwardly it was in a healthy condition as the amount of civil work in the high court was expanding. However, this concealed a distinctly worrying and significant imbalance between the experienced senior members and a rapidly contracting proportion of juniors. This growing imbalance was alleviated somewhat by the influx of several new juniors in 1968, but, as we have seen, by the end of 1969 over a third of the junior Bar was made up of those of five years standing or less.

As the end of the 1960s approached, there were a number of developments that proved to be the germ of significant changes that were to occur in the next two decades. First of all, it was gradually becoming apparent that the traditional immunity of barristers from being sued for professional negligence could no longer be taken for granted, and in 1968 it was unanimously agreed by a general meeting that professional indemnity insurance of £10000 should be compulsory for every member of the Bar.[125] However, as we shall see, the payment of premiums was to prove contentious in the early 1970s. A further sign of change was that in 1965 the Bar Council felt it necessary to make enquiries about sickness and prolonged disability insurance,[126] although nothing seems to have come of that at the time. Another was that the frequent differences between the

124 The fee was originally £200 in Irish pounds, and became £183 12s 4d sterling when the separate
    Irish currency was abolished in 1826, and the British and Irish currencies replaced with a single
    currency throughout the United Kingdom.
125 MGM, 27 June 1968.
126 BCM, 1 Feb. 1965.

Bar and the Government over issues such as fees for criminal cases, and the introduction of civil legal aid, rendered the position of the attorney general as a member of the government continuing to act as chairman of the Bar Council, and head of the Bar, whilst a member of the government, increasingly invidious. The inevitable tensions between the two roles became more apparent. As we have seen, the attorney general had been the *de facto* head of the Bar, presiding in that capacity as chairman of the Bar Council and general meetings of the Bar, although this position was not formally confirmed until a general meeting in June 1965. However, in December 1968 the attorney general, E.W. Jones QC MP, told the Bar Council that because of these conflicts he felt the attorney general should no longer be chairman of the Bar Council. He repeated this at a general meeting later that month.[127] His decision was accepted, the necessary constitutional amendments were made at a general meeting in June 1968,[128] and the first elections under the new constitution was held in on 30 January 1969 when F.A. Reid QC was elected chairman of the Bar Council for a two year term. However, the attorney general remained an *ex officio* member of the Bar Council until the dissolution of the Northern Ireland Parliament in 1972. Basil Kelly QC MP, who succeeded Jones as attorney general in March 1968 when Jones was appointed a high court judge, was an assiduous attender at Bar Council meetings until the abolition of his office in March 1972, despite the heavy demands upon him because of the dramatic increase in criminal prosecutions and other government business from 1968 onwards. A further harbinger of repeated government inquiries into the structures and practices of the legal professions throughout the next forty years or so was a questionnaire from the Monopolies Commission which the Bar Council prepared to respond to throughout the summer of 1967.[129]

However, unknown to anyone at the time, the Bar was soon to be faced with several challenges which were to severely tax both the Bar and the Inn of Court. The first was the enormous expansion in numbers that was to see the practising Bar grow to ten times its previous size over the next forty years, and in Chapter Six we have seen how the Inn grappled with the educational implications of this increase. The second was how to accommodate this number, a challenge that was responded to by repeated expansions in the size

127 BCM, 4 Dec. 1967, and MGM 12 Dec. 1967.
128 MGM 27 June 1968.
129 BCM 8 June and 26 Oct. 1967.

of the Bar Library, culminating in the construction of the New Bar Library. The third took the form of recurring public and governmental scrutiny of the legal system in Northern Ireland as part of the determination of government at various times to change the structures, practices and ethos of the legal profession. The Northern Ireland Bar was not unique in facing such critical scrutiny as the English, Scottish and Irish bars faced similar challenges throughout this period. What was unique to Northern Ireland was the fourth challenge, namely when the community was subjected to an unprecedented period of political turmoil and instability accompanied by more than thirty years of intense terrorist strife and communal upheaval. The clouds foreshadowing the political storm that was about to break were rapidly darkening during the second half of 1968 and the first half of 1969, and in succeeding chapters we shall see how the Northern Ireland Bar responded to these challenges.

In November 1966 there had been an early sign of the particular pressures these political developments were to impose upon the Bar. William Craig MP, a solicitor by profession, and as minister of home affairs responsible for the administration of the criminal law, the police, and the county and magistrates' courts, made extremely controversial remarks about Roman Catholic members of the legal profession in the Northern Ireland House of Commons. Replying to allegations about discrimination against Roman Catholics in legal and judicial appointments he said 'No doubt there are social and educational reasons' for there being only five Roman Catholics compared to nineteen of other denominations at the senior Bar.[130] In a rare, if not unprecedented, comment upon a political issue the Bar Council issued a statement rejecting these objectionable comments.[131]

130 HC Debates (NI) vol. 64, p. 2454.
131 BCM 21 Nov. 1966.

# CHAPTER NINE:

## 1969 to 2011-challenge and change

NINETEEN SIXTY NINE has been chosen as the starting point of this chapter for several reasons. The first is that it was the last year in which a small number of students were called to the Northern Ireland Bar. Starting with the large call in 1970 the number of students called each year thereafter was very much greater than had been the case before 1970. In the succeeding four decades that increase has not merely been sustained, but the numbers have continued to increase from time to time, with calls of more than 30 being the rule in recent years. Those students were trained through the Bar Course provided by the Inn itself, and then by the Institute of Professional Legal Studies. They have been supplemented by a numerically smaller, but cumulatively significant, increase in the number of members of the English and Irish bars who have been called to the Northern Ireland Bar, a significant number of whom practice in Northern Ireland from time to time. The effect of this has been that at the end of 2012 there were almost twelve times as many barristers in independent practice in Northern Ireland as there were in 1969. This has created great challenges for the Inn and the Bar in the areas of education[1] and accommodation,[2] and these topics are considered in other chapters.

The second reason is that in the spring and summer of 1969 the political uncertainty and unrest which had been an increasingly significant feature of public life in the province for some time boiled over into intensive and widespread violence and disorder. That speedily developed into what was to prove to be several decades of terrorism, communal division and antagonism on a very significant scale. Whilst the violence and political instability naturally affected the Bar, just as it affected every walk of life, in many ways the Bar, and the legal profession in general, was exposed to particularly severe stresses and strains. As we shall see the Bar was able to weather the stresses and strains created by the violence. Nevertheless, the changes to the legal and judicial system that were directly or indirectly the result of the sustained violence proved to be extremely significant and long lasting, and no account of the Bar during the last four decades would be complete without some reference to them.

1    Chapter 6.
2    Chapter 10.

A third reason is that the four decades covered by this chapter have also seen an unprecedented level of public and governmental scrutiny and examination of many parts of the legal system. The legal profession has not escaped critical, and often hostile, scrutiny during this time, and this has directly affected a number of important features of the practices of the Bar, and of its governance. This scrutiny, and the changes in the governance of the Inn of Court of Northern Ireland and the Bar which have resulted from it, are considered in Chapter Twelve. These decades were equally notable for many important changes in the relationships between the Inn and the Bar on the one hand, and King's Inns on the other, and changes in the manner of appointment of Queen's Counsel in Northern Ireland, changes which are dealt with in Chapter Eleven.[3]

Notwithstanding the many major challenges which we will consider elsewhere the everyday life of the Bar went on, and in this chapter we shall examine other challenges which the Bar has faced during that period, and how it responded to them. In 1969 the Bar was still a small and intimate profession. As we have seen the numbers at the Bar had fallen considerably in the early 1960s, and then had increased again somewhat in 1968 in particular, and this continued with four new barristers being called on various dates throughout 1969. When the author was called in September 1969 there were 60 members of the Bar Library, of whom about 20 were silks and 40 juniors, compared to rather more than 500 solicitors.[4] As in previous decades a newly called junior found a senior junior to act as his master. A pupil was expected to read his master's papers, draft pleadings, and sometimes opinions, under his supervision, as well as attending consultations and trials with his master.

As compulsory and non-practising pupillage was still some years in the future, a junior could find himself in court within days of call. This often meant being thrown in at the deep end before one of the seven judges of the Court of Appeal and the High Court. In the Friday morning Queen's Bench motion court before Mr Justice Jones one learnt the practical application of the hitherto somewhat puzzling rules of procedure, principally in personal injury cases. Undefended divorces were also

---

3    Chapter 11.
4    There were about 500 solicitors in private practice in 1967. Hewitt, *The Law Society of Northern Ireland A History* (Belfast, 2010) p. 142.

listed on Fridays, and to watch the lord chief justice, Lord MacDermott, minutely scrutinizing the facts and the law relating to the wreckage of a marriage was a fascinating experience for the onlooker, although it could be testing for the counsel and parties concerned. This was in marked contrast to Lord Justice Curran who despatched his divorce cases with the minimum attention to formality, recognising that the marriage had ended and not wishing to be kept too long in pronouncing its formal termination. The chancery motion court on Monday mornings was a completely different experience. Mr Justice Gibson presided with urbane, and justified, intellectual self-confidence, and the work was dealt with quietly and smoothly.

The increase in personal injury litigation towards the end of the 1960s was considerable. No doubt this reflected the arrival of new industries during the post War period, as well as the continued existence of traditional, and often dangerous, industries such as shipbuilding, and the effect of the recent introduction of legal aid. This increase meant the high court failed to keep up with the growth in litigation, despite the appointment of two extra judges in March 1968[5] to clear the backlog. 550 actions were set down and disposed of in 1967, and this increased to 832 actions in 1968.[6] Although 950 queen's bench actions were disposed of in 1971, by November 1972 the arrears had risen to 1145,[7]and by September 1973 had increased further to 1426.[8] These figures show that in the late 1960s and early 1970s there was a considerable, and increasing, amount of civil work in the high court for seniors, and for senior juniors.

On the criminal side indictable cases outside Belfast were divided between the county courts, whose judges dealt with the majority of the work, and the judges of the court of appeal and the high court, two of whom went out on assize twice a year. The assize judges devoted their time principally to criminal work, although they also dealt with a small number of civil appeals

5  E.W. Jones QC and A. McGonigal, MC and bar, QC were appointed puisne judges of the high
    court on 6 Mar. 1968.

6  *Report of the Committee on the Supreme Court of Judicature of Northern Ireland*, Mar. 1970,
    Cmnd. 4292, para. 60, (the MacDermott Report).

7  *Interim Report of the Joint Committee on Civil and Criminal Jurisdiction in Northern Ireland*, 1973.
    Cmnd. 5431, para. 17, (the Lowry Report).

8  *Report of the Committee on County Courts and Magistrates' Courts in Northern Ireland*, Cmnd. 5824.
    1974. para. 8, (the Jones Report).

from the county court.[9] A single lord justice or high court judge sat each year at the Northern Ireland Winter assize, which dealt with criminal cases only from all the counties outside Belfast, often sitting outside Belfast. In Belfast indictable work was divided between the Belfast City Commission, which dealt with the majority of indictable cases in the city, and the Belfast recorder's court. The city commission was the assize court for the city, and sat four times a year.[10] Again, the judges of the high court and court of appeal took it in turn to deal with this work. The lord chief justice also took his turn to sit at first instance in the high court, and on assize and the city commission.

The county courts (including the Belfast recorder's court) had a civil jurisdiction in the main limited to amounts up to £300. Judge Topping QC was the recorder of Belfast, and his was the busiest civil and criminal county court. Judge Brown QC was the judge for Co. Down, whilst Judge Conaghan QC was the judge for both Co. Armagh and Co. Fermanagh. Judge Johnson QC was the judge for Co. Tyrone, and for the southern division of Co. Antrim. Judge Little QC, the recorder of Londonderry, was the judge for the county borough of Londonderry, the county of Londonderry, and the northern division of Co. Antrim. By now senior juniors largely confined themselves to the high court, although they were seen more frequently in the recorder's court in Belfast than the other county courts. This meant that newly-called juniors might be passed cases by their masters, or other senior juniors, and would soon find themselves appearing in front of county court judges. This could help them to build up a lasting relationship with local solicitors in those counties who usually proved to be loyal supporters.

By this time it was much more common than before for junior counsel to find themselves appearing in the magistrates' courts, still commonly referred to as petty sessions. Small local courts were being gradually closed. Some were held once a month in small country towns or villages, and many had hardly changed in physical appearance since the nineteenth century. Visits to courthouses in Saintfield or Newcastle in Co. Down; Cushendall in Co. Antrim; Clogher or Castlederg in Co. Tyrone; Derrygonnelly or Letterbreen in Co. Fermanagh, were all possible. Some unusual venues were used as courts. Newtownbreda court was held in the function hall

---

9    See Appendix 9, Table II of the MacDermott Report. Appeals in civil matters in Belfast, and
     Counties Antrim and Down, went direct to a high court judge sitting in Belfast. Ibid., para. 209.
10   Ibid., Appendix 9, Table I.

of Malone Rugby Club, a modern building in the suburbs of Belfast. The court in Dromore, Co. Down was held in the local cinema. The resident magistrate (always known as the RM) sat at a table in front of the screen whilst counsel and solicitors sat in the stalls. In older buildings the resident magistrate was often the only person with the advantage of an open fire or a heater in cold weather.

Whilst the courts provided the main source of work for the Bar, there was a significant amount of work for some counsel in the Lands Tribunal, which had been set up in 1964,[11] and in planning applications. Junior counsel were often appointed as part-time chairmen of industrial tribunals. However, with the advent of 'the Troubles' as the decades of violence and political instability have become euphemistically known, there was also work for counsel in the commissions of inquiry set up under the chairmanships of Lord Cameron[12] and Mr Justice Scarman[13] respectively to examine the disturbances from October 1968 and in August 1969.

Although the main work of the Bar was centred in Belfast, junior counsel in particular travelled out of Belfast to country courts, and part of this involved appearing at the assize courts. By the late 1960s and the early 1970s the assize system had become increasingly outmoded, and although the assizes were not abolished until 1979 with the passage of the Judicature (Northern Ireland) Act 1978, the traditional assize circuit with members of the Bar travelling from assize town to assize town had, to all intents and purposes, already disappeared by 1979. As we have seen in the previous chapter, the circuit tradition had been weakening since at least the 1950s, and its ultimate demise was certainly hastened by the growth of work in other courts. This made it increasingly unattractive for even senior juniors to go on the assizes where the civil work had declined to very low levels, and the criminal work on the defence side was in the hands of a few counsel. The prospect of picking up briefs on circuit was less, although

11  By the Lands Tribunal and Compensation Act (NI) 1964.
12  The enquiry under the chairmanship of Lord Cameron had four counsel assisting it, but it did not conduct any public hearings or grant legal representation. See *Disturbances in Northern Ireland* Cmd. 532, p. 7.
13  The tribunal of inquiry chaired by Mr Justice Scarman was assisted by four counsel and did grant legal representation. Altogether 32 members of the Northern Ireland Bar (12 QCs and 19 juniors), and one junior member of the English Bar were engaged in the Scarman Inquiry. See *Violence and Civil Disturbances in Northern Ireland in 1969*, cmd. 566, vol. 2, Appendix VII, pp 59-60 for a list of counsel involved.

it was not unknown for solicitors to come to the hotel where the Bar were staying to see if there was anyone who could take on a case the next day, or even that day, usually in a civil bill appeal.[14] In addition the expense of staying in hotels for several days was significant, and one might well lose work in Belfast. Senior and junior Crown counsel were still appointed for each county by the attorney general,[15] and whilst these posts could be quite lucrative the prospects were less attractive for those who had few, or perhaps no, briefs in particular towns. However, although the tradition of newly called juniors joining the Circuit as probationers continued, the Circuit became increasingly anachronistic. This decline was illustrated by the Circuit records not being kept up to date. It also had an effect upon the finances of the Circuit. The structure of the Circuit depended upon the efforts of the Circuit steward, who was paid an honorarium out of the cess or levy imposed on those attending each town. However, this structure became increasingly difficult to sustain. In March 1975 the Bar Council had to step in to meet a shortfall of £436.11 in the Circuit income. Part of the shortfall represented non-payment of the circuit steward's honorarium for four sessions, or two years' arrears.[16]

Nevertheless, whilst the decline of the Circuit as an institution was inevitable, in the early 1970s its demise did not seem imminent. Despite the violence, the judges went out on circuit as they had done for hundreds of years, although security fears meant that the traditional pomp of inspections of guards of honour in each county town rapidly disappeared. Instead of travelling from one town to the next by car the judges sometimes had to travel in a military helicopter, and have an armed guard at their lodgings. Notwithstanding these constraints, they and the Bar kept up their respective traditions as best they could. The judges alternated as crown judge for each county, the crown judge being the senior judge during his time in that county. On the first night of the assize the judges would invite Crown counsel to dine in the judges' lodgings, when all concerned would usually dress for dinner in dinner jackets. If the assize lasted more than one day then defence counsel would be invited to dine on the second or on a subsequent night. In Londonderry the high sheriff gave a lunch in the

---

14  The author recalls one occasion when two Enniskillen solicitors came to the Bar hotel with briefs in civil bill appeals for the next day.
15  After the prorogation of the Northern Ireland parliament in 1972 these appointments were made by the director of public prosecutions.
16  BCM 11 Mar. 1965.

grand jury room in the courthouse to which the Bar were generally invited.

After the day's work was done there would be much conviviality amongst those members of the Bar who stayed to dine in a local hotel. The senior member present acted as the Father, and fines in the form of drink or cigars were levied by him for real or imagined breaches of protocol. The hotels varied in amenities and comforts, and as many of the traditional venues were blown up, or damaged by explosions, overnight stays became more difficult and less attractive. Circuit dinners to entertain the judges were rare. Perhaps the last was a large dinner held in Londonderry Courthouse in the mid-1970s at which the guest of honour was the newly-appointed Mr Justice Murray. Thereafter the role of the Circuit dinner was subsumed into the Bar dinners which were held from time to time in a hotel in, or near, Belfast. Sometimes dinners were held to mark a special occasion, as in 1971 when a dinner was held at the Culloden Hotel to mark the retirement of Lord MacDermott as lord chief justice, and the appointment of Sir Robert Lowry as his successor, when the principal guests were the Governor, Lord Grey of Naunton, and the lord chancellor, Lord Hailsham.[17] Other dinners were purely social events to which wives and girlfriends were invited. However, with the increase in size of the Bar, and the continuing terrorist violence, and the constraints the necessary security precautions inevitably imposed on every member of the community, such functions became less popular for a while. Nevertheless, occasional Bar dinners and dinners organised for students and pupils by the Inn of Court, together with the various clubs and societies that will be referred to later, have done much to encourage social contact amongst members of the Bar and the judiciary.

Throughout its history the Bar has had its particular traditions, sometimes adapting old practices to new developments. One that survived the disappearance of the Circuit has been the tradition of the Father, the position having continued as Father of the Bar rather than of the Circuit. This is a purely honorary position as the Father has no function other than to preside at Bar dinners when present. Although the post was an elective one in the past, the practice now is for the longest-serving practising member of the Bar to be appointed as the Father by the Bar Council. Thus when Ronald Appleton QC indicated in 2004 that he wished to stand down as Father, the chairman of the Bar Council wrote to J.D. McSparran QC to

17   BCM 26 Oct. 1971.

inform him that he was the most senior person and next in line as Father of the Bar, and McSparran accepted the position.[18] Another tradition that has had to be modified is that of a senior counsel presenting a red bag to a junior the senior has led in a case before the House of Lords. It seems that it was not considered necessary to note formally the disappearance of the judicial functions of the House of Lords when it was replaced by the Supreme Court in 2009. However, when the United Kingdom entered the then Common Market, and the European Court of Justice in Luxembourg became the ultimate court in certain circumstances, the Bar Council decided that red bags should be given for appearances before that court in the same way as had been done for appearances before the House of Lords.[19] Sometimes the traditions are of a less elevated variety, one being the habit of younger members who had little or no work to occupy themselves by playing cards, a practice the Bar Council felt in 1974 it had to prohibit before 4.30 pm.[20]

Despite the increasing tide of violence, and the many problems that created, the Bar still had to address other issues of concern to the profession. By the end of the 1960s the Bar recognised that the traditional immunity of the barrister from being sued for negligence was unlikely to survive much longer, and in 1968 a general meeting decided that professional indemnity insurance would be compulsory. Henceforth each member had to have insurance for a minimum of £10000. This was not a popular move with some, particularly as the premiums increased. In March 1971 the Bar Council noted the heavy cost of this insurance,[21] and in June of the same year the 'sharp increase' in premiums led to an unsuccessful attempt at a general meeting to rescind the requirement that professional indemnity insurance be compulsory.[22] The meeting instructed the secretary of the Bar Council to try to negotiate cheaper rates, especially for those who had been in practice for five years or less, but at the end of the year it was reported that this had not been possible.[23] Professional indemnity insurance has remained compulsory, and the level of cover that barristers have to have has increased from time to time, and by 1984 the levels were much higher

18   BCM 12 May and 9 June 2004.
19   BCM 29 Sept. 1978.
20   BCM 11 Feb. 1975.
21   BCM 1 Mar. 1971.
22   MGM 25 June 1971.
23   MGM 16 Dec. 1971.

than had been the case when such insurance became compulsory.[24] The premiums were often a cause for concern. For example, in 1976 the Bar Council noted concern about the level of premiums,[25] and over the years there have been occasions when the council was very worried about the number of members of the Bar who were in arrears with their premiums as well as their subscriptions.[26] The implications for aggrieved clients, and the implications for the Bar as a whole, if there were to be an unsatisfied judgment for damages for professional negligence against a barrister, were all too obvious, and each time the council took vigorous action to ensure that premiums were paid.

By the early 1970s it was increasingly evident that the vastly increased volume of serious crime due to widespread public disorder and terrorism was putting society as whole, the structures of government, the police and the criminal justice system under severe strain. These developments naturally had a profound effect upon the Bar. The growing backlog in civil cases in the high court already referred to was due to the dramatic increase in criminal work at all levels as a result of the civil disorder and terrorism.[27] This meant that more time had to be devoted to criminal trials in the magistrates' courts and on indictment. The county courts had to grapple with an immense increase in the number of compensation claims for injury to the person and damage to property. The number of judges increased substantially, particularly in the county court where nine additional county court judges were appointed between 1971 and 1978.[28] More resident magistrates were appointed, some of whom were barristers. These promotions in turn created opportunities for professional advancement for the senior Bar, and in turn this meant increased opportunities for senior and middle ranking juniors.

Violence on this scale inevitably meant that the Bar as a profession had to grapple with issues of acute sensitivity and concern. Some of these were relatively straightforward to resolve. In April 1970 the Bar Council resolved that 'Where in a criminal trial one of a number of defendants is separately

---

24  BCM 11 Jan. 1984. The minimum levels were increased to £100,000 for juniors of up to three
    year's standing, to £300,000 for juniors over three years, and to £500,000 for all seniors. These were
    minimum levels, many had insurance for higher amounts.
25  BCM 20 Sept. 1976.
26  BCM 18 May 1988 and 15 June 1988.
27  The Jones Report, para. 8.
28  One county court judge was a replacement for a murdered judge, the remainder were extra appointments.

represented no counsel appearing for him should appear for another defendant in the same trial'.[29] In October of that year the Bar Council acknowledged the shortage of counsel in criminal trials when it decided that there was no objection to an experienced junior leading another junior when senior counsel was unavailable.[30] Other issues were potentially very divisive. An illustration of the potential for acute political divisions to surface within the Bar Library occurred in April 1971 when the Bar Council met to discuss a meeting of members of the legal profession 'at which concern had been expressed both at the conduct of certain prosecutions and at an allegedly biased attitude to those prosecutions of some members of the judiciary'.[31] The minutes do not record the views expressed at the meeting, but the gravity of the matter, and perhaps the range of views expressed, may be inferred from the fact that the Council met on two consecutive days to discuss the matter.

The response of the Council was to set up a committee with the Law Society, but this seems to have been overtaken by events. A month later the Council considered a letter received from a solicitor containing the terms of two resolutions passed at a meeting of solicitors and barristers on 4 May 1971 which 'had been convened for the purpose of discussing public criticism which was said to have been made concerning the administration of the criminal law'. There is no reference in the minutes to what action (if any) was taken. The security situation worsened throughout 1971 and 1972. The response of the Government to the deteriorating security situation was to introduce internment without trial on 9 August 1971 by invoking section 12 of the Civil Authorities (Special Powers) Act (Northern Ireland) 1922. Members of the Bar were soon appearing before the 'Brown committee', a review body[32] which considered whether to order the release of detainees. One consequence of internment was that a number of English counsel were brought over to 'prosecute' detainees before the committee, the first example of a phenomenon that was to become more common, namely members of the English or Scottish Bar being brought over by the British Government, or by the chairmen of inquiries, to appear before tribunals or inquiries. Whilst this is permissible because it is not necessary to be a member of the Northern Ireland Bar to appear before a body or tribunal which is not a court, whether deliberate or not, this could often be seen as

29  BCM 20 Apr. 1970.
30  BCM 27 Oct. 1970.
31  BCM 3 and 4 Apr. 1971.
32  Chaired by Judge James Brown QC, county court judge for Co. Down.

indicating a lack of confidence in the Northern Ireland Bar. In the case of the detainees the decision to only use members of the English Bar to present the evidence for the Crown was taken to reduce the risks to the Northern Ireland Bar and the pressure which would be brought upon their limited numbers if they were instructed to appear on behalf of the Crown in these proceedings.[33] The shooting dead of 13 men in Londonderry on 30 January 1972 by members of the Parachute Regiment led to the appointment of Lord Widgery, the lord chief justice of England, to conduct an inquiry, and on 15 February the Bar Council decided that it was not improper for members of the Northern Ireland Bar to appear before Lord Widgery.

At the same meeting the Council considered a report in the London *Times* of 9 February that lawyers were losing faith in the judiciary in Northern Ireland. As was often the case when equally contentious views were considered by the Bar Council the minutes do not record the various arguments advanced. Reports of this nature revealed the enormous stresses that existed within both branches of the legal profession in Northern Ireland caused by external events.[34] The Northern Ireland (Emergency Provisions) Act 1973 which followed the report by Lord Diplock,[35] was another such event. The depth of feeling raised by the proposal to introduce non-jury courts and other aspects of the legislation can be seen from the 'considerable amount' of opposition expressed at a general meeting in March 1973 which discussed the proposals, and the acceptance by 16 votes to 14 of the proposition that resident magistrates should sit with judges.[36] The Diplock proposals were debated again at a further general meeting in May 1973[37] when the legislation was going through Parliament, and whilst four resolutions were passed opposing various provisions in the bill, as the number attending was small it was decided to hold a ballot on each of the resolutions in the Library on 17 May, but whether the ballot was held, or if it was, its outcome is unknown as there is no record of any ballot.[38]

---

33  *Report of a committee to consider, in the context of civil liberties and human rights, measures to deal with terrorism in Northern Ireland* (The Gardiner report), Cmnd. 5847, p. 39, para. 128.

34  The Law Society surmounted equally severe stresses, see Hewitt, *The Law Society of Northern Ireland A History*, pp 61-65.

35  (1907-85), a judge of the high court in England and Wales 1956-68, a lord of appeal in ordinary from 1968 until his death in 1985.

36  MGM 28 Mar. 1973.

37  MGM 16 May 1973. There had been an unsuccessful attempt to convene a meeting on 4 May which failed as inadequate notice had been given.

38  There is no reference to the meeting in subsequent Bar Council or General Meeting minutes.

Although there were to be many occasions in succeeding years when the Bar was faced with problems created by the continuing violence, this was the last general meeting which considered such divisive issues. It is to the credit of the Bar that despite the strains placed on its cohesion and collegiality by these external events, the Bar did not fracture into separate groups divided along religious and political lines, but continued to play a united and vital role in upholding the rule of law. One problem that arose within weeks of the May 1973 general meeting was symptomatic of the many practical difficulties faced by barristers and solicitors at that time. Barristers and solicitors alike were being searched and having their papers searched at the Maze prison when they went to consult clients.[39] Succeeding years have made every member of the community familiar with being searched at airports and elsewhere, but this was a new experience for the legal profession, one that irritated many. However, a much more serious matter was that counsel's papers were being searched, and attempts made to read them. The searching of papers, or attempts to read them, was clearly a significant inroad into the confidentiality of discussions between counsel and client. A difficulty of a more universal type later that year was caused by the huge increase in oil prices brought about by the Arab–Israeli war. As a result the Bar Council had to consider how members might be given access to petrol supplies to enable them to travel to various courts 'as the proper administration of justice required'.[40]

Nineteen seventy two was a year of exceptional violence, as can be seen from the following figures. There were 10,628 shooting incidents, 1,382 explosions, 467 deaths, of which 241 were civilians, 146 members of the security forces (the regular army, the Ulster Defence Regiment and the full-time and part-time Royal Ulster Constabulary).[41] Thousands of people, civilians and members of the security forces were injured, and many other grave crimes were committed. The Bar was not immune from the effects of this appalling level of terrorist violence, and on 11 October 1972 William Staunton QC RM was shot whilst leaving his daughter to school. He never recovered consciousness and died on 25 January 1973. Judge Rory Conaghan QC and Martin McBirney QC RM were shot dead in their homes on the morning of 16 September 1974. Not only were these murders an attempt

39  BCM 4 June 1973.
40  BCM 3 Dec. 1973.
41  The Gardiner Report, p. 61, Appendix B.

by the IRA to destroy the legal system and reduce the community to an even more lawless state, but all three had been close friends of many who were still at the Bar. Sadly, they were not to be the only members of the judiciary or members of the Bar to be murdered in succeeding decades. The murders of Judge William Doyle QC, shot on 16 January 1983 as he left church after Mass, and of Lord Justice Gibson and his wife Cecily, killed by a car bomb on 25 April 1987 as they crossed the border from the Republic of Ireland, were further assaults on the rule of law. Serving members of the judiciary were not the only victims of murder attempts, as can be seen from the death of Edgar Graham, a member of the Bar, a lecturer in the law faculty at Queen's University, and an Ulster Unionist member of the Northern Ireland Assembly, who was murdered at Queen's on 7 December 1983. Others survived terrorist attacks. Lord MacDermott, the former lord chief justice, was injured by a bomb concealed in a lectern at the University of Ulster at Jordanstown in 1977 when he was delivering a lecture. With characteristic determination he offered to return to complete the lecture. Sir Robert Lowry, his successor, narrowly escaped being shot in a sniper attack as he arrived at Queen's University for a meeting. Judge Garret McGrath QC suffered severe and lasting injuries which eventually forced him to retire from the county court bench. Other judges and resident magistrates had their homes wrecked by explosions. Given the intimacy of the Bar these murders and attacks on friends and former colleagues had a profound impact on the Bar. After various suggestions as to an appropriate form of memorial to Staunton, Conaghan and McBirney had been considered, in April 1976 the Bar Council noted that 79 members of the Library had entered into covenants in favour of the Corrymeela Community.[42] There were inconclusive discussions at the Bar Council from time to time about an appropriate form of memorial for members of the judiciary who had been murdered. In 1991 it was decided to erect a plaque to commemorate previous members of the Library who had been murdered. However, despite the decision to erect the plaque as soon as possible, nothing was done. It was not until 2000 that the benchers took the initiative to remedy this unpardonable omission by commissioning a memorial plaque. This was placed in the judges' corridor at the entrance to the Court of Appeal and unveiled at the end of 2000.[43]

---

42 The Community was set up in 1965 at Ballycastle, Co. Antrim to promote reconciliation between both sides of the community in Northern Ireland. Its founder, and first leader, was the Rev. Ray Davey, a Presbyterian minister.

43 BM 27 Oct. 2000.

Although former members of the Bar gave their lives to uphold the rule of law, and the Bar suffered the heaviest losses of life inflicted on the legal profession by terrorists, mostly republican but some by loyalists, grievous losses were also suffered by the solicitors' profession. Rory O'Kelly, a solicitor who had previously practised in Dungannon, was murdered in Coalisland, Co. Tyrone on 4 March 1977 because he was a member of the department of public prosecutions. Tom Travers RM, although gravely wounded, survived an attack on 8 April 1984 in which his daughter was murdered. Two prominent solicitors murdered by loyalist terrorists were Patrick Finucane, murdered in front of his wife and family on 12 February 1989; and Rosemary Nelson, killed by a booby trap bomb under her car on 15 March 1989.

The impact on the Bar of the Troubles was not confined to the murders of former friends and colleagues. The business of the courts had to continue. The persistent violence from time to time led governments of different political complexions to propose changes to the legal system in Northern Ireland, and we have already seen the reaction to the Bar in 1973 to the proposals in the Diplock report. Any proposal or comment upon the Bar or the legal profession generally, whether relating to the criminal law or other areas of the law, which could have significant impact on the legal system as a whole and the Bar as a profession, was a legitimate and traditional source of concern to the Bar Council, particularly where something was seen as a slight on the integrity of the Bar. One such occasion occurred in November 1978 when the *Times* newspaper carried a report of remarks by the then secretary of state for Northern Ireland, Roy Mason MP, which were seen as a reflection on the integrity of barristers in Northern Ireland. This created considerable resentment, and a general meeting of the Bar was held, at which a letter from the secretary of state was read saying that he was sorry if any barrister felt slighted by his remarks, and that he had every confidence in the probity of the Northern Ireland Bar. A critical resolution was carried by a large majority.[44] Unfortunately this was not the last occasion when it was necessary to protest to the government of the day about remarks by one of its members about the legal profession. In February 1989 the Bar Council expressed its sympathy to Mrs Finucane upon the tragic death of her husband, and decided to write to the attorney general 'expressing concern at the remarks made recently by Mr Douglas Hogg MP',[45] a home

44   MGM 17 Nov. 1978.
45   BCM 22 Feb. 1989.

office minister who had criticised a number of solicitors in Northern Ireland as being unduly sympathetic to the cause of the IRA.

One of the most significant changes to take place during the 1970s was the influx of women to the Bar. For many years after her call in 1948, Sheelagh Murnaghan was the only woman in practise at the Northern Ireland Bar. Phyllis Bateson was called in Michaelmas term 1972, followed by Judith Eve in in Michaelmas term 1973. Neither practised at that time, but in 1974 four women were called in Michaelmas term, each of whom entered practice. They were Patricia Kennedy, Mary Lenaghan, Eilis McDermott and Mayo Proctor. Mary Lenaghan had the distinction of becoming the first female member of the Bar Council a few months later. Appointed Reid Professor of Criminal Law at Trinity College, Dublin in 1975, Mary McAleese, as she became, went on to have a distinguished academic career. She became director of the Institute of Professional Legal Studies and a pro vice chancellor at Queen's University before being elected President of Ireland in 1997, serving as president until the end of her second seven year term in 2011. Eilis McDermott became a QC in 1989, and served as vice-chairman of the Bar Council in 2000-2001, taking over as chairman in 2002 for the unexpired portion of his two year term upon the death of the then chairman John Cushinan QC. Mayo Proctor later became the vice-president of industrial tribunals. Since 1974 the number of women at the Northern Ireland Bar has increased rapidly and women have played a full part in the Bar and reached the heights of the profession. Several have been appointed to judicial positions at all levels below the high court. Corrine Philpott QC was vice-chairman of the Bar Council from 1991 to 1993, and Noelle McGrenera QC was vice-chairman from 2004 to 2006, and chairman from 2006 to 2008.

Understandably a major preoccupation of any profession from time to time relates to its remuneration, particularly when it is subject to statutory regulation by government, or payments by government or public agencies remain unchanged for long periods, or when there are unacceptable delays in making payments. The Bar is no exception, and, whilst the general public can be expected to be unsympathetic to disputes about the payment of fees to barristers, this is to some extent explained by publicity given to very large payments from public funds from time to time to some successful practitioners. The unwillingness of the Bar to discuss, and attempt to justify, fees in public in the past has not helped either. The last forty years have seen numerous instances where issues relating to fees to counsel for civil, criminal, and family fees work have been a source of major concern to the Bar, and no account of the history of the Bar over the last four decades would be complete without some reference to the many problems in this area, problems that have a depressing familiarity as they reoccur every few years.

The fees for both barristers and solicitors in litigation in the county courts in Ireland have been have been subject to statutory regulation by the County Court Rules Committee since 1877, and this continues in Northern Ireland to the present day with scales which prescribes and limits the amounts that can be recovered by a successful party from the losing side.[46] If the statutory fees allowed to lawyers are not revised and increased from time to time to take account of changes in the pattern of litigation and inflation the real value of the fees can decline considerably. This was the case in 1971, when a general meeting complained that the county court scales had remained unchanged since 1957. In January 1972 the Bar Council noted the need for urgent action on the county court scale fees,[47] and they were increased later that year.[48] Thereafter they have been increased at reasonably frequent intervals to take account of inflation, although that is not to say that the scales have been increased as often, or by as much, as the Bar would have liked. As any changes in statutory fees requires government approval, the process can be prolonged if the government of the day is anxious to keep the cost of litigation, and hence lawyers' fees, as low as possible.

Whatever the appropriate fee should be, delays in payments by public bodies create acute problems for those barristers who are dependent upon those payments for their livelihood. In what was to be the first of many occasions that criminal practitioners were to face problems in this area, by 1974 it was apparent that defence counsel were experiencing delays in receiving payments of legal aid fees that they were due.[49] Given that the fees for barristers were paid to the solicitors who had instructed counsel by the legal aid authorities, and the solicitors were then responsible for paying the fees to counsel, this was not an easy matter to deal with. In some

46  See Hart, 'Complexity, delay and cost-The county courts in Northern Ireland', vol. 53 (2002), NILQ, pp 125-36.
47  BCM 17 Jan. 1972.
48  By the County Court (Costs) Rules (NI) 1972, SR & O (NI) 1972, No. 331.
49  BCM 7 Jan. 1974 and 4 Feb. 1974.

instances there were considerable delays by some solicitors in submitting fees for payment, as well as delays by the legal aid authorities in making the payments. The remedy eventually put in place was to persuade the legal aid department of the Law Society (as the Law Society was responsible for the administration of the legal aid system), to arrange for advance payments of a proportion of the fees that would be allowed. However, this did not resolve all the problems, because in 1976, and again in 1978, there were concerns that in some cases counsel were only getting the advance payments, and not the entire fee paid by legal aid.[50] This proved to be a recurrent problem, and after many years of representations and complaints to the legal aid authorities, a system of direct payments of fees in criminal cases to counsel was installed, although the introduction of this scheme proved to be remarkably protracted. By 1988 an agreement in principle had been reached with the Legal Aid Department whereby it would make direct payment of fees to counsel in legally aided criminal cases, and it said that it was working on the software to enable this to be done.[51] Despite this promise, fifteen months later a system of direct payments had still not been introduced.[52] Even when it was introduced, the direct payments system did not solve all the problems, and the 1990s were characterised by increasingly acrimonious disputes with the legal aid authorities over delays in payments, disputes compounded by disagreements over the levels of fees.

For example, in February 1994 there was concern over delays by the Legal Aid Department in meeting the targets fixed by the Northern Ireland Court Service for the payment of fees.[53] Although there was progress by September 1994 in reducing the backlog in payments,[54] as we shall see this was soon offset by severe delays in processing fees in matrimonial cases. By 1998 and 1999 there were again severe delays in payment of criminal legal aid fees. Although it was reported in April 1998 that the Legal Aid Department would not be up to date with payments until December,[55] by January 1999 there was still a backlog of 1444 cases in the Department.[56] Recurrent problems such as these caused anger on the part of those who

50  BCM 28 May 1977, 11 Jan. 1978 and 7 Feb. 1978.
51  BCM 10 Feb. 1988.
52  BCM 17 May 1989.
53  BCM 9 Feb. 1994.
54  BCM 21 Sept. 1994.
55  BCM 22 Apr. 1998.
56  BCM 13 Jan. 1999.

had to wait for a very long time for payment for work that may well have extended over an appreciable period of time, something that, admittedly with the benefit of hindsight, the Bar should have been prepared to emphasise earlier than it did when publication of amounts paid to counsel became common, something that led to a good deal of unfavourable, ill-informed, and often hostile, criticism.

Not only were there continuing problems with the payments of legal aid fees to defence counsel in criminal cases, but, from time to time, the Bar Council had to intervene when there were concerns about the low level of fees paid to prosecution counsel. The first instance of this during the period covered by this chapter occurred in the 1970s when extremely high inflation had an effect on counsel's fees in several areas of work, including fees paid to prosecution counsel in criminal cases. The effect of inflation led to negotiations to secure an increase of 30% in prosecution fees in the summer of 1975.[57] At the end of 1981 there were renewed problems with the level of prosecution fees.[58] A year later this problem was compounded by the unilateral introduction by one member of the department of public prosecutions of a cut off on the level of fees paid when more than four pleas were dealt with on one day in the Crown Court. The Bar had always objected to any attempt to impose a form of 'block' fee for any type of work, and this development was vigorously resisted in negotiations with the department over the level of fees paid by it to junior counsel. These negotiations proved to be difficult and protracted, and were not completed until the summer of 1984.[59] The result was an agreed increase in the scale fees of 20%, fractionally less than the rate of inflation of 21.5% since the last revision took effect on 1 July 1981. [60] As the increase only applied to cases since 1 April 1984 this illustrates the impact of inflation on fee scales. Unless increases are back-dated the government benefits from the delay in increasing the fees, and barristers have to absorb a reduction in income in real terms before the increase, a loss for that period which they never recover. Recurrent concerns about fees, as well as other issues that impacted on criminal practitioners more than others, played a part in the decision by a number of counsel who practised in the criminal courts to

---

57  BCM 6 May 1975.
58  BCM 7 Dec. 1981.
59  BCM 13 June 1984.
60  Undated memorandum by the author to the Bar Council.

form a Criminal Bar Association at the end of 1982.[61]

Problems with fees paid to prosecution counsel by the Department of Public Prosecutions, and its successor the Public Prosecution Service, as well as legal aid fees paid to defence counsel, have continued to pose severe problems for members of the Bar until the present day. In 1988 the Bar learnt of proposals to reduce defence fees to below the level of fees paid in 1982, leading a general meeting to recommend in March 1988 '...that no member of the Bar shall accept any brief in any legally-aided case for remuneration less than currently paid'.[62] The issue was referred to again at another general meeting the following year.[63] In February 1991 the Bar Council was informed that it was believed there were proposals to reduce the fees, possibly to a level 20 to 30% below the rates set in 1987.[64] In the event these proposals were not pursued, but developments in another area concerned the Bar Council in 1994[65] when it condemned a form which it believed was being issued by a firm, or firms, of solicitors requesting counsel to share the fees allowed by legal aid in the Magistrates' Courts on a 50/50 basis with the solicitors concerned. Young barristers doing defence work in these courts were vulnerable to be exploited in this fashion, and it cannot be a coincidence that the Council's action came less than two months after it approved the constitution of a Young Bar Association with membership open to those of seven years' call and under.

The year 1998 was also notable for the change in income tax law whereby professionals who had hitherto been assessed for income tax on income received were to be assessed in future on the basis of the fees that they charged.[66] Whilst this was a universal change, it clearly made life even more difficult for those who were not paid their fees promptly because they were required to pay tax on income they had not yet received. Given the major delays in payments of criminal legal aid fees to which reference has already been made, it is not surprising that suggestions that the fees might be reduced produced even greater ill-feeling. In the late 1990s problems with the delayed payment of fees in criminal cases were not confined to defence

---

61  BCM 13 Dec. 1982.
62  MGM 22 Feb. 1988.
63  MGM 8 Feb. 1989.
64  BCM 13 Feb. 1991.
65  BCM 8 Dec. 1993.
66  BCM 23 Feb. 1998.

practitioners. In January 1998 the Bar Council was told of delays in the payment of fees by the DPP. By this time prosecution fees were significantly less than the legal aid fees allowed to defence counsel, and although this differential was raised with the attorney general, Lord Williams of Mostyn QC, when he attended a Bar Council meeting in June 2000,[67] it was not until December 2003 that progress was made on resolving this issue. However, by January 2006 problems with prosecution fees was again reported to the Bar Council,[68] and in 2007 there were complaints that not only were prosecution fees being paid slowly, some senior counsel not being paid for one and a half or two years, but fees were also being reduced.[69] Difficulties with the level of prosecution fees continued thereafter. In 2009 a new scale of prosecution fees was still awaited. In 2010 the Bar Council decided that prosecution counsel should seek parity with the fees paid to defence counsel.[70] In March 2010[71] an extraordinary general meeting passed a motion that the fees paid by the Public Prosecution Service did not represent fair and reasonable remuneration. A year later discussions were still taking place between the Bar and the acting director of public prosecutions, with the Bar arguing for prosecution fees broadly equivalent to fees paid to defence practitioners.[72]

Barristers engaged in prosecution work were not the only practitioners to face difficulties over fees. A scheme for enhanced fees in what were known as Very High Cost Cases (VHCCs) had been introduced by the legal aid authorities to replace the previous scheme of fees in complex and lengthy criminal trials. By 2007 there were delays in the taxation of such cases,[73] and in late 2008 a general meeting altered the Code of Conduct for the Bar to permit counsel in such cases to withdraw from their cases. This had a significant impact on the most serious trials in the Crown Court. In January 2009 the Legal Services Commission put in place a system of interim payments and the backlog of payments was also tackled. These steps brought about some improvements, and later that year those counsel involved returned to their cases.

---

67  BCM 7 June 2000. This was one of the few occasions since 1972 when the attorney general attended a Bar Council meeting. Lord Goldsmith QC attended a meeting on 5 June 2002, and Baroness Scotland QC attended one on 16 Jan. 2008.
68  BCM 18 Jan. 2006.
69  BCM 17 Jan. 2007 and 14 Mar. 2007.
70  BCM 10 Mar. 2010.
71  MGM 25 Mar. 2010.
72  BCM 6 Apr. 2011.
73  BCM 14 Nov. 2007.

The continuing problems over the payment of defence fees, and the response of criminal practitioners, attracted considerable public attention, but they were not the only practitioners to suffer because of severe delays by the legal aid authorities in agreeing proper fees for legally aided cases, and by not making prompt payment. Practitioners in family law cases at all levels, who are predominantly women, were even more gravely affected. Their plight, and the length of time it took to get the legal aid authorities to agree, and then to make, proper payments for work done, was much greater than their criminal law colleagues. Acute difficulties with the legal aid authorities over the levels and payments of fees for various types of family work continued for over a decade, causing real hardship for many practitioners in this field, some of who were forced to leave the Bar as a result. A sign of the difficulties that were to come was seen in March 1996 when it became apparent that payments of legal aid fees in matrimonial cases were starting to fall behind payments for criminal cases, and delays of up to three years were not unusual.[74] By the beginning of 1997 an agreement had been reached with the court service over fees to be paid in cases under the Children (Northern Ireland) Order 1995.[75] By the spring of 1999 the position had deteriorated again, with the Bar pressing for interim payments, and by the summer of 1999 the feeling amongst family practitioners was that consideration was given to withdrawing from family cases. Nevertheless, protracted negotiations continued with the legal aid authorities, although it was to be several years before any real progress was made.

A major difficulty that contributed to these delays concerned the taxation of costs in cases under the Children Order. All concerned, including the legal aid authorities, had accepted that county court judges (who dealt with most of the cases under the Children Order) had the power to make orders for taxation of costs under the 1995 Order, but doubts arose as to the correctness of this view. In July 2002 Mr Justice Kerr ruled in a judicial review[76] that county court judges did not have such a power, and he suggested that amending legislation was required. This ruling (which effectively confirmed the reasoning of district judge Wells in a number of cases in which he declined to tax costs in such cases) was a major blow to the family Bar as it meant that there was no mechanism whereby costs could be assessed and paid in many family cases. A

---

74  BCM 13 Mar. 1996 and 17 Apr. 1996.
75  BCM 15 Jan. 1997.
76  *In the matter of an application by Thompsons solicitors* [2002] NIQB 39.

ruling by the then recorder of Belfast in September 2002[77] that county court judges did have power to certify in appropriate cases that the scales laid down twenty years before by the Legal Aid (remuneration of solicitors and counsel in county court proceedings) Order (Northern Ireland) 1981 did not provide adequate remuneration, and that appropriate fees could be assessed under Article 3 of the 1981 Order by a legal aid assessment committee, provided the prospect of some relief for hard-pressed family law practitioners. However, this ruling only applied to some cases. In addition, the large number of such cases, as well as the need to correct invalid orders that had already been made, meant that it would inevitably be some time before assessment committees could consider, and where appropriate certify higher fees in Article 3 cases than those laid down in 1981, and then for payments to be made.

By June 2003 the situation for many family law practitioners had become so bad that it was reported to the Bar Council that members of the Family Bar Association were leaving practice because they were not being paid. A year later the position had not improved, and it was estimated that around £100000 in unpaid fees was owed to members of the Family Bar Association.[78] By February 2005 it was believed that agreement had been reached with the legal aid authorities allowing direct payments to be paid to counsel in some cases, and for payments to be back dated.[79] Unfortunately, it soon emerged that what the legal aid authorities proposed was an 'all-in' fee for such cases, and that the figure was not a brief fee (that is only for the preparation and first day of any hearing) as the Bar thought, and the 'agreement' collapsed.[80] The situation became even worse in succeeding years. Despite efforts that were made in 2007 to agree an interim scheme for payments in Article 3 cases, by June of that year there had been no payments of fees in family cases for three years.[81] Although some progress had been made by 2008 over payments in Children Order cases, there had still been no payments for family cases in the magistrates' court, or appeals in such cases to the county courts.[82]

Given the deplorable delays by the authorities in making payments, as

---

77 South East Belfast HSST and TS and LC (19 Sept. 2002) County 94.
78 BCM 11 June 2003 and 9 June 2004.
79 BCM 9 Feb. 2005.
80 BCM 16 Mar. 2005.
81 BCM 7 Feb. 2007 and 20 June 2007.
82 BCM 29 Apr. 2008.

well as their failure to provide reasonable rates of remuneration for family law cases, difficulties that, as we have seen, had by then persisted for ten years, it is hardly surprising that in January 2009 members of the Family Bar Association decided to withdraw from Children Order cases.[83] No doubt this drastic action to which they had been driven resulted in some action by the authorities over these fees, and, although there were still some outstanding issues, in May the Family Bar Association decided to resume doing Children Order cases before county court judges in the family care centres.[84] Nevertheless, it was not until March 2010[85] that family practitioners were content with the fees suggested by the Legal Services Commission for cases heard in the family care centres, and the new system of fees was soon seen to be working well.[86]

If any lesson can be learnt from this unhappy saga, it is that government must be prepared to review at reasonable intervals the rates of remuneration paid by the state to lawyers to ensure that the rates provide fair remuneration for practitioners in the fields affected. This is not to say that practitioners are entitled to preferential treatment, only that unless they are paid a fair rate, and paid promptly, economic factors will inevitably force practitioners to give up the work. As a result clients who need the services of lawyers will suffer from being deprived of those services.

Unlike the practitioners that we have considered, for many years civil practitioners in the high court did not suffer comparable travails or hardships, and personal injury litigation in particular flourished. Broadly speaking, the system whereby the taxing master fixed interlocutory fees worked satisfactorily as he was prepared to increase interlocutory fees for pleadings from time to time to take account of inflation. A scale consisting of a number of bands for brief fees for senior and junior counsel (known as 'the Comerton Scale' after Alan Comerton QC who devised it), was widely accepted by defence solicitors and their insurance clients, and applied by both plaintiffs' and defendants' counsel. Updated versions were devised from time to time. However, that is not to say that there everything was plain sailing from the Bar's perspective, and there were disputes about civil fees from time to time. One such dispute concerned fees paid to senior

83 BCM 14 Jan. 2009.
84 BCM 24 June. 2009.
85 BCM 10 Mar. 2010.
86 BCM 21 Apr. 2010.

counsel in high court actions where cases fell within the county court jurisdiction. This had been increased from £5000 in 1982 to £10000 in 1992, and to £15000 in 1993, with the effect that a very significant transfer of litigation from the high court to the county court took place. By 2000 the number of civil bills dealt with in the county court had almost doubled, whilst the number of actions dealt with in the high court had declined by very nearly half. [87] This had perhaps been anticipated by the insurance industry following the abolition of juries in personal injury cases in 1987, something that the Bar vigorously opposed for many years[88] because it maintained that this would lead to a reduction in awards of damages in such cases, and so disadvantage plaintiffs. In any event in 1988 many insurers made it clear that they intended to refuse to pay the fees of senior counsel in any personal injury case which was settled and where the damages did not exceed £15000, a position reluctantly recognised by the Bar.[89] In 1990 many insurers went further, and indicated that they would refuse to pay any fee to senior counsel where the damages did not exceed £15000.

Further pressure by insurers on barristers doing personal injury work was evident in 1994 when the Bar Council was told of pressure on juniors appearing for defendants in the county courts to accept a lower fee than that which they were entitled to under the county court rules, a practice opposed by the Bar as it would undermine the 'swings and roundabouts' principle which is a fundamental principle of the county court cost scales.[90] That insurers continued to exert pressure on their counsel to accept less than the statutory scale fee was again reported in 2007.[91] The practice of insurers settling cases directly with plaintiffs' solicitors increased significantly around this time,[92] and has had a very significant impact on the Bar. Whilst insurers had approached solicitors directly to settle cases for many years, and some cases were settled by solicitors without counsel being briefed, the practice of insurers objecting to paying counsel a brief fee in such cases became more frequent as insurers attempted to drive down the cost of litigation. Provided clients were properly advised by solicitors as to the strength and value of their cases the Bar could not legitimately object to

87  Hart, ' Complexity, delay and cost, the county courts in Northern Ireland' Vol. 53 [2002] NILQ, p. 127.
88  For an example of the Bar's opposition see BCM 7 Dec. 1981.
89  MGM 24 June 1988 and 20 Oct. 1988.
90  See the judgment of Sir Robert Carswell LCJ in *Re C and H Jefferson* [1998] NI 404 at p. 409.
91  BCM 15 Jan. 1997.
92  BCM 1 June 1996.

being cut out completely from the process of negotiation. They could, and did, object to giving advice on the plaintiff's case and then not receiving a brief fee,[93] particularly when solicitors 'cherry picked' cases, settling the simpler cases direct with the insurers on the basis of counsel's opinion but not briefing counsel to negotiate. Faced with this challenge, in February 2009 the Bar Council sanctioned a major departure from traditional practice by permitting direct negotiations with an insurance company where the insurance company had not instructed any legal representatives. However, this was subject to two conditions. The first was that if the plaintiff client was present, then the barrister may only conduct such negotiations if attended by the instructing solicitor (or member of the solicitor's staff). The second condition was that provision had to made for counsel's fee.[94]

One area where the Bar fought a losing battle was the proposal to effectively abolish juries in personal injury cases in the high court. Although this had been done in England in the 1930s, jury trial remained an integral part of the high court in Northern Ireland for many decades, and was defended as ensuring that damages were in line with the views of the general public. Faced with criticism that the cost of litigation in Northern Ireland was higher because of higher awards by juries, under direct rule the Westminster government was unsympathetic to the continued use of juries in personal injury cases. Although the government did not proceed with a proposal in 1981 that juries be abolished in such cases,[95] it was evident that at some point the proposal would be brought forward again. At an extraordinary general meeting held in January 1982 to discuss the issue the chairman of the Bar Council reported that the Lord Chancellor, Lord Hailsham, was irrevocably convinced that jury trial in such cases was out of date. It was also reported that there was pressure from the Northern Ireland Office to speed up the disposal of, and to reduce the expense of, high court civil actions, and that although the Bar had suggested improvements these were felt to not go far enough by the judges.[96] In the event, the government did not renew its proposal until February 1987. In a final bid to rally political support at Westminster against the proposal the Bar Council even decided to employ a public relations firm to lobby on its behalf.[97] However, the

93   BCM 13 Feb. 2008.
94   BCM 11 Feb. 2009.
95   MGM 22 June 1981.
96   MGM 21 Jan. 1982.
97   MGM 21 Jan. 1982.

pressure to abolish what was seen by many as an anachronistic survival was irresistible, and to all intents and purposes civil juries in all but defamation and wrongful imprisonment cases were finally abolished later that year, bringing Northern Ireland into line with England and Wales.

It would be easy, but wrong, to infer from this lengthy review of the problems relating to fees and jury trials that the Bar was concerned only with its income, and standing in the way of change, and nothing else. Some of the other matters that were dealt with by the Bar Council over these years were less controversial. At the end of March 1973 the Bar said farewell to Sergeant Breheney who had attended all its members with impeccable courtesy and kindness since his appointment in 1954.[98] Another break with the days when the Library was a smaller, more close knit community, came in April 1980 with the retirement of Mrs Betty Steele who had run the servery with charm and kindness over the years.[99] Other matters were simply noted, as when in 1973 William Doyle QC resigned as a resident magistrate and returned to practice at the Bar for some years before being appointed a county court judge. In 1988 the resignation of A.E. Donaldson QC as a county court judge was also noted when he resumed practice. In returning to practice after resigning their judicial positions both were following the examples of those who, as we have already seen, took a similar course in the 1940s and 1960s.

A contentious issue with which the Bar was somewhat unexpectedly faced arose in the 1990s when it was faced with demands that it abandon its traditional costume of wig and gown, demands that seem to not to value the benefits of distinguishing members of a proud profession by their apparel. In 2005 and 2006 the family judge at the time pressed the Bar to dispense with wigs and gowns in family cases,[100] pressure resisted by young practitioners in particular. The lord chief justice issued a practice direction in 2006[101] saying that judges would not wear robes in such cases, save in exceptional circumstances, and encouraging members of the Bar not to wear wigs and gowns in such cases. The chairman of the Bar issued a tactful but firm memorandum to members later that year accepting that when children are giving evidence it would not be appropriate for barristers to wear wigs and gowns, but making clear that

98   BCM 2 Apr. 1973.
99   BCM 14 Apr. 1980.
100 BCM 11 May 2005, 18 Jan. 2006 and 15 Mar. 2006.
101 Practice Direction 4/2006.

The Bar Council remains committed to the wearing of a barrister's robes as a significant and tangible symbol of the unique role of the barrister in court proceedings and will support the wearing of wigs and gowns by members. It is the view of the Council that the fact that a Judge is not robed does not make it inappropriate for a barrister to robe.[102]

This clear statement of the Bar's justification for wearing the uniform of the profession is a dignified and appropriate response to iconoclasts who would like professional dress to be abandoned altogether, thereby rendering barristers indistinguishable from others in court. Barristers continue to wear wigs and gowns in the family courts. A similar challenge to the wearing of wigs in civil cases was brought before the annual meeting of the Bar in June 2010 but defeated,[103] reaffirming the rejection of a similar challenge in 1992.[104]

As can be seen from the chapters relating to education, accommodation, governance and call there were many other pressing and significant challenges with which the Bar has had to grapple over the decades from 1969 to the present day. Despite the gravity and multiplicity of these challenges, the Bar can point to areas where it took the initiative to bring forward proposals designed to improve the workings of the legal system, even though the responsibility for the implementation of changes in these areas was outside its control. A significant practical proposal made by the Bar was that Order 25 of the Rules of the Supreme Court be changed to require the pre-trial disclosure of medical reports in personal injury cases, and prohibiting a party from relying on medical evidence whose contents had not been disclosed. This procedural reform was designed to reduce the need for medical witnesses to attend to give evidence, and so reduce the cost of litigation and disruption to the health service. The idea had been discussed for some time, but no definite proposals had been brought forward by the Supreme Court Rules Committee, the statutory body responsible for the rules of the high court and court of appeal. In December 1983 the Bar Council requested that its proposals should be brought before the committee.[105] This led to the adoption of the main thrust of the Bar's proposals, although not all the Bar's suggestions were accepted by the committee, and the new rule came into effect on 1 April 1985.

102 11 Dec. 2006.
103 MGM 27 May 2010.
104 MGM 19 Nov. 1992.
105 BCM 14 Dec. 1983.

Another proposal initiated by the Bar about this time which brought about a major change in the court structure, albeit one that took a long time to reach complete fruition, was the creation of a specialist commercial court as part of the high court. Although there had long been such a specialist commercial court in England, the need for such court had not been felt in Northern Ireland. However, by the 1980s the growing volume and importance of commercial litigation, almost all of which was tried by a judge sitting without a jury, led to a feeling that such cases were not given sufficient priority because of the needs of the jury list, which was dominated by personal injury litigation. The Bar Council decided that the problem needed to be addressed. At its request, in 1985 Alan Comerton QC drew up proposals for the creation of a separate commercial court. This was accepted by the judiciary, but for many years one of its central features was not implemented. Whilst individual judges were appointed to case manage the pre-trial stages of commercial litigation in a separate list, it was not until the appointment of Mr Justice Weatherup as the commercial judge in January 2010 that the list finally received its own judge specifically allocated to try such cases.

The 1980s also saw a fundamental change in the way in which barristers could be instructed in certain types of litigation when the Bar changed its professional code of conduct to permit direct access by certain professions without the need to instruct a solicitor first. Direct professional access as it is known, had its origin in a report to the Bar Council in 1988 from a committee chaired by W.A. Campbell QC. This committee had been set up to consider how the Bar might modernise. It suggested that one area would be to permit direct access in certain categories of litigation where the client was a member of a profession recognised for this purpose, and the intervention of a solicitor was unnecessary. An example was where an accountant wished to instruct counsel in a tax matter. The committee reported in June 1988,[106] and, even though the proposal represented a major departure from the centuries old requirement that a barrister could only give advice to a client after being instructed by a solicitor, it was favourably received by the Bar. The necessary changes to the rules of the Bar were made by the end of 1990, and formally adopted in March 1991.[107] By May 1993 nine categories of profession had been recognised for this purpose.[108] By 22 June 1994 this had increased to 13,[109] and further increased

106 BCM 15 June 1988.
107 BCM 13 Mar. 1991.
108 BCM 19 May 1993.
109 BCM 22 June 1994.

to 16 by the time of the launch of the Bar Library Directory in 1996. The Directory was another initiative designed to bring the services that members could offer to the attention of the public and members of other professions by identifying individual barristers and their particular areas of interest.

An area where the Bar has supported initiatives designed to improve the range of legal services in the widest sense that are available to the legal profession and to the wider public was in the field of legal publishing. The market for locally published legal textbooks was so small in Northern Ireland that only a handful of such books were published from 1921 onwards. There was a tremendous need for an organisation that could provide legal publishing to lawyers and others concerned with the law and legal system of Northern Ireland. Accordingly, in 1980 the law faculty at Queen's set up the Servicing the Legal System Programme (SLS). SLS has delivered a tremendous range of legal publications and related services such as seminars, conferences and training courses through the medium of SLS Publications (NI) Ltd. Inevitably this needed considerable financial sponsorship from a range of sources, and from the inception of SLS in 1980 until its recent demise the benchers, the Bar Council, and then the Executive Council, played their part in providing financial support.

An inevitable consequence of the huge increase in membership of the Bar since 1969 has been that members of the Library of all ages are less familiar with many of their colleagues than was the case in the past, although with just over 700 barristers presently in practice it is impracticable to expect that every individual can hope to have the same degree of contact, personal as well as professional, with everyone else to the extent that was possible 40 or 50 years ago. Nevertheless, considerable efforts have been made to try to ensure that the personal friendships that play a vital part in augmenting the sense of professional camaraderie and respect that are essential to the effectiveness of any profession, especially the Bar, are maintained and strengthened wherever possible. One way has been to promote social gatherings. Dinners and dances of various kinds have been held for many years. The tradition of Bar dinners to entertain newly-promoted judges has been maintained despite the demise of the Circuit, but, by their nature, such dinners are occasional. One way of supplementing them was to introduce regular term dinners when members might dine together. These were introduced in 1985, and were held regularly for several years, but have fallen into disuse. Since 2006 the benchers have held two dinners each year at which they entertain students of the Inn, pupils and their masters.[110] Each student is therefore entertained twice, once when a student, and then as a newly-called pupil the next year. These dinners, and the dinner which the pupils give each year for their masters to mark the completion of their compulsory pupillage, and to which they invite members of the judiciary, provide a valuable means whereby the younger members can meet the senior members, and the judges, on an informal, social basis. Other functions are organised by the various sporting and social groups within the Bar. In 1982 there was a suggestion that a Bar Club be formed to which the various social and sporting groups would affiliate, with the proposed club having its own premises.[111] Whilst nothing came of this, there are several clubs and societies which provide the opportunity for those with similar interests to meet. The Bar Golfing Society is by far the oldest, but groups such as the rugby club, the hockey club, and fishing club wax and wane, allowing judges and barristers of different ages to mingle. The Bar Music and Drama Society provides a similar opportunity. Each year the Bar Council decides to support a particular charity nominated by members of the Bar, and this has enabled considerable sums to be donated to deserving charities each year, generated by donations and by social events such as dances. For example, in 2008 the Bar Charity Committee raised £82000 which was divided between two charities.[112]

As we approach the end of the present chapter it is appropriate to note some developments in recent years that may well have significant implications for the Bar in years to come. The first is the development of the solicitor advocate practising in both the criminal and civil fields. Quite understandably some solicitors wish to ensure that they can exercise their talents as advocates, and although they have long had a right of audience in the Crown Court (and before that at assizes), it is only in recent years that some solicitors have sought to act as advocates in criminal trials, and on occasions to be briefed as such by their own firms, or to be briefed by other solicitors. The latter practice in particular has been a source of considerable concern to the Bar. It was anxious that clients were told that they had the right to be represented by a barrister if they wished. The Bar was equally anxious that solicitor advocates would be bound by the same high standards of professional behaviour required of barristers. In other words that there should be 'a level playing field' between barristers on the one hand, and solicitors who were in effect acting as both

---

110 BM 28 Oct. 2005.
111 BCM 13 Dec. 1982.
112 MGM 1 Apr. 2009.

barristers and solicitors on the other.[113] To this end, the Bar Council made vigorous representations to the Law Society that there was a need for a satisfactory code of conduct governing solicitor advocates so that the latter did not have an unfair advantage over barristers, particularly when solicitors sought to be granted rights of audience in both the high court and the court of appeal. Whilst they have now been granted such rights by Part 8 of the Justice Act (Northern Ireland) 2011, solicitor advocates will be subject to various restrictions designed to ensure that there is such a level playing field. The Law Society is empowered to 'authorise' (i.e. licence) solicitor advocates, but it must also make regulations governing the education, training and experience of authorised individuals. Authorised individuals who are minded to retain another solicitor to represent a client before either the high court or the court of appeal must advise the client in writing of the advantages and disadvantages of representation by an authorised solicitor and by counsel, and must act in the best interests of the client when doing so, as well as advising the client that the choice of legal representation is solely a matter for the client to decide.

Another development in recent years has been the increasingly frequent appearance of barristers from England, and from the Republic, in both civil and criminal cases. Competition of this sort poses a number of challenges for the Bar. By Easter 2013 there were approximately 80 external members of the Bar based outside Northern Ireland, but who practise occasionally in Northern Ireland.[114] Whilst it is proper to ensure that such barristers are bound by the disciplinary and educational provisions that bind Northern Ireland barristers, legitimate completion cannot be avoided and must be faced. Some English counsel who specialise in particular fields, such as patent or tax law, where there is insufficient, or perhaps no, choice of specialist Northern Ireland counsel have always come over from time to time, and continue to do so. They provide a service for local clients that cannot be provided otherwise. Where there are local counsel who specialise in the relevant area, be it criminal law, judicial review or another field, local counsel have to provide their local clients with a service that is as efficient, economical and of equal intellectual calibre as their English counterparts if Northern Ireland barristers are to survive and prosper. Such competition is in the interests of both the public and the profession because it should help to keep standards at a high level.

113 BCM 10 May. 2006.
114 Information to the author from the Bar Council staff 28 Mar. 2013.

The last challenge comes from within the Bar itself, and has the potential to be the most significant challenge of all, and that is the growing number of barristers who practise from home and do not subscribe to the Bar Library. By November 2007 it was believed that 12 members of the Bar were now practising from home,[115] and in March 2013 it was thought that 12 were practising from home.[116] This tendency, if it continues, has significant implications for the health of the Bar. The Bar Library loses subscription income. In some cases the impetus for members leaving the Library but continuing to practise, may be because they may not be able to afford to pay their Library subscription, or may not regard it as value for money. Whatever the reason may be in each individual case, that so many barristers are practising outside the Library system is a cause for deep concern, and could create many problems in the future. For example there might be problems in maintaining professional standards, whether educational or disciplinary. Whilst membership of the Library has never been a formal requirement for practice at the Northern Ireland Bar, since 1921 almost all members of the Northern Ireland Bar have been subscribers to the Library. More than any other single factor that has given the Northern Ireland Bar its unique sense of collegiality, friendship and mutual professional and personal respect. These features have played a vital, and irreplaceable, role in sustaining, and holding together, the Northern Ireland Bar throughout its nine decades of existence as an independent Bar, and in particular during the long and dark years when society and the rule of law were constantly assailed by relentless, vicious and anarchic terrorists. It is therefore a matter of great concern when more than the occasional individual decides that he or she can practise without the cohesion that comes from daily contact with one's professional colleagues and opponents outside the courtroom, and without the research and support facilities provided to its subscribers by the Library.

115 BCM 14 Nov. 2007.
116 Information to the author from the Bar Council staff 28 Mar. 2013.

# CHAPTER TEN:

# Decades of physical expansion and new accommodation

Whilst the Bar Library provided sufficient space for the Bar when it opened in 1933, the increase in numbers after the Second World War placed an increased strain on the physical fabric and space of the Library. There was an increasing need for improved and modernised facilities for members, particularly for improved telephones, as well as an increasingly urgent need to increase the space to accommodate the dramatic and constant increase in numbers from 1970 onwards that has already been noted in Chapter Six. However, although in the early 1960s these problems were far in the future, there was still a need to find extra space for members to type, and to hold meetings of the Bar Council. This need, whilst obvious, was not one that could be easily met because the lay out of the Law Courts did not make it easy to provide extra space. No provision had been made in the original plans for later expansion, and when it became necessary to accommodate the huge expansion in numbers at the Bar that occurred from the 1970s onwards, initially this could only be done by moving into space hitherto used by other occupants of the building when they moved elsewhere. As we shall see, in the event each expansion only produced a short-lived amelioration of the acute shortage of space that was to be a feature of the Library for decades.

When the Bar Council sought some extra space in the early 1960s, the only way this could be provided by the public works department of the ministry of finance was to build a small, single floor, structure on one of the internal spaces on the ground floor of the building. In February 1961 the cost was estimated at £1650, and the lord chief justice approved an approach to the chief architect.[1] When the work was complete[2] this provided an extra 468 square feet[3] used to create a room named the Nicholson Room.[4] Although the decline in numbers at the Bar from 67 in 1962 to 56 in 1967 meant that there was a short period when the accommodation problem was eased, nevertheless there was still a shortage of desks. When the author was called in 1969 some of those called the

1    BCM 23 Feb. 1961.
2    BCM 6 Feb. 1964.
3    BCM 1 Mar. 1962 and 6 Feb. 1964.
4    In memory of Cyril Nicholson QC.

year before did not have their own seats, and those without seats had to find a vacant seat close to their master's desk where they could sit when its owner was not using it, or use their master's desk when he was absent.

The telephones could hardly be described as a system. Incoming calls were answered by Sergeant Breheney or one of the other members of staff, and the intended recipient called to the phone. This was a completely inadequate system, and one which was extremely frustrating, both for the Bar and for solicitors. As early as 1961 it was recognised that there was a need for more telephone lines, but the plans for what became the Nicholson Room prevented space being made available for more telephones.[5] Matters came to a head in November 1967. Prompted by a letter from a solicitor complaining about the inadequacies of the system, the Bar Council decided to engage a telephonist and install additional lines,[6] although it took nearly a year to install a separate booth for the telephonist.[7] The inadequate telephone facilities were to prove a continuing source of complaint, both from outside and inside the Library, for many years to come.

Although the Nicholson Room provided welcome additional space, it was obvious that further space would be desirable, indeed necessary, were the Bar to seek to improve its services to members by providing more shelving for books and room for the storage of members' papers. In 1965, when the prospect of the official assignee's office becoming vacant when the official assignee moved elsewhere arose,[8] the Bar Council did not hesitate to stake a claim to this space, as the official assignee's office in Room 13 adjoined the Smoke Room and offered an ideal route for expansion.[9] By November of that year the attorney general was able to report that the Bar's claim to Room 13 would be met, although economies in the department of works (which would deal with the matter) meant that there was no immediate prospect of this space becoming available.[10] In the event it was to be several years before this additional space became available to the Bar, and it was not until the early 1970s that the Bar Library expanded to incorporate Room 13, the extension being named the MacDermott Room.[11] This involved the construction of a new internal door

---

5    BCM 23 Feb. 1962.

6    BCM 4 Dec. 1967.

7    BCM 23 Sept. 1968 when it was noted that preparations were under way to install a booth for the telephonist, and racks in the ante room for solicitors' mail.

8    BCM 20 Sep. 1965.

9    BCM 16 May and 6 June 1966.

10   BCM 7 Nov. 1966.

11   The first reference to the extra space is in BCM of 7 May 1972.

giving access up steps into a large reading room of 850 square feet. In the mid-1970s additional male and female toilets were also constructed.[12]

The creation of the MacDermott Room resulted in a sizeable increase in the size of the Library but that was not the only extra space made available to the Bar in the early 1970s. In the 1960s the benchers explored the possibility of obtaining space within the Law Courts that could be used to provide a location for informal meetings. By November 1966 a scheme had been drawn up to allow the conversion of the first floor corridor adjoining the public galleries of the courts to be converted for this purpose,[13] although it was not until January 1972 that the work on what became known as the Long Gallery was complete and it became available for use by all members of the Inn, including students.[14] This was a commendable initiative that provided the first permanent space available for use by all members of the Inn, with newspapers and coffee available. Nevertheless, despite providing a welcome area where members of the Bar could go for a quiet conversation, or to read a brief, the Long Gallery was somewhat out of the way, and so it was never used a great deal by either the Bar or by the judges. Eventually it was closed and returned to the Court Service.

Although the addition of the MacDermott Room provided a respite to the pressure on accommodation in the Library, this proved to be only temporary because the growth in numbers in succeeding decades proved to be relentless, as can be seen from the figures below.

Barristers in private practice, 1969-2010.[15]

| Year | QCs | Juniors | Total |
|------|-----|---------|-------|
| 1969 | 22 | 39 | 61 |
| 1970 | 21 | 53 | 74 |
| 1975 | 21 | 93 | 114 |

12  Inn file I.A 1 1966-1971.
13  Ibid. Letter to J.A.L. McLean of 17 Nov. 1966.
14  Ibid. Note by J.A.L. McLean.
15  The figures for 1969-1975 are taken from Table 42.2 at p. 699 of the *Final Report of the Royal Commissionon Legal Services* (1979). Those for 1980-1983 are taken from Appendix A of the Submission to the Bromley Committee by the Executive Council, and those for 1990-2010 have been provided by the Executive Council.

| | | | |
|---|---|---|---|
| 1980 | 24 | 155 | 179 |
| 1983 | 27 | 221 | 248 |
| 1990 | 30 | 270 | 300 |
| 1996 | 40 | 356 | 396 |
| 2000 | 55 | 422 | 477 |
| 2005 | 63 | 517 | 580 |
| 2010 | 68 | 562 | 610 |

This dramatic and constant increase meant that for many years the Bar Council was engaged in an almost constant process of negotiation with the government to obtain more space in the Law Courts. Eventually, this process could continue no longer because there was no longer any available space in the building, and it became inevitable that new premises had to be found, a process that we shall trace in the final part of this chapter.

By September 1977 the pressure on space was again acute, for example whilst there were only 12 seats in the Nicholson Room, 22 were using the room, and 13 students were due to be called.[16] By December of that year the Bar Council was considering expansion into the premises occupied by the probate office on the first floor of the Law Courts, thereby obtaining a further 2000 square feet and almost doubling the size of the original Bar Library before the addition of the Nicholson and MacDermott Rooms.[17] That this expansion was urgent was obvious, because there was now severe overcrowding of the Library, and by February 1978 there were already 42 members without desks, and a further 30 members were expected.[18] Unfortunately the move by the probate office depended upon that office moving into part of the Law Courts to be vacated by the legal aid department, and as it could not move out until work was completed upon its new premises, the Bar had to wait until these other moves were complete before it could take possession of the probate office, resulting in a six month delay.[19]

16   BCM 6 Sept. 1977.
17   BCM 14 Dec. 1977.
18   BCM 22 Feb. 1978
19   BCM 22 May 1978.

Overcrowding meant that it was extremely difficult to work in the Library. If they were not in court that day, or when their cases were disposed of, more and more barristers went home to work. If necessary they returned to the Library later in the day for consultations. At this time as part of its examination of the legal professions throughout the United Kingdom the Royal Commission on Legal Services was examining every aspect of the Bar and the Inn of Court, and it is hardly surprising that in 1978 one of its sub-committees suggested that the setting up of chambers be considered as an experiment. Such a move would have brought about a seismic change in the structure of the Bar, but the Bar Council agreed that this would be considered by a sub-committee that would review the lay-out of the Library.[20] However, nothing seems to have come of the suggestion, no doubt because it was believed that the extra space in the probate office extension would render such a change unnecessary. However, as we shall see, the idea of chambers was to surface from time to time as pressure on space meant that the working conditions deteriorated. Another factor was that expansion projects resulted in substantial increases in annual subscriptions. In 1980 the Bar Council received requests from two members for their subscriptions to be reduced because they lived and worked outside Belfast. This was symptomatic of a growing trend whereby some members lived much further from Belfast than had been customary in the past, and, as their practices were almost completely located in country courts, the need of some members for the facilities provided by the Library was correspondingly less. The Bar Council refused the request because to grant it would lead to further requests and could encourage the setting up of chambers.[21] In its final report in 1979 the Royal Commission described the need for additional premises as 'urgently needed',[22] characterising the existing accommodation as 'cramped and inadequate'.[23] No doubt this gave added impetus to the initial expansion into the Upper Library as it became known.

Even before the work on the extension commenced there were fears that it might well prove inadequate. As the Bar Council noted in February 1979, although there would be another 60 spaces in the extension, there was little wastage of members leaving the Bar, and intakes of about fifteen a year were

20  BCM 24 Oct. 1978.
21  BCM 3 Mar. 1980.
22  *Final Report of the Royal Commission on Legal Services* (Oct. 1979), Cmd. 7648, p. 701,
23  Ibid., p. 700.

likely in the years ahead. Detailed planning of the new extension went ahead throughout the summer of 1979, and Library subscriptions for 1980 were increased by 40% to meet the anticipated capital repayments of £11000 a year, together with increased outgoings of £6000 a year.[24] The initial tenders proved to be well in excess of what had been hoped, and a revised tender of £73000 was accepted at the end of April 1980, the cost to be financed by a bank loan of £60000, interest free loans by some senior members of the Bar being offered to bridge the gap.[25] The work proceeded rapidly and the new extension was opened in the week of 12 January 1981,[26] although the eventual cost of £76000 was greater than anticipated.[27] A sign of the changing nature of the Bar was that now there were 25 lady members of the Bar, and the opportunity was taken to convert the secretary's room on the ground floor into a ladies robing room when a new room was provided for the secretary upstairs.[28] Several older members of the Bar decided to vacate their desks downstairs and move upstairs to ensure that there was a better mix of ages and experience in the Upper Library than might otherwise have been the case.

Despite this very significant increase in the overall size of the Library, the Upper Library provided what was to be a very brief respite from the serious overcrowding that had been a feature of the 1970s. We have already seen that there was concern the extension would prove to be insufficient even before the work started. As the work was under way it was suggested to the Bar Council in September 1980 that when, as anticipated, the Law Society moved out of the Law Courts into new premises in a couple of years' time, the Bar should try to acquire the space it would vacate.[29] By December 1983 there were 248 members, a 400% increase in 14 years, and it was reported to the Bar Council that the chairman and vice-chairman of the Executive Council (which had just come into existence a few weeks before) had written to the director of the Northern Ireland Court Service saying that 'a crisis point [had been] reached regarding space in the Bar Library'. In a letter to the director in January 1984 Michael Nicholson QC, the chairman of the Executive Council, pointed out the seriousness of the situation, explaining that 'even with the new extension, which provided desks for 60 members,

---

24   BCM 5 Nov. 1979.
25   BCM 14 Apr. and 28 Apr. 1980.
26   BCM 9 Jan. 1981.
27   BCM 16 Dec. 1981.
28   BCM 28 Oct. 1980.
29   BCM 11 Sept. 1980.

there are now 79 practising members without seats. Our need for extra accommodation is extreme'.[30] Nicholson suggested that if the Bar was to be allocated all of the rooms formerly occupied by the Law Society on the ground floor, it would give up the MacDermott Room in exchange, so that room could be turned into a court for the masters, and he also suggested some other changes in the usage of rooms in the Law Courts.

The accommodation position was complicated because for some years the Court Service insisted that the Bar should pay rent for the original Bar Library space on the ground floor, as well as charging for certain common services provided throughout the building. The Bar resisted the claim for rental of the ground floor on the basis that when the Law Courts were built the government of the day accepted responsibility for providing the common services for the supreme court, including the Bar Library, and that the Bar would thereby form an integral part of the administration of justice.[31] This dispute continued for some years. It was finally resolved in December 1984 on the basis of an agreement that whilst the Bar would not pay rent for the ground floor, as well as agreeing the rent for the first floor (which the Bar always accepted was due in principle), it would pay a fixed amount a year for 10 years (calculated to take account of projected inflation) for common services, and a fixed charge for heating calculated on the same basis, thus bringing to an end protracted, detailed, and at times tense, discussions.[32] Nevertheless, the Court Service, whilst vigorously pursuing its claim against the Bar, emphasised that it was 'well-disposed to assisting the Bar to achieve the objective of increased accommodation for the Library',[33] and during the rent dispute discussions went on to identify how further space could be found by expanding on the first floor beside the Upper Library. In May 1984 the Executive Council agreed to accept an offer from the Court Service of additional space which would have the effect of slightly more than doubling the size of the existing Upper Library,[34] although in the event some more space was found later.

A key element in the planning of this further expansion was an activity survey of the usage of the Upper Library carried out over five weeks in

30  13 Jan. 1984.
31  16 Mar. 1984. Nicholson to J.M. Steele, Director of the Court Service.
32  BCM 29 Nov. 1984.
33  11 June 1984. Steele to Nicholson.
34  ECM 22 May 1984.

September and October 1984. This revealed that only on one occasion did as many as 22 members use their desks in any period, and 'that generally desks are used as a base where as the necessity arises work is carried out but in the main as an area where papers are collated and stored'.[35] Based on this, Mr Proctor[36] suggested that whilst the proposed area of 92 feet by 25 feet could provide an additional 98 seats if furnished in the conventional manner, it would be possible to arrange the area in such a way that would provide additional much-needed facilities, although with fewer seats. By providing 74 seats, it would also be possible to provide a reference library, and an area which could be closed off by moveable partitions as required and used for meetings and functions by the Bar and the Inn of Court. The additional area would also be provided with suitable shelving, lockers for members, as well as tables and seats which would be used communally by all those who did not have seats in the Library. These tables and chairs could then be re-arranged as required, and by using the moveable partitions provide 'a much needed space in which to hold the various meetings of the Bar and the Inn and for entertaining guests'.

This imaginative and well-researched proposal was approved,[37] and it provided the foundation for the plans that were then drawn up by the Inn's architect, Stanley Devon of Dennis, McIntyre and Devon, although some additional features were incorporated.[38] These proposals were vital to relieve the chronic over-crowding of the Library. This had been alleviated to a minor degree by a rearrangement to give 17 more seats in the Upper Library, and 16 more in the Main Library. Whilst that meant that all of those called in 1980 and 1981, and four of the 1982 call, now had seats, the remainder of the 1982 call did not. In addition none of those called in 1983 or 1984 had seats,[39] and this meant that by December 1984 there 43 more members than seats.[40] The reference to a 'crisis' in 1983 had been fully justified.

However, despite the urgent need for further accommodation, various difficulties prevented the work from going ahead as rapidly as all concerned would have wished. In March 1985 a number of unforeseen problems

35  Bar Library-Additional Accommodation. Undated report by W.I. Proctor.
36  The full-time secretary of the Bar and Executive Councils.
37  Undated Finance Committee Minute. MGM 6 Dec. 1984.
38  Letter from Dennis, McIntyre and Devon to Proctor 17 Jan. 1985.
39  BCM 17 Oct. 1984.
40  MGM 6 Dec. 1984.

emerged during the demolition works in the extension. It was discovered that the floor was not level over the entire area; the ceiling beams and cornices were of varying sizes and heights, resulting in a recommendation that suspended ceilings be installed; and the contractors were reluctant to 'track' or cut into the ceiling to install lighting because of heating elements buried in the ceiling.[41] By September of that year it was reported that because of delays in design work, and in preparing details of the cost, the extension might not be ready until January or Easter 1986.[42] However, even this was to prove optimistic. One advantage of the delay was that in September 1985 agreement was reached for the addition of a small room at the Chichester Street end of the extension which would allow for the provision of catering services.[43] Whilst experience was to show that this was insufficient to provide a really useful catering facility as it was more in the nature of a transit station for food prepared elsewhere in the building, nevertheless, despite its limitations, it greatly enhanced the ability of the Bar and the Inn to have functions in the Bar Library, something that had not been practicable for many years.

Of course neither the Bar nor the Law Courts were immune from the serious terrorist violence that was a feature of life in Northern Ireland at that time. In 1986 further inconvenience was caused by delays in repairing or replacing bomb-damaged windows.[44] A less obvious, but equally serious, problem was the need for workmen to be vetted and obtain security clearance, and this too played a part in the delay. Despite the contract price for the necessary work being agreed at £140000 by November 1985, with a completion date of 31 March 1986,[45] that date was dependent upon the contractors, the long-established firm of H & J Martin, being in a position to start work by mid-December. It was already clear that there would be delay because of difficulties in obtaining security clearance for their workmen. The work started on 19 March 1986, even though not all the workmen had security clearance.[46] By mid-November 1986 the work on the extension was largely complete, with the new extension available for use,[47] although it proved to

41  ECM 26 Mar. 1985.
42  BCM 16 Sept. 1985.
43  ECM 25 Sept. 1985.
44  ECM 23 Apr. 1986.
45  ECM 27 Nov. 1985.
46  ECM 19 Mar. 1986.
47  ECM 10 Sept. 1986.

be some time before all of the minor works were completed.[48] In addition to the contract for the building work, a further £48345.26 was to be spent on chairs, tables, lighting and curtains for the extension, bringing the total cost to just over £188345.[49]

Whilst the main focus on these years was on the expansion of the Bar Library, many members of the Bar devoted their time, whether wholly or predominantly, to criminal work at the County Court House on the Crumlin Road. The numbers of those using the Bar Room there were such that it was, in effect, an extension of the Bar Library. By 1987 there was a need for much-needed structural improvements in the accommodation provided by the Court Service for the Bar at the courthouse. It was therefore a considerable blow to the Bar when it was learnt in March 1987 that these improvements had to be deferred due to lack of finance.[50] In March 1988 the Executive Council agreed to spend £4000 to provide telephones, bookshelves, text books and lockers for the Bar Room there, as well as leasing a photocopier for use by members of the Bar.[51] Whilst no doubt welcomed by those who worked there, this did not remove the need for other, more substantial, work.

By the time the work on the new extension to the Bar Library came to an end it was obvious that it was essential for the Bar to take stock of the developments of recent years. Whilst the emphasis in this account so far has been on the demand for extra accommodation, this was only a part of what was necessary, because there was also a need for greatly improved facilities. The Bar was slow to come to terms with the need for these facilities, in large measure because of a widely held belief that the expansion in numbers could not continue, and that the Bar might then shrink in size. Despite the growth in the numbers of members, and the increase in the number of law books and other legal publications, it was not until 1984 that a professional librarian was appointed. Miss Miriam Dudley took up her post in April of that year, [52] and she immediately introduced a long-overdue professionalism, and many welcome innovations, to this vital service. The reluctance on the part of many members of the Bar to adapt to the arrival of new technology also meant that the Bar was slow to provide essential equipment. As early

48   ECM 12 Nov. 1986.
49   ECM 19 Feb. 1986.
50   ECM 18 Mar. 1987.
51   ECM 16 Mar. 1988.
52   BCM 12 Mar.1984.

as 1972 a proposal to buy a photocopier was deferred,[53] and although the idea was discussed again in 1978,[54] it was not until 1984 that a photocopier was purchased.[55] Until then members used the photocopier in the Law Society premises. Given that the telephones and the photocopier were coin-operated, it is hard to see why it was decided not to buy a change dispensing machine in 1972.[56] Part of this reluctance to invest in new technology no doubt reflected doubts about the reliability of the equipment, or whether it would be sufficiently used to justify the expense. Nevertheless, it has to be accepted that there was a widespread conservatism amongst members of the Library that was unsympathetic to improving facilities that many saw as quite adequate for their individual practices. By the late 1980s there was a greater willingness to embrace technological advances. In 1989 it was decided that members could install fax machines for private use in their homes, and put their private fax and telephone numbers on their notepaper. However, the general meeting which approved these innovations balked at a proposal from the Bar Council that members could have business cards describing themselves as barrister at law, no doubt because it was felt to be a form of advertising, and hence unacceptable.[57]

For many years one of the greatest needs of the Bar was an updated telephone system. Long after the expansion of the Bar started in 1970 it remained the case that members who wished to make out-going calls had to use the coin-operated telephones in the Library. As these were in constant use, members had to resort to the telephone booths containing public telephones off the Main Hall. However, there were only a handful of these, and, although the telephones were in booths with doors, inevitably privacy was not absolute. Incoming calls from solicitors or others were routed through the switchboard to the internal booths in the Library, and an announcement was then made over the loudspeaker system that there was a call for the member concerned. The number of booths was wholly inadequate to provide a remotely acceptable service. The system was eventually upgraded to provide a new exchange and extensions on members' desks in 1984,[58] and this was regarded as providing

53   BCM 1 May 1972.
54   BCM 10 Apr. 1984.
55   ECM 18 Jan. 1984.
56   BCM 1 May 1972.
57   MGM 8 Feb. 1989.
58   ECM 18 June 1984.

a vast improvement upon the previous system.[59] However, it was not long before there were fresh complaints about the inadequacy of the telephone system. Early in 1986, after dissatisfaction with the telephone system was expressed by the Law Society at a liaison committee meeting, the Bar Council accepted that the majority of complaints from members, from solicitors and from clients about the difficulty in contacting counsel, and the lengthy delays in answering calls, were justified.[60]

No doubt because of this, and the pressures on staff created by the relentless rise in numbers and the constant need for more space, in November 1986 the Bar Council appointed a committee led by its chairman Anthony Campbell QC,[61] to look at the way forward for the Bar over the next decade.[62] That such a review was essential to ensure that the Bar provided a modern and efficient service to its clients was underlined by a highly critical motion passed at the annual general meeting of the Belfast Solicitors' Association in 1987 'that the administration of the Bar Library is no longer adequate for the modern needs of both professions and requires reform'.[63] Two years later that the Executive Council approved a suggestion by the Bar Council that management consultants be engaged 'to investigate the structure of management and its effectiveness, also the facilities provided by members and the Bar as a whole to solicitors and clients'.[64]

With the completion of the further extension it became clear that the wear and tear on the fabric of the remainder of the Library meant that it was essential to refurbish and upgrade the fabric and fittings of the downstairs area, and the original upstairs extension, of the Library. It was therefore decided to carpet the original Library, together with the reception area and corridors, the MacDermott Room, the Smoke Room and the original Upper Library. As well as carpeting, the opportunity was taken to provide six new seats and 64 lockers. It was estimated that the work could cost up to £200000, financed by a loan which would require an increase of 10% in subscriptions over three years.[65] William Dowling & Co were awarded the contract, and the

59   ECM 17 Oct. 1984.
60   BCM 12 Mar. 1986.
61   Later Lord Justice Campbell.
62   BCM 12 Nov. 1986.
63   BCM 18 Nov. 1987.
64   ECM 12 Dec. 1989.
65   MGM 12 May 1987.

work was to be carried out during the Long Vacation and September of 1987. Most of the work was completed within this period,[66] although some was not completed until the end of 1989.[67] In 1989 it was decided to complete the refurbishment by doing work to the servery, the reception area, the Nicholson Room, providing new telephone booths, and extending the robing rooms and toilets, all at a total cost of £120000.[68] Most of the work was done during the Long Vacation of that year,[69] although part of the work on the robing rooms and toilets had to be postponed to the same period in 1990 because of restrictions imposed upon the contractors by the Court Service, the historic monuments and buildings branch, and the works division of the department of the environment, one of the difficulties inherent in making substantial alterations to the fabric of a building of such significance.

Two further modest extensions were completed about this time. These improved the Library premises, but did not directly increase the space for members. The first was that in 1990 it was decided to create 480 square feet of extra space above the new toilet and robing facilities being built on the ground floor, and which had not been completed in 1989. This extra work increased the total spent on this refurbishment and extension to £110000.[70] Because of the considerable increase in the size of the Bar, and the complexity of its operations there had been a substantial increase in the size of the staff, and the extra space was used to provide office accommodation for them. It is an indication of the increase in the size and expertise of the staff that by 1993 staff costs amounted to just under £200000 out of a total budget for that year of just under £750000.[71] The second extension came about as a result of the decision of the Court Service to close the staff canteen on the third floor of the building, and remove the kitchen equipment. The canteen cooking facilities had been used by the Bar for functions and naturally this decision caused considerable dismay when it was conveyed to the Bar Council in January 1991.[72] Fortunately, it proved possible to agree that the Court Service would make available an area on the second floor that could be fitted out as a primary cooking facility to complement the existing

66   BCM 17 Sept. 1987.
67   BCM 6 Dec. 1989.
68   ECM 21 June 1989.
69   ECM 20 Sept. 1989.
70   ECM 21 Mar. 1990.
71   ECM 27 Jan. 1993.
72   ECM 23 Jan. 1991.

small facility on the first floor at a cost of some £20000. Although this did not materialise until the Spring of 1994,[73] it meant that the Bar was able to continue to have functions in the building, an essential adjunct to the corporate life of both the Inn and the Bar which would otherwise have had to have been abandoned.

A major difficulty not yet referred to was the effect of the dramatic growth of the Bar on the Bar car park immediately adjoining the Library on the west side of the building. This had been almost exclusively used by the Bar since the Law Courts were opened in 1933. The side door allowing members to come and go from the Library into the car park without going through the public parts of the building was very useful, particularly for those who wished to avoid importunate solicitors or clients. Whether W.F. McCoy QC suggested the creation of the Bar car park[74] by moving the building slightly to the east when it was being planned cannot be established, but whoever thought of this created a very valuable facility for the Bar.

With the huge growth in the size of the Bar that we have been considering, the car park was now completely inadequate for the Bar. Although various expedients were adopted from the 1970s, the Bar Council minutes throughout the 1970s and 1980s have many references to complaints about the inadequacy of the car parking arrangements, and about their misuse by present and former members of the Bar. Under the direction of Peter Smith QC in particular, repeated efforts were made to rent car parking spaces near the Library, something that was of great importance for those who had to travel to outlying courts. By 1992, in addition to the original Bar Library car park, additional spaces had been rented nearby at Gloucester Street and Oxford Street.[75] Subsequently, the Court Service needed the Bar Library car park when building work had to be carried out on the Law Courts, and the Bar agreed to move its car park onto the Variety Market site beside the Law Courts when that site was purchased by the Court Service. By 1996 this had become the Bar car park, but, as we shall see, it soon became earmarked for another use.

By the late 1980s the Bar Library had therefore more than doubled in

---

73   ECM 27 Apr. 1994 when it was noted that the new kitchen would be complete in a few weeks.
74   In a conversation with the author about the time the author was called to the Bar in September 1969.
75   BCM 9 Dec. 1992.

size from the original Bar Library of 50 years before, and considerable improvements had been made in the facilities to enable the Bar as a body through its individual members to provide an effective service to its clients. However, the seemingly inexorable increase in the size of the Bar meant that within a few years the Library had again become overcrowded and inadequate for the numbers in practice, with all of the strain on facilities that overcrowding created. This ultimately led to the most important decision the Bar had to make in its history, namely to build completely new premises outside the Law Courts building. By 1990 it was apparent that there was an urgent need to comprehensively review the entire working environment and accommodation needs of the Bar, and Coopers and Lybrand Deloitte management consultants were retained to provide a report. In the report they noted that the accommodation in the library amounted to approximately 10000 square feet, excluding passageways, toilets and staircases. Of the 300 members, approximately 200 had allocated seats, whilst the remaining 100 had to share 60 seats. Amongst the findings were that the layout and space was inadequate to carry out a professional business; the allocation of a seat to each barrister was not possible; there was a high level of background noise, and a lack of privacy and confidentiality. They concluded

> ...there are many unsatisfactory features of the current accommodation situation. However the low level of utilisation means that the present accommodation is not a high priority problem. Nevertheless if the weaknesses outlined are addressed then utilisation could increase and accommodation space could become inadequate.

Having reviewed the telephone, fax and post systems their conclusion was that

> The communications systems are outdated and give the perception of an unprofessional body to outsiders. In particular the solicitors, who are the members' main clients, are frustrated by their inability to contact barristers.[76]

Steps were taken to improve the telephone system when a decision was taken by the Executive Council in September 1993 to install a new system at

---

76 Coopers and Lybrand Deloitte report paras 311 and 324.

a cost of £102650 (plus VAT).[77] This was in use by March 1994.[78] However, necessary though this was, it was only one aspect of the increasingly urgent need to improve both the physical size of the Library and the various facilities. This was essential to enable the Bar as a body, and individual barristers, to provide a competitive service and to prepare for what a strategy paper prepared in 1991 by Coopers and Lybrand referred to as 'a changing legal services arena and increased competition'.[79] The report argued that 'There are serious shortcomings in current accommodation arrangements and these will worsen unless radical steps are taken to change direction',[80] and made an observation that was to prove of immense significance in the years to come. This was that

> Accommodation should be centrally located with convenient access to the courts. Accessibility to barristers is more important than for the client although the likely advent of Direct Professional Access may change this…If expansion outside the present Bar Library accommodation is contemplated as a likely prospect the Bar should start planning now for future accommodation requirements.[81]

The report pointed out that it was possible that the Library would have to accommodate 380 members by 1993-94, of whom 180 would be serviced by only 60 seats. Recognising that a root and branch review of the accommodation needs of the Bar was essential, an accommodation committee was set up for this purpose, and its report was considered by the Bar Council at a special meeting on Saturday 11 March 1995. The Bar Council accepted the general thrust of the report. Its proposals were circulated to every member of the Bar in May 1995. In his foreword to the proposals, the chairman of the Bar Council, Richard McLaughlin QC,[82] made two crucial observations about the need to address what he called 'an accommodation crisis'. The first related to the physical size of the Library. He pointed out that there were already 366 members of the Library but only 197 seats, and no one called since 1985 had a permanent desk. It was believed that within the next three years another 72 barristers would graduate from

---

77   ECM 22 Sept. 1993.
78   ECM 23 Mar. 1994.
79   Strategy Paper, (undated), p. 36.
80   Ibid., p. 37.
81   Ibid., pp 36 and 37.
82   Later Mr Justice McLaughlin.

the Institute, an increase in size of the Bar of 20%, leaving out of account those who might be called under the reciprocal arrangements with England and Wales, or from the Irish Bar under the provisions of the recent EC Directive.[83] With only approximately five desks a year being allocated the most recent intake could not hope to have a desk in less than 20 to 25 years. He also pointed to the need to ensure that the accommodation was of a sufficient quality to enable the Bar to improve the service it offered.

> The future needs of both professional and lay client should not be underestimated. With the backdrop of increased availability of legal services in firms of solicitors and large commercial organisations and the possibility of increased rights of audience for solicitors, barristers' clients will have greater expectations for a rapid, high quality service and value for money from counsel. This will be the case regardless of where counsel practice from. Almost all professionals now offer the client a full service. Full service means proper personal reception, comfortable office and meeting facilities, private and confidential consultations, professionally produced reports and correspondence as well as professional service in the given field of expertise. It must be considered whether the current library set-up, and anything modelled on it, can provide what is likely to be the required levels of customer service in the future for all levels of the Bar.[84]

The proposals identified three possibilities. The first was to develop a further extension by obtaining another 10000 square feet of accommodation within the Law Courts building that might become available to the Bar. The second would be to take approximately 50000 square feet of office space on the upper four floors of a five storey office building on a site provided by the Laganside Corporation on the east side of Oxford Street opposite the Law Courts. The third would be to develop a three or four storey building on a vacant site on the north side of May Street between the Law Courts and the Northern Bank site. These proposals drew on the recent expansion by the Irish Bar into additional accommodation close to the Four Courts, and it is significant that the Dublin example of providing individual rooms for occupation by one or more barristers was incorporated in the detailed proposals. There was a sizeable body of opinion within the Bar that saw the need for such accommodation. The proposal to have some individual rooms was so that those who required them could be accommodated within the Library structure, albeit in a form

---

83  89/48/ EC (The Diplomas Directive).
84  Foreword to Report on Proposals for Future Accommodation for the Bar, May 1995.

that departed from the traditional model of everyone working from individual desks in communal surroundings. Many feared that if some rooms were not offered a sizeable element of the Bar might leave the Library to form separate chambers on the English model. Such a development would have had grave implications for the collegiality of the Northern Ireland Bar and its continuance as a united body, with a risk of chambers forming on sectarian or structural lines. This might result in chambers consisting of counsel specialising in only doing work for plaintiffs or insurance companies, or for the prosecution or the defendant in criminal cases.

The report concluded with a proposal by the Bar Council that additional space be provided by a combination of the first and third possibilities designed to provide 120 spaces of reasonable standard, allowing for a degree of flexibility of use, by developing a further 10000 square feet extension within the Law Courts building that would provide approximately 60 spaces, and also building a 20000 square feet unit on the May Street site to provide approximately 60 spaces. An extraordinary general meeting of the Bar was held on Thursday 22 June at which the details of these proposals were discussed, and a ballot was held on 29 and 30 June 1995 asking whether the Bar agreed with this proposal, the question being whether

> ...the Bar agreed that the Bar Council should arrange a detailed investigation of construction, site acquisition, and running costs of the proposed new building at May Street or Oxford Street with a view to preparing a scale of proposed Library Subscriptions following completion of such a building.

The result of the ballot was that the proposal was decisively rejected by a margin of almost two to one, 152 voting no and 82 yes. The vote meant that no further work could be done to remedy the acute problems identified by Richard McLaughlin QC in his foreword to the 1995 report. However, these problems still had to be resolved, and when the annual general meeting of the Bar was held on 1 February 1996 it became apparent that there had been a significant shift of opinion within the Bar. A resolution proposed by Ian Tannahill and Jackie Orr calling on the Bar Council to re-open the accommodation debate and to investigate all possible equitable solutions to the accommodation problem, such investigations to cost no more than £9000, was passed after being amended to authorise the expenditure of £12000.

The Bar Council then explored a number of options which were presented to another general meeting on 25 June 1996. The information pack circulated to every member of the Bar at that time ruled out several options. The first was to place new desks in various parts of the existing Library. This would result in further deterioration of the facilities in the Library and was not cost effective. The second was to construct a mezzanine floor in the original ground floor of the Library, but as it is a fine historic room, and the Royal Courts of Justice is a listed building, it was felt that it was unlikely that the necessary statutory approval would be given. Obtaining additional space within the building was also ruled out because no spare accommodation would become available for at least four years. The Northern Bank was not prepared to sell its building on the corner of Victoria and May Streets. The final option that was ruled out was to build a new building on the Bar Library car park, part of which would be for the DPP or the Crown Solicitor's Office and part for the Bar. Whilst the Court Service was committed to developing this site in the longer term, this option depended on a feasibility study. In any event construction would also take four years. Although this option was ruled out, as we shall see it resurfaced later.

The first of the possible options identified at that time was to take extra accommodation in the Abercorn building on the corner of Anne Street and Victoria Street. This could provide up to 132 desks, 15 offices, nine consultation rooms, a Library research centre, as well ancillary facilities, but would divide the Library across two sites. The second and third options were two of those put forward in 1995, namely to move completely to a new building on the Laganside site opposite the Law Courts, or to construct an additional block on the Maysfield site. A referendum was held, and 154 voted in favour of pursuing the three options, of whom 152 voted in favour of the Laganside option. Of the 96 who voted against, 72 exercised no preference, 15 voted for the Laganside option, three voted for the Abercorn option, and six for the Maysfield option. That the proportions voting for or against the construction of a completely new building had changed so dramatically in a year demonstrated a realisation by a substantial majority that the Bar simply had no choice but to embark on a project to acquire new premises if it was to have satisfactory working conditions and offer an acceptable service to clients. Following the outcome of the vote, the Bar Council established a development committee chaired by John Gillen QC,[85] and appointed a leading Belfast estate agent, Ken Crothers, to act as their agent. Several sites were investigated, but

---

85   Now Mr Justice Gillen.

in October 1996 a new factor came into play when the Court Service indicated that the Variety Market site, currently the Bar car park, could now be available, although as we have seen this had been ruled out as a possible option earlier in the year, and this proved to be a decisive development.

However, the Bar Council did not have a mandate to pursue the Variety market option, and architects had been appointed to prepare detailed plans for the Laganside option should this prove to be the preferred option. The development committee explored the implications of both possibilities, and detailed discussions were held with the Court Service. The basic concept of the Variety Market option was that the Bar, either directly or by entering into an arrangement with a developer, would built a structure that would contain two parts. One part would be a new Bar Library. The other would be for the Department of Public Prosecutions. It would have to take a long lease on its part of the building because the government would not make the capital funding available to it to purchase a site or a building solely for its own use. The details of this option were reported to the Bar by the development committee in February 1997, and to a general meeting on 18 March 1997. The proposals were set out in a paper prepared by John Gillen QC and circulated to all members of the Bar before a referendum was held on 10 and 11 April 1997, when 164 voted in favour of building a new building and 150 voted against.

Members were also asked to express their preference between the Variety Market proposal and the Laganside proposal in the event that a majority voted in favour of building a new building. Both options could provide up to 400 desks, 40 offices, 20 consultation rooms, a public reception area, a server, and administration accommodation. The Variety Market building would be slightly smaller at 35000 square feet compared to the Laganside building's 37650 square feet. The Variety Market option was estimated to be significantly cheaper at £5,695,000, compared to £6,885,000 for the Laganside building. Both sites were also presented in alternative versions with 350 desks with no offices, but only at a slightly reduced cost in either case.[86] Two hundred and thirty five voted for the Variety Market proposal, 18 for the Laganside proposal, and 61 did not express a preference.

Although a majority had now voted to build a completely new Library, with

---

86   Memo 2 Apr. 1997 to all members of the Bar from J. Gillen QC.

the Variety Market site decisively endorsed, two major issues still remained. The first was that there remained a body of opinion who believed that the proposed development was unnecessary for those whose working lives were spent away from the Library, either at the Crumlin Road Courthouse, or at Crown or civil courts outside Belfast, and who therefore made less use of the Bar Library. The substantial increase in subscriptions that might be necessary to fund this proposal was an additional concern to many. These concerns were reflected in a resolution received on 7 September 1997 suggesting that the Bar recognise the right of members to remain in the original Library, those members only to be liable for subscriptions which would reflect a proper share of the administrative costs of the Bar and the limited facilities of the original Library, and have no liability for the capital and running costs of the new facility. This resolution was defeated by a substantial majority at an extraordinary general meeting held on 23 September 1997.[87]

The second issue related to the means of financing this project. Although careful husbandry meant that the Bar had accumulated reserves which would be used to help fund the work, it would still be necessary to obtain very substantial additional funds to enable the work to commence. Two options were explored before a final decision was made as to how the new building was to be financed. One was to finance part of the cost by means of a complex arrangement whereby the landlord of the new premises would be the pension fund of those members who chose to contribute. A considerable amount of time and effort was devoted to developing and explaining the intricacies of this approach by John Thompson QC and Stewart Beattie. However, it is unnecessary to go into the ramifications of this scheme because it required a total commitment of £1.5 million, and as only £1.4 million was pledged this approach was abandoned. The second approach, which was the one ultimately adopted, was a more conventional one whereby the Bar would borrow the total cost, and then repay that cost, plus interest, over a lengthy period, perhaps 20 years. It was estimated that this approach would require a one-off increase of 22% in Library subscriptions, and this would continue for the repayment period of the loan, irrespective of any inflationary increase or restructuring of subscriptions.[88] This would be a very heavy commitment on the part

87  MGM 23 Sept. 1997.
88  Chief executive to members of the Bar 6 Nov. 1997.

of the Bar for many years to come. This prospect was undoubtedly a major element in the concern which led to the resolution which was defeated in September 1997.

Once the momentous decision had been made to build a new Bar Library, there remained many twists and turns to be negotiated before building could start. Whilst the preparation of the specifications and plans for the part of the new building to be occupied by the Bar went ahead without any difficulty, the same was not the case for that part of the building to be occupied by the DPP. As the rental income from the DPP was essential to the financing of the entire project, this took some time to agree, and in turn meant that matters did not proceed as rapidly as the Bar would have wished. A second problem was that increases in site values in Belfast affected the negotiations with the Valuation and Lands Agency over the cost of the site. A complication arose as to whether the Bar Library part of the building would front on to Chichester street or not. Another difficulty related to the car parking spaces that would be lost when the Variety Market was redeveloped, and the Bar's wish to reclaim the car parking spaces in the grounds of the Law Courts. There were also technical issues relating to the terms of the lease. All of these difficulties contributed to a slower rate of progress than had been hoped.[89] The rental for the DPP building was not agreed until October 1998,[90] and it was not until 10 May 1999 that heads of agreement were signed with the lord chancellor.[91] Unfortunately, it then transpired that considerable investigations were still required into matters such as boundary lines and wayleaves, although the then chairman of the Executive Council, Brian Fee QC, was able to inform members of the Bar that it was anticipated that the final agreement would be signed in January 2000.[92]

It was significant that the onset of the new Millenium coincided with the stage being reached when the Bar was finally in a position to apply for planning permission, and, with the detailed design work proceeding in parallel, to look forward to the necessary piling starting in September 2000, although building work would take a further two years. After almost seven decades when the Bar was based within the Law Courts building, and after initially faltering when confronted with the case for a new building by

---

89   Letter from John Gillen QC to members of the Bar. 24 Apr. 1998.
90   Chairman's report to the AGM of Feb. 1999.
91   BCM 12 May 1999.
92   16 Dec. 1999.

Richard McLoughlin QC in 1995, the Bar had sufficient self-confidence as a profession to change its view. It now recognised the need for more accommodation created by the huge increase in numbers at the Bar over the previous 30 years, even though this meant moving outside the Law Courts. However, the Bar would then move into a building that would be an immense improvement on the overcrowded facilities it occupied in the Law Courts. The move would enable the Bar to preserve its collegiate character and ethos, whilst at the same time adapting to the needs of many by providing offices within the new building for those that wanted them. Nevertheless, the challenge presented by the continued increase in numbers and demand for offices led to the decision to incorporate a fifth floor in the building from the outset, although it had always been intended to allow for a fifth floor to be added in the future should that be necessary.[93]

The work on site started in October 2000. Although there were concerns in May 2002 that there might be a delay in completion of the building due to inclement weather and other factors,[94] the topping out ceremony was performed by Mr Justice Gillen (formerly John Gillen QC) on 14 June 2002. This recognised the major part he had played in steering the project through the crucial stages when the concept of the scheme had to be explained to the Bar, and then getting the design and construction underway. In November 2002 it was confirmed that the completion date would be Good Friday, 18 April 2003, and members moved in after Easter 2003. The official opening ceremony was performed by Professor Luzius Wildhaber, the President of the European Court of Human Rights, on 21 November 2003.

The design brief for the architects Robinson McIlwaine required an office development of approximately 120,000 square feet, of which the Bar Library would occupy approximately 50% facing onto Chichester Street, with the remaining 50% a commercial development facing May Street to be fitted out for the Department of Public Prosecutions. The Bar Library portion with its five stories over a basement car park is based around a central atrium space (as is the part of the building occupied by the DPP), with open plan library spaces on one side, and private offices for barristers on the other. The open plan part consists of open library desks with seating for 400 barristers. These desks are fitted with telephones and computer

93   Ibid.
94   ECM 22 May 2002.

terminals. Although considerably more commodious that the desks in the Old Bar Library, the desks deliberately echo evoke the concept of the Old Bar Library, whilst providing much more modern facilities than could be achieved in the old building. Sixty private rooms that could accommodate two or three barristers if necessary were also provided, thereby creating office facilities for those who wish to avail of them. Consultation rooms, administration facilities, and a restaurant on the top floor were also provided. At the front of the building facing Chichester Street there is an open, double-height entrance lobby finished in structural glass, and above this there is a glazed copper box, the lower portion of which contains staff offices, and the upper portion consists of a large room for meetings of the Bar Council. Both rooms have extensive views over the Royal Courts of Justice, Laganside Courts, and the Old Townhall building, the latter two being separated from each other by car park. It is unfortunate that the view is of the back of Laganside Courts, something that could have been avoided had the Court Service adopted the suggestion of the lord chief justice of the time, Sir Robert Carswell, that the Laganside Courts face the Royal Courts of Justice and not the River Lagan.[95]

The building has been furnished to a very high specification. The lobby is faced with Portland Blue stone cut in Northern Ireland, as are the staircases. The staircases are made of Portland Blue and of Whitbed stone, both polished where they are to be touched. The desks in the Library are finished in walnut, the full length doors throughout are of cherry wood, and extensive use is made of illuminated fibre optic lighting. In the architects' words, 'the concept was to create a modern library aesthetic as opposed to an office type environment', and 'the nature of the interior design reflects the client's conservative/modernist dichotomy'.[96] In an unusually enlightened move demonstrating the self-confidence of the profession, an art committee was set up. It purchased a significant number of art works 'not only to properly complete the spaces and architectural detailing of the building but also to increase the amenity of the barristers using the building and to recognise the role of artists in our society'.[97] These works are distributed throughout the building, but perhaps the most striking are the bronze panels created by Carolyn Mulholland for the wooden outer

95  Lord Carswell to the author.
96  McIlwaine 'The opening of the New Bar Library, November 21st 2003.'
97  Art Committee statement, 17 November 2003.

doors of the building. These, which she called 'Laws of God and Men' were chosen with the help of the Nobel Laureate poet Seamus Heaney.[98]

Once the new building was occupied there was a general recognition by many of those who had been sceptical of the scheme that it was a great success. However, despite a deliberate decision being taken to mix counsel of all ages when allocating seats, inevitably there is a feeling that some of the intimacy of the original Bar Library has been lost. Those barristers who work in the building are now spread over several floors, or immured within their offices in the case of those who have moved into one of the offices with one or two of their colleagues. However, this has been a necessary price to pay for the vastly improved facilities that now exist, and the success of the building as a modern, efficient and elegant working environment is a vindication of those whose vision and persistence led to its creation.

With the move of the Bar into the new Bar Library it became apparent that the wear and tear on the Old Bar Library was such that it needed a major refurbishment programme. In February 2004 a plan was prepared by Robinson Patterson architects to carry this out at an estimated cost of some £2 million.[99] This resulted in a significant change to the lay out of the Old Library. The Court Service was anxious to retrieve the MacDermott Room to provide much needed accommodation for the expanding staff required by the lord chief justice to support his new responsibilities as head of the judiciary. It was agreed to surrender the MacDermott Room, together with the store and staff kitchen on the second floor, to the Court Service. Although this would mean the loss of the kitchen facilities, these would be replaced in the newly refurbished area of the Old Bar Library because the decision was taken to create a new suite of rooms on the first floor of the Old Library. The major part of the first floor was to be one large room to be known as the Inn of Court. This would have a new and enlarged kitchen area attached at the Chichester Street end, replacing the existing staging area which was cramped and inadequate.[100] The new, large, room was to be larger than the dual purpose convertible space previously used for working, meetings and functions. The remainder of this floor was to be divided into a Members' Room at the May Street end, with a lobby between it and the Inn

98   See between pages 189 and 196.
99   BCM 11 Feb. 2004.
100 BCM 19 Mar. 2004.

of Court. The lobby would be reached from a landing on the first floor with adjoining toilets. The landing would be reached by a new staircase leading from a redesigned lobby and reception area on the ground floor beside the entrance door of the original Bar Library. In addition the very cramped staff offices on the upper level could be enlarged and improved.

This imaginative project was originally intended to take four months to complete, but the discovery of asbestos in the post room and servery extended the programme by three weeks, and it was not until January 2005 that the work was complete. The ground floor of the Old Library was completely restored to its previous elegance, and now serves as a working reference and research library. A fine new staircase leads to the first floor lobby in which now hang portraits of the judiciary, and where a cabinet has been built to display some of the silver owned by the Bar, the Inn and some of the Bar organisations such as the Bar Golfing Society. The Members' Room, lobby and the Inn of Court are each separated by full length glass windows, allowing the entire length of the Upper Library to be viewed as one space lit by matching modern chandeliers throughout, producing a fine effect at night. At the May Street end of the Members' Room stands the semi-circular wooden counter from the original servery. The Members Room can be used for dinners or small functions, whilst the Inn of Court is designed to be used for dinners or meetings, when the purpose-built tables are removed and the seating arranged as required. The original book cases have been retained, and the spaces between used to display some of the Bar and the Inn's collections of portraits, as well as copies of portraits of distinguished barristers and judges with Northern connections. These copies have been obtained from King's Inns and Trinity College, Dublin, others hang in the judges' corridor on the ground floor of the building. It was fitting that the official opening of this magnificent addition to the Inn of Court was performed by a former member of the Library and honorary bencher, Her Excellency Mary McAleese, President of Ireland, on 24 January 2005. Since then it has proved its worth by being extensively used for dinners, functions and lectures by the Inn, the Bar and other organisations such as the Judicial Studies Board.

It would be reassuring to close this chapter on this note of another major achievement on the part of the Bar in providing outstanding, and much-needed, accommodation for itself and the Inn. However, the continued increase in size of the Bar in the decade since the new Bar Library came into use has again generated something of the pressure on accommodation that existed in earlier decades. Some additional desk space has been provided in the new building by internal reorganisation. For example, a small satellite library had been provided in the new building, but it was found to be under-utilised, and was closed.[101] This re-organisation has been made necessary by a gradual increase in the number of members who do not have desks. By the end of 2010 it was acknowledged by the Bar Council that there was again a severe problem due to the lack of desks,[102] and that 'hot desking' (the sharing of desks) was again necessary. This was made permanent in 2011, although some relief was achieved in May 2011, by which time 121 members were without desks, when two resource rooms were converted to provide 23 new hot desks.[103] These problems will undoubtedly pose a significant challenge to the Bar in the years to come if the Bar continues at its present size, or continues to expand still further. At Easter 2013 there were 681 members of the Library, of whom 148 do not have desks of their own, and a further 12 members of the Bar are believed to be working from home.[104] How this can be resolved remains to be seen, but accommodation pressures again pose a significant challenge for the Bar.

101  BCM 16 Nov. 2005.
102  BCM 9 Dec. 2012.
103  BCM 6 Apr. 2011.
104  Information to the author from the Bar Council staff 28 Mar. 2013.

# CHAPTER ELEVEN:

## Call, Reciprocity and Silk

The 1970s proved to be a time when significant changes in several aspects of the structures of the Inn of Court and the Bar occurred. One of these related to reciprocity and relations between the Inn and King's Inns. As we have seen, in the early 1950s there had been something of a rapprochement between members of the Northern Bar and the Bar of Ireland because of the regular golf matches between the two bars, and occasional *ad hoc* meetings such as a cricket match held in 1971. However, it was not until 1975 that there was any significant thawing of relations between the Inn of Court of Northern Ireland and King's Inns. This process was initiated in Northern Ireland by a memorandum from Mr Justice O'Donnell to his fellow benchers in which he raised the issue of reciprocity between the two institutions. He drew attention to the absence of any provision for reciprocal recognition by the Inn of Court of Northern Ireland of barristers who were members of the Bar of Ireland. He suggested that the time had come to negotiate a proper reciprocal arrangement, particularly as both jurisdictions were now members of the European Community and, as he observed, 'the right of professional members of the Community to practise in the countries of the Community will assume greater importance as years go on'.[1] He pointed out that although the rules of King's Inns permitted a member of the Northern Ireland Bar of three years standing to be called to the Irish Bar, there was no corresponding rule in Northern Ireland. He also observed that the statutory requirement under s. 3 of the Legal Practitioners (Qualification) Act, 1927 that no one should be admitted to the Irish Bar unless he satisfies the chief justice that he possesses a competent knowledge of the Irish language would not apply to members of the Northern Ireland Bar if there was a reciprocity arrangement.

In Chapter Four we traced the dispute between King's Inns and the Northern Committee of Benchers that resulted in the severing of relations in 1925, and the subsequent decision by a meeting of Bench and Bar on 11 January 1926 to establish the Inn of Court of Northern Ireland. Following the creation of the Northern Inn, the benchers of the Inn adopted

---

1    Undated memorandum from O'Donnell J.

provisional rules relating to the admission and education of students to the Bar of Northern Ireland. As part of that process, the benchers included a provisional rule providing for the call of members of the Bar of the Irish Free State of three years standing who applied to be called to the Northern Ireland Bar. In October 1926 the under treasurer wrote to King's Inns suggesting that it might wish to introduce a similar rule of a reciprocal nature. This was followed by an exchange of letters, ending with a letter from Newton Anderson, the under treasurer of the Northern Inn, to the under treasurer of King's Inns of 27 June 1927. Nothing further was heard from King's Inns about the Northern proposal for reciprocity. It was not until January 1944 that the matter was raised again, when the under treasurer of King's Inns wrote to his Northern counterpart to ask what was the position about the provisional rule, only to be told that as nothing further had been heard from King's Inns after Newton Anderson's letter of 27 June 1927, the benchers revoked the provisional rule as they assumed that King's Inns did not wish to pursue the question of reciprocity. The under treasurer of King's Inns replied saying that

...the members of this Bench [i.e. the benchers of King's Inns] were shocked and surprised that no reply had been sent, expressed their sincere apologies, and would be very glad to re-open the matter with a view to arriving at a system of reciprocity.

However, on 1 June 1944 the benchers unanimously decided not to re-open the matter.[2] There the matter rested until 1958, when Mr Justice Murnaghan[3] wrote to the lord chief justice, Lord MacDermott, suggesting that a system of reciprocity be put in place. However, although the matter was considered at a number of benchers' meetings, this approach was not received any more favourably than the approach in 1944, and in December 1958 Lord MacDermott wrote to say that the benchers had decided to take no further steps towards reciprocity.[4]

Perhaps the benchers were still influenced by a feeling of resentment towards King's Inns because of the circumstances leading up to the split between King's Inns and the Northern Committee in 1925, and a continuing feeling that there should have been some division of the assets of King's Inns after

2    BM 1 June 1944.
3    A judge of the high court of Ireland 1953-79, and a native of Omagh, Co. Tyrone.
4    This passage is based upon a memorandum dated 24 March 1975 prepared for the benchers by J.A.L. McLean, under treasurer of the Inn of Court.

1921. Be that as it may, after 1958 no further official contact took place on this subject between the Inn of Court of Northern Ireland and King's Inns until the 1970s. Nor does it appear that any consideration was given by the benchers to establishing a system of reciprocity between the two inns, until Mr Justice O'Donnell raised the issue in 1975. However, it is worthy of note that by 1964 King's Inns made provision in its rules for call to the Irish Bar by members of the Bar of Northern Ireland of three years standing, subject to the production of a certificate of call and a certificate that the applicant was a proper person to be called to the Irish Bar.[5] This rule was in almost identical terms to the provisions in the King's Inns rules relating to call of members of the English Bar. It was also almost the same as Rule 28 of the rules of the Inn of Court of Northern Ireland governing the call of English barristers to the Northern Ireland Bar. However, there was no such provision in the rules providing for call of Irish barristers to the Northern Ireland Bar.

By 1975 there were much stronger bonds of personal friendship between many members of the judiciary and the bars of both jurisdictions, and those individuals now in positions of leadership represented a new generation less influenced by the experiences of the past. This was particularly so in the case of Sir Robert Lowry who, as lord chief justice and therefore chairman of the benchers, had excellent relations with his judicial colleagues in the Republic. In a spirit of professional amity 10 members of the Northern Bar were called to the Irish Bar on 27 November 1975.[6] Following Mr Justice O'Donnell's memorandum Lord Justice McGonigal prepared a report for the benchers on the question of reciprocity with the Irish Bar. In it he noted two significant matters. One was that, unlike the Northern Ireland Bar, King's Inns did not require an applicant for call to have a degree, and he observed that until recently the English Bar did not have such a requirement either. The other was that there was 'no requirement for an applicant under a reciprocal arrangement to take any examination in the Irish language', and that the requirement of three years' practice was a requirement of the English Bar for applicants from the Irish Bar who wished to be exempted from the regulations concerning pupillage and restricted practice. It appeared that King's Inns no longer required three years' practice from English barristers, nor did McGonigal understand that they would require it

---

5   Rules of the Honorable Society of King's Inns with regard to…the degree of Barrister-at-Law, July 1964, rule xxx (a).

6   *King's Inns Barristers*, p. 366.

of Northern Ireland barristers. However, as the three year requirement was a feature of the reciprocal arrangement between the Northern Ireland and English Bars he suggested that it be retained in any reciprocity arrangement with King's Inns.[7] He recommended that a reciprocal arrangement be entered into with the Irish Bar. The arrangement would be that a member of that bar who had three years' practice preceding his application for call to the Bar of Northern Ireland, and who had certificates from the chief justice or attorney general confirming that to be the case, and that he was a fit and proper person to be called to the Northern Ireland Bar, could be called without keeping terms, attending lectures or sitting examinations.

The benchers accepted the recommendation, and, in February 1976, passed a new Rule 28A substantially adopting McGonigal's proposals, with the slight modification that the applicant had to present a certificate from the chief justice of Ireland that the applicant had 'been actively engaged in practice' at the Irish Bar for three years immediately preceding the application. In a tangible demonstration of the new spirit of friendship between members of the Irish and Northern bars, 16 members of the Irish Bar were called to the Northern Ireland Bar by the lord chief justice on 10 June 1976, and a further five were called on 30 September 1976. These calls did much to cement a new feeling of professional friendship between both bars, and to place the relationship between the Inn and King's Inns on a new, and much more amicable, basis.

The reference by Mr Justice O'Donnell to the implications of the entry of the United Kingdom into the European Economic Community in 1975 was not the first time this topic had been raised. In 1973 the possibility of a proposed EEC directive allowing European lawyers to practise throughout the Common Market (as the European Economic Community was generally described at that time) was considered by the Bar Council, and it recognised the need for a common policy to be discussed with the English and Scottish Bars.[8] The entry of the United Kingdom and the Republic of Ireland into the EEC undoubtedly provided the stimulus for much greater liaison between the bars of both jurisdictions. In 1976 we find the first reference in the Bar Council minutes to the chairman attending a meeting of the

7   Report on proposed reciprocal arrangement with the Bar of the Republic of Ireland, 15 Dec. 1975.
8   BCM 15 Jan. 1973.

Standing Committee of Bars in Dublin.[9] However, the gestation period for the proposals from Brussels to permit legal professionals to practise throughout the EEC proved to be exceptionally prolonged, because it was not until December 1988 that provision was made by Directive 89/48/EEC for practitioners from one jurisdiction to practise in another.

The EEC Directive was to create several problems for the Bar and the benchers in years to come. Although some established practitioners at the Irish Bar have appeared in the Northern Ireland courts from time to time, usually for a specific case, they have usually not availed of the EEC Directive, but, rather, have been called under the conventional reciprocity rule already discussed. Where the individual concerned had been in practice at the Irish Bar for less than the three years required by Rule 28A there were concerns amongst the benchers and the Bar Council that applicants under the EEC Directive would be less experienced than newly-called members of the Northern Ireland Bar who received their training in Northern Ireland. At that time, unlike the Northern Ireland Bar, members of the Irish Bar were not required to undergo compulsory pupillage after call. In theory at any rate, members of the Irish Bar could apply to be called to the Northern Ireland Bar under the EEC Directive immediately after being called to the Irish Bar, and would be entitled to practice in Northern Ireland without undergoing pupillage.

As entry to the limited number of places for Bar students at the Institute of Professional Legal Studies at Queen's had become increasingly competitive, many unsuccessful applicants naturally explored the possibility of being called to the English or Irish Bars, and then sought to avail of the EEC Directive route as they would otherwise have to have had three years in practice at the Irish Bar to be called under the reciprocal arrangements. In the mid-1990s the benchers, the Executive Council, and the Bar Council each had reason to consider various aspects of the Directive provisions insofar as they affected the provisions for call. One issue was whether someone who was not a national of the jurisdiction in which he or she had qualified could rely on the Directive,[10] but the most difficult, and contentious, issue was that of pupillage. A lengthy, and inconclusive, discussion by the Executive Council of the issue in September 1996 encapsulated the different arguments

9   BCM 7 Oct. 1976.
10   ECM 11 Sept. 1996 and 25 Sept. 1996.

on this topic. Some took the view that, once an individual had passed the necessary exams that enabled them to practise at the Irish Bar, they were entitled to take advantage of the Directive. Others were concerned that this could be used as a back door method of coming to the Northern Ireland Bar, and that such individuals should undergo an aptitude test, as well as a period of pupillage in Northern Ireland, before they could practise in Northern Ireland.[11] The issue was again considered by the Executive Council a year later, and on that occasion the concerns were met by the two applicants volunteering to undergo pupillage in Northern Ireland if called under the Directive.[12] By 2002 King's Inns had amended its rules to require candidates for call to include in their memorials for call

> ...an undertaking that... if admitted to practise at the Bar of Ireland, they will not embark on practice as a barrister until they have been accepted as pupils for the normal period of pupillage by a practising barrister approved by the Bar of Ireland.[13]

This new requirement by King's Inns did much to alleviate the concern of the Northern Ireland Bar that applicants for call under the Directive were not subject to the same requirement to undergo pupillage as those who qualified in Northern Ireland, and, as we have seen in Chapter Six, compulsory pupillage is a requirement that the Northern Ireland Bar has required its own students to undergo from the 1970s.[14]

Not all those who wished to come to the Northern Ireland Bar having been called to the Bar elsewhere sought to do so from the Irish Bar. Since the 1990s the benchers, the Executive Council, and the Bar Council have had to grapple with many problems connected with applications from members of the English Bar to practise in Northern Ireland. Many applications were from individuals who had been brought up in Northern Ireland but went to the English Bar. Some had failed to get places in the Institute having studied law in Northern Ireland. Others studied law in Great Britain and were called to the Bar in England, but for various reasons wished to return to Northern Ireland and practise here. Some sought to return to Northern Ireland because of the difficulty of getting a place in chambers in England, others because

11  ECM 11 Sept. 1996.
12  ECM 23 Oct. 1997.
13  ECM 20 Nov. 2002 quoting Rule 19 of the Education Rules of the Honorable Society of King's Inns.
14  See p. 181.

of family or personal reasons. For those who had been in practice for three years in England there was of course the reciprocity provision which had existed since the Inn drew up its rules in the late 1920s. However, the 1990s saw a marked rise in the numbers of members of the English Bar who were originally from Northern Ireland applying to be called to the Northern Ireland Bar without having been in practice for three years. A complication was that many of these applicants had embarked on their legal studies after Rule 15A (relating to those of less than three years standing at the English Bar) was amended in 2001 to require applicants to have completed an English pupillage.[15] There were sometimes compelling personal and family reasons why applicants had changed their minds about wishing to practise in England. A further complication in some cases was that the period of pupillage had not been completed in England, or that the pupillage had been with an employed barrister, something that the rules of the Northern Ireland Inn of Court does not permit, as it requires pupillage in England and Wales to have been with a barrister in independent practice, as is the position in Northern Ireland.

One issue that was resolved relatively easily was the suggestion that members of the senior bar in England should be allowed the privileges accorded to their rank in their home jurisdiction without having to be called to the Inner Bar in Northern Ireland. This had been suggested by the Joint Committee of the Bars of the United Kingdom and Ireland in 1980,[16] and in 1998 the lord chief justice, Sir Robert Carswell, and his counterpart in England, agreed that henceforth the judiciary in each jurisdiction would afford all the privileges of the senior bar to members of the senior bars of the other jurisdiction when appearing before them without having to be called to the Inner Bar of that jurisdiction.[17] At the same time discussions were initiated to have a similar agreement with the Irish Bar, and one was agreed between the lord chief justice and the chief justice of Ireland in 2000.[18] These arrangements resolved what had become a cause of some dispute. Although it had been the invariable practice in Northern Ireland to award silk to an English silk, and, in 1985 to a senior counsel of the Irish Bar,[19] called to the Northern Ireland Bar, sometimes Northern Ireland silks

15  BM 5 June 2001, ECM 13 June 2001.
16  BCM 28 Oct. 1980.
17  BCM 18 Nov. 1998.
18  Information from the office of the lord chief justice to the author.
19  Patrick MacEntee SC was given silk in Northern Ireland on 29 Jan. 1985 when he was appearing in a criminal case.

wishing to be called to the senior bar in England or the Republic found that the same courtesy was not accorded to them. This naturally gave rise to resentment and ill-feeling.

Another issue related to the position of the pupil master, because the English Bar recognises employed barristers who are not in private practice as suitable to act as masters. The Northern Ireland Bar does not regard their work as suitable to provide experience for barristers in independent practice, because the *raison d'etre* of the Northern Ireland Bar is to be an independent referral Bar. Although many more barristers in Northern Ireland now follow legal careers outside the Bar, these are still very largely employed in the public service, particularly in the Public Prosecution Service and the Government Legal Service, whereas in England and Wales there are many more opportunities for employed barristers in large legal departments in the public, regulatory and private sectors. To reflect the position of the Northern Ireland Bar as an independent referral bar, Rules 15, 15A and 16 of the Inn of Court were amended to include the requirement that members of the English and Irish Bars who wished to be called under the reciprocity provisions had to have successfully completed not less than 12 months pupillage under the supervision of a member of the respective Bars 'in independent practice' who was duly qualified to provide such supervision under the rules of their respective Bars.

Whilst from time to time English counsel had been briefed in cases in Northern Ireland, usually in cases involving comparatively esoteric areas such as patent or tax law, or occasionally criminal cases of some notoriety,[20] for many years this was a rare occurrence. In the early 1990s there appeared a new phenomenon in the form of English counsel who had been retained in a single case, but, for whatever reason, did not wish to be called to the Northern Ireland Bar. Recognising that in such cases a client might otherwise be prevented from obtaining the services of the counsel of his choice, and that such counsel were sometimes specialists in areas of law where there might not necessarily be sufficient Northern Ireland counsel practising to give the client a reasonable choice of counsel, rules were introduced permitting the temporary call of counsel for a single case (and any appeal arising out of the case).[21] The majority of those who wished to appear more frequently in Northern

20   As in 1956 when Elwyn Jones QC, later Lord Elwyn Jones, lord chancellor, was called.
21   BCM 24 June 1992.

Ireland recognised that they should become members of the Bar and applied to be called in the usual way. However, a small number did not, and in some instances applied for temporary call on a number of occasions. This was felt to be undesirable for a number of reasons. It undermined the justification for a separate Northern Ireland Bar; such counsel were not necessarily subject to the same strict requirements for continuing professional development as their counterparts in Northern Ireland; it was unclear whether their professional indemnity insurance complied with the conditions required for a practising certificate in Northern Ireland; and there were doubts as to whether they were subject to any effective disciplinary sanction in the event that an individual might be subject to disciplinary proceedings in the same way that a member of the Northern Ireland Bar would be.

The benchers and the Bar Council each addressed aspects of this matter. In December 2010 the benchers accepted a recommendation that henceforth an applicant would be limited to a maximum of three temporary calls, and these applications would be considered by a committee of the Inn appointed for this purpose. Rules to that effect were approved by the Executive Council on 23 November 2011, and came into effect on 1 January 2012.[22] An important element of these rules is that the applicant for temporary call is now expressly required to acknowledge that he or she remains subject to the Code of Conduct and disciplinary powers and procedures of the Inn of Court of Northern Ireland, even after the conclusion of the case for which the applicant has been granted a temporary call certificate. Other requirements are that the applicant identifies the case, or group of cases for which he or she is to be briefed; has been in independent practice at the English Bar for at least three years before the application; has professional indemnity insurance that is valid in Northern Ireland and is equivalent to that required in Northern Ireland, and applies for a practising certificate in Northern Ireland. At the time of writing refinements of the procedural aspects of these rules are under consideration.

A matter that proved contentious for more than a decade and a half from the middle of the 1990s was the process for appointing Queen's Counsel (or 'senior counsel' as they are colloquially called in Northern Ireland, as opposed to 'leading counsel' in England and Wales). The office of Queen's Counsel has existed in England since the appointment of Francis Bacon in

22   BM 12 Dec. 2011.

1594 and in Ireland since the appointment of William Hilton in January 1613. The history and evolution of this office is outside the scope of this work, but whatever its origins and attributes in the past, Queen's Counsel now form the senior rank of the profession of barrister in each of the three jurisdictions of the United Kingdom. There is a corresponding senior rank in most common law jurisdictions, notably that of Senior Counsel in the Republic of Ireland. Although the office may be granted on an honorary basis, this is exceptional in Northern Ireland because the office is 'first and foremost a working rank in the profession of barrister', and is considered to be 'a mark of distinction as an advocate'.[23] Since the creation of the separate jurisdiction of Northern Ireland by the Government of Ireland Act of 1920 it has been the practice to confer the rank of King's or Queen's Counsel upon those members of the Bar who are considered to have demonstrated that they have the qualities to take their place in the senior rank of the profession, a rank correctly referred to as 'the Inner Bar' to distinguish it from the Junior or 'Outer' Bar, with the decision as to who should be granted 'silk' being made by the lord chief justice as the successor to the lord chancellor of Ireland.

Controversy over the selection of silks in Northern Ireland was not altogether a new phenomenon, because as early as December 1923 E.S. Murphy KC[24] raised with the Bar Council the

> ...question of a number of Government officials and other non-practising members of the Bar having latterly been given silk and of the probability of a considerable number of applications for silk being made by officials and non practising members of the Bar in the future.

After 'considerable discussion' it was resolved that the secretary write to the lord chief justice to convey the general opinion of the practising members of the Bar 'that silk should not be given on any ground other than that of professional standing and actual practice at the Bar'.[25] It would seem that these comments were made in anticipation of the imminent call to the Inner Bar of John Alexander Weir Johnston and Sir Arthur Scott Quekett which took place on 21 December 1923. Johnston had been a member of

---

23   These quotations are from the Guide cited by Kerr J in *The matter of an application by Seamus Treacy and Barry Macdonald for judicial review* [2000] NI 330.

24   Later Lord Justice Murphy.

25   BCM 17 Dec. 1923.

the North West Circuit.[26] Quekett had been legal assistant to the Local Government Board for Ireland, and in 1921 was appointed Parliamentary Counsel to the Government of Northern Ireland, a post in which he was to serve with distinction until his death.[27] However, the protests of the Bar Council were to no avail, and, as can be seen from the list of those called to the Inner bar between 1921 and 1939, several were in the Colonial Service and held, or were to attain, judicial office in the colonies. One such was David Thomas James Sherlock, who became chief justice of North Borneo in 1926. Another was Herbert Stronge, chief justice of Tonga 1917-25, and who was chief justice of the Leeward Islands when he was called in 1929. Many of those non-practising barristers who were called to the Inner Bar of Northern Ireland between 1921 and 1939 no doubt wished to show their solidarity with the new legal system in Northern Ireland. The practice of appointing non-practising silks remained controversial, and in 1938 the Bar Council passed a resolution objecting to such appointments.[28]

After the appointment of Sir James Andrews as lord chief justice in 1937 it became the practice for the lord chief justice to invite individuals to take silk, although very occasionally applications were made, rather than the person concerned waiting to be invited.[29] Basil Kelly was one of three who applied to Lord MacDermott in 1956. All three were 'postponed', but each was appointed two years later in November 1958.[30] By the 1970s the practice was firmly established whereby the lord chief justice invited those he regarded as suitable to take silk. This meant that the initiative was removed from the individual and placed solely in the hands of the lord chief justice. This was widely regarded by the Bar as unsatisfactory, because it meant that an individual could not choose for himself when it might be appropriate to take this crucial step in his career. If someone was invited to take silk at a time when he regarded the move as inopportune for personal or professional reasons, to refuse might mean that he would not be asked the next time, or by the next time his competitors would have established their practices to his disadvantage. At this time there was also renewed concern at the practice of appointing non-practising barristers as

---

26  *Thom's Irish Directory*, 1920, p. 934.
27  The author of *Constitution of Northern Ireland* (2 vols., 1928).
28  BCM 13 May 1938.
29  Evidence of Sir Robert Lowry LCJ to the Royal Commission on Legal Services, 5 Apr. 1979.
30  Letter from Sir Basil Kelly to T.V. Cahill QC of 7 Jan. 2007. I am indebted to Tom Cahill for making a copy of this letter available to me. The other applicants were Lloyd Moody and T.A. Blair.

silks. However, although the matter was discussed by the Bar Council in 1974, it decided not to raise its concerns with the lord chief justice.[31] The matter was considered by the Royal Commission on Legal Services, and in its final report in 1979 it recommended the adoption of the system in which candidates make formal application, with consultations with the judiciary and members of the profession on the same pattern as those undertaken by the Lord Chancellor in England and Wales. Lord Lowry LCJ implemented this recommendation for the next silk call in March 1983. Since then, those who wish to be considered for silk make an application when the lord chief justice decides that there should be another silk call. As can be seen from the dates in Part Two of this work, there has been no fixed pattern as to how often silk calls would be held.

For a time this system was uncontroversial, but in May 1995 some parts of the formal components of the procedure came under scrutiny for the first time.[32] At that time the procedure for appointment involved the lord chief justice notifying the secretary of state for Northern Ireland of the names of the successful candidates. The secretary of state as the successor to the governor of Northern Ireland, acting on behalf of the Queen and on the advice of the lord chief justice, then issued a warrant authorising their appointment. Before the successful candidate could be formally appointed to the office it was necessary for him or her to take the Oath of Allegiance, and also to make a declaration of office in the prescribed form. In May 1995 Philip Magee, a member of the Bar of Northern Ireland, made an application for judicial review of the requirement to take the Oath of Allegiance and to make the declaration of office in the then prescribed form. Before the application could be heard the secretary of state concluded that the requirement to take the Oath of Allegiance was in breach of the Promissory Oaths Act 1868 and the requirement was removed. At the same time he decided that henceforth the declaration of office would be in the form used in England and Wales, and the chairman of the Bar Council was so informed. Magee then consented to his application for judicial review being dismissed.

---

31  BCM 3 June 1974. This may have arisen because of the appointment of J.B. Fox and J.A.L. McLean in April 1974. Fox had recently retired as a resident magistrate, and McLean was permanent secretary of the supreme court of judicature and under treasurer of the Inn of Court of Northern Ireland.

32  Unless otherwise stated, this passage is based upon the judgment of Kerr J (as he then was) *In the Matter of an application by Seamus Treacy and Barry Macdonald for judicial review* [2000] NI 330 (hereafter referred to as '*Treacy and Macdonald's case*').

In April 1996 a notice inviting applications for silk was screened in the Bar Library, and Magee wrote to the chairman of the Bar Council and the principal secretary to the lord chief justice inquiring what form the declaration would take. Subsequent events are described in the judgment in *Treacy and Macdonald's case*, and a call to the Inner Bar took place in September 1996. It is sufficient for present purposes to note that in 1996 the Bar Council set up a committee under the chairmanship of Fraser Elliott QC[33] to investigate and report on all aspects of the appointment of senior counsel in Northern Ireland. As Mr Justice Kerr noted, the committee had been chaired by a highly experienced Queen's Counsel, it was comprised of a broadly based group of members of the Bar, and it had canvassed views from a wide spectrum of opinion both within and outside the Bar. The committee reported to the Bar Council in April 1997. At a meeting on 14 May 1997 the Bar Council accepted the recommendations of the Elliott committee with some minor alterations, and concluded that the process should be as follows.

(1) The function of making the appointment should remain with the Crown.

(2) The lord chief justice should make the necessary recommendations to the secretary of state.

(3) Before making his recommendations he should seek the views of the supreme court judges, the chairman and the immediate past chairman of the Bar Council (unless either was a candidate).

(4) Where the lord chief justice feels that the supreme court judges may not have an adequate opportunity to observe the candidate in practice, he should seek views from appropriate judicial or quasi-judicial office holders familiar with the candidate's abilities as a practitioner.

(5) The lord chief justice should always be free to consult whomsoever he thinks fit.

(6) The initiation of the process for appointment should be the responsibility of the lord chief justice.

(7) At least every two years the lord chief justice should review the

---

33   Chairman of the Bar Council 1989-1991.

desirability of making fresh appointments, and at that stage the chairman of the Bar Council should have an input.

(8) The lord chief justice should continue to retain the discretion to recommend appointment at any time.

(9) There should be no fixed number of Queen's Counsel, either as an absolute number or as a proportion of the number of barristers in practice.

A copy of the Elliott Committee report was sent to the lord chief justice, who sent a copy to the secretary of state. Following discussions between the lord chief justice and the lord chancellor, in October 1988 the lord chief justice wrote to the chairman of the Bar Council informing him of a proposal to bring the appointment arrangements for Northern Ireland more closely into line with those in England and Wales, the principal aspect of which would be that appointments would henceforth be made by the Queen acting on the advice of the lord chancellor. The Bar Council considered the matter at a meeting of 18 November. On 27 November the chairman wrote to the lord chief justice saying that the Bar Council 'was generally in favour of the proposals', but raising a number of matters about the application procedure. On 22 March 1999 the prime minister approved the transfer of powers relating to the appointment of Queen's Counsel in Northern Ireland from the secretary of state to the lord chancellor. On 31 March Her Majesty the Queen consented to the transfer of responsibilities, and on 19 April 1999 the lord chancellor wrote to the chairman telling him the new arrangements were now effective. The declaration issue was not raised during these exchanges between the lord chief justice, the lord chancellor and the chairman of the Bar Council.

Almost three years had now elapsed since the last call of Northern Ireland counsel to the Inner Bar, and at the end of April 1999 applications for silk were invited by the lord chief justice. As Mr Justice Kerr found, it appears that at about this time the lord chancellor decided that the wording of the declaration should not be changed so that harmony could be maintained between the systems in Northern Ireland and in England and Wales. The call was scheduled to take place on 21 December 1999. When Seamus Treacy and Barry Macdonald, two of the successful applicants, each learnt shortly before the call date about the form of the declaration, they requested that the Bar Council support their request that they be allowed to make the declaration of office in the terms recommended by the Elliott Committee, and accepted by the Bar Council at its meeting on 14 May 1997. The form that had been recommended by the Committee was

> I...do sincerely promise and declare that I will well and truly serve all whom I may lawfully be called to serve in the office of one of Her Majesty's Counsel learned in the law according to the best of my skill and understanding.

The terms of the declaration to which the successful applicants for silk were required to make was in the following terms.

> I..... do sincerely promise and declare that I will well and truly serve Her Majesty Queen Elizabeth II and all whom I may be lawfully called upon to serve in the office of one of Her Majesty's Counsel learned in the law according to the best of my skill and understanding.

On 20 December Treacy and Macdonald were granted leave to apply for judicial review of the decision of the lord chancellor, and the call of the remaining successful candidates took place as scheduled on 21 December 1999. As can be seen from the judgment Mr Justice Kerr delivered in May 2000 on the substantive application, a number of different grounds were advanced on behalf of the applicants and the interveners. Allegations of discrimination and bias against the applicant were not accepted by the judge, nor did he accept that the decision of the lord chancellor to require them to make the declaration breached their rights under Articles 9, 10 or 14 of the European Convention on Human Rights and Fundamental Freedoms, or of their common law rights of freedom of expression, or other international human rights standards relied on by the applicants' counsel. He did not accept that the applicants had a legitimate expectation that the declaration recommended by the Elliott Committee would be accepted, or that the Bar Council would be consulted before the lord chancellor took the decision to retain the declaration in its present form. However, the judge quashed the decision of the lord chancellor to retain the declaration in the impugned form because the decision was based on a mistaken understanding of the true facts. Mr Justice Kerr concluded that had the lord chancellor anticipated controversy about the declaration he would have consulted the Bar Council and the judges of the then supreme court of judicature of Northern Ireland.[34]

---

34  Since renamed the Court of Judicature of Northern Ireland to distinguish it from the Supreme Court of the United Kingdom.

Seamus Treacy and Barry Macdonald were called to the Inner Bar on 8 September 2000, having made the declaration in the amended form now used and which is set out later.

The ramifications of the judgment were not, however, confined to the successful applicants, because in the course of his examination of the historical background to the declaration, Mr Justice Kerr concluded that the lord chief justice had no power in relation to the declaration. As already noted, Her Majesty had agreed in 1999 that henceforth applications for silk in Northern Ireland would be granted by her on the recommendation of the lord chancellor. The effect of the conjunction of these circumstances was that a new system had to be devised to deal with applications for silk to take account of the role of the lord chancellor. Although another silk call took place on 21 December 2001, devising a new procedure for the future that would be acceptable to all was to prove a protracted exercise, and the procedure put in place to replace the old, and simple, procedure was widely believed to be unsatisfactory because it was seen to be cumbersome, expensive and took an inordinate length of time.

The Bar Council instituted a further review of the silk procedure by another committee, again under the chairmanship of Fraser Elliott QC, and the committee reported in April 2002.[35] The Bar Council took the view that the lord chancellor should not play any part in the silks process, but, if the office of Queen's Counsel was to be retained, the constitutional requirement that the Queen acted on the advice of her ministers meant that the lord chancellor had to be involved, even if only in a nominal capacity. The lord chancellor decided to issue a consultation paper on the appointment of silks, and in 2003 he made it clear that there would be no more calls until a decision was made. The Bar Council tried to obtain a final silk call before the consultation process was complete,[36] but in the event there was to be a gap of five and a half years between the 2001 call until the next call in 2006.

The process of devising an acceptable procedure for silk applications involved complex discussions. The lord chancellor naturally wanted to ensure that the procedures in both England and Wales and Northern Ireland were effectively the same, but the much smaller size of Northern

35   BCM 17 Apr. 2012.
36   BCM 11 June 2003.

Ireland meant that some of the steps proposed were seen as unnecessary in such a small jurisdiction. There was also an extremely strong feeling in the Bar that the administration of the process should not take place outside Northern Ireland.[37] Ultimately it was agreed that Northern Ireland would have its own scheme. A further complication was that for some years the lord chancellor had awarded silk to solicitors in England and Wales, and the Law Society wanted solicitors in Northern Ireland to be eligible. Deciding how the machinery would work proved exceptionally difficult. Although the outline of what was ultimately to be the structure and procedure had emerged by March 2005, it became clear by the end of that year that there were unlikely to be new silk appointments before Easter 2006,[38] and even that target was missed because the call did not take place until June 2006.

The structure of the system that had emerged by March 2005 had a number of principal elements.

- The applicant would be assessed as to how he or she met a number of 'competences'.
- There would be a lengthy application form with provision for reports from referees.
- A company would be set up to administer the process, and this would employ its own staff.
- The system would be self-financing, and each applicant would have to pay a substantial fee.
- The decision whether to grant silk would be made by a selection panel chaired by a senior retired judge, with two QCs, two solicitors, and two lay members.
- There would be a complaints panel to which unsuccessful applicants could apply, this would be chaired by a senior judge nominated by the lord chief justice, with a similar membership to the selection panel.

The system that came into being sought to implement these principles. A limited company, Queen's Counsel Appointments (Northern Ireland) Ltd, was set up to deal with the administrative aspects of the process. The selection panel and the complaints committee were also set up, and applications were

37   BCM 15 Sept. 2004.
38   BCM 16 Mar. 2005.

invited. When the process was complete 16 applicants were successful, and 20 were unsuccessful.[39] Although the successful candidates were called to the Inner Bar on 26 June 2006, it immediately became clear that there was widespread discontent with the outcome, and several disappointed applicants applied to the complaints committee. This was not an appeal committee because it was not empowered to substitute its own decision for that of the selection panel. The complaints committee's function was limited to deciding whether any of the unsuccessful candidates could show that the process in their case was unsatisfactory. In the event the complaints committee upheld a number of complaints, and referred all of the cases of those who had complained back to the selection panel. The selection committee then reconsidered all the complaints, and recommended a further six candidates for appointment who were called to the Inner Bar in June 2007.

Martin O'Rourke was one of the unsuccessful candidates, and he instituted judicial review proceedings which were unsuccessful. The judgments of Mr Justice Weatherup[40] at first instance, and Sir Brian Kerr LCJ[41] in the Court of Appeal, set out in the details of the appointments process in great detail, and the various issues that were considered, and those who wish to examine the history of these matters more closely can refer to the judgments. A number of significant matters emerge from the judgments. First of all, as the lord chief justice emphasised, the process was designed so that

> Ministers should no longer be involved directly in the identification of senior advocates, and that, in general, professional bodies should have complete independence from government. The only reason for the residual but limited part that the secretary of state played in the process was to allow the title of Queen's Counsel to be retained. Queen's Counsel is a Royal appointment and only Ministers can advise Her Majesty on appointments to that rank. But the government had determined that there should not otherwise be any ministerial involvement in substantive decisions as to who should become Queen's Counsel. To that end, the secretary of state had decided that he would not assess applications himself nor would he add or remove names from the list of those to be appointed silk.[42]

39   BCM 21 June 2006.
40   *In the matter of an application by Martin O'Rourke for judicial review* [2008] NIQB 50.
41   [2009] NICA 31.
42   Ibid., Kerr LCJ, [64].

The second matter was that the objectives of the process were 'the promotion of fairness, objectivity, excellence and diversity'. The third was that the means of establishing this was to make the process 'competency-based', and this identified seven competencies sub-divided into no fewer than 39 'behaviours'.[43] The fourth was that many of those taking part in the process as applicants, or as referees, were unable to complete the necessary forms correctly.[44]

Three further conclusions may be drawn. One is that the process took an inordinately long time to complete. Applications were invited by the selection panel on 6 June 2005, and were to be submitted by 30 September 2005. Candidates were informed whether they had been successful or unsuccessful on 6 June 2006. The successful candidates were called to the Inner Bar on 26 June 2006, and those who were successful after the reconsideration directed by the complaints committee were called on 1 June 2007, almost two years after the process had been initiated. The other conclusion is that the complexity of the forms which related to seven competences and 39 behaviours, with the demand for information on each, meant that the demands on those who had to participate in the process, the applicants, the referees, and, most of all, the members of the selection panel and complaints committee, in coping with the documentation required by the process were far greater than were reasonable. Finally, it is hard to avoid the conclusion that the result of all the effort put into designing this process was to produce an extremely cumbersome, complex, time-consuming, long drawn out, expensive and completely unsatisfactory process.

Such was the level of dissatisfaction with various aspects of the process that a general meeting of the Bar was held on 7 June 2007, when the whole process was severely criticised by many speakers. By then the Bar Council had already set up a review panel to look again at silk appointments. In view of the many deficiencies of the 2005 scheme it is not surprising that in succeeding years a great deal of effort was put into designing a fresh scheme that would avoid the deficiencies of the previous scheme, whilst preserving the fundamental requirements of a process that was fair, transparent, and with an independent element, a scheme that would identify those advocates whose qualities justified their being admitted to a rank that was widely seen as a 'kite mark' that demonstrated professional excellence.

---

43  Ibid, [2].
44  Ibid., [28].

Designing a new scheme was not easy, not least because it was necessary that any scheme had to be acceptable to the lord chancellor and to the Law Society of Northern Ireland. It was not until December 2010 that agreement was reached.[45] By now many matters relating to the administration of justice had been devolved to the Northern Ireland Assembly, and there was a minister of justice in the Northern Ireland Executive. In April 2011 applications were invited from those who wished to apply for silk, and the guide issued to applicants defines the title of Queen's Counsel 'as primarily a mark of quality and distinction in advocacy, both written and oral'. Applicants are expected to have sound intellectual ability and a thorough, comprehensive and up to date knowledge of legal principle and the relevant rules of law and procedure. He or she should have a high quality practice based on demanding cases of complex law and fact.[46] The guide makes it clear that there is no fixed quota for silks, and that, whilst no minimum period of years' experience is prescribed,

> ...it is unlikely that individuals with relatively few years' experience in legal practice will have acquired the necessary skills and expertise for appointment. A recommendation for appointment as Queens Counsel is made primarily on the basis of the applicant's performance as an advocate.[47]

The whole process was drastically revised. In 2011 the selection was made by a panel chaired by the lord chief justice, and consisting of a senior member of the Bar, a senior member of the Law Society, both nominated by their respective professional bodies, and an independent lay person. The application form, and the form to be completed by referees, had both been significantly shortened and simplified when compared to those of the 2005 scheme. Compared to the 2005 procedure, the 2011 process was much quicker. Applications had to be in by 13 May, and the successful applicants were notified by the end of June. The necessary formalities then had to be gone through whereby the minister of justice advised Her Majesty, and when her approval was forthcoming the minister, exercising the prerogative powers on behalf of the Queen, issued the necessary warrant to the lord chief justice to call the successful applicants to the Inner Bar. This process took somewhat longer than had been anticipated, but on 26 October 2011

---

45  BCM 9 Dec. 2010.
46  Guide for Applicants 2011, 4.4, 4.5 and 4.6.
47  Ibid., 4.7.

22 members of the junior Bar were called to the Inner Bar by the lord chief justice, each having made the form of declaration now required. The declaration is in the form recommended by the Elliott Committee, namely

> I... do sincerely promise and declare that I will well and truly serve all whom I may lawfully be called upon to serve in the office of Her Majesty's Counsel learned in the law according to the best of my skill and understanding.

Subsequently Peter Sefton, one of the unsuccessful applicants, sought to challenge a number of aspects of the 2011 process by way of an application to the Fair Employment Tribunal, but in May 2012, after a pre-hearing review, the application was dismissed by the tribunal for want of jurisdiction.[48] One can only hope that the problems that have beset the appointments process for the office of Queen's Counsel for the greater part of two decades will not be repeated in the future, and that this ancient office will continue to be filled by those who have reached the front rank of their profession, and will command the public respect that it has enjoyed in the past.

---

48  *Sefton v QC Appointments Ltd & others*, Case Ref. 112/11 FET 2144/11, decision 4 May 2012.

# CHAPTER TWELVE:

## Governance of the Inn and of the Bar from 1969 to the present day

A significant change in the manner in which the Bar conducted its affairs took place in September 1970 when it was decided to appoint someone who was not a barrister to the new post of part-time secretary to the Bar Council.[1] The first holder of this new post was appointed at the end of the year,[2] but only held it for a short time, resigning the following March to take up a full-time position elsewhere.[3] He was succeeded by W.J. Arthurs who served as secretary until his retirement five years later. Until the appointment of a part-time secretary the secretary to the Bar Council had always been a practising member of the Bar who combined the duties of secretary with his practice. However, the growing demands upon the secretary meant that it became more and more difficult for a practitioner to find the time to deal with the increasingly voluminous and demanding correspondence of the Bar Council. The need to have a paid secretary had been recognised for some time. Indeed at a general meeting in October 1965 a resolution had been passed by 16 votes to 11 in favour of appointing a paid secretary, but the decision was not implemented until five years later.

Despite the obvious benefits from having a part-time secretary who was not a practising member of the Bar, when Arthurs retired in March 1976[4] the Bar Council reverted to the traditional practice. J.P.B. Maxwell, a practising member of the Bar, was appointed part-time secretary to the Council. Maxwell served until May 1981 when he stood down. He was succeeded by W.I. Proctor. Proctor had been appointed to the new post of full-time Library administrator a month before[5] as it was recognized that the demands of supervising the growing number of staff required someone to perform this role on a full-time basis. With his appointment the Bar finally accepted that it was no longer possible for this role to be performed by a practising barrister. Proctor remained in his combined posts of secretary and Library administrator for a decade. As we have seen in the previous

1    BCM 26 Sept. 1970.
2    BCM 18 Nov. 1970.
3    BCM 112 Dec. 1975.
4    BCM 11 Nov. 1975 noted his intention to retire with effect from 31 Mar. 1976.
5    BCM 6 Apr. 1981, and 5 May 1981.

chapter, he performed a vital role in the expansion of the Upper Library. He also implemented a significant change in the administrative staff when long-serving employees, such as Sergeant Corr and Mr Roy, retired and were replaced by younger personnel. The transformation of the Bar's administrative staff from a small organisation, largely made up of retired policemen, to a larger and more professional complement, was taken a stage further with the appointment of Brendan Garland as the first chief executive of the Bar in June 1992,[6] and he worked in tandem with Proctor until the latter retired in July 1994.[7] Recognition of the need for further specialised staff resulted in the appointment of Mrs Lynn McMonagle as a senior secretary, and Miss Lorraine Lawlor as book'keeper, in September 1995.[8] The increase in the size of the Bar had brought about a significant increase in the administrative staff of the Library. There was also the work involved in dealing with an ever larger volume of correspondence, and the increased need to respond to a constant stream of issues of importance to the profession. These developments meant that it was no longer possible for members of the Bar to deal with these matters effectively as well as conducting their practice. The assistance of full-time, professional, staff led by a chief executive who could assist with policy matters, as well as acting in a managerial capacity, was essential.

Since the late 1960s a recurring phenomenon has been the frequency with which government has appointed outside bodies to examine the structures and practices of both parts of the legal profession, a process which has required the Bar and the Inn of Court to re-examine long-established practices and structures. The first manifestation of this attitude came in 1967[9] when the Monopolies Commision conducted an inquiry into restrictive practices in the professions throughout the United Kingdom. The Commission sent questions to the Northern Ireland and English Bars about a number of long-established rules of practice. The Bar Council considered the proposed memorandum prepared by the English Bar Council before settling its own statement to the Commission later in the year.[10] The Commission reported in 1970,[11] and in December 1971 a general meeting of the Bar accepted that the rule whereby a junior led by a senior must always mark a fee that was at least two thirds of the senior's fee (the

6   BCM 17 June 1992.
7   ECM 23 Mar. 1994.
8   ECM 20 Sept. 1995.
9   BCM 8 June 1967.
10  BCM 26 Oct. 1967.
11  Cmnd. 4463.

two thirds rule), and the rules governing a system of minimum fees, should be abandoned because the Commission considered both to be restrictive practices. As the equivalent rules had been abandoned in England and Wales[12] it was plainly impossible for the Northern Ireland Bar to maintain a different position once the English Bar had changed its rules. Although these rules were abrogated, it continued to be the case that juniors generally, though not invariably, marked fees on the brief and refreshers that were two thirds of the senior's fees. This meant that the change did not have as great an impact on the earnings of the junior Bar as might have been anticipated, particularly at a time when there was much more work available than had been the case in the past. A further report by the Monopolies Commission in 1976[13] on the two counsel rule (i.e. that a senior could never appear without a junior) led the English Bar to abolish its rule from 1 October 1977. At a general meeting in October 1977 the Bar decided to follow suit.[14]

As we have seen, since the formation of the Inn of Court of Northern Ireland in 1926, and indeed before that when the Northern Committee of benchers of King's Inns was in place, the governance of the Bar had been divided between the benchers and the Bar Council. The benchers controlled the education and admission of Bar students, as well as exercising the ultimate power of deciding matters of professional discipline. The Bar Council dealt with the administration of the Bar Library, as well as setting rules of professional conduct, and representing the interests of the Bar whenever that was necessary. That might involve defending a member who it felt had been unfairly criticised by a judge, or commenting on proposed legislation, or on matters such as fees paid by the state for criminal or civil legal aid. The great increase in size of the Bar which we have considered elsewhere inevitably led to a change in the age structure of the Bar as the number of young juniors increased very considerably. This was recognised as early as December 1971 when the composition of the Bar Council was changed by increasing the number of members of the junior Bar from four to six, at least one of whom had to be of less than three years standing at the time of election.[15] This change in the composition of the Bar, as well as the

---

12  BCM 11 Nov. 1971 and MGM 16 Dec. 1971.

13  Cmnd. 512

14  MGM 17 Oct. 1977. The minutes record the Bar Council's recommendation that the two counsel rule be abolished, but do not record the outcome of the vote. However, the resolution must have been passed as the rule disappeared from the Bar Rules.

15  MGM 16 Dec. 1971.

weakening of close relationships between individual barristers and judges that inevitably accompanied this change, gave rise to a growing feeling at the Bar that there should be a change in the relationship between the benchers and the Bar, even though senior members of the Bar were benchers. This feeling was exacerbated by unhappiness amongst many members of the Bar at what they perceived to be a lack of recognition by the benchers of the need for changes in the educational requirements of the Inn, notably by continuing the pre-Institute route of call to the Bar, and by being slow to introduce the requirement for non-practising pupillage that we have considered in Chapter Six. Illustrations of this feeling are the comment at the annual meeting in June 1976 that the relationship between the benchers and the Bar Council 'is not what it ought to be';[16] the observation by John Pringle QC, then chairman of the Bar Council, at the annual meeting in June 1978, that the Bar had been expressing the view for the past five years that there should be a period of compulsory non-practising pupillage;[17] and the statement by Francis O'Reilly at a general meeting in April 1980 that he and three other members of the Bar who lectured on the Old Bar Course were resigning their lectureships.[18]

The benchers, who were the ultimate governing body of the profession, by then consisted of the eight judges of the supreme court of judicature who were members *ex officio*, as was the attorney general (although as the attorney general was by now a member of the English Bar and a member of the government at Westminster his opportunity to play a significant part in the affairs of the Northern Ireland Bar was limited). There were also eight members of the practising Bar nominated by the other Bar benchers, and two other places filled by the benchers which customarily went to distinguished members of the Bar or judiciary. As well as the dissatisfaction of many members of the Bar with the benchers, and with their perceived remoteness from the Bar, many members of the Bar were also dissatisfied with the Bar Council. The appointment of the Royal Commission on Legal Services under the chairmanship of Sir Henry Benson, a distinguished accountant, provided the catalyst for a fundamental re-appraisal of the respective roles of the benchers and the Bar Council, and the entire governance of the Bar. The Benson Commission was required to examine

16   MGM 24 June 1976.
17   MGM 26 June 1978.
18   MGM 28 Apr. 1980.

the provision of legal services in Northern Ireland and in England and Wales. Its investigations and deliberations concerned not just the internal relations between the benchers and the Bar Council, and the administration of the Bar Library, but also the solicitors' profession and its governance. It also examined the relationship between the two parts of the legal profession in Northern Ireland, and in England and Wales, including whether there should be a fused legal profession.

This was the first time in the twentieth century that the Bars of Northern Ireland and of England and Wales had been subjected to a searching and comprehensive scrutiny of this type. It is beyond the scope of this work to examine in detail every aspect of the Benson Commission's work, and the response of the benchers and the Bar Council to its questions so far as they related to the provision of legal services in Northern Ireland. Nevertheless, any account of the Bar at this time would be incomplete without some reference to the Commission, and the issues considered by it. It is a measure of the importance the Bar attached to the issues raised by the Commission that the Bar Council prepared a submission in answer to the Commission's questionnaire that comprised two substantial A4 size volumes, the first of 158 pages, with a second volume of appendices of similar size.[19]

A fundamental question posed by the Commission was whether the Bar and the solicitors' profession should continue to exist as separate professions, or whether there should be a single, fused, legal profession offering the public all the services hitherto provided separately by barristers and solicitors. The Bar Council's response demonstrated the rationale of the Bar as a separate profession by pointing to the advantages to the public of the existence of separate professions in Northern Ireland, as the following extracts from the submission show.

> The function of the barrister is to give opinions on difficult questions of law and to conduct litigation in Court. He acts as a specialist and consultant. In a small community such as Northern Ireland, there are few firms of solicitors who would require the services of such a specialist on a full-time basis. It is to their advantage and therefore to the advantage of their clients that every firm

---

19  Submission to the Royal Commission on Legal Services from the General Council of the Bar of Northern Ireland in answer to the Royal Commission's Questionnaire, Apr. 1977 (hereafter 'the Submission').

of solicitors can select a barrister either to conduct litigation for their client or to research a point of law as required. If there were fusion, then such specialists would only be available to smaller firms of solicitors if they handed their client over to one of those firms providing such a service.

The Bar considers that it is giving a specialist service to solicitors and to the public, at a time when the administration of justice is under stress, which could not have been given by a fused profession.[20]

This statement of the fundamental justification for the existence of an independent Bar is equally valid today. Whilst the Royal Commission accepted that the interests of the public were best served by barristers and solicitors continuing as separate professions, it made a large number of detailed proposals for changes, some of which, so far as the Bar of Northern Ireland was concerned, were far reaching in their ramifications. In particular it approved the Bar Council's proposals for a fundamental change in the governance of the Bar, proposals which involved radical changes in the powers and functions of both the benchers and the Bar Council, and which were tactfully described in the submission as 'Proposals for discussion with a committee of benchers'. In its submission the Bar Council recognised that the increase in numbers at the Bar meant that the Library had become more impersonal, and that

Barristers called in recent years say that they find more senior members of the Bar somewhat remote. It is not surprising that the more junior members of the Bar find the Inn of Court to which they belong somewhat remote. Many of them do not appear in the High Court and are only known to the County Court Judges and Magistrates.

The submission continued in terms that clearly reflected criticisms of the benchers and the Bar Council of the type already described, whilst at the same time acknowledging the limitations of the powers of the Bar Council.

The Bar Council has always been criticised as being rather ineffectual. This criticism has grown in recent years because young members of the Bar consider that they work in inadequate accommodation and that arrangements for pupillage have become poor. Older members of the Bar feel that the Bar Council

20   Ibid., vol. 1, pp 27 –28.

has failed to play its part in ensuring compulsory pupillage and in maintaining the discipline of the profession. Members of the Bar Council find that their powers are very limited. It is the Benchers who decide who the Lord Chief Justice is to be invited to call to the Bar and the liaison between the Benchers and the Bar Council as to anticipated numbers has not been satisfactory. The Bar Council's disciplinary powers are very limited and do not include the power to disbar. The Council cannot decide upon compulsory pupillage and it has in general limited powers to deal with large problems.[21]

The Bar Council's proposal was that there should be a senate composed of four high court judges, two county court judges, the attorney general and the solicitor general *ex officio*, four members of the senior Bar, six members of the junior Bar (one under seven years in practice and one under three years in practice). There would also be five co-opted members, of whom one would be an employed barrister, and another a barrister holding office in a judicial capacity (other than in the high court or county court). Among the office bearers would be a chairman who would be a practising member of the Bar. The senate would have a full-time secretary. It would have a number of committees, e.g. an education committee, a finance committee and a library committee. It would also have a disciplinary tribunal with the power to disbar, suspend, reprimand or order a member of the Bar to repay or forego fees, subject to a right of appeal to the lord chief justice who would appoint a number of judges and senior members of the Bar to hear the appeal.[22]

Although the Bar Council sent its submission to the Royal Commission in April 1977, the benchers do not appear to have formally debated what form their submission should take until January 1979.[23] During what was clearly a lengthy and wide-ranging discussion, a number of significant points were made. One was that there was a considerable (though not universal) feeling that the proposal for a three–tier system of government was unnecessary. It was accepted that the existing system of discipline was disorganised, although there was far from general agreement that the Bar Council was ineffective. There was also much discussion about the composition of the benchers themselves and the various ways in which benchers could be elected. Whilst the benchers' submission to the Royal Commission also

21  Ibid, vol. 2, pp 1-2.
22  Ibid., pp 3-4.
23  BM 17 Jan. 1979.

dealt with education and training, its principal concerns related to the general structures, and the respective roles, of the benchers and the Bar Council.

The submissions of the benchers were prefaced by an explanation for the lack of formal negotiation between the benchers and the Bar Council, which was explained by 'the pressure of work on those who are in positions of sufficient authority for discussion to be worthwhile', and to the 'necessity during the whole of the last four years (and in particular the last 18 months) to devote a great deal of time to the new Judicature Bill'.[24] While there was undoubted force in each of these points, the considerable period of time that was later to elapse whilst the benchers and the lord chief justice considered the Bar Council's proposals that followed the report of the Royal Commission gives rise to a suspicion that throughout the entire period there was a lack of enthusiasm on the part of some of the benchers for any substantial change in the existing structure.

The benchers' submission avoided going into to detail, but made a number of important points. One was 'the respective disciplinary functions and procedures of the Benchers and the Bar Council are not properly defined and should be reorganised'. Other suggestions were that recruitment to the benchers could be widened by, say, including two county court judges and 'possibly two practising junior counsel nominated by the Bar Council', as well as changes to the procedure for nomination of Bar benchers. However, the judges of the supreme court of judicature and the attorney general would continue to be *ex officio* benchers because 'It is of great importance to preserve the status of the Benchers as a body standing above the fray and a little remote from the atmosphere of the hustings, albeit in close touch with reality'. The benchers suggested that there was no need for need for a senate, saying that 'It would be better...to reform, so far as may be necessary, the Benchers and the Bar Council instead of creating a Senate to the detriment of both traditional bodies'.[25]

The benchers had not prepared a further or final submission by the time Sir Robert Lowry LCJ and Sir Frank Harrison QC went to London to give

---

24  Submission on behalf of the Benchers of the Inn of Court of Northern Ireland. (hereafter the benchers' submision), p. 1.
25  Ibid., p. 3.

evidence to the Royal Commission on 5 April 1979. As Lowry conceded, this meant that he had to be careful not to go beyond what he considered could be delivered when he gave his evidence to the Royal Commission, and although he and Harrison were largely in agreement, they differed on some points. The Commission pressed both very hard on the Bar's proposal that a senate should be the governing body of the profession, and how it might be elected. Whilst he recognised that there were matters identified by the Bar which required a remedy, Lowry said that 'This can be applied, in my opinion, by reform, not by revolution'. He argued that 'disinterested persons are required who cannot be accused of any restrictive practice as to call or pupillage or anything of that kind'.[26] Whilst this was an admirable proposition, it is evident that Lowry was unsympathetic to the suggestion that the great majority of the governing body of the Bar should be elected by the practising members of the Bar, as can be seen from the following exchange.[27]

> Q.....I am still puzzled to see what your objection is in principle to the second proposition that the overwhelming majority of the governing body should be elected by those who carry on the profession. Are you contesting that principle?
> A. Yes. I think it is not a good principle.

Although elsewhere in the evidence Lowry accepted that '… practising barristers must be in the majority so that in the end what they say goes, no matter what the Lord Chief Justice says',[28] it is hard to avoid the conclusion that the benchers wished to concede little substantive change when it came to the principle that the Bar should be in the majority on whatever institution was the ultimate authority for entry into the profession. When the Royal Commission published its report in October 1979 it accepted the Bar Council's submissions, subject only to proposing that the new governing body should have a larger proportion of practising barristers than the Bar Council had proposed, thereby diluting the power of the benchers even further. The Commission did not mince its words.

> We consider that the present system is unsatisfactory because practising barristers, except for the few that are benchers, can take no effective part in

---

26  Note of a meeting of the Royal Commission on Legal Services 5 Apr. 1979, p. 7.
27  Ibid.
28  Ibid., p. 26.

the management of their profession. We have no doubt that a Senate should now be set up on the lines proposed by the Bar Council, though with a larger proportion of practising barristers than was proposed by the Bar Council. We consider that the Bar Council should remain in existence as a committee of the Senate to deal with matters affecting the interests of practising barristers. The functions of the benchers should be taken over by the Senate. We think the reorganisation of the governing body is overdue; it should not be further delayed and should be put into effect during 1980.[29]

The benchers had obviously anticipated the commission's conclusions, because at a meeting of representatives of the benchers and the Bar in June 1979 the benchers suggested that, rather than form a third body such as the proposed senate, the Inn itself should be reformed. The Bar took some time to reformulate its proposals, and in September 1980 sent its revised proposals to the benchers.[30] These would have seen the benchers transformed into a governing body comprising two main components. The judicial component would be composed of four judges nominated by the lord chief justice, the lords justices of appeal and the high court judges, two county court judges (nominated by county court judges who were members of the Inn); and a practising component composed of the attorney general and solicitor general (both *ex officio*) and 12 practising members of the Bar elected by the practising members of the Bar, one non-practising member of the Bar (who may be co-opted), and honorary members of the Bar who would co-opted by the benchers *honoris causa*. The chairman and vice chairman would be practising barristers, and there would be a number of committees dealing with finance, education, the Library and professional conduct. The Bar Council would consist of the Bar benchers elected by the Bar and would be an autonomous body for the purposes of its separate powers and functions, in the performance of which it would not be subject to any directions from the Inn, and its function would be '...to maintain the standards, honour and independence of the Bar and to act for the Bar generally in its relations with others and in matters affecting the administration of justice'.

The merit of these revised proposals was that, whilst they preserved the essential framework of the Bar's proposals which had been endorsed by the royal commission, they avoided the abolition of the Inn of Court, although

29  Cmd. 7648, 42.61, p. 703.
30  I.G. 1981-The government of the Bar.

the majority of senior judges would have ceased to be benchers, and the dual structure envisaged by the royal commission would remain. Despite the proposals having been sent to the Inn in September 1980, the benchers were slow to respond. Although the Bar Council had decided to delay its annual elections in order to accommodate the new body, and there were frequent references in the Bar Council minutes throughout 1981 and early in 1982 to delay on the part of the lord chief justice in preparing proposals for the benchers to consider,[31] it was not until March 1982 that it was reported that discussions had taken place with the benchers and that good progress had been made. There was a short-lived quickening of activity with two further meetings by April.[32] This proved to be short lived, and there was no further response from the benchers until they sent a request for further information a year later.[33]

A major stumbling block for the benchers appears to have been concern that the new arrangements would result in the power to determine rights of audience being removed from the judges and transferred to the Bar, thereby removing the ultimate power of the judges of the high court and court of appeal to decide who could appear before them.[34] This difficulty was dispelled by the judges of the supreme court of judicature resolving on 30 June 1983 that

> mindful that at common law the power and duty resides in them on behalf of Her Majesty of deciding to whom they shall grant and from whom they shall withdraw the right to practise and a right of audience as barristers in the Superior Courts in Northern Ireland, hereby resolve and determine that the power of prescribing and amending from time to time the qualifications for admission as a student of the Inn of Court and the qualifications for admission to the degree of barrister-at-law with a view to call to the Bar of Northern Ireland and of determining what persons shall be admitted as such students and approved for call respectively, hitherto exercised on behalf of Her Majesty's Judges and with their consent by the Benchers of the Inn may henceforth be exercised on behalf of Her Majesty's Judges and with their consent by the Executive Council the creation of which is provided for in the Constitution of the Inn to which this resolution is annexed.

31  BCM 9 Mar. 1981, 8 June 1981, 14 Oct. 1981, 7 Dec. 1981, 11 Jan. 1982, 8 Feb. 1982.
32  BCM 1 Apr. 1982.
33  BCM 11 Apr. 1983.
34  BCM 9 May 1983.

This resolution cleared the way for the creation of the present, tripartite, constitutional framework of the Bar and the Inn of Court which came into existence with the elections to the Bar Council held in the autumn of 1983. The resolution was based on the law as it was then considered to be in the light of the English decision in *Re S (a barrister)* in 1969.[35] *Re S* accepted the accuracy of the line of authority that held that the power to decide who should be admitted as barristers by, or disbarred from membership of, the inns of court in London had been delegated by the judges of the superior courts to the inns of court, and so was subject to the control of the judges as visitors. On the basis of that long line of authority, principally stemming from the words of Lord Mansfield CJ in *R v Benchers of Gray's Inn*, [36] the judges purported to delegate their powers to determine the admission of students to the Inn to the Executive Council. However, in the light of the subsequent decision of the English court of appeal in *R v Visitors to the Inns of Court, ex parte Calder*,[37] in which Lord Mansfield's dictum that the powers of the inns to call to the Bar had been delegated to them from the judges was doubted, *Re S* must be considered as being of questionable authority.[38] The assertion that the judges in Ireland delegated any powers to the benchers of King's Inns at any time is also at variance with what is now known of the history of King's Inns from the work of Dr Colum Kenny.[39] It is also inconsistent with what occurred at the joint meeting of bench and bar in January 1926 which created of the Inn of Court of Northern Ireland. The history of King's Inns, and of the Inn of Court of Northern Ireland, suggests that there was never any question of the judges delegating any powers over admission and call. The evidence suggests that the judges of the superior courts were and are equal partners in the only institution in Ireland, and subsequently in Northern Ireland, with the power to determine who should practise before those courts, namely King's Inns and the Inn of Court of Northern Ireland.

Be that as it may, the resolution cleared the last obstacle to the implementation of the new dispensation for the governance of the Inn and the Bar. The first meeting of the new Bar Council was held on 10 November 1983, and

---

35   [1970] 1 QB 160

36   (1780), 1 Doug. K. B. 353, (99 ER 227).

37   [1994] QB 1.

38   See the valuable discussion of this area by Sir John Baker 'Judicial Review of the judges as visitors to the Inns of Court' [1992] PL 411.

39   Kenny: *King's Inns and the Kingdom of Ireland,: The Irish 'inn of court', 1541- 1800* (Dublin, 1992).

that of the new Executive Council on 17 November. Although the new arrangements conformed to the general framework approved by the Royal Commission in 1979, it differed in certain details from that model. The Inn of Court was now divided into two bodies. The benchers were responsible for the formal decisions to admit students of the Inn and then to call them to the Bar. However, the benchers had very limited powers in these areas as decisions as to admission and call lay with the education committee of the Executive Council, although the benchers retained the discretion to dispense with the rules of the Inn in exceptional cases.[40] This power has been exercised from time to time, and any application for the exercise of the discretion is now considered by a committee of the benchers set up for this purpose. The benchers other principal role was to act in an appellate capacity in relation to certain disciplinary matters. Only they can disbar a barrister, or disbench a bencher, for misconduct. The chairman, vice chairman and bursar of the Executive Council are elected by the Bar, and the Executive Council consists of these officers, the lord chief justice *ex officio*, two judges of what is now the court of judicature elected by their colleagues, two county court judges who are members of the Inn elected by their colleagues. In addition, there are nine other members of the practising Bar.[41] It is responsible for the finances and administrative staff of the Bar, as well as for the property and fabric of the Bar Library and the Inn of Court. The Bar Council deals with all other matters relating to the Bar. As the chronology described above makes clear, the process which led to the creation of the new framework was prolonged, but the new dispensation worked very well for almost 30 years. However, as we shall see, if the recommendations of the Bain review of the legal profession in Northern Ireland are enacted this will bring about some significant changes in the structures of governance of the Bar. However, before turning to consider the Bain Committee report, it is appropriate to mention some changes in the composition and functions of the benchers since 1983.

The first change related to finance. The benchers handed over to the Executive Council the substantial funds which they had accumulated over nearly 60 years through prudent husbandry and shrewd investments, funds amounting to stocks and shares worth in the region of £133000, of which

---

40  Rule 29, Rules of the Inn of Court.
41  Three QCs, and six juniors, one of whom must be of no more than thee years standing.

about £110000 was available for general purposes.[42] The only funds now held by the benchers consist of the accumulated surplus of annual subscriptions paid by working benchers. The second change was that during his or her year of office the treasurer of the Inn has replaced the lord chief justice as chairman of the benchers, although if the lord chief justice is present he customarily chairs meetings in the absence of the treasurer, and is accorded precedence over all benchers except the treasurer. The other changes were in the composition of the benchers themselves. These were necessary because the expansion in the size of the high court in particular meant that all the *ex officio* judicial places were taken by judges of the high court and court of appeal. This meant that benchers appointed county court judges, or to other judicial positions, or positions in the administration of justice, had to resign as benchers upon their appointment.

The first initiative to address this problem came in 1983 when the new constitutional arrangements were brought into existence with the election of Judge J.P.B. Higgins QC and Judge Chambers QC as Bar benchers. Subsequently those county court judges who had been benchers before they had to resign when appointed as county court judges were restored to their positions as benchers. Despite this change, there were still perceived to be a number of anomalies, one of which was the under–representation of the county court judiciary, and the election of six county court judges as benchers by the Executive Council in June 1995 was to redress this problem.[43] However, in 1997 it was decided to set up a sub-committee of the benchers under the chairmanship of Mr Justice Sheil, the treasurer for that year, to consider revising the composition of the benchers.[44] After lengthy discussions the sub-committee recommended, and the benchers accepted, a scheme that meant that henceforth there would be seven categories of benchers. (1) The judges of the supreme court of judicature of Northern Ireland. (2) The attorney general for Northern Ireland, the solicitor general, and the chairman of the Executive Council. (3) Such persons who hold public office in the administration of justice as the benchers may elect. (4) Four county court judges elected by the benchers.[45] Benchers in categories (1) to (4) were only entitled to serve as benchers whilst holding their qualifying

42   ECM 18 Jan. 1984.
43   ECM 21 June 1995.
44   BM 15 Oct. 1997.
45   Save that any county court judge who was a bencher at 1 January 1999 shall remain a bencher with the right to vote at benchers' meetings.

office. (5) Bar benchers, that is barristers of at least 10 years standing in private independent practice elected by the Executive Council, provided that their number exceed those in categories (1), (3) and (4) by at least two. These provisions were to provide for various categories of individual, whilst ensuring that judicial benchers were always outnumbered by non-judicial benchers. (6) Those who had ceased to be 'working benchers' because they no longer held their qualifying offices, or had retired from practice, were henceforth to be non-voting benchers, but with all the other rights and privileges of benchers, (known as a 'bencher emeritus'), thus giving effect to the principle 'once a bencher, always a bencher'. (7) The final category consisted of those elected as honorary benchers. The necessary changes in the rules were enacted by the Executive Council on 19 May 1999.[46]

The constitutional tripartite structure of the benchers, the Executive Council, and the Bar Council, and their respective functions, remained otherwise largely unchanged for the next two decades. However, in the first decade of the twenty first century the Bar and the Inn were confronted with potentially the most serious challenge to the continued existence of the Northern Ireland Bar that it had faced since 1921. This decade was marked by demands throughout the United Kingdom and the Republic of Ireland for a fundamental and comprehensive review of every aspect of the way in which the legal professions operated, a mood reflecting a widespread, and vigorously articulated, view that the existing model of legal practice and regulation of professional standards was anti-competitive; increased costs to those who had to avail of legal services, whether they be individuals or businesses; and needed to be radically transformed and opened to new models of providing legal services, particularly by multi-disciplinary organisations. Various models were suggested. One was to allow barristers to form associations with other barristers. Another was to allow solicitors and barristers to join together in a single firm (known as Legal Disciplinary Practices or LDPs). A third would be to allow lawyers to enter into partnerships with non-lawyers, such as accountants, in what are known as Multi-Disciplinary Practices (MDPs). A further proposal, and that with the most far reaching consequences for the administration of justice, would be to allow non-lawyers to own law firms, the so-called 'Tesco Law' approach because it is widely believed that one of the likely results of allowing non-lawyers to own legal firms would be that supermarkets and

46 ECM 19 May 1998, BM 26 May 1999.

other organisations would begin to offer legal services.

The implications of each of these models are profound. Insofar as the Northern Ireland Bar and the Inn of Court were concerned, they would not merely transform the Bar, but, in all probability, would substantially undermine, or, if some of the more radical proposals were to be adopted, destroy the Bar as an independent profession. As a result the quality and range of legal services available to the Northern Ireland community would be severely restricted. There would be significant problems relating to the independence and regulation of such models. The professions would incur considerable additional costs as a result. These costs would inevitably be passed to the consumer, thereby increasing the cost of litigation and reducing competition. The implications for the administration of justice of such changes would be profound.

The first significant development was the report on competition in the professions issued in 2001 by the Office of Fair Trading (the OFT) in London which was critical of what it viewed as unjustified restrictions on competition in the legal professions. Following the OFT report the lord chancellor invited Sir David Clementi, a former deputy governor of the Bank of England, to carry out an independent review of the regulation of legal services in England and Wales. Clementi reported in December 2004.[47] At broadly the same time as the Clementi Review was carrying out its work, a similar exercise was conducted by the Scottish Executive, principally into complaints handling, and in May 2005 it issued a consultation paper on this topic.[48] This was followed by a report on the legal services market in Scotland published in May 2006.[49] This questioning of the existing systems was not confined to the United Kingdom, because in January 2005 the Competition Authority in the Republic of Ireland produced a preliminary report which, amongst other matters, proposed the removal, or amendment, of the rules requiring barristers to be sole traders, and of the restriction on partnerships between barristers and solicitors.[50]

Given these developments in the other jurisdictions it was inevitable that there would be consideration of the desirability of similar changes in

47  *Review of the Regulatory Framework for Legal Services in England and Wales*, Dec. 2004.
48  *Reforming Complaints Handling: Building Consumer Confidence.*
49  *Report by the Research Working Group on the Legal Services Market in Scotland.*
50  *Study of Competition in Legal Services*, January 2005.

Northern Ireland. In December 2005 the Northern Ireland government set up the Legal Services Review Group under the chairmanship of Professor Sir George Bain, a former vice-chancellor of Queen's University, Belfast, to recommend to the minister of finance and personnel how the legal professions in Northern Ireland should be regulated. By its terms of reference the Bain Committee, as the Group came to be known, was required to have regard to the Clementi Review and the proposals of the government in London that were due to be published in a subsequent White Paper; the emerging findings of the Scottish Executive's inquiry into regulation of the legal professions in Scotland; and the study of competition in legal services in the Republic of Ireland, as well as a number of other relevant reports.[51] In addition to Sir George Bain, the Committee was made up of not only practising lawyers but had representatives of consumers, small businesses and the voluntary sector among its members.[52] The breadth of its remit can be seen in the following extract from its terms of reference.[53]

> To bring forward firm proposals for the regulation of legal services in Northern Ireland that are consistent with:
> - Protecting and promoting consumer interests;
> - Promoting competition through the removal of unjustified restrictions;
> - Promoting public understanding of citizen's legal rights; and
> - Encouraging a strong, effective and independent legal profession.

The benchers and the Bar Council each made their own submissions to the Bain Committee, and as these were largely accepted in the Bain Report it is unnecessary to set them out in detail. Both argued that it was crucial to the health of the administration of justice that an independent referral Bar continued to exist. The proposals for the creation of partnerships between barristers, or barristers and solicitors, would result in a reduction in the availability of legal advice to the public. They would increase costs because of the additional burden of insurance and compliance with regulatory requirements for barristers, for example in the oversight of arrangements for the handling of client's money. A particular concern of the benchers was that membership of the Bar should not be influenced by government or its appointees, and that regulation of complaints should henceforth be

---

51  *Report of the Legal Services Review Group, Legal Services in Northern Ireland: Complaints, Regulation, Competition* (2006), (hereafter 'The Bain report'), p. 5, 1.19.

52  Ibid., p. 84, 8.1.

53  Ibid., p.5, 1.19.

the responsibility of the benchers, and not of the Bar. To achieve the latter objective the benchers proposed that, to ensure that the benchers were seen to be separate from the Bar, the benchers should no longer be numerically dominated by the Bar benchers, whose number should be reduced to place them in a minority. So far as education was concerned the benchers proposed that responsibility for determining admission to the Bar, qualifications and pupillage and training should be transferred to an admissions committee of the benchers, rather than the Executive Council.

After exhaustive consideration of the issues, the Bain Report largely accepted and vindicated the submissions of the benchers and the Bar Council. It accepted the principle of a continued independent Bar, upholding the division of the legal profession, and rejecting partnerships between barristers, between barristers and solicitors, and multi-disciplinary partnerships. Its conclusions on the continued existence of an independent referral Bar merit repetition.

> We start from the premise that competition is to be welcomed, and that consumers in Northern Ireland should have access to legal services that are provided on a competitive basis, with consumers receiving good quality legal advice and representation in as efficient and cost-effective a manner as possible. We believe that the Northern Ireland model, consisting of solicitors in general practice and an independent Bar Library, is a competitive model with a good range of choice available to the consumer. Indeed, we heard on many occasions of the advantage of the current system in allowing the most remote and poorest client in Northern Ireland the chance to be represented, subject to availability, by the finest Counsel, and we consider that is an advantage that should not be lost.[54]

> In summary, we consider that the current model of the independent referral Bar Library is one that works well in Northern Ireland and which offers consumers access to a wide choice of high quality, independent legal representation and advice. In our opinion, consumers have more to gain than to lose from retaining the prohibition on barristers forming partnerships.[55]

---

54   Ibid., p. 72, 6.36.
55   Ibid., p. 74, 6.43.

The Bain report also rejected the concepts of barristers forming partnerships with solicitors, multi-disciplinary practices between lawyers and non-lawyers, and external ownerships of law firms by non-lawyers.[56] The report accepted that the existing independent Bar was not anti-competitive, that alternative models would not work in Northern Ireland, and that such models would reduce competition and increase costs to the consumer, or at the least they had not been shown to work. The Bain report is of great importance. After careful and through analysis of the relevant arguments it accepted that, whatever might be appropriate elsewhere, in a small community like Northern Ireland the independent Bar serves the community well. Perhaps the core of the argument in favour of the continued existence of the Northern Ireland Bar as an independent body of practitioners is to be found in the passages where the report rejected the arguments in favour of Legal Disciplinary Practices (LDPs), considerations which encapsulate the rationale for the continued existence of the Bar as an independent profession.

> One of the advantages of the existing system is that consumers in Northern Ireland, even from the most remote part of the province, are able to secure the best legal representation by engaging with their local solicitor. If LDPs were established, small solicitors firms would have difficulty in competing with them. In addition, since most of the LDPs would probably be formed in larger cities – the majority of Queen's Counsel live in or near to Belfast – the advantage of being able to find a solicitor within a reasonable travelling distance would be lost. Instead of solicitors' firms in seventy-four locations, they would be replaced by fewer LDPs in fewer locations. Hence both geographical convenience and consumer choice would be reduced. In addition, since LDPs would have their own in-house Counsel, consumer choice would be even further reduced. Instead of having 560 barristers to choose from, consumers would probably find that their solicitors expected them to choose from the in-house barristers so that business remained within the practice. And these barristers might not have the same level of skill and experience, at least in the particular area of law required, as those in another LDP.

> We consider that access to justice and competition are essential in a jurisdiction such as Northern Ireland and that anything that has the potential to hinder the achievement of these twin goals should be avoided. We consider that Legal

---

56  Ibid., pp 74-76, 6.46-51.

Disciplinary Practices have that potential. Hence we believe that the current prohibition on LDPs being established here should remain.[57]

Although the Bain report vindicated the stance of the benchers and the Bar Council that the administration of justice and the interests of the public were best served by the continuance of the Bar as an independent profession, nonetheless it recommended rights of audience for solicitors in the higher courts, as well as substantial changes to the structures for dealing with complaints. The Northern Ireland minister of finance and personnel at the time accepted the recommendations of the Bain report, and rights of audience for solicitors in the High Court and Court of Appeal have since been conferred by s. 89 of the Justice Act (Northern Ireland) 2011. The necessary legislation to bring about some of the other changes has not yet emerged. Nevertheless, in anticipation of the legislation, both the benchers and the Bar Council have started work on the necessary constitutional and administrative changes that will be necessary. We now turn to consider the implications of these recommendations. Their overall effect, and of some consequential or related changes that were not mentioned in the report, but which inevitably flow from the recommendations, will be to remove the educational and disciplinary functions from the Executive Council and the Bar Council. These will be transferred to the benchers, thereby reversing some major elements of the 1983 constitution.

The first major consequence of the recommendations is that the non-Bar benchers must now be in a minority, overturning the principle that existed from the formation of the Inn of Court in Northern Ireland in 1926 that members of the Bar should always be in the majority. Indeed, this principle can be traced back to 1872 when the benchers of King's Inns resolved that at least half of the Bench should be practising members of the Bar.[58] This has come about because, although the Bain report did not refer to this in its recommendations, the submissions of the benchers proposed that the Bar benchers should henceforth be in a minority. It is implicit in the Bain report that the role of the Bar Council should be confined in future to representing the interests of the Bar, and that the benchers should be the ultimate disciplinary body for the Bar. In order that it will be seen to be the case, although the general regulation of the Bar will continue to be by

57   Ibid., pp 74–75, 6.46–47.
58   Hogan, *The Legal Profession in Ireland 1789-1922*, p. 62.

internal regulation, the ultimate responsibility for complaints will rest with a body in which the Bar representatives are in a minority.

The benchers therefore set in train a complete review of their composition. By December 2010 there were 44 working benchers, of whom 22 were Bar benchers, and a further four *ex officio* benchers[59] who were members of the Bar, but there were only 18 judicial benchers. A committee was appointed by the benchers to consider the constitution. After consideration of its report, and draft rules, it was decided that henceforth the following would be *ex officio* judicial benchers. (1) The judges of the court of judicature, and any justice of the supreme court who had been a member of the court of judicature of Northern Ireland. (2) Seven county court judges. (3) Such persons holding any other judicial office not otherwise provided for. (4) Any bencher appointed to a judicial office other than that of a judge of the court of judicature would remain a bencher whist holding such office, and retain his or her precedence as a bencher whilst holding such office. (5) Bar benchers, being barristers of at least 10 years standing in private independent practice elected by the Executive Council, provided that the number of judicial benchers exceeds the number of Bar benchers by at least two. (6) In addition, the chairman of the Executive Council and the attorney general for Northern Ireland Bar are *ex officio* Bar benchers. (7) As before, those who retire, whether from practice or from the judiciary, become benchers emeritii who have a voice, but not a vote, at all meetings. As they do not have a vote they do not pay the benchers' subscription. Transitional arrangements were put in place to provide for the continued membership of existing benchers, such as the advocate general and solicitor general, whose successors would not automatically be benchers.

These changes are designed to bring about the necessary changes to comply with the Bain submissions, and to provide for the election as benchers of other members of the judiciary, whilst rationalising a number of anomalies in the previous arrangements. The necessary rules were passed by the Executive Council on 23 November, 2011 and came into force on 1 January 2012.[60] Some appointments to a number of vacant places have since been made. At the date of writing[61] there are now 45 working benchers, 21 of

59   The chairman of the Executive Council, the attorney general for Northern Ireland, the advocate general for Northern Ireland and the solicitor general.
60   BM 12 Dec. 2011.
61   10 Feb. 2013.

whom are Bar benchers, together with three Bar benchers who are benchers *ex officio,* 24 benchers in all who are members of the Bar. There are 21 judicial benchers, so the transition to a state where the judicial benchers outnumber the Bar benchers is still in progress.[62]

The second major change which will come about as a result of the Bain report will be the transfer of responsibility for the admission of students to the Inn from the Executive Council back to the benchers. Before the creation of the Executive Council in 1983, in practice the Education Committee was the principal function of the benchers. This will, in all probability, become the position again, particularly as the number of students admitted, and the number of those from England and the Republic who are called under the reciprocal arrangements and the under the European Directive, has increased so much since 1983.

The third major change will be the transfer to the benchers of part of the disciplinary process. The benchers will be responsible for overseeing the client complaints procedure. They will also act in an appellate capacity from the proposed complaints and service committees. The Bar will continue to be responsible for the initial work of these committees. These committees will deal with client complaints, and have the power to award up to £3500 by way of compensation for professional negligence or complaints about the level of service by members of the Bar. These responsibilities will undoubtedly impose considerable administrative and financial burdens on the Inn and the Bar Council.

In addition, the Bain report recommended the creation of a new Legal Services Oversight Commissioner with the responsibility of overseeing the complaints procedures. The financial and administrative implications of this new office, which will have an equivalent role for the Law Society and the solicitors' profession, will also be considerable. As the draft legislation required to carry these proposals into law has not yet emerged at the time of writing, it is not yet possible to identify the detailed implications of how these changes will affect the Bar. Nevertheless, provided that the legislation follows the Bain proposals, it may be thought that whilst these changes are inevitable in an age of increased regulation of every profession, they represent significantly less intrusive regulation than might have been feared.

---

62   20 Sept. 2012.

# PART TWO

# PART TWO

## Calls to the Bar of Northern Ireland

Fifty two barristers signed the Roll of Barristers between October 1921 and January 1926, and a further 1859 signed the Roll of Members of the Inn of Court between January 1926 and 31 December 2012. To these have to be added two who are known to have been called but who did not sign the Roll, giving a total of 1913 individuals who have been called to the Bar of Northern Ireland from the time it came into existence in 1921 until 31 December 2012.

Those who are called to the Bar of Northern Ireland fall within one of six categories. The first, and the largest category amongst those listed below, consists of those who have been students of the Inn of Court. Since the Inn of Court of Northern Ireland drew up its own educational requirements it has required its students to possess a recognised university degree. As recently as 1980 it was not a necessary pre-condition of call to the Bar of England and Wales, or to the Bar of Ireland, to possess a university degree, although for many years most of those called to either bar did possess such a degree. The second category consists of those called under the present Rule 15 or its predecessors under the reciprocal call arrangements with the Bar of England and Wales. The third category consists of those members of the Bar of England and Wales who are called under Rule 15A because they are of less than three years standing at the Bar of England and Wales. The fourth category consists of those within Rule 16 who are members of the Bar of Ireland called under the reciprocal arrangements between the Inn of Court and the Bar of Ireland. The fifth category consists of former solicitors who have been in practice in Northern Ireland for not less than three years who are called under Rule 17. The sixth category consists of those called by virtue of EC Directive 89/48/EEC. So far only members of the Bar of Ireland have been called under this provision.

Although it is customary for the lord chief justice to refer to the rule under which the barrister is being called, in the list below no distinction is made between those members of the Bar of England and Wales called under Rule 15 or under Rule 15A, and similarly no distinction is made between those members of the Bar of Ireland who have been called under Rule 16 and those who have been called by virtue of the EC Directive. Because the Inn of Court of Northern Ireland requires its students to possess a degree, the university attended by those students of the Inn who have been called to the Bar of Northern Ireland is recorded below. However, in 1977 the Inn dispensed with its previous requirement that members of the English Bar seeking to be called to the Bar of Northern Ireland had to have a university degree, and when the reciprocity arrangements with the Irish Bar were put in place a year or two before no requirement was required of members of the Bar of Ireland seeking call to the Bar of Northern Ireland. Although the records of the Inn usually indicate the degree obtained by an English or Irish Barrister, this is not always the case. Similarly, a solicitor seeking to be called does not have to state his or her degree, and so this information has been omitted in the case of each of these three categories.

Since the lord chief justice of Northern Ireland agreed with the lord chief justice of England and Wales and England in 1998, and with the chief justice of Ireland in 2000, that each would extend to those who had already been called to the Inner Bar in their jurisdictions the courtesies and privileges accorded to those who had taken silk without requiring them to be called to the Inner Bar in the jurisdiction to which they were now being admitted, it has no longer been necessary for a QC in England and Wales, or a SC in Ireland, to apply to be called to the Inner Bar of Northern Ireland on call to the Bar of Northern Ireland. For that reason in the list below they are described as 'QC of the Bar of England and Wales' or 'SC of the Bar of Ireland' to denote their rank in those jurisdictions at the time of their call to the Bar of Northern Ireland.

A person who falls into one of the six categories above, and who has satisfied the relevant requirements, is required to present him or herself before the benchers of the Inn of Court in the Royal Courts of Justice on the date fixed for their call. This does not apply to those who are granted temporary call as there is no such procedure or ceremony in such cases because their call is temporary. The under treasurer introduces the candidate(s) by name to the treasurer and the benchers. The treasurer then addresses the candidate(s) in the following words which echo the form used in the similar ceremony used by King's Inns before the Bar of Northern Ireland came into existence in 1921.

The Benchers of the Inn of Court, having considered your application to be called to the Bar, have acceded to the prayer in your memorial, and if you will attend the [Nisi Prius] Court at [  ] the Lord Chief Justice shall call you to the Bar accordingly.

The candidates then attend before the lord chief justice in one of the court rooms, usually the Nisi Prius Court, where the lord chief justice calls the candidate(s) to the Bar in public on behalf of the benchers, thereby completing a two part process. In a handful of cases candidates have been called *in absentia*. In such cases the candidate's call papers are considered by the benchers and the candidate is recorded as having been called *in absentia*.

The public part of the call ceremony takes the form of the lord chief justice reading out the name(s) of the candidate(s) whereupon the candidate rises at his or her place in the row of seats reserved for junior counsel. When there is more than one candidate the lord chief justice calls the name of each candidate. When all the names have been called the lord chief justice then says:

The Benchers of the Inn of Court have resolved, pursuant to Rule [as the case may be] of the Rules of the Inn of Court of Northern Ireland, that you be admitted to the degree of barrister-at-law in Northern Ireland. I have pleasure, therefore, in calling each of you to the Bar of Northern Ireland and each of you will take your place accordingly.

The candidates then resume their seats. The lord chief justice then addresses the candidate by name, the candidate rises and the lord chief justice then asks 'Mr X' or 'Miss X', 'do you move?', the barrister does not reply, but bows and resumes his or her seat. The question 'Do you move?' signifies that the barrister is being invited to 'move' an application in court, thereby showing that he or she is now recognised to be a member of the Bar.

Sir Brian Kerr LCJ instituted the practice, which has been continued by the present lord chief justice Sir Declan Morgan, of taking the opportunity to address some general words of welcome to the newly-called barristers after the call ceremony before the lord chief justice (and his colleagues if other judges are present with him on the bench) rises and leaves the court.

The newly-called barrister signs the Roll of Barristers of the Bar of Northern Ireland, and the Roll of the Inn of Court of Northern Ireland.

Until 2012 this was done after the public part of the call ceremony, but the increase in numbers being called in recent years led the benchers to modify the procedure, and after the barristers have been presented to the treasurer they now sign the rolls before the ceremony in court.

The list of barristers called to the Bar of Northern Ireland has been compiled from the records of the Inn of Court of Northern Ireland, as have some of the biographical details, supplemented where necessary by details from reference works such as *Who Was Who*, *Who's Who*, *King's Inns Barristers*, or, in some instances, their official websites, or from barristers themselves or members of their families.

The list of King's and Queen's Counsel has been compiled from the Roll of Her Majesty's Counsel in Northern Ireland, and the records of the Inn of Court of Northern Ireland.

# Barristers called to the Bar of Northern Ireland between October 1921 and 31 December 2012

Aiken, Margaret Kathleen Miller. Trinity College, Dublin. M. 1928. Probate registrar, OBE.

Aldworth, Philip Joseph. Queen's University of Belfast. M. 1981. Disbarred to become a solicitor May 1993, called again H. 1994.

Alexander, John George. M. 1924. Died 16 Sept. 1946.

Alexander, Karon Sheilagh. Oxford University. M. 1995.

Algazy, Jacques Max. Bar of England and Wales. H. 2011.

Allen, David Stewart. Bar of England and Wales. M. 2000.

Allen, Jayne Adele. Queen's University of Belfast. M. 2004.

Allen, Mary Patricia. Queen's University of Belfast. M. 2009.

Allen, Michael John. Queen's University of Belfast. M. 1980.

Allen, Robert (Robin) Geoffrey Bruere. Bar of England and Wales. M. 2009.

Allister, James Hugh. Queen's University of Belfast. M. 1976. QC M. 2001. M (DUP) NI Assembly 1982-86, MEP 2004-09 (DUP 2004-07, Traditional Unionist 2007-09), leader Traditional Unionist Voice party 2007-.

Anderson, Alfred Hastings. H. 1926.

Anderson, David James Douglas. Queen's University of Belfast. M. 2011.

Aylmer, John Frances Michael. Bar of Ireland. M. 2007.

Anderson, Michelle Judith. Queen's University of Belfast. M. 2002.

Anyadike-Danes, Monyeazo Nnenna Mary (Moyne). Bar of England and Wales. M. 1997, QC T. 2007.

Anthony, Gordon Kennedy. Queen's University of Belfast. M. 2011.

Appleton, Ronald. Queen's University of Belfast. T. 1950, QC H. 1969.

Archbold, Patricia Claire. Queen's University of Belfast. M. 1992.

Archer, Peter Kingsley. QC of the Bar of England and Wales, solicitor general. T. 1974, QC T. 1974. MP (Lab) 1966-1992, solicitor general 1974-79, cr. Lord Archer of Sandwell 1992. Died 14 June 2012.

Armstrong, Christopher. Queen's University of Belfast. M. 1987.

Armstrong, Ivan. Queen's University of Belfast. M. 1976.

Armstrong, Michael. Cambridge University. M. 1948.

Ashe, Thomas Michael. Bar of England and Wales. T. 1993, QC T. 1998.

Askin, Leona Celine. Queen's University of Belfast. M. 1998.

Atchison, Wayne Thomas (b. 18 Sept. 1979). Queen's University of Belfast. M. 2002.

Auld, Robin. Member of the Bar of England and Wales. M. 1973. QC 1975, judge of the high court of England and Wales 1987-95, lord justice of appeal 1995-2007, author of report on reform of the criminal courts 2001.

Auret, Nicola Jane. Queen's University of Belfast. M. 1990.

Austin, Briege Frances. Queen's University of Belfast. M. 2007.

Babington, Andrew Hume. A former solicitor. T. 1985.

Babington, Robert John, DSC. Trinity College, Dublin. M. 1947. QC M. 1965, MP (U) North Down 1969-72, county court judge 1974-92. Died 17 Sept. 2010.

Bacon, John Paul. Queen's University of Belfast. M. 1999.

Balmer, Anne, Elizabeth. Queen's University of Belfast. M. 1987.

Baker, Garret Nicholas. Bar of Ireland. M. 1998.

Bamford, John (Ian) Law. Trinity College, Dublin. M. 1957 (*in absentia*). Disbarred to become a solicitor M. 1961. Resident magistrate 1980-98.

Banner, Charles Edward Raymond. Bar of England and Wales. H. 2010.

Barling, Gerald Edward. QC of the Bar of England and Wales. M. 1991, QC M. 1991, judge of the high court of England and Wales 2007-.

Barlow, Mark David. Bar of England and Wales. H. 2006.

Barr, Dane Alexander. Queen's University of Belfast. M. 2009.

Barr, Peter Eric Playfair. Bar of England and Wales. H. 2002.

Barr, William Queen's University of Belfast. M. 1979.

Barrett, Richard. Bar of Ireland. T. 1991.

Barrington, Donal Patrick Michael. SC Bar of Ireland. T. 1976. Judge of the high court of Ireland 1979-89, judge of the European Court of Justice 1989-95, judge of the supreme court of Ireland 1996-2000.

Basset, Mark Raymond. University College, Dublin. M. 2010.

Bateson, Philomena Lucy. Queen's University of Belfast. M. 1972.

Baxter, Adrian Terence Joseph. Queen's University of Belfast. M. 1987.

Beale, Judith Helen. Bar of England and Wales. H. 1988.

Beard, Daniel Matthew. Bar of England and Wales. M. 1998.

Beattie, Ian. Queen's University Belfast. M. 1989.

Beattie, Samuel Murdoch. Queen's University of Belfast. M. 1970. Disbarred to become a solicitor M. 1971.

Beattie, Thomas James Stewart. Queen's University of Belfast. M. 1986, QC T. 2007.

Beaumont, Benjamin. Bar of England and Wales. M. 2011.

Beck, Andrew Donald. Bar of Ireland. H. 2011.

Beggs, John Peter. Bar of England and Wales. M. 2007.

Belford, Alfred James. H. 1927, KC T. 1950. An umpire, and then a national insurance commissioner, under the National Insurance Acts, 1948-70.

Bell, Christine Mildred. Cambridge University. M. 1990 (*in absentia*). Professor of public international law, University of Ulster.

Bell, Helen Suzanne. Bar of England and Wales. M. 1990.

Bell, Eileen Siubhan. Queen's University of Belfast. M. 1975. Sometime private secretary to the lord chief justice.

Bell, Rosalind Scott. Bar of England and Wales. M. 2012.

Bell, Susan Josephine. Bar of England and Wales. H. 1998.

Bellamy, Christopher William. Bar of England and Wales. M. 1978.

Bentley, Ronald Lawrence. Queen's University of Belfast. M. 1974, QC M. 1993.

Bergin, Rachel. Queen's University, Belfast. M. 2012.

Bernard, Malachy Thomas. Queen's University of Belfast. M. 2005.

Berry, William Gregory Hamilton. University College, Cardiff. M. 1989, QC T. 2006.

Berry, Robert Marshall Michael. Queen's University of Belfast. M. 1980.

Best, Nicola. Queen's University of Belfast. M. 1996.

Best, Harold Alexander. Bar of England and Wales. H. 1999.

Best, Rachel. Queen's University of Belfast. M. 2006.

Birtles, William Jack. Bar of England and Wales. M. 1998.

Birts, Peter William. QC of the Bar of England and Wales. T. 1996, QC T. 1996. Circuit judge 2005-.

Black, Joelle Marie. University of Ulster. M. 2008.

Black, Louis. Queen's University of Belfast. M. 1934.

Black, William Henry. Queen's University of Belfast. M. 1978.

Black-Branch, Jonathan. Bar of England and Wales. M. 2002.

Blackburn, Alan David. Queen's University of Belfast. M. 1974.

Blackburn, Robert John. Bar of England and Wales. M. 2000.

Blackmore, Thomas Maitland. H. 1924.

Blair, Thomas Alexander. Queen's University of Belfast. T. 1946, KC M. 1958. Deputy commissioner of national insurance 1959-1969, chief national insurance commissioner (later chief social security commissioner) 1969-83.

Blake, Martin Lawrence. Queen's University of Belfast. M. 1972. Practised in California for many years, returned to practise in Northern Ireland 2012.

Blaney, John Joseph Patrick. Bar of Ireland. T. 1976.

Bleeks, Niall Thomas. King's College, London. M. 2012.

Bloch, Peter. Exeter University. M. 1982. Left to work in industry.

Blom-Cooper, Sir Louis Jacques. Bar of England and Wales. M. 1996, QC M. 1996.

Blyth, Earnan Padraig. Bar of Ireland. M. 1976. Irish Language editor of the *Irish Independent*.

Blythe, Rhyannon Aveen. Queen's University of Belfast. M. 2008.

Boal, Desmond Norman Orr. Trinity College, Dublin. M. 1952, QC H. 1973. MP (U) Shankill 1960-72. Disbarred at his own request T. 2002.

Boal, Kathleen Lindsay. Bar of England and Wales. M.1997.

Boal, William Harvey. Queen's University of Belfast. M. 1988.

Bonnar, Robert Gavin. Queen's University of Belfast. M. 1991.

Bonsu, Joseph Konaduh. Queen's University of Belfast. M. 1980.

Booker, Patricia Claire. Oxford University. M. 1997.

Booth, Michael John. QC of the Bar of England and Wales. H. 2001.

Boothman, Kieran. Queen's University of Belfast. M. 1975.

Bourke, Robert Emmett. Bar of Ireland. H. 2012.

Bowman, Hugh. Queen's University of Belfast. T. 1950, QC H. 1967. Died 1971.

Bowles, William. M. 1925.

Bowman, Shellee Catherine. Nottingham Trent University. M. 2009.

Bowsher, Michael Frederick Thomas. Bar of England and Wales. H. 2000.

Boyce, Timothy John. Trinity College, Dublin. M. 1998.

Boyd, Dennis. Queen's University of Belfast. M. 1982. Combined being a lecturer in law at Queen's University with practice.

Boyd, Michael John. Queen's University of Belfast. M. 2001.

Boyd, Patrick George Cardwell. Bar of Ireland. M. 1976.

Boyd, Stephanie Elizabeth. Queen's University of Belfast. M. 2001.

Boyle, Paul Charles Joseph. Queen's University of Belfast. M. 1985.

Boyle, Christine Lesley Maureen. Queen's University of Belfast. M. 1973 (in absentia).

Boyle, Catherine Patricia. Newcastle-Upon-Tyne University. M. 1985.

Boyle, Christopher Kevin. Queen's University of Belfast. M. 1971. Lecturer in law at Queen's University, later professor of law at University College, Galway, then professor of law at Essex University 1989-2010, director of the human rights centre there 1990-2003. Died 25 Dec. 2010.

Boyle, Gerard James. Bar of England and Wales. H. 2003.

Bradley, Conleth Michael. Bar of Ireland. M. 2007.

Bradley, Mary Suzanne. Queen's University of Belfast. M. 1978.

Brady, Alan. Bar of Ireland. M. 2010.

Brady, Amanda Mary. Queen's University of Belfast. M. 1986.

Brady, Anthony Bernard Gerard. Queen's University of Belfast. M. 1994.

Brady, Grainne. A former solicitor. M. 2011.

Brady, James Arthur Christopher. Bar of Ireland. M. 1997.

Brady, James Oliver. A former officer in HM Customs and Excise. Queen's University of Belfast. M. 1973, QC H. 1985, county court judge 1995-2004, died 11 July 2007.

Brangam, William Alva. Trinity College, Dublin. T. 1978, QC M. 2001.

Brannigan, Peter John (Sean). Bar of England and Wales. M. 2002.

Bready, Andrew John. Queen's University of Belfast. H. 1947.

Bready, Michael Gabriel Joseph. Bar of England and Wales. M. 2000.

Breen, John Harley. Queen's University of Belfast. T. 1949.

Breen, Michele Annette. King's College, London. A former solicitor. M. 2009.

Brennan, Daniel (Lord). QC of the Bar of England and Wales. M. 2001.

Brennan, Lara Caoimhe. Trinity College, Dublin. M.1994.

Brennen, Anthony. Bar of England and Wales. M. 2001.

Brennen, Paul Simon. University of Northumbria. M. 1999.

Breslin, John Arthur. Trinity College, Dublin. M. 1983. Disbarred to become a solicitor T. 1991. Called again T. 1995.

Brolly, Padraig Joseph. Trinity College, Dublin. M. 1992.

Brown, Andrew Stephen. University of Ulster. M. 2005.

Brown, Frederick George. Queen's University, Belfast. A former solicitor. M. 1988.

Brown, Herbert Macaulay Sandes Brown. M. 1921. The first person on the roll of barristers in Northern Ireland. Later a judge of the high court, eastern Nigeria. Died 19 Dec. 1987.

Brown, James Alexander. Oxford University (President of the Oxford Union 1936). M. 1946, QC M. 1956. County court judge 1967-82, recorder of Belfast 1978-82. Died 19 May 1999.

Brown, James Richard Charles. Bar of England and Wales. H. 2001.

Brown, Jillian Clare. Bar of England and Wales. M. 1997.

Brown, Lee Isabella. Queen's University of Belfast. M. 1997.

Brown, Michelle. Queen's University of Belfast. M. 2010.

Browne, Jonathan Paul. University of Ulster. M. 1997.

Browne, Trevor George. Queen's University of Belfast. M. 1981.

Brownlee, Shelley Victoria. Bar of England and Wales. H. 2010.

Brownlie, Andrew James. Queen's University of Belfast. M. 2005.

Bruce, Michael Robert. University of Oxford. M. 1937. Died 17 Nov. 1973.

Bruir, Rory de. Bar of Ireland. M. 1992.

Buckley, Denis Joseph Vaughan. Bar of Ireland. T. 1977.

Buckley, Elizabeth Deirdre (Lily). Bar of Ireland. M. 2010.

Buckley, Gordon Thomas. Queen's University of Belfast. M. 1977.

Bullick, Richard James. Queen's University of Belfast. M. 1996.

Bundell, Katherine Michelle. Bar of England and Wales. M. 1997.

Burchill, David Jeremy Michael. Queen's University of Belfast. M. 1974.

Burke, Andrew Robert. Queen's University of Belfast. M. 1994.

Burnett, Richard Adrian. Coleraine University. M. 1984.

Burns, Paul James. Queen's University of Belfast. M. 2009.

Burnison, Gordon. Queen's University of Belfast. Secretary of the Federation of Building Trade Employers of Northern Ireland. M. 1973.

Burnside, Jeffrey Stephen. Queen's University of Belfast. M. 1984.

Bunting, Jude James. Bar of England and Wales. M. 2009.

Bunting, Mairead Bernadette. Queen's University of Belfast. M. 2001.

Butler, Patrick Joseph. Queen's University of Belfast. M. 1998.

Byrne, Anthony Paul. Bar of Ireland. M. 2010.

Byrne, Conor Colman. Bar of England and Wales. M. 2002.

Byrne, Justin Martin. University College, Dublin. M. 1997.

Byrne, Michael Christopher. Officer in HM Customs & Excise. Queen's University of Belfast. M. 1975. Disbarred to become a solicitor M. 1981.

Byrne, Suzanne. Trinity College, Dublin. M. 1991.

Byrnes, Aisling Alice Elizabeth. Bar of England and Wales. T. 1996.

Cahalan, Michael James. Bar of England and Wales. M. 1999.

Cahill, Nessa Ann. Bar of Ireland. M. 2012.

Cahill, Thomas Vincent. Queen's University of Belfast. T. 1957, QC H. 1973.

Cairns, Gavyn Noel. Trinity College, Dublin. M. 2002.

Cairns, Timothy. A former solicitor. M. 2003.

Caldwell, John Foster. M. 1925. KC M. 1946. First parliamentary draftsman to government of Northern Ireland 1945-58, consolidator of statute law-Northern Ireland 1959-61. Chief parliamentary counsel, Jamaica 1956-61. Senior legal assistant, foreign and commonwealth office 1961-62. Died 8 May 1981.

Callaghan, Rosaline. Bar of England and Wales. M. 1999.

Callan, Paul. Bar of Ireland. T. 1976.

Calvert, Barbara Adamson. QC of the Bar of England and Wales. T. 1978, QC T. 1978. Honorary bencher 1995. (Married secondly Lord Lowry).

Campbell, Austin Seamus. Bar of England and Wales. M. 2001.

Campbell, Briege Michelle Anne. Queen's University of Belfast. M. 1999.

Campbell, Brenda Mary. Bar of England and Wales. M. 2002.

Campbell, Conagh Mary. Queen's University of Belfast. M. 2007.

Campbell, Conor Patrick. Trinity College, Dublin. M. 1990.

Campbell, David Robb. Bar of Ireland. H. 1928. Died 14 Jan. 1934.

Campbell, Francis Augustine (Gus). A former solicitor. H. 2005.

Campbell, Gerarda. Queen's University of Belfast. M. 2008.

Campbell, Gillian. Bar of England and Wales. M. 2002.

Campbell, James Dawson. University of Ulster. M. 2009.

Campbell, James Taylor. Queen's University of Belfast. M. 1981.

Campbell, Marie-Claire. Queen's University of Belfast. M. 2012.

Campbell, Michael Stuart. Queen's University of Belfast. M. 1990.

Campbell, William Anthony. Cambridge University. H. 1960, QC M. 1974, chairman of the Executive Council 1985-87. High court judge 1988-99, lord justice of appeal 1999-2008.

Canavan, Claire. Queen's University of Belfast. M. 2007.

Capper, Barbara Margaret. Bar of England and Wales. M. 2000.

Capper, David James. Queen's University of Belfast. M. 1984. Reader in law at Queen's University of Belfast 2002-.

Care, Vivian Arthur. Trinity College, Dublin. M.1948, QC H. 1983, a master of the high court.

Carlisle, David Windrum. Trinity College, Dublin. H. 1928 (*in absentia*).

Carlin, Fiona. Queen's University of Belfast. M. 1992.

Carlin, Seana Marie. University of Ulster. M. 2010.

Carney, Caroline Mary (b. 23 Jan. 1952). Bar of England and Wales. T. 1985. SC M. 2001.

Carpmael, Kenneth Sydney. KC of Bar of England and Wales. H. 1948. KC H. 1948.

Carroll, Mella Elizabeth Laurie. Bar of Ireland. T. 1976. SC M. 1976, judge of the high court of Ireland 1980-2005.

Carson, Margaret Emma. Cambridge University. M. 2008.

Carswell, Robert Douglas. Oxford University. T. 1957, QC M. 1971, high court judge 1984-93, lord justice of appeal 1993-97, lord chief justice 1997-2004, lord of appeal in ordinary 2004-09. Created Lord Carswell 2004.

Cartmill, David Hugh. Queen's University of Belfast. M. 1980.

Casey, Elizabeth (Lisa) Jane. Queen's University of Belfast. M. 2004.

Casey, Patricia Mary. Queen's University of Belfast. M. 1991. Disbarred to become a solicitor T. 1992.

Casey, Paul. Bar of England and Wales. H. 2000.

Casement, David John. Bar of England and Wales. H. 2007.

Caslin, Siobhan Rachel. Trinity College, Dublin. M. 2011.

Cassidy, Connor Patrick. Queen's University of Belfast. M. 2012.

Cassidy, John Price. M. 1925.

Cassidy, John Bernard. Bar of Ireland. T. 1976.

Cavanagh, Caroline Rose. Oxford University. M. 2009.

Cawley, Francis Joseph. T. 1924. Died 5 Nov. 1938.

Chambers, John Desmond. M. 1923, KC H. 1938, recorder of Belfast 1943-44, resigned and returned to practise at the Bar. Died 2 Apr. 1945.

Chambers, Jonathan. Oxford University. T. 1995.

Chambers, Linda. Queen's University of Belfast. M. 2002.

Chambers, Richard Rodney. Queen's University of Belfast. T. 1950. Capped 6 times for Ireland at rugby football. QC M.1964. County court judge 1972-1985, chief social security commissioner 1985-97.

Charleton, Peter. SC Bar of Ireland. H. 1998. Judge of the high court of Ireland 2006-.

Chambers, Michael James. Queen's University of Belfast. M. 2005.

Chapman, Stephen Ian. Queen's University of Belfast. M. 2005.

Cheshire, Lauren Elizabeth. Cambridge University. M. 2012.

Chesney, George Cecil. Bristol University. M. 1983.

Christie, Eric William Hunter. Bar of England and Wales. T. 1975.

Cinnamond, Anthony Moore. University College, Dublin. T. 1957. Left the Bar in 1960 and resumed practice in 1971. QC H. 1985.

Clancy, Herbert Edgar. H. 1925.

Clarke, Alexandra Jane. University of Ulster. M. 2009.

Clarke, Ciaran. Queen's University of Belfast. M. 2012.

Clarke, George Bernard Francis. SC Bar of Ireland. H.1990. Judge of the high court of Ireland 2004-12, and of the supreme court 2102-.

Clarke, Ernest Walker Thomas Gibson. Queen's University of Belfast. H. 1952. Died 19 Sept. 1965.

Clarke, Laura Mary. Queen's University, Belfast. M. 2011.

Clarkin, Joseph Patrick. University College, Dublin. M. 1971.

Clayton, John Patrick. Bar of Ireland. M. 2010.

Cleland, Conor Luke. Queen's University of Belfast. M. 1995.

Cleland, Eric William. Queen's University of Belfast. M. 2006.

Clohessy, Grainne Michele. H. 2008.

Clissman, Inge Fedelma. SC Bar of Ireland. H. 1996.

Clulow, Jill Edith. Queen's University of Belfast. M. 1996.

Coey, Leanne Elizabeth. Queen's University, Belfast. M. 2011.

Coffell, John Edward. Bar of England and Wales. M. 2001.

Coghlin, Patrick. Queen's University of Belfast. M. 1970, QC H. 1985, chairman of the Executive Council 1992-93, judge of the high court 1997-2008, lord justice of appeal 2008-.

Coghlin, Richard James. Queen's University of Belfast. M. 2006.

Coiley, Peter Alan. Dundee University. M. 2003.

Cole, Kirsty Louise. Queen's University of Belfast. M. 2011.

Coll, Laura. Queen's University of Belfast. M. 2012.

Coll, Kathryn Helen. Queen's University of Belfast. M. 2007.

Coll, Peter Gerard Joseph. University of Ulster. M. 1996.

Collins, Brian St John. University College, Dublin. M. 1981.

Collins, Claire Frances. Queen's University of Belfast. M. 1997.

Collins, Jonathan Thomas. Queen's University of Belfast. M. 1999.

Collins, Michael M. SC Bar of Ireland, sometime chairman of the Bar Council of Ireland. H. 2011.

Collins, Ruth Marie-Therese. Queen's University of Belfast. M. 1982. Disbarred to become a solicitor M. 1990, district judge (civil) 2000-.

Colmer, Adrian William Gibson. Nottingham University. M. 1994.

Colton, Adrian George Patrick. Queen's University of Belfast. M. 1983, QC T. 2006, chairman of the Executive Council 2010-12.

Colville, Iain David. Bar of England and Wales. M. 1997

Comerton, E. Alan. M. 1963, QC M. 1975. Author of *A handbook on the Magistrates' Courts Act* (Northern Ireland) 1964 (Belfast, 1968). Vice chairman of the Executive Council 1989-91.

Comerton, Julie-Anne. Bar of England and Wales. M. 2005.

Comerton, Jill Elizabeth. Queen's University of Belfast. M. 1993.

Conaghan, Roger Hugh (Rory). Queen's University of Belfast. H. 1943, KC M.1956. County court judge 1965-74, murdered by the IRA 16 September 1974.

Condron, Martin. Bar of England and Wales. M. 2009.

Condy, John Devenish. M. 1925. Killed in action in the Second World War.

Conlin, Richard George Thomas. Warwick University. M. 1988.

Conlon, Anne. Queen's University of Belfast. M. 1980.

Conlon, Kevin Thomas. Queen's University of Belfast. M. 1976, QC M. 1993.

Conlon, Mark James. Trinity College, Dublin. M. 2002.

Connell, Clive Albert. Trinity College, Dublin. M. 1985.

Connell, Ernest Russel. Queen's University of Belfast. M. 1979.

Connell, Paul James. Trinity College, Dublin. M. 1985.

Conner, George Ernest. Queen's University of Belfast. M. 1983. Resident magistrate (later district judge (magistrates' court)) 1999-.

Connolly, Fionnuala Anne. Queen's University of Belfast. M. 1996.

Connolly, Jennifer. Queen's University of Belfast. M. 2004.

Connolly, John Gerard Joseph. Trinity College, Dublin. M. 2002.

Connolly, Jonathan Graham. Queen's University of Belfast. M. 2003.

Connolly, Martina Antoinette. Queen's University of Belfast. M. 1997.

Connolly, Mary Elizabeth. University of Liverpool. A former solicitor. M. 2000.

Connolly, Oliver Joseph. Bar of Ireland. M. 2005.

Connolly, Patrick James. Queen's University of Belfast. M. 1978.

Connolly, Tara Maria. Birmingham Polytechnic. M. 1991.

Connor, Neil. Queen's University of Belfast. M. 1993.

Conway, John Edward. M. 1925.

Conway, Paul. Queen's University of Belfast. M. 2000.

Conway, John Brendan. Bar of Ireland. M. 1997.

Cooper, Gerard. Bar of Ireland. M. 2010.

Cooper, Joseph James. M. 1925. Chief superintendent of the Belfast Post Office. Died 19 June 1940.

Cooper, Samuel Ernest. Queen's University of Belfast. M. 1989.

Cooke, John Donal. SC of the Bar of Ireland. T. 1984. Judge of the court of first instance of the European Union 1995-.

Cooke, John Sholto Fitzpatrick. Oxford University. T. 1931. Clerk assistant of the Northern Ireland Parliament 1952-62. Died 15 August 1975.

Copeland, Michael John. Trinity College, Dublin. M. 1983.

Copeland, Paul Gerard. Queen's University of Belfast. M. 1977. Resident magistrate (later district judge (magistrates' courts)) 1993-.

Coppel, Jason Alastair. Bar of England and Wales. M. 1998.

Corbett, James, Patrick. Exeter University. M. 1994.

Corcoran, Charles. Bar of Ireland. M. 1990.

Corken, Heather Laurene. Queen's University of Belfast. M. 1986. Later joined the Northern Ireland Court Service.

Corkey, Matthew Colin. Dundee University. M. 2008.

Cormacain, Ronan Pol. Queen's University of Belfast. M. 1998.

Corrigan, Aidan Barry. University of Ulster. M. 2010.

Corrigan, Aiden Christopher. Queen's University of Belfast. M. 1980.

Coulter, Nicola Elizabeth. Queen's University, Belfast. M. 2010.

Cox, Michael William Gilbert. Queen's University of Belfast. M. 2007.

Cox, Rosemary Jennifer. Bar of England and Wales. T. 1990.

Coy, Stephen Gerard. Queen's University of Belfast. M. 1996.

Coyle, Christopher Patrick Martin. University of Ulster. M. 2007.

Coyle, John Joseph M. A former solicitor. T. 1990.

Craig, Alastair Trevor. Bar of England and Wales. M. 2006.

Craig, Robert Wilson. H. 1928.

Cranston, Ross Frederick. QC, Bar of England and Wales. MP, solicitor general. M. 1998, QC M. 1998. Judge of the high court of England and Wales 2007-.

Crawford, Damien Gerard Neil. Bar of Ireland. T. 1993.

Crawford, Fiona. Bar of Ireland. M. 2009.

Crawford, Richard Andrew. Queen's University of Belfast. M. 1990.

Crawford, William Ernest. M. 1923. City treasurer, Belfast Corporation 1933. Died 11 Jan. 1959.

Creaney, John Alexander. Queen's University of Belfast. T. 1957, QC H. 1971. Col. TAVR, OBE. DL.

Creed, Thomas Finbar. Bar of Ireland. T. 1991.

Creen, Dolores Maria. Queen's University Belfast. M. 1986. Disbarred to become a solicitor M. 1990. Called again M. 1994. Again disbarred to become a solicitor M. 2005. Called again T. 2007.

Cregan, Rosena Mary. Queen's University of Belfast. M. 2011.

Creighton, Dawn Marie. Queen's University of Belfast. M. 1986.

Cromie, Alfred Albert. M. 1923. Died in Sierra Leone in 1937 where he was junior crown counsel.

Crossey, Caoimhe. Queen's University of Belfast. M. 2012.

Crossey, Samuel Blair. Queen's University of Belfast. M.1968. Disbarred to become a solicitor H. 1980.

Crowe, Keith. Queen's University of Belfast. M. 1979.

Cullen, Padraig. Queen's University of Belfast. M. 1985. Disbarred to become a solicitor.

Cunningham, Adrian Anthony Bernard. Bar of Ireland. T. 1977.

Cunningham, Alan James. University of Ulster. M. 2003.

Cunningham, Bernard Christopher. Bar of England and Wales. H. 1984.

Cunningham, Catherine Louise (Kate). Trinity College, Dublin. M. 1997.

Cunningham, Robert Henry Thomas. Bar of England and Wales. M. 2001.

Cunningham, Samuel Knox (b. 3 Apr. 1919). Bar of England and Wales. E. 1942. MP (U) South Antrim 1955-70. Created a baronet 1963. *DIB*.

Curran, Breige Bernadette. Queen's University of Belfast. M. 1984.

Curran, Desmond Lancelot Edward. Queen's University of Belfast. T. 1952. Later ordained priest in the Roman Catholic Church and served in South Africa.

Curran, Luke Francis. Queen's University of Belfast. M. 2000.

Curran, John Joseph. T. 1960, QC M. 1974, county court judge 1981-2005.

Curran, Lancelot Ernest. Queen's University of Belfast. T. 1921, QC T. 1943. MP (U) Carrick 1945-49, parliamentary secretary to the minister of finance and chief whip 1945-47, attorney general 1947-49. Judge of the high court 1949-56, lord justice of appeal 1956-75. Died 20 Oct. 1984. *DIB*.

Currie, George Boyle Hanna. Trinity College, Dublin. Member of English Bar. H. 1948. MP (U) North Down 1955-70.

Cush, Michael Christopher. Bar of Ireland. T. 1990. SC M. 1998.

Cush, Peter John. Queen's University Belfast. M. 1971, chairman of the Executive Council 2003-05.

Cushinan, John Martin. Queen's University Belfast. M. 1978, QC M. 1999, chairman of the Executive Council 2000-01, died in office.

Daly, Michael Bernard. H. 1921.

Daly, Ronan John. Oxford University. M. 1994.

Danaher, John Gerard. Bar of Ireland. T. 1990. SC M. 1997.

Danaher, Maurice. H. 1926.

Darling, Gerald Ralph Auchlineck. Bar of England and Wales. M. 1957.

Darling, Paul Anthony. Bar of England and Wales. M. 2004

Dargan, Brenda Mary. Queen's University of Belfast. M. 1986.

Davey, Gerard Mary Joseph. Queen's University of Belfast. M. 1979.

Davidson, Wendy Elaine. Queen's University of Belfast. M. 2000.

Davison, Madge Margaret Elizabeth. Queen's University of Belfast. M. 1984. *DIB*.

Dawson, Norma Margaret. Queen's University of Belfast. M. 1976. Professor of law at Queen's University of Belfast 1995-.

De Blaghd, Earnan Padraig. Bar of Ireland. M. 1976.

De Bruir, Alison Orna. Bar of Ireland. M. 2010.

Deeny, Donnell Justin Patrick. Trinity College, Dublin. M. 1974, QC H. 1989, high court judge 2004-. SC H. 1996, high sheriff of Belfast 1983, and chairman of the Arts Council of Northern Ireland 1993-98.

Deery, Matthew Francis. Bar of Ireland. T. 1977.

Delany, Vincent Thomas Hyginus. University College, Dublin. M. 1958. Regius Professor of Laws at Trinity College, Dublin 1962-64. Died Jan. 1964. Author of *Christopher Palles lord chief baron of her majesty's court of exchequer in Ireland 1874-1916 his life and times (Dublin, 1960)*.

Dellow-Perry, Emma Jane. Durham University. M. 2010.

Dennison, Mervyn William. Queen's University of Belfast. M. 1945. Joined the colonial legal service in Southern Rhodesia, puisne judge Northern Rhodesia 1961. Later Secretary of Fermanagh County Council.

Denvir, Ciara Mary. Queen's University of Belfast. M. 1995.

Denvir, Kevin Michael. Queen's University of Belfast. M. 1979.

Deverell, Averil Katerine Statter. E. 1922. The second woman to be called to the Bar of Ireland where she practised for many years. Died 17 Feb. 1979. *DIB*.

Devine, Michael Buxton. Bar of England and Wales. M. 2000.

Devine, Sean. Bar of England and Wales. M. 2006.

Devlin, Alistair Francis William. Queen's University of Belfast. M. 1982, county court judge 2011-.

Devlin, Brendan. Queen's University of Belfast. M. 1995.

Devlin, Catherine Patricia. University of Ulster. M. 2011.

Devlin, Anne Eimear. Queen's University of Belfast. M. 1975. Disbarred to become a solicitor M. 1986.

Devlin, Eoghan Joseph. University of Ulster. M. 2001.

Devlin, Niamh Marie. John Moore's University of Liverpool. M. 2005.

Devlin, Una. Bar of Ireland. M. 2009.

Dickson, Christopher William. Cambridge University. M. 1970. Department of the DPP, later with the serious fraud office.

Dickson, Sidney Brice. Oxford University. M. 1976. Professor of law at University of Ulster 1991-99, chief commissioner Northern Ireland Human Rights Commission 1999-2005, professor of international and comparative law, Queen's University of Belfast 2005-.

Diffin, John. M. 1924. Died 28 May 1949.

Dillon, Francis. Queen's University of Belfast. M. 1978. Disbarred to become a solicitor M. 1990.

Dillon, Noel. Queen's University of Belfast. M. 1988.

Dingemans, James Michael. QC of the Bar of England and Wales. H. 2008.

Dinsmore, Claire. Queen's University of Belfast. M. 2004.

Dinsmore, Margaret-Ann. Queen's University of Belfast. M. 1980, QC M. 1996.

Dodd, David. Bar of Ireland. M. 2012.

Dodds, William. Queen's University of Belfast. T. 1948.

Dodds, Nigel, Alexander. Cambridge University. M. 1981. Lord Mayor of Belfast 1988-89, 1991-92. Minister of social development 1999-2000, 2001-02, of enterprise, trade and investment 2007-08 and of finance 2008-09. MLA (DUP) 1998-2010, MP (DUP) North Belfast 2001-, deputy leader DUP 2008-.

Doherty, Brian James. Queen's University of Belfast. M. 1996.

Doherty, Fiona Louise. Trinity College, Dublin. M. 1997.

Doherty, Kelly Marie. University of Ulster. M. 2006.

Doherty, Michael Patrick. Queen's University of Belfast. M. 2011.

Doherty, Sarah. A former solicitor. M. 2011.

Doherty, Sean Joseph. Queen's University of Belfast. M. 2001.

Doherty, Sean. University of Ulster. M. 2007.

Doherty, Tanya Marie. Queen's University of Belfast. M. 1998.

Doherty, Teresa Anne. University of Newcastle-Upon-Tyne. M. 1978. Principal magistrate Papua New Guinea 1987-88, judge of the supreme court of Papua New Guinea 1988-97, CBE 1997. A judge of the high court and the court of appeal of Sierra Leone 2003-05, subsequently a judge of the special court for Sierra Leone.

Doig, Alyn. Queen's University of Belfast. M. 1979. Disbarred to become a solicitor H. 1984.

Donaghy, Gareth Paul. Queen's University of Belfast. M. 2001.

Donaghy, Rory Michael. Bar of Ireland. M. 1996.

Donald, Denise Agnes. University of Ulster. M. 2008.

Donaldson, Andrew Ernest. Queen's University of Belfast. M. 1967, QC M. 1978. County court judge 1983 until 1987 when he resigned and resumed practice.

Donaldson, Alfred Gaston. Queen's University of Belfast. M. 1944. Parliamentary draftsman.

Donaldson, Honor. Trinity College, Dublin. M. 2002.

Donaldson, Marcus. Newcastle University. M. 2006.

Donaldson, Stephen Gerard Terence. Queen's University of Belfast. M. 2002.

Donnellan, Brice Hargrove. Queen's University of Belfast. M. 1974.

Donnelly, Bebhinn. Bar of England and Wales. M. 1999.

Donnelly, Catherine Mary. Bar of England and Wales. M. 2012.

Donnelly, Catherine Mary Goretti. Queen's University of Belfast. M. 1977.

Donnelly, John Joseph. Queen's University of Belfast. M. 1981.

Doran, Jon Michael Paul. University of Ulster. M. 2011.

Doris, Susan Deborah. Bar of England and Wales. M. 2001.

Dornan, Eamon. Bar of Ireland. M. 2012.

Dornan, William Philip. Queen's University of Belfast. M. 1978.

Dougan, James Hamilton. M. 1925.

Douglas, Colin Norman. Bar of England and Wales. M. 1998.

Douglas, Lisa Katrina. Queen's University of Belfast. M. 2007.

Dowd, Roger Michael. Queen's University of Belfast. M. 1991.

Dowling-Hussey, Arran. Bar of Ireland. M. 2006.

Downey, John Thomas. University of Ulster. M. 2005.

Downey, Roisin. Middlesex University. M. 2008.

Doyle, William Patrick. Queen's University of Belfast. T. 1948. QC H. 1968. Resident magistrate 1970-73, resigned and returned to the Bar. County court judge 1978-83. Murdered by the IRA 16 Jan. 1983.

Drennan, Neil Patrick Cecil. Queen's University of Belfast. M. 1976, QC M. 2001. A full-time chairman of industrial tribunals, and of the Fair Employment Tribunal of Northern Ireland 2003-.

Drew, Sandhya. Bar of England and Wales. M. 2003.

Duddy, Malachai. Bar of Ireland. M. 2008.

Duffy, Gavan Patrick. Queen's University of Belfast. M. 1991. QC M. 2011.

Duffy, Michael Gerard. Queen's University of Belfast. M. 1989.

Duffy, Peter Joseph Francis. Bar of England and Wales. T. 1995.

Dunford, Gregory Craig. A former solicitor. M. 2000.

Dunlop, Andrea Patricia. Bar of England and Wales. H. 2002.

Dunlop, Jonathan Lawrence. Queen's University of Belfast. M. 1996.

Dunlop, Robert David. Queen's University of Belfast. M. 1998.

Dunn, Campbell John McLaughlin. Queen's University of Belfast. M. 1978.

Dunn, Darren William. Bar of England and Wales. M. 2004.

Dunn, Michael John. Queen's University of Belfast. M. 1987.

Dunne, Anne-Marie Therese. Bar of Ireland. T. 1984.

Dunwoody, Clare Lisa. Queen's University of Belfast. M. 1991.

Dunseath, Laura Ann. Dundee University. M. 2000.

Durkan, Mary Louise. Queen's University of Belfast. M. 2004.

Dutt, Dhan Raj. T. 1924.

Eady, Jennifer Jane. Bar of England and Wales. M. 1994.

Early, Thomas Lawrence. Queen's University of Belfast. M. 1976.

Eastwood, Luke. Queen's University of Belfast. M. 2012.

Eastwood, Sinead Marie. Queen's University of Belfast. M. 1990.

Edington, Fiona Anne Rider. Bar of England and Wales. M. 2001.

Edmondson, James Douglas. Bar of England and Wales. M. 1997.

Edwards, John Gerard. Queen's University of Belfast. H. 1950. Resident magistrate Kenya 1958-63. Disbarred to become a solicitor M. 1963. Resident magistrate 1974-1999. Called again T. 1986.

Egan, Alexander Howard. Trinity College, Dublin. T. 1935. Judge in the New Hebrides, 1940.

Egan, Michael Desmond. Queen's University of Belfast. M. 1989.

Elesinnla, Ayoade. Bar of England and Wales. H. 2009.

Elliott, Elizabeth Julie-Ann. Bar of England and Wales. M. 2001.

Elliott, Daphne Anne. Queen's University of Belfast. M. 1984.

Elliott, Fraser Caldwell. Trinity College, Dublin. M. 1966, QC M. 1978, vice chairman 1987-89, and chairman of the Executive Council 1989-91.

Elliott, Stephen. Trinity College, Dublin. M. 1984.

Ellis, Rosalind Thelma. Queen's University of Belfast. M. 2007.

Ellis, William Roche Denny. Bar of Ireland. M. 1976.

Ellison, Julia Barbara. Queen's University of Belfast. M. 2011.

Elvin, David. QC of the Bar of England and Wales. H. 2009.

English, Roy Cummins. Queen's University of Belfast. T. 1951. Died 19 May 1955.

Ervin, Noreen Ann. Queen's University of Belfast. M. 1976.

Esdale, Alan John. Oxford University. M. 1977.

Eve, Judith Mary. Queen's University of Belfast. M. 1973. Lecturer in law at Queen's University.

Fahy, Patrick Desmond. Edinburgh University. M. 1999.

Falconer of Thoroton, Lord. QC of the Bar of England and Wales. T. 1997, QC. T. 1997. Solicitor general 1997-98, minister of state at the cabinet office 1998-2001, at the department of transport, local government and the regions 2001-02, and the home office 2002-03, secretary of state for constitutional affairs and lord chancellor 2003-07.

Farell, Donal Joseph. Queen's University of Belfast. M. 2002.

Farell, Mark. University of Northumbria. M. 1994.

Farell, Mary Theresa. Bar of Ireland. H. 2003.

Farrelly, Francis Justin Joseph. Queen's University of Belfast. M. 1978.

Fee, Brian Francis. Queen's University of Belfast. M. 1978, QC M. 1996, chairman of the Executive Council 1996-98.

Fee, Dermot Patrick. Queen's University of Belfast. M. 1975, QC M. 1999.

Fee, Fiona Mary. Bar of England and Wales. M. 2009.

Fee, Geraldine Roberta. Queen's University of Belfast. M. 1988. Joined Northern Ireland Court Service.

Fee, Nessa Cassidy. Trinity College, Dublin. M. 2006.

Fee, Rory Dermot. University College, Dublin. M. 2007.

Feenan, Dermot Kevin. Queen's University of Belfast. M. 1989 (*in absentia*).

Fee, Tom. Trinity College, Dublin. M. 2012.

Feeney, Kevin Timothy. Bar of Ireland. T. 1989.

Fegan, Conan. Bar of Ireland. H. 2008.

Fennell, Sarah Jane. Bar of Ireland. M. 2012.

Fennelly, Michael Patrick (Niall). Bar of Ireland. SC H. 1978. T. 1988. Advocate general, European Court of Justice 1995-2000, judge of the supreme court of Ireland 2000-.

Ferguson, Niall. Bar of England and Wales. M. 1999.

Ferguson, Richard. Queen's University of Belfast. M.1956, MP (U) South Antrim 1968-69. QC H. 1973. Vice chairman Bar Council 1980-83. Left the Northern Ireland Bar in 1985 to practise at the English Bar. QC (Eng.) 1986. Died 26 July 2009.

Ferguson, Samuel William. Queen's University of Belfast. M. 1975.

Ferguson, William Barry. Queen's University of Belfast. M. 1974.

Ferguson, Stephen Michael. Bar of England and Wales M. 1991.

Ferran, Paul Anthony. Queen's University of Belfast. M. 1977.

Ferriss, Timothy Terence. Oxford University. M. 1968, QC H. 1989.

Ferrity, Patrick Joseph Anthony. Queen's University of Belfast. M. 1980.

Fidler, Ami. Queen's University of Belfast. M. 2004.

Finegan, Anne Frances. Queen's University of Belfast. M. 1978.

Finlay, Kathleen. Queen's University of Belfast. M. 1982.

Finnegan, Kevin James. Queen's University of Belfast. M. 1973, QC H. 1985, county court judge 2001-.

Fisher, Sian Lee Margaret. University of Ulster. M. 2008.

Fitzgerald, Edward Hamilton CBE. QC of the Bar of England and Wales. H. 2012.

Fitzpatrick, Bernard James Louis. Queen's University of Belfast. M. 1986.

Fitzpatrick, Thomas John P. Queen's University of Belfast. M. 1994.

Fitzmaurice, Bernadette. Northern Ireland Polytechnic. M. 1985.

Fitzpatrick, Edward James. Bar of England and Wales. H. 1998.

Fitzpatrick, Gerald Joseph. Queen's University of Belfast. M. 1982.

Fitzpatrick, Stephen Colbert. University College, Dublin. M. 2010.

Fitzsimon, Samuel Ernest Sydney. Bar of England and Wales. M. 1926.

Fitzsimons, Catherine Mary Ann. University of Ulster. M. 2008.

Fitzsimons, Wendy-Ann. Queen's University of Belfast. M. 1981.

Flanagan, Colm. University of Ulster. M. 2003.

Flanagan, Donal Thomas. Trinity College, Dublin. M. 1997.

Flanagan, Julie Marie. Queen's University of Belfast. M. 2002.

Fogarty, Kenneth Christopher. Bar of Ireland. H. 1996.

Foley, Brendan Anthony. Bar of Ireland. H. 2011.

Foot, Sir Dingle Mackintosh. Oxford University. Bar of England and Wales. M. 1969, QC M. 1969. Solicitor general 1964-67.

Foote, Jeffry Ian. Queen's University of Belfast, where he was a lecturer in law. T. 1971, QC H. 1985, county court judge 1997-2004, died 18 Apr. 2004.

Forde, Barry George. Dundee University. M. 1998.

Forde, Michael Brian. Queen's University of Belfast. M. 2009.

Forman, Ian Douglas. Bar of England and Wales. M. 1994.

Forte, Mark Julian Carmino. Bar of England and Wales. H. 1996.

Fortune, Malcolm Donald Porter. Bar of England and Wales. M. 2009.

Fosdick, David John. Bar of England and Wales. H. 2012.

Foster, Eamon Martin. University of Ulster. M. 2008.

Foster, Paul. A former solicitor. M. 2000.

Foster, Simon Michael. Queen's University of Belfast. M. 1993.

Fowler, Stephen Alexander. Ulster Polytechnic. M. 1984, QC T. 2006, county court judge 2011-.

Fox, John Gerard. Queen's University of Belfast. H. 1945. Resident magistrate. QC T. 1974.

Fox, Neil. Queen's University of Belfast. M. 2000.

Fraser, Alasdair MacLeod. Trinity College, Dublin. M. 1970. Department of Public Prosecutions 1973, deputy director 1988-89, director of public prosecutions 1989-2010. QC H. 1989. CB 1992, knt. 2001. Died 16 June 2012.

Freeman, David Anthony. Queen's University of Belfast. M. 1973.

Friedman, Daniel Simon. Bar of England and Wales. M. 2001.

Friel, Osisin Ruari. Queen's University of Belfast. M. 2011.

Friers, Fiona Therese. University of Ulster. M. 2004.

Fysh, Robert Michael Leslie. Bar of England and Wales. H. 1975.

Gallagher, Frances Catherine Adrianna. Queen's University of Belfast. M. 1983.

Gallagher, James Alexander. Queen's University of Belfast. M. 1972, QC M. 1996.

Gallagher, John Alexander. Bar of Ireland. M. 2008.

Gallagher, Paul. SC of the Bar of Ireland, attorney general of Ireland 2007-11.

Gallagher, Roisin Catherine. Queen's University of Belfast. M. 2004.

Gallagher, Suzanne Mary. Queen's University of Belfast. M. 2005.

Gallagher, William Alan. Queen's University of Belfast. M. 1973. Lecturer at the Institute of Professional Legal Studies 1977-2009.

Garnier, Edward Henry. Bar of England and Wales, QC, MP, solicitor general. M. 2010

Geoghegan, Hugh. Bar of Ireland. SC M. 1977. T. 1989. Judge of the high court of Ireland 1992-2000, of the supreme court of Ireland 2000-2010.

Geoghegan, Mary Finlay. Bar of Ireland. SC M. 1988. T. 1989. Judge of the high court of Ireland 2002-.

George, Mark McHallam. Bar of England and Wales. M. 2011.

Gervin, Colin. University of Ulster. M. 2012.

Gibb, Thomas Alan. Queen's University of Belfast. M. 1970.

Gibbins, Brian Richard. Bar of England and Wales. M. 1994.

Gibbons, Charles Christopher. Bar of England Wales. M. 1983.

Giblin, Patrick Martin. Bar of Ireland. M. 2007.

Gibson, Christopher. Queen's University of Belfast. M. 2009.

Gibson, George Peter Henderson. Cambridge University. T. 1968, QC M. 1978, county court judge 1983-2010.

Gibson, Heather Anne. Queen's University of Belfast. M. 1983, QC T. 2006.

Gibson, John James. Trinity College, Dublin. M. 1935. District probate registrar in Londonderry.

Gibson, Joseph John Laughlan. Trinity College, Dublin. M. 1927.

Gibson, Keith Charles Gordon. Dundee University. M. 1999.

Gibson, Lauren Jayne. Bar of England and Wales. M. 2001.

Gibson, Maurice White (b. 1 May 1913). Queen's University of Belfast. H. 1938, KC M. 1956. High court judge 1968-75, lord justice of appeal 1975-87. Murdered with his wife Cecily by the IRA 25 April 1987. *DIB*.

Gibson, William Robert Barry. Nottingham University. M. 1983.

Giffin, Nigel Dyson. QC of the Bar of England and Wales. QC. M. 2008.

Gifford, Anthony Maurice (Lord). QC of the Bar of England and Wales. H. 1984, QC H. 1984.

Gilert, Dennis Malcolm. Bar of England and Wales. H. 2001.

Gillan, Aileen Margaret. Queen's University of Belfast. M. 1992.

Gillan, Dominique Lye Ping. Queen's University of Belfast. M. 1993.

Gillen, John de Winter. Oxford University. M. 1970, QC H. 1983, judge of the high court 1999-.

Gillespie, Conor. University of Glamorgan. M. 1994.

Gillespie, John Christopher. Queen's University of Belfast. M. 1980.

Gilkeson, Janice Emma Shirley. Dundee University. M. 2009.

Gilmore, Mary Seanin. Bar of England and Wales. M. 2002.

Gilmore, Stephen Michael. Queen's University of Belfast. M. 2007.

Girvan, Frederick Paul. Cambridge University. M. 1971, QC H. 1983, high court judge 1995-2007, lord justice of appeal 2007-.

Girvan, Karen Elizabeth. Queen's University of Belfast. M. 1975.

Girvan, Peter Michael. Bar of England and Wales. M. 2005.

Glass, Mary Patricia. Bar of England and Wales. M. 2001.

Glyn, Caspar Hilary Gordon. Bar of England and Wales. H. 2011.

Gogarty, Alain Patrice. Queen's University of Belfast. M. 1979.

Goldsmith, Peter Henry (Lord). QC of the Bar of England and Wales. M 2001. Chairman of the Bar Council of England and Wales 1995, attorney general 2001-07.

Good, Patrick Simon. Trinity College, Dublin. M. 1983. QC M. 2011.

Gormley, Barry George. Trinity College, Dublin. M. 1998.

Goss, Craig Gerard. University of Ulster. M. 2004.

Gourley, Laurence Patrick. Queen's University of Belfast. M. 1990.

Gowdy, William Thomas. Oxford University. M. 2006.

Graham, David Charles. Queen's University of Belfast. M. 1991.

Graham, Edgar Samuel. Queen's University of Belfast. M. 1980. Lecturer in law at Queen's University and member (UU) of the Northern Ireland Assembly 1982-83, murdered at Queen's University by the IRA 7 Dec. 1983. *DIB*.

Grainger, Thomas James Gerald. Queen's University of Belfast. M. 1981.

Grange, Hugh. Trinity College, Dublin. M. 1970. Went to practise in England, later joined the Treasury Solicitor's Office and the Law Officers Department.

Grant, Charles Hugh. Queen's University of Belfast. M. 1991.

Grant, Gerard. Queen's University of Belfast. H. 1932.

Grant, John Eugene. Queen's University of Belfast. M. 1975, QC M. 1996, chairman of the Executive Council 1996-98.

Grant, Marie-Therese (b. 17 Oct. 1977). Bar of Ireland. M. 2009.

Grant, Martin Alistair Piers. Queen's University of Belfast. M. 1975, county court judge 2005-.

Grattan, Sheena. Lecturer in law at Queen's University. M. 1999. Author of *Succession law in Northern Ireland and Drafting trusts* and *Will Trusts in Northern Ireland*.

Gray, George Thomas Alexander. Queen's University of Belfast. M. 1972.

Gray, Margaret Olivia. Bar of England and Wales and Bar of Ireland. H. 2009.

Gray, Richard John. Queen's University of Belfast. M. 1989. Disbarred to become a solicitor H. 1992.

Gray, Robert Michael Ker. QC of the Bar of England and Wales. T. 1984, QC T. 1984.

Grealy, Clare Mary Frances. Bar of Ireland. M. 2000.

Green, Samuel. Bar of England and Wales. M. 2007.

Greene, Brian Joseph. Queen's University of Belfast. M. 1978. A full time chairman of industrial tribunals 2007-.

Greene, Richard. Bar of England and Wales. M. 1994.

Greer, Desmond Sproule. Professor of common law at Queen's University of Belfast 1973-2004. M. 1996. QC (hon.) M. 1996.

Greeves, Carolyn Robyn. Queen's University of Belfast. M. 1987.

Gregan, Haley Angela. Liverpool University. M. 1995.

Gregg, James Reali. T. 1923. Attorney general of Uganda Mar. 1944, judge of the supreme court of Nigeria, 1948, puisne judge Hong Kong 1953-61.

Gregg, Richard Wallace. Queen's University of Belfast. H. 1953. Worked for British Petroleum, then as a member of the Dept of the DPP for Northern Ireland.

Gribben, Kyle. University of Ulster. M. 2011.

Grier, Elaine. University of London. M. 2003.

Grieve, Dominic Charles Roberts. QC of Bar of England and Wales. M. 2010. MP, attorney general, advocate general for Northern Ireland 2010-.

Griffin, Nicholas John. Bar of England and Wales. M. 2011.

Grindle, Tessa Louise. Bar of England and Wales. M. 1998.

Haddick, Barbara Joan. University of Ulster. M. 2003.

Hagan, Colm. Queen's University of Belfast. M. 2003.

Haggan, Nicholas Somerset. Bar of England and Wales. M. 1986.

Haines, Florence Olive. Portobello College, Dublin. M. 1996.

Hale, Julian Michael. Bar of England and Wales. H. 2002.

Hall, Peter Stephen. Manchester University. M. 1987.

Hallerton, Damien Francis. Queen's University of Belfast. M. 2011.

Halliday, David Ross. Bar of England and Wales. H. 1999.

Ham, Stephen Robert. Queen's University of Belfast. M. 1999.

Hamill, Conor Michael Patrick. Queen's University of Belfast. M. 1990.

Hamill, Karen Elizabeth. Queen's University of Belfast. M. 1999.

Hamill, Mark Aidan. Queen's University of Belfast. M. 1977. Resident magistrate (later district judge (magistrates' courts)) 1999-.

Hamill, Michael Joseph. Queen's University of Belfast. M. 1977.

Hamilton, Eleanor Warwick. QC of Bar of England and Wales. M. 1999.

Hann, Kieran Patrick. Queen's University of Belfast. M. 1988.

Hanna, George Boyle. Queen's University of Belfast. M. 1927, QC M. 1946. MP (U) Duncairn. Minister of home affairs 1953-56, and of finance 1956. County court judge for Co. Down from 1956 until his death on 1 Mar. 1964. *DIB*.

Hanna, Robert Nicholas Harvey. Cambridge University. M. 1973, QC H. 1989.

Hanna, Ronan Gearoid. Bar of England and Wales. H. 2010.

Hannigan, Joanne. Queen's University of Belfast. M. 1998.

Hannin, Thomas John Berchmans Steen. SC Bar of Ireland. T. 1976.

Hansen, Sarah Louise. Cambridge University. M. 2012.

Harbinson, James Magoffin. H. 1923.

Hardiman, Adrian Patrick. SC of the Bar of Ireland. M. 1993. Judge of the supreme court of Ireland 2000-.

Hardy, Martin Joseph. Queen's University of Belfast. M. 2002.

Hare, Herbert Hamilton. H. 1924. Editor of the *Irish Law Times and Solicitors' Journal*, 1931-49.

Hargan, John Carl. Bar of England and Wales. M. 2001.

Harkin, Aidan Mario. Queen's University of Belfast. M. 1980.

Harkin, Orla Mary. Queen's University of Belfast. M. 2001.

Harkness, Ethne Elizabeth. Queen's University of Belfast. Lecturer in law at Queen's University 1977-1998. M. 1999. Director of law reform for Northern Ireland 2003-07.

Harper, Catherine Sarah. Trinity College, Dublin. M. 2004.

Harrison, Francis Alexander Lyle. Trinity College, Dublin. M. 1937, MBE 1943, KC T. 1948. President of the lands tribunal 1965-83. Knt. 1974. Died 19 Aug. 2002.

Harrison, Gareth Roy. Queen's University of Belfast. M. 1993.

Hart, Anthony Ronald. Trinity College, Dublin. M. 1969, QC H. 1983, county court judge 1985-1997, recorder of Belfast 1997-2005, presiding judge of the county courts 2002-05, high court judge 2005-2012.

Hart, Michael Christopher Campbell. Bar of England and Wales. H. 1994, QC H. 1994.

Harty, Francis Gerald. Queen's University of Belfast. T. 1950. Left the Bar but resumed practice before joining DPP. Resident magistrate 1980-95. Died 28 May 2009.

Harvey, Arthur Daniel. Queen's University of Belfast. M. 1972, QC H. 1989.

Harvey, Ciaran Stephen. Queen's University of Belfast. H. 1999.

Harvey, Deborah Alexandra. Queen's University of Belfast. M. 2006.

Harvey, Sinead. Queen's University of Belfast. M. 1988.

Hatton, Lee David. Queen's University of Belfast. M. 2000.

Haughey, Caroline Philipa. Bar of England and Wales. H. 2012.

Haughey, John Joseph. Bar of Ireland. M. 1998.

Havers, Sir Robert Michael Oldfield. Bar of England and Wales. QC, MP, solicitor general 1972-74. M. 1972, QC M. 1972. Attorney general 1979-87, created Lord Havers when appointed lord chancellor 1987, held that office for five months. Died 1 Apr. 1992.

Hayes, David. Bar of Ireland. H. 2000.

Hazlett, Thomas John. Bar of Ireland. T. 1984.

Heaney, Mark Anthony. Queen's University of Belfast. H. 2001.

Hedworth, Alan Toby. QC of the Bar of England and Wales. H. 2012.

Heffernan, Helena Mary. Bar of Ireland. T. 1984.

Henderson, Lois Amanda Laird. Queen's University of Belfast. M. 1981. Resident magistrate (later district judge (magistrates' court)) 2005-.

Henderson, Roger Anthony. Bar of England and Wales. H. 2009.

Hendron, Gerald James. Bar of England and Wales. H. 2006.

Hendron, Marie-Therese. Bar of England and Wales. M. 2001.

Hendron, Roisin. Trinity College, Dublin. M. 2001.

Heneghan, Margaret. Bar of Ireland. H. 2006.

Henry, Colin John William. Queen's University of Belfast. M. 1983.

Henry, Enid Margaret Lawrence. Queen's University of Belfast. M. 1931.

Henry, Herbert George. M. 1923.

Henry, Sir James Holmes, Bt. Bar of England and Wales. E. 1938.

Henry, Kathleen Teresa Elizabeth. Bar of Ireland. M. 2004.

Henry, Philip. Queen's University of Belfast. M. 2003.

Henry, Philip Ivan. Bar of England and Wales. M. 1990.

Henshaw, Andrew Raywood. Bar of England and Wales. H. 2011.

Heraghty, David Andrew Paul. Bar of England and Wales. M. 2003.

Herron, Charles. Queen's University of Belfast. M. 1970.

Hewson, Barbara Mary. Bar of England and Wales. H. 2000.

Hewson, Joseph Bushby. Bar of England Wales. H. 1953.

Heyes, Adam Scott. Queen's University of Belfast. M. 2005.

Hicks, William David Anthony. QC of the Bar of England and Wales. H. 2000.

Hibbert, William John. Bar of England and Wales. M. 2012.

Higgins, Adrian Patrick. Bar of England and Wales. M. 1999.

Higgins, John (Eoin) Patrick Basil. Queen's University of Belfast. T. 1948. QC M. 1967. County court judge 1971-84, recorder of Belfast 1982-84, high court judge 1984-93. Appointed a lord justice of appeal but died 2 Sept. 1993 before he was sworn in. *ODNB*.

Higgins, Malachy Joseph. Queen's University of Belfast. M. 1969, QC H. 1985, county court judge 1988-93, judge of the high court 1993-2007, lord justice of appeal 2007-.

Higgins, Margaret Mary. Oxford University. M. 1984, QC T. 2006.

Higgins, Nichola Claire Lesley. Bar of England and Wales. H. 2007.

Hill, Fiona Mary Tamar. Queen's University, Belfast. M. 2010.

Hill, Norman Leonard Alexander. Queen's University of Belfast. M. 1984.

Hill, Niall Benjamin Morrison. Bar of Ireland. M. 1997.

Hill, Richard David. Queen's University of Belfast. M. 2009.

Hill, Robert Charles. Queen's University of Belfast. H. 1959, QC M. 1974.

Hilling, Anthony. Queen's University of Belfast. M. 1975.

Hillis, James Gerard Thomas. Queen's University of Belfast. M. 1994.

Hindley, Stewart Frederick. Queen's University of Belfast. M. 2005.

Hogg, Christopher Andrew. University of Ulster. M. 2009.

Hogg, the Hon. Mary Claire. QC of the Bar of England and Wales. T. 1993 *(in absentia)*. Judge of the high court of England and Wales 1995-.

Holyroyd-Pearce, James Edward. England and Wales. M. 1974.

Holland, Robert Smith. H. 1926.

Holmes, Christopher Richard. Queen's University of Belfast. M. 1990.

Holmes, Conor John Michael. Queen's University of Belfast. M. 2009.

Hoolahan, Anthony Terence. QC of the Bar of England and Wales. T. 1980, QC T. 1980.

Hopkirk, Francis Cecil. Queen's University of Belfast. T. 1949.

Hopkins, Peter Michael. A former solicitor. M. 2007.

Hopley, David James. Queen's University of Belfast. M. 1979, QC T. 2006.

Horner, Thomas Mark. Cambridge University. M. 1979, QC T. 1996, judge of the high court 2012-.

Houston, Margaret Denise. Queen's University of Belfast. M. 1984.

Houston, John James. M. 1925. Died 1938.

Howe, Gerald Lewis. E. 1924. Went to Kenya, knt. 1949, chief justice Hong Kong Nov. 1950. Died 25 May 1955.

Howland, John Mary (b. 17 Sep. 1952). Queen's University of Belfast. M. 1981.

Huddlestone, Karl James. Queen's University, Belfast. M. 2010.

Hudson, Ronald. Bar of Ireland. M. 2011.

Hughes, Cathy. Dundee University. M. 2001.

Hughes, Deirdre. Bar of Ireland. M. 1998.

Hughes, Jonathan. Queen's University of Belfast. M. 2012.

Humphreys, Michael Robert. Oxford University. M. 1994. QC M. 2011.

Humphreys, Richard Francis. Bar of Ireland. H. 2001.

Humphreys, Richard William. Bar of England and Wales. M. 1997 (*in absentia*).

Humphries, Michael John. Bar of England and Wales. M. 2011.

Hunt, Denise Marie. Queen's University of Belfast. M. 1985.

Hunt, Niall Joseph. Queen's University of Belfast. M. 1987.

Hunt, Nigel Joseph. Oxford University. M. 1994.

Hunter, David William. Oxford University. M. 1971, QC H. 1985.

Hunter, Herbert Alan. Queen's University of Belfast. M. 1984. Joined the Northern Ireland Court Service 1990, chief executive of the Northern Ireland Judicial Appointments Commission 2005-07, and of the Law Society of Northern Ireland 2007-.

Hunter, John Kevin. Queen's University of Belfast. M. 1979.

Hunter, Mary Geraldine. Queen's University of Belfast. M. 1989.

Hunter, Norman John. Queen's University of Belfast. M. 1986.

Hunter, Victoria Natalie Bryony. Dundee University. M. 2008.

Hutton, Desmond Michael Denis. Queen's University of Belfast. M. 1998.

Hutton, James Brian Edward. Oxford University. T. 1954, QC H. 1970. High court judge 1979-88, lord chief justice 1988-97, lord of appeal in ordinary 1997-2004. Created Lord Hutton 1997.

Hutton, Rachel Kathleen Julia. Oxford University. M. 1997.

Hyland, Laura. Queen's University of Belfast. M. 2007.

Hyndman, Kelly Anne. Queen's University of Belfast. M. 2007.

Ifonlaja, Angela. Bar of England and Wales. M. 2007.

Irvine-Geddis, Jason Francis. Queen's University of Belfast. M. 1994.

Irvine, Malcolm Richard John. Trinity College, Dublin. M. 2005.

Irvine, Peter Charles. Queen's University of Belfast. M. 1982. QC M. 2011.

Irwin, Charles David Alfred. Queen's University of Belfast. M. 1971. Estate duty office, disbarred to become a solicitor M. 1973.

Irwin, Glenn Alexander. Queen's University of Belfast. M. 1979.

Irwin, Stephen John. Bar of England and Wales. H. 1997. A high court judge in England and Wales 2006-.

Irwin, William Henry. Trinity College, Dublin. M. 1932. Joined colonial legal service, puisne judge Trinidad, member of West Indies court of appeal, judge of high court of Western Nigeria.

Iyer, Koduvayur Subramanian Venkateswaran. Bombay University. H. 2003.

Jackson, Claire Oonagh. Bar of Ireland. T. 1991.

Jackson, John Dugald. Durham University. M. 1977. Professor of public law at Queens' University 1995-2008, dean and professor of law University College, Dublin 2008-11, professor of criminal law and procedure Nottingham University 2011-. Author of numerous publications on the law of evidence

Jackson, Joseph Gerard. Bar of Ireland. H. 1993.

Jackson, Peter John Edward. Bar of England and Wales. H. 1982 (*in absentia*).

Jaffa, Ronald Mervyn. Bar of England and Wales. M. 2008.

Jamison, Robert Nigel. Queen's University of Belfast. M. 1978.

Jebb, Timothy Robert Alexander. A former solicitor. M. 2012.

Jenkins, Simon Gilbert. University of Ulster. M. 1999.

Jenkinson, Angela Ruth. Queen's University of Belfast. M. 1984.

Jennings, Anthony Francis. Warwick University. M. 1987.

Jennings, Colin. Bar of Ireland. M. 2010.

Jennings, Lisa. Bar of England and Wales. H. 2002.

Johnson, William. Trinity College, Dublin. T. 1924, QC M. 1946. County court judge for Co. Tyrone and South Antrim 1947-78. Author of *History and customs of the Bar and Circuit of Northern Ireland, a personal recollection* (Belfast, 1985), and *The Irish legal scene glimpses of the past* (Belfast, 1987). Active in the Scout movement throughout his life, culminating in his service as chief commissioner for Northern Ireland 1955-65. Died 26 July 1993.

Johnston, Christopher George. Bar of England and Wales. H. 2003.

Johnston, William Denis. H. 1926. Playwright and writer, and father of Jennifer Johnston, the novelist. *DIB*.

Johnston, James Michael. Portabello College, Dublin. M. 1997.

Johnston, Jean Michele. Wolverhampton Polytechnic. M. 1987.

Johnston, Jill. Bar of England and Wales. H. 1998.

Johnston, Natalie. University of Ulster. M. 2010.

Johnston, Nicole Elizabeth. Bar of Ireland. M. 1997.

Jones, Andrew Kenneth Robert. Queen's University of Belfast. M. 1973.

Jones, Ashleigh Margaret. Queen's University of Belfast. M. 2008.

Jones, Daniel Oskar. Bar of England and Wales. M. 2002.

Jones, Edward Warburton. Trinity College, Dublin. H. 1936, QC T. 1948. MP (U) Londonderry City 1951-68, attorney general 1964-68, high court judge 1968-1975, lord justice of appeal 1973-1984. Author of *Jones LJ his life and times the autobiography of the Rt Hon Sir Edward Jones* (Enniskillen, 1987). Died 17 Mar. 1993.

Jones, Frederick Elwyn. Member of the Bar of England and Wales. H. 1958, QC H. 1958. Lord chancellor 1974-79. Died 4 Dec. 1989.

Jones, Gregory Percy. Bar of England and Wales. H. 2008.

Jones, Jonathan Guy. Bar of England and Wales. M. 2006.

Jones, Melanie. A former solicitor. M. 2012.

Jones, Nicolas Con Thomas. University of Ulster. M. 2004.

Jones, Peter William Warburton. Bar of England and Wales T. 1975. Practised in Northern Ireland from 1994 until his death on 29 Mar. 2001. *DIB*.

Jones, Susan Heather. Queen's University of Belfast. M. 2010.

Jones, Timothy Arthur. Bar of England and Wales. H. 1998.

Jordan Jowett, Deborah. Bar of England and Wales. M. 1994.

Jordan, Katie Suzanne. Queen's University of Belfast. M. 2009.

Jowett, Cristina Samanta Hustwait Frias. Bar of England and Wales. M. 1997.

Junkin, William Roy. Queen's University of Belfast. M. 1971. Law lecturer at Queen's University. Department of the DPP, deputy director of public prosecutions 1998-2008, also served as acting director for a time during that period. CB.

Kane, Alan James. Queen's University of Belfast. M. 1981, QC T. 2007. Member (DUP) Northern Ireland Assembly 1982-86, member Cookstown DC 1981-93 (chairman 1986-91).

Kane, Maxine Sharon. Queen's University of Belfast. M. 1991.

Kavanaugh, Claire Alison. Bar of England and Wales. H. 2000.

Keane, Desmond St John. QC of the Bar of England and Wales. M. 1993, QC M. 1993.

Keaney, Damien Gerard. Bar of Ireland. M. 2009.

Keaney, Francesca Maria Theresa. Queen's University of Belfast. M. 2006.

Kearney, Brendan. Queen's University of Belfast. M. 2012.

Kearney, James Martin (Sean). Bar of England and Wales. M. 2002.

Kearney, John Joseph. Queen's University of Belfast. M. 1989. QC M. 2011.

Kearney, Paul. A former solicitor. M. 2011.

Kearns, Martin Joseph. Bar of Ireland. M. 1999.

Keating, Alan Jude. Bar of Ireland. M. 2012.

Keegan, Brian McMurrough. University of Leicester. M. 1998.

Keegan, Patrick Gerard. Queen's University of Belfast. M. 1992.

Keenan, Colm Joseph. Queen's University of Belfast. M. 1980. QC M. 2011.

Keenan, Rachel Elizabeth. Trinity College, Dublin. M. 2008.

Keery, Neil William. Bar of England and Wales. H. 1998.

Kell, Stephen James. Queen's University of Belfast. M. 1984.

Kelley, Severina Frances. Queen's University of Belfast. M. 2011.

Kelly, Caroline. Bar of Ireland. M. 1997.

Kelly, Brendan Damien. Bar of England and Wales. H. 2011.

Kelly, Elaine Isabella. Queen's University of Belfast. M. 1991.

Kelly, Gerard Francis. Bar of Ireland. M. 2010.

Kelly, John William Basil. Trinity College, Dublin. T. 1944. QC M. 1958. MP (U) Mid Down 1964-72, attorney general 1968-72, judge of the high court 1973-84, lord justice of appeal 1984-95. Died 5 Dec. 2008.

Kelly, Leanne. Dundee University. M. 2001.

Kelly, Marie Margaret. University College, Dublin. M. 2010.

Kelly, Marie-Therese (Maxine). Bar of Ireland. M. 2002.

Kelly, Michael Patrick. Queen's University of Belfast. M. 1980.

Kelly, Matthias John. Bar of England and Wales. M. 1983.

Kelly, Peter Augustine. Bar of Ireland. T. 1983, judge of the high court of Ireland 1996-.

Kelly, Patricia Margaret Agnes. Queen's University of Belfast. M. 1983.

Kelly, Robert James. H. 1924.

Kelly, Shaun Patrick. Queen's University of Belfast. M. 1977.

Kelly, Teresa Josephine. Bar of England and Wales. M. 1999.

Kelly, Thomas Andrew. Bar of England and Wales. H. 1982.

Kelso, Stephen. Manchester Polytechnic. M. 1993.

Kennedy, Bernard Charles (Brian). Queen's University of Belfast.
M. 1978, QC M. 2001.

Kennedy, Beresford Roland George. Bar of England and Wales. H. 1999.

Kennedy, Denise Margaret. Exeter University. A former school teacher. M. 1977. Private secretary to the lord chief justice 1990-93, master of the high court 1993-2000, county court judge 2000-2012.

Kennedy, Fiona Mary Patricia. Sheffield University. M. 1992.

Kennedy, Hugh Paul. Queen's University of Belfast. H. 1956, QC H. 1973, chairman of the Bar Council 1980-82.

Kennedy, Irnya. University of Odessa. M. 2005.

Kennedy, James Alexander. Queen's University of Belfast. M. 1999.

Kennedy, John Andrew Dunn. Bar of England and Wales. H. 1989. Head of the office of law reform 1976-82, Clerk to the Northern Ireland Assembly 1979-99.

Kennedy, Joseph Michael. Queen's University of Belfast. M. 2003.

Kennedy, Mary Clare. Bar of Ireland. M. 2011.

Kennedy, Martin Joseph. Bar of Ireland. T. 1976.

Kennedy, Patricia Anne. Queen's University of Belfast. M. 1974.

Kennedy, Robert Thomas Quin. Cambridge University. M. 1980. Disbarred to become a solicitor M. 1985.

Kennedy, Roisin. Bar of England and Wales. M. 2009.

Keogh, Michael John. Bar of Ireland. H. 1989.

Kerr, Brian Francis. Queen's University of Belfast. M. 1970, QC H. 1983, judge of the high court 1993-2004, lord chief justice 2004-2009. Lord of appeal in ordinary and created Lord Kerr of Tonaghmore 28 June 2009, a justice of the supreme court of the United Kingdom Oct. 2009-.

Kerr, Gordon William. Queen's University of Belfast. M. 1976, QC M. 1996, a county court judge 2012–

Kerr, Linda Patricia. A former solicitor. M. 1999.

Kerr, Nicola Jane. Queen's University of Belfast. M. 1993.

Kerr, Margaret. Bar of England and Wales. M. 1999.

Kerr, Patrick Brian. Bar of England and Wales. M. 2008.

Kerrin, Andrew. Queen's University of Belfast. M. 2006.

Kessler, James Richard. QC of the Bar of England and Wales. M. 2003.

Khan, Shaukat Ali. Bar of England and Wales. M. 1994.

Kidd, Julia Helen. Trinity College, Dublin. M. 2005.

Kierans, Catherine. Bar of England and Wales. H. 2005.

Kiley, Denise Charlotte. Queen's University of Belfast. M. 2008.

Killen, Orla Claire. University College, Dublin. M. 2010.

Killen, Shona Marie. Queen's University of Belfast. M. 2011.

Killops, Nigel. Queen's University of Belfast. M. 1976.

Kilpatrick, Alyson. Bar of England and Wales. H. 1998.

Kimber, Katherine Anne. Queen's University of Belfast. M. 2001. Disbarred to become a solicitor H. 2006.

Kinder, Ann Catherine. Trinity College, Dublin. M. 1993. Disbarred to become a solicitor T. 1995.

Kinkead, Michael Glencross. University of Ulster. M. 2010.

King. Leo Aloysius. T. 1924. Died 28 July 1935.

King, Peter. Manchester University. T. 1994.

Kinnear, Jonathan Shea. Bar of England and Wales. M. 1996.

Kinnen, Jeremy James William. Queen's University of Belfast. M. 2007.

Kinney, Marie Clare. Queen's University of Belfast. M. 1993.

Kinney, Sara Elizabeth. Queen's University of Belfast. M. 1991.

Kinsella, Gareth James. Bar of Ireland. M. 2010.

Kirkwood, Jennifer Eileen. Dundee University. M. 2008.

Kirwan, Samuel Valentine. T. 1923.

Kitchin, David James Tyson. Bar of England and Wales. M. 1987.

Kitson, Raymond Andrew. Trinity College, Dublin. M. 1975.

Kitson, Mrs Theresa Bridget (Tessa). Queen's University of Belfast. M. 1978.

Knight, Brian Joseph. Bar of England and Wales. M. 1979.

Knox, Charles William. Queen's University of Belfast. M. 1979.

Kok, Khee Wee. Queen's University of Belfast. M. 1977.

Kraehling-Smith, Julia. Bar of England and Wales. H. 2001.

Kraehling-Smith, Marcus Andrew Charles. Bar of England and Wales. H. 1999.

Kyne, Louise Marie. Queen's University of Belfast. M. 2005.

Lamb, Benjamin. M. 1925. Died 1955.

Lamb, Ian Stuart. Bar of England and Wales. H. 1981.

Lamont, Mary Fiona. Queen's University of Belfast. M. 1978.

Landau, Toby Thomas. Bar of England and Wales. H. 2000.

Landy, Vincent Andrew. SC Bar of Ireland. T. 1976.

Langstaff, Brian Frederick James. QC of the Bar of England and Wales. H. 1999. Judge of the high court of England and Wales 2005-.

Lannon, John Michael. Queen's University of Belfast. M. 1980.

Lannon, James Bernard Edward (Seamus). Wolverhampton University. M. 2002.

Larkin, Aidan Joseph. University College, Dublin. (SDLP) Member of the Northern Ireland Assembly 1973-74, member, Magherafelt DC 1973-77. M. 1976.

Larkin, Eileen. Queen's University of Belfast. M. 1995.

Larkin, John Francis. Queen's University of Belfast. M. 1986. Reid Professor of law at Trinity College, Dublin 1989-91, editor of *The trial of William Drennan* (Dublin, 1991). QC M. 2001. Attorney general 24 May 2010-.

Larkin, Mary Josephine. The Queen's University of Belfast. M. 1988.

Lasok, Karol Paul Edward. QC of the Bar of England and Wales. M. 2001.

Lavery, Charles Michael. Queen's University of Belfast. M. 1956, QC M. 1971, chairman Executive Council 1988-89.

Lavery, Catherine Ruth (nee Trimble). Queen's University of Belfast. M. 1980. Lecturer in law at Queen's.

Lavery, Colum Stephen. Dundee University. M. 2012.

Lavery, David Alexander. Queen's University of Belfast. M. 1980. Principal secretary to the lord chief justice 1993-2001 (seconded to the multi-party talks chaired by Senator George Mitchell 1996-98, and to be principal secretary to the first minister 1998-2001), director of the Northern Ireland Court Service 2001-. Author of *Road Traffic Law in Northern Ireland* (Belfast, 1989).

Lavery, Finbar Jurgen. Bar of England and Wales M. 2000.

Lavery, James Patrick. Trinity College, Dublin. M. 1973, QC M. 1993.

Lavery, Joanne Eileen Mary. A former solicitor. M. 2002.

Lavery, Laurence. Bar of England and Wales. M. 2003.

Lavery, Melissa Geraldine. Queen's University of Belfast. M. 2005.

Lavery, Mary Josephine. Queen's University of Belfast. M. 1988.

Lavery, Michael Charles William. University College, Galway. M. 1990.

Lavery, Naomh Marie. Queen's University of Belfast. M. 2003.

Lavery, Neasa Maire. Queen's University of Belfast. M. 1996.

Lavery, Ronan Ulrich. Trinity College, Dublin. T. 1993. QC M. 2011.

Law, Stephen James. Queen's University of Belfast. M. 1993.

Lawlor, Eoin Fintan. Bar of Ireland. M. 2010.

Leahy, Eamon. Bar of Ireland. T. 1990.

Leckey, David Hamilton Alexander. Queen's University, Belfast. M. 1992.

Lee, Richard Thomas. Queen's University of Belfast. M. 1985.

Lehane, Sheila. Bar of Ireland. M. 2007.

Lenaghan, Clare Patricia. Queen's University, Belfast. M. 1991.

Lenaghan, Mary Patricia (Mrs Mary McAleese). Queen's University of Belfast. M. 1974. Reid professor of criminal law, Trinity College, Dublin 1975-79 and 1981-87, director of the Institute of Professional Legal Studies 1987-97, and pro vice-chancellor, Queen's University 1994-97. President of Ireland 1997-2011.

Lennon, Karen Jane. Bar of England and Wales. M. 2003.

Lennon, Mark Joseph Paul. Queen's University, Belfast. M. 1982.

Lennox, Susan Victoria. Bar of Ireland. H. 2006.

Lenny, Paul Matthew. Bar of England and Wales. M. 1998.

Leonard, Catherine Martine. Bar of England and Wales. M. 2002.

Lester, Anthony Paul. QC of the Bar of England and Wales. T. 1984 QC T. 1984. Created Lord Lester 1993.

Lever, Jeremy Frederick. Bar of England and Wales. H. 1987, QC H. 1987.

Lewis, Alun Kynric. QC of the Bar of England and Wales. M. 1988, QC M. 1988.

Lewis, David Alexander Gower. Bar of England and Wales. M. 2010.

Lewis, Francis William. M. 1925. Died 22 Sept. 1937.

Lewis, Robert Paul. Queen's University of Belfast. T. 1978, died 8 Mar. 2012.

Lewis, Philip Stephen. Bar of England and Wales. H. 1998.

Leyden, Kyle Martin. Bar of Ireland. M. 2006.

Lieven, Natalie Marie Danielle. Bar of England and Wales. H. 2011.

Lincoln, Fredman Ashe. QC of the Bar of England & Wales. M. 1963, QC M. 1963.

Lindsay, Jennifer-Ann. University of Ulster. M. 1993.

Lindsay, Joel Alexander. Queen's University of Belfast. M. 1992.

Lindbrom, Keith John. QC of the Bar of England and Wales. M. 2002.

Lissack, Richard Anthony. Bar of England and Wales. M. 2007.

Little, David John. Trinity College, Dublin. H. 1938. MP (U). KC H. 1964. Recorder of Londonderry 1965-79. Died 17 Apr. 1984.

Little, Emma Louise. Queen's University of Belfast. M. 2012.

Little, Emma Mary Jean. Queen's University of Belfast. M. 2003.

Litvack, Margaret Anne. Queen's University of Belfast. M. 2000.

Livingstone-Ievers, Laura. Trinity College, Dublin. M. 1997.

Lockhart, Robert Edward Brett. University College, Cardiff. M. 1982, QC T. 2006.

Lockie, David Norman. Queen's University of Belfast. M. 1974, master of the high court 1998, county court judge 1998-2011.

Logan, Eileen Elizabeth. Bar of England and Wales. H. 2001.

Logue, Emma-Louise. Queen's University of Belfast. M. 2006.

Logue, Kathryn Margaret. A former solicitor. M. 2004.

Long, John William Michael. Queen's University of Belfast. M. 1975, QC M. 1996. Author of *The Law of Adoption in Northern Ireland: the annotated legislation* (Belfast, 2002), and co-author (with Gemma Loughran) of *The Law of Children in Northern Ireland: the annotated legislation* (Belfast, 2004).

Long, John Oliver Horner. M. 1924. Died in an air raid in Malta 12 Sept. 1941. *ILT&SJ* lxxv (1941), 242, 248.

Loughran, Gemma Mary. Queen's University of Belfast. M. 1989, county court judge 2004-. Co-author (with Michael Long QC) of *The Law of Children in Northern Ireland: the annotated legislation* (Belfast, 2004).

Loughran, Paul Vincent. Queen's University of Belfast. M. 1976.

Loughrey, Michael William. A former solicitor. M. 2012.

Lowe, Rita Ann. Queen's University of Belfast. M. 1985. Disbarred to become a solicitor H. 1992.

Lowry, Jonathan William Eric. Ulster Polytechnic. M. 1988.

Lowry, Robert Lynd Erskine. Cambridge University. M. 1947, QC M. 1956, judge of the high court 1964-71, lord chief justice 1971-88, a lord of appeal in ordinary1988-94. Created Lord Lowry 1979. Died 15 Jan. 1999. *ODNB, DIB.*

Lucas, Edward Allan. Bar of England and Wales. M. 1994.

Lundy, Brian Patrick. Queen's University of Belfast. M. 2001.

Lundy, Laura Mary. Queen's University of Belfast. M. 1989.

Lunny, Conor Anthony Martin. Queen's University of Belfast. M. 2005.

Lunny, Donal Thomas. Trinity College, Dublin. M. 1998.

Lunny, Eilis Mairead. Bar of Ireland. M. 2012.

Lunny, Patrick Anthony. Queen's University of Belfast. M. 1983.

Lyell, Sir Nicholas Walter. QC of the Bar of England and Wales. T. 1987, QC T. 1987. MP (C) 1979-2001, parliamentary under secretary, department of health & social services 1986-87, solicitor general 1987-92, attorney general 1992-97. Created Lord Lyell 2005.

Lyle, Rachel Helen Laura Louise. Nottingham University. M. 2001.

Lyle, Robert. York University. M. 1995.

Lynas, Peter Robert. Dundee University. M. 1998.

Lyness, Scott Edward. Bar of England and Wales. H. 2000.

Lynch, James Dominic. Bar of Ireland. T. 1976.

Lynch, Patrick Thaddeus. Queen's University of Belfast. M. 1975, QC M. 1999, county court judge 2004-.

Lynch, Patrick Valentine. Queen's University of Belfast. M. 1968.

Lynch, Frances Bernadette. Queen's University of Belfast. M. 2002.

Lyness, Scott Edward. Hull University. H. 2000.

Lynn, Alexander. Queen's University of Belfast. M. 1921. Died 11 Apr. 1958.

Lynn, Gerald Cunningham. Queen's University of Belfast. M. 1933. Resident magistrate.

Lyttle, Patrick. Queen's University of Belfast. M. 1978, QC M. 1999.

McAleavey, Katherine Anne. Cambridge University. M. 2004.

McAleenan, Fiona Mary Patricia. Queen's University of Belfast. M. 1995.

McAleer, Fintan Martin. Queen's University of Belfast. M. 2006.

McAleer, James Joseph. Bar of England and Wales. H. 1998.

McAleer, Michael Sherrard. Portobello College, Dublin. M. 1997.

McAlinden, Barry O'Neill. Cambridge University. M. 1992.

McAlinden, Gerald Joseph. Queen's University of Belfast. M. 1986. QC. M. 2011.

McAlinden, James Paul. Bar of England and Wales. M. 2003.

McAlister, David William Richard. Queen's University of Belfast. M. 1976.

McAlister, Colette Bowman. Queen's University of Belfast. M. 1993.

McAlister, Marie Katrina. Queen's University of Belfast. M. 1977.

MacAllister, James Connolly. Queen's University of Belfast. M. 1976.

McAllister, Ryan John. Queen's University of Belfast. M. 2005.

McArdle, Eamonn Terence. Bar of England and Wales. M. 1996.

McArdle, James Gerard. Queen's University of Belfast. M. 2000.

McAreavey, Louise. Queen's University of Belfast. M. 1986.

McAteer, Ivor Columba. Queen's University of Belfast. M. 1990.

McAteer, Philip Rory. Queen's University of Belfast. M. 1997.

McAughey, David Francis. Queen's University of Belfast. M. 1986.

McAuley, Mark Howard. Queen's University of Belfast. M. 1994.

McAuley, Ruaidhri Patrick. Queen's University of Belfast. M. 2007.

McBirney, Robert Martin. Trinity College, Dublin. E. 1941, QC H. 1964. Resident magistrate 1969-74. Murdered by the IRA 16 September 1974.

McBride, Connell Martin. A former solicitor. M. 2012.

McBride, Denise Anne. Queen's University of Belfast. M. 1989. QC M. 2011.

McBride, Eileen Rosemary. Queen's University of Belfast. M. 1979. A full-time chairman of industrial tribunals and the fair employment tribunal 1994-2005, president of industrial tribunals and of the fair employment tribunal 2005-.

McBride, Paul Martin. Queen's University of Belfast. M. 1990. Disbarred to become a solicitor M. 1991.

McBride, Stephen Philip John. Queen's University of Belfast. M. 1988.

McBride, Thomas Gamble. Queen's University of Belfast. M. 1928.

McBrien, Edward Johnston David. Queen's University of Belfast. M. 1982. Author of *The Liquor licensing laws of Northern Ireland*, 1997 and 2007.

McBrien, Mary Alice. Bar of Ireland. M. 2008.

McBurney, Rosemary Sarah. University of Ulster. M. 2004.

McCaffrey, Jessica Anne Elizabeth. Queen's University of Belfast. M. 2006.

McCain, Sara Joanne. Queen's University of Belfast. M. 2009.

McCabe, Thomas Peter. Bar of England and Wales. M. 2009.

McCall, William Martin Dominica McGrath. Trinity College, Dublin. H. 1935. Magistrate in Singapore, 1941.

McCall, Andrew Bradley. Queen's University of Belfast. H. 1938. KC T. 1950. Resident magistrate.

McCann, Aoife. Bar of England and Wales. H. 2001.

McCann, David John. Nottingham University. M. 2001.

McCann, Joseph Peter Mark. Queen's University of Belfast. M. 2003.

McCann, Martin Bernard. Queen's University of Belfast. M. 1981.

McCarney, Damian John Malachy. University of Ulster. M. 2002.

McCarroll, John Johnston. Bar of England and Wales. H. 2002 (*in absentia*).

McCartan, Ciara. Bar of England and Wales. M. 2001.

McCarthy, Captain Andrew J, MBE. T. 1924.

McCarthy, Niall St John. Bar of Ireland. M. 1976. Judge of the supreme court of Ireland 1982-92. DIB.

McCartney, Brian Gerard. New University of Ulster. M. 1983, QC T. 2006.

Macartney, Brian Wilfred. Queen's University of Belfast. M. 1975.

McCartney, Niamh Aine. Queen's University of Belfast. M. 2004.

McCartney, Patrick Joseph M. Bar of Ireland. T. 1991.

McCartney, Robert Law. A former solicitor. M. 1968, QC M. 1975. MP (UKU) N Down, 1995-2001, MLA (UKU) 1998-2007.

McCaughey, Ronan. Bar of Ireland. M. 2009.

McCaughley, Ann Patricia. Queen's University of Belfast. M. 1992.

McCausland, Sara Donna. Queen's University of Belfast. M. 2009.

McCausland, Robert Cleeland. Northumbria University. M. 2011.

McCavana, Emma Louise. Queen's University of Belfast. M. 2003.

McClean, David William. Queen's University of Belfast. M. 1996.

McLean, Ronan James. Queen's University of Belfast. M. 2011.

McCleave, Terence Andrew. Queen's University of Belfast. M. 2010.

McCloskey, John Bernard. Queen's University of Belfast. M. 1979, QC M. 1999. Author of *Human Rights Act 1998 and the European Convention*, (Belfast, 2008), judge of the high court 2008-.

McCloskey, Caroline Marie. Queen's University of Belfast. M. 2001.

McClure, Brian David. Bar of England and Wales. M. 2002.

McColgan, Donna. Queen's University of Belfast. M. 1986. QC M. 2011.

McCollum, Ciaran Michael. Queen's University of Belfast. M. 1998.

McCollum, Liam Gerard. Queen's University of Belfast. M. 1985, QC M. 2001.

McCollum, William Pascal (Liam). University College, Dublin. T. 1955, QC M. 1971, high court judge 1987-97, lord justice of appeal 1997-2004.

McComb, Nigel Jeremy Wasson. Queen's University of Belfast. M. 1983.

McComb, Michael Colin Clive. Oxford University. H. 1973.

McConkey, Richard John. Queen's University of Belfast. M. 2001.

McConnell, Jane Sara. Bar of England and Wales. M. 1999.

McConnell, Lorna. Queen's University of Belfast. M. 1983.

McConnell, Robert William Brian. Queen's University of Belfast. H. 1948. MP (U) S Antrim 1951-70, parliamentary secretary ministry of health and local government 1963-64, minister of home affairs 1964-66. A national insurance commissioner and president of the industrial court 1968-81. Created Lord McConnell 1995. Died 25 Oct. 2000. *DIB*.

McCorkell, Peter George Alexander. University of Ulster. M. 2006.

MacCormack, John Anthony. Bar of Ireland. H. 2012.

McCormack, Patrick Thomas. Queen's University of Belfast. M. 1990.

McCormick, Rachael Anne. Queen's University of Belfast. M. 2011.

McCormick, Roseanne. Queen's University of Belfast. M. 1989.

McCorry, Cathal Joseph. Queen's University of Belfast. M. 1981, master of the high court 2001-.

McCoy, John Gerard. Bar of Ireland. M. 1995.

McCracken, James Ivan Priestly. M. 1929.

McCracken, Michael Harold. A former solicitor. M. 2005.

McCrea, Michael Edward. Queen's University of Belfast. M. 1983.

MacCreanor, Charles Camillius. Queen's University of Belfast. M. 1989. QC M. 2011.

McCreanor, Thomas. Queen's University of Belfast. M. 1988.

McCrissican, Patricia Louise. University of Ulster. M. 2008.

McCrisken, Joseph Anthony. University of Ulster. M. 2002.

McCrory, Francis Gerald. Queen's University of Belfast. M. 1976, QC M. 1996.

McCrudden, John Christopher. Bar of England and Wales. M. 2005. Professor of human rights law at Oxford University, currently professor of law at Queen's University of Belfast.

McCrudden, John Francis. Queen's University of Belfast. M. 1975, QC M. 1993.

McCrudden, Laurence Patrick. Queen's University of Belfast. M. 1977, QC M. 2001.

McCrudden, Samuel Gary. Queen's University of Belfast. M. 1977.

McCullagh, Ciara Sara Alice. Queen's University of Belfast. M. 1992.

McCullagh, Gareth Peter. Queen's University of Belfast. M. 1999.

McCullough, Adrian. Queen's University of Belfast. M. 1976.

McCullough, Denise Susan. Bar of England and Wales. H. 1993.

McCullough, Geraldine. Queen's University of Belfast. M. 2001.

McCusker, Fergal. Bar of England and Wales. H. 2004.

McCutcheon, Oliver William. Trinity College, Dublin. H. 1931. Disbarred to become a solicitor.

MacDermott, John Clarke MC. Queen's University of Belfast. M. 1921. KC 1936. MP (U) Queen's University 1938-44. Minister of public security, attorney general, judge of the high court 1944-47, created Lord MacDermott 1947, a lord of appeal in ordinary 1947-51, lord chief justice 1951-71. Survived an IRA murder attempt in 1977. Died 13 July 1979. *ODNB, DIB.*

MacDermott, the Hon. John Clarke. Cambridge University. M. 1949, QC H. 1964, chairman Bar Council Aug-Dec. 1971, high court judge 1973-87, lord justice of appeal 1987-1998.

McDermott, Eilis Maire. Queen's University of Belfast. M. 1974, QC H. 1989 chairman of the Executive Council 2001.

McDermott, Marie-Claire. Leeds Metropolitan University. M. 2002.

McDevitt, Henry Morris Brian. Queen's University of Belfast. H. 1948. QC H. 1968, later a resident magistrate. Died 1979.

Macdonald, Barry. Southampton University. M. 1979, QC M. 2000. SC M. 2000.

Macdonald, Eoin Barry. University of Ulster. M. 2008.

Macdonald, James Alistair. Queen's University of Belfast). M. 2012.

McDonald, Peter Terence. Queen's University of Belfast. M. 1976, QC M. 1993.

McDonald, Jane Elizabeth. Queen's University of Belfast. M. 1980.

McDonald, James William. Bar of England and Wales. M. 1967.

McDonald, Neal Michael. Bar of Ireland. M. 2002.

McDonald, Melanie Sharon. Bar of England and Wales. H. 2011.

McDonnell, John Martin. Queen's University of Belfast. M. 1981.

McDonnell, Martin James. Bar of England and Wales. H. 1999.

McDowell, Alison Jane. University of Durham. M. 1998.

McDowell, David Arnott Craig. Bar of England and Wales. M. 2003.

McDowell, Iris Edith. Trinity College, Dublin. Senior lecturer in law at the Ulster College. M. 1976.

McDowell, Michael Aneurin Fitzgerald. Queen's University of Belfast. M. 1988.

McEleavy, Peter Eugene. Bar of England and Wales. M. 1999.

MacEntee, Patrick. SC of the Bar of Ireland. T. 1984, QC H. 1985.

McEntee, Francis Richard. Bar of England and Wales. H. 2003.

McElhenny, Michele Anne. Queen's University of Belfast. M. 1988.

McElhenny, Siobhan Alice. Queen's University of Belfast. M. 1993.

McElholm, Brian Patrick. Queen's University of Belfast. M. 1981. Disbarred to become a solicitor M. 1986. Resident magistrate (later district judge (magistrates' courts)) 1998-.

McElvanna, Claire Marie. Queen's University of Belfast. M. 1999.

McEnroy, Felix James. Bar of Ireland. T. 1990.

McEvoy, Leona. Queen's University of Belfast. M. 2010.

McEvoy, Mark John Anthony. Bar of England and Wales. M. 2001.

McEvoy, Martin Patrick. Queen's University of Belfast. M. 1997.

McEvoy, Joseph Francis. Queen's University of Belfast. M. 1985.

McEvoy, Philip. Trinity College, Dublin. M. 2000.

McEwen, Robert Mark. Sheffield University. M. 1986.

McFarland, Paul. Queen's University of Belfast. M. 1993.

McGaffin, Joanne Jean. University of Ulster. M. 2012.

McGahan, Orlagh Frances. Queen's University of Belfast. M. 2003.

McGahon, Hugh Bradbury. Bar of Ireland. T. 1983.

McGarrity, Mark Patrick. Queen's University of Belfast. M. 2004.

McGarvey, Michael James. Queen's University of Belfast. M. 2003.

McGinley, Helen Patricia. Queen's University of Belfast. M. 2001.

McGill, Austin John. Oxford University. M. 1985.

McGill, Laura Aileen. Dundee University. M. 2004.

McGinn, Paul Joseph. Queen's University of Belfast. M. 1981.

McGinty, Kevin Charles Patrick. Bar of England and Wales. Attorney general's office. H. 1998.

McGivern, Anne Frances. Queen's University of Belfast. M. 1989.

McGivern, Oonagh. Bar of England Wales. M. 1999.

McGleenan, Sean Anthony. Bar of Ireland. M. 1997. QC M. 2011.

McGonigal, Ambrose Joseph MC and bar. M. 1948. QC M. 1956, judge of the high court 1968-75, a lord justice of appeal 1975-1979, died 22 Sept. 1979. *DIB*.

McGonigal, Eoin Patrick. Bar of Ireland. T. 1976. SC H. 1984.

McGonigal, Richard. M. 1925. SC H 1940, judge of the European Court of Human Rights 1959. *DIB*.

McGowan, Aidan Francis Robert. Cambridge University. M. 2011.

McGowan, James Christopher Finbar. Bar of Ireland. M. 1996.

McGowan, Malachy John Patrick. Cambridge University. M. 2007.

McGrade, Paul Joseph Michael. Oxford University. M. 1997.

McGrane, Catherine Anne-Marie. Trinity College, Dublin. M. 2007.

McGrath, Henry Garrett. Queen's University of Belfast. M. 1947, QC M. 1965. Resident magistrate 1967-13 Sept. 1968, returned to practice at the Bar, elected a bencher 16 Sept. 1968. Chairman of the Bar Council 1972, county court judge 19 Mar. 1973. Suffered grave and permanent injuries as the result of a murder attempt by the IRA in April 1974. Later retired from the county court bench due to ill-health caused by his injuries and briefly resumed practice before retiring permanently. Died June 2009.

McGrath, Imogen. Bar of Ireland. M. 2012.

McGrath, John Patrick. Queen's University of Belfast. M. 2010.

McGrath, Karen Marie. Queen's University of Belfast. M. 2011.

McGrath, Margaret Mary. Queen's University of Belfast. M. 1976.

McGregor, William Roy. Queen's University of Belfast. Officer in the RUC. M. 1973. Supt RUC until May 1975.

McGregor, Helen Barbara Ruth. Queen's University of Belfast. M. 1996.

McGrenera, Noelle Bernadette Patricia. Queen's University of Belfast. M. 1978, QC M. 1999, chairman of the Executive Council 2006-08.

McGrory, Clodach Margaret Mary. Trinity College, Dublin. M. 1990.

McGrory, Patrick James Barra (b. 23 June 1960). The first solicitor to become a QC in T. 2007. Called H. 2009. Director of public prosecutions 2011-.

McGuckin, Karl David Peter. Bar of Ireland. M. 2011.

McGuckin, Sarah Brigid. Queen's University of Belfast. M. 2010.

McGuigan, Derval Majella. Queen's University of Belfast. M. 1989.

McGuigan, Gregory. Queen's University of Belfast. M. 1991. QC M. 2011.

McGuinness, Donal. Bar of Ireland. H. 2004.

McGuinness, Andrew Joseph. Queen's University of Belfast. M. 1998.

McGuinness, Sonya Mary. Queen's University of Belfast. M. 1995.

McGuiness, Anne Marie. Queen's University of Belfast. M. 1985, QC T. 2006.

McGurk, Una Therese. University of Ulster. M. 2002.

McHugh, Anna Cait. Queen's University of Belfast. M. 2011.

McHugh, Gareth Paul. Queen's University of Belfast. M. 1993.

McHugh, Mary Catherine Patricia. A former solicitor. M. 2001.

McIlroy, Julie Elizabeth. Queen's University of Belfast. M. 2007.

McIvor, Daren Mary. A former solicitor. M. 2008.

McIvor, Frances Jill. Queen's University of Belfast. M. 1980.

McIvor, William Basil. Queen's University of Belfast. H. 1950. MP (U) Larkfield 1969-72, minister of community relations 1971-72. Member (UU), Northern Ireland Assembly 1973-74, minister of education, 1974. Resident magistrate 1974-93. Author of *Hope deferred experiences of an Irish unionist* (Belfast, 1998). Died 5 Nov. 2004.

Mackay, Irene Leslie. Bar of England and Wales. M. 1998.

McKay, Charles Alexander. Queen's University of Belfast. M. 1976, QC T. 2007.

McKay, Catherine Mary. Queen's University of Belfast. M. 1988.

McKay, Randal Joseph. Queen's University, Belfast. M. 1970. QC H. 1989, county court judge 1994-2009.

McKeag, Thomas Benedict Oliver. Queen's University of Belfast. H. 1950.

McKeagney, Sinead Anne. Trinity College, Dublin. M. 1994.

McKee, David John Brian. Cambridge University. M. 1990.

McKee, James Brian. Trinity College, Dublin. H. 1953. Disbarred to become a solicitor H. 1956.

McKee, John. H. 1960, QC M 1974, a county court judge 1981-1998, combined with being president of industrial tribunals and president of the industrial court 1981-89.

McKee, Katherine. Bar of England and Wales. H. 1999.

McKee, Michael William. Queen's University of Belfast. M. 1984. Disbarred to become a solicitor M. 1991.

McKeever, Catherine Mary Christine. Bar of England and Wales. M. 2011.

McKeever, John. Queen's University of Belfast. M. 2006.

McKelvey, Alice Elizabeth (b. 12 Oct. 1978). Dundee University. M. 2003.

McKelvey, Ross Oscar. Liverpool Polytechnic. M. 1987.

McKenna, Barry Anthony Gerard. Queen's University of Belfast. M. 2003.

McKenna, Francis Michael. Queen's University of Belfast. M. 1984.

McKenna, Marie Therese Siobhan. Bar of Ireland. M. 1998.

McKenna, Tara Ann Marie. Queen's University of Belfast. M. 1996.

McKeown, Guillaume. Queen's University of Belfast. M. 2009.

McKeown, Philip. University College, Dublin. M. 2012.

MacKenzie, Claire. Cambridge University. M. 1997.

MacKeown, Robert Francis. H. 1927.

McKeown, David Francis. Queen's University of Belfast. M. 2008.

McKeown, Paul Michael Gerard. Queen's University of Belfast. M. 1988.

McKernan, Paula. Queen's University of Belfast. M. 2005.

McKillop, Thomas Gerard. Queen's University of Belfast. M. 1980.

McKnight, Kathleen Margaret. A former solicitor. M. 2005.

McLarnon, Anna. Queen's University of Belfast. M. 2012.

MacLaughlin, William Hopkins. Trinity College, Dublin. H. 1952. Disbarred to become a solicitor H. 1960.

McLaughlin, Brian. Queen's University of Belfast. M. 1996.

McLoughlin, George Leeke. Queen's University of Belfast. M. 1945. Deputy director of public prosecutions 1982-87. CB.

McLaughlin, Laura Marie. Queen's University of Belfast. M. 2011.

McLaughlin, Kieran Patrick. University of Ulster. M. 2010.

McLaughlin, Paul Christopher. Trinity College, Dublin. M. 1997.

McLaughlin, Richard. Queen's University of Belfast. M. 1971, QC H. 1985, chairman of the Executive Council 1994-96, judge of the high court 1999-2012.

McLean, John Alexander Lowry. Queen's University of Belfast. T. 1949. QC T. 1974. Principal secretary to the lord chief justice and permanent secretary of the supreme court of judicature of Northern Ireland 1966-1993. Under treasurer of the Inn of Court 1966-97.

MacLynn, Adrian Geoffrey Simon. Bar of Ireland. M. 1979.

MacMahon, James Hugh. Queen's University of Belfast. M. 1987.

McMahon, Arlene. Bar of England and Wales. M. 2002.

McMahon, Laura Margaret. Bar of England and Wales. M. 2005.

McMahon, Kenneth Robert More. Queen's University of Belfast. H. 1969, QC H. 1985.

McManus, Mairin (Maureen). Bar of Ireland. M. 1996.

McMeekin, Audrey Moyra. Trinity College, Dublin. M. 1928.

MacMenamin, John. Bar of Ireland. T. 1983. SC M. 1991, judge of the high court of Ireland 2004-12, judge of the supreme court 2012-.

McMillan, Katherine (Karen) Rose. Bar of England and Wales. M. 1996.

McMillan, Robert James. Bar of England and Wales. H. 1983.

McMillen, David Michael. Queen's University of Belfast. M. 1984. QC M. 2011.

McMillen, Jonathan George. Queen's University of Belfast. M. 2001.

McMullan, Eunan Hugh Padraigh. Queen's University of Belfast. M. 1983.

McMullan, Jeremy John. QC of the Bar of England and Wales. M. 1994, QC T. 1996. Circuit judge in England and Wales Nov. 2001-.

McMullan, Manus Anthony. Bar of England and Wales. M. 2007.

McMullan, Victoria Elizabeth. Queen's University of Belfast. M. 2010.

McNally, Aisling Brigid. Queen's University of Belfast. M. 2011.

McNally, Geralyn. Queen's University of Belfast. M. 1994.

McNally, Philip. Queen's University of Belfast. M. 2011.

McNamara, Michael James. Bar of Ireland. M. 2008.

McNamee, Rory Michael. A former solicitor. H. 1997.

McNeill, Seamus Joseph. Queen's University of Belfast. M. 1985.

McNerney, Margaret Mary. Bar of Ireland. M 1990.

McNicholl, Emer Louise Daniele. University of Ulster. M. 2011.

McNulty, Fiona Majella. Bar of England and Wales. M. 2001.

McNulty, James Oliver. Queen's University of Belfast. M. 1968, QC H. 1983.

McPhillips, Patrick Boyle. Queen's University of Belfast. Inspector, RUC. M. 1974.

McPolin, Laura Maureen. Queen's University of Belfast. M. 1994. Joined Northern Ireland Court Service.

McQuitty, Steven John. University of Ulster. M. 2005.

McQuitty, James Lloyd. Cambridge University. Bar of England and Wales. M. 1941, QC H.1960. Left the bar to become a director of Ulster Television.

McReynolds, Melody Jane. Queen's University of Belfast. M. 1982, master of the high court 1999-2004, county court judge 2004-.

McSparran, James Desmond. Queen's University of Belfast. M. 1951, QC H. 1967.

McStay, Liam Hugh. Queen's University of Belfast. M. 1993.

McTaggart, Stuart. Bar of England and Wales. M. 2001.

McVeigh, Stephen Daniel James. Queen's University of Belfast. M. 2012.

McVeigh, Herbert Andrew. Queen's University of Belfast. H. 1931, KC T. 1948, high court judge 1956-64, lord justice of appeal 1964-73. Knt. 1964, died 3 Oct. 1977.

McVeigh, Paula Claire. Queen's University of Belfast. M. 2009.

McVeigh, Joanne. Queen's University of Belfast. M. 2005.

Macaulay, Andrew Alfred. M. 1923. Died 1926.

Macaulay, Maurice Scott. T. 1925. Assistant to the parliamentary counsel. Died January 1947.

Mack, Geoffrey Alexander. Durham University. M. 1979.

Mackey, Irene Leslie. Bar of England and Wales. M. 1998.

Madden, Patricia Mary. Queen's University of Belfast. M. 1986. Full time chairman of industrial tribunals 2002-07, vice president of industrial tribunals and of the fair employment tribunal 2007-10, county court judge (Her Honour Judge Smyth) 2010-.

Magee, Andrew Mannix. Queen's University of Belfast. M. 2000.

Magee, Eamon Anthony. Queen's University of Belfast. M. 1979.

Magee, Philip Patrick. Queen's University of Belfast. M. 1975. Lecturer in law University College Cork. SC Bar of Ireland H. 2003.

Magee, Samuel Cairns. Bar of England and Wales. M. 2006.

Magennis, Brendan Patrick.University of Ulster. M. 2002.

Magill, Andrew Philip. Trinity College, Dublin. H. 1927. Civil servant 1901-1925, served as private secretary to several chief secretaries for Ireland before becoming an assistant secretary in the ministry of home affairs in Northern Ireland in 1921. CB 1919. Died 21 Apr. 1941. *ILT&SJ* lxxv (1941) 111.

Magill, Daniel. Queen's University of Belfast. M. 1971. Department of Public Prosecutions 1976-97, deputy director 1989-97, resident magistrate (later district judge (magistrate's courts) 1997-.

Magill, Peter. Queen's University of Belfast. M. 1978.

Magill, Kevin Diarmid. Bar of England and Wales. H. 1997.

Maginness, Alban Alphonsus. University of Ulster. M. 1976. Lord mayor of Belfast 1997-98, MLA (SDLP) 1998 -.

Maginess, William Brian. Trinity College, Dublin. H. 1923, QC M. 1946. MP (U) Iveagh 1938-64. Parliamentary secretary ministry of agriculture and ministry of public security 1941-43, and of ministry of commerce 1943-44. Minister of labour 1945, minister of home affairs 1945-53, and minister of finance 1953-56, acting prime minister Nov. 1954-Mar. 1955, acting attorney general Aug-Oct 1952 and attorney general 1956-64, county court judge 1964-67. Died in office 16 Apr. 1967. *DIB*, *Belfast Telegraph* 17 Apr. 1967.

Maguire, Andrew James. Bar of England and Wales. M. 2011.

Maguire, Conor Martin. Queen's University of Belfast. M. 2000.

Maguire, Tara Jane. Liverpool University. M. 2007.

Maguire, Jayne. Bar of Ireland. M. 2004.

Maguire, John Edward. Queen's University of Belfast. Served in the Inland Revenue. M. 1973. Lecturer Institute of Professional Legal Studies 1977-82, chairman of industrial tribunals 1982-89, president of industrial tribunals 1989. President of industrial tribunals and of the fair employment tribunal 1990-2005. CBE 1996.

Maguire, Paul Richard. London School of Economics. Lecturer in law at Queen's University. M. 1978. QC T. 2006, high court judge 2012-.

Maguire, Richard. Bar of England and Wales. M. 1999.

Maguire, Roderick Malachy. Bar of Ireland. M. 2012.

Maguire, Kieran Ross. Bar of Ireland. M. 2002.

Maguire, William Joseph. Trinity College, Dublin. M. 1925.

Mahaffey, Sheena Martina. Queen's University of Belfast. M. 1992.

Mahood, Emma Jane. Bar of England and Wales. M. 2001.

Mairs, Brian John. Queen's University of Belfast. M. 1980.

Major, John. Bar of Ireland. H. 1997.

Malcolm, Charles Barry. Queen's University of Belfast. M. 1970. Lecturer in law at Queen's University.

Mallon, James Joseph. Queen's University of Belfast. M. 1977.

Mallon, John Oliver. Queen's University of Belfast. M. 1998.

Mallon, Kieran Anthony Joseph. University College, Dublin. M. 1985. QC M. 2011.

Mallon, Paul Andrew. Queen's University of Belfast. M. 1992 (*in absentia*).

Mallon, Terence Joseph. Bar of England and Wales. M. 1999.

Maloney, Michael Anthony. Bar of Ireland. M. 1989.

Managh, Patricia Sara. King's College, London. M. 1996.

Manning, Dermot Philip. Bar of Ireland. H. 1999.

Mannis, Glenn Robert. Queen's University of Belfast. M. 2009.

Marks, Rosemary Joanne. Dundee University. M. 1999.

Marquand, Charles Nicholas Hilary. Bar of England and Wales. H. 2001.

Marlow, Ronan Sean Kevin. Queen's University of Belfast. M. 2010.

Markey, Patrick Ivan. Queen's University of Belfast. H. 1962, QC M. 1978, county court judge 1994-2009.

Marrinan, Desmond Patrick. A former solicitor. T. 1985.

Marrinan, Desmond Patrick James. Queen's University of Belfast. M. 1972, lecturer in law at Queen's University 1971-77, county court judge 2003-.

Marrinan, Patrick Alyosius. M. 1925. Sometime county inspector, RIC. Died 8 Oct. 1940.

Marrinan, Patrick Aloysius. Trinity College, Dublin. M. 1977. Called to the Bar of Ireland H. 1981, SC M. 2000.

Marsh, Alison. Bar of England and Wales. M. 2002.

Martin, Aisling Mary. Bar of Ireland. M. 2004.

Martin, Derek Henry. Queen's University of Belfast. M. 1970.

Martin, Gay Madeleine Annesley. Bar of England and Wales. M. 1980.

Martin, John Alfred Holmes. Queen's University of Belfast. M. 1970, chairman of industrial tribunals 1988-89, vice president of industrial tribunals and of the fair employment tribunal 1990, QC H. 1989, county court judge 1990-1997, chief social security commissioner 1997-2011.

Martin, Nigel Gregory. Queen's University of Belfast. M. 1985.

Martin, Roisin Marie. Queen's University of Belfast. M. 2003.

Martin, Robert (Roy) Logan. QC of the Bar of England and Wales. QC of the Bar of Scotland, dean of the Faculty of Advocates 2004-2007. M. 2010.

Martin, Trevor McDonald. Queen's University of Belfast. M. 1980.

Martin, Vincent P. Bar of Ireland. M. 2002.

Mason, John Gerard. Queen's University of Belfast. M. 1981.

Masterson, Kenneth William. Queen's University of Belfast. Chief inspector RUC. M. 1978. Deputy chief constable of the RUC 1993-94 Died 18 Sept. 1994.

Mateer, Philip Alexander. Queen's University of Belfast. M. 1981, QC T. 2007.

Matier, Colin Paul. Queen's University of Belfast. M. 2000.

Matthews, Agnes-Jane Mary. Queen's University of Belfast. M. 1985.

Matthews, Angela. Queen's University of Belfast. M. 2011.

Matthews, Michael Kenneth. Queen's University of Belfast. M. 1970.

Matthews, Neale Edward. Queen's University of Belfast. M. 1987. Disbarred to become a solicitor M. 2000. Called again T. 2002.

Maurici, James Patrick. Bar of England and Wales. M. 2009.

Maxwell, Andrew John Samuel. Trinity College, Dublin. M. 1984.

Maxwell, John Philip Barklie. Trinity College, Dublin. M. 1971. Under treasurer 2009-.

Maxwell, Michael Edmond. Trinity College, Dublin. M. 1973.

Mayhew, Patrick Barnabas Burke. QC of the Bar of England and Wales. T. 1983. QC T. 1983. MP (C) 1974-97, parliamentary under-secretary department of employment 1979-81, minister of state at the home office 1981-83, solicitor general 1983-87, attorney general 1987-92, secretary of state for Northern Ireland 1992-97. Created Lord Mayhew 1997.

Meade, John Joseph. Trinity College, Dublin. M. 1984. Disbarred to become a solicitor M. 1992.

Meares, Eric Ivor. Trinity College, Dublin. T. 1951.

Meares, Keith Munro. T. 1924. Disbarred by King's Inns to become a solicitor.

Meenan, John. Queen's University of Belfast. M. 1947.

Megaw, John. Bar of England & Wales. T. 1937. A high court judge in England 1961-69, and a lord justice of appeal 1969-89. Died 1997.

Melvin, James Warren. Bar of England and Wales. M. 2000.

Mercer, Jonathan Robert. Queen's University of Belfast. M. 1982.

Middleton, Christopher Michael. Bar of England and Wales. M. 2004.

Micks, Edward Christopher. M. 1925. SC 1948. Died 1973.

Millar, Gavin James. Bar of England and Wales. H. 2010.

Millar, Robert Thomas. London University. A first class clerk in the Supreme Court. M. 1976. Legal secretary to the lord chief justice 1982-89, a master of the high court 1989-1997.

Millar, Robert William. Queen's University of Belfast. M. 1987.

Millar, William McCrum. Queen's University of Belfast. M. 1927. Resident magistrate in Co. Tyrone for many years.

Millen, Patrick. Bar of Ireland. M. 2002.

Miller, Geoffrey Biddal. Queen's University of Belfast. M. 1983, QC T. 2006, county court judge 2009-.

Miller, Gillian Elizabeth. Queen's University of Belfast. M. 1988.

Miller, Rosemary-Jayne. Queen's University of Belfast. M. 1980.

Milliken, James Richard David. University of Ulster. M. 2008.

Millinson, Christopher. University of Kent at Canterbury. M. 1981.

Mills, Barbara Jean Lyon. QC of the Bar of England and Wales, T. 1991, QC T. 1991. Director of the serious fraud office 1990- 92, director of public prosecutions in England and Wales 1992-98.

Mills, Diane. Queen's University of Belfast. M. 1998.

Mills, George Arthur Charles. Bar of England and Wales. H. 2000.

Mills, Richard Louis Kenneth. SC of the Bar of Ireland. T. 1976.

Milner, Christopher William. Queen's University of Belfast. M. 1971, resident magistrate 1986-2003.

Miskelly, Vincent James. University of Ulster. M. 2009.

Mitchell, Andrew Robert. Bar of England and Wales. M. 2007.

Mitchell, Eithne Catherine. Queen's University of Belfast. M. 1997.

Moeran, Fenner Orlando. Bar of England and Wales. M. 2012.

Molloy, Steven Gerard. Bar of England and Wales. M. 2001.

Molony, Patrick Martin Joseph. Bar of England and Wales. H. 1999.

Molony, Timothy John. Bar of England and Wales. M. 2010.

Monroe, Hubert Holmes. QC of the Bar of England and Wales. T. 1963.

Montgomery, Andrew. Queen's University of Belfast. M. 1994.

Montgomery, Clare Patricia. QC Bar of England and Wales. M. 2001.

Moody, Lloyd. Trinity College, Dublin. T. 1941, QC M. 1958. Crown counsel in Palestine, returned to Northern Ireland due to ill-health. A national insurance commissioner 1958, and then president of the industrial court.

Moody, Sean-Alistair. Bar of England and Wales. M. 1999.

Moon, Phillip Charles Angus. QC of the Bar of England and Wales. H. 2009.

Mooney, Dean Gerard John. Queen's University of Belfast. M. 2004.

Mooney, Gerard Patrick. Trinity College, Dublin. M. 1984.

Mooney, Niall Patrick. Bar of Ireland. M. 2009.

Mooney, Philip. Trinity College, Dublin. M. 1965, QC H. 1983.

Mooney, Patrick Terence. Queen's University of Belfast. M. 1971, QC H. 1985.

Mooney, Stephen. Queen's University of Belfast. M. 2003.

Moore, Neil Ross. Queen's University of Belfast. M. 1996.

Montague, Turlough Marius. Ulster Polytechnic. M. 1982, QC T. 2006.

Moran, Edward Patrick Augustus. Queen's University of Belfast. M. 1975.

Moran, Lisa Maria. Queen's University of Belfast. M. 1997.

Morgan, Austen Jude. Bar of England and Wales. H. 2000.

Morgan, Charles Declan. Cambridge University. M. 1976, QC M. 1993, judge of the high court 2004-09, lord chief justice 2009-.

Morgan, Edward Patrick. Bar of England and Wales. H. 2000.

Morgan, John. Bar of England and Wales. M. 2009.

Morgan, Martin Samuel Anthony. Queen's University of Belfast. M. 1995.

Morgan, Rachel Mary. Queen's University of Belfast. M. 1997.

Moriarty, Andrew Joseph. Bar of England and Wales. M. 1998.

Morris, John, QC of the Bar of England and Wales, attorney general. T. 1997, QC T. 1997. MP (Lab) 1959-2001, secretary of state for Wales 1974-79, attorney general 1997-99. Created Lord Morris of Aberavon 2001. KG 2003.

Morrissey, John Thomas. Queen's University of Belfast. M. 1987.

Morrissey, John Joseph. Bar of Ireland. M. 2006.

Morrison, Anne Elizabeth. Queen's University of Belfast. M. 1991.

Morrison, Robert Ivor Moss. Queen's University of Belfast. M. 1970.

Morrison, Captain Thomas Dawson. District inspector RUC. H. 1927.

Morrow, Harriet Anne. Queen's University of Belfast. Former lecturer in English literature at Queen's University. M. 1991.

Morrow, Mervyn Alexander. Queen's University of Belfast. M. 1970, QC H. 1983.

Morton, Rosemary Caroline Patricia. Queen's University of Belfast. M. 1985.

Mortimer, William Jamison. Trinity College, Dublin. Former lecturer in the College of Technology. M. 1978.

Moss, Peter Redfern. Queen's University of Belfast. M. 1971.

Mulgrew, Marcus James. Portobello College, Dublin. M. 2000.

Mulholland, Lee-Anne. Queen's University of Belfast. M. 2003.

Mulholland, Mark. Queen's University of Belfast. M. 1993. QC M. 2011. Chairman of the Executive Council 2012-.

Mulholland, Maria Catherine. Queen's University of Belfast. M. 2010.

Mulholland, Seamus Joseph. Queen's University of Belfast. M. 2012.

Mullaly, Maria. University of Ulster. M. 1993.

Mullan, Conor Charles. Liverpool University. M. 2003.

Mullan, Grainne Ann. Trinity College, Dublin. M. 2001.

Mullan, James Anthony. Bar of England and Wales. H. 1996.

Mullan, John Boyd. University of Ulster. M. 2006.

Mullan, Maeve Denise. University of Ulster. M. 2007.

Mullan, Sean Paul. Queen's University of Belfast. M. 2010.

Mullen, Yvonne. Bar of Ireland. M. 2010.

Muller, Franz Joseph. QC of the Bar of England and Wales. M. 1982 (*in absentia*).

Mulrine, Daniel John Chrysostom. Member of the Bar of Ireland and the Bar of England and Wales. M. 1965.

Mulqueen, Barry Joseph. University College, Galway. M. 1995.

Mulvenna, Michael Edward. University of Ulster. M. 2012.

Murnaghan, Sheelagh Mary. Queen's University of Belfast. M. 1948. MP (Lib) Queen's University 1961-69. Died 14 Sept. 1993. *DIB*.

Murphy, Brian Joseph. Queen's University of Belfast. M. 2008.

Murphy, Ciara. Bar of England and Wales. M. 2001.

Murphy, Ciaran Michael. Liverpool University. M. 1985, QC T. 2006.

Murphy, Daire Padraig. Queen's University of Belfast. M. 1995.

Murphy, Francis Dominic. SC Bar of Ireland. Chairman council of the Bar of Ireland, judge of the high court of Ireland 1982-96, judge of the supreme court of Ireland 1996-2002.

Murphy, Grainne Mary. Trinity College, Dublin. M. 1992.

Murphy, Louise. Queen's University of Belfast. M. 2000.

Murphy, Ruairi. Queen's University of Belfast. M. 1997.

Murphy, Timothy Desmond. Bar of Ireland. M. 1991.

Murphy, Yvonne. Bar of Ireland. T. 1993.

Murray, Anne-Marie. Queen's University of Belfast. M. 1987.

Murray, Blaithin Aine. Queen's University of Belfast. M. 2006.

Murray, Dolores Colette. Queen's University of Belfast. M. 1978.

Murray, Donald Bruce. Queen's University of Belfast. Member of the Bar of England and Wales. T. 1953, QC M. 1964, chairman of the Bar Council 1973-May 1975, high court judge 1975-1989, lord justice of appeal 1989-93.

Murray, Kathryn Alison. Queen's University of Belfast. M. 2012.

Mynors, Charles Baskerville. Bar of England and Wales. M. 2002.

Napier, James Patrick Anthony. Queen's University of Belfast. M. 1988.

Nash, Raymond Anthony. University of Glamorgan. A former quantity surveyor. M. 1995.

Neeson, Laura. Queen's University of Belfast. M. 2006.

Neeson, Maurice Gabriel. Queen's University of Belfast. M. 1977.

Neeson, Michael James. Trinity College, Dublin. M. 2007.

Neill, Emily Charlotte. Bar of England and Wales. H. 2012.

Nerney, Margaret Mary. Bar of Ireland. M. 1990.

Nesbitt, Richard Law. Bar of Ireland. T. 1988.

Newark, Francis Headon. Oxford University. Lecturer in law 1937-46 and then professor of civil law 1946-73 at Queen's University, Belfast. Editor of the Northern Ireland Law Reports 1947-73. CBE. T. 1972, QC T. 1972.

Ni Chulachain, Sinead. Bar of Ireland. M. 1999.

Nicholl, Grace Anne. University of Ulster. M. 2007.

Nicholson, Cyril Anthony de Lacy. H. 1927, KC H. 1945. Died 1 May 1963. Sometime high sheriff for Co. Londonderry, president of the Irish Cricket Union and served on many public bodies.

Nicholson, James Michael Anthony. T. 1956, QC M 1971, chairman of the Executive Council 1983-85, high court judge 1986-1995, lord justice of appeal 1995-2006. President of the Irish Cricket Union 1978.

Nicholson, Thomas Edward Cyril. Bar of England and Wales. M. 2003.

Nixon, Benjamin. Queen's University of Belfast. M. 2005.

Nixon, Diane Eleanor. Bar of England and Wales. M. 2008.

Nixon, Elaine Violet. Bar of England and Wales. H. 2009.

Nixon, Suzanne Patricia. Queen's University of Belfast. M. 1995.

Nolan, Michael Patrick. QC of the Bar of England and Wales. M. 1974, QC M. 1974. High court judge in England and Wales 1982-91, lord justice of appeal 1991-93, a lord of appeal in ordinary 1994-98. Created Lord Nolan 1994. Died 2007.

Nugent, Blaine Peter. University of Ulster. M. 2009.

Nugent, Plunkett. University of Ulster. M. 2006.

O'Boyle, Michael Patrick. Queen's University of Belfast. M. 1973.

O'Brien, Dermod Patrick. QC of the Bar of England and Wales. M. 2002.

O'Brien, Desmond. Queen's University of Belfast. M. 2008.

O'Brien, James. A former solicitor. M. 2012.

O'Brien, Luke David. Queen's University of Belfast. M. 2010.

O'Brien, Kathleen Jeannie Horner. Queen's University of Belfast. H. 1952. Joined the English Bar in 1955, a law reporter in England, returned to practice in Northern Ireland in the 1970s.

O'Brien, Martin Gerald. Queen's University of Belfast. M. 1989.

O'Brien, Michael. National University of Ireland. H. 1926.

O'Brien, Susan. M. 1976. Disbarred H. 1978 to become a solicitor in England.

O'Connell, Gareth. Bar of Ireland. H. 2011.

O'Connell, James Daniel Gerard. Queen's University of Belfast. M. 1982.

O'Connor, Andrew Mark. Trinity College, Dublin. M. 2002.

O'Connor, Hugh Patrick. Queen's University of Belfast. M. 1990.

O'Connor, John Edward. Queen's University of Belfast. M. 2002.

O'Connor, John Peter. University of Ulster. M. 2001.

O'Connor, Michael Columba. Bar of Ireland. H. 2012.

O'Connor, Siobhan Marie Louise. Queen's University of Belfast. M. 2004.

O'Donnell, Donal Gerard. Bar of Ireland. T. 1989. Judge of the supreme court of Ireland 2010-.

O'Donnell, Turlough. Queen's University of Belfast. T. 1947, QC H. 1964, chairman of the Bar Council Jan. 1970-Aug 1971, high court judge 1971-79, lord justice of appeal 1979-89.

O'Donnell, Turlough Joseph. Bar of Ireland. T. 1983. SC H. 1997.

O'Donoghue, Francis Philip. Queen's University of Belfast. M. 1985, QC M. 2001.

O'Donovan, Diarmuid Brian Dominck. SC Bar of Ireland T. 1976. Judge of the high court of Ireland 1996-2007.

O'Flaherty, John. Bar of England and Wales. H. 2009.

O'Flaherty, Sinead. Bar of England and Wales. M. 2000.

O'Grady, Adele Maria. Queen's University of Belfast. M. 1992.

O'Hagan, Patrick Gabriel. Queen's University of Belfast. M. 1987.

O'Hagan, Bronwyn Mary. Queen's University of Belfast. M. 1995.

O'Hagan, Fergus McKenna. SC Bar of Ireland. H. 1996.

O'Hagan, Siobhan Roisin. Queen's University of Belfast. M. 1994, QC (Mrs. Siobhan Keegan) T. 2006.

O'Hanlon, Patrick Michael. University College, Dublin. Independent MP 1969-72, founder member SDLP, member (SDLP) Northern Ireland Assembly 1973-74. M. 1986. Died 7 Apr. 2009.

O'Hanrahan, Sean Desmond Mary. SC Bar of Ireland. T. 1976. Judge of the circuit court 1982-92.

O'Hara, John Ailbe. Queen's University of Belfast. M. 1979, QC M. 1999, chairman of the Executive Council 2008-10, high court judge 2013-.

O'Hare, Brendan Gerard. Former lecturer in physics. Queen's University of Belfast. M. 1989.

O'Hare, John Francis. Trinity College, Dublin. M. 1988.

O'Hare, Kevin. Bar of Ireland. M. 2007.

O'Hare, Kevin Joseph. Trinity College, Dublin. M. 1985.

O'Hare, Paula. Bar of Ireland. T. 1991.

O'Hare, Sean Thomas. A former solicitor. M. 1998.

O'Higgins, Michael Liam. Bar of Ireland. M. 2012.

O'Kane, Conor David Joseph. University of Liverpool. M. 1991.

O'Kane, Fiona Marie. A former solicitor. M. 2005.

O'Kane, Garrett Jude. Bar of England and Wales. M. 2002.

O'Kane, Patrick Eoin. Bar of England and Wales. M. 2000.

O'Kane, Paula Mary Colette. Queen's University of Belfast. M. 1982.

O'Keefe, Joseph Boyd Philip. Queen's University of Belfast. M. 2004.

O'Keefe, Peter Anthony. Queen's University of Belfast. M. 1976.

O'Kelly, Anne Frances. Queen's University of Belfast. M. 1980.

O'Kelly, Sile Proinsias. Bar of Ireland. T. 1991.

O'Leary, James Francis. Bar of Ireland. T. 1991.

O'Neill, Andrew Colm. Cambridge University. M. 2007.

O'Neill, Catherine. University of Dundee. M. 2002.

O'Neill, Cathryn Mary. Queen's University of Belfast. M. 2012.

O'Neill, Conn Gerald Francis. Queen's University of Belfast. M. 2005.

O'Neill, Damien. Bar of England and Wales. M. 2004.

O'Neill, John Brendan. A former solicitor. M. 1948. Disbarred 1953 to become a solicitor again.

O'Neill, John Duncan. Queen's University of Belfast. M. 1977.

O'Neill, Kerri Anne. Queen's University of Belfast. M. 2009.

O'Neill, Kerri Marie. Bar of England and Wales. M. 2012.

O'Neill, Patrick. Bar of Ireland. H. 2008.

O'Neill, William John Barry. Queen's University of Belfast. M. 1991.

O'Rawe, Mary Brigid Frances. University of Kent at Canterbury. M. 1991.

O'Rawe, Christopher Donal. Bar of England and Wales. M. 2002.

O'Reilly, Cormac Anthony. Trinity College, Dublin. M. 2000.

O'Reilly, Francis Edward Patrick. Queen's University of Belfast. M. 1972.

O'Reilly, Garett Edward. A former solicitor. H. 2006.

O'Reilly, James Patrick. T. 1925.

O'Reilly, James. SC Bar of Ireland. M. 1989.

O'Reilly, Mary Carmel. Queen's University of Belfast. M. 1976.

O'Reilly, Paul Mary. Bar of Ireland. M. 2000.

O'Reilly, Sarah Anne Kathleen. Queen's University of Belfast. M. 2004.

O'Rourke, Martin. Liverpool Polytechnic. M. 1987. QC M. 2011.

O'Rourke, Mary Bernadette. Bar of England and Wales. H. 2003.

O'Sullivan, Brian Patrick. Open University. M. 2009.

O'Sullivan, David Kevin Timothy. A former solicitor in England and Wales, then a member of the Bar of England and Wales. M. 2001.

Oakey, Patrick Lauri. Queen's University of Belfast. M. 1956. Disbarred to become a solicitor M. 1962.

Oertzen, Ashling Christine. Queen's University of Belfast. M. 2012.

Okyere, Kwame Amponsah. Queen's University of Belfast. M. 1973.

Orbinson, William James. Queen's University of Belfast. M. 1988, QC T. 2006. Author of a number of works on planning law and practice.

Orr, Jacqueline. Trinity College, Dublin. M. 1976, QC M. 2001.

Orr, John. Queen's University. M. 1973, QC M. 1996.

Orr, Hugh Mark. Trinity College, Dublin. M. 1980, QC M. 1996.

Ouseley, Duncan Brian. QC Bar of England and Wales. M. 1997, QC M. 1997, judge of the high court of England and Wales 2000-.

Oughton, Richard Donald. Bar of England and Wales. H. 1999.

Overing, Tracey Tanya Marie. Queen's University of Belfast. M. 2004

Paines, Nicholas Paul Billot. Bar of England and Wales. T. 1996.

Park, Andrew Edward Wilson. QC of the Bar of England and Wales. H. 1992, QC H. 1992, judge of the high court of England and Wales 1997-2006.

Park, Jonathan Samuel. Bar of England and Wales. M. 1993.

Parker, Christopher James. Queen's University of Belfast. M. 1994.

Parker, Kenneth Blades. Bar of England and Wales. H. 1987. QC 1992.

Passmore, John William. Bar of England and Wales. M. 2003.

Patterson, Brenda Margaret Hale. Trinity College, Dublin. Northern Ireland Civil Service. M. 1976. (Lady Sheil).

Patterson, William Reginald Lambert. E. 1923. Disbarred by King's Inns to become a solicitor.

Patterson, Sean Joseph. Queen's University of Belfast. M. 1995.

Patton, Craig James. Bar of England and Wales. M. 2004.

Patton, William Francis. M. 1921, KC H. 1945. Served as a deputy county court judge for several years until he retired from that post in 1972. CBE 1975, died 20 June 1976.

Pauley, Jacqueline Wendy. Queen's University of Belfast. M. 1989.

Payne, Jennifer Susan Bar of Ireland. T. 1990.

Pearce-Higgins, Daniel. QC Bar of England and Wales. M. 2001. Circuit judge in England 2004-.

Pearson, Christopher. Bar of England and Wales. M. 1996.

Pearson, John Michael. Bar of England and Wales. H. 1969.

Perceval, Sir Walter Ian. QC of the Bar of England and Wales, MP (C), solicitor general. T. 1979, QC T. 1979.

Perry, Desmond Lawrence . Queen's University of Belfast. M. 1974. Resident magistrate (later district judge (magistrates' courts)) 1992-.

Peters, Nigel Melvin. Bar of England and Wales. T. 1985.

Petrie, John. Queen's University of Belfast. M. 1947. Resident magistrate 1973-85, QC M. 1985, county court judge 1985-2000. Died 30 July 2009.

Phelan, Diarmuid Rossa. SC of the Bar of Ireland. H. 2012.

Phelan, Michael Vincent. Queen's University of Belfast. M. 1936.

Phillips, Heather Elizabeth. Queen's University of Belfast. M. 2004.

Phillips, James Neil. Dundee University. M. 1999.

Phillips, Rory Andrew Livingston. Bar of England and Wales. M. 2006.

Philpott, Corrine Elizabeth. Queen's University of Belfast. M. 1977, QC M. 1993, vice-chairman of the Executive Council 1992-93, county court judge 1998-.

Pilcher, Rebecca Charlotte. Bar of England and Wales. M. 1995.

Pitchford, Lauren Rae. Bar of England and Wales. H. 2008.

Pittaway, David Michael. QC of the Bar of England and Wales. H. 2011.

Platts-Mills, Mark Fortescue. Bar of England and Wales. H. 1980.

Pollock, Elisabeth Alexandra. Dundee University. M. 2008.

Pollock, George Keith. Trinity College, Dublin. H. 1957. Joined Colonial Service. Disbarred to become a solicitor 1968.

Porter, Robert Wilson. Queen's University of Belfast. T. 1950, QC M. 1965. MP (U) Queen's University 1966-69, Lagan Valley 1969-72, parliamentary secretary to minister of home affairs 1969, minister of health and social services 1969, minister of home affairs 1969-70. Knt. 1971. County court judge 1978-95, recorder of Belfast 1993-95.

Potter, Donald Charles. Bar of England and Wales. H. 1967.

Potter, Gary Rankin. Queen's University of Belfast. M. 1982.

Potter, Michael Alexander. Queen's University of Belfast. M. 1988.

Power, John Mel. Queen's University of Belfast. M. 1985.

Power, Lewis Niall. Bar of England and Wales. H. 1996 (*in absentia*).

Power, Lawrence Imam. Bar of England and Wales. M. 2005.

Preston, Kenneth James. Queen's University of Belfast. M. 1976.

Pringle, Alfred Denis. H. 1926. SC, judge of the high court of Ireland 1969-74. Died 22 Aug. 1998.

Pringle, John Kenneth. Queen's University of Belfast. M. 1953, QC H. 1970, chairman of the Bar Council 1975-80, recorder of Belfast 1984-93, judge of the high court 1993-99.

Proctor, Gerda Mary Elizabeth (Mayo). Trinity College, Dublin. M. 1974. Resident magistrate Kenya 1976-82 and judge advocate Kenya 1981-82. Returned to practice in Northern Ireland. Full time chairman of industrial tribunals 1989-90, vice-president of industrial tribunals and of the fair employment tribunal 1990-2007. OBE 2007.

Purdy, Heather Margaret. Queen's University of Belfast. M. 2004.

Purvis, Gareth John. Queen's University of Belfast. M. 1992.

Quigley, Bernadette. Bar of Ireland. M. 2012.

Quin, Michael Joseph Kelleher. T. 1924.

Quin, Charles George. Southampton University. M. 1978. Took up a post as crown counsel in Bermuda, a judge of the grand court in the Cayman Islands.

Quinlivan, Karen Marie. University College, Dublin. M. 1993. QC M. 2011.

Quinn, Aine Fionnuala. Queen's University of Belfast. M. 1994.

Quinn, Declan Patrick. Queen's University of Belfast. M. 2000.

Quinn, Lauren Louise. Queen's University of Belfast. M. 2008.

Quinn, Nigel Goddard. Queen's University of Belfast. M. 1982.

Quinn, Patrick Fintan. Queen's University of Belfast. M. 1981.

Quinn, Paulyn Marrinan. Bar of Ireland. M. 1992. SC H. 2000.

Quinn, Stephen Gillespie. Queen's University of Belfast. M. 1977, QC T. 2006.

Quigley, Conor. Bar of England and Wales. M. 2009.

Rafferty, Charles Emmet Pearse. Queen's University of Belfast. M. 1985.

Rafferty, Francis James. Queen's University of Belfast. M. 1992.

Rafferty, John Francis. Queen's University of Belfast. M. 2011.

Rafferty, Laura. Bar of Ireland. M. 2012.

Rafferty, Louise Emma. Bar of England and Wales. M. 2010.

Rafferty, Neil Sinton. Queen's University of Belfast. M. 1990.

Rafferty, Steffan Patrick. Queen's University of Belfast. M. 2009.

Rainey, Paul Joseph. Queen's University of Belfast. M. 2010.

Ramsey, Michael. Bar of Ireland. H. 1999.

Ramsey, Paul Eugene. Queen's University of Belfast. M. 1977, QC M. 2001.

Ramsey, Sarah Louise. Queen's University of Belfast. M. 1993.

Ranaghan, Paula Florence. Queen's University of Belfast. M. 1984.

Randolph, Fergus Mark Harry. Bar of England and Wales. M. 1991.

Rawlinson, Sir Peter Anthony Grayson. QC, MP T. 1972, QC T. 1972. Attorney general for England and Wales 1970-74, and (under direct rule) for Northern Ireland 1972-74. MP (C) 1955-78, solicitor general 1962-64. Created Lord Rawlinson of Ewell 1978, died 28 June 2006.

Rea, Conan. Queen's University of Belfast. M. 1997.

Rea, John Michael. Trinity College, Dublin. M. 1983.

Rea, Robert Kevin. Bar of England and Wales. H. 1997.

Reade, James Derek. M. 1972.

Redpath, Charles William Grant. Queen's University of Belfast. M. 1981. Master of the high court 2005-.

Reed, Piers Knowle Moorehouse. Bar of England and Wales. M. 1988.

Reel, Mark Francis. Queen's University of Belfast. M. 1996.

Reichert, Nicholas (Klaus) George Gerard. Bar of Ireland. M. 1998.

Reid, David James. Queen's University of Belfast. M. 2003.

Reid, David John. Cambridge University. M. 2006.

Reid, Francis Alexander. Queen's University of Belfast. H. 1938. Practised in Malaya, served in the armed forces there during the Second World War and was a prisoner of the Japanese. Resumed practice in Northern Ireland after the War. QC M. 1956. First elected chairman of the Bar Council 1969. National insurance commissioner (later social security commissioner) 1969-1983, chief social security commissioner 1983-85.

Reid, Simon Patrick. Queen's University of Belfast. M. 1994.

Reilly, Dale Arnold. Queen's University of Belfast. M. 1996.

Reilly, Thomas Edward Martin. Bar of England and Wales. H. 1997.

Reynold, Frederic. QC of the Bar of England and Wales. H. 1989, QC H. 1989.

Reynolds, James. H. 1931. Crown counsel, Hong Kong 1940, high court judge, Eastern Nigeria 1956.

Reynolds, Miriam. Bar of Ireland. T. 1993, SC H. 1998.

Rice, Melanie Naomi Sophia. Queen's University of Belfast. M. 2004.

Richards, Neil Kwadwo. Reading University. M. 2007.

Ringland, Christopher David. Cambridge University. M. 2010.

Ringland, David Alexander. Queen's University of Belfast. M. 1978, QC M. 1999.

Ringland, John Terence. Southampton University. M. 1984.

Ritchie, Stephen Kirkwood. Queen's University of Belfast. M. 1978.

Ritchie, Timothy John. Queen's University of Belfast. M. 2000.

Robinson, Cathal Mark. Queen's University of Belfast. M. 1999.

Robinson, Claire Joanne. Queen's University of Belfast. M. 2001.

Robinson, Gavin James. University of Ulster. M. 2004. Lord mayor of Belfast 2012-2013.

Robinson, Linda Mary. Bar of England and Wales. T. 1996.

Robinson, Keith Liam Hamilton. Oxford University. M. 1996.

Robinson, Michelle Pansy Panchetta. Bar of England and Wales. H. 2002.

Roe, Patrick Joseph. M. 1925. Judge of the circuit court 1948-57.

Rodgers, Paul Anthony. Queen's University of Belfast. M. 1996.

Rodgers, Hugh Martin. Queen's University of Belfast. M. 1975. QC M. 2011.

Rogers, John. SC Bar of Ireland, attorney general of Ireland 1984-87. T. 1989.

Rogers, Michael William. Newcastle University. M. 2005.

Rogers, Neil Anthony. Queen's University of Belfast. M. 2012.

Rogers, Sarah Elizabeth. Queen's University of Belfast. M. 2006.

Rooney, John. Bar of England and Wales. H. 2000.

Rooney, Kevin James. Queen's University of Belfast. M. 1983. Lecturer in law at Queen's University 1984-87. QC M. 2011.

Rooney, Lesley. Queen's University of Belfast. M. 1990. Joined the Office of Law Reform in 1992.

Rooney, Orla. Queen's University of Belfast. M. 2012.

Ross, Victoria Gabrielle Anne. Queen's University of Belfast. M. 2002.

Rothwell, Jane Anne. Bar of Ireland. M. 2012.

Roughton, Ashley Wentworth. Bar of England and Wales. M. 2000.

Rountree, Nicola Catherine Ann. Queen's University of Belfast. M. 2009.

Rowan, Anna Elizabeth Marion. Bar of England and Wales. M. 2012.

Rowland, Robert Todd. Queen's University of Belfast. H. 1949, QC H. 1969. Vice chairman of the value added tax tribunal for Northern Ireland 1972-1974, county court judge 1974-90, president of the lands tribunal 1983-90.

Ruddell, George Sidford. Queen's University of Belfast. M. 1989.

Russell, David. Queen's University of Belfast. M. 1991.

Russell, James Francis Buchanan. Queen's University of Belfast. H. 1952, QC M. 1968, county court judge 1978-97, recorder of Belfast 1995-97. Died 27 Jan. 2013.

Ruth, Adrian Christopher James. Queen's University of Belfast. M. 1997.

Ryan, Eithne Mary Catherine. Bar of England and Wales. M. 1996.

Ryan, John Gerard. Bar of Ireland. M. 1989.

Ryan, Oonagh Patricia. Queen's University of Belfast. M. 1980.

Ryan, Roisin Finnuala Moll. Bar of England and Wales. M. 2001.

Sales, Philip James. Bar of England and Wales. H. 2004. Judge of the high court of England and Wales 2008-.

Sands, Aidan James. Queen's University of Belfast. M. 1998.

Sands, Phillipe Joseph. Bar of England and Wales. M. 1994.

Savage, Brendan. Bar of Ireland. M. 2011.

Savage, Patrick Owen. Queen's University of Belfast. M. 2009.

Savill, Mark Ashley. Bar of England and Wales. M. 2006.

Sayers, Donal Peter. Queen's University of Belfast. M. 1997.

Scholes, James. Queen's University of Belfast. M. 1973. Department of the DPP. Deputy director of public prosecutions 2008-09, acting director 2009-11, deputy director 2011-12.

Scoffield, David Alister. Oxford University. M. 1999. QC M. 2011.

Scotland, Baroness Patricia. QC of the Bar of England and Wales. M. 2008. Parliamentary under- secretary, foreign and commonwealth office 1999-2001, parliamentary secretary lord chancellor's department 2001-03, minister of state at the home office 2003-07, attorney general 2007-2010.

Scott-Bell, Rosalind Sara. Bar of England and Wales. M. 2012.

Scullion, Andrew. Queen's University of Belfast. M. 2011.

Sefton, Peter Stewart. Queen's University of Belfast. M. 1983.

Seymour, Colin Brian. Bar of Ireland. H. 1996.

Seymour, David. Bar of England and Wales. T. 1997.

Shannon, William Norman. Queen's University of Belfast. M. 1976. Disbarred to become a solicitor T. 1982.

Shannon, David Stanley. Queen's University of Belfast. M. 1977.

Sharpe, David Robert Kitson. Queen's University of Belfast. Practised medicine (MRCP, FRCS), before being called to the Bar. M. 1999.

Shaw, Charles Barry. Queen's University of Belfast. M. 1948, QC M. 1964. Director of public prosecutions 1972-89. CB 1974, knt. 1980. Died 30 Sept. 2010.

Shaw, Michael. Queen's University of Belfast. M. 1984.

Shaw, Stephen James. Queen's University of Belfast. M. 1980, QC M. 2001.

Shea, Timothy Bertrand. Queen's University of Belfast. M.1974. Practised in the Cayman Islands 1984-96 when he died.

Sheehan, Dermot. Bar of Ireland. M. 2010.

Sheeran, Nuala Mary. Queen's University of Belfast. M. 1996.

Sheil, John Joseph. Trinity College, Dublin. M. 1964, QC M. 1975, high court judge 1989-2004, lord justice of appeal 2004-06.

Sheil, Mary Kathleen Antonia (Moya). M. 1930. Died 14 Jan. 1942.

Sheil, Michael Forde. Queen's University of Belfast. M. 2004.

Sheilds, Jonpaul. Queen's University of Belfast. M. 1995.

Sheils, Claire Mary Petra. Ulster Polytechnic. M. 1984. Joined the Equal Opportunities Commission Aug. 1990.

Sheridan, Francis Anthony. Bar of England and Wales. M. 1994.

Sheridan, Paul Adrian. Queen's University of Belfast. M. 1977.

Sherrard, Brian George. Queen's University of Belfast. M. 1992. Northern Ireland Court Service 1998-2006. Coroner 2006-2012, county court judge 2012-.

Sherrard, Christopher. University of Dundee. M. 2001.

Sherry, Eamon Martin. Bar of England and Wales. H. 1998.

Shields, Richard Gerard. Trinity College, Dublin. M. 2002.

Shipley, Norman Graham. Bar of England and Wales. M. 1999.

Shipley-Dalton, Duncan Edward. University of Essex. M. 1996. MLA (UUP) 1998-2003.

Shipsey, William Edward. Bar of Ireland. T. 1989.

Sholdis, Sarah Carole Denise. Queen's University of Belfast. M. 1986.

Sidhu, Jagdeep Kaur. Bar of England and Wales. H. 2002.

Silkin, Samuel Charles. QC of the Bar of England and Wales, attorney general. T. 1974 QC T. 1974. MP (Lab) 1964-83, attorney general 1974-79, created Lord Silkin of Dulwich 1985. Died 17 Aug. 1988.

Simcock, Sarah Louise. Bar of England and Wales. M. 2009.

Simpson, Carl Alexander. Queen's University of Belfast. M. 1975, QC M. 1996.

Simpson, Gerald Eric John. Queen's University. M. 1974, QC M. 1999.

Simpson, Jacqueline Anne. Oxford University. M. 1987.

Simpson, Noreen Mary (Mollie). Queen's University of Belfast. M. 2000.

Simpson, Suzanne Elizabeth. Manchester University. M. 1998.

Singer, Andrew Michael. Bar of England and Wales. M. 1997.

Singer, Jacqueline Victoria. Queen's University of Belfast. M. 2011.

Sinton, William Henry. Durham University. M. 2009.

Skelt, Ian Stuart. Bar of England and Wales. M. 2008.

Skelton, Peter. Bar of England and Wales. M. 2006 (*in absentia*).

Slade, Edwyn Alick Frank Hobart. Queen's University of Belfast. T. 1930. Appointed secretary to Londonderry Education Committee July 1930.

Slevin, Patrick Charles. Bar of England and Wales. H. 2005.

Sloan, Emma Catherine Veronica. Queen's University of Belfast. M. 2004.

Smith, Anthony Noel. A former solicitor. H. 1999.

Smith, Christine Anne. Queen's University of Belfast. M. 1985. QC M. 2011.

Smith, Ciaran Edward. Bar of Ireland. M. 2007.

Smith, Marcus Andrew Charles. Bar of England and Wales. H. 1999.

Smith, Peter David. Queen's University of Belfast. Lecturer in law at Queen's University. M. 1969, QC M. 1978, deputy high court judge 2002-08, judge of the courts of appeal of

Jersey and Guernsey 1996-2009, chairman of the life sentence review commissioners 2002-08, and of the parole commissioners 2008-11. Member of the Independent Commission on Policing for Northern Ireland 1998-99 (The Patten Commission). CBE 2008.

Smyth, Aileen (Ann). Queen's University of Belfast. M. 2007.

Smyth, David William. M. 1972 (*in absentia*), QC H. 1989, county court judge 1990-.

Smyth, James Corry Fraser. Member of the Bar of England and Wales. H. 1955. Judge advocate's department, resumed practice c. 1972.

Smyth, John Gerard Patrick. Queen's University of Belfast. M. 1984.

Smyth, Laura Jane. University of Ulster. M. 2005.

Smyth, Lynn Catherine. Queen's University of Belfast. M. 2010.

Smyth, Michael David. Queen's University of Belfast. M. 2001.

Smyth, Moira Bernadine. Queen's University of Belfast. M. 1995.

Smyth, Paul Anthony. Queen's University of Belfast. M. 2009.

Smyth, Richard. Trinity College, Dublin. M. 2003.

Smyth, Thomas Clement. Bar of Ireland. T. 1983. A solicitor and assistant secretary of the Law Society of Ireland 1963-68. Bar of Ireland M. 1968, SC 1977, judge of the high court of Ireland 1996-2007.

Snow, Darren Mark. Bar of England and Wales. H. 2009.

Solomon, Montague Philip. Bar of England and Wales. M. 1969.

Soloman, Richard James Norman. A former solicitor. M. 2011.

Southey, David Hugh. QC of the Bar of England and Wales. M. 2010.

Spellman, Jarlath Anthony. Bar of Ireland. T. 1996.

Spence, Stuart Adrian. Queen's University of Belfast. M. 1981.

Spencer, Sir Derek Harold. QC of the Bar of England and Wales, solicitor general. T. 1992, QC T. 1992. MP (C) 1983-87 and 1992-97, solicitor general 1992-97.

Spens, David Patrick. QC Bar of England and Wales. H. 2012.

Spring, Linda. Bar of England and Wales. M. 1999.

Sreenan, Paul. Bar of Ireland. M. 2012.

Stallworthy, Nicolas Kyd. Bar of England and Wales. M. 2010.

Stanbury, Matthew Francis. Bar of England and Wales. M. 2010.

Staunton, William James. Queen's University of Belfast. T. 1948, QC M. 1971. Resident magistrate 1 Feb. 1972, shot by the IRA Oct. 1972 and died of his injuries 25 Jan. 1973.

Steele, Caroline Jayne. Queen's University of Belfast. M. 2000.

Steele, John. Trinity College, Dublin. M. 1931.

Steele, Edward Richard Alexander. Queen's University of Belfast. Lecturer in law at Queen's University. M. 1984.

Steer, Robin William. University of Leicester. M. 1994.

Stephens, Denis Synge. Trinity College, Dublin. Member of the Bar of Ireland. Registrar of the supreme court of judicature of Northern Ireland M. 1978, QC M. 1978. Died 17 Apr. 1999.

Stephens, William Benjamin Synge. Manchester University. M. 1977, QC M. 1996, judge of the high court 2007-.

Stevenson, Colin Pedlow. Trinity College, Dublin. M. 1984.

Stevenson, Douglas Clarke. A former solicitor. M. 2009.

Stevenson, John Alexander. Queen's University of Belfast. M. 1983.

Stewart, Alan James. Queen's University of Belfast. M. 2006.

Stewart, Alexander. Solicitor to the department of health and social services 1973-83. T. 1984.

Stewart, Charles. Queen's University of Belfast. T. 1938, KC 1950. MP (Ind) Queens University 1958-66, chief justice of Cameroons 1966-67, resumed practice Sept. 1967, resident magistrate 1968-83.

Stewart, Emma Jane. Queen's University of Belfast. M. 2006.

Stewart, Ercus Gregory. Bar of Ireland. T. 1976.

Stewart, John Howard. University of Bristol. M. 1980.

Stewart, Richard Paul. Bar of England and Wales. T. 1991.

Stitt, Michael William. Trinity College, Dublin. M. 1975, QC M. 1996.

Stockman, Odhran. Queen's University of Belfast. M. 1987. Social security commissioner 2011-.

Stuart, Archibald. M. 1924.

Stuart, Diana. Bar of Ireland. M. 2011.

Sullivan, Paul John. Bar of England and Wales. M. 2001.

Summers, Christopher James. University of Ulster. M. 2012.

Sweeney, Honoria (Noreen) Pauline Mary. Queen's University of Belfast. M. 1986.

Swift, Felix (b. 17 July 1969). Bar of England and Wales. M. 2000.

Swift, Felix. Bar of England and Wales. M. 2000.

Swift, Jonathan Mark. Bar of England and Wales. M. 2008.

Symons, John Maurice. QC of the Bar of England and Wales. M. 1990, QC M. 1990.

Taggart, Patrick Joseph. Bar of England and Wales. M. 1997.

Talbot, Gordon Albert. Queen's University of Belfast. M. 1974.

Tannahill, Ian David Robert. Queen's University of Belfast. M. 1990.

Taylor, Patrick Joseph. Trinity College, Dublin. M. 2005.

Teevan, Thomas Leslie. Queen's University of Belfast. T. 1952. MP (U) for West Belfast Nov. 1950-Oct. 1951. Died 11 Oct. 1954. *DIB*.

Tennyson, Lauren. Bar of Ireland. H. 2012.

Thom, William Ian Hamilton. Cambridge University. M. 1985.

Thomas, Cheryl Diane. Bar of England and Wales. H. 1998.

Thomas, Natalie Louise. Bar of England and Wales. M. 2001.

Thompson, Aaron David Coulter. Queen's University of Belfast. M. 2002.

Thompson, Benjamin Robert. University of Ulster. M. 2012.

Thompson, Johanna Jane Elizabeth. Manchester University. M. 1994.

Thompson, Josephine. Queen's University of Belfast. M. 1974.

Thompson, John David. Queen's University of Belfast. M. 1977, QC M. 1993. Died as the result of a yachting accident in the Caribbean 2007.

Thomas, Cheryl Diane. University of Hull. H. 1998.

Thomas, Natalie Louise. London University. M. 2001.

Thomlinson, Peter Robert. Bar of England and Wales. T. 1993.

Tierney, Caoimhe Brighid. Queen's University of Belfast. M. 2009.

Tierney, Michael James. University of Ulster. M. 2010.

Timmins, Shane Brabazon. Queen's University of Belfast. M. 1971.

Todd, Eamon Paul. Queen's University of Belfast. M. 1996.

Toner, Henry Gerard John. Queen's University of Belfast. M. 1976, QC M. 1999.

Tookey, Geoffrey William. QC of the Bar of England and Wales. T. 1954, QC T. 1954.

Toolan, James Celsus. Queen's University of Belfast. M. 1980.

Topping, Walter William Buchanan (Ken). Queen's University of Belfast. M. 1930, KC M. 1946. MP (U) Larne 1945-1960, parliamentary secretary ministry of finance and chief whip 1947-56, minister of home affairs 1956-60. Recorder of Belfast 1960-78, died 26 July 1978. *DIB.*

Torney, Gerald Patrick. Queen's University of Belfast. M. 1932. Called to the Bar of England and Wales M. 1935, died 1936.

Torrens, Barry Ian. Bar of England and Wales. H. 1999.

Toulmin, John Kevin. QC of the Bar of England and Wales. M. 1989. Offical referee and senior circuit court judge 1997-98, judge of the technology and construction court 1998-.

Trainor, Aisling. Queen's University of Belfast. M. 2007.

Trainor, Shauna. Bar of England and Wales. H. 2001.

Travers, Hugh. Cambridge University. M. 1995.

Treacy, James (Seamus) Mary Eugene. Queen's University of Belfast. M. 1979, QC M. 2000, high court judge 2007-.

Trimble, Marilyn Teresa. Bar of Ireland. M. 2000.

Trimble, William David. Queen's University of Belfast. T. 1970. Lecturer in law at Queen's University 1968-1990 and editor of the Northern Ireland Law Reports 1975-90, author of *Northern Ireland Housing Law* (1986). Member Northern Ireland Constitutional Convention 1975-76, MP (UU) 1990-2005, MLA 1998-2007, leader of the Ulster Unionist Party 1995-2005 and first minister of Northern Ireland 1998-2002. Joint winner of Nobel Peace Prize 1998, created Lord Trimble 2006.

Troop, Paul Benjamin. Bar of England and Wales. H. 2010.

Tweedale, John Piers. Queen's University of Belfast. M. 1973.

Turkington, Ian Bernard. Manchester University. M. 1995.

Turriff, Derrick Edward William. Birmingham University. H. 1987.

Turner, Kerry Siobhan. Bar of England and Wales. M. 1998.

Tyner, Patrick Hugh. Bar of England and Wales. M. 1979.

Vajda, Christopher Stephen. Cambridge University. T. 1996.

Valentine, Barry James Allen Charles. Queen's University of Belfast. M. 1974. Author of *County Court Procedure in Northern Ireland* (1985); *Criminal Procedure in Northern Ireland* (1989, 2nd ed. 2010); *Civil Proceedings in the Supreme Court* (1997); *Civil Proceedings in the County Court* (1999); an online annotated version of the Northern Ireland Statutes, and *Cricket's Dawn that Died: The Australians in England 1938* (1991). Honorary bencher.

Valentine, Donald Graham. Bar of England and Wales. M. 1980.

Valera, Eamon de. Bar of Ireland. M. 1976. Judge of the high court of Ireland 2002-.

Vance, Laura Ann. Trinity College, Dublin. M. 2006.

Vasey, Patricia Margaret. University of Sydney. M. 1978.

Vaughan, David Arthur John. QC of the Bar of England and Wales. M. 1981, QC M. 1981.

Vaughan, Kieran Patrick. Bar of England and Wales. M. 2007.

Vials, Cora Ann Elaine. Bar of England and Wales.

Village, Peter Malcolm. Bar of England and Wales. M. 1997.

Wall, Gavan James. A former solicitor. M. 2001.

Wall, James Benedict. Queen's University of Belfast. M. 2009.

Wallace, Christopher. Queen's University of Belfast. M. 2010.

Walls, Damian Thomas. Queen's University of Belfast. M. 1984.

Walker, Suzanne. Bar of England and Wales. M. 2007.

Walkingshaw, Sarah Jayne. Trinity College, Dublin. M. 2003.

Walsh, Dermot Patrick Joseph. Queen's University of Belfast. M. 1983.

Walsh, Edward Michael. SC Bar of Ireland. T. 1976. Judge of the high court of Ireland 1981-82.

Walsh, Margaret Mary. Queen's University of Belfast. M. 1979, QC M. 2001.

Walsh, Rosemary Gemma. Bar of England and Wales. M. 2011.

Ward, Barry Martin. Bar of Ireland. M. 2010.

Ward, Orla Mary. Bar of England and Wales. M. 2004.

Ward, Michael Gerard. Queen's University of Belfast. M. 2011.

Warnock, Andrew Ronald. Bar of England and Wales. H. 2005.

Warnock, Timothy Mark Victor. Queen's University of Belfast. M. 2004.

Watson, Margaret Mary. Queen's University of Belfast. M. 1985.

Watt, Elizabeth Jane. Dundee University. M. 1978.

Watt, Graeme William. Oxford University. M. 2001.

Watt, Robert. Queen's University of Belfast. T. 1946, QC H. 1964, county court judge 1971-89.

Waters, Michael. Bar of Ireland. H. 2004.

Watters, Rosemary. Queen's University of Belfast. M. 1982. Resident magistrate (later district judge (magistrates' court)) 1998-.

Watterson, Brian John. Queen's University of Belfast. M. 1980.

Watterson, Rebecca Isobel. Trinity College, Dublin. M. 2010.

Weatherhead, Louise. Bar of England and Wales. H. 1998.

Weatherup, Ronald Eccles. Queen's University of Belfast. M. 1971 *(in absentia)*, QC M. 1993, high court judge 2001-.

Webb, Henry Robert James. Queen's University of Belfast. M. 1992.

Webster, Richard Colin. Queen's University of Belfast. M. 1988.

Weir, Alan Anthony. Queen's University of Belfast. M. 1990.

Weir, Claire. Bar of England and Wales. M. 1998.

Weir, Marion. Bar of England and Wales. M. 2001.

Weir, Peter James. Queen's University of Belfast. M. 1992. MLA (UU) 1998-2001, MLA (DUP) 2002-.

Weir, Reginald George. Queen's University of Belfast. M. 1970, QC H. 1985, chairman of the Executive Council 2002-03, judge of the high court 2003-.

Weir, Richard Keenan. Queen's University of Belfast. M. 1979, QC M. 2001.

West-Knights, Laurence James. Bar of England and Wales. M. 2000.

Whelan, Roma Felicity. Queen's University of Belfast. M. 1982. Went to practise in England in 1985.

Whelan, Sorcha. Bar of Ireland. M. 2012.

Wells, Nathan Ernest John. Bar of England and Wales. H. 2010.

White, Alan Thomas George. Queen's University of Belfast. M. 1974. Department of the DPP 1980-2000, resident magistrate (later district judge (magistrates' court)) 2000-.

White, Ciaran James. Bar of Ireland. H. 2003.

Whiteside, Richard John. Queen's University of Belfast (degrees in medicine and former general practitioner). M. 1995.

Whyte, Gillian Clare. Bar of England and Wales. M. 1999.

Widdis, Hugh. University College, Dublin. M. 1994.

Willis, Aaron John. Queen's University of Belfast. M. 2009.

Wilkinson, David Rankin. Cambridge University. M. 1947. Died 14 Apr. 1982 whilst on a Bar holiday in Portugal.

Wilkinson, Hiram Parkes. Member of the Bar of England and Wales 1889, judge of the high court at Weihaiwei (China) 1916-1925. M. 1926, QC M. 1928. Died 1 Apr. 1935.

Williams, Rhodri John. Bar of England and Wales. H. 2009.

Williams of Mostyn, Lord. QC of the Bar of England and Wales. H. 1993, QC T. 1993, attorney general 1999-2001, leader of the House of Lords 2001-03, died 20 Sept. 2003. Created Lord Williams of Mostyn 1994.

Williamson, Jonathan Eric. Queen's University of Belfast. M. 2010.

Williamson-Graham, Anita. University of Ulster. M. 2003.

Willis, Aaron John. Queen's University of Belfast. M. 2009.

Willis, Claire Colettine. Queen's University of Belfast. M. 2006.

Wilson, Alastair James Drysdale. QC of the Bar of England and Wales. H. 1989, QC H. 1989.

Wilson, Charles. Trinity College, Dublin. M. 1923. Went to the Straits Settlements (Singapore), where he was registrar of the high court.

Wilson, Crozier Terence. Queen's University of Belfast. T. 1948. Died 1963.

Wilson, Daniel Martin. Bar of England and Wales. M. 1936. Killed in action in the Second World War, MC.

Wilson, Gordon Crymble Spencer. Queen's University of Belfast. M. 1974.

Wilson, Josephine Olivia. Queen's University of Belfast. M. 1999.

Wilson, John Willoughby. Cambridge University. M. 1960. Private secretary 1966-79, then legal secretary 1979-80, to the lord chief justice, master of the high court 1985-93, master (Queen's Bench and Appeals) 1993-06. QC T. 1988. Under treasurer, Inn of Court of Northern Ireland 1997-08. Honorary bencher.

Wilson, Kenneth James Ashcroft. Bar of England Wales. M. 1999.

Wilson, Rosemary Helen. Nottingham Trent University. M. 1997.

Wilson, Stephen Elijah. Bar of Ireland. M. 2011.

Wolfe, Martin Judge. Queen's University of Belfast. M. 1994.

Woods, Cathy Leanne. Bar of England and Wales. M. 2009.

Workman, Ian William. Oxford University. M. 1949. Went to Canada in 1952.

Wright, Elizabeth Anne. Queen's University of Belfast. M. 1989.

Wright, Frederick George Ian. Bar of England and Wales. H. 1998.

Wright, Rosalind. Bar of England and Wales M 1999. Director of the serious fraud office 1997-2003, and of the office of fair trading 2003-07.

Wright, Stephen John. Queen's University of Belfast. M. 1978.

Wyeth, Mark Charles. QC of the Bar of England and Wales. H. 2010.

Young, George Vaughan Chichester. A former solicitor, a member of the colonial service. T. 1949. Later assistant attorney general, Sarawak.

Young, Jennifer Claire (b.14 Aug. 1976). Queen's University of Belfast. M. 2002

# King's Counsel and Queen's Counsel
# by date of call since 1921

* Members of the Bar of England and Wales
** Members of the Bar of Ireland  *** Solicitor

**24 May 1922**
James Alexander Pringle
William McAfee
James Sinclair Baxter

**2 December 1922**
David Thomas James Sherlock[1]
James Ambrose Rearden
(*in absentia*)

**21 December 1923**
John Alexander Weir Johnston
Sir Arthur Scott Quekett

**3 November 1924**
Thomas John Day Atkinson

**1 November 1926**
John Clarke Davison
William Lowry

**17 June 1927**
John Charles Weir [2]

**14 November 1928**
Hiram Parkes Wilkinson

**13 February 1929**
Arthur Black
Edward John McKean

**22 February 1929**
Percy Alexander McIlwaine[3]
(*in absentia*)

**18 March 1929**
Herbert Cecil Stronge
(*in absentia*)

**3 February 1933**
Samuel Clarke Porter
Walter Oakman Hume
George Boyle Hanna
John Edmund Warnock

**15 April 1936**
Marin Gore Ellison
John Clarke MacDermott MC

**1 June 1938**
John Desmond Chambers

**7 June 1938**
Oscar Bedford Daly[4]
(*in absentia*)

**1 June 1939**
William Frederick McCoy
Bernard Joshua Fox
John Hugh Hamilton Campbell

---

1   Chief Justice British North Borneo 1926, Judge
    of the court of appeal, Jamaica, Sept. 1935.
2   Died Allahabad, India, 17 Feb. 1936.

3   Chief Justice of the Straits Settlements.
    Called in person 11 May 1934.
4   Chief Justice, Bahamas.

**10 June 1943**
Thomas Wallace Dickie
Charles Leo Sheil
Lancelot Ernest Curran

**1 March 1945**
William Francis Patton
James McSparran
Issac Copeland
Cyril Anthony De Lacy Nicholson

**25 October 1946**
Brian Maginess
William Johnson
John Foster Caldwell
George Boyle Hanna
Walter William Buchanan Topping

**26 January 1948**
Kenneth Sidney Carpmael*

**6 July 1948**
Herbert Andrew McVeigh
Edward Warburton Jones
Francis Alexander Lyle Harrison

**5 July 1950**
Alfred James Belford
John Gerard Agnew
Thomas Andrew Bradley McCall
Charles Stewart

**23 April 1954**
John Megaw*
Geoffrey William Tookey*

**31 March 1956**
Frederick Elwyn Jones*

**2 November 1956**
Maurice White Gibson
Francis Alexander Reid
Roger Hugh Conaghan
James Alexander Brown
Robert Erskine Lynd Lowry

**28 November 1958**
Andrew Lloyd Giles Moody
John William Basil Kelly
Thomas Alexander Blair

**16 March 1960**
James Lloyd McQuitty

**10 December 1963**
Fredman Ashe Lincoln*

**10 March 1964**
David John Little
Robert Martin McBirney
Robert Watt
Turlough O'Donnell
The Hon John Clarke MacDermott

**18 December 1964**
Charles Barry Shaw
Richard Rodney Chambers
Donald Bruce Murray

**13 December 1965**
Robert John Babington DSC
Henry Garrett McGrath
Robert Wilson Porter

**16 January 1967**
John Patrick Basil Higgins
Hugh Bowman
James Desmond McSparran

**15 January 1968**
Henry Morris Brian McDevitt
William Patrick Doyle
James Francis Buchanan Russell

**20 January 1969**
Robert Todd Rowland
Ronald Appleton

**2 December 1969**
Sir Dingle Mackintosh Foot*

**26 January 1970**
John Kenneth Pringle
James Brian Edward Hutton

**29 September 1971**
William James Staunton
William Pascal McCollum
James Michael Nicholson
Charles Michael Lavery
Robert Douglas Carswell

**17 April 1972**
Sir Peter Rawlinson AG*

**1 June 1972**
Professor Francis Headon Newark
CBE

**28 November 1972**
Sir Robert Michael Oldfield Havers
SG*

**26 January 1973**
Desmond Norman Orr Boal
Hugh Paul Kennedy
Richard Ferguson
Thomas Vincent Cahill

John Alexander Creaney

**18 April 1974**
John Bernard Fox
John Alexander Lowry McLean

**26 April 1974**
The Hon Samuel Charles Silkin AG*
Peter Kingsley Archer SG*

**23 September 1974**
Robert Charles Hill
William Anthony Campbell
John McKee
John Joseph Curran

**12 November 1974**
Michael Nolan*

**12 November 1975**
E Alan Comerton
John Joseph Sheil
Robert Law McCartney

**6 April 1978**
Barbara Adamson Calvert*

**9 November 1978**
Patrick Markey
Fraser Caldwell Elliott
Andrew Ernest Donaldson
George Peter Henderson Gibson
Peter David Smith

**10 November 1978**
Denis Synge Stephens

**22 June 1979**
Sir Walter Ian Perceval SG*

**19 June 1980**
Anthony Terence Hoolahan*

**15 September 1981**
David Arthur John Vaughan*

**24 March 1983**
Vivian Arthur Care
Philip Mooney
James Oliver McNulty
Anthony Ronald Hart
John de Winter Gillen
Brian Francis Kerr
Mervin Alexander Morrow
Frederick Paul Girvan

**28 June 1983**
Sir Patrick Barnabas Burke Mayhew
SG*

**13 April 1984**
Anthony Maurice Gifford (6th Baron)

**14 May 1984**
Anthony Paul Lester*
Robert Michael Ker Gray*

**14 January 1985**
Anthony Moore Cinnamond
Kenneth Robert More McMahon
Malachy Joseph Higgins
Jeffry Ian Foote
Patrick Coghlin
Reginald George Weir
David William Hunter
Richard McLaughlin
Terence Mooney
James Oliver Brady
Kevin James Finnegan

**29 January 1985**
Patrick MacEntee**

**6 September 1985**
John Petrie

**3 February 1987**
Jeremy Frederick Lever*

**25 June 1987**
Nicholas Lyell SG*

**30 June 1988**
John Willoughby Wilson

**8 November 1988**
Alun Kynric Lewis*

**17 January 1989**
Alastair James Drysdale Wilson*

**28 January 1989**
Frederic Reynold*

**6 March 1989**
Timothy Terence Ferris
Randal McKay
John Alfred Holmes Martin
Arthur Daniel Harvey
David William Smyth
Robert Nicholas Harvey Hanna
Donnell Justin Patrick Deeny
Eilis Maire McDermott

**3 April 1990**
Alasdair Macleod Fraser

**26 October 1990**
Robert Richard Fysh*

**8 November 1990**
Christopher Symons*

**21 June 1991**
Bruce Mills*

**27 November 1991**
Gerald Ralph Auckinleck Darling*

**27 February 1992**
Andrew Edward Wilson Park*

**25 June 1992**
Sir Derek Spenser SG*

**26 November 1992**
Kenneth Parker*

**18 June 1993**
Lord Williams of Mostyn*

**25 October 1993**
Desmond St John Keane*

**11 December 1993**
Ronald Eccles Weatherup
James Patrick Lavery
Charles Cecil Adair
John Francis McCrudden
Kevin Thomas Conlon
Charles Declan Morgan
Peter Terence McDonald
Corrine Elizabeth Philpott
John David Thompson
Ronald Lawrence Bentley

**21 March 1994**
Michael Hart*

**11 June 1996**
Jeremy McMullen*

**25 June 1996**
Peter Birts*

**5 September 1996**
James Alexander Gallagher
John Orr
John Eugene Grant
John William Michael Long
Michael William Stitt
Carl Alexander Simpson
Gordon William Kerr
Frederick Gerard McCrory
William Benjamin Synge Stephens
Brian Francis Fee
Thomas Mark Horner
Margaret Ann Dinsmore
Hugh Mark Orr

**11 December 1996**
Sir Louis Jacques Blom-Cooper*
Professor Desmond S. Greer (Hon)

**20 May 1997**
John Morris AG*
Lord Falconer of Thoroton SG*

**24 October 1997**
Duncan Ousley*

**29 May 1998**
Michael Ashe*

**25 September 1998**
Ross Cranston SG*

**21 December 1999**
Gerald Eric John Simpson
Dermott Patrick Fee
Patrick Thaddeus Lynch
Henry Gerard John Toner
John Cushinan
Patrick Lyttle
Noelle Bernadette Patricia McGrenera
David Ringland
Bernard Mary McCloskey
John O'Hara

**8 September 2000**
Barry McDonald
James (Seamus) Mary Eugene Treacy

**21 December 2001**
James Hugh Allister
Neil Patrick Cecil Drennan
Jacqueline Orr
Laurence Patrick McCrudden
Paul Eugene Ramsay
William Alva Brangam
Bernard (Brian) Charles Kennedy
Richard Keenan Weir
Stephen Shaw
Margaret Mary Walsh
Liam Gerard McCollum
Francis O'Donoghue
John Larkin

**26 June 2006**
Stephen Quinn
Paul Richard Maguire
David James Hopley
Robert Brett Lockhart
Turlough Montague
Adrian Colton
Heather Anne Gibson
Brian Gerard McCartney

Geoffrey Miller
Stephen Alexander Fowler
Margaret Mary Higgins
Anne Marie McGuiness
Ciaran Murphy
William Orbinson
Gregory Berry
Siobhan Roisin Keegan

**1 June 2007**
Charles Alexander McKay
Moyne Anyankide-Danes
Alan James Kane
Philip Alexander Mateer
Thomas James Stewart Beattie
Barra McGrory***

**26 October 2011**
Hugh Martin Rodgers
Colm Joseph Keenan
Peter Charles Irvine
Patrick Simon Good
Kevin James Rooney
Kiernan Anthony Joseph Mallon
David Michael McMilllan
Christine Anne Smith
Gerard Joseph McAlinden
Donna McColgan
Martin O'Rourke
John Joseph Kearney
Denise Anne McBride
Charles Camillus MacCreanor
Gavan Patrick Duffy
Gregory McGuigan
Ronan Ulrich Lavery
Mark Mulholland
Karen Quinlivan
Michael Robert Humphreys
Sean Anthony McGleenan
David Alister Scoffield

# Attorneys General for Northern Ireland

# from 1921[1]

Rt Hon Richard Best KC, MP
31 May 1921[2]-5 November 1925

Rt Hon Sir Anthony Brutus Babington KC, MP
24 November 1925[3] – 2 December 1937

Edward Sullivan Murphy KC, MP
3 December 1937 – 13 April 1939

Arthur Black KC, MP
14 April 1949 – 5 November 1941

Rt Hon John Clarke MacDermott KC, MP
10 November 1941 – 3 November 1944

Rt Hon William Lowry KC, MP
3 November 1944 - 5 June 1947

Lancelot Ernest Curran KC, MP
6 June 1947 – 4 November 1949

Rt Hon Edmund Warnock KC, MP
9 November 1949 – 10 April 1956

---

1   From the prorogation of the Northern Ireland parliament in 1922, and the devolution of justice powers in 2010, the attorney general for England and Wales was also attorney general for Northern Ireland.
2   The list outside the attorney's chambers in the Royal Courts of Justice in Belfast gives the date of Best's appointment as 27 September, 1921. However, St John Ervine in his biography of Lord Caigavon, *Craigavon Ulsterman* (London, 1949), states at p. 403 that Best was appointed before the election of 24 May, but gives no date. At p. 417 he includes Best in the government announced on 31 May, and that date is preferred to 27 September 1921 as the date of Best's appointment.
3   The list referred to at fn 2 above gives the date of Babington's appointment as 11 November 1925, but the Belfast Gazette of 27 November 1925 contains a notice that Babington was sworn in on 24 November, and the latter date is therefore technically correct. Babington was knighted in the New Year's Honours List 1937.

Rt Hon William Brian Maginess QC, MP
14 April 1956 - 20 March 1964

Rt Hon Edward Warburton Jones QC, MP
20 March 1964 – 11 March 1968

Rt Hon John William Basil Kelly QC, MP
11 March 1968 – 29 March 1972

Rt Hon Sir Peter Rawlinson QC, MP
30 March 1972 – 4 March 1974

Rt Hon Samuel C. Silkin QC, MP
6 March 1974 – 9 May 1979

Rt Hon Sir Michael Havers QC, MP
9 May 1979 – 17 June 1987

Rt Hon Sir Patrick Mayhew QC, MP
17 June 1987 – 14 April 1992

Rt Hon Sir Nicolas Walter Lyell QC, MP
14 April 1992-1 May 1997

Rt Hon John Morris QC, MP
1 May 1997 – 29 July 1999

Rt Hon Lord Williams of Mostyn QC
29 July 1999 – 14 June 2001

Rt Hon Lord Goldsmith of Allerton QC
14 June 2001 – 26 June 2007

Rt Hon Baroness Scotland of Asthal QC
26 June 2007 – 24 May 2010

John F Larkin QC
24 May 2010 -

# Chairman and Vice Chairman of the Bar Council

## 1969-2012

The date on which the chairman assumes office has varied slightly over the years. Before the creation of the Executive Council in 1983 the chairman was usually elected in January. From 1983 onwards both the Chairman and Vice Chairman are elected for a two year term. Initially they took up office on 1 December, but in more recent years they are usually elected in January and take office shortly afterwards. The Chairman for the appropriate term is named first in the list below, followed by the vice chairman.

| | |
|---|---|
| 1969 | F.A. Reid QC, W.P. Doyle QC. |
| 1970- August 1971 | T. O'Donnell QC, J.C. MacDermott QC. |
| August 1971[1]-January 1972 | J.C. MacDermott QC. |
| 1972-March 1973 | H.G. McGrath QC, J.C. MacDermott QC,[2] |
| | D.B. Murray QC. |
| March 1973[3]-May 1975 | D.B. Murray QC, J.K. Pringle QC.[4] |
| June 1975-1980 | J.K. Pringle QC, H.P. Kennedy QC. |
| 1980-November 1983 | H.P. Kennedy QC, Richard Ferguson QC. |
| November 1983-1985 | J.M.A. Nicholson QC, W.A. Campbell QC. |
| 1985-1987 | W.A. Campbell QC, C.M. Lavery QC. |
| 1987-1989 | C.M. Lavery QC, F.C. Elliott QC. |
| 1989-1991 | F.C. Elliott QC, E.A. Comerton QC. |
| 1992-1993 | P. Coghlin QC, Corrine Philpott QC. |
| 1994-1995 | R. McLaughlin QC, J.E. Grant. |
| 1996-1997 | J.E. Grant QC, B. Fee QC. |
| 1998-1999 | B. Fee QC, J. Cushinan. |
| 2000-2001 | J. Cushinan QC, Eilis McDermott QC. |
| September 2001 –December 2001 | Eilis McDermott QC[5], Henry Toner QC. |

1 MacDermott became chairman upon the appointment of O'Donnell as a high court judge.

2 D.B. Murray succeeded MacDermott as vice-chairman in January 1983.

3 Murray succeeded McGrath as chairman when McGrath was appointed a county court judge.

4 Pringle became vice-chairman in January 1974, and succeeded Murray as chairman in May 1975 when Murray was appointed a high court judge.

5 Eilis McDermott became chairman for the unexpired portion of Cushinan's term upon Cushinan's death, and was succeeded by Toner as vice chairman.

| | |
|---|---|
| 2002–2003 | R.G. Weir QC, P. Cush. |
| September 2003–December 2003 | P. Cush,[6] J. Thompson QC. |
| 2004–2005 | P. Cush, Noelle McGrenera QC. |
| 2006–2007 | Noelle McGrenera QC, W.B.S. Stephens QC, J. O'Hara QC.[7] |
| 2008–2009 | J. O'Hara QC, G. Berry QC. |
| 2010–2011 | A. Colton QC, Mark Mulholland. |
| 2012– | Mark Mulholland QC, Denise McBride QC. |

6    Cush became chairman for the unexpired portion of Weir's term when Weir was appointed a high court judge, and was succeeded by Thompson as vice chairman.

7    O'Hara became vice chairman in 2003 upon the appointment of Stephens as a high court judge.

# Benchers of the Honorable Society of the Inn of Court of Northern Ireland

Treasurer for 2013: The Hon Mr Justice Weir

| | Appointed or elected | Treasurer |
|---|---|---|
| C.M. Lavery Esq QC | H 1979 | 1987 |
| F.C. Elliott Esq QC | H 1984 | 1996 |
| T.V. Cahill Esq QC | T 1988 | |
| R.C. Hill Esq QC | M 1988 | |
| The Rt Hon Lord Kerr | T 1990 | 1999 |
| The Rt Hon Lord Justice Higgins | M 1993 | 2001 |
| The Rt Hon Lord Justice Coghlin | T 1993 | 2003 |
| J.O. McNulty Esq QC | T 1994 | 2004 |
| T.T. Ferriss Esq QC | T 1994 | 2006 |
| Ms E. McDermott QC | T 1994 | |
| The Rt Hon Lord Justice Girvan | T 1995 | 2005 |
| His Honour Judge Smyth QC | T 1995 | 2009 |
| The Hon Mr Justice Gillen | M 1997 | 2011 |
| B.F. Fee Esq QC | H 1999 | 2008 |
| His Honour Judge Finnegan QC | M 1999 | |
| K.R. McMahon Esq QC | M 1999 | |
| M.A. Morrow Esq QC | M 1999 | 2010 |
| The Hon Mr Justice Weir | M 1999 | 2013 |
| Peter Cush Esq | M 1999 | 2012 |

Dominic Grieve QC MP  (*ex officio*) HM Advocate General

John F. Larkin QC  (*ex officio*) Attorney General for Northern Ireland

M Mulholland QC (*ex officio*)
Chairman of Executive Council 2012-2014

| | |
|---|---|
| The Hon Mr Justice Weatherup | T 2001 |
| D. Hunter Esq QC | M 2001 |
| The Hon Mr Justice Deeny | M 2001 |
| Ms N. McGrenera QC | M 2003 |
| The Rt Hon Sir Declan Morgan, Lord Chief Justice | T 2004 |
| N. Hanna Esq QC | T 2005 |
| K. Conlon Esq QC | T 2005 |
| T. McDonald Esq QC | T 2005 |
| The Hon Mr Justice Stephens | T 2005 |
| The Hon Mr Justice O'Hara | T 2005 |
| Her Honour Judge Philpott QC | M 2005 |
| The Hon Mr Justice Treacy | H 2007 |
| G. Simpson Esq QC | T 2008 |
| D. Fee Esq QC | T 2008 |
| H. Toner Esq QC | T 2008 |
| The Hon Mr Justice Horner | T 2008 |
| Mrs M.A. Dinsmore QC | T 2008 |
| The Hon Mr Justice McCloskey | M 2008 |
| The Hon Mr Justice Maguire | T 2012 |
| His Honour Judge Lynch QC | T 2012 |
| His Honour Judge Grant | T 2012 |
| Her Honour Judge McReynolds | T 2012 |
| Her Honour Judge Loughran | T 2012 |

# BENCHERS EMERITII

| | | |
|---|---|---|
| The Rt Hon Sir John MacDermott | M 1968 | 1972 |
| The Rt Hon Turlough O'Donnell | T 1969 | 1973 |
| His Honour Richard Chambers QC | M 1969 | 1995 |
| The Rt Hon Sir Donald Murray | M 1970 | 1974 |
| The Rt Hon Sir Robert Porter QC | H 1973 | 1976 |
| R. Appleton Esq QC | T 1973 | 1982 |
| Sir John Pringle | T 1973 | 1984 |
| The Rt Hon Lord Hutton | T 1974 | 1981 |
| The Rt Hon Sir Liam McCollum | M 1975 | 1985 |
| The Rt Hon Lord Carswell | H 1979 | 1988 |
| The Rt Hon Sir Michael Nicholson | H 1979 | 1990 |
| H.P. Kennedy Esq QC | M 1979 | 1989 |
| The Rt Hon Sir Anthony Campbell | M 1983 | 1993 |
| His Honour Patrick Markey QC | H 1984 | 1994 |
| The Rt Hon Sir John Sheil | T 1988 | 1997 |
| P.D. Smith Esq QC | M 1988 | 2000 |
| P. Mooney Esq QC | T 1994 | 2002 |
| His Honour John McKee QC | T 1995 | |
| His Honour John Curran QC | T 1995 | |
| Sir Anthony Hart | T 1995 | 2007 |
| Sir Richard McLaughlin | M 1999 | |
| His Honour John Martin QC | M 2001 | |
| His Honour Randal McKay QC | M 2005 | |
| His Honour Norman Lockie | M 2009 | |

# HONORARY BENCHERS

| | |
|---|---|
| The Hon Thomas A Finlay | H 1985 |
| The Rt Hon Lord Mackay of Clashfern FRSE | M 1987 |
| His Honour Robin Rowland QC | T 1990 |
| The Rt Hon Lord Mayhew of Twysden QC | M 1992 |
| The Rt Hon Lord Hope of Craighead | H 1995 |
| Mrs Barbara Calvert QC (Lady Lowry) | H 1995 |
| The Rt Hon Lord Irvine of Lairg | T 1998 |
| President Mary McAleese | M 1999 |
| The Hon Mr Justice Keane | H 2000 |
| The Rt Hon Lord Cullen of Whitekirk | H 2002 |
| The Rt Hon Dame Elizabeth Butler-Sloss | M 2004 |
| The Hon Mr Justice John L Murray | T 2005 |
| The Rt Hon the Lord Woolf | T 2005 |
| His Honour Thomas Burgess | M 2005 |
| J.W. Wilson QC | M 2008 |
| B.J.A.C. Valentine | M 2009 |
| Adrian Whitfield QC | H 2010 |
| The Hon Mrs Justice Susan Denham | M 2011 |

# Lords of appeal in ordinary, and from October 2009 justices of the Supreme Court, who were members of the Bar of Ireland, or of the Bar of Northern Ireland, from the foundation of the Northern Ireland Bar in 1921.

The Rt Hon Lord Atkinson
    19 December 1905-11 February 1928
The Rt Hon Lord Carson
    1 June 1921[1] -11 November 1929[2]
The Rt Hon Lord MacDermott, MC
    23 April 1947-6 April 1951
The Rt Hon Lord Lowry
    8 August 1988-7 January 1994
The Rt Hon Lord Hutton
    6 January 1997-12 January 2004
The Rt Hon Lord Carswell
    13 January 2004 - 26 June 2009
The Rt Hon Lord Kerr of Tonaghmore.
    29 June 2009 -

# Judges of the Supreme Court of Judicature, and now the Court of Judicature, of Northern Ireland from 1921.

## Lord Chief Justice

The Rt Hon Sir Denis Stanislaus Henry, Bt
    15 August 1921 - d. 1 October 1925
The Rt Hon Sir William Moore, Bt
    2 November 1925 - ret. 1 December 1937
The Rt Hon Sir James Andrews, Bt
    1 December 1937 - d. 18 February 1951
The Rt Hon Lord MacDermott, MC
    6 April 1951 - ret. 31 July 1971

1   [1921] 2 AC.
2   [1929] AC.

The Rt Hon Sir Robert Lynd Erskine Lowry (created Baron Lowry 18 July 1979)
    2 August 1971 - 8 August 1988
The Rt Hon Sir James Brian Edward Hutton
    8 August 1988 - 6 January 1997
The Rt Hon Sir Robert Douglas Carswell
    6 January 1997 – 12 January 2004
The Rt Hon Sir Brian Francis Kerr
    12 January 2004 – 29 June 2009
The Rt Hon Sir Declan Morgan
    3 July 2009 –

## Lord Justices of Appeal

The Rt Hon William Moore
    17 October 1921 - 1 November 1925
The Rt Hon James Andrews
    17 October 1921 - 30 November 1937
The Rt Hon Richard Best
    5 November 1925 - d. 23 February 1939
The Rt Hon Sir Anthony Brutus Babington
    2 December 1937 - ret. 26 February 1949
The Rt Hon Edward Sullivan Murphy
    13 April 1939 - d. 3 December 1945
The Rt Hon Samuel Clarke Porter
    15 March 1946 - d. 10 July 1956
The Rt Hon Arthur Black
    3 March 1949 - ret. 31 August 1964
The Rt Hon Sir Lancelot Ernest Curran
    28 September 1956 - ret. 31 August 1975
The Rt Hon Sir Herbert Andrew McVeigh
    7 September 1964 - ret. 10 January 1973
The Rt Hon Sir Edward Warburton Jones
    11 January 1973 - ret. 5 January 1984
The Rt Hon Sir Ambrose Joseph McGonigal MC
    28 May 1975 -d. 22 September 1979
The Rt Hon Sir Maurice White Gibson
    12 September 1975 – murdered by the IRA 25 April 1987
The Rt Hon Turlough O'Donnell

15 October 1979 - ret. 31 October 1989

The Rt Hon Sir John William Basil Kelly
6 January 1984 - ret. 21 April 1995

The Rt Hon Sir John Clarke MacDermott
30 July 1987 – ret. 1 September 1998

The Rt Hon Sir Donald Bruce Murray
7 November 1989 - ret. 31 August 1993

The Rt Hon Sir Robert Douglas Carswell
8 November 1993 - 6 January 1997

The Rt Hon Sir James Michael Anthony Nicholson
24 April 1995 – ret. 31 December 2006

The Rt Hon Sir William Paschal McCollum
8 January 1997 – ret. 1 September 2004

The Rt Hon Sir William Anthony Campbell
16 September 1998 – ret. 31 August 2008

The Rt Hon Sir John Joseph Sheil
6 September 2004 – ret. 31 December 2006

The Rt Hon Sir Malachy Joseph Higgins
8 January 2007 –

The Rt Hon Sir Frederick Paul Girvan
8 January 2007 -

The Rt Hon Sir Patrick Coghlin
5 September 2008 -

# Judges of the High Court

The Hon Daniel Martin Wilson
17 October 1921 - d. 5 January 1932

The Rt Hon Thomas Watters Brown
8 February 1922 - d. 7 October 1944

The Hon Robert Dick Megaw
11 February 1932 - ret. 6 November 1943

The Hon Arthur Black
20 November 1943 - 2 March 1949

The Rt Hon John Clarke MacDermott MC
3 November 1944 - 22 April 1947

The Rt Hon William Lowry
5 June 1947 - ret. 11 October 1949

The Hon Charles Leo Sheil
 3 March 1949 - d. 5 September 1968
The Hon Lancelot Ernest Curran
 3 November 1949 - 27 September 1956
The Hon Herbert Andrew McVeigh
 28 September 1956 - 6 September 1964
The Hon Robert Lynd Erskine Lowry
 7 September 1964 – 2 August 1971
The Rt Hon Edward Warburton Jones
 6 March 1968 - 10 January 1973
The Hon Ambrose Joseph McGonigal MC
 6 March 1968 - 27 May 1975
The Hon Maurice White Gibson
 18 November 1968 - 27 May 1975
The Hon Turlough O'Donnell
 2 August 1971 - 14 October 1979
The Rt Hon John William Basil Kelly
 11 January 1973 - 5 January 1984
The Hon John Clarke MacDermott
 11 January 1973 - 30 July 1987
The Hon Donald Bruce Murray
 28 May 1975 - 7 November 1989
The Hon Sir James Brian Edward Hutton
 5 September 1979 - 8 August 1988
The Hon Sir John Patrick Basil Higgins
 6 January 1984 - d. 2 September 1993[3]
The Hon Sir Robert Douglas Carswell
 6 January 1984 - 8 November 1993
The Hon Sir James Michael Anthony Nicholson
 27 May 1986 - 24 April 1995
The Hon Sir William Paschal McCollum
 1 September 1987 - 8 January 1997
The Hon Sir William Anthony Campbell
 21 September 1988-16 September 1999
The Hon Sir John Joseph Sheil
 7 November 1989 - 6 September 2004

---

3 Appointed a lord justice of appeal but died the night before he was to be sworn in to that
 office.

The Hon Sir Brian Francis Kerr
    30 March 1993 – 12 January 2004
The Hon Sir John Kenneth Pringle
    6 September 1993 –ret. 31 August 1999
The Hon Sir Malachy Joseph Higgins
    8 November 1993 – 8 January 2007
The Hon Sir Frederick Paul Girvan
    24 April 1995 – 8 January 2007
The Hon Sir Patrick Coghlin
    9 April 1997 – 5 September 2008
The Hon Sir John de Winter Gillen
    6 January 1999 –
The Hon Sir Richard McLaughlin
    6 September 1999 – ret. 4 September 2012
The Hon Sir Ronald Eccles Weatherup
    4 June 2001 –
The Hon Sir Reginald George Weir
    5 September 2003 –
The Hon Sir Declan Charles Morgan
    5 May 2004 – 3 July 2009
The Hon Sir Donnell Justin Patrick Deeny
    6 September 2004–
The Hon Sir Anthony Ronald Hart
    6 January 2005 – ret. 5 January 2012.
The Hon Sir William Benjamin Synge Stephens
    29 January 2007 –
The Hon Sir James (Seamus) Mary Eugene Treacy
    29 January 2007 –
The Hon Sir Bernard Mary McCloskey
    5 September 2008 –
The Hon Sir Paul Richard Maguire
    14 May 2012 –
The Hon Sir Thomas Mark Horner
    5 September 2012 –
The Hon Sir John Ailbe O'Hara
    8 April 2013 –

## Judges of the county courts in Northern Ireland

Whilst the Court of Appeal and the High Court in Northern Ireland were brought into existence by the Government of Ireland Act, 1921, and the Lord Chief Justice and the judges thereof (with the exception of Moore LJ who transferred from the High Court in Dublin) were new appointees appointed in 1921, the existing county courts in that part of Ireland that fell within the new jurisdiction of Northern Ireland, and the judges thereof, continued largely unaffected by the structural and jurisdictional changes brought about by the 1921 Act.

The exceptions were those judges who were judges of more than one county, and who now found themselves judges of counties in both Northern Ireland and Southern Ireland. Two judges were in this dilemma, and they were permitted to elect to serve only in Northern or Southern Ireland. Judge Green KC, who had been appointed the judge for Armagh and Louth in 1909, became the judge for Armagh and Fermanagh, and continued in post until his death in 1940.[4] Judge Johnston, judge for Fermanagh and Monaghan, transferred to Southern Ireland where he was later promoted to the High Court, ultimately becoming a judge of the Supreme Court of the Irish Free State.

The remaining judges simply continued as county court judge of their counties. Judge Matheson, the Recorder of Belfast and chairman of quarter sessions for Co. Antrim since 1919,[5] died in the early part of 1921 and was succeeded by D.M. Wilson KC. Wilson was appointed to be one of the judges of the new High Court in Northern Ireland later that year, and was succeeded as Recorder by H.M. Thompson KC.

Interestingly, several of the judges who had been appointed before 1921 continued to live in Dublin, or outside Northern Ireland, and presumably came to Northern Ireland only when their duties required. Judge Bates, the judge for Co. Down since 20 September 1919, lived in Dublin until the late 1920s when he is recorded in the *Belfast and Ulster Directory* as living in Greenisland, Co. Antrim. However, the *Directory* records Judge Linehan KC, the judge for Tyrone since 12 September 1912, as living in Dublin until 1926

---

4    *ILT&SJ* lv (1921) 297; *ILT&SJ* lxxiv (1940) 49.
5    Hart, *A history of the King's serjeants at law in Ireland*, p. 176.

when a London address appears. He was not alone in living outside Northern Ireland. By 1925 Judge Osborne KC, Recorder of Londonderry, appears in the *Directory* with an address at Dalkeith, Midlothian, near Edinburgh.

Unlike their English counterparts who only exercised a civil jurisdiction (save in a few cases where a judge was also appointed as chairman of quarter sessions until after 1938 when the practice of combining both posts became more common[6]), under the County Courts (Ireland) Act, 1877 county court judges were also the chairman of quarter sessions of the county or county borough of which they were judge or recorder, and so from that date also exercised a criminal jurisdiction. Until 1939 the Recorder of Belfast also was the county court judge and chairman of quarter sessions for Co. Antrim, but in that year the business of Co. Antrim was divided amongst other judges, although for a while the Recorder continued to be styled the judge and chairman of the county. Judge Begley KC, the judge for Co. Down, became the judge for the Ballymena Division covering the north of Co. Antrim as well as continuing in Co. Down, and Judge McGonigal KC, the judge for Co. Tyrone, also assumed responsibility for the Belfast Division, that is the southern part of Co. Antrim outside the City of Belfast.

This division of Co. Antrim persisted until the restructuring of the county courts and the criminal jurisdiction of the assize and criminal courts with the creation of a unified Crown Court to deal with all indictable business in Northern Ireland by the Judicature (Northern Ireland) Act, 1978. The South Antrim Division as it came to be known remained linked to Co. Tyrone, and the same judge dealt with both divisions until 1979. The Ballymena Division later became the responsibility of the Recorder of Londonderry, and remained so until 1979. In the following lists the Co. Antrim Divisions and their judges appear separately.

Before 1979 a county court judge was appointed to a county and could not be required to sit outside that county or division without his consent, although a rapid increase in business from 1969 onwards meant that between 1971 and 1979 a number of additional judges were appointed who were not appointed to any particular county or division, but were assigned to individual courts as the business of those courts required.

---

6   Patrick Polden, *A history of the County Court, 1846-1971*, (Cambridge, 1999), pp 257-58.

It was otherwise unknown for a judge to move to another county, especially as the Recorder of Belfast was always appointed directly from the Bar until 1978 when Judge Brown QC was promoted from Co. Down to be Recorder. Thereafter, only Judge Pringle QC was appointed Recorder from the Bar, and an existing judge has been promoted to be Recorder whenever a vacancy occurred.

The Recorder of Belfast, although a more recent creation than the office of Recorder of Londonderry which was created in 1613, is the senior county court judge in Northern Ireland, and since the creation of the post of presiding judge of the county courts in 2002 the Recorder of Belfast has also held that post. The remaining county court judges are now allocated from time to time to different divisions by the lord chief justice, and for the sake of simplicity all other appointments to the county court bench since 1971 are listed in order of their appointment, and assignments to individual divisions omitted. Where the exact date of appointment can be ascertained this is given. Since October 1974 each judge signs a roll upon appointment, and the dates of all appointments commencing with that of R.T. Rowland QC are taken from that roll. Occasionally when there was a vacancy some time could elapse before a replacement was appointed, and when a temporary judge is known to have been appointed his name is given in brackets.

| Recorders of Belfast | Recorders of Londonderry |
|---|---|
| Herbert M. Thompson KC | R.E. Osborne KC[1] |
| (1921-1941) | (Retired-14 May 1938) |
| Rt Hon Arthur Black KC | J.C. Davison KC |
| (1941-1943) | (1939-1946) |
| J. Desmond Chambers KC | (M.G. Ellison KC) |
| (1943-1944) | (1956-1948) |
| Bernard J. Fox KC | Issac Copeland KC |
| (1944-1959) | (1946-1965) |
| Rt Hon W.W.B. Topping QC | J.D. Little QC |
| (1960-1978) | (1965-1979) |
| James A. Brown QC | The Rt Hon Sir Robert Porter QC |
| (1978-1982) | (1979-1982) |
| J. (Eoin) P.B. Higgins QC | J.J. Curran QC |
| (1982-1984) | (1982 -1985) |

J.K. Pringle QC
(30 Jan. 1984-1993)
Rt Hon Sir Robert Porter QC
(1993-95)
J.F.B. Russell QC
(1995-1997)
A.R. Hart QC
(1997-2005)
T.A. Burgess
(2005-2012)
D.K. McFarland
(2012-)

A.R. Hart QC
(1985-1990)
M.J. Higgins QC
(1990-1993)
J.A.H. Martin QC
(1993-1997)
T.A. Burgess
(1997-2004)
Corrine E. Philpott QC
(2002-2007)
D. Marrinan QC
(2007-2010)
Piers Grant
(2011-)

Co. Antrim
H.M. Thompson KC
(1921-1942)

Co. Down
A.H. Bates[2]
(1919-1 Sept. 1939)

| Belfast/South Antrim Division | Ballymena Division | Co. Down |
|---|---|---|
| J. McGonigal KC | A.H. Bates | M.D. Begley KC[3] |
| (28 Dec. 1938-1943)[4] | (1938-1939) | (Sept. 1939-1958) |
| | M.D. Begley KC | |
| | (Sept. 1939-1958) | |
| C.L. Sheil | Issac Copeland KC[5] | G.B. Hanna KC[6] |
| (14 Aug.1943)[7] | | |
| T.J. Campbell KC | | |
| (1945-1946) | | |
| W. Johnson KC | D.J. Little QC | W.B. Maginess QC |
| (1947-1978) | (1965-1979) | (20 Mar. 1964- |
| | | 16 Apr. 19670 |
| | | J.A. Brown KC |
| | | (1967-1978) |

Co. Tyrone

J. Linehan KC

(9 Sept. 1912-1938)

G.B. Hanna KC

(7 May 1937-1938)

J. McGonigal KC

(29 Dec. 1938-1943)

C.L. Sheil KC

(14 Aug. 1943-Nov. 1944)

T.J. Campbell KC

(3 Dec. 1944-3 May 1945)

Issac Copeland KC

(acting judge until 1947)

W. Johnson KC

(15 Sept. 1947[10]-1978)

Co. Armagh & Co. Fermanagh

G.C. Green KC

(25 Sept. 1909 and Co. Fermanagh from 1921 until 1941)

M.G. Ellison KC

(acting county court judge until August 1943)

J.H. Robb KC

(10 May 1943[8]-1954)

J. G. Agnew QC

(1 Jan. 1954-6 May. 1965)[9]

R. H. Conaghan QC

(1965-murdered by the IRA  16 Sept. 1974)

J.P.B. Higgins QC

(1974-1978)

R.R. Chambers QC

## County Court Judges appointed since 1971 with the dates of their being sworn in.

(Female judges' names are shown in italics, and solicitor judges marked *)

R. Watt QC 18 May 1971.

J.P.B. Higgins QC 18 Sept. 1971

R.R. Chambers QC 14 Feb. 1972.

H.G. McGrath QC 19 Mar. 1973.

R.T. Rowland QC 10 Oct. 1974.

R.J. Babington DSC QC 20 Nov. 1974.

The Rt Hon Sir Robert Porter QC 9 Oct. 1978.

W.P. Doyle QC 9 Oct. 1978 (murdered by the IRA 16 Jan. 1983)

J.F.B. Russell QC 9 Oct. 1978.

J.J. Curran QC 16 Feb. 1981.

J. McKee QC 3 Mar. 1981.

A.E. Donaldson QC 18 Apr. 1983.

G.P.H. Gibson QC 18 Apr. 1983.

A.R. Hart QC 12 June 1985.

J. Petrie QC 9 Sept. 1985.

M.J. Higgins QC 30 Apr. 1988.
D.W. Smyth QC 5 Mar. 1990.
J.A.H. Martin QC 16 May 1990.
T.A. Burgess 30 Nov. 1992.*
P.I. Markey QC 4 Jan. 1994.
R. McKay QC 4 Jan. 1994.
J.O. Brady QC 27 June 1995.
D. Rodgers 5 Mar. 1997.*
J.I. Foote QC 19 Mar. 1997.
*C.E. Philpott* QC 22 Apr. 1998.
D.N. Lockie 8 Sept. 1998.
D.K. McFarland 8 Sept. 1998.*
*D. Kennedy* 22 Sept. 2000.
K. J. Finnegan QC 1 June 2001.
D. Marrinan 3 July 2003.
*M. McReynolds* 6 Sept. 2004.
P. Lynch QC 6 Sept. 2004.
*G. Loughran* 6 Sept. 2004.
P. Babington 6 Sept. 2004.*
P. Grant 27 June 2005.
G.B. Miller QC 11 May 2009.
*P. M. Smyth* 1 Feb. 2010.
S.A. Fowler QC 20 Jan. 2011.
A.F.W. Devlin 20 Jan. 2011.
G. W. Kerr QC 28 Feb. 2012.
B.G. Sherrard 10 Sept. 2012.
P.J. Kinney 10 Sept. 2012.*

1    *ILT&SJ* lxxii (1938) 297.
2    *ILT&SJ* lxxiv (1940) 4.
3    *ILT&SJ* lxxiii (1939) 270.
4    *ILT&SJ* lxiii (1939) 7.
5    *ILT&SJ* lxxx (1946) 127
6    Son of Judge G. B. Hanna KC, county court judge of Co. Tyrone 1937-1938.
7    *ILT&SJ* lxvii (1943) 200.
8    *ILT&SJ* lxvii (1943) 129.
9    Note on his Inn of Court file.
10   Warrant of appointment. PRONI/D4022/A/7.

# The

# LAWS AND RULES

## of the Society of the

# NORTH EAST BAR

# 1875

******

### I. Constitution and Membership.

1.     The Society of the North East Bar consists of such Barristers as have been regularly admitted Members of the Society, and have complied with its Laws and Rules.

2.     The Member of longest standing on circuit shall be THE FATHER of the Society, and shall receive the respect and attention paid from time immemorial to THE FATHER, and in the absence of THE FATHER of the Society, the Senior Member shall be THE FATHER for the time being.

3.     The election of Members shall be by ballot, which shall take place at a meeting of the Society in Dublin.   The Town Steward or a deputy named by THE FATHER, shall conduct the ballot in the most secret manner.   The ballot shall commence when nine Members are present, and not sooner; and shall conclude when the then present FATHER shall direct.   One black ball in seven shall exclude.

4.     Before any gentlemen joining the Society for the first time can be balloted for, he must have been proposed by one Member of the Society and seconded by another at a Meeting of the Society in Dublin, not more than four terms preceding his probationary circuit; and he must have subsequently gone a probationary circuit, during which he must appear as a Barrister in three Assize towns at least, and dine with the Society in each town, in which he shall so appear, if there be a Bar-Dinner. Every new Member who shall join the Society shall, upon his admission, pay the sum of Two Guineas to the Treasurer.

5.    Any Member, who shall have absented himself for three successive circuits, shall, before the next succeeding circuit, cease to be a Member, unless he shall, in the meantime, have paid to the Treasurer the sum of One Pound for each of the three circuits during which he shall have so absented himself. Any Member who, by reason of his absence from the circuit, shall have ceased to be a Member of the Society, shall not be re-admitted until he shall have been proposed and seconded, and again balloted for, at a meeting of the Society in Dublin. Upon his re-admission he shall pay the sum of Three Guineas to the Treasurer, and he shall thereupon rank in the Society according to his former seniority.

6.    The Treasurer shall officially erase from the list of Members the name of any Barrister who has ceased to be a Member.

## II.  General and Special Legislative Powers of the Society.

1.    No Law or Rule of the Society shall be made, repealed, or altered, except at the meetings of the Society in Dublin; and notices of motion for the same, with the names of the proposer and seconder shall be given at the meeting of the Society in Dublin, previous to the one at which the same shall be decided upon or passed, and shall be entered on the Minutes of the Meeting; but the consideration of any such notice of motion may, by leave of the meeting, be adjourned or postponed to a future meeting.

2.    When notice shall have been given of any motion to make, repeal, or alter any Law or Rule, the Town Steward shall post a copy of same, or of any adjournment or postponement thereof, one clear week before the meeting at which it is to be moved; otherwise it shall not be proceeded with.

3.    The Society, at a meeting to be specially convened for the purpose on circuit, by the then present FATHER of the Society, and consisting of at least twelve members, shall have power to dispense with any of the Laws or Rules of the Society during the continuation of that circuit, or any part thereof; but this power shall not extend to enable business expressly directed to be transacted at a meeting in Dublin, to be transacted at a meeting on circuit.

4.    THE FATHER of the Society shall, on a requisition in writing, signed by not less than twelve members, summon a special meeting of the Society to consider any definite question embodied in a proposed resolution and to be handed in writing to THE FATHER with the requisition. Such special meeting shall have no power

to transact any other business, and one fortnight's notice thereof in writing shall be posted in the Library of the Four Courts.

5.   The Society, at any meeting, or at any Assize town, may, as always has been its undoubted right, on a Bar-Day, impose any Fine or Congratulation to any amount, for any cause whatsoever which to the Members of the Society may see a fit one for either Congratulation or Fine.  Any person fined or congratulated at any meeting of the Society, either in town or on circuit, and refusing or neglecting to pay any such Fine or Congratulation, shall be held by the Society in contempt.

### III.  Bar Committee.

1.   At the General Meeting of the Society in Dublin, held immediately before the Summer circuit, a Standing Committee of Five for the ensuring year shall be chosen, one of whom shall be appointed Treasurer, and another Auditor.  Such Committee shall have the control and management of all matters relating to the arrangements of the Society on circuit, and shall be authorized to purchase in Dublin or elsewhere a sufficient stock of wine, to be sent to the towns on circuit where suitable cellarage can be procured, and to select, or authorize the selection of the wine and wine merchant for the Annual Dinner; and such Treasurer shall discharge the various duties, hereinafter prescribed.

2.   A Bar-Waiter or Bar-Waiters may be hired by the Committee to attend the Society on circuit; to be paid by the day as long as he or they shall be employed, giving him or them a reasonable time for going and returning.

3.   The Committee shall at least once a-year settle the Treasurer's account, and shall lay a full statement thereof, together with their general Report, before the Bar at their General Meeting in Dublin, held immediately before the Summer circuit; and such statement shall be entered on the Bar-Book by the Steward of such Meeting of the Society.

### IV.  Appointment and Duties of Town Steward.

1.   THE FATHER of the Society, previous to each Summer circuit, shall appoint such Member as he shall think fit, to be Town Steward for the Society for the ensuing twelve months.  Upon his appointment he shall take possession of, and be accountable for, the Bar-Book, and the several articles belonging to the Bar which are mentioned in the first page prefixed to the Bar-Book; he shall duly

enter the minutes of the Meetings of the Society in the Bar-Book, and he shall discharge the various duties in relation to the Annual Dinner, and also in relation to the conduct of the ballot, and to the posting of notices of motion to make, repeal, or alter any law or rule or adjournment or postponement thereof as herein respectively prescribed. THE FATHER shall have power to name a deputy, in case such Steward shall at any time be unable to act.

2.    In case all the Members shall have reserved the office of Town Steward, then the Member who shall have served the said office at the most distant period of time shall be re-appointed, THE FATHER of the Society only excepted.

## V. Annual Dinner in Dublin.

1.    The Society shall meet annually at half-past six o'clock to dine together in Dublin, or in the neighbourhood (which shall be considered as a Meeting in Dublin), on the first Tuesday after the last day of Trinity Term, with power to THE FATHER to fix specially any other hour, or any other day, if he shall so think fit.

2.    The Town Steward shall, previous to the Annual Dinner in Dublin, collect the sum of Fifteen Shillings from each Member, to defray the expense of such dinner, and all expenses exceeding the sum so collected shall be defrayed by the members present at such meeting; and he shall provide such Annual Dinner at any place he shall appoint, of which he shall give notice, of a week at least, to each Member then in Dublin.

3.    In future the Town Steward shall only forward invitations for the Annual Dinner to the presiding Judges of Assize, at the immediately preceding Spring, and the next ensuing Summer, Assizes on the North East circuit and to their respective Registrars, and to such persons as, having been Members of the Society, shall have accepted judicial appointments in the Superior Courts.

4.    If any Member shall entertain at dinner, on the day appointed for the Annual Dinner of the Society, any other Member by which his absence may be occasioned, he, and every Member so entertained, shall forfeit to the Society Two Guineas, to be paid to the Steward of the next meeting for the use of the Society.

## VI. The Father on Circuit, and his Powers.

1.    The senior Member of the Society who shall be in the Bar-Room on circuit, when dinner is served each day, shall be the FATHER for that evening.

2.     All questions arising between Members of the Society in Court or in the Bar-Room on circuit, shall be finally and immediately decided and adjusted, by the then present FATHER; and any member of the Society refusing to abide by, or disobeying the said FATHER'S order or award on such occasion, shall be expelled.

### VII. Bar-Towns and Bar-Rooms.

1.     All the towns on the North East circuit, in which the Assizes are held, shall be considered Bar-Towns; but the regulations with regard to Dinners, Bar Costume, and Probationers shall not apply to Drogheda.

2.     The day on which the Commission is opened in each town, and every day on which the Judges or either of them, shall be sitting in any town on circuit, shall be a Bar-Day in such town or towns respectively.  When the Commission shall be opened in any town earlier than three o'clock, the previous day shall be a Bar-Day in that town, and when the Commission shall be opened in any town upon a Monday earlier than three o'clock, the previous Saturday shall be a Bar-Day in such town.

3.     Lists of the Members (with a column for their addresses) shall be prepared by the Treasurer from the books, and a sufficient number shall be printed; and the Steward of each Bar-Town shall fix one of the lists in the Bar-Room, and one of them in the Court-house, in each town.

4.     No person whatsoever shall be admitted into the Bar-Room, to associate with the Members on circuit, unless he shall first have been regularly admitted a Member of the Society, except gentlemen desirous of becoming Members, and then going their probationary circuit, and during that one circuit only, and such other Barristers as THE FATHER in each town shall, in his discretion, think proper to invite.

5.     Any Member making a bet in the Bar-Room, either in town or on circuit, shall forfeit for each bet there made one gallon of Claret, or the value thereof, to be paid instantly.

6.     The Society shall cease to sit as a Bar-Club on circuit, at ten o'clock pm or so soon after as THE FATHER of that day shall leave the Chair.

## VIII.  Briefs on Circuit.

1.    No Barrister on circuit shall take any Record brief, unless a Fee shall have been marked thereon.

2.    No Member shall receive any Record brief on circuit, after the rising of the Court which shall sit latest on the first day of business in each Assize town, and if he shall do so he shall forfeit and pay immediately to the use of the Society the Fee received with, or marked upon, such brief, and a further sum out of his own pocket, of the same amount, or, upon refusing or neglecting to do so, shall be expelled; and no docket or writing whatsoever, other than a brief, with a Fee marked thereon, shall exempt any Barrister from incurring this penalty and forfeiture.

3.    In conformity with the most ancient and undoubted laws and usages of the  Society, Members shall not act professionally in the Civil Court on circuit with Barristers who are not Members, except with Probationers, and in the usual manner with Counsel specially retained.

## IX.  Circuit Stewards and Dinner Arrangements.

1.    In each Bar-Town a Member of sufficient experience shall be appointed by THE FATHER to act as Steward for such town, to whom all contributions of the Bar-Mess-Fund for that town shall be paid.  Such Steward shall direct the Junior of the day in his duties, shall inform him of what sums he is to collect, and what payments he is to make; and shall supply him with the proper funds for making such payments.

2.    The Steward of each town shall keep an account, in a book to be provided for the purpose by the Treasurer, of the receipts and expenditure in each town, including the quantity and particulars of the wine consumed in the town, and shall also keep an account in another book, to be provided for that purpose by the Treasurer, of the wine used out of, and remaining in, the cellar in such town as well as any additions made to the stock of wine during the Assizes.  And such Steward shall hand over such books dated and signed by him to the Steward of the next town; and at the end of the Assizes the Steward of the last Bar-Town shall give such books to the Treasurer, to be kept by him till the next circuit.

3.    In every Bar-Town (except on the first day of an Assizes on which the Commission shall be opened after twelve o'clock, and except on days which are not

Bar-Days), a list of the Members shall be daily posted up in the Bar-Room in the Court-house, by the Steward for that town, at the sitting of the Court, containing the name of every Member. And every Member intending to dine shall, before one o'clock affix his initials to his name in the said list, which list shall be taken down at one o'clock by the Steward, who shall order dinner in his discretion (as to numbers) accordingly. Any Member absenting himself, after having so signified his intention of dining, shall pay to the Bar-Mess-Fund a fine of Two Shillings, or any Member who shall have been in the Assize town previous to one o'clock, and who shall appear at dinner without having expressed intention, as mentioned above, shall pay to the Bar-Mess-Fund a fine of One Shilling.

4.     The Steward, in ordering dinner, shall direct the number of assistants the hotel waiter shall have in attendance on that day; and shall pay the hotel waiter such sum for attendance as he shall consider proper.

### X. Duties of Junior for the day.

1.     It is the duty of the Junior to sit at the foot of the table at dinner, to open the wine, settle the account thereof, and to do all matters and things relating thereto; to collect the amount of the bill of the day on which he shall act as Junior; and to execute the office of Junior in all respects as he shall be directed by the Steward of the town, subject, nevertheless, to the final control and directions of the then present FATHER. The Junior Member of the Society who shall be in the Bar-Room on circuit, when dinner is served each day, shall be the Junior for that day.

2.     The Treasurer shall supply the Steward in each Bar-Town with dockets, to be used by the Junior at dinner for ascertaining the quantity of wine used each day by the Society at dinner. And the Junior shall produce to the Steward, on passing his account, a docket for each bottle of wine so used.

3.     Any Junior who shall in any manner neglect his duties, shall be fined in such a quantity of wine as THE FATHER shall think fit.

### XI. Circuit Bar-Mess-Funds and General Wine Stock.

1.     Every Member on circuit, and every Probationer, shall be obliged, as soon as he shall appear in any Bar-Town, to pay to the Steward a sum to be specified by THE FATHER, not exceeding in any town the sum of Thirty Shillings; and, in addition to such general payment, each Member and Probationer who shall dine

in the Bar-Room on a Bar-Day, shall pay a further sum of Three Shillings every day he shall so dine. Such several payments shall be collected into one fund, to be called the BAR-MESS-FUND for that town. Out of such fund the proportion of the expense of the Bar-Waiter, and the expenses connected with the Bar-Room (if any there be in that town), shall in the first instance be paid and then the Bar-bills for dinner, wine, waiter, etc, from day to day as long as the fund shall last. If the fund be exhausted before the Assizes shall have terminated in that town, then the wine bills and other expenses of the dinners, each day after the fund shall be so exhausted, shall be paid by those who dine in that town on such day. But if there be a surplus, the same shall be paid to the Treasurer, to be added to the general fund.

2.    In order to keep up the stock of wine, the Society shall be charged for all such wine as they shall consume on circuit such prices as the Committee shall direct; and the Treasurer shall supply the Steward in each Bar-Town with a scale of prices which the Steward is to charge the Society for the wine; and which he shall pay to the Treasurer.

## XII. Miscellaneous Provisions.

1.    No charge shall be permitted in the Bar-bill for supper or tea, or for beer or other liquor used at luncheon; and each Member who shall order any of those matters shall be individually responsible for the payment thereof.

2.    When any Member or Members shall dine in any Bar-Town during the circuit, on any day which shall not be a Bar-Day, he or they shall be permitted to use the wine of the Society, on paying to the Steward of the town the proper price for the same; but in no case shall any wine given to the Society in payment of any Congratulation or of any Fine be used except on a Bar-Day.

3.    The Members shall wear Bar Costume on circuit.

4.    A book, containing the Laws and Rules of the Society, shall be delivered to THE FATHER for the time being, the Treasurer, and the Steward of each town, for the purpose of bringing the same on circuit.

# Bibliography

## MANUSCRIPT SOURCES

Council of Legal Education (Northern Ireland)

CLE AC/R/79/7/XV
CLE/M/02/5

Office of the Lord Chief Justice of Northern Ireland

File S.C. L/23
File S.C. L/24

Public Record Office of Northern Ireland

T.2855/1, Willes, Miscellaneous observations on Ireland 1750-60
CAB/4/92
CAB/4/182
CAB/4/187
CAB/6/57
CAB/11/102
FIN/18/6/6
SCH/524/3A/1/11

The General Council of the Bar of Northern Ireland

Album of photographs of the North East Bar
Circuit Minute Book
Circuit Account Book
Minutes of the Bar Council
Minutes of General Meetings
Report on Proposals for Future Accommodation for the Bar, May 1995
Submission to the Royal Commission on Legal Services from the General
Council of the Bar of Northern Ireland in answer to the Royal Commission's
Questionnaire, April 1977

The General Council of the Bar of Ireland

Law Library Minute Book 1816-1836

Law Library Treasurer's Accounts 1837-1843

The Honorable Society of the Inn of Court of Northern Ireland

Admission records
Box 4 (File 'Erection of memorial to Solicitors and Barristers 1939-45')
Box 23
Box 26
Box 34
Draft Petition to His Grace the Governor of Northern Ireland
File 3 (Inn) 'Royal Commission on Legal Services'
File I.A 1 1966-1971
File S. 2
Copy minutes of the last meeting of the North East Circuit
Minutes of benchers
Minutes of the Northern Committee of Benchers
Minutes of the Executive Council of the Inn of Court of Northern Ireland
Note of a meeting of the Royal Commission on Legal Services held on Thursday 5 April 1979
Roll of subscribers to the Bar Library, robing room and luncheon room
Roll of Barristers
Roll of members of the Honorable Society of the Inn of Court of Northern Ireland
Submission on behalf of the Benchers of the Inn of Court of Northern Ireland to the Royal Commission on Legal Services

The Honorable Society of King's Inns

Minutes of Benchers
The reminiscences of Lord Shandon, lord chancellor of Ireland

The National Archives

30/89/2    A memoir by the Honourable William Evelyn Wylie KC
30/89/14   Fee books of the Honourable William Evelyn Wylie KC
WORK 27/7/1

In private ownership

Babington, Sir Anthony. *Personal Reminiscences*. 1966
Judges of assize for North West Circuit

## PRINTED SOURCES

*Analecta Hiberniae, including the reports of the Irish Manuscripts Commission.*
*'A volley of execrations' The letters and papers of John Fitzgibbon, earl of Clare 1772-1802.* ed. D.A. Fleming and A.P.W. Malcolmson. Dublin, 2005.

*Belfast and Ulster Directory.*

*Calendar of the state papers relating to Ireland.*

*Calendar of the patent rolls (Ireland).*

*Dublin University Calendar* 1916-17.

*Interim Report of the Joint Committee on Civil and Criminal Jurisdiction in Northern Ireland,* 1973. Cmnd. 5431.

*Liber munerum publicorum Hiberniae.* ed. Rowley Lascelles. 2 vols. London, 1770.

*Memoirs of the life and times of the Rt Hon Henry Grattan.* ed. Henry Grattan junior. 5 vols. London 1839-46.

*Reforming Complaints Handling: Building Consumer Confidence.*

*Report from the select committee on legal education, together with the minutes of evidence...*1846. H.C. 1846 (686).

*Report of the proceedings at a meeting of the bench and Bar...at which an Inn of Court was established.*

*Report of the Committee on County Courts and Magistrates' Courts in Northern Ireland.* Cmnd. 5824. 1974.

*Report of a committee to consider, in the context of civil liberties and human rights, measures to deal with terrorism in Northern Ireland.* Cmnd. 5847.

*Report by the Research Working Group on the Legal Services Market in Scotland.*

*Report of the Committee on Legal Aid and Advice in Northern Ireland.* 1960. Cmd. 417.

*Report of the Committee on Legal Education in Northern Ireland.* Cmd. 1973.

*Report of the Committee on Professional Legal Education in Northern Ireland.* 1985

*Report of the Committee on the Supreme Court of Judicature of Northern Ireland* 1970. Cmd. 4292.

*Report of the Royal Commission on Legal Services.* Cmd 7648.

*Report of the Legal Services Review Group, Legal Services in Northern Ireland: Complaints, Regulation, Competition.* (2006).

*Rules of the Honorable Society of King's Inns with regard to...the degree of Barrister-at-Law,* July 1964.

*Study of Competition in Legal Services,* January 2005.

*The correspondence of Daniel O'Connell.* Ed. M. O'Connell. 8 vols. Dublin

*The laws and rules of the Society of the North East Bar.* 1875.

*The letters of Lord Chief Baron Willes to the earl of Warwick 1757-62: an account of Ireland in the mid-eighteenth century.* ed. J. Kelly. Aberystwyth, 1990.

*The state letters of Henry, earl of Clarendon.* 2 vols. Oxford, 1765.

*Thom's Irish almanac and official directory.*

*Wilsons's Dublin Directory.* 1761.

## SECONDARY SOURCES: BOOKS

Ball, F.E. *The judges in Ireland 1221-1921*, 2 vols. London, 1926.

Baker, J.H. *An introduction to English legal history* 3rd. ed. London, 1990.

----------- *Legal Education in London 1250-1850.* London, 2007.

----------- *The order of the serjeants at law.* London, 1984.

Blackburne, Edward. *Life of the Rt Hon Francis Blackburne, late lord chancellor of Ireland.* London, 1874.

Bodkin, M. McD. *Recollections of an Irish Judge.* London, 1914.

Bolton, G.C. *The passing of the Irish Act of Union: a study in parliamentary politics.* Oxford, 1966.

Bourke, O.J. *Anecdotes of the Connaught Circuit from its foundation in 1604 to close upon the present time.* Dublin, 1885.

Brand, P. *The origins of the English legal profession.* Oxford, 1992.

Brett, C.E.B. *Court Houses and market houses of Ulster.* Belfast, 1973.

----------- *Long Shadows Cast Before, nine lives in Ulster, 1625-1977.* Edinburgh, 1978.

Brunkner, T. *Digest of cases in the courts of common law in Ireland.* Dublin, 1865.

Campbell, T.J. *Fifty years of Ulster.* Belfast, 1941.

Clarke, A. *The Old English in Ireland, 1635-42.* Cornell, 1966.

Costello, K. *The Court of Admiralty of Ireland 1575-1893.* Dublin, 2011.

Curran, J.A. *Reminiscences of John Adye Curran KC.* London, 1924.

Davies, J. *Le Primer Report des Cases en les Courts del Roy en Ireland.* Dublin, 1615

Delaney, V.T.H. *Christopher Palles, lord chief baron of her majesty's court of exchequer in Ireland 1874-1914, his life and times.* Dublin, 1960.

*Dictionary of Irish Biography.*

*Dictionary of Irish Literature.* Ed. R. Hogan. 2nd. ed. Connecticut and London, 1996.

Ellis, S.G. *Reform and Revival, English government in Ireland, 1470-1534* Royal Historical Society studies in history, vol. 47, London, 1986.

Ervine, St. John. *Craigavon Ulsterman*. London, 1949.

Ferguson, K (ed.) *King's Inns Barristers 1868-2004*. Dublin, 2005.

Garham, N. *The courts, crime and the criminal law in Ireland, 1692-1760*. Dublin, 1996.

Gray, J. *The great Cave Hill right of way case*. Belfast, 2010.

Hand, G.J. *English Law in Ireland*. Cambridge, 1967.

Hand, G.J. and Treadwell, V.W. *His Majesty's Direction for settling the courts within the kingdom of Ireland, 1662* in *Anal. Hib*. 26 (1970).

Harbinson, J.F. *The Ulster Unionist Party, 1882-1973 its development and organisation*. Belfast, 1973.

Hart, A.R. *A history of the king's serjeants at law in Ireland: honour rather than advantage*. Dublin, 2000.

Healy, M. *The Old Munster Circuit a book of memories and traditions*. 3rd. impression, London and Dublin, 1948.

Hewitt, A. *The Law Society of Northern Ireland-A History*. Belfast, 2010.

Hogan, D. *The legal profession in Ireland 1789-1922*. Dublin, 1986.

----------- *The Honorable Society of King's Inns*. Dublin, 1987.

Hopkinson, M. (ed.) *The last days of Dublin Castle: the diaries of Mark Sturgis*. Dublin, 1999.

Johnson, W. *History and customs of the Bar and Circuit of Northern Ireland*. Belfast, 1985.

Jones, E.W. *Jones LJ, his life and times the autobiography of the Rt Hon Sir Edward Jones*. Enniskillen, 1987.

Kenny, C. *King's Inns and the kingdom of Ireland: the Irish 'inn of court' 1541-1800*. Dublin, 1992.

----------- *Tristram Kennedy and the revival of Irish Legal training 1835-1885*. Dublin, 1996.

----------- *King's Inns and the battle of the books, 1972 – cultural controversy at a Dublin library*. Dublin, 2002.

King, William. *The state of the protestants in Ireland under the late King James' government*. 3rd. ed. London, 1692.

Kotsonouris, M. *Retreat from revolution: the Dail courts, 1920-24*. Dublin, 1994.

*The winding up of the Dail Courts, 1922-1925: an obvious duty*. Dublin, 2004.

Lawrence, R.J. *The government of Northern Ireland public finance and public services 1926-1964*. Oxford, 1965.

Lynch, D. *Northern Circuit Directory 1876-2004*. Liverpool, 2005.

MacAnnaidth, S. *Fermanagh books, writers and newspapers of the nineteenth century*. Enniskillen and Belfast, 1999.

MacDermott, Lord. *An enriching life*. 1979.

McDonnell, A.D. *The life of Sir Denis Henry Catholic Unionist*. Belfast, 2000.

McDowell, R.B. *Grattan, a life. Dublin*. Dublin, 2001.

McDowell, R.B. and Webb, D.A. *Trinity College Dublin 1592-1952 an academic history*. Dublin, 2004.

O'Broin, L. *W.E. Wylie and the Irish Revolution 1916-17*. Dublin, 1989.

O'Carroll. *Mr Justice Robert Day (1746-1841) The diaries and addresses to grand juries 1793-1829*. Tralee, 2004.

O'Flanagan, J.R. *The Irish Bar*. 2nd ed. London, 1879.

---------- *The Munster Circuit. Tales, trials and traditions*. London, 1880

Osborough, W.N. *Studies in Irish History*. Dublin, 1999.

Otway-Ruthven, A.J. *A history of medieval Ireland* 2nd ed. London, 1980.

*Oxford Dictionary of National Biography.*

Marjoribanks, E. *The life of Lord Carson*. London, 1932.

Pawlisch, H.S. *Sir John Davies and the conquest of Ireland: a study in legal positivism*. Cambridge, 1985.

Plunkett, D. *The life letters and speeches of Lord Plunkett*. London, 1867.

Prest. W.R. *The Inns of Court under Elizabeth 1 and the Early Stuarts 1590-1640*. London, 1972.

Quinn, A.P. *Wigs and guns: Irish barristers in the Great War*. Dublin, 2006.

Rhadamanthus. *Our Judges*. Dublin, 1890.

Richardson, H.G. and Sayles, G.O. *The Irish parliament in the middle ages*. Philadelphia, 1952.

Robinson and McIlwaine, *The opening of the New Bar Library*, November 21st 2003.

Ross, J. *The years of my pilgrimage*. London, 1924.

Sainty, J. *A list of English law officers, king's counsel and holders of patents of precedence*. London, 1987.

Sheehy, E. *May it please the court*. Dublin, 1951.

Sheil, R.L. *Sketches of the Irish Bar*. (ed.) R.S. Mackenzie, New York, 1854.

Smith, G.H. *The North East Bar, a sketch historical and reminiscent*. Belfast, 1910.

---------- *Sketch of the Supreme Court of Judicature of Northern Ireland*. Belfast, 1926.

Smyth, C.J. *Chronicle of the law officers of Ireland*. London and Dublin, 1839.

Sullivan, A.M. *Old Ireland reminiscences of an Irish KC*. London, 1927.

----------- *The last serjeant*. London, 1952.

Walsh, Louis J. *The yarns of a country attorney being stories and sketches of life in rural Ulster*. 2ⁿᵈ. impression, Dublin, 1918.


# SECONDARY SOURCES:
## ARTICLES AND COMPOSITE WORKS


Aiken, M. 'The Bar of Northern Ireland's first lady'. Inn of Court Newsletter vol.1, no. 3.

Baker, J.H. 'The inns of court and chancery as voluntary associations', and

----------- 'Counsellors and barristers' in *The legal profession and the common law: historical essays*. London, 1986.

---------- 'Judicial Review of the judges as visitors to the Inns of Court'. [1992] PL.

----------- 'The degree of barrister' in *The common law tradition: lawyers, books and the law*. London, 2000.

Barnard, T.C. 'Lawyers and the law in later seventeenth-century Ireland'. *IHS* xxviii (1993).

Brand, P. 'The birth and early development of a colonial judiciary: the judges of the lordship of Ireland, 1210-1377' in W.N. Osborough (ed.), *Explorations in law and history: Irish Legal History Society discourses 1988-1994*. Dublin, 1995.

----------- 'The early history of the legal profession in Ireland' in Daire Hogan and W.N. Osborough (ed.), *Brehons, serjeants and attorneys, studies in the history of the Irish legal profession*. Dublin, 1990.

----------- 'Ralph de Hengham and the Irish common law'. *Ir Jur*, xix (1984).

----------- 'Ireland and the literature of the early common law'. *Ir Jur*, xvi (1981).

----------- 'Irish law students and lawyers in late medieval England'. *IHS*, xxxii (2000-2001).

Clancy, T. 'The Four Courts building and the development of an independent Bar of Ireland' in C. Costello (ed.) *The Four Courts: 200 years*. Dublin, 1996.

Cregan, D.F. 'Irish catholic admissions to the English inns of court 1558-1625'. *Ir Jur* v (1970).

Curran, C.P. 'Cooley, Gandon and the Four Courts' in C. Costello (ed.) *The Four Courts: 200 years*. Dublin, 1996.

Delaney, V.T.H. 'Legal studies in Trinity College, Dublin, since the foundation'. *Hermathena*, lxxxix.

---------- 'The gold collar of SS of Ireland'. (1961) 77 *LQR*.

Greer, D.S. 'The development of civil bill procedure' in J. McEldowney and P. O'Higgins (ed.) *The common law tradition: essays in Irish legal history*. Dublin, 1990.

---------- 'A security against illegality? The reservation of crown cases in nineteenth century Ireland' in N.M. Dawson (ed.) *Reflections on Law and History Irish Legal Hsitory Society Discourses and other papers, 2000-2005*. Dublin, 2006.

Griffin, C. 'Post Gandon at the Four Courts' in C. Costello (ed.) *The Four Courts: 200 years*. Dublin, 1996.

Hart, A.R. 'Fighting Fitzgerald: mad, bad and dangerous to know, an eighteenth century murder trial'. *NILQ* 49 (1998).

---------- 'Complexity, delay and cost-The county courts in Northern Ireland'. *NILQ* 53 (2000).

Heuston, R.F.V. 'Legal history and the author: some practical problems of authorship' in W.N. Osborough (ed.) *The Irish Legal History Society: Inaugural Addresses*. Dublin, 1989.

Keane, R. 'A mass of crumbling ruins: the destruction of the Four Courts in June 1922' in C. Costello (ed.) *The Four Courts: 200 years*, Dublin, 1996.

Kelly, R.J. 'The Connaught Bar from 1604 to 1904', *Journal of the Galway Archaeological and Historical Society*, vol. iv (1905).

Kenny, C. 'The exclusion of catholics from the legal profession in Ireland, 1537-1829', *IHS*, xxv (1986).

--------- 'The Four Courts at Christ Church, 1608-1796' and

--------- 'Irish Ambition and English preference in chancery appointments, 1827-1841: the fate of William Conyngham Plunket' in W.N. Osborough (ed.) *Explorations in Law and History Irish Legal History Society Discourses, 1988-1994*. Dublin, 1995.

--------- 'Adventures in training-the Irish genesis of the 'remarkable and far-sighted' Select Committee on legal education, 1846' in P. Brand, K. Costello and W.N. Osborough, (ed.) *Adventures of the Law-proceedings of the sixteenth British Legal History Conference 2003*. Dublin, 2005.

McLean, J.A.L. 'Some developments in Northern Ireland since 1921-the Supreme Court of Judicature in Northern Ireland'. (1972) *NILQ*.

Osborough, W.N. 'The admission of attorneys and solicitors in Ireland, 1660-1866' in Daire Hogan and W.N. Osborough (ed.), *Brehons, serjeants and attorneys: studies in the Irish legal profession*. Dublin, 1990.

--------- 'The title of the last lord chief justice of Ireland' in W.N. Osborough

*Studies in Irish Legal History*. Dublin, 1999.

Power, T.P. 'Conversions among the legal profession in Ireland in the eighteenth century' in Daire Hogan and W.N. Osborough (ed.), *Brehons, serjeants and attorneys: studies in the Irish legal profession*. Dublin, 1990.

Johnston, W.J. 'The first adventure of the common law'. *LQR*, xxxvi (1920).

McCavitt, J. "Good planets in their several spheares'-the establishment of the assize circuits in early seventeenth-century Ireland'. *Ir Jur* xxiv (1989).

McParland, E. 'The Old Four Courts, at Christ Church'

\--------- 'The early history of James Gandon's Four Courts', both in C. Costello (ed.) *The Four Courts: 200 years*. Dublin, 1996.

Strahan, J.A. 'The bench and bar of Ireland', *Blackwood's Edinburgh Magazine*, January 1920.

Towey, T. 'Hugh Kennedy and the constitutional development of the Irish Free State' in *Ir Jur* xxii (1977).

## THESIS

P.E. Leonard. *The contribution of Thomas Joseph (T.J.) Campbell KC MP (1871-1946) to Nationalist politics in Northern Ireland.*

## NEWSPAPERS AND LEGAL JOURNALS

*Armagh Guardian*
*Belfast Gazette*
*Belfast Newsletter*
*Belfast Telegraph*
*Down Recorder*
*Fermanagh Times*
*Irish Law Times and Solicitors' Journal*
*Irish News*

# INDEX